Eurozone Dystopia

Groupthink and Denial on a Grand Scale

William Mitchell

Professor of Economics, Centre of Full Employment and Equity, University of Newcastle, Australia

Edward Elgar
PUBLISHING

Cheltenham, UK • Northampton, MA, USA

Published by
Edward Elgar Publishing Limited
The Lypiatts
15 Lansdown Road
Cheltenham
Glos GL50 2JA
UK

Edward Elgar Publishing, Inc.
William Pratt House
9 Dewey Court
Northampton
Massachusetts 01060
USA

A catalogue record for this book
is available from the British Library

Library of Congress Control Number: 2014959497

This book is available electronically in the **Elgar**online
Economics subject collection
DOI 10.4337/9781784716660

MIX
Paper from
responsible sources
FSC® C013056
FSC
www.fsc.org

ISBN 978 1 78471 665 3 (cased)
ISBN 978 1 78471 666 0 (eBook)

Typeset by Servis Filmsetting Ltd, Stockport, Cheshire
Printed and bound in Great Britain by T.J. International Ltd, Padstow

Contents

PART III THE OPTIONS FOR EUROPE

Preface

This book is written for laypersons that are interested in economic ideas but haven't studied the subject in any formal manner. While economic terms (jargon) are used throughout, every attempt has been made to simplify and explain them to maximise meaning and comprehension. The book aims to provide an alternative viewpoint to empower people with a progressive bent to challenge the current austerity mantra that is causing the European nations to stagnate with high unemployment and increasing poverty rates. The underlying assumption is that the political process has been captured by powerful and wealthy elites, who exploit our lack of understanding of economics to impose policies that undermine prosperity and redistribute income and wealth to the few at the top. Without a thorough exposure of the neo-liberal economic myths relating to deficits and debt, there is little chance that progressives will be able to gain traction against this neo-liberal attack on people's rights and prosperity.

Special acknowledgement for the valuable administrative and editorial assistance received from Melinda Hannan (at CofFEE). Special thanks also go to Dr Louisa Connors who has offered valuable editorial review and criticism of the draft. Kind thanks go to Dr Natalie Doyle who has provided helpful advice and discussion about various nuances of European history, specifically the Franco-German rivalry. Thanks also to Thomas Fazi who provided instigation and support throughout the Project. I have also benefited from my long-standing academic collaboration with Professor Joan Muysken at Maastricht University and the long periods I have spent working there thinking about European history and related economic developments.

The overall project is dedicated however to the millions of nameless unemployed workers who have been denied the opportunity to live fulfilled lives by the implementation of flawed neo-liberal economic policy abetted by orthodox economists who unfortunately bear none of the costs of their folly.

While many have offered help and advice, all errors remain the responsibility of the author.

William Mitchell
Newcastle, Australia
August 2014

Conventions

References to official documents, reports and press releases from the Commission of European Communities are listed under European Commission irrespective of the date they were released. Similarly, the European Council is used to document all references that were associated with its role.

Where a reference is cited but no page number is provided the citation is from a non-paginated document, usually an internet page.

The citation style is to cite the document initially and, if further specific citations follow, then only the page number is given as long as that is not ambiguous.

Quotations from non-English documents are translations of the original by the author.

Abbreviations

BBG	Bundesbankgesetz (Bundesbank Act)
BIG	Basic Income Guarantee
BIS	Bank of International Settlements
BVerfG	German Federal Constitutional Court
CAP	Common Agricultural Policy
CDU	Christian Democratic Union (Germany)
CSU	Christian Social Union of Bavaria (Germany)
CJEU	Court of Justice of the European Union
CofFEE	Centre of Full Employment and Equity
ECB	European Central Bank
ECOFIN	Economic and Financial Affairs Council
ECU	European Currency Unit
EDP	Excessive Deficit Procedures
EMS	European Monetary System
EMU	Economic and Monetary Union
EU	European Union
FFA	Federal Fiscal Authority
GDP	Gross Domestic Product
GFC	Global Financial Crisis
IGC	Intergovernmental Conference
JG	Job Guarantee
MMT	Modern Monetary Theory
NAIRU	Non-Accelerating Inflation Rate of Unemployment
OCA	Optimal Currency Areas
OMF	Overt Monetary Financing
PIIGS	Portugal, Italy, Ireland, Greece and Spain
QE	Quantitative Easing
REER	Real Effective Exchange Rate
SGP	Stability and Growth Pact 1997
SMP	Securities Market Program
TINA	There Is No Alternative
Troika	Collective comprising the EU, the ECB and the IMF

1. Introduction

GROUPTHINK

> . . . a pattern of thought characterized by self-deception, forced manufacture of consent, and conformity to group values and ethics. (Merriam Webster online dictionary)

> We bouwen op drijfzand [We are building on quicksand]. (André Szász, former Director of the De Nederlandsche Bank, 1999)

This book critically examines the options that the Eurozone nations have to address the social and economic crisis that has bedevilled them since 2008. The book elucidates these options within an historical understanding of the path taken to create the Economic and Monetary Union (EMU). The historical experience highlights the difficulties that nations with very different economic structures and a lack of cultural solidarity face when they try to fix exchange rates and adopt a common currency. It also allows us to understand how the growing dominance of neo-liberal economics in the 1980s intersected with the post World War II Franco-German rivalry to create a destructive Groupthink that undermines prosperity, denies reality, and rejects viable solutions to the crisis on ideological grounds.

There are superior options to austerity, even within the common currency arrangement. But if sustainable prosperity is to be achieved then the Eurozone should be dismantled in an orderly fashion and national currencies restored. If such a development cannot be brokered between the Member States, then the superior option for nations such as Italy, Greece, Spain and such is to unilaterally exit the EMU and restore their own sovereignty.

The great European visionaries in the immediate post World War II period did not desire to put the European economies into a straitjacket of austerity and hardship. Rather they aimed to achieve peacetime prosperity. Europe's political leaders devised the 'European Project' as an ambitious plan for European integration to ensure that there were no more large scale military conflicts fought on continental European soil. The Project began at a time when the advanced nations had embraced a broad

Keynesian economic policy consensus with governments committed to sustaining full employment.

The Keynesian era emerged out of the Great Depression, which taught politicians that without major government intervention, capitalism is inherently unstable and prone to delivering lengthy periods of unemployment. Full employment came only with the onset of World War II as governments used deficit spending to prosecute the war effort. The Keynesian era of macroeconomic policy that followed was thus marked by government deficits supplementing private spending to ensure that all workers who wanted to work could find jobs. The broad political and economic consensus that emerged after the war brought very low levels of unemployment in most Western nations, which persisted until the mid 1970s, although some European nations had bouts of sustained higher unemployment as a consequence of having to defend their weaker currencies.

Within this broad policy consensus, the discussions about integration were conditioned by Franco-German rivalry. France was determined to create institutional structures that would stop Germany from ever invading it again. It saw an integrated Europe as a way of consolidating a dominant role in European affairs but was determined to cede as little national sovereignty as possible to achieve these aims. France was also resentful of the influence that the US was exerting in Europe, particularly through the Marshall Plan, which intrinsically tied West Germany to the US.

The Germans, suffering a deep shame for their past militarism and associated deeds, had only their economic success including the 'discipline' of the Bundesbank to generate national pride. As well as a need to expand its export markets, Germany wanted to be part of the 'European Project' to demonstrate a rejection of its ugly history. But an obsessive fear of inflation meant that this participation had to be on German terms, which meant that the new Europe had to eventually accept the Bundesbank culture. This became a grinding process. Within the German 'stability' environment, it was seemingly overlooked that Germany, in fact, relied on robust import growth from other European nations for its prosperity. The fact that not all nations in a Bundesbank centric 'stability environment' could have balance of trade surpluses was ignored.

After World War II, the advanced nations also agreed to fix their exchange rates relative to the US dollar, which in turn was linked to the price of gold, because they believed this would bring economic stability. But the so-called Bretton Woods system, established in July 1944, was under pressure from the start because countries with trade deficits always faced downward pressure on their currencies. In order to maintain their exchange rates they had to: buy their own currencies in the foreign exchange markets using their foreign currency reserves; push up domestic interest rates to attract capital inflow; and constrict government spending to restrain imports. The nations with weaker currencies were thus often faced with recessed growth rates, higher unemployment, and depleted foreign reserves, and this created political instability. The effective operation of the system required the nations to have more or less similar trade strength, which was of course an impossibility and ultimately proved to be its undoing.

The Franco-German rivalry structured a series of less than effective compromises on the way to monetary union. The 1957 Treaty of Rome was heavily biased in favour of the occupied France at the expense of the aggressors Germany and Italy. But Germany's growing industrial and export strength became an increasingly significant threat to the French economy. German industrial ambition eventually required France to compromise on its own fierce resistance to ceding any national sovereignty to a European level entity. The early experience with the Common Agricultural Policy (CAP), introduced in 1962 as the first major initiative of the newly formed EEC, should have taught the European nations that entering a currency union would be a fraught exercise. France wanted to protect French farmers and Germany wanted to expand its industrial export market. To achieve their goals, the Germans agreed to provide subsidies through the CAP to French farmers: a gnawing tension that remains today. But the administrative viability of the CAP required a very stable exchange rate environment because a multitude of agricultural prices had to be supported across the Community. Once the Member States locked in the CAP they were also trapped into pursuing the impossible task of maintaining fixed exchange rates. The German mark became the strongest currency in the 1960s as Germany's export strength grew, which put France and Italy under constant pressure of devaluation and domestic stagnation and undermined the CAP. The various agreements to maintain fixed parities between the European currencies all largely failed because of the different export strengths of the Member States. But instead of taking the sensible option and abandoning the desire for fixed exchange rates, the European political leaders accelerated the move to a common currency when the Bretton Woods system collapsed in 1971. The lessons from the Bretton Woods fiasco were not learned.

The 1970 Werner Report outlined a comprehensive timetable for the creation of a full economic and monetary union by the end of the decade. It was clear the Committee wanted monetary and fiscal policy to be centralised with the 'centre of decision of economic policy . . . [to] . . . be politically responsible to a European Parliament' (Werner Report, 1970: 13). A later study by the MacDougall Committee in 1975 also emphasised that an effective economic and monetary union would require a strong fiscal presence at the federal level. They assessed that 'It is most unlikely that the Community will be anything like so fully integrated in the field of public finance for many years to come as the existing economic unions we have studied' (MacDougall Report, 1977: 11).

There are many competing explanations as to why Werner's plan failed to materialise, but the basic reason is that in an era of growing currency instability the French fear of German dominance and their unwillingness to cede power to supranational institutions, combined with the German inflation obsession, stood in the way. The two nations could clearly find ways to cooperate on a political level but trying to form an economic and monetary union was difficult. In 1972, the Governor of the Danish Central Bank said, 'I will begin to believe in European economic and monetary union when someone explains how you control nine horses that are all running at different speeds within the same harness' (McAllister, 2009: 58).

In 1972, social psychologist Irving Janis identified group behaviour he termed 'Groupthink', which is a 'mode of thinking people engage in when they are deeply involved in a cohesive in group, when the members striving for unanimity override their motivation to realistically appraise alternative courses of action' (Janis, 1982: 9). It 'requires each member to avoid raising controversial issues' (Janis, 1982: 12). Groupthink drives a sort of 'mob rule' that maintains discipline within the group or community of decision makers. These communities develop a dominant culture, which provides its members with a sense of belonging and joint purpose but also renders them oblivious and hostile to new and superior ways of thinking. Groupthink becomes apparent to the outside world when there is a crisis or, in Janis's words, a 'fiasco', such as the Global Financial Crisis (GFC).

What eventually allowed the 'nine horses' to be harnessed together was not a diminution in Franco-German national and cultural rivalry but rather a growing homogenisation of the economic debate. The surge in Monetarist thought within macroeconomics in the 1970s, first within the academy, then in policy-making and central banking domains, quickly morphed into an insular Groupthink, which trapped policy makers in the thrall of the self-regulating, free market myth. The accompanying 'confirmation bias', which is 'the tendency of people to only notice information consistent with their own expectations and to ignore information that is inconsistent with them' (IEO, 2011: 17) overwhelmed the debate about monetary integration. The introduction of the Monetarist-inspired Barre Plan in 1976 by French Prime Minister Raymond Barre, under President Valéry Giscard d'Estaing, showed how far the French had shifted from their Gaullist 'Keynesian' days. Across Europe, unemployment became a policy tool aimed at maintaining price stability rather than a policy target, as it had been during the Keynesian era up until the mid 1970s. Unemployment rose sharply as national governments, infested with Monetarist thought, began their long-lived love affair with austerity.

The Delors Report (1989), which informed the Maastricht conference, disregarded the conclusions of the Werner and MacDougall Reports about the need for a strong federal fiscal function because they represented 'old fashioned' Keynesian thinking, which was no longer tolerable within the Monetarist Groupthink that had taken over European debate. The new breed of financial elites, who stood to gain massively from the deregulation that they demanded, promoted the re-emergence of the free market ideology that had been discredited during the Great Depression. The shift from a Keynesian collective vision of full employment and equity to this new individualistic mob rule was driven by ideological bullying and narrow sectional interests rather than insights arising from a superior appeal to evidential authority and a concern for societal prosperity.

The Monetarist (neo-liberal) disdain for government intervention meant that the EMU would suppress the capacity of fiscal policy and no amount of argument or evidence, which indicated that such a choice would lead to crisis, would distract Delors and his team from that aim. Delors knew that he could appease the French political need to avoid handing over policy discretion to Brussels by shrouding that aim in the retention of national responsibility for economic policy making. He also knew that the harsh fiscal rules he proposed that restricted the latitude of the national governments would satisfy the Germans. Monetarism had bridged the two camps.

The whole process had a surrealistic air about it at the time.

To fully appreciate the options available for the Eurozone, the discussion has to be framed within a valid economic framework. While poor political motivation cannot be ignored, a major part of the problem that currently besets the Eurozone nations arises from the application of a flawed macroeconomic framework that has been used by officials and their political masters since the 1980s.

The Eurozone is now locked down in a straitjacket of economic austerity, driven by an economic ideology that is blind to the evidence of its own failure. The neo-liberal policies of deregulation and the demonisation of the use of discretionary fiscal deficits (government spending greater than tax revenue) created the crisis in the first place, and now the same sorts of policies are prolonging it. The current policy approach has institutionalised economic stagnation, widespread retrenchment, and the deterioration of working conditions and retirement pensions. Millions of European workers are now unemployed, youth jobless rates are around 60 per cent in some advanced nations, inequality and poverty rates are rising, and massive daily losses of national income are being endured. The dramatically high youth unemployment rates will ensure that the damage will span generations and undermine future prosperity as a cohort of jobless youth enter adulthood with no work experience and a growing sense of dislocation from mainstream societal norms.

The Eurozone political elites claim that there is no alternative (TINA) but to impose more austerity by cutting fiscal deficits and enforcing widespread cutbacks to social welfare systems. The major political parties in most nations, whether in government or opposition, have unquestionably accepted the dominance of neo-liberal ideology, which has not only homogenised the political debate but also obscured the only credible routes to recovery. A correct assessment of the current state indicates that fiscal deficits have to increase. Austerity is exactly the opposite of the policy response that is required. A sustained recovery in the Eurozone and elsewhere requires a categorical rejection of mainstream macroeconomic theory and practice and a reorganisation of the institutional structures to allow deficits to increase. The assessment is that this can only be done if the union is dismantled.

This book rejects the TINA mantra that has been a powerful organising framework for conservatives to promote the myth that fiscal discipline and widespread deregulation will allow a free market to maximise wealth for all. The argument rehearsed in the book is fairly simple even if the concepts that underpin it are not. The neo-liberal economic framework, promoted vigorously by many economists, the multinational agencies such as the International Monetary Fund (IMF) and the Organisation for Economic Co-operation and Development (OECD), and conservative politicians including the Eurozone establishment in Brussels and Frankfurt, blinds the public eyes to realistic alternatives by confining the boundaries of the public debate through the use of selective priorities, wrongful causalities, and scandalous misrepresentations of reality. Thus before one can really appreciate the alternatives, the underlying economics needs to be reframed. The actual and superior alternatives to the current fiscal austerity are too easily dismissed as being naïve, unrealistic or just downright crazy, if they are viewed and assessed through the neo-liberal economic lens.

The major conjecture in the book is that the European policy-making elites – the politicians, the supporting bureaucracies, the central bankers and expert consultants – remain trapped in neo-liberal Groupthink that created the euro monster in the first place. It is a group dynamic that resists change and explains the arrant disregard of viable alternative policy paths that could restore growth.

American biologist Joseph Altman specialised in neurobiology and discovered adult neurogenesis in the 1960s. He showed that adult brains could create new neurons but the idea was fiercely denied by contemporary thought at the time. It wasn't until the phenomenon was 'rediscovered' by another scientist (Elizabeth Gould in 1999) that the proposition became fashionable. Neurogenesis is now one of the most significant areas in neuroscience. Why were Altman's discoveries ignored for almost 30 years? Charles Gross wrote in 2008 that 'the dogma of "no new neurons" was universally held and vigorously defended by the most powerful and leading primate developmental anatomist of his time' (Gross, 2008: 331).

Altman's experience helps us understand the enduring crisis within the EMU. First, academic disciplines (such as neurobiologists, economists and so on) work within organised 'paradigms', which philosopher Thomas Kuhn identified as 'universally recognized scientific achievements that for a time provide model problems and solutions for a community of practitioners' (Kuhn, 1996: X). Typically, the body of knowledge that defines the paradigm are 'recounted . . . by science textbooks, elementary and advanced' (Kuhn, 1996: 10). Kuhn challenged the notion that 'scientific' activity is a linear process, whereby scholars add new empirically supported facts to the knowledge base to replace previously accepted notions. Rather, Kuhn said that dominant viewpoints persist until they are confronted with insurmountable anomalies, whereupon a revolution (paradigm shift) occurs. The new paradigm exposes the old theories as inapplicable, introduces new concepts, asks new questions and provides students with a new way of thinking with a new language and explanatory metaphors. Once supplanted, the old theories are no longer considered valid knowledge. Kuhn also noted that there is a sort of mob rule among practitioners within a dominant paradigm and they vehemently hold onto their views even in the face of logical or empirical anomaly. The dominant group becomes trapped in Janis's Groupthink and initially vilifies those who propose new ways of thinking. Altman's work represented the potential for a paradigm shift and was resisted by the mob until change became ineluctable.

Imre Lakatos extended Kuhn's notion of a scientific community by introducing the concept of a 'research programme', which consisted of a hard core (theories that define the paradigm), auxiliary assumptions (the 'protective belt') and methodological rules or heuristics (Lakatos, 1970). The hard core is akin to a religious belief in that it is never subjected to empirical scrutiny by the group and is protected by the heuristic. It defines what the group stands for. The positive heuristic defines the day to day research activities, the allowable questions that can be explored, and the research methods that are acceptable. It is permissible to challenge some of the auxiliary hypotheses, which in themselves, plausible or not, provide no threat to the core theories. The core is protected by the negative heuristic, which essentially bans certain questions from being asked and forms of enquiry or evidence being admitted, even when strong contrary evidence is produced. One might think of this as denial. For a time, a research program maintains dominance because it adds content, which is considered to advance knowledge and is of interest to the group. At some point a research program may become degenerative in that its content diminishes in the face of increasing empirical anomaly, that is, the theory no longer provides an adequate explanation of what people know and see. But a degenerating research program can maintain its hold on a professional group for an extended period, such is the resistance to change among those within it.

Just before the GFC revealed its worst, Olivier Blanchard, the chief economist at the IMF, reviewed the understanding that macroeconomists had of the real world and claimed that the 'state of macro is good' (Blanchard, 2008: 2). He asserted that a 'largely common vision has emerged' (p. 5) in macroeconomics, with a 'convergence in methodology' (p. 3) such that research articles in macroeconomics 'look very similar to each other in structure, and very different from the way they did thirty years ago' (p. 21). They now follow 'strict, haiku-like, rules' (p. 26). He also noted that the dominant 'New Keynesian' approach in macroeconomics had 'become a workhorse for policy and welfare analysis' (p. 8) because it is 'simple, analytically convenient . . . [and] . . . reduces a complex reality to a few simple equations' (p. 9). It didn't seem to matter to these economists that in the 'basic NK model . . . there is no unemployment' (p. 12), such that all fluctuations in measured joblessness are characterised largely by workers choosing whether or not to work as part of a so-called optimal choice between work and leisure.

The mainstream macroeconomists, who have an abiding faith in the ability of the self-regulated market to deliver optimal outcomes, which we will refer to as the neo-liberal approach, had declared some years before the crisis, with an arrogance common to the discipline, that the 'business cycle is dead'. That is, the large swings in macroeconomic performance (recessions and mass unemployment and boom and inflation) that had dominated the attention of economic policy makers in the post World War II period and led to fiscal policy (the manipulation of taxation and government spending) being the primary tool governments used to maintain full employment and price stability were now being denied. University of Chicago professor Robert Lucas Jnr gave an extraordinary address to the American Economic Association in 2003 where he claimed 'that macroeconomics in this original sense has succeeded: Its central problem of depression-prevention has been solved, for all practical purposes, and has in fact been solved for many decades' (Lucas, 2003: 1). A year later, the US Federal Reserve Bank Governor Ben Bernanke claimed that as a result of the policy shift away from governments attempting to manage total spending in the economy by varying fiscal policy settings in favour of using monetary policy (interest rate setting by central banks) to concentrate purely on price stability and the pursuit of fiscal surpluses, the world was enjoying the Great Moderation (Bernanke, 2004).

Allegedly, damaging recessions were a thing of the past and low inflation and steady growth were now the norm. The public was led to believe that these mainstream economists had triumphed over the old Keynesian interventionists who had over regulated the economy, sucked the enterprise out of private entrepreneurs, allowed trade unions to become too powerful, and bred generations of indolent and unmotivated individuals who only aspired to live on income support payments. The dominant narrative was that with the economic cycle now under control, economic policy should concentrate on deregulating labour and financial markets and reducing income support payments to reduce the subsidy to the unemployed so that the 'market' can work more efficiently. This was denial writ large. Paul Krugman (2009) said these alleged 'successes' defined a self-styled 'golden era for the profession'. The mainstream paradigm in economics was blind 'to the very possibility of catastrophic failures in a market economy' (Krugman, 2009), and its policy prescriptions, based on an unjustified belief in the efficiency of markets, created the circumstances that would lead to the crisis. The worst economic crisis in 80 years was building while most economists waxed lyrical in their own world of self-aggrandisement and self-congratulation.

This view of economics dominates the academy, which then feeds into the domain of policy making. But the GFC has made it starkly obvious to all that mainstream economics is a degenerative research program with little empirical validity. Krugman (2009) said that 'the economics profession went astray because economists, as a group, mistook beauty, clad in impressive-looking mathematics, for truth.' The American institutional economist David Gordon (1972) wrote that whenever the mainstream economics paradigm is confronted with empirical evidence that appears to refute its basic predictions, it creates an exception by way of response to the anomaly and continues on as if nothing had happened. As a result, the mainstream macroeconomics textbooks, which students are forced to use, contain very little that is useful for understanding how the real world actually works. Students are given false accounts of how the financial sector, including banking, works; are taught a number of myths about the impact of the government on the private markets; and, above all, are taught that if markets are left to their own devices, the outcomes will be superior to those that involve regulation or government oversight. As the gap between theory and outcome has become obvious to all, it is easy to cast those who hang onto the mainstream theoretical propositions as cult worshippers who have lost all 'scientific' credibility.

These cult worshippers maintain their hegemony in a number of ways, including control of teaching programs in universities; control of hiring processes within the academy; control of key publication outlets; control of major research funding bodies; and dominating the linkages between the academy, business and government. Much of the control is implicit and accomplished through networks to get around external oversight such as anti-discrimination legislation. Jack Barbash discussed the way in which the economics profession protects its belief system from criticism and avoids, as far as possible, addressing real world problems. He notes that there is 'no formally coercive apparatus' but 'the equivalent of an "old boy" network' in operation (Barbash, 1982: 51). Advantages (publications, research grants, promotions, consulting opportunities, influence, etc.) accrue to those who conform to the rules. Socialisation begins in one's student days where the masters of the paradigm control the curriculum; the grading systems; and who gets postgraduate scholarships to pursue doctoral studies. The indoctrination intensifies when one enters the postgraduate stages. In economics, the graduate student learns that 'rigor is more important than substance' and 'method is more important than result' (p. 52). Remember those haiku-like rules that govern an economics paper's chance of publication success.

More insidious is that neo-liberal economics privileges the interests of capital and the financial elites. To understand why there is so much resistance to abandoning failed economic theories, we need to understand that the mainstream economics paradigm is much more than a set of theories with which economics professors indoctrinate their students. Blyth (2013: 100) notes that these mainstream economic theories 'enshrine different distributions of wealth and power and are power resources for actors whose claims to authority and income depend upon their credibility', which explains, in part, why there is such resistance to abandoning them, even though it is clear that they are bereft of any evidential standing.

Historically, the body of theory that now represents neo-liberal economics was first developed in the late 19th century as an antidote against the rising influence of Marxism, particularly in Europe. Marx's message that profits were the reward for ownership of capital, not a reward for any contribution to production, resonated strongly with workers. The capacity of owners of capital to take the surplus labour of the workers for nothing was an inflammatory idea. Workers considered this essential feature of capitalism to be patently unfair and increasingly violent protests threatened the capacity of capital to maintain its elite position relative to the vast bulk of the population. Clearly a solution was needed. Industrialists recruited economists to develop theories that made capitalism look as though it was fair and rewarding productive input in proportion to its contribution to final output. Later this was refined as attacks on government policy aimed at redistributing national income. Yet all the time, the interests of those who owned or served capital were being advanced at the expense of the less advantaged.

Which leads us to the second reason why the Altman case is of interest to anyone seeking to understand why the EMU is in such a mess. The neo-liberal Groupthink, which dominates economic policy making in Europe, is a case of denial on a grand scale. It not only created economic structures and policy frameworks that spawned the crisis, but has also led to a policy response which has ensured the massive costs will endure for generations while the problems remain unsolved. It was obvious that the Eurozone was doomed from the start and now the same neo-liberal ideology is masquerading as the solution. Groupthink suppresses alternative thinking and evidence that is contrary to the dominant viewpoints.

In 2011, the IMF's Independent Evaluation Office (IEO) released a scathing assessment of the institution's performance in the lead up to the GFC (IEO, 2011). The IEO said, 'Warning member countries about risks to the global economy and the build up of vulnerabilities in their own economies is arguably the most important purpose of IMF surveillance' (IEO, 2011: vii). However, the IEO identified neo-liberal ideological biases at the IMF and determined that the IMF failed to give adequate warning of the impending GFC because it was 'hindered by a high degree of groupthink' (p. 17), which among other things suppressed 'contrarian views' where an 'insular culture also played a big role' (p. 17). The report said, 'Analytical weaknesses were at the core of some of the IMF's most evident shortcomings in surveillance' (p. 17) as a result of 'the tendency among homogeneous, cohesive groups to consider issues only within a certain paradigm and not challenge its basic premises' (p. 17).

> The prevailing view among IMF staff – a cohesive group of macroeconomists – was that market discipline and self-regulation would be sufficient to stave off serious problems in financial institutions. They also believed that crises were unlikely to happen in advanced economies, where 'sophisticated' financial markets could thrive safely with minimal regulation of a large and growing portion of the financial system. (p. 17)

The External Evaluation Report says that 'IMF economists tended to hold in highest regard' (p. 18) economic models of the world proven to be inadequate (so-called Dynamic Stochastic General Equilibrium models).

Willem Buiter (2009) described these economic models as useless 'self-referential, inward-looking distractions at best', which exclude 'everything relevant to the pursuit of financial stability'.

Economist Robert Schiller (2008), who says Groupthink tells us why 'panels of experts could make colossal mistakes', also implicates central bankers in this self-censoring behaviour where 'mavericks' are put under intense pressure if they question the 'group consensus'. For example the US Federal Reserve Bank 'through its extensive network of consultants, visiting scholars, alumni and staff economists, so thoroughly dominates the field of economics that real criticism of the central bank has become a career liability for members of the profession' (Grim, 2009). Not only does the Federal Reserve fund a huge amount of non-staff economic consultancies but also 'keeps many of the influential editors of prominent academic journals on its payroll' (Grim, 2009). By controlling what gets published in the key journals, the bank also influences the career trajectory of economists, and thus suppresses independent research that might be critical of the way the central bank operates. The Federal Reserve has an 'intolerance for dissent', something that well-known economist Alan Blinder found out quickly, when he joined the bank as a vice chairman. He lasted around 18 months after 'a lot of senior staff . . . were pissed off . . . [because he was] . . . not playing by the customs that they were accustomed to' (Grim, 2009). His sin? He asked too many questions and challenged too many assumptions. Even a moderate critic of the bank, Paul Krugman, reported that he was 'blackballed from the Fed summer conference at Jackson Hole . . . ever since I criticized Governor Alan Greenspan' (*Democracy Now!*, 2007).

Some economists (rightly) observed that the lack of a federal fiscal capacity and the binding restrictions on national governments' fiscal policy would bias the EMU towards low growth and persistently high unemployment, and ultimately ensure that the system was incapable of withstanding a large spending collapse of the type that hit the world economy in 2008. But the Groupthink erected a wall of denial and the European politicians successfully convinced people that by maintaining price discipline, economic growth would be maximised. The GFC exposed how ridiculous that mantra was. But those who dared question the Monetarist supremacy at the time, and instead advocated Keynesian remedies to reduce the entrenched European unemployment, were met with derision from the bulk of the profession who had embraced the new economic theory and its policy implications.

Further, by insisting on economic and monetary union under these terms and then imposing self-defeating austerity onto the nations suffering the most from that dysfunctional design, the European political elites have undermined the long-standing European Project. Germany had successfully reinvented itself as a good European citizen, after its disastrous and criminal behaviour during World War II. But as the perceived 'enforcer' of austerity, Germany is now vilified again: the 'ugly German' has returned. The unelected economic mandarins in Brussels and Frankfurt, aided and abetted by the unaccountable officials from the IMF, now have influence on who remains in political office in some nations (for example, the appointment of Lucas Papademos in Greece). The citizens were initially bullied into accepting the euro and all that went with it by their political leaders and now the same leaders are seen to go cap in hand to the Troika to preserve their hegemony, while imposing untold social and economic hardship on their citizens. Open expressions of racism are proliferating (for example, the 'lazy Greek' narratives). The media and politicians now regularly engage in the language of retribution, with cooperation giving way to hostility, resentment, and a breakdown in the social order.

These tensions expressed themselves at the 2014 European Parliament elections, with the anti-austerity parties at the extremes of the political spectrum enjoying stunning success in several countries. The majority of the Parliament remains pro EU but the shift away from that position at the 2014 poll was monumental. The French press carried headlines like 'séisme', 'éruption volcanique' to express the view that the anti EU vote was a 'political earthquake'. Similar sentiments were expressed in many different languages across the European media. The new leftist party in Spain has driven a wedge into the two main political parties' hold on power and the stunning success of the far right in France tells us that the French people are sick of austerity and the bullies from Brussels, Frankfurt and Washington. The success of anti EU parties in Denmark (Danish People's Party), Britain (UKIP) and Greece (Syriza) are also symptomatic. The right wing parties have also promoted anti-immigration policies, which are becoming increasingly popular. Economic austerity has morphed into a very nasty confection.

The current policy options are thus not working and will not underpin sustained prosperity. Eventually, the European economies will stabilise and start growing again, but the residual damage from the austerity will be massive and span generations. Millions will be poorer and without reasonable opportunities as a result. The neo-liberal political leaders will rejoice and claim success but they won't advertise the low base from which the growth has resumed. The EMU is a flawed system. It has to change and the question that this book addresses is the form that change should take.

Three main options are considered in detail. First, the viability is assessed of establishing a true federation, with a European level fiscal capacity to ensure that total spending in the Eurozone is sufficient to generate enough jobs to satisfy the desire of the workers. Various hybrid schemes that have been proposed by economists in Europe and beyond are considered. However, the differences between the European nations are so great that such a choice is highly unlikely despite the fact that the EMU could function effectively if there was such a capacity.

Second, the proposal known as Overt Monetary Financing (OMF) is advanced. OMF would require the ECB to use its currency issuing capacity to underwrite the fiscal deficits of the Member States in order that they create growth and employment in their domestic economies without encountering the restrictions that private bond markets place on their spending. OMF, erroneously called the 'printing money' option, is universally considered to be taboo among neo-liberals because they wrongly claim it will lead to inflation, and perhaps hyperinflation. Our analysis shows that it can be a very effective way for governments to responsibly manage economic growth without having to issue public debt. OMF is a strategy that could render the EMU workable. It also represents a desirable operational option should the euro be abandoned by one or more nations, in which case the OMF would be facilitated by the newly empowered central banks in the exiting countries.

The third option considered in detail is the so-called exit option. This is the preferred option, since it accords with the historical and cultural realities of Europe. It would be ideal if the Eurozone nations agreed to an orderly dismantling of the common currency and a restoration of the individual currency sovereignty for each nation. In lieu of such an unlikely turn of events, exit remains the superior option for an individual nation such as Greece or Italy, acting unilaterally. In fact, given the size of the Italian economy in relation to the overall Eurozone economy, Italy should demonstrate leadership by finalising a negotiated exit with Brussels that minimises the damage for all parties. This would provide the blueprint for other nations such as Greece, Spain, Portugal and others to follow.

In one sense, the story of this book is black and white. The choice is stark, abandon this neo-liberal nightmare or continue the suffering. An orderly exit with policy choices that stimulate growth rather than entrench stagnation and suffering is a superior route for most European citizens, notwithstanding the substantial costs that would be involved in recreating national currencies. This matches the dichotomous nature of the TINA strategy employed by the neo-liberals: that the euro is the salvation and is irrevocable, and that abandoning it would be catastrophic. There are no nuances to the TINA approach.

The book is in three parts. Part I provides a detailed critique of the historical decisions that led up to the Maastricht Treaty in 1991 and the decision to introduce the single currency. This decision had very little economic basis and was largely driven by the French desire to be a dominant European force interacting with the obsessive fear of inflation among German policy makers. This dysfunctional Franco-German dynamic took a turn for the worse when it intersected with the resurgent neo-liberal economic ideology in the late 1980s. The Treaty of Maastricht was a direct result of this combination of factors.

Part II examines the period after the inception of the common currency up to the crisis. Despite the claims by the political leaders that the introduction of the euro had been a great success, the preconditions for the crisis were being put in place. The attack by Germany on workers' capacity to enjoy real wages growth, and their mercantile obsession with increasing export surpluses, created dangerous imbalances in other parts of Europe, which would intensify the crisis once started. But the crisis could have been minimised and a speedy return to growth guaranteed if the Stability and Growth Pact (SGP), an essential part of the neo-liberal attack on the capacity of governments to pursue responsible spending policies in the face of external shocks, had not been enforced. The ECB could have used its currency issuing capacity to ensure the Member States did not run foul of private bond markets. The ECB's reluctance to act responsibly ensured that the private debt crisis became a public debt crisis.

Part III provides a detailed analysis of the options outlined above. It is clear that there are two realities that have to be addressed. The first relates to the intrinsic politics of Europe, which is exemplified by the decades-long Franco-German rivalry. The second relates to the stranglehold that the neo-liberal economists have on the policy debate. The exit proposal is consistent with the first reality: breaking the economic union will help restore the effectiveness of the political aspects of the 'European Project'. There is no suggestion that the European Union needs to be dismantled to jettison the euro. Whether the Union is functional is a separate discussion, which is outside the ambit of this book. But for exit to be a superior option, governments need to abandon their neo-liberal pretensions and more fully understand the opportunities that they have when they restore their own currencies, float them on international currency markets, and re-establish their own central banks with the capacity to set their own interest rates.

There is a detailed discussion debunking the neo-liberal myths that have constructed austerity as the only alternative. That part of the narrative provides the reader with an adventure into a new way of thinking about economics, one that requires the economics profession to realise that the current economics 'paradigm' has failed and needs to be replaced. That task alone will be massively resisted by the entrenched interests that derive their power from maintenance of the economics status quo, no matter how disastrous it has been for the ordinary citizens.

At the moment, Europe is trapped in a destructive neo-liberal Groupthink, which represents denial on a grand scale.

A major jail break is required to restore prosperity and hope.

PART I

The Early Years

2. Early attempts at monetary union and the Hague Summit

EARLY ATTEMPTS AT EUROPEAN MONETARY UNION

The idea of a common currency in Europe or parts of Europe has long been entertained. In the 19th century, when Europe was undergoing the unification of states, the introduction of a common currency was seen as an essential element of nationhood. Germany united its states in 1834 and formed the German Customs Union (or Zollverein) with a common currency, the Vereinsmunze. In 1876, the Reichsmark became the national currency, once the German Reichsbank took control of all currency issuance (Holtferich, 1993). Similarly, the Italian unification of 1861 was also accompanied by the acceptance of the lira by all states.

Other common currency arrangements formed in Europe in the 19th century collapsed. Upon attaining independence in 1830, Belgium adopted the French franc, which formed the 'franc zone'. In 1848, France and Belgium formed the Latin Monetary Union (LMU) with Switzerland. Italy joined in 1861 with Greece and Bulgaria joining in 1867. In terms of our quest to understand modern developments, the motivation for the formation of the LMU came from France, which was concerned about its declining colonial power and loss of economic power (see Flandreau 1995, 2000; Einaudi 2000; Flandreau and Maurel, 2005).

The LMU was a bi-metallic (gold and silver) currency arrangement with each nation retaining its own currency (gold and silver coins), which were exchanged at parity across the union (apart from a small transaction charge). The respective central banks guaranteed convertibility of gold and silver into minted coins at the fixed parity. When silver lost value, the central banks suspended convertibility. The onset of World War I saw the gold standard abandoned as governments started funding their war spending by selling their gold stocks, which drove the gold price down. This finally brought the system to an end after years of dysfunction. It was formally abandoned in 1926.

A similar, multinational currency experiment was formed in 1873 when the Scandinavian Currency Union (SCU) was established between

Sweden and Denmark, with Norway joining two years later. It was a monetary union based on gold where each nation 'introduced the decimal system and adopted a common unit of currency', the Scandinavian krona (Bergman, 1999: 365). The currencies of the member nations (gold coins and other silver and bronze tokens) were fixed against the price of gold and would remain freely exchangeable at parity for a period of eight years, whereupon the common currency unit would prevail (Bergman, 1999; Bergman et al., 1993; Henrikson and Kaergard, 1995). Political developments undermined the system. For example, when Norway broke with Sweden in 1905, the Swedes limited convertibility. But, as with the LMU, the monetary instability associated with the onset of World War I was the last straw. The formal arrangement was terminated in 1921. Bordo and Jonung (2003) document other unsuccessful attempts at establishing monetary unions in Europe in the 19th century.

What lessons do we learn which help us understand the options for Europe in 2014? First, the adoption of a common currency by previously separate states can be successful if it is part of a national unification. It is important to note that the formerly independent states that agreed to unify had quite diverse economic structures (types of industry, sources of employment) and considerable income disparities. The formerly independent states also had distinct cultural differences. So we cannot conclude that cultural homogeneity or major economic disparities undermine the possible success of a currency union. The common element is that these previously independent states agreed, politically, to forego their differences and create a single national state, which then established, among other things, national economic policy machinery that would work to improve the prosperity of all citizens in the new nation.

Second, the multilateral arrangements such as the LMU and the SCU failed because there was no political agreement to merge the independent governmental structures into a national entity. Throughout the life of these unions, each government only agreed to participate in the currency union inasmuch as it advanced its own national goals. These conflicting aims were exposed at times of extreme monetary instability (World War I) when the abandonment of the gold standard was clearly a reflection of independent national interests being exercised.

The idea of a European currency was revived in 1929 when the German Foreign Minister, Gustav Stresemann, who had worked assiduously in the inter-war period to reconcile Germany and France, petitioned the League of Nations on 9 September 1929 with the following question, 'Where are the European currency and the European stamp that we need?' (European Commission, 2012a). The New York Stock Exchange collapsed on Black

Friday just six weeks later, which put paid to any idea of international currency cooperation in Europe for the indefinite future.

Of significance though for understanding the current state of play, you will note that Stresemann saw the need to bring France and Germany into a closer economic working relationship, a theme that dominated and motivated discussions in the post World War II period and culminated in the adoption of the euro.

After World War II, the 44 allied nations agreed to return to a type of gold standard because they believed this would bring economic stability. The so-called Bretton Woods system was established in July 1944 and required the central banks of participating nations to maintain their currencies at agreed fixed rates against the US dollar. The newly created International Monetary Fund (IMF) was empowered (with contributions from the member states) to offer short-term funding to any nations that could not earn sufficient foreign currency reserves via trade to maintain the agreed exchange rate parities. The US government, in turn, agreed to convert US dollars into gold at a fixed price.

THE BRETTON WOODS EXCHANGE RATE SYSTEM AND THE BARRE REPORT

After the Treaty of Rome 1957, which established the European Economic Community (EEC), there was regular discussion about the need for closer economic cooperation between the Member States. In February 1969, the so-called Barre Report reaffirmed the European preference for fixed exchange rates and a move to a common monetary policy (Barre Report, 1969). The Europeans were concerned about developments in world currency markets and the depletion of US gold reserves, in the context of the commitment by the US government under Bretton Woods to guarantee US dollar convertibility into gold. During the 1960s, a large quantity of gold reserves shifted from the US to Europe as a result of persistent US balance of payments deficits.

The use of the US dollar as a reserve currency exposed the instability of the Bretton Woods system. The economist Robert Triffin warned in the early 1960s that the system required the US to run balance of payments deficits so that other nations, who used the US dollar as the dominant currency in international transactions, were able to acquire them. In the 1950s, there had been an international shortage of US dollars available as nations recovered from the war and trade expanded. But in the 1960s, the situation changed. Nations started to worry about the value of their growing US dollar reserve holdings and whether the US would continue to maintain gold convertibility. These fears led nations to increasingly exercise their right to convert their US dollar holdings into gold, which significantly reduced the stock of US-held gold reserves. The so-called Triffin paradox was that the Bretton Woods system required the expansion of US dollars into world markets, which also undermined confidence in the dollar's value and led to increased demands for convertibility back into gold. The loss of gold reserves further reinforced the view that the US dollar was overvalued and, eventually, the system would come unstuck (Triffin, 1960).

The way out of the dilemma was for the US to raise its interest rates and attract the dollars back into investments in US denominated financial assets. But this would push the US economy into recession, which was politically unpalatable. It was also increasingly inconsistent with other domestic developments (the War on Poverty) and the US foreign policy obsession with fighting communism, which was exemplified by the build up of NATO installations in Western Europe and the prosecution of the Vietnam War. The US spending associated with the Vietnam War had overheated the domestic US economy and expanded US dollar liquidity in the world markets further. The resulting inflation was then transmitted through the fixed exchange system to Europe and beyond because the increased trade deficits in the US became stimulatory trade surpluses in other nations. These other nations could not run an independent monetary policy because their central banks had to maintain the exchange parities under the Bretton Woods agreement.

It is important to note that the US balance of payments deficits were also a reflection of choices made by other nations. In the growth period after World War II, other nations demonstrated a strong desire to accumulate US dollar reserves, which required them to run external trade surpluses against the US.

THE POST WORLD WAR II 'EUROPEAN PROJECT'

In the immediate post World War II period, the 'European Project' was devised as an ambitious plan for European integration. The 'European Project' was largely about detente after two very fracturing wars and lots of smaller disputes in the 20th century. It was thought that by creating a political union, the historical enmities would fade and cordial relations could be fostered. It was an extension of the logic that led to the Entente Cordiale in 1904 between the French and British, which ended their long history of military conflicts.

It was logical that the EU would also seek to harmonise certain economic parameters as a way of working together for the betterment of all. Thus during the early post World War II period, the sense of deep antagonism towards the Germans was actively discouraged as Germany grew out of the wreckage that it had wrought on itself and the rest of Europe to become a strong economy. A major impetus to the growth in Europe was the Marshall Plan, which provided a substantial fiscal injection into the European economies from the US. While the overall contribution of the Marshall Plan has been debated for decades, there is a broadly held view that it helped to kick-start the European economy, which was floundering with ravaged infrastructure, low rates of investment, major food and other shortages, and a general air of pessimism. The Marshall Plan was also an early part of the plan for European integration in that it removed trade barriers within Europe and established European level institutional structures to facilitate the socio-economic recovery. It is interesting to note that if the current fiscal austerity mentality and obsession with fiscal rules had prevailed in the immediate post World War II period, the Marshall Plan would have been impossible and Europe would have wallowed in the stagnant growth, high unemployment and food shortages that marked the late 1940s.

The first significant achievement of the newly formed EEC was the Common Agricultural Policy (CAP), which was introduced in 1962 and constituted a major step towards the goal of integration. The policy removed tariffs on agricultural products and introduced common prices, although this took some time to achieve given the parochial resistance of rural communities in the participating nations. At the heart of the policy design were the competing interests of France, which wanted to protect its farmers, and Germany, which wanted to expand its industrial export market. The CAP, more or less, provided for a German subsidy to French farmers, which was the compromise required for each nation to achieve its domestic political needs.

While the CAP embodied these political tensions, it also relied on the Bretton Woods fixed exchange rates for administrative ease given the multitude of agricultural prices that had to be supported across the Community. The CAP could not function effectively with sudden or significant fluctuations in the currency values of the Member States. The uncertainty with the Bretton Woods system in the 1960s accelerated the idea that a common currency within the Community was necessary.

Conservatives long to return to gold standard type monetary systems, but the reality was that the Bretton Woods system functioned poorly. After full convertibility between the US dollar and gold was finally achieved in 1959, it went downhill from then onwards as the Triffin paradox became clear to all. There were various ad hoc efforts, the specifics of which do not concern us here, to avoid the inevitable collapse of the system (for example, the rise of currency swaps between central banks). None of these band-aid measures could, however, eliminate the intrinsic contradictions of the system.

THE BRITISH DEVALUATION

Some events stand out in the 1960s, which are highly relevant to our current task. The first major event was the UK devaluation against the US dollar in November 1967 by 14.3 per cent to $2.40. The British government had struggled throughout the 1960s to maintain the pound at $2.80 in the face of ongoing trade deficits. 1967 was a year of world economic crisis, the largest since 1949. Cost pressures were rising and translating into persistent inflation in many nations. In 1966 and into 1967, Britain ran very large balance of payments deficits and there was a substantial associated loss of foreign currency reserves as the Bank of England intervened to maintain the exchange rate. British industry was also less able to exploit the growing export markets relative to the more competitive French and German economies.

Confidence in sterling plummeted. A government spending contraction, accompanied by a wage and prices freeze in mid 1966, led to a decline in imports and an improving trade position. There was a slight slowdown overall and unemployment edged up. This provided temporary respite from the speculative pressures on the pound, which was also strengthened by interest rate cuts in the US and Europe, which encouraged net capital inflows into Britain in search of higher yields. Britain used this windfall to repay various international debts, including reducing its outstanding debts to the IMF.

The calm was short lived. The first disruption came on 5 June 1967, when the Six Day War between the Arab States (United Arab Republic, Jordan and Syria) and Israel broke out after Israeli military aggression (air strikes into Egypt). The war impeded British exports, increased the cost of oil and saw a sterling sell off. Second, the US increased interest rates to quell its credit boom and this boosted the value of the dollar as funds flowed into the US in search of the higher interest returns. Third, Europe entered recession, which further damaged UK exports, and its trade account moved deeper into deficit. The loss of export revenue also led to rising British unemployment and plunged Britain into a policy quandary.

The pound was under pressure from the increasing external deficit and net capital outflow, which would normally have led to some domestic policy contraction given the fixed exchange rate. But with a recession looming, the British government needed to bolster domestic demand. It opted to avoid the political cost of further rises in unemployment and the Bank of England cut interest rates, while the Treasury expanded its spending, which pushed the trade deficit up. The Wilson government also imposed capital controls to stem the outflow of pounds with limited success.

There was considerable debate as to whether the British government was committed to maintaining currency stability given these expansionary domestic policy interventions. Additionally, despite initial wage restraint in 1967 on the back of the 1965–66 wage freeze, wages growth was rapid in the latter part of 1967 and outstripped productivity growth, thereby undermining Britain's international competitiveness. This was exacerbated by industrial unrest on the waterfront (in May 1966 and again in September 1967), which further constrained Britain's exports.

The British government had to face the reality that to defend the mounting pressure on the pound it would have to invoke a harsh recession and drive unemployment up further. The stop-go growth pattern of the 1960s, which was typical for nations running trade deficits under the Bretton Woods system, had come firmly up against the political constraints. This conflict between economics and politics is one of the major reasons fixed exchange rate systems fail and clearly has relevance for the EMU.

The British government also knew that earlier efforts in the 1960s to deal with a weak balance of payments situation had resulted in lost national income but didn't really solve the underlying problem. It was obvious that the pound was overvalued and, try as they might to preserve that value for reasons of national prestige, it had to be devalued. That occurred on 18 November 1967.

This was the first rather significant nail in the Bretton Woods coffin and reflected the tensions that had been building up throughout the decade. The British devaluation created a massive surge in demand for gold as speculators anticipated that the US would also devalue the dollar. The strain on US gold reserves was reaching a crisis point and foreign exchange markets were behaving nervously (Toniolo, 2005). The continued weakness of the pound was mirrored across the Channel in the growing strength of the German mark as its industrial might created ongoing trade surpluses.

FRENCH CIVIL UNREST CAUSES PROBLEMS IN EXCHANGE RATE PARITY

The second major event that precipitated the end of the Bretton Woods system began in May 1968 when the French franc came under extreme pressure as a result of the civil unrest led by the student strike. Investors quickly moved funds from France to Germany, which undermined the capacity of their central banks to maintain the agreed exchange rate parities. The Bundesbank responded by dropping interest rates to encourage capital outflow. Further, and interesting in the context of today's malaise and associated narratives in Europe, the Bundesbank also purchased significant volumes of German government bonds to ensure their yields were low, thus further encouraging investors to sell marks in the foreign exchange markets and reduce the need for any revaluation (BIS, 1969: 10).

THE UNDERVALUED MARK

The speculation about the mark continued throughout the second half of 1968 as German competitiveness continued to rise as a result of its relatively low inflation (particularly against the US which was trying to absorb its Vietnam expenditure). To quell the growing rumours that the mark would be revalued, the Bundesbank facilitated rather large purchases of US dollars over a very short period in September 1968. This action was repeated in November and, while the Bundesbank's foreign reserves soared, the speculation continued. Everyone believed the mark was grossly undervalued. The bank also feared that inflation would result from its foreign exchange market purchases because they involved pushing more marks into the system in exchange for other currencies.

The three related circumstances: the belief that the mark was undervalued; the ongoing trade deficits in Britain and the capital outflows; and internal strife in France, caused what the Bundesbank called 'an exceptional surge of international speculation' (Bundesbank, 1968: 3). This led to the closure of foreign exchange markets on 21 and 22 November, a sign that the international monetary system was incapable of dealing with the situation.

Just before the closure, the Bank of International Settlements (BIS), the central bank of the central banks, held its normal meeting in Basel on 17–18 November 1968, and negotiations led to an agreement among the German and French central banks that they would ask 'their respective government for a simultaneous 5% revaluation of the mark and 5% devaluation of the French franc' (Toniolo, 2005: 427). The German government refused to revalue because they believed their economy would continue to strengthen (leading to rising imports) and argued that the French, UK and US governments would have to rein in the inflationary surge with restrictive policy (leading to a decline in imports). They considered that these changes would reduce the pressure on the mark as the trade surplus fell. Their view was that an irreversible realignment of the mark would 'have posed a severe budget problem for the government because of the large increase in support to agriculture that would have been required' (BIS, 1969: 11). Once again the macroeconomic policy debate was closely related to the implications of fluctuating exchange rates for the viability of the CAP.

THE FARCICAL 1968 BONN MEETING

As the foreign exchange markets closed, the finance ministers and central bank governors of the Group of Ten nations met in Bonn at the request of the German government. The other nations clearly believed that the topic of the discussion was to be the revaluation of the mark and the devaluation of the French franc. They were wrong. On 20 November 1968, the day before the scheduled meeting in Bonn, the German government unilaterally introduced a series of contractionary policies, in lieu of a formal revaluation, which were described by the Bundesbank (1968: 3) as a 'resort to de facto revaluation'. These included trade duties (except for agricultural produce) and other credit restraints on the banks.

The meeting itself has been described as a farce (see Tonioli, 2005: Capie, 2010). There was the 'petty, mischief-making, and garrulous' chair overseeing the meeting who set up conflict between the central bankers and the finance ministers (Capie, 2010: 421). Bi-lateral animosities were the norm. The British claimed the meeting had stipulated that Germany would have to revalue. Conflict ensued and the Germans provided 'anti-British' briefings to the press corps (Capie, 2010: 421). The British threatened retaliation in the form of unspecified withdrawal of support for NATO if they were forced to devalue the pound further (Capie, 2010: 420).

Forest Capie (2010: 422) summarised the situation: 'The Bonn meeting of 1968 undoubtedly marked a low point in international monetary affairs in the post war era. And there was little recovery in relationships over the next few years. The unilateral changes in parities in 1969 simply continued the poor feeling that pervaded the atmosphere.'

After the meeting, the French and British governments increased taxes and introduced other policies aimed at reducing imports to avoid having to devalue.

The BIS characterised the international atmosphere in 1969:

> . . . the focus of attention generally was not on output trends but on the feverish atmosphere that characterised the situation. The state of crisis which prevailed at times in the international monetary situation contributed to this atmosphere, though happily, calm had been restored by the beginning of this year. (BIS, 1970: 3)

Curiously, the calm was due to the French and German governments rejecting major currency realignments, which blighted any speculative fever. But it was to be a short-lived break in hostilities. France continued to run an external deficit, thus placing continued downward pressure on its exchange rate, while Germany's external surplus remained large. Taken together, it was clear that the trade fundamentals expressed in the balance of payments were at odds with the fixed currency parities of both nations, the franc was significantly overvalued and the mark undervalued. Further, Britain's currency devaluation in November 1967 had also done little to correct its external deficit.

The resignation of French President De Gaulle in April 1969 led to huge currency outflows from France to Germany as speculators bet on the mark revaluing even though the German government continued to deny the inevitable. The French government was the first to recognise that the market predictions were realistic and on 8 August 1969, it finally devalued the franc against the price of gold by 11.1 per cent.

Across the border, Germany was getting set for a federal election and it was considered unlikely that the new government would resist revaluation. The Bundesbank, facing massive pressures to keep the currency within the agreed limits was buying US dollars in the foreign exchange markets 'on an accelerating scale' (BIS, 1970: 4). They even closed the Frankfurt currency market on the Friday before the election to avoid what is referred to as a 'Black Friday'. Often currency realignments are performed over weekends to minimise the disruption that last minute speculation can cause to the economy and financial system. The foreign currency exchanges remained closed the day after the election in recognition of the massive instability that the fixed exchange rate system was generating.

The pro-revaluation Willy Brandt won the September election, and to manage the transition, in the face of massive currency bets being made on revaluation, the Bundesbank suspended 'its intervention in the foreign exchange market at the former upper and lower limits' (Bundesbank, 1969: 5). This simply meant that they stopped buying US dollars once the mark had reached the upper limit allowed for under the Bretton Woods agreement. This effectively floated the mark, which immediately was revalued by around 5 per cent to DM3.84 per US dollar, on the first day the currency markets reopened. The BIS called this an 'excellent tactical move' (BIS, 1970: 4) because it ensured the speculative inflow of funds to Germany would slow and that it could stop selling marks to defend the indefensible DM4 parity.

The official statement at the time indicated the German government was intending 'to return to a fixed parity for the mark within a short time, even though this is unlikely to be the old parity, still legally in force, of one dollar to four marks' (Bundesbank, 1969: 6). This suspension of official Bundesbank intervention was contrary to the IMF Articles of Agreement, but the Fund tolerated it because it was the only way to restore stability in the international monetary system. A new parity was established on 27 October 1969, some 9.3 per cent above the previous fixed parity, and Germany resumed its place in the system. But that would not last for much longer.

Interestingly, the revaluation by the German government was heavily criticised by the Bavarian farmers. Under the CAP, all agricultural prices were paid in US dollars and the revaluation meant that German farm output became more expensive to outsiders. The strength of the agricultural lobby and, particularly, the political support that the Bavarian farmers gave to the Finance Minister in the conservative CDU/CSU alliance Franz Josef Strauss had been a principle reason why the German government had refused to revalue prior to the election. The new government was also sensitive to the power of this lobby and sought a special deal with the EEC, whereby the previous domestic price level would be maintained for farm output despite the lower rates for foreign currencies. The EEC agreed, under German pressure, 'to sanction the levying of a compensatory surcharge equivalent to the degree of appreciation of the Deutsche Mark on imports of those agricultural products' that were part of the EEC common market (Bundesbank, 1969: 6).

The tolerance of the IMF and the relaxation of the EEC rules for German farm output were all signs that the design of the monetary system was at odds with the reality of the situation. One could say the same thing about the way the authorities in Europe act in relation to the euro. Rules are continually relaxed or amended to meet whatever financial emergency arises as a result of the intrinsically unworkable system.

THE 1969 HAGUE SUMMIT

On 2 December 1969, the Heads of State or Government of the Member States convened at The Hague in the 13th-century Ridderzaal (Hall of Knights) for a summit. The gathering was not a response to the currency turmoil but was influenced by it. The main agenda driving the summit was the vexed issue of Community enlargement, in particular Britain's inclusion, which could not be accomplished while De Gaulle had remained President of France. The Dutch and German members were keen for enlargement. There were three main perspectives surrounding their preference, which bear on our discussion of the development of the common currency. First, the inclusion of Britain would open markets for Dutch and German exports. Second, the relative instability of the British pound would require progress to increased monetary cooperation once Britain joined the Community. Third, a Community that included Britain would give Europe increased power in world financial markets and redress the growing concern that the US was too dominant. But this latter view was almost in denial of the fact that the Bretton Woods system required a dominant America to run continuous external deficits. Remember the Triffin Paradox!

Politics and the CAP were at the core of the enlargement debate. The Dutch Prime Minister Piet de Jong summarised the tension in Europe during a Cabinet meeting on Friday, 27 October 1967. In relation to the inclusion of Britain, he said that he was not:

> . . . justified in leading the Netherlands towards a European satellite state under the French, and after the death of President De Gaulle, under German hegemony. History teaches us that democratic principles under either French or German hegemony are not in safe hands. The accession of Great Britain and the Scandinavian countries, especially for the preservation of democracy in Europe, is of the greatest importance. (Notulen Ministerraad, 1967: 10–11; see also van der Harst, 2003, for more discussion of the Dutch attitude leading up to the 1969 summit)

The summit came at the end of a decade when the European Project had floundered. The tensions had been clear throughout the 1960s and were exemplified by the French promotion in 1961 of the Fouchet Plan, which would have replaced the emerging supranational European institutions with a system of intergovernmental bodies to run Europe and be dominated by France. The proposed 'Union of States' was also motivated by President de Gaulle's increasing hostility towards US involvement in European affairs under the Atlantic alliance (NATO). The tensions increased as France twice rejected Britain's applications to join the Community (because they feared Britain would undermine the CAP). The situation worsened in 1965 with the stand off concerning funding for the CAP among other matters, which became known as the Empty Chair Crisis, where France effectively boycotted the Commission. This crisis in turn led to the Luxembourg Compromise, which entrenched the torturous political processes that still prevent speedy progress being made in current day Europe. France clearly wanted to become the most powerful nation within the Community, if not the world, and to keep Germany and the US in check.

There was the famous private conversation between De Gaulle and the French government minister Alain Peyrefitte on 22 August 1962 about the Fouchet Plan (Soutou, 1996: 131):

> 'What is the point of a Europe?' he confided to Alain Peyrefitte on August 22nd 1962. 'It should serve to prevent us from being dominated by America or Russia . . . France could be the strongest of the six members. We could control this lever of Archimedes. We could carry away the others. Europe represents the first opportunity France has to regain what she lost at Waterloo: world dominance.'

The 1969 Hague summit was held at the end of this less than optimistic decade for European integration at the initiation of Georges Pompidou, who replaced De Gaulle in April 1969. On 6 June 1969, Pompidou enunciated his plans at Mülhausen for 'continuite et overture' during the French presidential campaign. In trying to distance himself from De Gaulle's European hostility, Pompidou stated that he wanted the EEC political leaders to develop a common market with financial integration, to more closely cooperate on economic matters, and to enlarge the membership to include Britain, Ireland, Denmark and Norway. What he really wanted to ensure was that the very favourable system of cross subsidy under the CAP would continue. It is moot that he wanted Britain and the other nations to complicate French designs for supremacy in Europe. The CAP was a source of tension for Germany, which predominantly funded 'the Community's surplus production' of agricultural output (Hiepel, 2003: 65; see also European Commission, 1974 for a breakdown of the contributions and reimbursements under the European Agricultural Guidance and Guarantee Fund, which demonstrates the advantages France gained under the policy).

Pompidou's Statement to the Hague summit prioritised the issues of 'price disturbances caused by parity changes jeopardizing the future of the common market in agriculture' and 'the growing burden of farm surpluses' (European Commission, 1970c: 33). He later said that in terms of enlargement 'Now is the time . . . to discuss it without preconceived ideas but without giving anything away' (European Commission, 1970c: 34). By way of contrast, Brandt's Statement noted that the central issue was the 'enlargement of the Community'.

While there were complex and, at times, conflicting political agendas underpinning each nation's motivations for participating at the summit, Pompidou's willingness to abandon the long-standing French veto on the issue of enlargement was matched by Brandt's signals that Germany would allow the concept of a joint monetary policy to be put on the agenda. Germany had long opposed the idea of monetary integration unless the other countries agreed to follow the policy set by the Bundesbank, which prioritised a low and stable inflation rate. We should, however, not overstate the willingness of Pompidou to accept enlargement. A more realistic account is that he was 'persuaded' by

Brandt's 'skilful mixture of demands and concessions' (Hiepel, 2003: 63) to accept enlargement as a necessary evil to further his agricultural policy designs.

Marie-Thérèse Bitsch (2007: 165) called the Hague summit the 'nouveau Messine' referring to the 1955 Messina Conference in Italy, which saw the members of the European Coal and Steel Community (ECSC) commit to creating the European Economic Community (EEC). After a series of studies and reports, which informed the Treaty of Rome, the EEC was formed in 1958. The concept of integration was centre stage at Messina and manifested in the agreement to create a customs union. Bitsch also considered the Hague summit was the 'beginning of the revival of the integration process'. While the final outcome of the summit could support that conclusion, the story is more complex.

It is clear that the summit did not introduce the idea of European integration. That had been part of the European Project since recovery began after World War II. In 1968, key long-term decisions were taken about the funding of the CAP and the operations of the customs union (Moravcsik, 1998; van der Harst, 2003). But the idea of an economic and monetary union (common currency) was seriously advanced for the first time at the Hague summit conference. While the Final Communiqué is silent, the summit's supporting documents reveal that the push for the creation of an economic and monetary union came surprisingly from the newly elected Brandt, who in Pompidou had found a much more pragmatic French leader to deal with. The summit also agreed to admit Britain, which signalled a clear ambition for enlargement (Allers, 2013).

But, in order to understand why Europe is where it is now it is important to recognise the way in which intergovernmental arrangements were largely eschewed as the way forward in favour of supranational institutions. The tensions between the Commission bureaucrats and the politicians representing national interests were clear (Ludlow, 2003). The very fact that Germany and France had realigned their exchange rates without consulting Brussels was an illustration of who was running the agenda. The Commission clearly wanted to make itself the institutional hub of the integrated Europe (see Ludlow, 2003).

The Final Communiqué of the summit (European Council, 1970) spoke of the Community arriving at 'a turning point in history' and the 'irreversible nature of the work' towards a 'united Europe'. It talked about the 'completion of the Communities' which as a 'final stage' would 'lay down a definitive financial arrangement for the common agricultural policy by the end of 1969'. As an integral part of this financial arrangement, the Communiqué said that 'a plan in stages should be worked out during

1970 with a view to the creation of an economic and monetary union. The development of monetary co-operation should depend on the harmonisation of economic policies.'

They agreed to investigate the possibility of setting up a European reserve fund, which would lead to a joint economic and monetary policy.

3. The Werner Report and the collapse of Bretton Woods

THE WERNER REPORT

The follow up meeting of the Council of Ministers of the Six Member States in Paris on 6 March 1970 placed the creation of an economic and monetary union at the top of their agenda. This meeting formalised the rather vague statements in the Final Communiqué of the Hague summit about union by appointing an expert group under the direction of the Prime Minister of Luxembourg, Pierre Werner, which would flesh out the details of how this union would be achieved.

The so-called Werner Plan was submitted to the Commission as an interim report on 20 May 1970 with the Final Report (Werner Report, 1970) presented on 13 October 1970. It outlined a comprehensive timetable for the creation of a full economic and monetary union by the end of the decade. The Council of Ministers formally endorsed Werner's three-stage implementation plan on 22 March 1971. Willy Brandt told the Bundestag on 6 November 1970 that the Werner proposal was the 'great common task of the 1970s' and that it represented a 'new Magna Carta for the Community' (Deutscher Bundestag, 1970: 4269).

The main features of the Werner Plan are worth dwelling on. The aim was 'to determine the elements that are indispensable to the existence of a complete economic and monetary union' (Werner Report, 1970: 9). These elements constituted the 'minimum that must be done' and included:

> . . . the total and irreversible convertibility of currencies, the elimination of margins of fluctuation in exchange rates, the irrevocable fixing of parity rates and the complete liberation of movements of capital. It may be accompanied by the maintenance of national monetary symbols or the establishment of a sole Community currency. (p. 10)

Significantly, the Report said:

> . . . only the global balance of payments of the Community vis à vis the outside world is of any importance. Equilibrium within the Community would be

> realized at this stage in the same way as within a nation's frontiers, thanks to the mobility of the factors of production and financial transfers by the public and private sectors. (p. 10)

The conceptualisation of the newly created economic and monetary union as a new 'nation' where the member countries effectively become states of a federation was clearly thought elemental. That conceptualisation did not emerge until around two decades later in the Treaty of Maastricht.

The Report considered short-term economic policy would be 'decided in its broad outlines at a Community level' and that the 'principal decisions of monetary policy should be centralized' (p. 10). The Report was in keeping with the times where fiscal policy, that is, government spending and taxation decisions, was given a higher priority than monetary policy, which involved interest rate setting. The Report was clear that national budgets would not be responsible for addressing asymmetric development (p. 11).

There was an extremely powerful statement in the Report (pp. 12–13), which echoes today:

> The centre of decision for economic policy will exercise independently, in accordance with the Community interest, a decisive influence over the general economic policy of the Community. In view of the fact that the role of the Community budget as an economic instrument will be insufficient, the Community's centre of decision must be in a position to influence the national budgets, especially as regards the level and the direction of the balances and the methods for financing the deficits or utilizing the surpluses.

In summary, the Werner Report concluded that an effective economic and monetary union would require, among other elements (p. 12):

- the creation of liquidity throughout the area and monetary and credit policy will be centralized . . . ;
- monetary policy in relation to the outside world will be within the jurisdiction of the Community;
- the policies of the Member States as regards the capital market will be unified;
- the essential features of the whole of the public budgets, and in particular variations in their volume, the size of balances and the methods of financing or utilizing them, will be decided at the Community level . . .

Of further importance, it was emphasised that the 'transfer to the Community level of the powers exercised hitherto by national authorities will go hand-in-hand with the transfer of a corresponding Parliamentary responsibility from the national plane to that of the Community. The centre of decision of economic policy will be politically responsible to a European Parliament' (p. 13). The Parliament would be elected on the basis of universal suffrage thereby recognising that economic policy should be democratically determined and those responsible for the policy should be held accountable to the will of the people. There was no hint that this level of intervention would be the domain of officials centred in Brussels who would do deals with unaccountable bodies such as the IMF that would result in millions of Europeans being made unemployed, which is the norm in Europe in 2014.

The intent of the Werner Report was that:

- There should be a Community wide central bank, which acts as the lender of last resort and is responsible for regulation and oversight.
- That monetary policy will be centralised.
- That there should be centralised capital market access.
- That the 'federal' fiscal operations – size of deficits, debt issuance etc. – will dominate national and regional budgets, which will be retained to ensure localised initiatives are effective.

These characteristics are present in a number of functioning federations such as Australia, Canada, and the USA.

The EEC Council and the representatives of the Governments of the Member States met on 22 March 1971 to consider the Werner Report and confirmed their political agreement to the ten-year phased plan to establish an economic and monetary union by 1 January 1981. However, a careful comparison of Werner's recommendations and the subsequent official Council resolution (European Commission, 1971) reveals a major omission in the latter (see Vedel, 1972).

On 22 July 1971, the European federalist Georges Vedel, a French constitutional lawyer, was appointed by the European Commission to chair an 'ad hoc Working Party of independent experts to examine the whole corpus of problems connected with the enlargement of the powers of the European Parliament' (Vedel, 1972: 7). They tendered their report to the European Parliament on 25 March 1972.

As part of their enquiry they considered the political will of the Community to create a full economic and monetary union; the initiative, they concluded, had come from the 'Governments themselves' (Vedel, 1972: 16) at the 1969 Hague summit, so could not be conceived as a move by Brussels for more supranational power.

Vedel (1972: 18) noted:

> The resolution does not, incidentally, refer to certain institutional proposals in the Report, one of which was that there should be set up a 'centre of decision for economic policy' to 'exercise independently, in accordance with the Community interest, a decisive influence over the general economic policy of the Community'. Concerning the European Parliament, the Werner Report added: 'The centre of decision for economic policy will be politically responsible to a European Parliament. The latter will have to have a status corresponding to the extension of the Community's tasks, not only from the point of view of the extent of its powers, but also having regard to the method of election of its members.'

The European Parliament's own resolution (European Commission, 1970b) had expressed support for the outline presented in the Werner Report but emphasised that democratic control of the transfer of powers from member states to the federal level required strengthening the powers of the European Parliament (see also Vedel, 1972: 8).

THE 'MONETARIST-ECONOMIST' (FRANCO-GERMAN) STRUGGLE

The differing reactions from France and Germany to the Werner Report were conditioned by the stark differences between their approaches to economic policy, which reflected the historical and cultural development of each nation and its role in Europe in early parts of the 20th century. Their respective responses to the Werner Report echoed the way each nation approached the Treaty of Rome deliberations in the late 1940s, which eventually saw the creation of the European Coal and Steel Community, the precursor to modern Europe. The 'two contrasting ways of thinking' (Danescu, 2013a: 2) remain today and the shortcomings of the EMU reflect, in part, the compromises that were required to accommodate these two rather opposing perspectives.

The clash of views was popularly known as the 'economists v. monetarists'. The latter were led by France and joined by nations with typically weak currencies and external deficits, while the former were led by Germany and joined by nations with similar trading and currency strength (Danescu, 2013a; Howarth and Loedel, 2003). The dichotomised typology along national lines is a simplification because within, say, France and Italy, there were political forces reflecting both ways of thinking, each with demonstrated influence on the overall shape of the resulting monetary union. But the dichotomy works as a simple framework to understand basic dynamics that have dominated the move to monetary union. We should note that the term 'monetarist' in this context is quite different to the more common usage associated with the free market economics of 'Monetarism', which rose to international dominance in the late 1970s under the championship of Margaret Thatcher. We consider the role of Monetarism in Chapter 5.

The differences among policy makers in Germany and France reflected 'fundamental characteristics of their history and society' (Maes, 2002: 2). The French attitude to the Werner Report and integration, in general, was conditioned by 'la tradition républicaine', which emerged after the French Revolution had disposed of the monarchy. The strong secular state that was created assumed a central role in economic management from education and training through to final production and sale. State elite institutions (the 'Grandes Ecoles') were formed, and provided the private sector with cadres trained in the tradition that politics rather than the market would drive economic policy. Similarly, the powerful State Planning Office exercised control over industrial policy (starting with 'Le Plan' under Jean Monnet 1947–53).

The French embrace of the creation of European level institutions was more about ensuring Germany would never again go to war with them than any grand desire for a supranational entity. In 1950, the Planning Office, under Monnet's directorship, published the final draft of the proposal to establish the European Coal and Steel Community (French Planning Office, 1950). The draft said, 'The French government proposes immediate action on one limited but decisive point'. The reference to a limited step was significant. The proposal indicated that the 'solidarity in production thus established will make it plain that any war between France and Germany becomes not merely unthinkable, but materially impossible'.

Keynesians dominated the French Planning Office and prioritised domestic objectives (such as full employment and a high wage economy), which meant they would allow the exchange rate to adjust (through devaluation) if international competitiveness became an issue. But the 'powerful Finance Ministry' was more pragmatic and supported policies that delivered 'a strong French franc, wage moderation and sound public finances' (Maes, 2002: 4). They were more in line with the German thinking on these matters. The tension between these two approaches within France played out in the post World War II period in several ways. In periods when 'la tradition républicaine' dominated French politics, there was hostility towards the relinquishment of power to the supranational level and willingness to establish intergovernmental institutions to advance a sense of Europe. The more pragmatic approach, however, was pro Europe and sympathetic to the creation of supranational institutions (Maes, 2002: 4). The fact that France participated in the 'currency snake' in 1972, then joined the European Monetary System (EMS) in 1979, and ended up supporting the Delors Plan to create the EMU is evidence that the pragmatists ultimately held sway in France. But these decisions were not without compromises aimed at assuaging the tension between the rival approaches to economic policy.

In relation to the Werner Report, the French Keynesians (the 'monetarists') wanted a single currency and a European central bank established as the first step towards an economic and monetary union. They would then support a transition period established to achieve convergence in fiscal and industrial policy (Tsoukalis 1977; Howarth and Loedel, 2003). But they were implacably opposed to the loss of sovereignty that would accompany the full implementation of Werner's recommendations.

The French media expressed alarm when the Werner Report was released. On 18 October 1970, ten days after its presentation in Luxembourg, the conservative French daily *Le Figaro* carried headlines such as 'Les yeux ouverts' ('Eyes wide open') and warned its readership that this:

> . . . is a fundamental change of direction, which no one can decide apart from the President of the Republic . . . We insist on no decision being taken on this issue without a clear debate involving public opinion . . . Only with its eyes wide open may France decide what sacrifices it is prepared to take and what losses it must refuse. (Danescu, 2013b: 2)

Somewhat at variance with that view, the centre-left daily *Le Monde* claimed that the financial markets were already global and compromising national sovereignty. It said the real problem would be the risks of inflation arising from the creation of a European reserve currency along the same lines that the US dollar had encountered as the sole reserve currency under Bretton Woods (Danescu, 2013b).

Germany represented the so-called 'economists'. It had a federal tradition and had recoiled from centralisation (after the Nazi period). It did not embrace the broad Keynesian consensus that emerged among advanced nations after the Great Depression. The most influential group in the post World War II period in relation to economic policy making was associated with the so-called Freiburg School (Hagemann, 2000). This group developed two strands of thought, which define modern German approaches to economic and monetary matters. On the one hand, they supported the German free market tradition of Ordoliberalism, which in modern parlance is very much like conventional neo-liberalism and indeed most people simply refer to Ordoliberalism as 'German neo-liberalism'. But, unlike the harsh social views embedded in neo-liberal free market thinking, the Freiburg School supplemented Ordoliberalism with the concept of the Social Market Economy or 'Soziale Marktwirtschaft'.

Ordoliberalism stresses the need for tight monetary policy to ensure price stability and tight fiscal positions. Government industry policy should be directed at enhancing competitiveness by freeing the market. The Ordoliberal tradition began in the 19th century and fused with the events of the 1920s and 1930s in Germany to become a form of 'German Monetarism' (in the Thatcher sense). The Freiburg School further developed the concept during the Second World War years. The Germans were scarred by the hyperinflation of the 1920s and the nationalist socialist era that followed. The Ordoliberals eschewed Keynesianism because they feared it would be inflationary and they wanted to avoid any hints of government intervention (the hangover from the disastrous Nazi period). They also aimed to build a strong private sector driven by investment in traded goods industries. In general, free markets were held out as the optimal way to allocate resources. Thus while other nations were pursuing 'Keynesian full employment' economic policies after World War II, Germany mostly ran tight budgets and maintained growth by keeping the value of the currency low to boost exports. Ironically, they benefited from the Keynesian policies elsewhere that allowed for strong economic growth and strong import demand for German goods and services.

The promotion of the Social Market economy separates the German approach from laissez faire (free market) capitalism. Indeed, the combination of the Social Market economy and Ordoliberalism reflects repugnance towards both unregulated laissez faire and Marxian socialism. Under the Social Market, economic activity should be organised on the basis of free choice and competitiveness, and state intervention is approved as long as it maintains fair competition, ensures the private sector maintains decent working conditions and wages, and provides a social welfare net for those who cannot provide adequately for themselves. The 'social welfare' leanings were heavily influenced by the solidaristic Catholic notion of 'All Souls', which set it apart from the broader social democratic visions of the welfare state. That is, they were saturated with conservative morality rather than with aspirations for social freedom.

In this type of economy, the state sets rules and monitors compliance (Maes, 2002). The Germans did experiment with a more traditional Keynesian approach in the 1960s (for example, the Stability and Growth Law in 1967) but it was always tightly controlled by the all powerful and independent central bank. The emphasis on price stability dominated German macroeconomic policy. While the Bundesbank always dictated the deficit limits, it was not until the OPEC oil price hikes in the early 1970s and the resulting stagflation (simultaneous high inflation and unemployment) that the macroeconomic debate in Germany shifted back towards the Ordoliberal tradition.

In relation to the Werner Report, the 'economists' (Germany and the Netherlands) wanted the process to begin with the convergence in economic policies, including strict fiscal rules about deficits and public debt and then move onto setting up supranational institutions like a European central bank and a common currency. The currency would be the 'finishing touch' (Danescu, 2013a: 2). The Germans trusted decentralised decision making as a result of the success of the independent Bundesbank, which had become, along with the stable mark, an icon in the post World War II German resurgence (Howarth and Loedel, 2003). As long as there were strict rules and compliance procedures in place, the Germans were not opposed to 'European integration and the transfer of sovereignty to supranational European institutions' (Maes, 2002: 8).

The Werner Committee was thus comprised of members who came from different backgrounds and had very different views on what an economic and monetary union would look like, how it would be implemented, how it would function, and what goals it would advance.

The Dutch supported the 'economist' views of the German Finance Minister, Karl Schiller (Danescu, 2013b). The Italians appeared to span both the 'economist' and 'monetarist' camps, and moved over time from a position supporting the retention of the fixed exchange rate system to one of flexible exchange rate advocacy (Verde, 2004). The French, supported by the Belgians, wanted the process to move to establish mechanisms to limit exchange rate movements between the European currencies and ensure there was an adequately supported central fund to ensure the CAP was secured (Danescu, 2013b).

The controversies that persist in the modern debate about the future of the Eurozone were on display as the Werner Committee sought some sort of compromise between the different camps. Even the appointment of Werner himself was an international intrigue that reflected complex dealings between the major players. The Belgians and French wanted their respective nominations to succeed and came up with Werner as a compromise, largely because they thought he would be sympathetic to their monetarist leanings. In the process, the French reneged on a previous Franco-German agreement to recommend a joint chair. The fact that Werner was also the Prime Minister of Luxembourg meant that subtle diplomacy had to be involved to avoid an international incident. The final agreement to appoint Werner was largely 'thanks to Germany – which managed to bypass the double dealing by France and bring the Netherlands on board' (Danescu, 2014a: 5).

At the first meeting in Luxembourg (20 March 1970), 'the main objective was clear and all parties were in agreement on this' but 'determining its exact details gave rise to bitter clashes between the "economists" and the "monetarists"' (Danescu, 2014b: 4). The Germans wanted 'prior convergence of economic policies' whereas the Belgians, French and Italians wanted monetary union before any economic convergence was anticipated. The French clearly were aiming for currency stability and eschewed handing over national sovereignty for fiscal policy (spending and taxation) to a supranational body. The Germans discounted the French position as wanting to 'get access to European reserves which would basically be German reserves' (Danescu, 2013a: 3, quoting Lefèvre, 2002).

The 'intellectual disagreements between monetarists and economists in the Werner Group grew more and more acrimonious' (Danescu, 2014b: 5) at subsequent meetings, which led Pierre Werner to arrange a meeting between the representatives of Belgium, Luxembourg and the Netherlands to try to reach a common Benelux position. That initiative failed because the Dutch 'sided clearly with the German economists' (Danescu, 2014b: 5). They did manage to agree that it would be beneficial to establish a European exchange stabilisation fund to reduce the dependence of the European currencies on the US dollar. This fund would support currencies in trouble and reduce the fluctuations deemed damaging to the effective operation of the CAP.

For important periods of the deliberations, 'no minutes, even summary minutes' (Danescu, 2014b: 8) were made public, not due to 'negligence on the part of the secretariat' but rather because there remained 'profound differences of opinion among the members' of the working party (Danescu, 2104b: 8). There was even dispute about the wording in the Interim Report published on 22 May 1970. The Germans believed the wording was changed to weaken the 'transfers of responsibility' (Danescu, 2014b: 8–9) that would be required for a fully functioning economic and monetary union. As the disagreements continued, Werner held private meetings with Jean Monnet in Paris in early July. There are no documents available, but it is considered 'highly likely that the two men discussed how to exert influence – especially on the Germans and the Dutch – to make sure that the work of the group produced an outcome' (Danescu, 2014b: 14).

The Germans adopted a 'rigid attitude' and were 'not encouraging when it came to finding a compromise solution' (Danescu, 2014b: 16). Werner realised that a European level stabilisation fund could not be established immediately if German support was to be achieved. Further, it was recognised that if there were no 'innovation on the monetary front' (Danescu, 2014b: 16) in the first three years, then proposals for 'harmonising economic and budgetary policies' (Danescu, 2014b: 16), the German position, would fail. The final Report was thus a compromise, and was soon overtaken by the monetary disruption that followed the breakdown of the Bretton Woods system.

The nature of the compromise was 'obtained by opting for the lowest common denominator' (Danescu, 2013a: 4). The Werner Report considered the proposal to be the 'minimum that must be done' (Werner Report, 1970: 9) but chose only to detail the first three-year stage, thus baulking at the difficult decisions. It claimed that it was not 'feasible' to lay down 'a precise and rigid timetable for the whole of the plan by stages' preferring to 'maintain a measure of flexibility' (p. 27). It also maintained faith with the Germans by leaving the 'total and irreversible convertibility of currencies, the elimination of margins of fluctuation in rates of exchange, the irrevocable fixing of parity ratios and the total liberation of movements of capital' (p. 26) as the last act, a decade into the future, without a coherent pathway being defined. Just as ambiguous was the recommendation of a European reserve fund, a major aim of the French. While noting that integration would require new 'links in monetary matters' (p. 29), the Report indicated that the establishment of a European Fund for monetary cooperation as a forerunner of the Community system of central banks 'must be effected as soon as possible' but avoided committing to whether this should be done in the first stage.

Hans Tietmeyer, former Bundesbank President and an original member of the Werner Committee, noted that (2003: 6):

> After the Werner Group had presented its final report it rapidly became evident that precisely this transfer of powers and the emergence of supranational structures were the sticking point for the French. Owing particularly to pressure from the Gaullist parliamentary party, President Pompidou and his government felt obliged to refrain from endorsing a concrete phased plan including a clear definition of the final stage. For the German delegation, on the other hand, any greater curtailment of national and monetary sovereignty without binding definition of the requisite supranational structures was unacceptable.

As a consequence, the joint resolution of the Council of Ministers was adopted in March 1971, which approved general goals for union, chose to defer the 'concrete definition of stages II and III of the phased process' (Tietmeyer, 2003: 7) outlined in the final report.

The Werner proposals were clearly more in line with what the Germans desired and the French knew it. The rivalry within French politics between the republicans who eschewed handing over national sovereignty to European level decision making units and other leading officials (Barre, Marjolin, d'Estaing, and later Delors) who were sympathetic to the German position was played out within the French government. Pompidou faced major opposition within his Gaullist party to the Werner preference for establishing supranational institutions. He had to effectively renegotiate the French position before it went to the Commission for ratification (Tsoukalis, 1989: 108–10). The French, particularly Finance Minister Giscard d'Estaing, wanted the process to produce more exchange rate cooperation to reduce fluctuations against the US dollar, rather than closely coordinated economic policy. The Germans desired to break out of the currency instability by floating the mark. At the time it was facing massive capital inflows, largely from the US as a result of the currency uncertainty, and this was straining its capacity to both maintain economic growth and defend the fixed parity.

Against that background, the French and German leaders (Pompidou and Brandt) met in January 1971 to work out a compromise agreement that could go to the European Council the following month. Gone were any concrete plans to transfer power to any supranational institutions. The French gained some traction by getting Brandt to agree to the creation of the European level reserve fund to reduce exchange rate fluctuations.

On 22 March 1971, the Member States passed a political resolution to accept the proposals that the European Commission had distilled from the Werner Report (Werner Report, 1970), which would establish an economic and monetary union (European Commission, 1971). The Resolution recognised that the union could be achieved over the decade 'provided it has the permanent political support from the governments' and would mean that the 'major economic policy decisions will be taken at the Community level and therefore the necessary powers will be transferred from the national to the Community level'. They were somewhat conditional, however, saying that the final outcome 'may be the adoption of a single currency' which would ensure the exercise would be irreversible (European Commission, 1971: 1). The Resolution noted that an economic and monetary union would require, among other things, that fiscal policy would be determined at the Community level (European Commission, 1971: 2).

While the Werner Report had been somewhat diffident about the establishment of a European level fund to be used to militate against currency instability between the member nations, the Resolution invited the Monetary Committee of the Community and the Committee of Governors of the Central Banks to work towards establishing a European Monetary Cooperation Fund (EMCF), 'possibly' in the first three years of the plan (European Commission, 1971: 4). As it turned out, the Fund would be the only real development that came out of the compromised Werner process.

The rather weak outcome from the Werner process was in France's favour and satisfied its growing dislike for the idea of a common currency. What emerged from this compromise was an agreement to allow the currency fluctuations to 'snake' within a defined band (the 'tunnel'). With growing fears about the stability of the US dollar value and the sustainability of its convertibility into gold, the European leaders were keen to take some initiative to provide more certainty to European trade.

But first, we need to backtrack a little in time.

BRETTON WOODS COLLAPSES AS THE SNAKE APPEARS

Tensions in the International Monetary System Mount

Desperate to retain the Bretton Woods system of fixed exchange rates, world political leaders introduced a series of ad hoc initiatives in the 1960s to defer its inevitable collapse. The US made various attempts to economise on gold (for example, the US Federal Reserve Bank eliminated the need for private banks to hold a proportion of their reserves at the Federal Reserve in the form of gold). Various other strategies were introduced in the second half of the 1960s.

In 1969, the US increased interest rates to rein in the strong growth and rising inflation that had resulted from the massive public spending associated with the prosecution of the Vietnam War. The tighter policy reduced the supply of US dollars to the international monetary system, which placed strains on international trade and finance. The IMF responded by introducing a new type of foreign exchange reserve asset called the Special Drawing Rights (SDRs). It was intended to be a vehicle to broaden the available international reserve assets and save the Bretton Woods system from the Triffin paradox. Recall that the Bretton Woods dilemma centred on the US dollar's status as the international reserve currency, which required the US to run increasing external trade deficits in order for world trade and finance to grow. But these deficits undermined the confidence in the value of the US dollar and increased the demand for gold convertibility. The growing shortage of US gold stocks in the late 1960s thus endangered the viability of the monetary system. The tightening US monetary policy at the end of the decade exacerbated this problem.

The creation of the SDRs was meant 'to supplement dollars in official reserve holdings' (Boughton, 2001: 926) by giving nations an alternative asset to use in international transactions. They were initially issued at par to the US dollar (1 SDR = 1 US dollar) and allocated by the IMF to member nations in proportion to their total contribution to the Fund. They were meant to allow nations 'to settle a financial obligation or to acquire another good or asset' (Boughton, 2001: 925). SDRs could be voluntarily exchanged between IMF member nations for currency or the

IMF could tell 'members with strong external positions to purchase SDRs from members with weak external positions' (IMF, 2013a: 1).

Upon their introduction, the SDRs were immediately referred to as 'paper gold' (Boughton, 2001: 924) because it was intended they would allow the US to economise on the gold transfers. The European nations, which were holding significant stocks of US dollars, also thought the SDRs would overcome their own fears and this led to a slowdown in the loss of US gold stocks. With the rapidly declining US gold stocks, the European governments had feared that the US government would either devalue the US dollar against gold or would abandon convertibility altogether. But they also knew that if they attempted to cash out their US dollar holdings into gold, the end of the system was guaranteed.

Soon after the SDRs were introduced, the US cut interest rates to revive its recessed economy, which turned the international tap of US dollars back on and the SDRs were effectively rendered redundant. The SDRs were never seen as a viable reserve currency alternative to the US dollar. When the Bretton Woods system collapsed a few years after the SDRs were introduced, the SDRs were revalued in terms of a basket of currencies rather than just the US dollar. This prompted one IMF official in 1989 to say that the IMF's '"basket currency" had become a "basket case"' (Boughton, 2001: 924). Like many of the IMF innovations and interventions, the SDRs failed to achieve their purpose because they were poorly conceived and were band aids to an international system in terminal decline as a result of its basic design flaws.

As the US cut its interest rates, the Bundesbank increased German rates in order to slow its economy. The interest rate differentials that developed encouraged capital flows out of the US and this exacerbated the US shortage of foreign reserves. The mark also came under renewed pressure to revalue. The heavy capital inflow to Germany from the US continued and 'produced a US external deficit of a size never before seen, though soon to be dwarfed by that of 1971' (BIS, 1972: 23). To reduce the overwhelming upward pressure on their currency, the Bundesbank was selling the mark in the foreign exchange markets 'on a substantial scale' (BIS, 1971: 13).

The 'Snake in the Tunnel' is Proposed and Fails – An Early Warning Ignored

On 6 March 1971, the Committee of Governors of the Central Banks of the Member States met as currency pressures continued to mount in the face of huge capital inflows into Europe from the US, which forced the central banks, particularly the Bundesbank, to sell large volumes of their currency to defend the fixed parity. The meeting sought to devise a way to reduce the fluctuations between the European currencies. Under the Bretton Woods system, the IMF allowed currencies to fluctuate by plus or minus 1 per cent with respect to the US dollar. This meant that European currencies could, in principle, fluctuate by as much as 4 per cent against each other because a plus or minus 1 per cent against the US dollar translated into a range of plus or minus 2 per cent against each other. The Member States considered that degree of variation to be too large and in the European Monetary Agreement, signed in 1958, they had agreed to limit fluctuations against the US dollar to plus or minus 0.75 per cent and plus or minus 1.5 per cent against each other. At the March meeting, the Governors agreed they would experiment with a narrowing of allowable margins in value between the Member State currencies from 1.5 per cent (plus or minus 0.75 per cent) to 1.2 per cent (plus or minus 0.6 per cent), thus defining a new 'snake' for the currencies to follow. The meeting also sought to establish a 'Community-wide level of the US dollar' (Committee of Governors of the Central Banks, 1971: 8), which would define the 'tunnel' that the 'snake' might move within. After considerable discussion nothing was agreed, except to defer the question and seek more technical input to later meetings.

Events, however, overtook them. The system of fixed exchange rates relied on nations having gold resources to meet temporary balance of payments deficits and the US guaranteeing US convertibility into gold. The IMF also played an important role in extending loans to nations who were short of the foreign currency needed to defend their exchange rates at times of considerable pressure. The reality of world trading relations was that these requirements could not be sustained.

By early May 1971, the scale of the US dollar purchases by the Bundesbank had become massive and various German commentators (for example, leading research institutes) started to advocate the floating of the mark (BIS, 1972). There were also other European discussions about the need to create more flexibility between the European currencies and the US dollar.

The crisis came to a head on 5 May 1971, when the Bundesbank suspended further foreign exchange market intervention (that is, they stopped selling the mark and buying US dollars) and closed the foreign exchange market. The central banks in Austria, Belgium, the Netherlands and Switzerland 'followed suit' (BIS, 1971: 13). The Germans had a tainted choice: either alter domestic policy settings by cutting interest rates with the risk of worsening inflation, imposing capital controls and revaluing the mark or free themselves from the external constraint imposed by the Bretton Woods system by floating. The German government, in defiance of the Bundesbank, actually proposed a joint float of all the Member State currencies against the US dollar, a proposition that only the Dutch supported (Hoffmeyer, 2000: 30).

The Council of Ministers were determined to maintain the fixed parities claiming that '"under normal circumstances" a system of flexible exchange rates within the Community was not compatible with the efficient operation of the Community' (Bundesbank, 1971: 9). Of course, these were anything but normal circumstances and so the Germans were begrudgingly allowed 'for a limited period' to 'extend the margins of fluctuation of the exchange rate of their currency' (Bundesbank, 1971: 9). Four days later, Germany and the Netherlands floated their currencies and both immediately appreciated. In addition, Austria revalued by 5.05 per cent and Switzerland by 7.07 per cent (BIS, 1972). The French steadfastly refused to abandon the parity and discontinued 'further negotiations on monetary questions' with the other Member States (Hoffmeyer, 2000: 30), thus putting paid to the agreement of the Committee of Governors of the Central Banks to experiment with a more restricted snake.

The European currency pandemonium and the widening US trade deficit in 1971 as its economy came out of recession tolled the death knell for the Bretton Woods system.

The Final Collapse

The final bell rang on Sunday, 15 August 1971 when US President Nixon effectively ended the Bretton Woods system of fixed exchange rates by suspending US dollar gold convertibility. Nixon's decision meant that national currencies no longer had any gold backing. This was the only way to resolve the unsustainable tensions within international monetary markets. The US dollar quickly devalued against gold and most of the other major currencies were revalued. The Bretton Woods system was formally abandoned in February 1973 after further major US dollar devaluation. This historic shift established the modern era of fiat currencies, which provide no guaranteed convertibility into any other commodity (such as gold). These currencies are given legal status by dint of a legislative fiat at the imprimatur of the national government. The world of economics had changed and governments were no longer financially constrained in their spending. We consider the implications of this historic change more fully in Chapter 17.

Various currency arrangements followed the formal abandonment of Bretton Woods. Most nations freely floated their currencies, which meant that the forces of supply and demand in foreign exchange markets determined their values against other currencies. That situation persists today. Other nations opted to peg their currency to another currency or perhaps to a basket of other currencies, while others adopted a foreign currency outright (for example, nations that 'dollarised' by accepting the US dollar as their domestic currency). Against all logic and evidence, the Europeans chose to press on with a fixed exchange rate system.

The lesson that the Europeans should have learned from all this was that nations with very different economies and export strengths will always find it difficult tying their exchange rates together in any fixed arrangement and jointly prospering in the process.

4. The 'snake in the tunnel' reappears

THE SMITHSONIAN AGREEMENT 1971 – CLUTCHING AT STRAWS

When President Nixon refused the demands by countries to convert dollars into gold (principally from the UK) on 15 August 1971, the dollar became a non-convertible fiat currency. If all nations had followed suit and floated at that point the world would have been a better place. The unilateral action by the US gave the other nations in the Bretton Woods system three options: (a) fully float their currencies against the US dollar and all other currencies; (b) jointly float against the US dollar, that is, maintain fixed parities between themselves but allow for flexibility against the dollar; or (c) continue to peg to the now non-convertible US dollar.

During the mark crisis in May 1971, the Germans had proposed that the EEC Member States arrange a joint float against the US dollar but the French rejected the plan. They were steadfast in their desire to maintain the peg, and used capital controls to reduce the currency fluctuations. The French saw danger in anything resembling a float because it would threaten the subsidies they enjoyed from Germany under the CAP. Before the foreign exchange markets reopened again following the shock announcement by the US to close the gold window and abandon convertibility, the Germans once again proposed a joint float and the French continued their resistance.

A few days before the collapse (13 August 1971), the widely read German weekly newspaper *Die Zeit* wrote that the German Economic and Finance Minister Karl Schiller was unhappy with the policy of the Bundesbank and wanted it to place the US dollar under more pressure (*Die Zeit*, 1971a). It also said that the experience of the last three months made it clear that floating the mark would ease the concerns of having to defend the parity (*Die Zeit*, 1971a). Two weeks later (27 August 1971), *Die Zeit* covered the acrimonious and closed meeting of Finance Ministers (Ecofin) in Paris on 19 August 1971 where the Germans repeated their desire for a joint European float and the French again vetoed the idea. *Die Zeit* said the 'differences in Paris were to be regretted' and reflected, in part, a return of the 'personal animosity between Schiller and his French counterpart Giscard d'Estaing' (*Die Zeit*, 1971b). It also suggested it was difficult to understand the French fear of German 'superiority' and that other nations had seen the sense of floating with the mark.

Giscard d'Estaing reaffirmed to the French National Assembly on 13 May 1971 the Government's 'determination not to change the current parity of the franc and thus leave, in this respect, no illusions and no hope for speculators' (Assemblée Nationale, 1971: 1818). He indicated that the Government would 'remain faithful to the spirit and letter of the Bretton Woods agreement, which provides for fixed exchange parities' (p. 1819). The French clearly were sticking to the hope that they could somehow make some progress towards a monetary union, which would see stable exchange rates and a funding mechanism for the CAP. Their heads were firmly buried in sand!

The foreign exchange markets reopened a week later on Monday, 23 August 1971 and only France held onto its fixed parity against the US dollar but only for official and commercial transactions (BIS, 1972: 27). All other European currencies were floated and appreciated against the US dollar. The Japanese initially tried to maintain the parity against the US dollar but this required massive intervention by the Bank of Japan. The BIS (1972: 27) noted that the 'Bank of Japan had to absorb dollars on a scale so massive . . . that on 28th August the yen too was allowed to float'. The reality was that all currencies were left to find their own value against the obviously overvalued US dollar in accord with their relative trading performances and domestic economic strengths.

But leopards don't easily change their spots, or rather fools seldom differ! It was clear that 'all the main countries wished to restore fixed exchange rates' (BIS, 1972: 27) but recognised the arrangements under the Bretton Woods system were unsustainable. Many of the appreciating nations, especially Germany, were worried that their currencies would go too high and, as a consequence, resumed buying US dollars and selling their own currencies to limit the scope of the float. The export lobbies in these nations were powerful and feared they would be priced out of their markets as a result of the currency appreciating too far. Further, the various rates of appreciation altered the relative competitiveness of nations in terms of their own currencies, which introduced further political tensions. Speculators exacerbated the political problems by betting on differential movements.

The US government was also reluctant to alter its value against gold, which the Europeans considered violated the 'IMF rules by being unwilling to devalue' (BIS, 1972: 28). The Europeans argued that the US balance of payments was at a point of fundamental disequilibrium, which meant that the capital outflow from the US would continue indefinitely because all speculators would consider the dollar to be overvalued. Despite being the 'big kid on the block', the US had to finally bow to international pressure. The task was to work out new parities that might hold given the huge US balance of payments deficits.

At the end of November 1971, the G10 Finance Ministers and central bank Governors met in Rome to advance that task. These discussions moved to Washington and on 18 December 1971 the G10 parties met at the Smithsonian Institute and signed the so-called Smithsonian Agreement. It was obvious that the US dollar would have to devalue in order to restore the system of fixed exchange rates. The agreement established a new set of parities, although, unlike the Bretton Woods system, there would be no US dollar convertibility. It would remain a fiat currency that the other nations pegged against. The major components of the agreement were that the US agreed to devalue the US dollar to $38.00 per ounce of gold (from the Bretton Woods parity of $35 per ounce). Most other nations agreed to revalue their currencies and the average upward revision was around 10 per cent, a significant realignment. France and Britain were passive and their parities altered in line with the US devaluation (about 1 per cent) (BIS: 1972: 29). The US made no commitment to intervene in foreign exchange markets to maintain the value of the now non-convertible dollar. The new international monetary system was no longer a gold standard but rather an unanchored US dollar standard. The technicalities of the differences between the two systems are beyond the scope of our discussion, but, essentially, the responsibilities among the parties (the US and the rest of the world) were reversed, with the US now required to use its monetary policy settings to maintain price stability given the absence of a gold anchor. On the other hand, the pegging nations had to ensure their balance of payments were in equilibrium to avoid any pressures on their currencies against the US dollar. The nations also agreed to widen the band within which their currencies could fluctuate against the US dollar from plus or minus 1 per cent to 2.25 per cent, meaning there could now be a spread of 4.5 per cent against each other.

The Smithsonian Agreement had two major aims: (a) to quickly calm down the foreign exchange markets and stop the massive flow of funds out of the US into Europe so that the fixed exchange rates could be managed; and (b) to progressively allow the revised exchange rate parities (devalued US dollar and revalued European currencies) to alter trade patterns to facilitate the reduction of the US balance of payments deficits and nations such as Germany to reduce their massive balance of payments surpluses.

The initial responses 'to the Smithsonian agreement were generally very positive, reflecting relief that the period of floating exchange rates was over' (BIS, 1972: 30). But, by early 1972, the revaluations led to further speculative attacks on the US dollar, which pushed several currencies (mark, guilder, Belgian franc and yen) to their upper limits within the allowable, but widened 'tunnel'. It soon became obvious that the system was not viable. Facing an election, the US government was keeping interest rates low, which led to inflationary pressures in Europe. The latter were enduring very strong balance of payments surpluses as a result of their higher interest rates attracting massive capital inflows from the US. It was a case of 1971 revisited.

THE 'LE SERPENT Á L'INTÉRIEUR DU TUNNEL' AND THE BASEL ACCORD 1972

With renewed currency instability in early 1972, currency traders formed the view that the Smithsonian Agreement was unsustainable. There had to be massive central bank intervention in the form of US dollar purchases in the foreign exchange markets to keep it functioning (BIS, 1972: 32). The BIS said the developments 'in the rather battered international monetary system may be said to come under the heading of unfinished business left over from the upheaval of 1971. In broader perspective, they constituted a further instalment of the more or less permanent crisis which has prevailed since 1967' (BIS, 1973: 20). In terms of the aims of the Agreement, the BIS concluded, 'the more immediate aim was not achieved, nor were any real signs evident during 1972 of progress towards the longer term adjustment process' (p. 20). A renewed crisis was building.

The Europeans were intent on modifying arrangements in their own eccentric way to reduce their internal currency fluctuations. Their devotion to the impossible was persistent to say the least. The Smithsonian bands were also at odds with the sentiment expressed in the Werner Report, which had recommended 'the elimination of margins of fluctuation in rates of exchange' (Werner Report, 1970: 26) as the final goal of the economic and monetary union, and narrowing the fluctuations during the adjustment phase. So while the EEC nations had signed up to the Smithsonian Agreement, the Council agreed in March 1972 to significantly alter the terms. On 13 December 1971, the Committee of Governors of the Central Banks of the Member States established a 'group of experts' presided over by M. Théron. Their report, submitted on 2 February 1972, set out a system that formally became known as the 'snake in the tunnel' system even though the concept had already been tried (Théron, 1972). This system represented the first European specific attempt to maintain fixed exchange rates between the currencies and was the extension of work done previously by an expert group under the direction of Belgian central bank governor, Baron Ansiaux, in 1970, which had informed the Werner Report.

For a very short period in early 1972, foreign exchange markets were calm and the European polity thought it was apposite to return to the Werner plan to map out the adjustment phases towards complete economic and monetary union (BIS, 1973). The Council met on 21 March 1972 and resolved to introduce the first coordinated step towards economic and monetary union along the Werner path. After considering the Théron Report, they resolved to gradually reduce the margins for currency fluctuations within Europe, while 'fully utilising the margins of fluctuations allowed for' by the Smithsonian Agreement (European Commission, 1972). The 'snake in the tunnel' thus became the first specific element of an otherwise vague Werner implementation process. The Council Resolution indicated that from 1 July 1972, the fluctuations between currencies of the Member States would not exceed 2.25 per cent, which was a rather skinnier snake than the 3 per cent recommended by the Théron Report but still consistent with the hope of returning to stable exchange rates. On 10 April 1972, the Committee of Governors of the Central Banks of the Member States met in Basel to map out the practicalities of the March Council Resolution. At that meeting, the central banks of the Member States and those of Denmark, Ireland and the United Kingdom (the latter three were due to join the EEC in January 1973) agreed to the Council resolution. They also retained the Smithsonian band of 4.5 per cent against the US dollar. This agreement became known as the 1972 Basel Accord.

The central bankers also agreed to intervene in foreign exchange markets if their currencies were in danger of breaching the new more restricted 'snake'. To facilitate cooperation in this intervention, they agreed to swap their currencies to ensure that they had sufficient funds to sustain this commitment. The Basel Accord took effect on 24 April 1972.

THE 'SNAKE' ESCAPES ITS 'TUNNEL' AND BRETTON WOODS BECOMES HISTORY

Hans Tietmeyer (2003: 7) described the snake as a 'relatively loose exchange-rate arrangement' that 'experienced not only a good many tensions, but also withdrawals and re-entries on several occasions, not least by the French franc'. Howarth and Loedel (2003: xv) referred to it as the 'ill-fated snake'.

The snake started slithering out of control a few months after the Basel Accord. The British floated the pound and withdrew from the arrangement in June 1972, following a period of massive instability in international currency markets. The increased volatility began in February 1972, as speculators renewed the bets against 'weak' currencies. It was generally considered that the US dollar remained overvalued even though it had been devalued by 7.9 per cent against gold, and other nations had revalued as part of the Smithsonian Agreement. This was in the context of the ongoing US balance of payments deficits and the unwillingness of the US government to drive unemployment up through domestic monetary and fiscal restraint (BIS, 1973: 21). The speculative activity saw significant fund movements out of the US dollar into marks, the Benelux currencies and the yen (BIS, 1973: 22). In the case of the European currencies, the upward pressure pushed them to the upper limits renegotiated as part of the Smithsonian process and forced their respective central banks to sell their currencies and buy US dollars to soak up the strong demand.

The speculative attacks reached a peak in June–July 1972, and the British pound was particularly targeted as a result of the widening British balance of payments deficit. While the so-called 'sterling crisis' led to massive Bank of England and Banque de France intervention in an attempt to halt the sale of the pound in international currency markets, the British government was ultimately forced to float on 23 June 1972. The Basel Accord, in fact, worsened things, because the central bank intervention by France, Belgium and Germany (selling their currencies to buy the pound) had contained the slide of the pound against the US dollar, but weakened their own currencies. As the BIS (1973: 22) noted, 'These currencies therefore looked relatively cheap'. And when the dam broke and the pound floated, there was massive buying of these currencies, which pushed them up to the upper limits against the US dollar. This renewed speculation that the European currencies would float against the dollar and forced the Finance Ministers in mid July 1972 to reaffirm 'their determination to adhere to the existing rate structure' (BIS, 1973: 23).

The first fault line in the Smithsonian Agreement had thus opened. While various measures were taken to ease the currency crisis, it was clear that the balance of payments adjustments envisaged when the nations signed the Agreement were not forthcoming. The US balance of payments deficits, which were undermining confidence in the US dollar were not abating quickly; German and Japanese trade surpluses continued to grow; the higher European interest rate persisted; all of which meant that large currency flows were undermining the capacity of the central banks to maintain parities within the agreed limits. There was no doubt that investors were coming to the realisation that the Smithsonian attempt to shore up the failed Bretton Woods fixed exchange rate system was doomed.

The international currency crisis intensified in January 1973, when Italy was forced to partially float the lira (segmenting commercial transactions from the rest) to stem the capital outflow. A full float came on 14 February 1973 but the decision to partially float meant Italy had to quit the 'snake'. The Swiss franc floated on the same day for similar reasons. In early February, the US published an 'enormous trade deficit for 1972' (BIS, 1973: 24) and this prompted a renewed speculative selling of the US dollar of greater volumes than in the previous attacks. The Bundesbank and the Bank of Japan, in particular, were forced to engage in massive US dollar buying to maintain the agreed parities. On 9 February 1972, the foreign exchange markets were closed because 'the situation had become untenable' (BIS, 1973: 24). Four days later, after some frenzied discussions between governments, the US dollar was devalued by 10 per cent and 24 hours later, the yen and the lira floated.

The crisis deepened in early March as the US dollar hit its revised lower limits against the other major currencies. On 1 March 1973, the foreign currency markets closed again to give the authorities time to meet and determine the next step. It was obvious that any attempt to fix exchange rates against the US dollar (even within bands) would fail given the disparities in economic policies and outcomes. The BIS wrote that 'the market was in disarray' (BIS, 1973: 24) and the only course of action was to abandon the fixed exchange rate regime and float the US dollar, which occurred when the currency markets opened again on 19 March 1973. The Bretton Woods system of fixed exchange rates had finally been terminated despite the efforts to salvage it under the Smithsonian Agreement.

The remaining Basel Accord partners (Benelux, Denmark, France, Germany and the Netherlands), however, chose to ignore the 'sword of Damocles', such was their fear of floating exchange rates, and on 12 March 1973, announced they would jointly float against the US dollar, effectively keeping the 'snake' (Basel Accord) but abandoning the 'tunnel' (the Smithsonian Agreement). There were a series of ad hoc decisions taken to control capital flows and to realign currencies (for example, the mark was revalued by 3 per cent immediately and then by 5.5 per cent in June 1973) as part of this decision. Norway and Sweden also decided to become part of the joint float.

Despite early optimism, mainly from politicians seeking to give an impression of stability, the trouble was far from over. The underlying economic fundamentals in Europe meant that the currency pressures were unstable. Germany faced continual upward pressure on its currency and France the opposite. This meant that the Bundesbank continually had to purchase the 'snake' currencies and the other central banks were continuing to intervene on a significant scale to stabilise currency movements.

Various events later in 1973 further disrupted the world economy and the currency markets. The outbreak of hostilities in the Middle East in October 1973 (the 1973 Arab–Israeli War) was accompanied by the oil embargo imposed by the Organization of the Petroleum Exporting Countries (OPEC). A few days later, on 16 October, the Arab nations increased the price of oil by 17 per cent and indicated they would cut production by 25 per cent as part of a leveraged retaliation against the US President's decision to provide arms to Israel. The price of oil rose by around three times within eight months (US Energy Information Administration, 2013). The BIS (1974: 30) assessed at the time that the US, 'despite the embargo placed on it . . . was in a better situation than Europe or Japan to withstand both the internal and external effects of the OPEC countries' actions owing to its lesser dependence on oil imports.' The result, the US dollar appreciated by 17 per cent in the six months to February 1974, basically taking it back to the December 1971 value at the time of the signing of the Smithsonian Agreement. Further, the European currencies suffered major depreciation, as did the yen. On 19 January 1974, the French government decided to float and exit the 'snake' because it was facing a major strain on its foreign exchange reserves as a result of its dependence on imported oil. The 'snake' was looking decidedly Germanic by this stage leading commentators to refer to the residual 'snake' system as a mark zone (Maes, 2002: 15).

The confidence in the US dollar didn't last long though and by February 1974 a major reversal was underway. The BIS (1974: 30) assessed that there was an initial overreaction by the foreign exchange markets as the OPEC price hikes and the embargo came into force. It was also clear that while the US was less dependent on oil imports than the European nations, the oil price hikes would still have a substantial impact on its balance of payments. As a result, the US dollar lost ground in the currency markets. The European story was the opposite. Less energy was required in the mild winter of 1973–74 and the German export locomotive continued to build even bigger trade surpluses (BIS, 1974).

The world was back to the sort of setup that created the crisis less than a year earlier, in mid 1973. After abandoning the 'snake' in January 1974, the French franc re-entered the arrangement on 10 July 1975 at the original parity agreed in the Basel Accord. The Swiss government negotiated an entry in September 1975 but by November, it decided not to exercise that option given ongoing instability. Then on 15 March 1976, the French franc again exited the 'snake' never to return, and in October 1976, the mark was revalued by a further 2 per cent as it became difficult for the Bundesbank to keep the currency within the agreed limits.

Less than six months later (April 1977), most of the remaining members of the 'snake' devalued against the mark, further revealing the unviable nature of the arrangement. After Sweden pulled out on 28 August 1977, the Norwegian and Danish currencies devalued again. Early in 1978, Norway was forced to devalue by a further 8 per cent (13 February 1978). A further realignment occurred in October 1978 as the mark was revalued against all the other 'snake' currencies. Ultimately, Norway could not stay in the arrangement such was the pressure on its currency, and it exited on 12 December 1978.

THE EUROPEAN MONETARY COOPERATION FUND 1973: WERNER'S ONLY LEGACY

The growing currency instability meant it was difficult to advance the move to economic and monetary union. While 1973 was largely a year of chaos on international currency markets, there was one development that could be traced to the Werner proposals. On 3 April 1973 the European Monetary Cooperation Fund (EMCF) was established. The Council decision indicated that the Fund would 'be integrated at a later stage into a Community organization of central banks' (European Commission, 1973a), a precursor to establishing a European central bank. The Fund was meant to progressively narrow 'the margins of fluctuation of the Community currencies against each other' (European Commission, 1973a) and encourage cooperation between central banks to ensure each had sufficient reserves to defend their own currencies within the scope of the 'snake'.

When the Fund was announced, the EEC said 'a first step toward the European Community's goal of economic and monetary union by 1980 became a reality today' (European Commission, 1973b). The Council decision introduced a new 'European monetary unit of account of a value of 0.788867088 grammes of fine gold' (European Commission, 1973b), which was designed to replace the US gold convertibility abandoned in August 1971. Each participating currency would be defined in terms of its parity against gold and the unit would be used to settle transactions within the group.

The deliberations leading to the establishment of the Fund were, as usual, vexed, with both France and Germany adopting passive negative standpoints, albeit for quite different reasons. The French were reluctant to agree to any supranational authority and considered the 'monetary decisions fell within the purview of the government' (Danescu, 2014c: 3), a consistent position that had hampered progress towards the economic and monetary union since the inception of the idea. The Germans were reluctant because they didn't want to become the paymaster, especially if funds were being given to governments who had no economic policy discipline. The records show that the other Member States (and the three new candidates for membership, Denmark, Ireland and Norway) were positive about the development, seeing the advantages in using the new unit of account to settle internal balance of payments imbalances (thus avoiding the use of the US dollar).

The Italian position was unique (European Commission, 1973c). In the context of the currency crisis in early 1973, the Italian members of the EC Monetary Committee urged the Council to 'give the European Fund real powers' and to strengthen the 'Community's credit potential' and progressively pool reserves (p. 1). The Italian members said that 'the pooling of reserves does not mean the transfer of ownership to a common pool' but rather 'joint management' (p. 2). The intent was to ensure the Fund would have the capacity to maintain the agreed currency parities to 'facilitate a joint float of the EEC currencies against the currencies of the rest of the world' (p. 3). In effect, the Italians were proposing a European version of the pre 1971 IMF.

The French and German resistance ensured that the pooling proposal didn't see the light of day. The EMCF was poorly provisioned from the start and was 'purely an accounting body', with 'its transactions . . . conducted by the Bank for International Settlements' (Danescu, 2014c: 6).

WHY THE WERNER PLAN FAILED

While the Werner Report optimistically talked about 'a monetary union', the vague plan it presented never materialised and was finally abandoned in 1977. The only artefact of the many meetings and interchanges between national leaders, high level ministers, central bankers and others was the EMCF, which was nothing much more than an accounting organisation. The 'snake', which was the first step in reducing currency fluctuations within Europe, shrank to become a mark zone, and the economic and philosophical differences between the aspirant nations showed no signs of diminishing.

The popularised assessment is that it was the 1971 'Nixon Shock' and the resulting turbulence in international currency markets, followed by the OPEC oil price hikes, that caused the proposed transition to economic and monetary union to come unstuck. There is truth in that narrative and it is certainly a more soothing explanation than the other reality. The basic reason it failed is because the economies involved were too disparate and the French fear of German (military) dominance in Europe remained, as did their fierce notion of sovereignty that militated against delegation of power to supranational institutions and the German inflation obsession.

Recognising the impact of both the breakdown of the international fixed exchange rate monetary system and the inherent national disparities, McAllister (2009: 63) concluded that the Werner Committee had to 'pick its way through the minefield of "monetarists" . . . and the "economists"' and the resulting conception was 'built on shifting sand in being based on the very Bretton Woods' mechanisms that were fast foundering . . . all the knitting unravelled'. On 23 January 1972, Frede Sunesen, the Governor of the Danish Central Bank, wrote in the *Financial Times*, 'I will begin to believe in European economic and monetary union when someone explains how you control nine horses that are all running at different speeds within the same harness' (cited in McAllister, 2009: 58).

These reflections resonate strongly with the views expressed at the time of the Maastricht deliberations by those who warned that the proposed EMU was flawed and would expose the system to failure.

5. Monetarism arrives amidst currency turmoil

THE RISE OF MONETARISM AND FREE MARKET IDEOLOGY

While the traditional rivalries between France and Germany and the desire to maintain fixed exchange rates were at the centre of the Eurocentric negotiations about economic and monetary union in the late 1970s, a new, even more insidious factor, the increasing dominance of free market economics entered the picture. This factor was a major catalyst for the sequence of events that took Europe to Maastricht and resulted in the flawed EMU that exists today.

In the 1970s, the high inflation that followed the OPEC oil price hikes was accompanied by high unemployment as governments tried to suppress economic activity to control the inflation. This era of stagflation provoked a major shift in economic thinking. The Keynesian macroeconomic orthodoxy, that dominated the post World War II period, was predicated on the view that the total spending in the economy determined the level of unemployment. Firms employed people if they had sales orders. After the cessation of the war and with the mass unemployment of the Great Depression of the 1930s still firmly etched in the minds of policy makers and the population, governments generally committed to using fiscal and monetary policy to maintain states of full employment where everybody who wanted a job could find one. This led to an acceleration of prosperity across the advanced world.

Accompanying this approach was a view that inflation would only result if the spending outstripped the capacity of the firms to produce goods and services, leaving them no option but to increase prices. Accordingly, high unemployment should be associated with low inflation and vice versa. Stagflation thus presented a new situation. Most economists understood that inflation could also emerge as a result of sudden cost pressures (for example, imported oil price rises) which then squeezed existing profit margins and the real value of the workers' wages, and under certain circumstances, could trigger a struggle between labour and capital over who would bear this loss. Inflation would result if workers gained wage rises and firms responded by pushing up prices or vice versa. The correct policy response was to address the incompatible demands for more national income from labour and capital by seeking some sort of consensual approach to sharing the costs of the imported raw material price rise.

However, this understanding was lost on policy makers when responding to the OPEC oil price hikes and they sought to stifle the accelerating inflation by suppressing spending using policy measures we now refer to as fiscal austerity (public spending cuts and/or tax increases) and tight monetary policy (increasing interest rates). The resulting stagflation created a perception that Keynesian policies had failed and bestowed a sense of legitimacy on the free market approach, which had claimed that inflation was the result of lax government policy. This view had been wholly discredited during the Great Depression by the work of John Maynard Keynes and others, but remained alive and well in the more conservative academic departments.

The long-standing dominance of Keynesian policy was thus abandoned by a large number of economists in the 1970s. Alan Blinder (1987: 278) said by 'about 1980, it was hard to find an American macroeconomist under the age of 40 who professed to be a Keynesian. That was an astonishing turnabout in less than a decade, an intellectual revolution for sure.' The resurgence of the free market approach, which we now rather roughly refer to as neo-liberalism, manifested initially as Monetarism, and Milton Friedman and his University of Chicago colleagues championed the entry of these ideas back into the mainstream policy debate. While Raymond Barre was the first to implement these ideas in France in 1976, Margaret Thatcher's government became internationally known as the political spearhead of this conservative academic resurgence.

The rise of Monetarism was not based on an empirical rejection of the Keynesian orthodoxy, but 'was instead a triumph of *a priori* theorising over empiricism, of intellectual aesthetics over observation and, in some measure, of conservative ideology over liberalism' (Blinder 1987: 278). It represented a shift from those who consider that state intervention, regulation and spending is crucial for the achievement of a balanced and equitable economy, to those who eschew state involvement and believe, with religious passion, that a self-regulating free market can provide increasing wealth and opportunity for all.

The core Monetarist idea was that excessive growth in the money supply associated with excessive government spending and lax monetary discipline by the central banks (interest rates too low) caused inflation. Further, price stability required the imposition of deflationary policies, which involved tighter credit policies and cutbacks in fiscal deficits. The Monetarists introduced the concept of the natural rate of unemployment, to combat the view that the austerity would generate higher unemployment. Put simply, they argued that a free market would deliver a unique unemployment rate that was associated with price stability and that government attempts to manipulate that rate using fiscal and/or monetary policy would only lead to accelerating inflation. The prescription was for policy makers to concentrate on price stability and let unemployment settle at this 'natural' rate, ignoring popular concerns that it might be too high. By this time, any Keynesian remedies proposed to reduce unemployment (such as increasing the fiscal deficit) were met with derision from the bulk of the economics profession who had wholeheartedly embraced Monetarism. Despite the predominance of Monetarist thought at the time, there was very little factual evidence presented to substantiate their policy approach. In fact, it flew in the face of all reasonable logic. It was a triumph of free market ideology over the facts.

But with policy makers increasingly loath to use discretionary fiscal and monetary policy to stimulate the economy, unemployment rose and persisted at high levels. The battle against high unemployment was abandoned in order to keep inflation at low levels. This major shift in macroeconomic policy paradigms was going on as the 'snake' was slithering into dysfunctional oblivion and the political elites in Europe were plotting their next strategy in the pursuit of monetary union.

THE EUROPEAN MONETARY SYSTEM (EMS)

In 1950, Jacques Rueff, who was a trusted economic advisor to De Gaulle and a French central banker, wrote that 'L'Europe se fera par la monnaie ou ne se fera pas' ('Europe will be made by money or it won't be made'), which provided the mantra for those who believed that the European Project would ultimately require a single currency (Rueff, 1950).

As the 'snake' was falling apart, the President of the Commission of European Communities, Roy Jenkins, delivered the first Jean Monnet lecture in Florence on 27 October 1977. He described the demise of the Werner plan as a 'retreat rather than an advance' (Jenkins, 1977: 3). In making the case for a renewed push to monetary union he said that there would be advantages in 'creating a major new international currency backed by the economic spread and strength of the Community, which would be comparable to that of the United States, were it not for our monetary divisions and differences' (p. 5). He also claimed that eliminating currency fluctuations within Europe would improve economic welfare. Rueff's agenda was back on track.

The economic situation across the 'snake' membership was disparate.

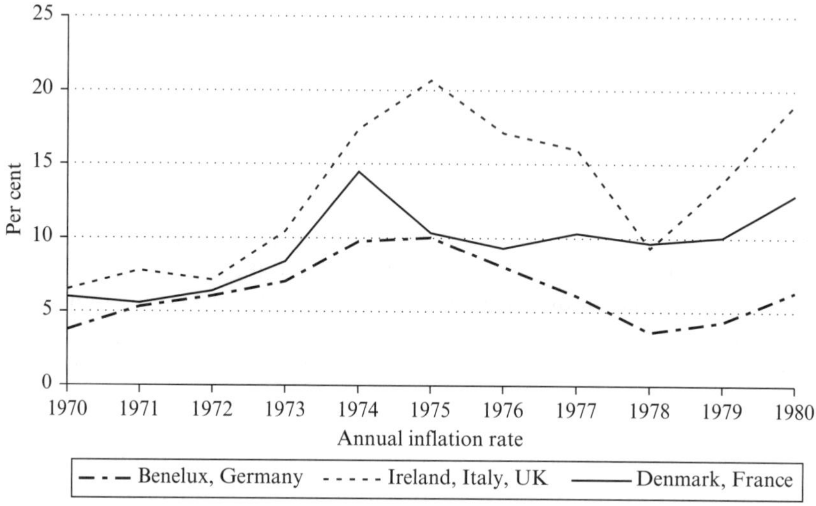

Source: European Commission, Annual Macroeconomic Database (AMECO).

Figure 5.1 Comparative inflation rates among original 'snake' membership, 1970–80, per cent per annum

The withdrawal of the French franc in March 1976 exemplified the problem facing the non-German membership: either they had to continually devalue their currencies or create high domestic unemployment to reduce imports. Neither option was politically tenable. Even after the revaluation of the mark in October 1976, the remaining currencies were under pressure.

Figure 5.1 shows the average annual inflation rates between 1970 and 1980 of the low inflation nations (Benelux, Germany), the mid inflation nations (Denmark and France), and the high inflation nations (Ireland, Italy and the United Kingdom). The widening fluctuations in the latter half of the 1970s reflected the different struggles the nations had in dealing with the oil price rises.

Figure 5.2 shows the respective current account balances as a per cent of GDP. The low inflation nations had strong trade positions and continually faced upward pressure on their currencies, particularly Germany. The rest of the nations had weak trade positions and faced the opposite pressures in foreign exchange markets. These disparities made it virtually impossible for the fixed parities embedded in the 'snake' arrangement to be maintained.

Further, the CAP was causing further tensions, particularly in France.

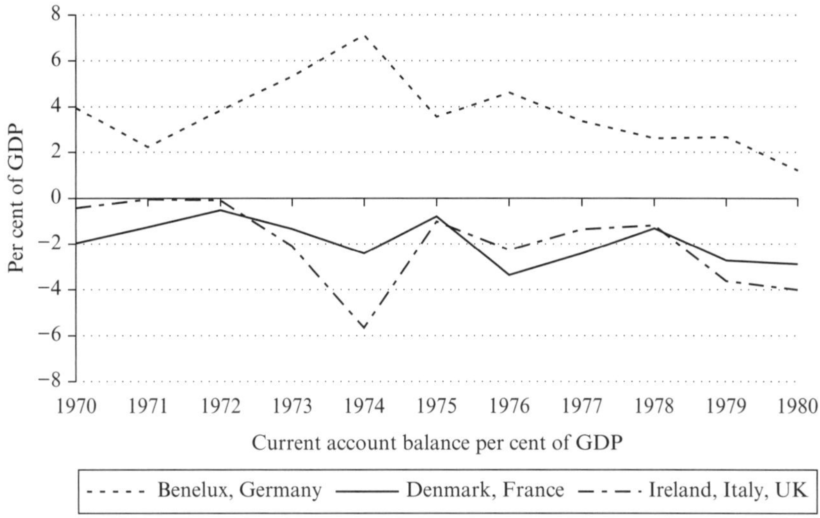

Source: European Commission, Annual Macroeconomic Database (AMECO).

Figure 5.2 Comparative current account balances among original 'snake' membership, 1970–80, per cent of GDP

The CAP became more complicated in 1969 when the mark was revalued and the French franc devalued. The CAP required that the EC harmonise agricultural prices expressed in terms of a common 'Agricultural Unit of Account' (AUA), which was set in terms of gold parity of the US dollar as used in the Bretton Woods system and introduced in 1962. One AUA corresponded to one US dollar. In turn, these common CAP prices were converted into national currencies using the exchange rate parities. Stability of the fixed agricultural price system across the membership thus depended on the stability of national currencies because if one currency depreciated, the fixed prices would yield a competitive advantage to that nation's farmers and vice versa.

A relatively simple solution would have been to adjust the national currency price upwards for devaluing nations and downwards for revaluing nations. In the former instance, the French argued that:

> . . . such a sharp rise would not have been desirable either internally, where it would have aggravated the inflationary trends which had given rise to the devaluations and would have put the farmers concerned in a more privileged position than other social and professional categories, or in the European context, where it would have provoked over production of certain agricultural products. (European Commission, 1974: 6)

In the latter case, the strength of the farm lobby in Germany made it politically impossible to cut farm incomes. The system was already pitched in favour of the less efficient farming nations such as Italy and Germany who wanted the harmonised agricultural prices to be higher than otherwise. Despite the opposition from France, the less efficient farming nations won the day.

To cope with the 1969 realignment in the French and German currencies, the European Commission introduced a complex system of so-called 'green exchange rates' or simply 'green rates'. These rates were designed to insulate farm prices from the fluctuations in the market exchange rate. They were set at the parities that ruled prior to the realignment. Without them, farmers in Germany, for example, would have experienced a drop in farm income each time the mark was revalued because a given AUA price would translate into less marks. By expressing the AUA in terms of the 'green rates', farm incomes were stable against currency fluctuations. If the national currencies were stable against each other, then the 'green rates' would be equal to the actual exchange rates. Once the 'green rates' were introduced the 'EU effectively abandoned common agricultural prices' (von Cramen-Taubadel and Thiel, 1994: 263). There were also equity issues involved. In the case of a revalued mark, while the German farmers received the same mark payment for their farm output, their mark income was now more valuable against all other currencies. Other nations resented this inequity.

The 'green rates' were accompanied by the system of Monetary Compensatory Amounts (MCAs), which were introduced 'to correct any distortions in competition that might emerge between the EEC Member States as a result of fluctuations in exchange rate parities' (Fauvet, 1979). The system involved levies being imposed on intra EU farm exports that had become more competitive as a result of devaluation and subsidies paid to intra EU farm exports that had been damaged as a result of revaluation. The impact of both was to protect farmers 'in strong currency countries that would otherwise have suffered from revaluation induced CAP price reductions' (von Cramen-Taubadel and Thiel, 1994: 263). After France left the 'snake' in 1976, the French farmers lobbied to have the MCAs terminated, given the implications of the system for their overall farm incomes in the context of a weakening French franc.

Carchedi (2001: 205) considered the MCAs to be 'a flagrant violation of the EEC principles' (which prohibited any duties being imposed on trade within the common market) and 'both reflected and fostered from the very beginning the interests of Germany, that is, of the German conservative ruling classes'. Such was the complexity and opaqueness of the system, that the German chancellor emerged 'from a meeting of the Council complaining that he had only one official who understood the system of green exchange rates but could not explain it, and one official who could explain it but did not understand it' (Eichengreen, 2007: 184).

Within this context, big changes were also underway in French politics, which significantly altered economic policy, not only domestically, but also with respect to the European Project. Valéry Giscard d'Estaing was elected President in 1974. In the traditional struggle between the French policy makers in the Planning Ministry and the technocrats in the Ministry of Finance (who were more amenable to the German position on integration and economic management), Giscard d'Estaing was in the latter camp.

Canadian philosopher and writer John Ralston Saul, who examined the role played by Giscard d'Estaing in France during the 1970s, told *The Guardian* that the French President 'first verbalised the idea that economics was the prism through which we should see civilisation' (Jeffries, 2005) at the initial G7 meeting in 1975. Saul also said that Giscard d'Estaing 'believed free markets would establish natural international balances' and that 'Boom and bust was over' (Jeffries, 2005).

Initially, he had to share power with the Gaullist Prime Minister Jacques Chirac as part of a strategy to resolve internal conflicts in the parliamentary majority. However, this proved untenable and Chirac quit in 1976 in order to rebuild the Gaullist power base in French politics and position himself for a tilt at the Presidency at the next election. When Giscard d'Estaing appointed Raymond Barre as Chirac's successor in 1976, he proclaimed him to be the 'meilleur économiste de France' (best economist in France). Barre was also appointed as Minister of Economy and Finance, a position he held until 1978. The pair promoted a powerful anti-Gaullist position with respect to domestic economic policy, reflecting their neo-liberal views, and moved the French perspective on 'Europe' closer towards the German 'economists' viewpoint.

Barre presented the 'Declaration of the Government', which outlined the new policy plan to the National Assembly on 5 October 1976 (Journal Officiel de La République Française, 1976). The rhetoric and objectives were in stark contrast to the 'Planification' associated with the French Planning Office and 'la tradition républicaine' that had dominated the Chirac era. Gone was the former Keynesian emphasis, tinged with the 'engineering tradition in economic thought in France' (Maes, 2002: 4). Barre's linguistic content and flourish were consistent with what we now hear from politicians in today's neo-liberal era. It is also worth noting that Barre was neither a career politician nor a member of a political party when he took office, which again resonates with the trend during the recent crisis to appoint technocrats to assume leadership positions and inflict austerity on nations at the expense of democratic choice.

The 'Barre Plan', introduced in 1976 and consolidated in 1977, involved a combination of tax increases on fuel, tobacco and alcohol, wage freezes to fight inflation, fiscal austerity, attacks on trade unions and industrial restructuring, particularly in the steel industry. Barre claimed, 'the fight against inflation is now a prerequisite for national ambitions' (Journal Officiel de La République Française, 1976). This was the 'economist's' approach whereby government focused on maintaining a strong currency by suppressing domestic costs. The focus shifted from regarding the fiscal balance as a reflection of the pursuit of functional ends, such as a strong domestic economy with low unemployment, to one where the balance became an objective in its own right and deficits were vilified. Barre claimed that harsh fiscal austerity was necessary and that the economy would emerge stronger, with lower unemployment. The 'bitter pill now, better future health' message he preached is strikingly similar to the policies and narratives imposed on Europe by the Troika in 2010. His plans were met with strong resistance, not the least because the austerity was targeted at workers, leaving those who could evade taxes and who enjoyed high incomes relatively unscathed. Giscard d'Estaing and Barre thus beat the British Tories under Thatcher by a few years to the questionable fame of being the first Monetarist government along the lines espoused by Milton Friedman and the so-called University of Chicago boys.

Barre's rhetoric and policies, the so-called 'Barrisme' (Fuerxer, 2003), was, like Thatcher's Monetarist purge, unpopular with the trade unions, the disadvantaged and social democrats. In 1978, he vilified the trade unions as poster carriers ('les porteurs de pancartes') who wasted time staging protest marches to serve their vested interests and said that this behaviour was a strange way to serve the national interest (*Le Figaro*, 2007). He used the term 'microcosme' to deride the opponents of austerity, a reference to those who were complacent and failed to see the realities confronting the nation (*Le Figaro*, 2007). He said the unions only 'write, babble and chatter and are accompanied by a procession of complaining wits that revel in intrigue and gossip' (*Le Figaro*, 2007). In the same way that Thatcher seemed to celebrate being unpopular, Barre told the rising pool of unemployed to start their own businesses and suggested that those 'complaining do not make a nation' (*Valeurs actuelles*, 2007).

But the unpopularity extended beyond his confrontational language. Like Thatcherism, Barrisme failed to achieve its stated purpose. The economy deteriorated just as his Keynesian opponents had predicted. Economic growth came in well under the forecasts. The unemployment rate, which in 1976 was just over 4 per cent, rose to 5.2 per cent in 1978, and by the end of his Prime Ministership it had risen to 7.4 per cent. Further, inflation was not reduced substantially and the currency continued to depreciate. One commentator noted on the third anniversary of his Prime Ministership that, after three years of anti-inflation austerity, 'Everything is more expensive, even the price of a baguette' (*The Spectator*, 1979). It is true that the French economy, like much of the oil dependent world, was caught up in the second oil crisis in 1979, after the demise of the Shah of Iran upset oil supplies and world financial markets overreacted by pushing prices up far higher than was warranted by the actual contraction in supply. But the Barre Plan had failed long before 1979 and the oil crisis just sealed his political fate (along with that of Giscard d'Estaing) and paved the way for Chirac to return.

The Germans had started to embrace Keynesian policies in the mid 1960s after the nation was shocked by recession in 1965 and 1966. In 1963, the government created the 'Sachverständigenrat' or Council of Economic Experts to advise it on macroeconomic policy setting. One of the early 'Fünf Weisen' (or 'five wise men' as the Council members were known), Olaf Sievert (2003) reflected that Germany had not followed the standard Keynesian macroeconomic policy path that most advanced western nations in the period after World War II. In the early period of the Council, the Austrian school liberalism of Ludwig Erhard, who was the CDU Chancellor between 1963 and 1966 and an early member of the conservative free market Mount Pelerin Society, dominated German macroeconomic policy. The recession changed perceptions and Willy Brandt increasingly used Keynesian spending stimulus to maintain Germany's strong economic performance in the late 1960s. Sievert (2003: 35) noted that by the early 1970s, the 'wise men' were not free of Keynesian thought, but, equally, were not dominated by it.

German monetary policy was caught between its prioritisation of domestic price stability and the obligations of the central bank under the Bretton Woods agreement to defend the currency parity. Hurt by the experience of the 1920s when the gold-backed mark lost all value and by the further nominal wealth losses in 1948 when the Reichsmark was abandoned as part of the currency reforms, Germans placed a high priority on price stability. This fear of inflation became a cultural obsession in Germany and has influenced the design of their monetary institutions and the interaction between monetary and fiscal policy ever since. The new German Constitution in 1949 set in process the establishment of the Bundesbank, and the resulting 1957 Bundesbank Act clearly stipulated that the bank has 'the primary objective of maintaining price stability' (Section 12) and that it is 'independent of instructions from the Federal Cabinet [Government]' (Section 12) (Bundesbankgesetz, 1997).

But the Bundesbank was also required to defend the exchange rate, principally by expanding the money supply through the sale of marks to keep its value down. This responsibility was often in conflict with its basic charter to maintain price stability. Rising inflation as the currency strengthened in the latter part of the 1960s reflected this compromised position. Inflation also accelerated in 1973 as the oil price rises impacted, a common trend across the advanced world. The 1973 oil crisis was accompanied by significant real wage rises in Germany that were in excess of productivity growth and thus squeezed profits. Fiscal policy at the time was also expansionary, reflecting the continuing Keynesian emphasis on strong domestic growth and high employment levels. The oil crisis soon changed all that.

When the Bretton Woods system collapsed and Germany floated against the US dollar in March 1973, the Bundesbank was freed to concentrate on domestic price stability commitments, although that freedom wasn't absolute given the nation's membership and obligations under the 'snake'. Further, the Council of Economic Experts morphed into a supply side (neo-liberal) organisation after the first oil price hikes in 1973 (Sievert, 2003: 34).

Helmut Schmidt succeeded Brandt as German Chancellor on 16 May 1974, and while he maintained the 'social–liberal coalition' between his own SPD and the liberals of the Free Democratic Party (FDP), there were clear signals that the policy position was hardening to a more conservative 'fight inflation first' strategy. In Schmidt's inaugural speech on 17 May 1974 to the Bundestag, he maintained that 'Das Modell Deutschland' (the German Model) was the way forward, a mix of hard line attitudes to inflation with social policies to take the pressure off the collective bargaining process. He sought to contain real wages growth and redistribute national income back to profits to encourage investment, which he claimed would stimulate employment growth in the long term. The bitter pill approach! He then delivered his famous call 'Without investments there is no growth; without investments there is no job security, no higher wages and no social progress' (Schmidt, 1974). Although this marked an end to the Keynesian embrace, he did stress the necessity for both private and public investment for future prosperity, in marked contrast to the extreme Monetarist position that eschewed significant public investment.

At the same time, the Bundesbank temporarily drank the worst Monetarist kool-aid. Beyer et al. (2009: 18) argued that while the Bundesbank initially accepted the Monetarist views of Milton Friedman and others in 1974 and rejected fine tuning the economy with interest rate adjustments in favour of formal targeting of the money supply, 'the honeymoon with leading monetarists came soon to an end' when the

Bank admitted that the 'experiment' failed and that it could not control the money supply. It is a major doctrine of mainstream macroeconomics that the central bank controls inflation by controlling the money supply. Experience shows that the central bank is unable to do the latter and must use interest rate management if it desires to influence the state of the economy and have any impact on inflation. In later chapters, it is argued that the extent to which the central bank can influence price stability is limited anyway and always involves major output losses. But the Bundesbank still defined its role as maintaining long-term price stability, while recognising that short-term growth imperatives were the responsibility of fiscal and industry policy administered by the government in conjunction with the roles played by industry and unions (the so-called 'social partners') in wage negotiations (see Beyer et al., 2009).

While Barre was ridiculing the French trade unions, the German government was busy implementing innovative policies such as 'Mitbestimmung' (participatory management or codetermination), which allowed trade unions to elect worker representatives to sit on the management board of German companies. It complemented Germany's long tradition of 'Betriebsrat' (Works Councils), which allowed workers to form bargaining units at the shop floor level to adjust the national collective bargains agreed between the peak employer and worker bodies to suit local circumstances. These initiatives were part of the anti-inflationary strategy. It was argued that if the workers had a stake in the enterprise management they would better appreciate the consequences of their bargaining demands.

Apart from dealing with the Bader–Meinhof gang, Schmidt's other concerns were then focused on the increasing strength of the mark in the context of continued lack of confidence in the US dollar and the difficulties this posed for managing the shrinking 'snake' membership and maintaining the competitiveness of Germany's export industries.

Some would say that Germany avoided most of the economic upheaval that beset the advanced world following the first oil crisis in 1974 as a result of Schmidt's 'abandonment' of Keynesian policies. But the reality was that in all Monetarist-tinged policy regimes, rising unemployment was the price that was paid. In 1974, before the policy position hardened, the unemployment rate in Germany was 2.8 per cent. By 1987 it was 10.5 per cent, having risen year by year over Schmidt's tenure. Further, Keynesian ideas were not entirely cast aside. The government combined increased investment in worker education and training with public sector job creation strategies, the so-called Arbeitsbeschaffungsmaßnahmen (ABMs), in response to rising unemployment. Further, unemployment benefits and other pensions were increased to help prevent the fall in total spending. A fully Monetarist state would not have supported these demand boosting initiatives and unemployment would have been much higher as a consequence.

The other legacy of the tight monetary policy approach adopted by the Bundesbank was that Germany came under increasing criticism, particularly from the US, which was continuing to suffer balance of payments difficulties and a weakening currency. It wanted Germany to ease interest rates and thus reduce the incentive for capital flows to move out of US dollars into marks. The Bundesbank was forced in late 1977 and early 1978 to engage in substantial selling of the mark in international currency markets to reduce upward pressure on it. The bank's Monthly Report for February 1978 said, 'The mood among German exporters was . . . depressed at the turn of 1977/78, primarily . . . because of the persistent rise in the mark, particularly against the US dollar' (Bundesbank, 1978a: 6). Within this context, Schmidt increasingly started to look beyond domestic policy as a way to resolve Germany's major headache, the instability of its strong currency among weaker, neighbouring currencies. The rising mark was making it very difficult to retain the 'snake' and this motivated Schmidt to pursue his European initiative with a sympathetic (pro European) Giscard d'Estaing. Schmidt and Giscard d'Estaing both came to office in 1974 at a time when the global economy was in chaos as a result of the oil crisis, stagflation and ongoing currency speculation. For the first time, the Germans found a French ally who was willing to advance the 'European' issue on their own terms. Once again the heightened motivation for monetary integration was directly related to the weakening of the US dollar. In the period after the abandonment of the Smithsonian Agreement, the US government had allowed the US dollar to devalue and the Europeans interpreted this as a lack of concern for the problems that currency instability caused for their customs union and the CAP.

Schmidt decided that the creation of an economic and monetary union would not only silence the critics of German monetary policy but, in helping to stabilise the German currency, would deliver benefits to German exporters. But Schmidt had to deal with the simmering conflict between the German government and the Bundesbank. The popularity of German politicians in the post World War II period was dependent on its record of low inflation and unemployment. The Bundesbank focused on keeping inflation low at the expense of unemployment, given that inflation was controlled by restricting total spending in the economy. When Brandt began the Keynesian era, which Schmidt maintained for a while, the conflict between government and bank was never far from the surface. The government was more interested in currency stability in the world foreign exchange markets while the bank was more focused on domestic price stability, and the two ambitions were not necessarily consistent at all times

(Hetzel, 2002). Hetzel cites Johnson (1998: 70) who said a Bundesbank official considered this struggle to be 'a Glaubenskrieg (religious war) of Wagnerian proportions' (Hetzel, 2002: 40).

Schmidt's European ambitions inflamed these tensions within Germany's economic policy circles. The stagflation that followed the first oil crisis consolidated the Bundesbank's domestic price stability priorities and the Federal government swung away from Keynesian policies and all but abandoned low unemployment rates as an objective. But the Bundesbank saw the growing pressure towards increased economic and monetary integration within Europe as a threat to its independence (Hetzel, 2002).

Throughout the 1970s, the mark appreciated against the US dollar and the French franc. The strains reached breaking point when the mark appreciated strongly against the US dollar in 1977 and early 1978, and the French franc simultaneously weakened against the mark. The perverse currency movements were imposing costs on the German export industries and provided the motivation for Germany to seek a better way of shifting some of the adjustment burden from its economy onto the weaker currencies of its European trade partners. In other words, it wanted to reduce the asymmetry in the system that was biased against Germany.

The idea of asymmetry itself was contestable. The German view was supported by Denmark and the Netherlands and was focused on avoiding import price inflation from higher inflation nations under a fixed exchange rate system, a problem that beset the latter years of the Bretton Woods system. Further, the Bundesbank feared that a lack of discipline in the weaker currency nations would force it to take responsibility for maintaining exchange rates, and in the context of an appreciating mark, this would compromise its capacity to control the money supply and expose Germany to higher inflation. Conversely, the weaker currency nations (France, Italy, the United Kingdom) were concerned that they would have to accept the restrictive Bundesbank monetary policy settings or else face major capital outflows. Under the 'snake', the dominance of German monetary policy (higher interest rates) forced its trading partners to endure higher unemployment than they desired (Houben, 2000). The upshot was that all parties had incentives, for different reasons, to move to a more symmetrical system of exchange rate management.

Both Schmidt and Giscard d'Estaing also considered currency instability to be a drag on the growth in European industrial production, which they considered a major cause of the persistently high unemployment that had beset Europe after the first oil price shock (Loriaux, 1991). They might have also implicated the excessively tight monetary policy and the lack of fiscal expansion, but the growing dominance of the neo-liberal ideology in this period precluded such wisdom (see Modigliani, 2000).

Further, currency instability within the customs union meant that exporters encountered costs by having to continually adjust their foreign currency prices and created incentives to engage in cross-border arbitrage (buying cheap in one currency on one side of the border and selling for profit in another currency on the other side of the border), which undermined local suppliers. Further, without currency stability, the setting of common agricultural prices was vexed and the ad hoc solution introduced was the complex system of green rates.

The currency instability combined with the persistent balance of payments deficits in many European nations led nations such as Italy, Denmark and the United Kingdom to defy EEC rules regarding free trade (under the customs union) and impose import restrictions. The introduction of the Italian import deposit (which required importers to place funds in advance with the Italian Foreign Exchange Office) in 1976, ostensibly in response to its balance of payments problems caused by the oil price rises, was seen as a basic challenge to the concept of freedom of movement of goods and services, a foundation stone of the customs union. The policy caused consternation among its European exporters and raised accusations of a return to the 'beggar thy neighbour' strategies that haunted world trade during the Great Depression. Unilateral imposts such as the deposit scheme were self-defeating if all nations followed suit. The global result would be a decline in overall trade and no change in the capacity of the nation to deal with the deficits caused by the need to pay higher prices for oil.

The matter led to Commission v Italy (Case 95/81, 1982) in the European Court where Italy argued the deposit scheme was in fact 'part of monetary policy' (p. 2191) and therefore legal under Article 104 of the Treaty. The Italians also argued it was allowable under 'the concept of public policy' (Article 36) (p. 2192), which related to the government's right to protect its currency sovereignty. The French government supported Italy in its claim that a nation 'must be able to combat' speculative attacks on its currency using methods such as the deposit scheme in question (p. 2194). While the Italian government lost the case, the general point was that the currency instability was undermining the legal framework of the European Project, in this case the customs union.

Schmidt and Giscard d'Estaing met in relative secrecy in early 1978 to develop a joint strategy to replace the ineffectual 'snake' with a more integrated level of monetary cooperation. The UK were early participants in these discussions but dropped out quickly. Notably, the Bundesbank Council and the European Council (apart from Roy Jenkins) were not privy to these meetings (Kaelberer, 2001). After working out a deal that both nations could live with, the two leaders unveiled their plan for a renewed attempt to introduce a European Monetary System (EMS) at the European Council summit in Copenhagen on 7 and 8 April. The proposal became reality at the European Council meeting in Bremen on 6–7 July 1979, when the leaders decided to push ahead with the creation of the EMS along the lines laid out in Copenhagen. The Council argued that the 'serious disruptions of the world economy, especially since the end of 1973' required Europe to take a 'common approach . . . to achieve . . . a considerably higher rate of economic growth and thus reduce the level of unemployment by fighting inflation' (European Council, 1978a: 17). This would be achieved by 'establishing a greater degree of monetary stability' (p. 17) and would require 'the creation of a closer monetary cooperation' (p. 18). In effect they wanted to bolster the 'snake', which they confirmed would 'remain fully intact' (p. 18).

Annex IV of the Council conclusions outlined the proposed design of the EMS, which would be 'at least as strict as the "snake"' (p. 20). Interventions to stabilise currencies within the snake would 'be in the currencies of participating countries' and changes 'in central rates' would be mutually agreed in advance. This represented a change to the existing 'snake', which allowed individual nations to alter their own parities.

The EMS introduced the European currency unit (ECU), which was effectively identical to the previously created European Unit of Account (EUA). The ECU was intended to be the benchmark accounting value against gold, which other currencies would be paired against. It was also to be 'used as a means of settlement between the EEC monetary authorities' (p. 20). The ECU was to reflect a basket of European currencies with each participating central bank subscribing 20 per cent of its US dollar and gold reserves to the initial pooled ECU fund. Initially, this allocation of ECUs to the Member States was to be administered through the EMCF, established in 1972 as part of the 'snake'. The proposal also extended the European credit facilities available to central banks to make it easier to maintain the agreed parity ranges. For example, the Very Short Term Financing (VSTF) facility was designed to automatically extend credit to any nation that required funds to defend its currency.

On the question of symmetry, the so-called 'bi-lateral parity grid' was created with the individual currency values expressed in terms of the ECU. This meant that the individual currency parities against the ECU also defined their values against each other. The French, particularly, wanted the ECU to be 'at the center of the system' (European Council, 1978a: Annex, 5) and be used as the intervention unit because they assessed it would reduce the importance of the mark. Germany opposed the use of ECU as the basis for intervention for various reasons, which need not concern us here. Essentially, it wanted a system that would free the Bundesbank from having to bear all the responsibility of maintaining parities in the face of ongoing upward pressure on the mark (Piodi, 2012). In this context, there were ongoing disputes about the creation of a central fund (that is, a central bank) that could use the ECUs to intervene to maintain parities.

The 'Belgian compromise' to the Franco-German impasse was the so-called Exchange Rate Mechanism (ERM) based on the 'bi-lateral parity grid' and supplemented by a 'divergence indicator', an 'early warning' threshold, which created, in a formal sense, the appearance of symmetry in the new system. The agreed plan was that currencies could fluctuate against each other by plus or minus 2.25 per cent. When either the upper or lower limit was reached the central banks of the relevant Member States would have to undertake foreign exchange transactions to bring the bi-lateral parity back into the acceptable range. The proposed intervention was to be triggered by the 'divergent indicator' (set at 75 per cent of the divergence margin).

So, for example, if the French franc reached the lower band of its parity against the mark the latter would have reached the upper band of its agreed parity against the franc. This would mean that both the Bundesbank and the Banque de France would have to simultaneously sell marks and buy francs in the foreign exchange markets. In theory, there would be less pressure on any one currency to adjust and less monetary disturbance in the respective economies. In reality, the adjustment process was not symmetric because the liquidity effects of the respective interventions were quite different.

If, for example, a nation's currency was depreciating against the mark, it either had to have mark reserves or access to funds through the VSTF facility. Some interventions were made using US dollars but mostly bi-lateral interventions were the norm early on in the arrangement (Ungerer et al., 1983). VSTF calls were recorded as a debt that had to be paid back in foreign currencies within 45 days. To ensure solvency, therefore, nations facing depreciating currencies had to effectively increase their interest rates or devalue. Germany was, however, favoured by the accounting rules of the system. While it had to sell its own currency and acquire, say, French francs to push its parity down below the upper limit against the franc, the rules gave the Bundesbank a VSTF credit and this was debited against the Banque de France in the same way as the French intervention. But the important point was that this placed no pressure on the Bundesbank to alter its interest rates. In other words, just as the adjustment under the Bretton Woods system always fell on the nations with balance of payments deficits (weaker currencies) and required them to reduce domestic growth and increase unemployment in order to ease the downward pressure on their currencies, the same asymmetric biases were built into the EMS.

Piodi (2012: 38) notes that the European Parliament gave the Bremen proposal 'a cool reception' and emphasised that the establishment of a ECU fund was 'not sufficient for the success of the European Monetary System' and did not constitute a viable path to full economic and monetary union unless it was accompanied by a common economic policy across the Member States. This concern repeats itself throughout the several decades of debate in Europe about the viability of the economic and monetary union. It was also ignored at Maastricht in 1991.

On 5 December 1978, the European Council met in Brussels and agreed to set up the EMS along the lines outlined at the Bremen summit (European Council, 1978b). The system was crisis prone from the outset, and instead of abandoning the almost impossible task of tying these disparate European economies together into a fixed exchange rate currency zone, the European political leaders began the rocky road to Maastricht with a compromised EMS and plenty of neo-liberal verve.

From the outset, the December agreement was less than complete and was concerned 'primarily with the initial phase of the EMS' (European Council, 1978b: 114). The all-important issue of the creation of a European central bank was thus deferred for two years because deep disagreement remained between the French and the Germans. As history tells us, the implicit next phase in the Council resolution was never implemented. The Germans didn't want the European Monetary Fund to have central banking functions given that this would compromise the Bundesbank capacity to maintain price stability. Other nations feared the creation of an independent fund would also compromise their sovereignty. Piodi (2012: 41) says, 'There was the fear that the European Monetary Fund would create international liquidity' and this could be inflationary. The compromise was to defer these issues for the second phase, which then raised issues as to what responsibility the Bundesbank and the Banque de France would have in ensuring the currency parities were maintained (Hetzel, 2002).

The Bundesbank exploited these vagaries and firmly defined its place in the EMS on its own terms. That strategy was important for what was to come post Maastricht.

THE EMS STARTS . . . AFTER A DELAY

The EMS came into operation on 13 March 1979 despite it being agreed at the December Council Meeting that it would start on 1 January 1979

(European Council, 1978b). The delay was caused by the French disagreeing with the decision to retain the MCAs as part of the CAP. The French wanted the MCAs to be abandoned because their farmers were forced to make payments to the system given the adverse movement of the franc against the previously determined ‘green rates’. In the official Statements by the Heads of State or Government at the Brussels Council Meeting in December 1978, Giscard d’Estaing emphasised the need to ‘return to a system of uniform pricing on agricultural markets, since the divergences which existed at present were anomalous’ (European Council, 1978c: 13).

While the delay was only three months, the dispute, once again, emphasised that France’s motivation for economic and monetary union was driven strongly by its desire to ensure the agricultural subsidies paid to its farmers by Germany via Brussels would continue.

THE BUNDESBANK ASSERTS ITSELF EARLY

The beginning of the EMS was marked by two ‘stand out’ facts, ‘an oil price rise which in real terms has been of the same order of magnitude as that of 1973–74, and an acceleration of inflation in all industrial countries’ (BIS, 1980: 3). Within this context, the uncertainty left by the failure to create a European level central bank was soon resolved by the aggressive action of the Bundesbank.

To maintain its price stability charter, the Bundesbank introduced formal monetary targets in 1975 as a response to the growing influence of Monetarism in the academy and the rising inflation arising from the oil price shock in that year. The introduction of monetary targets enabled the central bank to distance itself from real issues such as unemployment by signalling ‘that monetary policy will not be available as an instrument of discretionary aggregate demand management’ (von Hagen, 1989: 54). This policy shift was the beginning of the abandonment of the commitment by national governments to full employment (Mitchell and Muysken, 2008). Central bankers increasingly claimed their only role was to maintain price stability and that fiscal policy should not compromise the central bank’s commitment. The predictable result was stagnant growth and persistently high unemployment.

The Bundesbank’s money growth target in 1975 was 8 per cent. By 1985 it had narrowed this to a 3–5 per cent range, which reflected its ‘growing intolerance of inflation’ (Kahn and Jacobson, 1989: 21). Sometimes it would publish a single money supply growth target as the goal, while at other times a range was provided.

When the EMS was finally put into operation on 13 March 1979, the Bundesbank announced a tougher approach to its quest for price stability. From 1975 to 1979, Germany's money supply grew well above the 8 per cent. In 1979, it announced a new money growth range of 6 to 9 per cent per annum, which was designed to give it flexibility depending on 'further domestic and external economic developments' (Bundesbank, 1979: 5). In other words, it wanted to be tougher or easier depending on economic growth rates. Pointedly, the Bundesbank noted that while it was having 'difficulties' in 'meeting such objectives' the announcement of the targets was, among other things, intended to 'facilitate a certain coordination of monetary policies in the countries of the European Community' (Bundesbank, 1979: 5). In 1980, the range was reduced to 5 to 8 per cent and in 1981 from 4 to 7 per cent.

While the Bundesbank's primary focus was on price stability, it also continued to be jointly responsible under the EMS for exchange rate stability, which at times compromised its capacity to maintain its target growth in the domestic money supply. For example, to stop the mark from breaching the upper value limit, the Bundesbank was often forced to sell marks, usually in return for US dollars or other currencies. This pushed more marks into circulation, which the Bundesbank considered exposed the German economy to an excessive inflation risk. This sense of compromise was an important factor in the way the Bundesbank operated within the EMS.

As a result of the jostling between France and Germany, the EMS was effectively just an agreement to limit currency fluctuations between the Member States and provided no real scope for an economic and monetary union as presented in the Werner Report. The decision to consider the establishment of the European Monetary Fund (EMF) was effectively abandoned by the end of 1980. Already the transfer of US dollar and gold reserves held by the participating central banks to the EMCF as part of the creation of the ECU base was a compromised arrangement, driven by the Bundesbank concern that it would build up excess stocks of the relatively useless ECU. The compromise saw the central banks depositing the assets through short-term 'swap' contracts, which meant they did not cede ownership. Limitations on the use of ECUs in settling debts between central banks were also put in place and the EMCF was prevented from creating ECUs in its own right. All these arrangements/restrictions were designed to ensure the EMCF could not act like a central bank.

This environment of distrust meant it was obvious that the Bundesbank would prevent the creation of the EMF, which had been originally envisioned as the European counterpart to the US Federal Reserve Bank. The Germans raised legal complexities as a means of undermining the introduction of the Fund, while the French Gaullists rehearsed their usual preoccupation about losing sovereignty to a supranational body (Hoffmeyer, 2000). All talk of the Fund evaporated in France once the socialists were elected in 1981. The EMS then remained a voluntary arrangement between central banks to reduce currency fluctuations, which had limited political support. Further, the economic divergences among the signature nations were of such magnitudes that this arrangement would be constantly stressed to breaking point. Hoffmeyer (2000: 55) concluded 'the visions were again in shambles'.

The shambles was quick to manifest. Between March 1979 and March 1983, there were seven currency realignments and 11 up to January 1987 (Table 5.1). Respective governments requested several of the realignments to restore lost competitiveness as inflation differentials widened. Others were required to maintain the overall integrity of the system given the difficulty the central banks were having keeping within the 'parity grid'. The fourth realignment, on 5 October 1981, followed the May 1981 election of François Mitterrand, the first socialist President in France's Fifth Republic. Speculation against the franc in the second half of 1981 forced the Banque de France to buy the currency in large quantities in international exchange markets to stop it breaching the agreed lower bound. Mitterrand considered this unsustainable and it was agreed that the mark

Table 5.1 Currency realignments in European Monetary System, March 1979 to January 1987, per cent against the ECU

Date of realignment	Belgian Lux Franc %	Danish Krona %	D-Mark %	Dutch Guilder %	French Franc %	Irish Punt %	Italian Lira %
24 Sep. 1979	–	−2.86	+2.00	–	–	–	–
30 Nov. 1979	–	−4.76	–	–	–	–	–
23 Mar. 1981	–	–	–	–	–	–	−6.00
5 Oct. 1981	–	–	+5.50	+5.50	−3.00	–	−3.00
22 Feb. 1982	−8.50	−3.00	–	–	–	–	–
14 Jun. 1982	–	–	+4.25	+4.25	−5.25	–	−2.25
21 Mar. 1983	+1.50	+2.50	+5.50	+3.50	−2.50	−3.50	−2.50
22 Jul. 1985	+2.00	+2.00	+2.00	+2.00	+2.00	+2.00	−6.00
7 Apr. 1986	+1.00	+1.00	+3.00	+3.00	−3.00	–	–
4 Aug. 1986	–	–	–	–	–	−8.00	–
12 Jan. 1987	+2.00	–	+3.00	+3.00	–	–	–

Note: Lux refers to Luxembourg, D-Mark refers to Deutsche Mark.

Source: Bank of International Settlements, various Annual Reports.

would be revalued by 5.5 per cent and the franc and lira would be devalued by 3 per cent, a massive swing against the mark.

The French government sought two further devaluations in June 1982 and March 1983, mostly to deal with the strengthening mark and the diverging economic policies between the two nations. These realignments were of such a scale that it was clear that the EMS could not continue unless the non-German Member States reoriented their domestic economic and monetary policies to follow the restrictive stance taken by the Germans.

The French experience is particularly interesting. After indulging in the early Monetarist experiments under Giscard d'Estaing and Barre, the political fallout associated with the sharply rising unemployment demonstrated the poverty of that policy framework and led to Mitterrand's election. His government immediately set about doing what a sovereign government should do: use fiscal and monetary policy to expand employment, reduce unemployment and expand the social wage. But the French were still intent on remaining in the EMS. They wanted everything: political popularity associated with the lower unemployment and improved living conditions, a straitjacket on perceived German pretensions to European power, and continued German subsidies to the CAP. On the one hand, domestic policy sovereignty was crucial if it was to lower unemployment and this predicated against participating in the EMS. On the other hand, the desire to undermine German influence and to find a way to subsidise their farmers under the CAP forced them to engage in the European dialogue. They were caught betwixt!

By the third currency realignment in March 1983, the French were at the crossroads and the incompatibility of these competing ambitions was obvious. At that point, France had a choice. It could retain its policy sovereignty and pursue its legitimate domestic objectives by floating the franc or remain within the EMS and subjugate its domestic policy freedom to the dictates of the Bundesbank. Unfortunately, for the French and for Europe in general, they chose the neo-liberal path, however culturally alien this was to them (Balleix-Banerjee, 1997).

Accordingly, the French government fell lock step into the increasingly dominant Monetarist policy approach that involved using rising unemployment as a policy tool to discipline the inflation process. That political reality was too stark for the public to accept and necessitated a smokescreen being erected to disassociate the rising unemployment from macroeconomic policy choices. The rising unemployment was reconstructed by the political and bureaucratic spin doctors as a 'structural' problem reflecting a failure of individuals to be self-reliant and assiduous in job search and skill development. A bevy of securely employed and highly paid economists pumped out a massive number of 'research' papers, which served to give authority and legitimacy to this ideologically tainted and empirically bereft view. Most of this 'authority' lacked credibility, but then mainstream economics has never really been concerned with its theoretical inconsistencies or lack of empirical traction.

The shift in policy in March 1983, the so-called 'tournant de la rigueur' (turn to austerity), took France back to the 'fight inflation first' policies of Giscard d'Estaing in the late 1970s and ended the few years of social advance in France. The shift in language, from 'd'austérité' (as coined by Raymond Barre) to the softer 'la rigeur' was just window dressing. The socialists were abandoning their principles to become part of the neo-liberal political convergence that captured social democratic parties in most advanced nations during this period. While the so-called 'désinflation competitive' (Fitoussi et al., 1993) aimed to break the repeating cycles of devaluations and high interest rates, it was heavily motivated by the long standing preoccupation among the French politicians and their industrial support base to stay competitive against the Germans as a sort of one-upmanship (Howarth and Loedel, 2003).

The sudden shift in policy in March 1983 should also be seen in the context of the longstanding intellectual battle between the planners and the Finance Ministry economists as to the pros and cons of the free market and the growing obsession among economists in the Banque de France with the primacy of price stability in economic policy making. The tensions were there before March 1983 and each time that France was forced to devalue (October 1981 and June 1982), the Banque de France demanded fiscal policy cutbacks. Duchaussoy (2010) confirmed the hostility of the Banque de France to the Mitterrand government's growth policy. Its governor, Renaud La Genière, wrote to the Economics and Finance Minister Jacques Delors in 1981 urging him to pay more attention to price stability and to cut public deficits. The correspondence between the two institutions revealed that a real enmity had developed between the monetary and fiscal policy makers in France over this period.

In 1983, Delors, as the Economics, Finance, and Budget Minister (1983 to 1984), strengthened the neo-liberal program that Barre had begun. The reduction in domestic inflation that resulted from the 'scorched earth' approach was celebrated as the first serious sign towards a convergence reality, while the sharp rises in unemployment were brushed under the carpet and forgotten. Various bureaucrats, supported by free market orientated academics worked overtime to convince everyone that the unemployment was not a result of a lack of jobs created by excessively restrictive fiscal and monetary policy, but rather a sign that people were not searching for work hard enough and were lulled into a welfare-dependent lassitude. The war on the victims of this folly in macroeconomic policy gathered pace through the 1980s and culminated in the 1994 release of the OECD *Jobs Study*, which became the bible for those intent on ignoring the fact that the unemployed cannot search for jobs that are not there.

There was also a distinct shift in attitudes among the socialists towards Europe from March 1983. For example, the ultimately tragic French socialist politician Pierre Bérégovoy wanted France to leave the EMS when he was Minister for Social Affairs in 1981. By the time he became the Minister of the Economy and Finance in 1984 he was a champion of austerity and a strong French franc, and even more assertive about these matters than Delors (Guigo, 2013).

On 16 May 1983, the European Council extended '4000 million ECU or the equivalent amount in other currencies' to France, on the condition that it tighten fiscal policy 'in accordance with the adjustment programme which it has presented' (European Council, 1983: 44–45). The French had agreed to limiting the fiscal deficit to 3 per cent of GDP in 1983 and 1984, restraining social security and unemployment insurance payments and cutting the capacity of state-owned enterprises to borrow. Further, the Banque de France was required to reduce the money growth target to create a 'marked reduction in the rate of domestic credit expansion'.

The decision was brazen. For being compliant and abandoning its 'Keynesian' desires the French government was given some short-term funds to bolster the exchange rate. The tone of the discussion and the wording in the official resolution (European Council, 1983) were akin to the paternalistic statements issued by the IMF when it extended harshly conditional loans to struggling nations, which undermined the governments' capacities to advance the wellbeing of their citizens.

The result was also similar to the experiences of the poorest nations who have been given these conditional IMF loans. France's output gap (the difference between actual output and the maximum potential output) nearly trebled between 1982 and 1985 as economic growth, household consumption and private investment slumped and more than half a million workers joined the jobless queues over the three year period. The official unemployment rate rose from 7.4 per cent in 1982 to 10.2 per cent in 1985 and continued to increase after that. Not surprisingly, the saving ratio (household saving out of disposable income) fell from 16.4 per cent in 1982 to 13.5 per cent in 1985 as a result of the failing economic growth and rising unemployment undermining household incomes.

However, the bureaucrats judged the outcome to be a success and applauded the French for adopting the German solution. Everyone was pursuing 'Modell Deutschland' now!

THE EMS'S 'SECOND LIFE' MARKED BY INCREASING FRANCO-GERMAN ACRIMONY AS THEY MARCH TOGETHER TOWARDS MAASTRICHT

The Bundesbank effectively forced the devaluations on the French franc in the early years of the EMS by refusing to reduce its own interest rates to quell the outflow of capital from France. By giving primacy to the Monetarist position on inflation, Germany became the de-facto monetary authority in Europe. In effect, the decision by the EMS Member States to peg against the mark and subjugate their own policy independence meant that the Bundesbank became the central bank for the EEC (Hetzel, 2002: 50). For all of France's historical concerns about sovereignty and rejecting supranational European institutions, it took the socialists in 1983 to give up that freedom, and then not to Brussels but to Germany, of all nations. Once the Germans had won that 'war', the French became increasingly motivated to support a separate European central bank to wrest some control back from Germany. Perversity seemed to have no end.

It was argued that the growing acceptance of the primacy of 'price stability' among French politicians on both sides of politics was a reflection of their desire to regain the semblance of French domination in Europe (Baun, 1996). De Boissieu and Pisani-Ferry (1995: 23) noted that 'only a low-inflation, stable-currency France could pretend to some form of leadership in Europe' and 'maintaining France's status within the EC and within the so-called French-German couple' required them to fall into line. So for the French political class, the connection 'rigueur: power' (p. 23) became an objective in itself and the costs to the citizens in the form of suppressed real wages and rising unemployment was subsidiary, at best. Mitterrand 'made the choice of giving priority to France's European commitments over his own initial economic program in 1983' (p. 23). This divergence in motivations of the political class and the wellbeing of the population is now the norm in modern Europe.

After France began to toe the 'correct' ideological line, the longed-for 'convergence' in economic policies and outcomes began to emerge and the currency instability reduced. There were also external developments that helped reduce the pressure on the mark and hence the other European currencies. The election of Ronald Reagan to the US Presidency in 1981 warmed the cockles of the neo-liberal ideologues. The reality was that his Administration introduced an old fashioned 'Keynesian stimulus', which promoted strong economic growth following the severe recession in 1982. The ideologues were seemingly blind to the fact that what was working for the US was exactly what they loathed. The smoke and mirrors was a reversal of the old adage 'do as I say not as I do'.

The US dollar strengthened through the first years of the 1980s and there were large capital inflows to the US in response to the favourable investment climate, supported by an 'expanding "structural" component of the US budget deficit' (BIS, 1985: 8). While there were some adverse effects in Europe as imports became more expensive, they were 'more than offset by the benefits bestowed on the rest of the world by the locomotive role of the US economy, without which there would have been no recovery in world trade' (BIS, 1985: 9). Given the restrictive policies in Europe, the rise in European unemployment would have been much worse if the US had not introduced the large fiscal stimulus to its economy.

The promoters of the EMS, however, declared it a success. In the sense that inflation rates moderated and converged, one might concede that the objectives were attained. Figure 5.3 shows the evolution of annual inflation rates in the EMS member nations between 1970 and 1995. The nations are divided into the high inflation (Ireland, Italy and the UK), medium inflation (Denmark and France), and low inflation (Benelux and

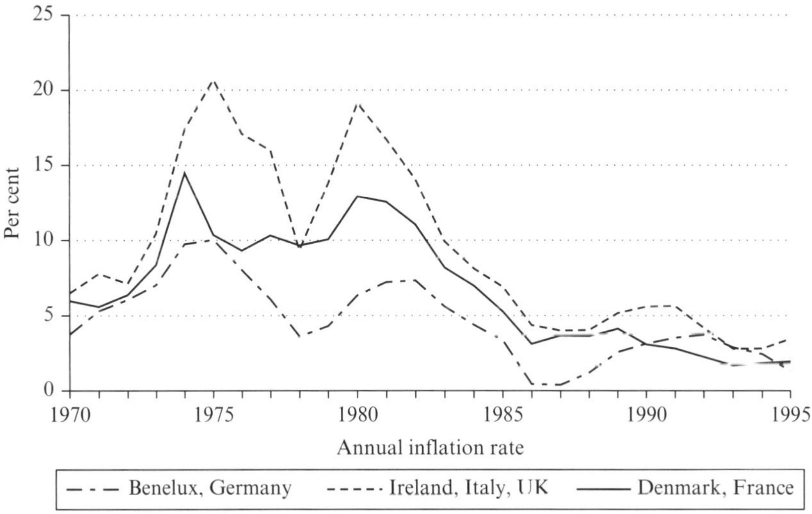

Note: The UK joined the EMS late in 1980 and left soon afterwards (1982). Group averages are shown.

Source: European Commission, Annual Macroeconomic Database (AMECO).

Figure 5.3 Annual inflation rates, EMS member nations, 1970–95, per cent

Germany) at the inception of the EMS in March 1979. The spike in the early 1980s corresponded with the second oil price hike in 1979, which coincided with the demise of the Shah of Iran. It is clear that inflation rates fell during the 1980s in all nations and convergence was nearly absolute by the mid 1980s.

But equating the convergence of inflation rates with economic success is only possible if the economic goals are narrowly specified. The Council Resolution on 5 December 1978 had stated that the EMS should be seen 'within the context of a broadly based strategy aimed at improving the prospects of economic development' (European Council, 1979: 9, Annexe 1) and expressed a desire 'to strengthen the economic potential of the less prosperous countries of the Community' (p. 9, Annexe 1). It is hard to reconcile these grand ambitions with the later self-congratulatory back-slapping among the political classes that declared the EMS a success and motivated them to pave the way to Maastricht. Figure 5.4 gives a glimpse of what happened to the people in Europe over this period. Unemployment rates rose sharply in the first several years of the Monetarist economic policy onslaught and remained at elevated levels as the politicians were busy putting further nails in the coffin of European prosperity in the

Source: European Commission, Annual Macroeconomic Database (AMECO).

Figure 5.4 Annual unemployment rates, EMS member nations, 1970–95, per cent

form of the Single European Act in February 1986, the Basel/Nyborg Agreement in September 1987, and then the 1989 Delors Report.

Baun (1996: 607) noted that the EMS produced 'declining rates of economic growth in Europe throughout the 1980s' as a result of the 'built-in deflationary or antigrowth bias of the system . . . dominated by the conservative monetary priorities of Germany and its independent central bank'. One could argue that even though the EMU has made things more complicated, nothing has fundamentally changed in Europe today. Further, while Germany's inflation obsession can be clothed in a philosophical argument that inflation is intrinsically anti-democratic in the sense that it is a 'non voted tax', the ceding of economic sovereignty under the EMS by the other Member States to the Bundesbank was the beginning of the loss of democracy in Europe, which has accelerated over the course of the current crisis.

Once the French realised that instead of a European level body compromising their policy sovereignty it was the Bundesbank that was in control, their attitude to fast tracking a full European monetary union changed. The acrimony between France and Germany broke out openly in 1987. Things were more manageable in the early years of the EMS because the US dollar had been regaining strength and the nations maintained capital controls, which attenuated the flow of funds into and out of their nations. Throughout this period, the IMF, true to form, had been urging the nations to liberalise capital flows, which of course, once achieved would further tighten the Bundesbank policy straitjacket for the other nations in relation to defending their parities. However, the US dollar started to depreciate again towards the end of 1986 and this put new pressure on the mark to revalue. In the fallout, the French franc fell to the lower end of the agreed EMS parity range. The French government did not wish to devalue nor could they reasonably maintain the parity without worsening the unemployment that the fiscal austerity had wrought.

The French and Italians knew that the Bundesbank effectively set the interest rates for all EMS nations, irrespective of whether the rates were appropriate elsewhere outside Germany. Further, while the formal EMS understanding placed equal burden on the central banks to maintain currency stability, the reality was that the nations facing downward pressure on their currencies had to shoulder the adjustment burden because the Bundesbank increasingly refused to do its share, given that the mark was stronger. For the Germans, intervention would mean selling marks in currency markets, which they feared would ignite domestic inflation as a result of the expanding money supply. Ungerer et al. (1990: 10) concluded, 'the hegemonic role of German economic policy . . . narrowed the choice of economic strategies for its partner countries, impeded growth oriented policies on their part, and thus perpetuated unemployment problems' and was 'contrary to the community character of the EMS'. This problem remains one of the intractable issues facing Europe today.

The first attempt to nullify the German dominance of the EMS, which had effectively become a mark zone, came in the mid 1980s, with the failed attempt by Delors, in his role as European Commission President, to promote the French demand that a European monetary authority be included within the wording of the European treaties. This manoeuvring was part of the debate associated with the introduction of the Single European Act (SEA). The SEA was signed in February 1986 and was the first major revision since the 1957 Treaty of Rome. The aim was to reform the 'Common Market' to ensure that free trade in theory meant free trade in practice. It also aimed at improving the speed of decision making in the EEC (by implementing qualified majorities for certain Council decisions) and empowering the European Parliament. Notably, the unanimity rules and the veto powers were maintained for many matters relating to economic and monetary policy, although what issues were demarcated in this way was unclear and legally contestable (Good, 1988). As expected, the process was controversial with strident disagreement about how much power to give the European Parliament.

Apart from generalities in the preamble to the SEA that noted the 'objective of the progressive realization of Economic and Monetary Union', the 'introduction of the European Monetary System (EMS)', and that the 'Community and the Central Banks of the Member States have taken a number of measures intended to implement monetary cooperation' (European Council, 1988), there was no explicit recognition of a European level monetary institution. The French attempt failed. A new strategy was needed if they were to counter the German economic policy dominance within the EEC.

A number of separate developments after 1986 pushed Europe towards monetary union and promoted the French intentions. In 1986, the EMS veterans Giscard d'Estaing and Schmidt re-entered the debate by setting up the 'Committee for the Monetary Union of Europe', which had its first meeting in Brussels in December of that year. In April 1987, the Committee released 'A Programme for Action' which included the creation of a European central bank, use of the ECU for private sector transactions, increased convergence of economic policies, and the liberalisation of capital controls (Committee for the Monetary Union of Europe, 1988). This Report was influential at the European Council meeting in Hannover on 27–28 June 1988.

At the end of 1986 and into 1987, there were major speculative attacks on the European currencies as the US dollar weakened. The EEC

Economic and Finance Ministers agreed to realign the currencies on 12 January 1987 because the central banks could not hold the existing parities in the face of the speculative capital flows. There was a general concern that the German domination of the EMS was forcing unwanted realignments within the EMS and stifling growth prospects (Tsoukalis, 1989). It was obvious that there was neither stability nor growth!

In 1986, the famous French cohabitation began, with the socialist Mitterrand as President appointing the right wing neo-Gaullist Jacques Chirac as his Prime Minister. The latter, who as the majority holder in the Assembly was given oversight of the domestic economy, didn't waste any time in picking up the deregulation and privatisation agenda from the previous regime. Chirac wanted to be France's Margaret Thatcher. Chirac appointed Édouard Balladur as the Minister of Economy, Finance, and Privatisation, the last responsibility reflecting the penetration that the neo-liberal ideology had made into the affairs of the state. Balladur started selling off public companies and abolishing the wealth tax as part of the much vaunted, but never to materialise, 'trickle down' growth strategy. He was also the vanguard for France's now very pro European stance.

Balladur pressured the Ecofin members about the need to usurp the Bundesbank's deflationary policy bias. This concern led the Ministers to call upon the Committee of Governors of the Central Banks to formulate a plan to improve the intervention mechanisms within the EMS. The result was a meeting of the Governors in Basel on 8 September 1987, which sent a plan for strengthening the EMS to the Economics and Finance Ministers (Committee of Governors of the Central Banks, 1987). The day before, the 'Alternates' to the EEC Monetary Committee met to review the document that would be considered by the Governors. At that meeting, the Bundesbank representative stressed that it 'could not accept rules that weaken its stability oriented policies' and that it was up to the other EMS countries 'to work further towards greater stability so as to have other strong currencies in the system which could acquire reserve status and thereby reduce the relative role of the Deutsche Mark' (European Council, 1987: 1). This was a rather 'Marie Antoinette' style denial of what was happening to say the least. Richter (1999: 3) notes that 'To experts on German affairs it must have been clear from the beginning that the Bundesbank would not yield to political pressure and that no Bonn government in its right mind would get the idea of changing Section 3 of the BBG' (the BBG being the Bundesbank Act, in which Section 3 defines the price stability responsibilities).

What became known as the Basel/Nyborg Agreement was based on the recognition that large scale intervention in the currency markets was not sufficient to maintain currency stability and that both increased cooperation (meaning: more symmetrical intervention burdens) and differential interest rates were required. The French, supported by the Belgians and Italians, demanded that bilateral obligations on currency market intervention be enforced (Renard, 1987). The Dutch and German representatives wanted to avoid being forced to expand the supply of their own currencies to defend the weak currencies because they feared this would be inflationary.

Unsurprisingly, the Bundesbank won! The bankers, recognising that investment funds were now more mobile, not to mention the ideological preference to abandon capital controls, agreed to allow currencies to move more freely within the set bounds and to expand the flexibility of the VSTF capacity to fund intervention in situations where the lower limits of a parity were threatened (BIS, 1988: 196). The Germans argued that nations should abandon capital controls and rely more on interest rate differentials to manage the currency parities, which would reduce the need to call on the VSTF. The 'easy credit' implied by the VSTF was repugnant to the Germans (Gros and Thygesen, 1992). The agreement reached was intended to result in less frequent currency realignments (BIS, 1988: 196). The Governors' proposal was signed off at a meeting of the European Council in Nyborg on 12 September 1987.

But Balladur was just getting started on the French government's new anti-Bundesbank strategy. On 8 January 1988, he released his 'Mémorandum sur la construction monétaire européenne' for discussion among the Ecofin Ministers (Balladur, 1988). He realised immediately that without capital controls, the French economy would be more sensitive to the Bundesbank's deflationary stance and that France would have to continue to use higher interest rates to maintain the franc parity. French politics, let alone national pride, would not tolerate that reality.

Statements coming from the Banque de France were reinforcing these developments. Deputy Governor of the Banque de France Philippe Lagayette wrote in 1988 that while the EMS had been a success (stabilising inflation) it was not well geared to promoting and sustaining growth (Lagayette, 1988: 444). He proposed three major changes: make the intervention system more symmetric, broaden the EEC membership, and develop the use of the ECU as a European currency (p. 444). He specifically said that the external surpluses of Germany were a source of tension for the weaker currencies and there was no adjustment mechanism to correct the imbalances (p. 445).

The point was that there was a corrective mechanism in place, but because of the Bundesbank intransigence, all the adjustment was forced onto France and the other weaker nations. In recognising that the trade imbalances were problematic for the EMS, Lagayette said that the values of the European currencies could not be set by the economic situation of the nation with the largest external surplus (Lagayette, 1988: 445). He called for a return to the vision in the Werner Report, and the logical necessity of a single currency and a European central bank, all code for reducing the power of Germany.

Balladur, once again, promoted the French concern about the EMS on the grounds that the intervention criteria forced the nation with the weaker currency to assume the adjustment burden. He indicated French support for a common European currency, a strategy designed to eliminate the mark forever. What the French thought would happen if they succeeded in gaining a common currency and the creation of a European central bank, which would replace the Bundesbank, is another matter. They clearly found out in 2008!

In February 1988, the Italian Finance Minister Giuliano Amato responded supportively with his own memorandum accusing the Germans of stifling growth and operating with an undervalued currency. The Italians upped the ante by threatening 'to invoke escape clauses in the process of capital liberalization . . . as well as implement various protective domestic regulations' if the asymmetries were not eliminated (Moravcsik, 1998: 433). While the two memoranda were strident in their attacks on the system, they failed to outline a process towards economic and monetary union. Piodi (2012: 52) said they were 'vague when it came to the solutions for achieving monetary union'.

But Germany was also very sensitive to the growing anti-German sentiment in Europe. They saw the European Project in terms of restoring its place in Europe. In 1995, former German Chancellor Schmidt reflected on the accusations of German bullying or intimidation in relation to the evolution of the economic and monetary union and the reactions of leading German policy makers to these accusations. He said, 'the creation of the monetary union is in the first instance eminently a task for foreign policy' (Schmidt, 1995). He noted that Germany had conducted three wars with France over the last 125 years and that without a full economic and monetary union, the mark and the German financial institutions would dominate Europe. This would spark increased fear and envy against Germany, and lead, for the third time in the 20th century, to a coalition of almost all other European nations against Germany (Schmidt, 1995).

In this context, the German Foreign Office took the diplomatic decision to push for the union to quell the ongoing criticism of the ugly German, which threatened to derail the progress that the nation had made in restoring its image in the post World War II period. The situation had been reached where the French pushed for monetary union to undermine the dominance of the Bundesbank despite their historical distaste for ceding domestic policy discretion to supranational bodies and the Germans supported the union as part of their vision of a place in Europe, which less than half a century before they had devastated with their extreme politics of anthropological supremacy. The German willingness to advance the common currency was highly conditional, however, and reflected the dominance of the Bundesbank. Neither the French nor German motivations encouraged confidence in what would be created.

While the French and Italian memoranda were 'vague' on detail, it was left to the Germans to articulate in fine print how the economic and monetary union might emerge and operate. Two separate German memorandums were issued in early 1988. The author of the first, issued on 26 February 1988, was Helmut Kohl's Minister of Foreign Affairs, Hans-Dietrich Genscher. It was an exercise in German precision, balanced, to be fair, by a concern to placate the concerns of the French so that a truly 'federal' solution could be achieved. The essence of Genscher's input was to recommend the establishment of a single currency mediated by a European central bank. Genscher knew he had to walk the fine line between old 'economist' and 'monetarist' positions that had separated the French and the Germans for decades (Genscher, 1998). He also knew that the political balance within France had swung towards the 'economist' position under Chirac, which was much more closely aligned with the hard line German position on inflation. Further, he had to bring the German 'economists' along and they were hostile to anything that would diminish the dominant position of the Bundesbank.

Genscher knew that a recommendation to increase the use of the ECU as an intervention currency would find favour with the French, who wanted to diminish the importance of the US dollar and the mark in currency markets. He also knew that he could reduce opposition within Germany from the Bundesbank and economists in the Ministry of Finance, if the proposal effectively rehearsed the Bundesbank Act, such that there should be no compromise against the fight against inflation irrespective of what the democratically elected polity might desire by way of domestic growth strategy. So instead of the deflationary strategy of the Bundesbank dominating European policy and bringing Germany into conflict with the other nations, Genscher proposed that a new European Central Bank would dominate policy even though the policy would remain the same. German concerns about inflation would thus be assuaged and they could shift the responsibility for the policy stance to a supranational body. It was largely an exercise in smoke and mirrors though.

Genscher's memo was followed soon after by a statement by German Finance Minister and Chairman of the Council of European Communities, Gerhard Stoltenberg, to the Interim Committee of the IMF (Stoltenberg,

1988), which concentrated on increasing the freedom of capital flows and divorcing the issue from balance of payments problems. This was a direct challenge to the Italian position, which, while favouring capital liberalisation, still suggested that capital controls could be used if the EMS asymmetries persisted. Stoltenberg and the Bundesbank President, Karl Otto Pöhl, were not enamoured with the creation of a European central bank, but were persuaded by Genscher's emphasis on price stability as the priority policy goal.

As an aside, Stoltenberg made a statement to the IMF on 14 April 1988, which further elaborated the German position. He indicated that the challenge in maintaining exchange rate stability was to reduce major balance of payments discrepancies between surplus and deficit nations and that an 'important element of this strategy is the maintenance of an adequate rate of growth in domestic demand' (Stoltenberg, 1988: 38). Modern Germany might take heed!

A recent reflective piece published by the Bundesbank (Lindenlaub, 2011) considered the different ideas about integration within Europe that had to be reconciled. Lindenlaub (2011: 1) said, 'France was aiming only for a European reserve fund, the intended aim of which was to stabilise the exchange rates between the European currencies at an average value and to minimise exchange rate fluctuations against the US Dollar. For a long time, price stability was of secondary importance'. By way of contrast, Germany was 'prepared to go a comparatively long way in meeting French aims' but could only conceive of a union where there was a 'matching institutional design', a 'prior orientation to stability' and 'a system of fixed exchange rates only if it did not jeopardise price stability in Germany' (Lindenlaub, 2011: 1).

On the Genscher proposal, Lindenlaub said (2011: 2):

> In the end, Germany presented a proposal, in consultation with the Bundesbank, which went far beyond what the French had in mind: a single currency and common central bank preceded by further advances in convergence in the reduction of inflation rates and budget deficits as well as in the liberalisation of capital flows, and progress towards a political union.

Genscher's proposal was considered at the European Council meeting in Hannover on 27–28 June 1988, which established a working party headed by Jacques Delors to develop a detailed implementation plan for the creation of an economic and monetary union.

6. The Delors Report

THE COMMITTEE IS STACKED

The Delors Committee deliberately excluded the Economics and Finance ministers at the suggestion of Delors himself. He wanted the Committee to 'consist of the governors of the central banks, who were more independent than the governments' (Danescu, 2013c: 4). Delors (1989a: 63) noted 'The creeping paralysis of the Community was the result of the Member States calling into question the Community method for the progressive and limited transfer of national powers to common institutions possessing a real power to make decisions.'

Delors knew that the Bundesbank would not budge at all on the independence of a new European central bank and that it would have been difficult to get agreement if the Ecofin Ministers were involved. Howarth and Loedel (2003: 36) said, 'National treasury officials from several countries balked at German demands on autonomy and focused a great deal more on the economic side of EMU'. Further, the central bankers had been explicitly excluded from the design of the EMS in 1979, which Delors considered had rendered the system prone to failure. Delors thus constituted his Committee to minimise any (legitimate) discussions of Member State sovereignty and to push through a homogenised Monetarist vision for the new united Europe. By excluding the diversity of opinion, Europe was setting itself up for monumental failure, which manifested in 2008.

Verdun (1999: 308) asked how the 'consensus on the creation of EMU in the Community could have been reached so easily'. He concluded that the Delors Committee constituted an 'epistemic community', defined by Haas (1992: 3) as 'a network of professionals with recognized expertise and competence in a particular domain and an authoritative claim to policy-relevant knowledge within that domain or issue-area'. This network also shares normative and causal beliefs and is engaged in a 'common policy enterprise' (p. 3), which means they agree on 'common practices associated with a set of problems' (p. 3). The central bankers met regularly and held a similar worldview about the primacy of monetary policy and the need for fiscal policy to be a passive support to the deflationary strategy defined by the Bundesbank. The neo-liberal Groupthink was consolidating.

In simple terms, the exclusion of the Ecofin Ministers meant that the Monetarist-orientated central bankers would come up with a consensus fairly quickly. The addition of a conservative mainstream economics professor (Niels Thygesen from Copenhagen), and some other bankers (Alexandre Lamfalussy, BIS; and Miguel Boyer, President Banco Exterior de España) also reinforced the lack of diversity. All members of the Committee were firmly wedded to the new era of neo-liberalism and the abandonment of Keynesian macroeconomic policies in favour of the hard line pursuit of price stability.

DELORS ABANDONS THE WERNER PLAN

Prior to the publication of the Delors Report, the European Council had reasserted, at its December meeting in Rhodes, that its focus would be on the 'progress made in establishing the single market' (European Council, 1988: 2) and 'the irreversible nature of the movement towards a Europe without internal frontiers' (p. 2). The Delors Report reiterated that focus and noted the seminal nature of the 1970 Werner Report (Delors Report, 1989a). Delors said, in a 1999 documentary produced by the European Commission (1999), that 'the overall philosophy behind what we proposed and even the structure of the Delors Report were very heavily influenced by the Werner Report'. For example, the three-phase implementation plan was 'taken over from the Werner Report'.

Needless to say that circumstances had changed considerably in the period between the two reports. When the Werner Committee considered economic and monetary union, the European Community was made up of six member states. Delors was considering a union of 12 states. Tietmeyer (2003: 13) noted that the 12 nations were economically more diverse than the earlier six and that the 'political ideas about the goal of integration diverged distinctly more' with 12 than six. He also noted that there had been a 'paradigm shift in economic policy' (p. 13) in the 1980s with Monetarism dominating policy makers and offering a 'more supply-side oriented economic policy' (p. 3).

The reality was that the Werner Report influence on the Delors Report was relatively superficial and extended to the acceptance of Werner's 'three necessary conditions for a monetary union' (Delors Report, 1989a: 14–15):

- the assurance of total and irreversible convertibility of currencies;
- the complete liberalisation of capital transactions and full integration of banking and other financial markets; and

- the elimination of margins of fluctuation and the irrevocable locking of exchange rate parities.

The Delors Committee also said the 'replacement of national currencies by a single currency should therefore take place as soon as possible after the locking of parities' (p. 13).

However, as we saw in Chapter 3, the Werner Report vision went far beyond those 'necessary conditions'. It clearly stressed, in addition to the creation of a European central bank as the issuer of the new single currency, that 'transfers of responsibility from the national to the Community plane will be essential' for the conduct of economic policy (Werner Report, 1970: 10). Moreover, the Werner Report noted that on:

> . . . the institutional plane . . . two Community organs are indispensable: a centre of decision for economic policy and a Community system for the central banks. These institutions, while safeguarding their own responsibilities, must be furnished with effective powers of decision and must work together for the realization of the same objectives. The centre of economic decision will be politically responsible to a European Parliament. (p. 26)

The Werner Plan thus considered an economic and monetary union would push Europe towards political union, with the European Parliament at centre stage. The Werner Report said, 'these transfers of responsibility represent a process of fundamental political significance which implies the progressive development of political cooperation. Economic and monetary union thus appears as a lever for the development of political union, which in the long run it cannot do without' (Werner Report, 1970: 12).

Conversely, the Delors Report (1989a: 13) constructed the economic and monetary union in terms of the continuation 'of individual nations with differing economic, social, cultural and political characteristics' and the 'existence and preservation of this plurality would require a degree of autonomy in economic decision-making to remain with the individual member countries.'

The Delors Plan deviated starkly from Werner's vision for a European level fiscal policy function. Modern federations align the primary fiscal responsibility at the level of the currency issuer. But the Delors Committee concluded that the primary fiscal policy responsibility would remain at the Member State level, that is, at the level of the currency user rather than currency issuer. The European level oversight would be limited to imposing arbitrary, but binding, fiscal rules, and importantly, prohibiting the newly created central bank from directly supporting Member State governments in times of need. The Delors Plan ignored the Werner conclusion that the European Parliament should take responsibility for economic policy decisions at the Community level.

There were several reasons cited for the change in thinking in the Delors Report, not the least being the fact that the French had rejected Werner's vision, which involved significant economic policy-making capacity being transferred to the supranational level. But the shift was typically justified by appealing to changes that had occurred in the world economy in the decade following the release of the Werner Report, including the demise of the Bretton Woods system; the introduction of the EMS; the inflation spikes that followed the two oil price hikes in the 1970s; and the opening up of global financial markets. But all these 'reasons' just provided a smokescreen to what had really changed. The fact is that the Monetarist disdain for discretionary fiscal policy being used to smooth out fluctuations in private spending and maintain low levels of unemployment was now dominant. The promotion of the sanctity of the free market and the dislike for state involvement in the economy beyond setting property rights had completely transformed the way policy makers conceived options.

This homogeneity of thinking or cognitive bias is referred to as Groupthink, which refers to 'the tendency among homogeneous, cohesive groups to consider issues only within a certain paradigm and not challenge its basic premises' (IEO, 2011: 17). As noted in Chapter 1, the group dynamics within the IMF that were exposed during the GFC were common among all mainstream economists, including those advising the national governments and Brussels. These economists and policy makers were trapped by the peer group belief that self-regulated private markets would always adjust to avoid any economic crisis. Within that intellectual prison, there was simply no need for strong fiscal agency or regulative structures.

By the end of the 1980s, this view was dominant in the academy and had infiltrated the major multilateral institutions (for example, the IMF, World Bank, OECD), treasuries and central banks across the advanced world. Economists and policy makers were trapped by 'confirmation bias', which 'refers to the tendency of people to only notice information consistent with their own expectations and to ignore information that is inconsistent with them' (IEO, 2011: 17). Groupthink dominated the Delors Committee as they ignored the persistently high unemployment that the deflationary biases in economic policy across Europe had caused.

The Nobel Prize winning macroeconomist Franco Modigliani reflected on European macroeconomic policy and the persistently high unemployment in the period after the oil price rises:

> Unemployment is primarily due to *lack of aggregate demand*. This is mainly the outcome of erroneous macroeconomic policies . . . [the decisions of Central

> Banks] . . . inspired by an obsessive fear of inflation . . . coupled with a benign neglect for unemployment . . . have resulted in systematically over tight monetary policy decisions, apparently based on an objectionable use of the so-called NAIRU approach. The contractive effects of these policies have been reinforced by common, very tight fiscal policies. (Modigliani, 2000: 3; emphasis in original)

THE DELORS PLAN AND THE EMPEROR'S NEW CLOTHES

The Delors Report's treatment of fiscal policy was relatively brief and reflected the dominance of the Monetarist macroeconomics, which wanted strict fiscal rules to limit discretionary government spending. The Report recommended that:

> . . . binding rules are required that would . . . impose upper limits on budget deficits of individual member countries of the Community . . . exclude access to direct central bank credit and other forms of monetary financing . . . limit recourse to external borrowing in non Community currencies . . . [which] should enable the Community to conduct a coherent mix of fiscal and monetary policies. (Delors Report, 1989a: 20–21)

In other words, the 'Delors Plan' constructed counter-stabilisation policy purely in terms of central banks adjusting interest rates to maintain price stability irrespective of the impact on economic growth and unemployment. Historically, counter-stabilisation policy described the way governments offset the fluctuations in private spending, which, in the absence of such intervention, would create boom and bust cycles. The aim was to maintain satisfactory economic growth and full employment without inflation. It was recognised that government deficits would at times have to rise significantly to counter major declines in private spending. The Delors Plan was in contradistinction to that Keynesian orthodoxy.

The Delors Plan mirrored the plans laid out by Genscher in his February 1999 memo and the statement released by the Bundesbank President, Pöhl (1989a: 131–55). Pöhl rejected the idea they should just pick up the 'ideas contained in the Werner Report' (p. 132). He wanted a 'new start' and stated that no progress could be made until there is 'agreement . . . that stability of the value of money is the indispensable prerequisite for the achievement of other goals' (p. 132). The Werner Report was considered to be an artefact of the Keynesian macroeconomic policy years with the emphasis on full employment and government intervention, which was anathema to the Monetarist dogma that had become dominant in the late 1980s.

As a result, the Bundesbank model triumphed with only an independent central bank being the macroeconomic policy institution deemed necessary at the federal level. An independent central bank would allow it to ignore political demands to compromise its monetary policy stance in recognition of rising unemployment, for example. The word 'unemployment' does not appear at all in the Delors Report despite it being persistently high across Europe at the time and the single largest cause of poverty. While there is some reference to the need to promote economic growth, the Report repeats the Monetarist mantra that the attainment of price stability will ensure stable, long-term growth.

However, the Delors Committee did try to justify why the emperor would have new clothes. On the question as to whether regional disparities in economic performance challenged the concept of a monetary union, Delors (1989a: 81) wrote that the creation of a monetary union 'eliminates the instrument of exchange rate adjustment between the regions of the economy' and raises the issue of how disparate regions will converge in economic performance. He said, 'disparities within the EC at present are considerable, but not incomparably greater than in some mature federations such as the United States, Canada or Switzerland' (p. 81). His conclusion was that 'the problem of regional disparities . . . would not seem to be an obstacle to a furthering of the EC's economic and monetary integration' (p. 81).

On the vexed issue of 'how the mature federal monetary unions' handle these regional disparities, Delors noted (p. 82):

> The experience of all federal economic and monetary unions is that a diversity of budget mechanisms combine in assuring an important 'shock absorber' function between regions and states with respect to the impact of cyclical and structural shocks . . . It would thus seem plausible to expect a substantial development of the budgetary function of the EC in the case of a monetary union.

In other words, all mature federal monetary unions have a federal fiscal capacity that allows the union to distribute public spending in an asymmetric way, not only to help poorer regions make structural transitions (for example, with public infrastructure development), but also to address the consequences of negative private spending movements, which impact disproportionately across regions as part of the economic cycle. Delors might have also said that this 'federal' fiscal capacity is a prerequisite for an effectively functioning economic and monetary union, and while the 'states' might retain some fiscal functions, they are dwarfed in magnitude by the capacity inherent at the currency-issuing federal sphere.

Delors seemed aware of this in his closing remarks, which reiterated the 'powerful "shock absorber"' capacity of a federal fiscal function. He also said that using fiscal policy to dampen 'the amplitude of economic difficulties or of surges in prosperity of individual states' was 'both the product of and source of the sense of national solidarity which all relevant economic and monetary unions share' (Delors, 1989a: 89).

This idea that fiscal policy can redress cyclical difficulties across all regions in a federation, legitimised by a sense of 'federal' solidarity, is highly significant for an effective monetary union. Citizens of California or New South Wales refer to themselves as Americans and Australians, respectively. By contrast, citizens of Germany and Greece refer to themselves as Germans and Greeks, respectively. There is a crucial difference in those self-assignments that no economic or monetary infrastructure can usurp.

Pöhl (1989a: 136) also understood the requirements of a functioning monetary union:

> A monetary union presupposes considerable shifts in the responsibility for economic policy to a central authority and hence a far reaching reshaping of the Community in political and institutional terms in the direction of a broader union. Although complete political union is not absolutely necessary for the establishment of a monetary union the loss of national sovereignty in economic and monetary policy associated with it is so serious that it would probably be bearable only in the context of extremely close and irrevocable political integration. At all events, within a monetary union, monetary policy can only be conducted at a Community level. A substantial transfer of authority will also be necessary in the field of fiscal policy.

But even though these key members of the Delors Committee obviously recognised the importance of a federal fiscal capacity for a functioning federation, it was also clear that ideology prevented the Committee from including that capacity in their Plan. The BIS representative on the Delors Committee, Alexandre Lamfalussy, noted that most federal systems conducted their macroeconomic policy 'in the context of their sizeable federal budgets' but that:

> This solution . . . is out of the question for a prospective European EMU because its central budget is not expected to exceed 3 per cent of GDP . . . The size of the Community budget would clearly be too small to provide for an adequate *masse de manoeuvre* for an effective macro fiscal policy. (Lamfalussy, 1989: 95; emphasis in original)

Lamfalussy also recognised 'the relatively small present and prospective role of budgetary transfers in the Community is ultimately a reflection of the lack of political unity, which imposes major constraints on the acceptability of redistributional transfers between member countries' (p. 108).

At that point, the political leaders involved in this venture should have concluded that the creation of an effective economic and monetary union was non-viable. Events have proven that to be the case, but it was obvious, even in 1989, that there was not a sufficient commitment nor 'sense of national solidarity' to create a single functional European economy.

The Delors Committee thus eschewed any notion of a central fiscal authority on ideological grounds. Without a federal fiscal function, it was very likely the Member State fiscal deficits would exceed 3 per cent of GDP during major recessions. Thus the fiscal positions of the Member States would have to be very flexible if they were to adequately offset fluctuations in private spending of the magnitude that occurred in 2008. Yet the Delors Committee proposed tight fiscal rules, which were formalised later in the SGP and put the EMU into an unworkable straitjacket from day one. Further, there is normally a close correspondence between the fiscal authority in a federation (the 'treasury') and the nation's central bank, which is usually given the role of currency issuance. In the absence of a federal fiscal capacity, the Member States would have to enjoy central bank support to ensure that fiscal policy was not constrained by the lack of currency issuing capacity. The Delors Plan deliberately dislocated these two essential arms of macroeconomic policy and banned any central bank support.

The proposal that went to Maastricht was thus deeply flawed from the start. Interestingly, this decision was not driven by the historical Franco-German disputes about loss of sovereignty to Brussels, but was rather a reflection of the dominance of the Monetarist obsession with limiting the discretionary spending capacity of the elected state. The false belief that a self-regulating private market would deliver the best outcomes and be resilient enough to withstand cyclical events had infested the European integration process. It was a blind ideological intervention.

THE MISAPPLICATION OF SUBSIDIARITY

The Delors Committee mainly relied on the concept of subsidiarity to justify the absence of a European level fiscal function in the Plan. Ungerer (1997: 204) concluded that the:

> Delors Committee did not see a need for a decision center for economic policy, and referred, instead, to already existing institutions. This may have reflected consideration for the desire of countries to safeguard their sovereignty but was also in line with the Delors Committee's support for the principle of subsidiarity.

The term subsidiarity, a long standing concept in political theory (as far back as Aristotle), entered the European dialogue in 1989 as part of a new 'Eurolanguage' as the political leaders were intent on pushing through the economic and monetary union (Millon-Delsol, 1992; Endo, 2001). The Oxford Dictionary defines subsidiarity as '(in politics) the principle that a central authority should have a subsidiary function, performing only those tasks which cannot be performed at a more local level'. The concept was popularised by the Roman Catholic Church in the 1931 encyclical, Quadragesimo Anno, which pronounced that 'It is a fundamental principle of social philosophy, fixed and unchangeable, that one should not withdraw from individuals and commit to the community what they can accomplish by their own enterprise and/or industry' (Pope Pius XI, 1931). The idea is thus generally taken to mean that in a federal structure, issues should be managed at the most decentralised level that is effective. The principle has been referred to as a 'golden rule' for allocating functions between various tiers of European governments.

The concept formally became part of European Law when it was included in the wording of the Treaty of the European Union (also known as the Maastricht Treaty) adopted in December 1991. The wording in the Preamble noted that the signatories resolved to create 'an ever closer union among the peoples of Europe, in which decisions are taken as closely as possible to the citizen in accordance with the principle of subsidiarity' (European Commission, 2012b: 16). The term appears again in Article 5 and Article 12. Article 5 notes that:

> Under the principle of subsidiarity, in areas which do not fall within its exclusive competence, the Union shall act only if and in so far as the objectives of the proposed action cannot be sufficiently achieved by the Member States, either at central level or at regional and local level, but can rather, by reason of the scale or effects of the proposed action, be better achieved at Union level. (p. 18)

Endo (2001: 8) claims there is 'built-in confusion within the Treaty' in the way it constructs the term. In the Preamble, decentralisation is emphasised ('closely as possible to the citizen'), whereas in Article 5, Brussels 'simply might continue its business of integration, by finding a few justifications for such actions'. He notes that the term is ambiguous, having both a negative and a positive connotation, depending on the perspective adopted. The former emphasises the limits of competence of the central body and the right of lower bodies to look after themselves, if they can; while the latter focuses on the rights and necessity of responsible central intervention if the lower entity cannot effectively function.

Delors (1991: 7–8) said subsidiarity is about '. . . the development of each individual. But, as we all know, steps in this direction presuppose that there are men and women capable of taking on the responsibilities in order to achieve the common good.'

Further on, he said (1991: 9):

> Subsidiarity is not simply a limit to intervention by a higher authority vis-à-vis a person or a community in a position to act itself, it is also an obligation for this authority to act vis-à-vis this person or this group to see that it is given the means to achieve its ends.

The emphasis on the common good and its link to subsidiarity was also echoed in the Preamble to the European Parliament's 1994 'Resolution on the Constitution of the European Union', where it is stated that there is an awareness on 'behalf of the peoples of Europe' that there is a 'need for decisions concerning them' to be 'taken at a level as close as possible to the citizens themselves, with powers delegated to higher levels only for reasons of the common good' (European Parliament, 1994: 156).

The debate turns on the meaning of common good but there is little doubt if one examines the daily public statements of the European politicians that communitarian perspectives are inherent in their visions. This also resonates with the statement from Delors that 'all relevant economic and monetary unions' share a 'sense of national solidarity'. In terms of the common good, we regularly hear concerns expressed about the European unemployment problem and the need for more growth in Europe. While these concepts are not without contest, a broad consensus would suggest that the common good is not being advanced if there are 60 per cent of a nation's youth unemployed or over 10 per cent of Europe's willing workers without jobs.

British economist John Maynard Keynes used the concept of compositional fallacy to expose the flaws in conservative mainstream economics during the Great Depression. We examine this concept again in Chapter 16. Keynes demonstrated that the mainstream free market economics approach was prone to these fallacies, which are logical errors that arise when something is claimed to be true in general by dint of some specific part of the whole being true. The important point in relation to the allocation of competencies across the levels of government is that there are some functions that have to be performed at the aggregate level in a federal system if the overall system and its components are to function effectively. The fiscal policy capacity to offset major asymmetric private spending fluctuations is one such function and is intrinsic to the ability of the overall system to achieve common good, however broadly that is defined.

When the Delors Committee was invoking subsidiarity they were so infested with neo-liberal economic thinking that they failed to understand the imperative for a federal fiscal or treasury competency. Lower entities in a federal system cannot achieve desirable ends if they are denied access to support from the currency issuing level of the system and further constrained in the size of deficits they can run.

FRANCO-GERMAN SHENANIGANS GIVE WAY TO BUNDESBANK RULE

The reporting timetable set by Delors was delayed because there was debate within the Committee on 'whether a parallel currency could be introduced' (Verdun, 1999: 318) and about the specific mechanisms required for transiting to a complete economic and monetary union. The historical antagonisms were out in force. France and Italy wanted the ECU to be elevated as a parallel currency (see Larosière, 1989). French central banker Jacques de Larosière outlined a gradual transition emphasising the creation of a European Reserve Fund (ERF), which would aim to resolve currency fluctuations as a precursor to introducing a common currency in a 'third phase'. Through these transitory phases, the 'development of the ECU' would be important (Larosière, 1989: 182).

The idea of a parallel currency was opposed by Germany and the Netherlands, who wanted a tightly controlled single currency (see Pöhl, 1989a). Dutch central banker Wim Duisenberg argued that a 'parallel currency implies the absence of a monetary union' (Duisenberg, 1989: 185). He also argued that the nations had to accept the fact that 'economic convergence' was essential and would require 'the loss of sovereignty implicit in the abolition of the exchange rate as an adjustment mechanism' (p. 189). The Germans and Dutch also refused to accept the idea of an ERF. The vision set out by Pöhl (1989a) dominated the final agreed Delors position. Given the ideological constraints on the process, Modell Deutschland was really the only serious show in town (Dyson, 1994).

The Delors Report settled on a three-stage plan for achieving monetary union without tight deadlines although it stressed that 'the creation of an economic and monetary union must be viewed as a single process', by which they meant that once it was agreed to enter the first stage, there was no going back (Delors Report, 1989a: 27). In the first stage, the Delors Committee determined that the '1974 Council Decision on economic convergence' (p. 30; see also European Council, 1986: 19–24) would be replaced by tighter coordination of fiscal policy 'with precise quantitative guidelines and medium term orientations' (Delors Report: 1989a: 30). Further, all the nations would join the ERM and currency realignments would be discouraged in favour of using other policy options (for example, interest rate movements) to maintain the parities. The mark would thus remain the benchmark currency. The permissible fluctuations around the agreed parities would be narrowed. Most significantly, the central banks would play a greater role in overseeing domestic policies chosen by each Member State and 'consistency between monetary and economic policies would be facilitated' by ensuring that the Central Bank Governors were represented at Ecofin meetings (Delors Report, 1989a: 30).

In other words, fiscal policy discretion would be subjugated to dominant 'Bundesbank style' monetary discipline. The domination of the unelected and largely unaccountable central bankers was almost complete. They had openly stated that if the pursuit of price stability was accompanied by strong employment growth and low unemployment, then well and good. But they would never compromise the pursuit of price stability (as they saw it) even if it meant stagnant growth and rising unemployment.

The second stage would begin once the Treaty was revised and the nations had agreed on the design of the economic and monetary union. The new institutional structure would initially provide macroeconomic monitoring and analysis to facilitate common decision making. Delors saw stage two as an irrevocable step towards union with policy convergence across the membership being 'strengthened', even though the 'ultimate responsibility for policy decisions would remain at this stage with national authorities' (Delors Report, 1989a: 33).

In the second stage, the 'European System of Central Banks would be set up and would absorb the previously existing institutional monetary arrangements' (p. 34). This would be the precursor to the final institutional innovation, the creation of the European Central Bank. During stage two, the central banks of the Member States would move towards a position of greater independence from the political processes, as in the case of the Bundesbank, and participate in the formulation of 'general monetary orientations' for the overall Community, implemented by the individual central banks. At that point, national sovereignty and democratic oversight would be further reduced although that was not emphasised in the Delors rhetoric.

The third stage would see the introduction of the single currency issued by the European Central Bank. At that point, the Member States would cede sovereignty and adopt the use of a foreign currency, with all the limitations that go with that status. We will return to that in Part III. Policy flexibility would be lost because the 'rules and procedures of the Community in the macroeconomic and budgetary field would become binding' (p. 35). Thus, democratically elected national governments would no longer be able to defend the wellbeing of its citizenry in the event of a major collapse in total spending of the sort we saw in 2008. It was explicitly stated that the European institutions (in this case Ecofin) would 'have the authority . . . to impose constraints on national budgets to the extent to which this was necessary to prevent imbalances that might threaten monetary stability' (p. 36).

In other words, fiscal policy would lose any correspondence with its underlying capacity and purpose, which up until then had been seen as providing a strong counter-stabilising policy tool to maintain low unemployment and strong economic growth. The Delors Committee was proposing a Europe that would be united in the sense that it had adopted the Bundesbank culture, but which would soon be demonstrating very disparate outcomes in terms of economic growth and unemployment.

Delors delivered his Report to the European Commission in April 1989 and the European Council accepted it at the Madrid summit on 26–27 June 1989. The Council resolved to launch the first stage on 1 July 1990. They also resolved to hold an 'Intergovernmental Conference' to help map out the subsequent stages outlined in the Delors Report, although no date was specified for this meeting (European Council, 1989a). The Council said that the 'realization' of the Delors Plan 'would have to take account of the parallelism between economic and monetary aspects, respect the principle of subsidiarity and allow for the diversity of specific situations' (p. 10).

THE WALL COLLAPSES – 'I LOVE GERMANY SO MUCH, THAT I PREFER THERE TO BE TWO OF THEM'

The French novelist François Mauriac wrote during the Cold War: 'I love Germany so much, that I prefer there to be two of them' (*Le Monde diplomatique*, 2011). Before the European Council were able to convene their conference to map out the second and third phases on the Delors Plan, political events in the East overtook them. On 9 November 1989, the Berlin Wall came down and immediately an unanticipated new agenda cut across the plans for monetary union. The Cold War had dampened the sensitivity elsewhere in Europe about Germany under the security blanket provided by the establishment of the North Atlantic Treaty Organisation in 1949. The post World War II institutional developments made it difficult for West Germany to have any further military ambitions. The French, in particular, were ever wary, if not paranoid, about this issue. The 'Them' (Communist world) versus 'Us' (the 'free world') narrative, constantly spun by the US and its allies, also diverted attention away from the threat of German domination.

But that all changed when the 'Wall' collapsed and with German reunification back in vogue, the rest of Europe started to ask what life would be like if Germany became 'too powerful'. It revived the 'German question' (Delors, 1989b). A scan of the French press at the time reveals a deep national insecurity about an enlarged Germany (Lind, 2011). Even at the political level, this suspicion was evident. On 17 October 1989, Delors gave a speech to the College of Europe in Bruges, which berated the 'embittered', the 'fatalistic', and those 'shackled by resignedness' (a reference to the increasing paranoia about a possible German reunification) (Delors, 1989b: 11). He concluded that 'the only acceptable and satisfactory answer to the German question' was to strengthen the 'federalist traits of the Community' (p. 11).

But there was some way to go before France and Britain would accept that. Mitterrand, using his prerogatives as the French President of the European Commission, called an informal summit of the heads of government at the Élysée Palace on 18 November 1989. Delors was also invited in his capacity as European Commission President. At that meeting, Mitterrand demanded that German Chancellor Kohl clarify the policy objectives of Germany, in particular with respect to borders.

The British were similarly hostile to the prospect of an enlarged Germany. Margaret Thatcher, who attended the November Paris meeting, later recalled that Mitterrand has posed a 'number of questions, including whether the issue of borders in Europe should be open for discussion' (Thatcher, 1993: 759). Kohl responded by saying that 'there should be no discussion of borders but that the people of Germany must be allowed to decide their future for themselves' (Thatcher, 1993: 793). In her response, Thatcher said, 'There must be no question of changing borders' (Thatcher, 1993: 793–94). Thatcher also admitted to extreme anti-German views in her 1993 memoirs. She wrote that she eschewed the notion of a 'collective guilt' among the Germans but that Germany's 'national character' was 'by its very nature a destabilizing force rather than a stabilizing force in Europe' (Thatcher, 1993: 791).

On 28 November 1989, just ten days after the Paris meeting, Kohl unilaterally announced in a speech to the Bundestag, that Germany would pursue a 'Ten-Point Program to overcome the division of Germany and Europe' (Deutscher Bundestag, 1989). Mitterrand and Thatcher then met informally in Strasbourg on Friday, 8 December during the European Council meeting. Thatcher recalled two meetings with Mitterrand, in which he was openly hostile towards Kohl's ten-point plan (Thatcher, 1993: 796–97). She said, 'It seemed to be that although we had not discovered the means, at least we both had the will to check the German juggernaut. That was a start' (Thatcher, 1993: 797).

Mitterrand also scheduled a hasty trip in December 1989 to meet with

Mikhail Gorbachev in Kiev, who he knew was opposed to the German reunification. Lind (2011: 140) quotes Stanley Hoffmann, who said the Kiev meeting 'could not help but invoke the ghosts of Franco-Russian allegiances against the German danger and of German obsessions about encirclement.' She also quotes Edouard Husson as saying that 'François Mitterand's entire European policy can be explained by one simple motive: the obsessive fear of German power' (Lind, 2011: 140). Judt (2005: 640) noted that Mitterrand initially sought to stop the reunification by 'trying to convince Soviet leaders that as traditional allies, France and Russia had a common interest in blocking German ambitions. Indeed, the French were banking on Gorbachev to veto German unity'.

The Belgian Prime Minister, Wilfried Martens, who was 'strongly' in favour of German reunification, recalled, 'the fall of the Berlin Wall required a mental readjustment' and Kohl's Bundestag announcement 'encouraged everyone . . . to get a move on' (Martens, 2009: 100). Martens stood apart from the anti-German hysteria spouted by his colleagues and said 'Kohl wanted to embed German reunification with a united Europe. This concurred with his deepest convictions. He wanted to strengthen and broaden the Community with all that this implied at the time: the EMU and the Social Charter, and further in the future, the European Political Union . . .' (Martens, 2009: 100). He also noted that the Strasbourg European Council meeting on 8–9 December 1989 was firmly focused on European integration, and that the Council report managed to construct the German reunification within 'the principle of "not a German Europe, but a European Germany"' (Martens, 2009: 101).

Mitterrand eventually fell into line with the idea that German reunification was part of the broader European integration. Garton Ash (1994: 390) concluded that 'This Franco-German understanding was the single most important driving force behind the inter-governmental conferences on what was loosely called the European political and monetary union, and hence of the Maastricht treaty'. Germany was becoming a 'European Germany' although the discussions about economic and monetary union would reasonably support the conclusion that a 'German Europe' was being developed.

This was clearly the view of the British. Thatcher could not accept that Mitterrand had fallen into line on a 'European Germany'. Clearly, there were ongoing tensions within the British government about the reunification. In July 1990, the British paranoia became starkly evident in an interview conducted by the editor of the conservative British magazine, *The Spectator*. Dominic Lawson interviewed the British Trade and Industry Secretary, Nicholas Ridley, who was a close confidant to Thatcher. The interview was published in the magazine's 14 July 1990 issue (Lawson,

1990). It led to the forced resignation of Ridley but disclosed the inner sentiments of the Thatcher government. It was so explosive that Lawson subsequently clarified that Ridley was sober and knew the tape was rolling (Stead, 1990). The Germans called the views expressed 'scandalous and incomprehensible' (Longworth, 1990). Lawson noted that at the time, Pöhl was about to visit 'England to preach the joys of a joint European monetary policy' (Lawson, 1990: 8).

The following is an edited version of the interchange that followed:

> Ridley: This is all a German racket designed to take over the whole of Europe. It has to be thwarted. This rushed takeover by the Germans on the worst possible basis, with the French behaving like poodles to the Germans, is absolutely intolerable.
> Lawson: Excuse me, but in what way are moves toward monetary union, 'The Germans trying to take over the whole of Europe'?
> Ridley: The deutschmark is always going to be the strongest currency, because of their habits (last phrase was emphasised in original).
> Lawson: But Mr. Ridley, it's surely not axiomatic that the German currency will always be the strongest?
> Ridley: It's because of the Germans (last word emphasised).
> Lawson: But the European Community is not just the Germans.
> Ridley: When I look at the institutions to which it is proposed that sovereignty is to be handed over, I'm aghast. Seventeen unelected reject politicians . . . with no accountability to anybody, who are not responsible for raising taxes, just spending money, who are pandered to by a supine parliament . . . I'm not against giving up sovereignty in principle, but not to this lot. You might just as well give it to Adolf Hitler, frankly . . .
> Lawson: But surely Herr Kohl is preferable to Herr Hitler. He's not going to bomb us after all.
> Ridley: I'm not sure I wouldn't rather have . . . the shelters and the chance to fight back, than simply being taken over by . . . economics (the last word emphasised) . . .
> [Later Ridley attacked the Bundesbank again]
> Ridley: I don't know about the German economy. It's the German people (last word emphasised). They're already running most of the Community. I mean they pay half of the countries. Ireland gets 6 per cent of their gross domestic product this way. When's Ireland going to stand up to the Germans?

The decision to reunite Germany also had significant economic ramifications. First, well-educated, German speaking Ostlanders boosted West Germany's available labour supply. This resulted in an increased domestic demand for housing and consumer durables and put upward pressure on the German price level. Second, in early 1990, Kohl announced that the mark would exchange one for one with the ostmark (with exceptions for large debts and loans) and become the single currency for the united Germany. At the time, the ostmark traded in Berlin at about 5 to 1 marks. The inflated one for one peg was, in fact, a massive West–East subsidy to facilitate the German monetary union but it also reduced the productive capacity in the East, as the former East German firms were no longer competitive given their lower productivity and wage levels. It also provided an immediate boost to the real purchasing power of East German consumers in terms of West German goods.

The Bundesbank wanted to increase interest rates to quell any inflationary surge, which would have pushed the value of the mark up against the other European currencies. Pöhl told the Banking Federation in Bonn on 6 October 1989 that Germany's 'most important partners' (that is, France) would oppose such a move (Pöhl, 1989b). The Ecofin ministers were adamant the 1987 Basel–Nyborg agreement meant that currency stability would be managed without significant realignments. In the autumn of 1989, French Prime Minister Rocard called Kohl and demanded he oppose any realignment, which would be tantamount to a devaluation of the French franc. Bonn then told the Bundesbank President that realignments were off the agenda, a decision that demonstrated that despite the vaunted 'independence' of the German central bank, the politicians typically ruled (Henning, 1994: 215).

The upshot was that German inflation rose more quickly than that of its European partners, which led the Bundesbank to finally increase interest rates in 1990. The stable, but undervalued mark and the reduction in the German inflation rate, then presented problems for Germany's trading partners. To remain competitive against Germany they had to drive their inflation rate down below Germany's. This required harsh cutbacks in domestic spending, which would certainly invoke a recession. European political nuances were at the same time opposing currency movements that would provide competitive adjustments for each nation but forcing nations to endure the domestic costs of recession.

In other words, even before the delegates arrived in the lovely Limburg city of Maastricht, the European nations were rehearsing the problems that come with a fixed exchange rate system, where one nation is economically dominant and the other members of the system struggle to maintain international competitiveness. In 1990, they had a vision of what would come in 2008, but the leaders and their advisors were so besotted with neo-liberal ideology that they couldn't identify the future vulnerability of the monetary system they were set on creating. They certainly had no perception of the enormous costs their citizens would incur when that vulnerability was breached.

7. Onward to Maastricht

ONWARD TO MAASTRICHT: THE MARCH OF THE IDEOLOGUES

While the Economic Council meeting in Madrid on 16 and 17 June 1989 accepted the Delors Plan and resolved to begin the first stage on 1 July 1990, it was not until the meeting in Dublin on 25 and 26 June 1990 that the Council agreed that the 'Intergovernmental Conference' (IGC), which would consider the changes to the Treaty of Rome necessary to implement stages two and three, would meet on 14 December 1990. It was intended to coincide with another meeting between governments on advancing political union. In between the meetings in Madrid and Dublin, an Ecofin Committee working party considered how the Delors Report could be rendered acceptable to the Member States, bearing in mind that the Delors Committee had deliberately excluded the 'politicians' from the process to that point. The vehement opposition from the British brought home the need to render something that would be politically acceptable.

French politician Élisabeth Guigou was charged with leading this 'high level' EMU group. A preliminary agenda setting meeting between European Council members and Ms Guigou was held in Paris on 15 September 1989 (European Commission, 1989c). The minutes show that the Commission should 'be ready to explain and advocate the need for binding rules in the budgetary field (in October's meetings for the Group)' (European Commission, 1989c).

On 27 September 1989 the group produced an issues paper on the 'role of the Community Budget' (European Commission, 1989d: 6), in which they sought to separate so-called structural and macroeconomic issues, and determined that the IGC should consider whether a federal fiscal capacity in the proposed economic and monetary union was warranted. They also wanted consideration of the possibility that federal fiscal policy could be used for discretionary changes in spending to help complement Member State policies, in pursuit of commonly agreed macroeconomic objectives.

The European Council meeting in Strasbourg on 8–9 December 1989 considered the Group's report, ratified the 1 July 1990 starting date agreed to in Madrid, and determined that the IGC would meet, 'under the auspices of the Italian authorities, before the end of 1990' (European Council, 1989b: 8). The IGC would thus meet after the starting date of stage one, which signalled that attention would be focused on the transition to stages two and three, as part of the 'single process' conceived by Delors. Accordingly, once stage one had begun, nations, by implication, were committed to seeing the process through. The Council also committed to presenting a new 'composite paper on all aspects of the achievement of Economic and Monetary Union which will take into account all available analyses and contributions' (p. 8). The paper would be considered at a special meeting of the European Council in Dublin on 18 April 1990. Standing alone was the United Kingdom, which opposed any treaty change to facilitate a single currency.

Economists Daniel Gros and Jean Pisani-Ferry (1989) argued at one of the informal EMU workshops run by the European Commission in late 1989 that the central issue to be decided related to fiscal policy. They recognised that the standard view among economists considered that 'a monetary union is politically acceptable only if it provides at least some "insurance" scheme in the form of automatic income transfers among participating regions' (Gros and Pisani-Ferry, 1989: 14). That is, effective federations provided a federal fiscal capacity to provide relief when states within the federation were in recession. They concluded that this 'raises the issue of the appropriate level and role of the Community budget' and that such transfers could be achieved via a 'Community wide unemployment insurance scheme or via some sort of fiscal equalisation mechanism' (Gros and Pisani-Ferry, 1989: 14).

There was no consensus on that point though. On 27 November 1989, the Danish Government released its 'official report on the EMU', and while they agreed with the Bundesbank stipulation 'that monetary financing of budget deficits cannot take place' (Ministry of Economic Affairs, 1989: 2), they were 'sceptical' about the proposals in the Delors Report concerning binding rules on budget deficits. They argued that 'such rules are not necessary as budget deficits in the future will be financed in the market' (Ministry of Economic Affairs, 1989: 2), which was based on their view that nations would soon run out of money if they were running deficits that were larger than the market assessed they could bear. There was no mention of the role of fiscal deficits in countering aggregate demand slumps and protecting employment. Those 'functional finance' considerations, which we will return to in Chapters 17–19, had disappeared from the debate. It was all about rules and constraints so as not to 'compromise' spending discipline.

Throughout 1990, various workshops were organised by the European

Council, which handpicked economists to present papers. The academy had, however, fallen so tightly under the spell of Monetarism, that there was little room for disagreement. The Commission published a collection of these so-called 'background studies' in its own journal, European Economy, in 1991. Three papers covered the topic 'Macroeconomic policy and public finance'.

Van Rompuy et al. (1991: 109) defined a federal system in terms of 'a multi-level public sector' including the 'supply of public goods and services, taxation, redistribution and stabilization functions'. They asked which level of 'government should stabilize the economy' when there are 'nation-wide positive or negative shocks' (p. 112) and concluded that the 'way out of this dilemma is a coordinated stabilization policy' (p. 113). To reduce the 'coordination costs' this capacity should be assigned to the central government. They concluded, 'a federal stabilization function necessitates the exclusive use of some fiscal instruments in such a way that it cannot be disturbed by the independent action of lower-level governments' (p. 113). They should have gone further and noted that this federal function is intrinsic to the way in which federal treasuries and central banks coordinate their actions in mature federations. It makes little economic sense to centralise the currency issuance capacity but then leave fiscal policy mainly to 'state' governments. In the end, they concluded that this issue 'remains a delicate question' and failed to endorse a large federal fiscal function.

In the same volume, Frederick van der Ploeg (1991: 136) noted that once exchange rates are fixed between nations, 'stabilization policy is more difficult to conduct in the face of country-specific shocks'. He proposed to establish a 'European Federal Transfer Scheme (EFTS)' to provide fiscal transfers to member states, where the independent central bank exerts deflationary discipline, which 'leads to too low inflation' (p. 136). He also summarised the problems that the proposed system would face if, for example, there were a shift in spending away from British goods towards French goods. In a non-EMS world, the pound would drop in value as the franc rose and the governments would adjust their fiscal positions (British deficit up, French down) to attenuate the effects of such a spending shift on output and employment. He concluded that 'there is a danger that politicians will go along with the idea, advanced by the Delors Committee, that there should be constraints on too high budget deficits' (p. 144) which would prevent such discretionary responses to the rising unemployment in Britain and the risk of inflation in France. He noted under the Delors Plan fiscal policy was 'likely to be pro-cyclical' (p. 144), which means that it would reinforce the direction of the private spending cycle. Normally a nation's fiscal deficit automatically rises during a slowdown in economic activity because of the loss of tax revenue. But with fiscal rules constraining the size of the deficit, the government may have to impose discretionary cuts to spending and/or raise taxes if the deficit breached the allowable thresholds. In other words, governments would have to cut net spending at the same time as the economy was deteriorating, which is the anathema of sound fiscal policy practice. His proposed EFTS, which would transfer income from expanding nations to declining nations, represented a minimalist federal fiscal function. He speculated that Delors didn't consider such a scheme because it would reduce the incentive of unemployed individuals in a declining region (nation) to shift to growth areas. His overwhelming conclusion was that an EMU without some form of federal fiscal role would perform 'badly when Member States are hit by country-specific shocks' (p. 146).

The final paper by Charles Wyplosz focused on two questions: (a) should there be fiscal rules, which would 'limit national fiscal policy independence', and (b) does the EMU 'require an EC-wide fiscal policy?' (Wyplosz, 1991: 165). He noted the bias among economists to couch these questions 'under the code-name of fiscal discipline' and talk about 'reasonable' fiscal positions (p. 165). But he noted that it 'is not clear . . . what reasonable, or indeed disciplined, fiscal policies really are' (p. 165). Wyplosz concluded, 'budget deficits – possibly even long-lasting ones – do not necessarily form an indication of fiscal laxity. There exist a large number of reasons which make public deficits and debts socially desirable' (p. 172). Overall his rather conservative advice to the European Council was that 'extreme caution should be exercised before setting binding rules . . . [and] . . . Without the exchange-rate instrument, fiscal policies may well be called upon to provide a substitute way of dealing with national shocks' (p. 182).

The prescient analysis of these experts was clearly ignored. On 22 May 1990, the Economic Policy Committee of the Council published the 'principles', which should govern fiscal policy under an EMU. They were (European Council, 1990a: 1):

- the avoidance of monetary financing of budget deficits;
- the avoidance, or at least reduction, of excessive budget deficits;
- the reduction of excessive levels of public debt;
- the improvement of the structure of budget revenue and expenditure;
- the reduction of excessively large ratios of public expenditure to national product.

A statistical annexe was provided presenting the 'Relevant macroeconomic variables' to guide discussion (p. 1). The unemployment rate or employment growth rates were not considered to be relevant. In fact, there was no mention of the persistently high unemployment rates in the Member States at the time the paper was presented. This paper exemplified the way in which the Monetarist doctrines had excised the responsibilities of government to maintain high employment rates from any discussion of fiscal policy parameters. The discussion of fiscal policy had become a stand-alone exercise with an internal logic defined by the ad hoc fiscal rules. The discussions at the time rarely focused on the 'functions' of government deficits. Instead, there was an obsession about whether deficits were 'reasonable', 'excessive' or otherwise, with little definition on how we might demarcate those assessments.

With the IGC approaching, the Commission presented its own position paper for the December IGC on 21 August 1990 (European Commission, 1991c). The so-called Christophersen Report basically rubber stamped the Delors Plan and emphasised the need for a single currency. The primary macroeconomic function exercised at the Community level would be an independent monetary policy 'committed explicitly to the objective of price stability' (p. 19). National state bodies would, by dint of new national legislation, be prevented from compromising 'the fundamental stability objective' (pp. 19–20).

Thus, in the long intellectual battle between the 'monetarists' (France, Belgium, Italy) and the 'economists' (Germany and the Netherlands), the latter had won out handsomely. The model of economic policy that was emerging was clearly 'Modell Deutschland' with the Bundesbank culture to be defined in the proposed legal framework of the new monetary union. Even the Italian submission to Monetary Committee of the Council reflected the dominance of the new Monetarist paradigm in macroeconomics. The Italians said:

> As a matter of fact, there is universal agreement that price stability is an essential prerequisite for any sound economic policy and that central banks are the institutions best equipped to pursue it. Thus a prerequisite for the effective working of the ESCB is that other macroeconomic policies do not endanger price stability. (European Council, 1990c: 1–2)

The Italian submission appealed to 'recent developments in economic theory' (that is, the new Monetarist literature) to eschew 'activist macroeconomics policies' (p. 3), which is a reference to discretionary fiscal interventions by government. While supporting 'budgetary discipline' through the imposition of 'binding rules' (p. 8), they also recognised that these rules should not 'unduly constrain . . . growth, employment and external balance' (p. 8). There is the devil and the Italians provided no solution to the problem that such 'discipline' would, inevitably, bias the Eurozone to stagnation.

Their claim to 'universality' of viewpoint is a common neo-liberal tactic to give the impression that there are no contested ideas in macroeconomics. Margaret Thatcher often used the phrase that she had derived from the 19th-century libertarian Herbert Spencer that 'there is no alternative' (TINA) to free markets as she sought to justify the harsh economic changes she wrought in Britain in the 1980s. The current European policy obsession with fiscal austerity has used the same rhetoric. As Europe was about to enter monetary union, it was similarly held out that economists all agreed on these basic 'facts' – an independent central bank with no remit for employment or growth and rule constrained fiscal policy confined to the state level.

The Christophersen Report also claimed that discretionary fiscal policy was a 'threat to monetary stability' and as a result of the 'potential threat of budget deficits and their financing . . . additional provisions' were required (European Commission, 1991c: 24). These include the familiar provisions that were written into the Maastricht Treaty:

1. no monetary financing of public deficits or market privileges for the public authorities concerning the placing of public debt;
2. no bailing out; in the case of imbalances, a Member State could not benefit from an unconditional guarantee concerning its public debt either from the Community or from another Member State.

Further, 'excessive deficits must be avoided' (p. 24) although when a deficit would become 'excessive' was not specified. Despite this vagueness, the Report concluded, 'some yardstick would seem necessary for the identification of excessive deficits' (p. 24). As we will see, the yardstick that was finally accepted was an arbitrary deficit-to-GDP ratio written on the 'back of an envelope' one night by an advisor to François Mitterrand.

American economist Alan Blinder (1987) presented a compelling critique of the dominance of Monetarism and concluded that the political importance of inflation had been blown out of all proportion to its economic significance. After dismissing the arguments that inflation imposes high costs on the economy, Blinder (p. 33) noted:

> The political revival of free market ideology in the 1980s is, I presume, based on the market's remarkable ability to root out inefficiency. But not all inefficiencies are created equal. In particular, high unemployment represents a waste of resources so colossal that no one truly interested in efficiency can be complacent about it. It is both ironic and tragic that in searching out ways to

improve economic efficiency, we seem to have ignored the biggest inefficiency of them all.

The dilemma recognised by the Italians, that binding fiscal rules could 'unduly constrain the potential contribution of fiscal policy' to maintaining output and employment growth, was put to one side by the ruling Monetarist ideology. It was claimed, as an article of faith, that by running a tight monetary stance to maintain price discipline, economic growth would be maximised. The reality was that tight monetary policy and strong growth might only be expected if net exports were very strong, as in the German case, and then only if spending growth in the rest of the world was strong. Certainly, the other European partners to this folly were not in the same position as Germany to withstand the deflationary policy stance that the Bundesbank specialised in.

The costs of this blindness were demonstrated during the GFC and persist in its aftermath. But anyone who dared question the Monetarist supremacy at the time and, instead, advocated Keynesian remedies to reduce the entrenched European unemployment, was met with derision from the bulk of the economics profession who had embraced the new economic theory and its policy implications. While the TINA brigade dominated, the fact was that the rise in acceptance of Monetarism was not based on an empirical rejection of the Keynesian orthodoxy, but 'was instead a triumph of a priori theorising over empiricism, of intellectual aesthetics over observation and, in some measure, of conservative ideology over liberalism' (Blinder, 1988: 278). The European political Groupthink embraced the ideology wholeheartedly and the consequences for ordinary citizens would be severe.

THE FRENCH SHIFT POSITION ON MONETARY UNION

The path was now set for Rome where the economic and political IGCs would be simultaneously held on 15 December 1990. The conjunction of conferences was not coincidental. A crucial part of the restoration of the Franco-German accord on economic and monetary union after the rift over German reunification came in March 1990 after the East German elections, which brought victory for Kohl's Christian Democrats. If anyone was ever in doubt about the intention and public acceptance in Germany for reunification, then the 18 March poll dispelled that doubt. The French had no option but to accept that they had failed to stop the process and so the strategy then was how to make the best of that failure (Riding, 1990). The revised French position emerged as early as 20 March 1990, when the French Foreign Minister, Roland Dumas, urged the Germans in a radio interview to not only focus on reunifying its own borders but also to maintain a firm commitment to economic and monetary union. Dumas said that the task ahead was 'to advance further, faster and more deeply toward building Europe' in both political and economic terms (Riding, 1990). Baun (1996: 617) argued that the bringing together of the economic ambitions (the 'key objective of France') and the political aspirations ('Germany sought a stronger European parliament and more cooperation in foreign and defense policy') gave Kohl 'something in return for agreeing to surrender the D-mark and German monetary sovereignty' to appease domestic political concerns.

THE ITALIANS BECAME IMPATIENT – ROME, OCTOBER 1990

The Italians considered that German federal elections scheduled for December 1990 might have created uncertainty about the German position on economic and monetary union. Accordingly, the Italian Prime Minister Giulio Andreotti, who was also the President of the European Council, decided not to wait for the December IGCs and called an unscheduled European Council summit in Rome on 27–28 October to advance the monetary union agenda. The summit 'decided to take a further step towards European unity' although the British delegation preferred 'not to pre-empt the debate in the Intergovernmental Conference' (European Council, 1990b: 2). The further step was to announce that the 'second phase' of the Delors Plan would 'start on 1 January 1994', after 'the Treaty has been ratified'. This would 'ensure the independence of the new members of the new monetary institution . . . [and that] . . . monetary powers have been transferred'. Further, the Treaty change would ensure that 'the monetary financing of budget deficits . . . [was] . . . prohibited' and that no bailouts were allowed (p. 6). The third phase was foreshadowed to begin within a reasonable time after the Commission and the Council had reflected on the 'functioning of the second phase' (p. 6).

At this stage there was no mention of the European Parliament despite the Christophersen Report having made it clear that if the responsibility for monetary policy was to be handed over to an unelected group who would not be answerable to the governments of the Member States, then there had to be some 'democratic oversight'. This, apparently, would be accomplished by the national governments ratifying its creation and the 'method of appointment of its president and the board members'

(European Commission, 1991c: 20). Further, the central bank would have to report to the European Parliament.

The European Parliament had been mostly compliant since the release of the Delors Report. Its 14 April 1989 resolution on economic and monetary union (two days after the release of the Delors Plan) contained no major divergences from the 'Monetarist party line'. The Parliament wanted to speed up the process of monetary integration by broadening membership of the EMS and requiring all Member States to pursue a common economic policy, despite the significant structural variations across these economies. They proposed a starting date of 1 January 1995, a much more truncated phase-in than the European Council had considered possible.

It promoted the Monetarist mantra about central bank independence and the need for 'fixing money supply targets' (European Parliament, 1989: 334) despite the fact that central banks cannot fix such targets. This fact was evident in the 1980s, after central banks found it was impossible to closely target money supply growth. That failure exposed the poverty of Monetarist theory but didn't quell the enthusiasm for it among those who had adopted it by way of 'religious' affiliation.

The European Parliament thus became part of the Monetarist 'cheer squad' and supported the central bank being legislated to adopt as its sole charter an inflation first policy with no responsibility for economic growth and full employment and no capacity of elected governments to influence that policy. In particular, the Resolution claimed the 'European Central Bank would be federal in nature' and 'based on what are long-established national central bank structures' (p. 335). It failed to note that in long-established federal structures, the central banks and the treasuries cooperated closely on monetary matters, which ensured that federal fiscal policy could maintain prosperity across the federated states. In the Parliament's vision, Europe didn't need a federal treasury. How wrong they were.

By October 1990, nuances had appeared in the European Parliament's 'Resolution on Economic and Monetary Union' (European Parliament, 1990), which effectively stated the position of the Parliament in the lead up to the IGC, scheduled for December 1990 (Piodi, 2012). This Resolution was based on a report presented by Belgian member M. Fernand Herman, who sat on the Committee on Economic and Monetary Affairs and Industrial Policy. Under Article 1, the term 'autonomous European Central Bank' was used (European Parliament, 1990: 63), whereas the 'Resolution on the process of European monetary integration' passed on 14 April 1989 had indicated that the European Central Bank would be part of a system of European central banks and that the 'Central Bank of each Member State of the European Monetary Union should

. . . be independent of the corresponding political authority' (European Parliament, 1989: 335). Piodi (2012: 59–60) notes that the term 'autonomous' was 'fully illustrated' in the Herman Report and refers to the 'ability to decide for itself and the freedom to act that allows the politically agreed objectives of monetary policy to be achieved'. Those objectives were dominated by the exclusive focus on price stability.

THE GOLDEN RULE OR NOT – THE CIRCUS MARCHES INTO ROME, DECEMBER 1990

Intergovernmental Conferences are designed within the European political context to be vehicles for proposing treaty changes. Decisions taken at these conferences have to be reached unanimously by the Member States and become formal additions to the treaty once they are ratified by the Member States individually. The Intergovernmental Conference in Rome or the Assizes as it became known was hosted by the Italian parliament as part of Italy's six-month presidency of the European Council. It began on 15 December 1990 and was tasked with producing agreed amendments to the Treaty of Rome, so that stages two and three of the Delors Plan could be implemented. The conference had around 12 months to come up with the proposed changes. The proposed treaty changes would then be ratified at the meetings in December 1991 to be held in Maastricht.

The important 'preparatory' documents that informed this process were the Delors Committee Report, the Guigou Report, the Christophersen Report (reflecting the Commission's official view) and the Herman Report (and subsequent Resolution) from the European Parliament. Other contributions from the various workshops and committees were also considered including the 'draft statute' for the new central bank provided by the Committee of Governors of the Central Banks (European Commission, 1991c: 34–35).

All these 'inputs' sang from the same hymn sheet, which meant that the die was already cast. The deals had been done by the time the Member States converged on Rome. The Committee of Governors of the Central Banks had rubber stamped the sections of the Delors Plan relating to the creation of an independent central bank in a report delivered on 27 November 1990. Germany had won. It demanded that if it was to surrender the mark and relegate the Bundesbank to being part of the European System of Central Banks with the newly created European central bank at the helm, then the latter would have to be constituted and act as if it was the Bundesbank: independent of the politicians, singularly focused on price stability, and unable to offer any funding assistance to the Member

States in economic strife. The French resistance to this had faded in the 1980s as its policy makers had been seduced by the now dominant Monetarist views among macroeconomists.

The recommendation from the Delors Report that 'no new institutions' be created 'in the economic sphere' (meaning no new European level treasury fiscal function) was accepted without debate. Even the French hope that Ecofin might be bolstered to act as a European fiscal authority was abandoned because the Germans considered this would compromise the focus of the new European central bank on inflation control. Thus, fiscal policy was left as the responsibility of the Member States, albeit with the plan to impose tight 'binding' limits on what the national governments could do (Gerbet, 2014). These limits would bias Europe towards stagnation, but that wasn't fully revealed until the GFC, and is still not widely understood or admitted.

The European Commission noted in the lead up to the IGC that there was 'unanimity that certain rules (no monetary financing, no automatic bail outs) and a principle (the avoidance of excessive budget deficits) should be enshrined in the Treaty' (European Commission, 1991c: 36). However, despite this 'unanimity' there were still differences on matters of detail that had to be settled before there could be a change to the Treaty. Among the outstanding issues was the nature of the binding fiscal rules, which would be imposed 'to prevent the appearance of imbalances which might compromise monetary stability' (p. 35). The other major issue related to the rules and criteria that would govern the transition from stage two to stage three. There were some token words about 'democratic responsibility', which had become an issue because monetary policy and the fiscal rules would be determined by unelected and largely unaccountable bodies, the new central bank and the European Council. It was proposed that these bodies would have to be 'clearly and directly responsible before the Parliament' (p. 36) an ambition that was never fulfilled.

In terms of the binding rules, the EMU Working Group had considered the formulation of an 'Excessive Deficits rule', which would be built into Member State legislative frameworks before the nation could receive its 'entry ticket' to the EMU (EMU Group, 1990: 1). The group recommended the so-called 'golden rule', which limited fiscal deficits to the rate of public investment in productive capital. The 'golden rule' essentially means that over some defined economic cycle (from the peak of activity to the next peak) the government deficit should match its capital (infrastructure) spending. All 'recurrent' spending (that is, spending which exhausts its benefits within the current year) should be 'funded' through current revenue (taxes and fines, etc.).

The 'golden rule' reflects the mainstream economics view that governments have to 'fund' their spending just like a household. We will consider the fallacies of this view in Chapters 17 and 18 because they impinge on the way we construct the future options for Europe. But within the flawed mainstream framework, any excess in government spending over taxation receipts has to be 'financed' in two ways: (a) by borrowing from the private sector; and/or (b) by 'printing money' (borrowing from the central bank). The latter funding source, the so-called 'monetary financing of deficits by central banks', is considered taboo because neoliberal economists claim it causes accelerating inflation as a result of 'too much money chasing too few goods for sale'.

Chapter 21 considers that argument in detail, but for now we conclude that the proposition is generally preposterous because economies that are constrained by spending that is insufficient to generate full employment of available productive resources respond to increases in spending by expanding the production of goods and services rather than increasing prices (which could lead to inflation). There is an extensive literature that shows that when governments expand their own spending to offset a decline in private sector spending, the spare capacity available is brought back into productive use without any inflation response.

But, given these fears, mainstream economists argue that a better (but still poor) solution is for governments to issue debt (bonds) to the private sector to 'finance' their deficits. However, there are also alleged costs associated with this option, which is why mainstream economists advocate governments should run fiscal surpluses whenever they can. These costs include alleged increases in short-term interest rates and higher future tax rates because the debt has to be 'paid back'.

For the present discussion, we note that the golden rule logic may be legitimately applied to governments that do not issue their own currency, such as state governments in a federal system. Similarly, under the proposed EMU, Member States were to cede their currency issuing capacities to the European Central Bank and effectively use a foreign currency. In that regard, the EMU Member States were to become equivalent to the states in the US or Australia.

In that context, the 'golden rule' is considered equitable across generations because the current taxpayers 'pay' for the public benefits they receive now, while the future generations have to pay for the benefits that the infrastructure delivers to them in the years to come. Thus, day to day spending that benefits the current taxpaying public should be covered by taxation revenue and capital infrastructure should be funded through debt. The fiscal balance would thus always be zero net of public investment spending.

Germany was already implementing the 'golden rule'. The Financial

Reform Act of 1969 was a major change to the German 'Basic Law' or 'Grundgesetz' and 'created a mandatory, standardised framework for the budget law of central and regional government' (Lübke, 2008: 134) by revising Articles 109 to 115 of the 'Basic Law' and introducing the 'Budgetary Principles Act' ('Haushaltsgrundsätzegesetz'). While the details do not need to concern us here, the 'golden rule' was given authority under Article 115 (Limits of Borrowing), such that 'Revenue obtained by borrowing shall not exceed the total expenditures for investments provided for in the budget; exceptions shall be permissible only to avert a disturbance of the overall economic equilibrium' (Federal Law Gazette I, 2010).

The Christophersen Report concluded that: 'Despite its definitional shortcomings, the golden rule of public finance . . . appears the most satisfactory from an analytical point of view and is the only one widely applied in existing federations' (European Commission, 1991c: 24).

The European Commission was unclear on the need for 'binding rules' as proposed by Delors. They noted that one couldn't really judge the 'sustainability of the fiscal position . . . in isolation from an overall assessment of the economic situation and development' (p. 24). In other words, imposing a 'one size fits all' set of rules would likely be excessively punitive in certain circumstances. They instead advocated a system of 'multilateral surveillance' with the Ecofin at the helm to help coordinate economic policies to ensure they did not pose a 'threat to monetary stability' (p. 24). Within the system the 'golden rule' was proposed as the overarching framework for fiscal control.

THE 'BACK OF THE ENVELOPE' RULES

Despite these insights, the 'golden rule' was not adopted. As it turned out, it was not the Germans who led the way in defining the binding rules at the IGC. Mitterrand's government had introduced a fiscal regime in 1983 that was stricter than the 'golden rule'. Mitterrand told his Prime Minister Pierre Mauroy, at the outset of his third government in March 1983, that he had to 'bring down inflation to a rate compatible with our competitors . . . [and maintain] . . . the public budget deficit within its current levels' (quote from Le Point, 28 March 1983, translated by Sachs et al., 1986: 296). The 'current levels' were around 3 per cent. It was left to the Minister of the Economy, Finance and Budget, Jacques Delors, to invoke the radical shift in policy by abandoning the 'Programme commun' (the joint policy focus on inflation and unemployment) and instead pursue the so-called 'tournant de la rigueur'. Their concept of rigour was guided by events that had occurred on an evening in June 1981.

In 2010, Guy Abeille, who was a project manager in the French Ministry of Finance when Mitterrand came to power in 1981, explained how the 3 per cent deficit rule entered European political parlance (Abeille, 2010). His tasks included writing a monthly briefing to the Minister on economic developments including the fiscal position. This briefing came through the Director of Budget. Each year he would make handwritten notes about politically acceptable alterations to the fiscal policies from the previous year. In 1981, the French Ministry of Finance had become concerned with the inflationary consequences of the oil price rise associated with the Yom Kippur War. Abeille said that up to that point, the French government had been running a deficit of around 1 per cent of GDP but no particular ratio was considered when designing fiscal initiatives. Rather, functional outcomes were the centre of the discussion (for example, reducing unemployment).

Giscard d'Estaing believed that the fiscal deficit would start to garner negative political impacts if it exceeded 30 billion francs, and the Ministry of Finance engaged in financial 'gymnastics' to deliver an outcome below that ('fetish') threshold. In 1981, the fiscal deficit rose to around 55 billion francs and forecasts for 1982 revealed the fiscal deficit would be above 100 billion francs, which according to Abeille was 'a figure that even the most fearless would not dare to whisper in secret'.

One night in June 1981, Abeille was summoned by the deputy director of the Budget Department, Pierre Bilger, along with some other 'economists', who Abeille noted were considered a 'rare species' in the bureaucracy as a result of their mathematical training and their capacity to handle numbers and appear knowledgeable. The economists were told that Mitterrand (elected 21 May 1981) wanted a simple, practical deficit rule, which would project an aura of fiscal discipline and would be seen as authoritative by dint of the endorsement by economists. This would allow him to resist the demands for more funds from his government ministers. Abeille noted that they quickly decided that a deficit-to-GDP ratio would suffice because it was a clear target and the nuances and shortcomings of such a measure, which any reasonable economist would recognise, would evade the understanding of the public.

For example, how does one interpret a rising deficit-to-GDP ratio? It could mean the government is deliberately expanding the gap between its spending and revenue at a faster rate than the economy is growing, or it could mean that the economy is contracting and the government is losing tax revenue (and could even be cutting spending). These ambiguities, which we will consider in later chapters, are typically not understood by the public and allow movements in fiscal measures to be misrepresented in the public debate to advance ideological agendas that aim to cut the scope of government activity.

Abeille said that their agenda was politically motivated rather than driven by economic concerns. They quickly did some 'back of the envelope' calculations, which showed that the projected deficit and GDP estimates would deliver a deficit-to-GDP ratio of around 3 per cent. The figure had 'no other foundation than the circumstances of the day' but ticked all the boxes. He said that a rule of 1 per cent would have been too restrictive and not able to be sustained given that the movements in economic activity would lead it to be violated in the normal course of an economic cycle, and 2 per cent would also be too restrictive.

Abeille emphasised that the 3 per cent 'number was not based on economic theory' (*Le Parisien*, 2012a). In another interview, Abeille added that (*Le Parisien*, 2012b):

> We imagined the 3% figure in less than an hour, it was a 'back of an envelope' calculation, without any theoretical reflection . . . Mitterrand wanted us to quickly provide him with an easy rule, which sounded economic, with which he could confront the ministers who marched into his office asking for more money . . . We needed something simple . . . 3%? It was a good figure, a figure that has stood the test of time, it was reminiscent of the Trinity . . . Mitterrand wanted a standard, we gave it to him. We did not think it would endure beyond 1981 . . . [the] . . . Minister of Finance, who was the first to talk about the deficit as a percentage . . . 100 billion francs was huge . . . he preferred to speak of 2.6% . . .

So France came to the December 1990 IGC with its arbitrary fiscal rule of 3 per cent intending to outdo Germany's 'golden rule' in terms of 'fiscal toughness'. But over the previous decade or so, with the 3 per cent rule in operation, France's unemployment rate had risen from around 5.2 per cent to around 8.4 per cent, and would continue to rise into the 1990s as austerity madness gripped Europe. In the years since the IGC, the unemployment rate in France has dipped below the 1990 level only briefly. But with the Monetarist mania focused on inflation control, the massive costs associated with unemployment had become a distant concern.

THE CIRCUS LEAVES ROME AND HEADS FOR MAASTRICHT

The first several months of 1991 were busy ones for the Finance Ministers supported by a phalanx of treasury bureaucrats and other relevant committees within the European Commission. The Economic and Social Committee of the European Community held a meeting on 21 February 1991 and subsequently noted that while there had been progress towards the goal of an economic and monetary union up until then, there were 'still considerable *objections* and *doubts* to be overcome' (Economic and Social Committee, 1991: 31; emphasis in original).

They documented the lack of political will among Member States to surrender sovereignty to the extent required to make the system function. They noted the wide disparities in inflation rates among the EMS nations and the fact that some 'Member State **budget deficits** which continue to be financed by central bank borrowing can only be successfully tackled by addressing national resource allocation problems' (p. 32; emphasis in original). The Committee questioned whether it made any sense to pursue a common monetary policy across 12 countries (Denmark, Netherlands, Germany, Ireland, France, Belgium, Italy, Luxembourg, Spain, Britain, Portugal and Greece):

> . . . there is no tangible *proof* either that the economic policies of the twelve different countries can actually be *subordinated to common guidelines* or that the national measures deemed necessary to successfully overcome unemployment, structural weaknesses and regional imbalances are in fact compatible with the common goal of general price level stability. (p. 32; emphasis in original)

They also documented the concerns that an 'independent' monetary policy would have for 'democratic accountability' (p. 32).

Somewhat pointedly they noted that these 'objections and doubts are largely unknown to the wider *public* in the majority of Member States. The discussion of economic and monetary union options is often oversimplified and frequently limited to the question of timing and institutional arrangements' (p. 32; emphasis in original). The public could not appreciate the disadvantages of proposed union, which were 'not explained clearly enough in the Commission's report' (p. 32). In particular, the public could not appreciate the costs to nations of abandoning their currencies and accepting a common monetary policy. Further, the abandonment of the capacity of central banks to fund deficits 'would be painful for many countries' (p. 32). By painful, they meant that unemployment would be higher than necessary, governments would be unable to provide essential public services, and there would be increased poverty rates and social exclusion. All of which have come to pass in recent years.

The hardline Monetary Committee of the Council, a major source of the 'over simplified' and 'process oriented' information that was pumped out to the unknowing public as part of the political massaging of the move to economic and monetary union, had no such reservations. They released a report on 12 April 1991, which signalled their agreement on the 'criteria for excessive deficits' (European Council, 1991: 1), that is, the binding rules that would stop Member States, subsidiarity principle notwithstanding, from running deficits beyond a certain limit. They said there had been 'considerable' but not 'unanimous' support (p. 2) for 'three independent criteria' (p. 2):

1. A 'debt-to-GDP ratio in excess of a reference value with inadequate action to stabilise or reduce it', or
2. 'Breach of the golden rule and a deficit-to-GDP ratio in excess of a (low) reference value', or
3. 'Deficit-to-GDP ratio in excess of a (higher) reference value'.

The number 60 per cent was noted as the reference value under Criterion 1, while 0.5 per cent and 2 per cent were bandied about for Criteria 2 and 3, respectively. The discussion that followed was a labyrinthine exercise in how many 'fish' they would 'catch' in the excessive deficit 'net'. There was no discussion of the role of fiscal policy and the context in which it might be exercised to keep unemployment low in the face of significant shifts in private spending. The concerns of the Economic and Social Committee's 'Opinion' were thus well founded. The Monetary Committee econocrats happily played around with spreadsheets inserting different levels of the respective 'reference values' to work out the 'fish' harvest (where the fish were nations where humans lived and worked)!

The Report's Annexe documented the scale of nations in breach at various 'reference values'. In some simulations, where the 'reference values' were very low, nine of the twelve nations would breach the rules if implemented. The reality was that there was a wide disparity in deficit outcomes across the original EMS nations, which became larger once twelve nations became the focus. For example, in 1990, France was running a deficit of 2.5 per cent of GDP and so was comfortable advocating a 3 per cent rule. Of the original EMS nations, Belgium recorded a deficit of 6.8 per cent of GDP in 1990, Denmark 1.3 per cent, Germany 2.9 per cent (which would soon rise sharply as a result of the reunification outlays), Ireland 2.8 per cent, Italy 11.4 per cent, Netherlands 5.3 per cent and the United Kingdom 1.5 per cent. Luxembourg was an exception and was recording a fiscal surplus in 1990 of 4.3 per cent of GDP.

But unemployment was elevated in all these nations relative to the situation encountered at the beginning of the EMS in 1979. It was clear that these deficits were not large enough given the rising unemployment across these nations. But with Monetarist ideology blurring this understanding, and instead promoting a series of myths about fiscal deficits, policy makers were blithe, if not blind, to that reality. The Monetary Committee seemed to be focused on whether the sanctions for breaching the proposed rules would be automatic or not and other arcane matters of process within the punitive regime they were designing and forgot that there is a direct link between the size of the deficit and unemployment.

The discussions mostly concerned what could be done about Italy (with concern over Belgium and the Netherlands simmering). Concerns were also focused on the new EMS entrants including the peseta (entered 19 June 1989); the pound (6 October 1990) and the escudo (4 April 1992), and finally, the prospect that Greece might join the economic and monetary union.

On 4 July 1991, the Commission published an updated 'Communication' to the Council, which expressed the concerns that it had for the lack of progress towards economic convergence, given that Stage II of the transition to economic and monetary union was 'only two and a half years away' (European Commission, 1991a: 1). The 'worrying set-backs' among some countries were defined in terms of rising deficits in the face of an acknowledged 'less favourable economic situation' (p. 1). Extraordinarily, the Commission claimed that it was appropriate for Member States to enact harsh fiscal cutbacks in this recessed environment because 'the policies required to strengthen growth fundamentals are also those necessary to improve convergence'. This is an early statement of the 'fiscal contraction expansion' mantra that has been at the forefront of the imposition of fiscal austerity during the current crisis.

Neo-liberals claim that by cutting public spending, total spending in the economy will rise. Where did this sophistry come from? A basic rule of macroeconomics is that spending equals income, which leads to output and employment. Someone's spending is another person's income. There has to be growth in spending for income and output to grow. If there is unemployment it means that total spending is insufficient to generate enough output and hence jobs to satisfy the preferences for work of the unemployed. The Keynesian solution was for the government to either directly increase spending to lift sales in the private sector and stimulate further income and/or to cut taxes, which might lead to higher private spending.

The Monetarists rejected this approach claiming that government spending and deficits were inflationary and wasteful. As an alternative, they introduced the rather bizarre turnaround in logic that said that when there is unemployment the correct strategy for government is to cut its spending, that is, introduce what is now popularly known as 'fiscal austerity'. This policy view was based on an arcane theoretical notion that economic textbooks promote called 'Ricardian Equivalence'. It sounds scientific, but in simple terms it refers to the assertion that private spending is weak during a recession because households and firms form the view that the government will have to increase taxes in the future to pay back the debts it incurs due to the higher deficits. As a consequence, the households and firms deliberately stop spending and save up to ensure they can pay the higher taxes. Once the government starts to cut the deficit, the theory claims that a signal is sent to the private sector that future taxes will be lower and so they start spending again. Problem solved.

There has never been any credible empirical evidence produced by anyone to show that private households and firms behave in this way when deficits rise. The overwhelming evidence shows that firms will not invest while consumption spending is weak and households will not spend because they are scared of becoming unemployed and try to minimise their outstanding debt obligations. Ricardian agents only exist in the rarefied world of mainstream macroeconomic textbooks and have never been observed at large in the real world.

But in 1991, the European Commission was introducing this notion into the debate about economic and monetary union. The wheels had starting falling off back then.

THE DUTCH START TO WORRY ABOUT FAILURE

On 25 October 1991, some Council members (President in Office Wim Kok, President Delors and Vice President Christophersen) made statements to the European Parliament in Strasbourg. Kok told the gathering that 'Maastricht . . . was just seven weeks away' (European Commission, 1990b: 1) yet major issues were unresolved including final agreements on the reference values for the binding fiscal rules and the mechanisms that would curtail the yet to be specified excessive budgetary deficits. Even the single currency was not yet unanimously accepted. Further, there was no agreement as to how an unelected and politically independent European Central Bank would be consistent with democratic ideals. In that regard, there 'was no consensus among Member States over executive decisions and the role of the European Parliament' (p. 2). Delors also muddied the waters by urging the discussion not to adopt a 'solely arithmetical appreciation of deficits' (p. 2). In other words, universally binding numerical rules would unlikely be in the public interest.

The Dutch, in particular, were getting anxious about what might happen if the Maastricht Council meeting failed to reach agreement on the Treaty revisions. By the end of the 1990s, the former Executive Director of the Dutch Central Bank, André Szász, was despairing of the process that led to the Maastricht meeting, even though he had played an important role at the time. He wrote that the 'early prospect of German unification came as a shock' (Szász, 1999: 144) for the British and French. The French responded to the implied loss of power within Europe by accelerating their call for monetary union, while the British increasingly distanced themselves from continental Europe. France also tried to use the simultaneous Intergovernmental Conferences to argue for a supranational '"Economic Government" in parallel to the European Central Bank', which would be a 'democratic' institution that would 'execute the main elements of economic policy' (p. 157). But the French were not united on this demand (Howarth, 2000). The Dutch and German negotiators differed from the French and favoured an independent supranational economic policy-making body to parallel the new central bank, but didn't want this to be part of a 'reinforced Ecofin Council', which would have been subordinate to the European Council (Szász, 1999: 157). Germany and the Netherlands considered, in Szász's view, that such a body could run excessive deficits and then divert political pressure onto the ECB if the latter raised interest rates in the pursuit of its price stability goals.

The political implications of German reunification, however, concentrated minds. In November 1991, Szász urged the parties to forge an agreement because he believed that the new Germany, already a successful federal state, might go it alone (Baun, 1996: 620). *The New York Times* ran a story on 16 November 1991, which quoted Helmut Kohl as saying that the upcoming Maastricht meetings were 'a fateful hour for Europe' (Kinzer, 1991a) and that it would be 'a catastrophe for European development . . . the beginning of the collapse of our community' (Kinzer, 1991a) if the Treaty talks failed.

8. The Maastricht Treaty

BY THE TIME THEY GOT TO MAASTRICHT . . .

On 11 December 1991, the troupe rolled into Maastricht for the European Council meeting that would finally take the decision to recreate the European Community with a new treaty centred on the introduction of the economic and monetary union. Nations who joined the EMU would cede their currency issuing capacities to a newly created and independent European Central Bank, prevent that institution from playing a defensive role in times of crisis ('monetary financing of deficits') and agree to constrain their own fiscal freedoms to such a degree that they could no longer exercise their responsibilities to consistently maintain strong economic and employment growth. They also agreed to expose themselves to the whims of the private bond markets that existed only to make profits without regard for national goals such as full employment. The Council meeting effectively determined that the deflationary bias of the Bundesbank became the dominant policy paradigm for Europe at large, except that Germany's export strength was not shared.

The Germans and the Dutch held their position on the need for binding fiscal rules with sanctions for breaches. The British wanted no rules because they understood, correctly, that they compromised the democratic legitimacy of the national governments. There were curious conflicts among conservatives over this question. The liberals said there was no need for rules because once the governments lost their currency-issuing capacity (and many were still selling bonds to their central banks in return for cash) the private bond markets would stop lending to any profligate government. The alternative view was that once a nation encountered 'funding' constraints, the pressure for bailouts would be intense. The central bankers were leading the charge for tight fiscal constraints to avoid 'overburdening monetary policy' (Szász, 1999: 159).

Going into Maastricht, the 'golden rule' was still on the table given it allowed for differences in national commitments to the provision of public infrastructure. But the 'golden rule' also ran foul of the neo-liberal preference for private infrastructure provision over public outlays. Szász (1999: 159) said that 'in the end the golden rule proved unacceptable' and attention then turned to using arbitrary ceilings on deficits and public debt ratios. He concludes that the agreement to set the reference values to 3 per cent (deficits to GDP) and 60 per cent (gross public debt to GDP) 'was a compromise' (p. 159) to bring together those who wanted a higher allowable deficit figure and others who wanted a legally binding balanced budget. The public debt ratio appeared to be a reflection of the current situation and had no science backing it.

Whether it was France's long-standing 3 per cent limit that ruled is unclear although during the negotiation phase the French had opposed the implementation of the 'golden rule' (Schönfelder and Thiel, 1994). Other claims (aired on the Franco-German TV channel ARTE) concluded that at the time of the Maastricht Council meeting, the 3 per cent limit was around the deficits currently being run by Germany at 2.8 per cent and France at 3 per cent.

While there was no economic theory endorsing the 3 per cent rule, it was obvious that the threshold did not reflect the scales of deficits that might reasonably be encountered in a major recession. Szász speculated that the 3 per cent limit would be breached 'as soon as an adverse cyclical situation presents itself' (Szász, 1999: 160). If that happened across the union, then any sanctioned process would lose meaning. It was clear that as they went into Maastricht the potential for the union to collapse under its own compromised and flawed design was high. But the political careers had to be maintained or made! The folly that masqueraded as responsible leadership would within a decade inflict untold misery on the most disadvantaged citizens in many European countries. But in 1991, as December approached, the bluster and rhetoric was pushing the throng in one direction only. The cliff would come later.

ITALY AND THE ITALIANS AT MAASTRICHT

Italy received particular focus in the lead up to the Maastricht meeting. There was great dispute about its capacity to meet the strict convergence criteria demanded by the Germans. The historical instability in Italian politics, marked by short lived coalitions, was considered to be a major reason why the Italians had devalued more than the other EMS nations and run consistently larger deficits (Della Sala, 1997). The claim was that the political cycle was so short relative to the economic cycle that there was little incentive to worry about the consequences of imprudent economic policy. The claim doesn't bear scrutiny because despite a pattern of short-lived coalitions in the two-decade period leading up to the Maastricht meeting, Italy had actually exhibited quite stark changes in the conduct of its economic policy and by the early 1990s was embracing the neoliberal approach, albeit not as closely as the Bundesbank would have liked (Walsh, 1999).

Within this increasing 'Bundesbank' focus, Italy had halved its inflation rate in the period 1988–91, but as Maastricht approached it still remained at around 6 per cent, which was high relative to other nations. Its fiscal deficit remained around 10 per cent, a figure that had persisted throughout the 1980s in response to persistently high unemployment. As a member of the EMS, the government was always prepared to devalue the lira and it frequently did, although the extent of the fluctuations against the mark was reduced towards the end of the decade. But Italian industry enjoyed the fact that the nation's international competitiveness was maintained by the exchange rate adjustments, which avoided damaging internal deflationary strategies (wage cuts) being imposed.

While the Italians were small players relative to the might of Germany and France, they nevertheless played a significant role in the Maastricht process. Before 1987, the Italians had clearly been among the nations that wanted Germany to take more responsibility for adjusting the mark upwards within the EMS rather than force devaluation and higher interest rates onto the external deficit nations. But after the Basel-Nyborg Agreement in 1987, when the EMS nations agreed to rely more on interest rate adjustment rather than currency realignments to maintain the agreed parities, internal policy tensions within Italy started to reveal themselves. By 1990, Italy was running significant fiscal deficits in an effort to boost domestic demand and stave off the rising unemployment. This macroeconomic stance was at odds with the emerging Monetarist culture in Italy promoted by the central bank officials in tandem with the Finance Minister, Guido Carli, who had previously been the Governor of the Banca d'Italia and was one of the key Italian negotiators at the IGCs and at Maastricht.

Giavazzi and Pagano (1988: 304) posed the question: 'why should a high inflation country ever want to belong to an agreement such as the EMS?' in relation to the fact that high inflation nations such as Denmark and Italy had endured a loss of competitiveness in the first half of the 1980s as a result of tying their nominal exchange rates to the EMS parities. They could only devalue infrequently and in between such realignments their industries lost out to external competitors. One line of argument was that France and Italy were able to piggyback on Bundesbank discipline if they stayed in the EMS, albeit at the expense of higher interest rates and persistently high unemployment. These nations knew that if they joined the EMS then there would be a 'transfer of responsibility for . . . monetary policy from . . . [their central bank] . . . to Germany's Bundesbank' (p. 304). Thus for a nation joining the EMU, its central bankers would have a strong incentive to keep inflation down, given that exchange rate adjustments would no longer be able to be used to maintain competitiveness.

Building on this argument, Dyson and Featherstone (1996) argued that by the end of the 1980s, the EMU narrative within Italy was being exploited by officials in the Department of Treasury (Tesoro), the Banca d'Italia, the Foreign Ministry, and the Prime Minister's Department to prioritise German-style monetary discipline and reduce the discretion of economic policy makers. The so-called 'vincolo esterno (external ties) concept, whereby the introduction of the EMU would restrict domestic policy makers and modernise the structure of the Italian economy, its income support systems and industrial practices, became a major motivation for Italian support of EMU. Carli, in particular, promoted the 'vincolo esterno' aspects of the EMU (Carli, 1993).

Fiscal deficits were blamed for the higher interest rates but the connection between the two was a direct result of Italy fixing its exchange rate, which meant that the Banca d'Italia often had to push up interest rates to stop the lira from devaluing. Thus it was its membership of the EMS that was the problem. Any domestic spending, public or private, would increase imports and place downward pressure on the lira. Carli knew that if Italy were to join the EMU, then the Banca d'Italia would effectively be forced to accept the Bundesbank culture and prioritise price stability (Carli, 1993). This resonated with his ideological preferences towards smaller government. As a result, the Italians accepted the German approach to transition to the EMU, which would require both fiscal and monetary discipline being imposed domestically for a number of years.

The major losers would be those who had long benefited from the system of 'partitocrazia' in Italy. 'Partitocrazia' is a pejorative term describing the dominance of the political party machines over civil society in decision making in Italy. The parties had long manipulated the proportional representation system in Italy to ensure party favourites were able to retain office despite being unpopular. Party leaders had also occupied powerful and very visible positions in Italian society. Such a system was open to corruption and patronage, especially since the Italian political parties retained extensive capitalist interests in sectors such as the media, health, and education.

Della Sala (1997: 15) argued that Italy had been seen as a 'weak' state 'lacking the capacity to aggregate demands into coherent policy programmes', which was exposed once capital controls were eliminated as part of the Single European Act in the late 1980s and economic interdependence between nations increased. He made the usual neo-liberal claim that this required a 'hollowing out' of the state, which was code for transferring resources into the hands of financial and other elites via privatisation, and labour market and financial deregulation. These changes are combined with a reduction in democratic oversight that arises from reducing the flexibility of fiscal policy and increasing the 'independence' of the monetary authority.

This agenda was certainly embraced by the technocrats in Italy leading into Maastricht. Della Sala (1997) argued that the Italian state had become a 'non-state' (p. 19) as a result of being '"captured" by . . . a broad range of societal interests' (p. 19). This was especially the case in relation to economic policy making which he described as 'incremental, serving micro-sectional interests, and without any clarity or coherence' (p. 19). The political parties pursued their own interests rather than a 'national' interest.

Della Sala (1997) argued that a 'state with weak economic management capacity should be susceptible to the transforming forces of markets and supranational authority' (p. 19) that the EMU would bring. This would especially be the case given that the Maastricht negotiations had been ideologically corralled by a 'few widely shared assumptions' (p. 20) – the neo-liberal Groupthink. These assumptions were, of course, that macroeconomic policy would concentrate largely on price stability with strict rules on deficits and that the changes to the Treaty would ensure Member States would accomplish a convergence in their economic policies.

The 'vincolo esterno' was seen by a growing number of technocrats in Italy as a way to break this party domination. They wanted an independent central bank because it would escape the politicisation of Italian party politics, which they considered promoted the narrow interests of the party elites at the expense of prudent monetary discipline (Dyson and Featherstone, 1996). The external discipline argument was not confined to Italy but was embraced by the new neo-liberal central banking and finance elites throughout Europe as a means of leveraging their own power to advance their own agendas (Dyson and Featherstone, 1996).

The lure of the EMU thus brought out a new elite of technocrats with support from both the right and left of Italian politics as the TINA mantra that Margaret Thatcher had used to bulldoze her way through Britain permeated across the Channel.

The EMU gave these new elites a chance to place Italy into their version of a 'modern' Europe and they took this pro European approach to the IGCs in 1990. The Italians wanted to be seen as a serious player in the 'new' Europe rather than part of the rabble or periphery. After all, between 1950 and 1990, Italy led Europe in per capita income growth (second in the world to South Korea), which brought Italy up to France and Germany. As a result, the 'Italians thought they had made it back into the fold of the developed world . . . and they looked forward, as members of the Exchange Rate Mechanism of the European Monetary System (EMS), to European monetary unification' (De Cecco, 2007: 763).

But even though the Italians went along with the Germans and the popular perception was that the Maastricht Treaty represented a German victory, the reality is more nuanced. The reality was that 'the German position had been considerably watered down by the group led by France and Italy' (Fratianni, 2000: 158). In particular, the Dutch had proposed that the European Council would set the date for Stage III at which time the list of qualifying countries would be determined. Carli was implacably opposed to this and the date was left in abeyance (Carli, 1993; Fratianni, 2000).

Further, Carli led the way in 'softening' the fiscal convergence criteria so that a literal interpretation would give way to what Fratianni called a 'dynamic' interpretation (Carli 1993: 158) whereby Italy could claim to have qualified as long as its public debt ratio was moving in the right direction, even though it would certainly remain above the 60 per cent ceiling that was defined in the Treaty (see also Cangelosi and Grassi, 1996).

But despite Italy's exploitation of the strength of Germany's desire to be part of Europe and hence its willingness to compromise on key 'monetary' principles, there was still a widespread scepticism questioning whether Italy and Greece could ever meet the convergence criteria that would be required to ensure all nations entered the EMU on a viable footing. The German Finance Minister, Theo Waigel, led the chorus of critics. By the time the details of the Maastricht Treaty were being consolidated this scepticism had significant ramifications for internal politics in Italy and the fiscal rules that would lead to the SGP. The SGP, adopted by the European Council in 1997, was based on Waigel's 1995 submission, which was, in part, targeted at Italy. After Italy had put in a draconian fiscal package of spending cuts and tax increases in 1998, Waigel said, 'Italy has achieved remarkable success' (James and Friedman, 1998). He might have also mentioned that the unemployment rate was already above 11 per cent and continued rising during that year.

Italy's other impact during the Maastricht process related to Britain's position on Europe. While the simmering relations between the two European powerhouses France and Germany attracted a lot of attention in the negotiations leading up to Maastricht, another bilateral intrigue was going on. This related to Thatcher's disdain for Italy and the skilful manoeuvring by the Italians that effectively cost Thatcher her Prime Ministership. Bindi (2011, 2013) relates how in the second half of 1990, Mario Andreotti used his Presidency of the European Community to push his pro European case. At the informal (out of schedule) Council meeting he called in Rome in October 1990, Carli's proposals were accepted despite fierce opposition from Thatcher. When Thatcher returned to London, she made a negative statement about the meeting to the House of Commons on 30 October 1990 (House of Commons Hansard, 1990a). Opposition leader Neil Kinnock said that 'her tantrum tactics will not stop the process of change' but just 'strand Britain in a European second division without the influence over change that we need' (House of Commons Hansard, 1990a).

Thatcher replied by attacking France and Germany and argued that EMU would be an imposition on Britain's sovereignty. Her Government 'would not be prepared to have a single currency imposed upon us, nor to surrender the use of the pound sterling as our currency' (House of Commons Hansard, 1990a). She then delivered her famous tirade, which produced the headline in the Sun tabloid newspaper two days later 'Up yours, Delors' (House of Commons Hansard, 1990a):

> Yes, the Commission wants to increase its powers. Yes, it is a non-elected body and I do not want the Commission to increase its powers at the expense of the House, so of course we differ. The President of the Commission, Mr. Delors, said at a press conference the other day that he wanted the European Parliament to be the democratic body of the Community, he wanted the Commission to be the Executive and he wanted the Council of Ministers to be the Senate. No. No. No.

The strident anti-European sentiment expressed by Thatcher created further dissent within her own party and two days later, on 1 November 1990, the Foreign Minister, Geoffrey Howe, resigned from the Cabinet, citing Thatcher's poor handling of British interests in Europe as the reason. On 13 November 1990, he made a farewell speech to the House of Commons and disclosed that Thatcher had defied advice from the Chancellor of the Exchequer and the Bank of England on the EMU and that her stance on Europe was a 'tragedy' and 'that the Prime Minister's perceived attitude towards Europe is running increasingly serious risks for the future of our nation' (House of Commons Hansard, 1990b). Michael Heseltine challenged for leadership two days later and, with mounting pressure, Thatcher quit as Prime Minister on 22 November 1990.

In her memoirs (Thatcher, 1993) scolded Howe for being 'either disloyal or remarkably stupid' for suggesting that Britain should not oppose the 'principle of a single currency'. But it was Rome that was the final blow. Andreotti and Carli were significant players in isolating Thatcher from the European debate and, ultimately, from her position of power in Britain.

As we will see, Italy and Britain also featured in a major crisis just seven months after the Maastricht Treaty was signed, which threatened to undermine the whole EMU process. Not only would Black September 1992 rock Italian pride as it was thrown out of the EMS, but it would also confirm Britain's tenuous European credentials.

But we are moving ahead of ourselves.

WHAT WAS AGREED AT MAASTRICHT AND WHAT WAS NOT

Despite the huge expense that resulted from flying high paid officials around Europe to attend countless meetings and briefings and paying various consultants top rates to provide advice to these officials, the European Council meeting in the Limburg Statenzaal in Maastricht on 9 and 10 December 1991 virtually rubber stamped the Delors Report which had been made public in April 1989. Essentially, the Maastricht Treaty took the existing yet doomed EMS; tweaked it a bit with the hope of some, yet to be agreed, fiscal constraints that would make it even more unworkable; and added the creation of an undemocratic policy unit (the European Central Bank) which absorbed and, hence, negated the most basic function of any responsible government, the capacity to issue its own currency. And this was hailed as the grand vision for a modernised Europe. But, of course, all of these changes were still less than precise and would take the rest of the decade to implement. Further, typical of European politics, the timing and nature of the transitional stages laid out in the Delors Plan were not without controversy.

But the Treaty on European Union that emerged inserted 'Title VI – Economic and Monetary Policy', which contained four separate 'chapters': Chapter 1 Economic policy, Chapter 2 Monetary policy, Chapter 3 Institutional provisions, and Chapter 4 Transitional provisions. The plan was for a complete economic and monetary union by the end of the 1990s. I am sure a few Dutch delegates in the Statenzaal muttered 'eindelijk' ('finally') when the signatures of the relevant Member State leaders crossed the paper.

Four protocols were established to flesh out the legal details for the chapters in Title VI.

- Chapter 1 – Protocol 5 on the excessive deficit procedure;
- Chapter 2 – Protocol 3 on the Statute of the European System of Central Banks and of the European Central Bank;
- Chapter 4 – Protocol 4 on the Statute of the European Monetary Institute;

- Chapter 4 – Protocol 6 on the convergence criteria referred to in Article 109j of the Treaty establishing the European Community.

Under Economic Policy, it was clear that governments would now be under 'multilateral surveillance' (Maastricht Treaty, 1992: 17), which would coordinate policies across the Member States to ensure that 'Member States . . . avoid excessive government deficits' (p. 19). Excessive is defined according to a 'reference value' defined under the excessive deficit protocol.

Specifically, these values were (p. 29):

- 3% for the ratio of the planned or actual government deficit to gross domestic product at market prices;
- 60% for the ratio of government debt to gross domestic product at market prices.

A punitive regime was specified whereby the European Council could 'impose fines of an appropriate size' on a nation that has 'excessive deficits', thus ensuring that perverse fiscal dynamics would be the norm. That is, a fiscal deficit could easily exceed the 3 per cent ceiling if there was a major recession and taxation revenues fell. The appropriate policy response would be to inject a spending stimulus into the economy, push the deficit out further, and watch both the economy recover and the deficit-to-GDP ratio fall again as the increased employment delivered more tax revenue and GDP grew. The rule after all is a ratio: the size of the deficit on the top (numerator) and the market value of GDP on the bottom (denominator). The ratio falls in a recovery because the numerator falls and the denominator increases.

The logic of the excessive deficits rule was to bully governments into taking exactly the opposite action to what responsible fiscal practice would specify. In other words, it forces governments to pursue 'pro cyclical' fiscal policy changes, which just means that governments are forced to cut spending at a time that private spending is weak. The policy thus compounds the problem by making the economic cycle worse. Responsible fiscal practice is counter cyclical: governments should increase their deficits when the economic cycle is deteriorating. As if encouraging governments to adopt ill-advised fiscal strategies wasn't enough, the protocol of imposing fines on a nation that was caught in recession represented lunacy to anyone who wasn't blinded by the Monetarist ideology.

Further restrictions on the flexibility of economic policy for democratically elected governments were specified in Article 104 which prohibited 'Overdraft facilities or any other type of credit facility with the ECB or with central banks of the Member States . . . governments . . .' as the direct purchase 'by the ECB or national central banks of debt instruments' issued by governments (Maastricht Treaty 1992: 18). The noose was well and truly tightened and it was only a matter of time before it would start causing damage.

The chapter on 'Monetary Policy' canonised the primacy of the price stability objective as an article of deep religious faith. The Bundesbank culture was now successfully embodied into European law. While Article 2 in the Treaty suggested that the aim of the Community was to foster 'a high level of employment and of social protection' (p. 6) the decision to create a dominant central bank, separated from democratic oversight, that had no responsibilities to promote growth if there was any 'prejudice to the objective of price stability' (p. 21) was telling. Piodi (2012) notes that the European Parliament was concerned that there was 'disconnect between monetary policy and the other Community's policies' (p. 64). Further, the European Parliament raised the lack of clarity on what 'price stability' actually meant. What would the price stability target be?

The main sources of contention then were the transitional provisions. The Treaty ratified the decision of the Rome Council meeting in October 1991 to introduce Stage II of the EMU transition on 1 January 1994. Accordingly, the vehicle that would finally become the European Central Bank, the European Monetary Institute (EMI) would be established and put into operation, even though monetary sovereignty would remain at the Member State level. The EMI was intended to start the process of coordination of national monetary policies and set up the machinery that would take over the individual monetary policy operations of the Member State central banks.

This set in motion a new struggle. On 29 October 1993, the European Council held an unscheduled meeting in Brussels, which announced that Stage II would begin just two months later. The EMI would thus begin operation on 1 January 1994 and be headed by Baron Alexandre Lamfalussy, who at the time was the general manager at the BIS. They decided to locate the EMI in Frankfurt, very near to where the Bundesbank had been located since 1972. The EMI initially worked out of Basel (where Lamfalussy was located) while it acquired office space in what was to become known as the Eurotower. The building was the original home of the old German 'Bank für Gemeinwirtschaft', which was a very powerful bank owned by the trade unions and aimed to provide services on a cooperative basis to workers to give capitalism a 'human face'. Ironic really!

There was an almighty struggle among the political leaders to win the location of the EMI, which played out along familiar lines. The candidates included London, Amsterdam, and Frankfurt am Main. Britain didn't want Frankfurt to be the location because it feared London would lose its financial dominance to Germany (Ungerer, 1997: 273). There was some talk of it being located in Bonn, given that Berlin was about to become the seat of the Federal German government and there would be plenty of office space available. The Dutch wanted it to be in Amsterdam even though there wouldn't have been much office space available. There was some talk that the European institutions should be spread around, across the 12 member states. But it was the urgings of Kohl that won the day. He was determined to situate the EMI (and then the ECB) in Frankfurt as 'compensation' to the German people for losing their beloved mark, which had been their 'symbol of post-war stability' (Ungerer, 1997: 273). It seemed to slip the attention of the Germans that every other nation that was entering the EMU was also losing its own, presumably beloved, currency!

The decision on location and choice of Lamfalussy was also referred to the European Parliament, even though matters relating to EMU were among the excised areas from the new 'codecision' powers (with the Council of Ministers) that were bestowed on the European Parliament under the Maastricht Treaty, which came into force on 1 November 1993 (European Commission, 2009). The appointment of Lamfalussy was thus not within the scope of powers held by the European Parliament but the Council considered it a courtesy to make the referral. It did establish a new procedure, however, where the European Parliament now runs 'hearings' where candidates nominated by the European Council appear and make their case for appointment. This process is meant to inject some democratic element into the appointment system for the head of the ECB but is another of those talk fests that have no legal status, unlike the appointments process in the US where the Congress can reject a Presidential nomination for Federal Reserve Governor.

THE MAASTRICHT TREATY FORMALISES THE ABANDONMENT OF FULL EMPLOYMENT

It is interesting to juxtapose the lack of any commitment to growth and full employment in the Maastricht Treaty with the grand policy statements that accompanied the peace at the end of World War II. The overwhelming challenge for each nation was how to turn their war-time economies, which had high rates of employment as a result of the spending associated with the war effort, into peace time economies without sacrificing the high rates of labour utilisation. Concerns about full employment were at the centre of these policy frameworks released by governments in most nations at the end of the Second World War.

Britain, for example, released its White Paper on Employment Policy in May 1944, which was an important statement on the Government's Post War policy agenda. Its opening statement said (Minister of Reconstruction to Parliament, 1944: 3):

> The Government accept as one of their primary aims and responsibilities the maintenance of a high and stable level of employment after the war . . . A country will not suffer from mass unemployment so long as the total demand for its goods and services is maintained at a high level . . . the Government believe that widespread unemployment in this country can be prevented by a policy for maintaining total internal expenditure.

The basic rule of macroeconomics that spending equals income was intrinsically related to the desire to maintain a high level of employment. British economist William Beveridge said that full employment (Beveridge, 1944: 18):

> . . . means having always more vacant jobs than unemployed men, not slightly fewer jobs . . . It means that the jobs are at fair wages, of such a kind, and so located that the unemployed men can reasonably be expected to take them; it means, by consequence, that the normal lag between losing one job and finding another will be very short.

Even the conservative weekly *The Spectator* applauded the sentiment at the time. It welcomed the White Paper on Employment because it represented 'a complete break with the old delusions which came to a head in the economic fallacies propagated and acted upon in 1931 . . . [and] . . . accepts the responsibility of the Government for averting mass unemployment by maintaining total expenditure on goods and services' (*The Spectator*, 1944).

The 'old delusions' was a reference to the conservative British Treasury line during the Great Depression that less government spending and wage cuts would solve the mass unemployment. The alternative that required government to take responsibility for ensuring expenditure was adequate to generate jobs for all those who desired them was proposed by John Maynard Keynes and others, and eventually held sway.

The old British Treasury line was resurrected as the Monetarism of the 1970s and permeated the economic thinking that went into the Maastricht Treaty and led to the design of the EMU. The imposition of fiscal austerity during the current crisis reflects the 'old delusions' that initially made the Great Depression worse before Keynesian policies were introduced.

9. Converging to crisis and austerity

THE CONVERGENCE CRITERIA

The fiscal rules relating to excessive deficits and associated fines were to become binding in Stage III. Chapter 4 of the Maastricht Treaty dealt with the 'transitional provisions' governing the move to full economic and monetary union. After the first stage commenced on 1 January 1990 it was intended that the liberalisation of capital would be accomplished before the Treaty was signed. This process had not been completed by the time the Treaty was signed in February 1992 and Article 73b required this to be achieved before the second stage would begin on 1 January 1994. Further, any nations still allowing their central banks to provide overdraft facilities or purchase treasury debt (and there were several) had to curtail this practice before Stage II was to begin. Article 109E also required Member States to 'avoid excessive government deficits' (Maastricht Treaty 1992: 18) as preparation for Stage II.

The onset of Stage II would also see the coordination of European monetary policy, previously 'managed' by the Committee of Governors of the Central Banks, devolved to the newly created EMI. The EMI would prepare for the introduction of the common currency (including its design and name) and the absorption of the individual Member State central banks into the ECB system. None of this work was particularly transparent to the citizens of Europe.

But the early pain would come with the so-called 'convergence criteria', which were laid out in Article 109j. The point of these conditions, in the minds of the Treaty signatories, was to ensure all participating nations would not threaten the hallowed 'price stability' objective after Stage II was completed. The Germans and the Dutch maintained the line that 'admission to the third Stage' should not be at the discretion of any Member State (Szász, 1999: 161). There was clear suspicion that the Italians and the Greeks, at least, would not be able to meet the criteria by the time the nations were ready to enter the irrevocable Stage III. While the system of fines proposed for deficits that exceeded the arbitrary reference values in the Treaty (3 per cent of GDP) would not apply until Stage III, nations were expected to treat the rules as binding during this transition phase. Each nation would also have to introduce appropriate legislation, which would render their central banks independent of the political process.

Article 109j of the Maastricht Treaty (1992) was supported by more detailed conditions set out in Protocols 3 and 6, which required Member States to:

- Achieve a high degree of price stability, which was defined in Protocol 6 to mean 'an average rate of inflation, observed over a period of one year before the examination, that does not exceed by more than one and a half percentage points that of, at most, the three best performing Member States' (p. 30).
- Act in accordance with Protocol 3 on the excessive deficit procedure, which established the 3 per cent and 60 per cent rules for fiscal deficits relative to GDP and public debt to GDP, respectively.
- Under Protocol 6, maintain an exchange rate 'for two years before the examination' within the 'normal fluctuation margins provided for by the Exchange Rate Mechanism' of the EMS (2.25 percentage) 'without severe tensions', which was taken to mean not having 'devalued its currency' against the currency of any Member State (p. 30).
- Under Protocol 6, maintain interest rates such that in the year before 'the examination . . . an average nominal interest rate . . . does not exceed by more than 2 percentage points that of, at most, the three best performing Member States in terms of price stability' (p. 30).

The 'convergence criteria', which in the eyes of the political and bureaucratic class in Europe defined an appropriate economic state, failed to mention anything about unemployment rates, poverty rates or notions of social inclusion. The whole discussion was about 'sacrifice' to the 'deity' represented by these financial ratios. The tainted reasoning was based on the Monetarist notion that full employment would arise automatically if price stability were achieved. Economists use terms like the 'natural rate of unemployment' to describe their belief (which they hold out as fact) in the ability of the market system to deliver a unique unemployment rate that is consistent with price stability.

The Member States were put on notice that they would be 'examined' over a one or two year period before they could expect to enter Stage III. The sense of pressure, which accompanies all examination processes, was added during the Maastricht deliberations to Article 109j. But consistent with the whole exercise there were inconsistencies and dysfunction. Article 109j (clauses 2 and 3) laid out the rather complicated 'time path' and decision rules that would be applied to get the nations to Stage III.

The 'examination process' would involve the European Council informing the Council of Ministers whether 'each Member State' and a 'majority of the Member States' had fulfilled 'the necessary conditions for the adoption of the single currency' (Maastricht Treaty 1992: 20). Then by 31 December 1996, the Council of Ministers would, 'decide . . . whether it is appropriate for the Community to enter the third Stage' (p. 20). If this decision were taken, then they would be required to set a date for the 'beginning of the third Stage' (p. 20). Clause (4) added some conditionality such that if 'by the end of 1997, the date . . . has not been set, the third Stage shall start on 1 January 1999' (p. 20).

What did that mean? First, the politicians were trying to fast track the convergence process so that nations such as Italy and Greece would quickly implement fiscal austerity. Second, it was clear that Clause (4) would set the Stage III date as 1 January 1999, if the Council hadn't already decided on a different date before the end of 1997. Does that mean they thought that things could move more swiftly than specified under Clause (4)? It is hard to imagine given that Clause (4) also said that before 1 July 1998, the Council would meet with the Council of Ministers 'after a repetition of the procedure' (checking compliance to the convergence criteria) to satisfy themselves that the Member States had met the required standards to proceed. Third, in April 1991, during the IGC process, Jean Claude Trichet, the French delegate, had won the day with his 'three principles': no veto, no coercion, and no arbitrary exclusion (Bini-Smaghi et al., 1994: 17). In the light of those guiding principles, a nation could sign the Treaty yet still claim it gave 'no undertaking to move to the third Stage' (p. 17).

Leading into the Maastricht Council meeting, the Dutch proposed a way around this dilemma by proposing a voluntary, multi-speed transition to EMU. Accordingly, the Council would meet at some given time and decide which Member States had satisfied the convergence criteria and then any Member State would have the option of joining Stage III or not and choose when. As long as at least six states met the criteria, they could go ahead to Stage III while other aspirants would play catch up if they wanted to do so. While the Germans were supportive, presumably because only 'like' nations would join the new system, there was 'violent opposition' to this 'multi-speed approach' (Szász, 1999: 162), coming from Italy and the Commission itself (Delors). It was obvious that if they had continued along this path, the 'treaty would have been downgraded to the level of a mere declaration of intent' (Bini-Smaghi et al., 1994: 18), which seemed contrary to all the narratives that had been spun about the proposed union since the Hague summit in 1969.

Szász (1999: 161) says that, in fact, the 1 January 1999 date (Clause 4) was added 'at the last minute and at the highest level' to 'impose time pressure on convergence'. He surmised that convergence would not have progressed quickly without this pressure. But there lay the danger. A fixation on a particular date was 'likely to prevail' (p. 162) over the accompanying economic criteria. If the economic criteria were the only part of the 'examination', nations who wanted to be included but knew they would fail the test would simply stall the process or exploit nuances to be admitted, in which case, they would undermine the viability of the system. While the Council of Ministers thought the viability of the EMU rested on these criteria being sustained, they were more motivated by the urgency to achieve political rather than economic goals.

The negotiators decided that there could be no 'opt out' clause if there was to be a viable transition to EMU but still had to assuage the open hostility of the British and the polite resistance of the Danish. Clearly they had to limit any 'opt out' clause and in truly European style, that typically leads to dysfunction, they introduced two selective 'opt out' protocols for Britain (Protocol 11) and Denmark (Protocol 12). They were separated because the Council knew Britain would never join but still wanted to hold out some path, and in the case of Denmark, the Council thought it would join but needed a different time path.

THE RATIFICATION DEBACLE – 1992–93

On 7 February 1992 the amended Treaty of Rome was signed and the EMU became European law. As the leaders left Maastricht there were 'winners' everywhere. The French thought they would finally get rid of the Bundesbank and create something they might have more control over. The Germans knew that by playing the European card they would look less scary and they also understood that the terms of the Treaty would ensure the Bundesbank would morph into the ECB with no loss of 'German' discipline. Eventually, the euro would become the new 'mark', except that everyone would be using it. There was a lot of optimism and delusion among the political classes.

Upon returning to Germany from Maastricht, Kohl announced to the Bundestag that:

> The way to European unity is irreversible ... The member states of the European Community are now bound in such a way that it is impossible for

> them to split apart and fall back into the concept of the nation-state . . . That means that we have achieved a key goal of German policy toward Europe. (Kinzer, 1991b)

He was not entirely happy that Maastricht had only concentrated on the economic and monetary union at the expense of advancing the political union, in particular, 'strengthening the European Parliament' (Kinzer, 1991b). But, it was enough, at that stage, to gain the agreement regarding the EMU.

Szász (1999: 115) noted the signing came not 'a moment too soon' given that the 'political momentum' for implementing the Delors Plan was 'starting to dissipate'. He speculated that the final push to secure the EMU agreement by the European political elite had 'failed to carry their constituents along with them' (p. 115). The general public had a sense that great change was coming but were almost totally ignorant as to what the implications of that would be. There was a sense of denial among those driving the change as well. The system they had conceived and put into place could not possibly withstand a major world recession. But their zealous adherence to Monetarism blinded them to that possibility and a bevy of economists 'back filled' during the 1990s with all sorts of spurious 'research' reports that seemed to justify and give authority to the design and the fiscal rules that came with it.

In addition, by 1991, the mini growth surge that Europe had enjoyed during the EMU negotiation phase was well and truly over and a major recession was approaching. Germany was at the centre of the shifting fortunes. Its reunification spending had created favourable spillovers across Europe but had driven the German inflation rate up to around 5 per cent. Any reasonable interpretation of this would have suggested that the inflation rate would soon fall again once the abnormal spending patterns ended. But the Bundesbank's inflation impatience saw them prematurely hike interest rates and, within a few months, Europe was in recession.

Within this context it did not take long for the debate to revert back into parochialism. The Maastricht Treaty still had to be ratified by each of the individual signatory nations and the ratification process varied across the nations. The politicians thought this would be a relatively quick matter and the Treaty could become operational on 1 January 1993 (Baun, 1996: 622). How wrong they were.

Denmark was the first nation to go through the ratification process. The rules in Denmark were that a national referendum had to be held, which unfortunately for the political elites meant the people would have their say directly on the EMU, vote by vote. The Danish politicians and bureaucrats had been operating in their own cocoon, attending too many EMU working groups, Council meetings and IGC meetings, and had become trapped in the Groupthink. As a result, they confidently set 2 June 1992, just four months after the Treaty was signed, as the referendum date. The result was a disaster for the EMU proponents. There was a turnout of 82.9 per cent of eligible voters but only 49.3 per cent were in favour.

The Danish government thought it would win the day by distributing half a million copies of the Treaty ('a large number', Szász, 1999: 166) to the population of 5 million. In the end it 'only served to convince voters they were being asked to enter into obligations of an impenetrable character' (p. 166). The result meant that under the existing rules, Denmark would scupper the whole show. Szász (1999: 166) said, 'it was hard to imagine that one small country could prevent the Treaty from coming into force . . . yet such were the rules'. Something had to be done. The solution came at the European Council meeting in Edinburgh on 11–12 December 1992, which considered, among other things, the 'problems raised by Denmark in the light of the outcome of the Danish referendum on 2nd June 1992 on the Maastricht Treaty' (European Council, 1992: 2).

The Memorandum produced in Part B of the Council's conclusions was devoted to 'Denmark and the Treaty on European Union' and was the result of some very heavy negotiation to overcome the obvious problem the Community faced. Denmark had submitted a document 'Denmark in Europe' to the Council on 30 October 1992, which was a statement of demands that should be met if it was to play ball and not bring the EMU down. There were four major 'opt outs' required for Danish support and the Council met each one of them, which was no surprise to anyone given the stakes. Accordingly, among other concessions granted, Denmark did not have to participate in Stage III, which meant they did not have to surrender their currency sovereignty. After gaining these concessions and assuaging the public hostility towards the EMU, the Danish government held a new referendum on 18 May 1993 and achieved a turnout of 85.5 per cent with 56.8 per cent voting affirmative. Not a substantial ratification by any means. But the problem in that corner of Europe was solved.

But we jump ahead. After the Danish rejected the first referendum, politicians elsewhere remained in denial and blithely went about their own ratification processes, hoping that the Danish problem would go away. On 3 June 1992, the day after the Danish rejected the first vote, President Mitterrand announced that France would hold a referendum on 20 September 1992 to ratify the Treaty. He didn't, strictly speaking, have to call a referendum. A majority in the Assembly would have been enough to carry the ratification process in France. Various explanations in the literature seek to explain his decision, ranging from noble statements that Mitterrand thought the people should have their say to more devious motives concerning his electoral unpopularity at the time (Szász, 1999). The general view is that he didn't believe the French would follow the Danish sentiment.

Whatever the motives, on 20 September the people did speak and Mitterrand achieved the barest victory with 51.1 per cent in favour on a 69.7 per cent turnout – the so-called 'petit oui'. The antagonists rehearsed all the concerns in the lead up to the poll: worry that loss of policy sovereignty would entrench unemployment, worries that the Germans would remain dominant, but more so, given the loss of sovereignty.

Things were not calm in Germany either. Getting the German people to give up their beloved mark would take some doing and the public hostility towards the EMU proposal was growing. Ratification in Germany involved a decision of the Bundestag, but that decision had to be constitutional. It was clear that Kohl would carry the vote in the Parliament but not before he had to agree to some 'concessions' relating to the necessity of adopting 'a strict interpretation' (Szász, 1999: 169) of the convergence criteria when it came to admitting Member States to the final Stage. The German politicians clearly didn't want any 'riff raff' joining the EMU.

Before long a number of litigiously minded souls decided to test the constitutionality of the Maastricht Treaty in terms of the German Basic Law. The German Federal Constitutional Court was asked to determine the validity of the Treaty and on 12 October 1993 rejected the petitions and ruled the Treaty was constitutional (German Constitutional Court, 1993).

Despite the confident hubris from the politicians and their apparatchiks, the ratification process turned out to be:

> . . . a painful and protracted process, causing considerable embarrassment to many governments. Strong opposition manifested itself not only in countries where the governments had been more or less pushed along, like Britain and Denmark, but also in those where the governments had taken the lead, France and Germany. (Szász, 1999: 170)

It is also clear that a sense of denial had formed among the political classes and separated them from reality, a common feature of Groupthink. The European Commission put out a brochure in May 1991 entitled 'Economic and Monetary Union: Europe on the Move', which was a political exercise aimed at convincing the public that things were heading in a direction that would benefit all (European Commission, 1991b). It was glossy and expensive to produce but failed to grasp any of the realities that would be realised once the full EMU plan was implemented and confronted with a serious economic downturn, such as that imported from the US sub-prime collapse in 2007.

Szász (1999: 171) provided a stark account of how the political authorities 'themselves were unclear . . . and lacked an overall view'. He recounted a meeting he attended in May 1990 in his role as the Executive Director of the Dutch central bank with members of the 'Dutch cabinet most involved in European issues' (p. 171). The Dutch were fervent advocates of 'European integration in general and of EMU in particular' (p. 171). He noted that during the discussion he formed the view that 'the ministers were looking at the implications of EMU seriously for the first time, and did not at all like what they saw' (p. 171). The Dutch Prime Minister, evidently when summing up, 'wondered whether the political authorities realised what they were doing' (p. 171). Wim Kok, the Finance Minister, reminded the gathering that it was 1990 and the discussions about the EMU 'had been going on for quite some time' (p. 171).

The ratification process did not provide positive reinforcement for the political manoeuvres that had ensued since the Delors Plan was released in 1989. There was uncertainty, dissent and, in retrospect, a sense of foreboding of what was to come.

And then along came Black September, which was partially caused by the negativity coming from the flawed ratification process.

THE SUMMER OF '92 – THE 1992/93 MONETARY CRISIS

While the *Summer of '42* was a comedy-drama film with European connections, the summer of 1992 in Europe was anything but comedic and threatened to stop the transition to the EMU before it had really started. But the politicians and European Commission bureaucrats managed to construct the near meltdown of the EMS as a demonstration of why a single currency was needed rather than a reason to abandon their half-baked plan before any more damage was done. Any reasonable interpretation, based on an understanding of what happened and why, would conclude that a single currency would be very destructive for some, if not most, of the 12 nations that were in the process of surrendering their currency sovereignty to join the EMU.

Once the ratification process was completed, attention turned to meeting the convergence criteria. Table 9.1 provides a snapshot of where the nations were in terms of the major convergence criteria in 1992. The unemployment rate, ignored as a desirable criterion, is also shown. To put a finer point on it, the policy makers considered the unemployment rate (via its link to the economic growth rate) to be the 'adjustment variable' as they pursued policies designed to meet the demands of the convergence

Table 9.1 Convergence criteria data, 1992

	UN rate	Inflation rate	Interest rates		Fiscal balance		Gross public debt	Current account
			Nominal	Real	Total	Golden rule		
	%	%	%	%	% GDP	% GDP	% GDP	% GDP
Belgium	7.1	2.4	9.38	5.76	−8.16	−6.31	128.5	2.69
Denmark	8.6	2.1	11.71	9.87	−2.64	−0.75	68.0	2.11
Germany	6.6	5.1	9.46	3.85	−2.45	0.30	42.0	−1.08
Ireland	15.4	3.1	12.37	9.30	−2.84	−0.79	90.4	0.36
Greece	7.9	15.9	23.54	7.61	−11.03	−8.05	79.1	−0.16
Spain	16.3	5.9	13.34	6.21	–	–	45.9	−3.69
France	9.3	2.4	10.35	8.26	−4.60	−1.01	39.7	−0.29
Italy	8.8	5.2	14.01	9.24	−10.32	−7.42	104.7	−2.38
Luxembourg	2.1	3.6	–	–	−0.18	4.22	4.8	14.45
Netherlands	4.9	3.7	9.35	6.69	−4.16	−0.87	77.3	2.26
Portugal	4.1	9.0	16.18	6.57	−4.37	−0.80	50.0	−6.94
UK	9.8	4.3	9.68	6.58	−6.43	−4.24	37.8	−1.65

Note: UN is the unemployment rate. – Data unavailable.

Source: Eurostat, Annual Macroeconomic Database.

criteria. They knew that to reduce public debt ratios and fiscal deficits and bring inflation rates into line they would have to reduce domestic activity, given their undertakings under the EMS in terms of maintaining narrow exchange rate bands. The logic of forcing the heavy adjustment work onto the domestic economy rather than the exchange rate was obvious: unemployment rates would have to rise. And so they did.

As policy makers imposed policy austerity in an effort to meet the criteria, unemployment rates rose from 1992 to 1995 as follows: Belgium from 7.1 per cent to 9.7 per cent; Greece from 7.9 to 9.2 per cent; Spain from 16.3 per cent to 20 per cent; France from 9.3 to 10.6 per cent; Italy from 8.8 to 11.2 per cent; the Netherlands from 4.9 to 7.1 per cent; and Portugal from 4.1 to 7.2 per cent.

The significant disparity between the 12 economies was further demonstrated by the behaviour of the so-called 'real effective exchange rates'. The BIS have published these special measures of international competitiveness on a monthly basis since January 1964. Real effective exchange rate measures are compiled by adjusting the actual exchange rate (called the nominal parity) by relative inflation rates. To understand the concept, consider the case of two nations with the same inflation rate, which means the prices of goods and services in each country are rising by the same rate. If the exchange rate in Country A starts to depreciate against the Country B (which means that B's rate is appreciating against A's rate), then goods and services offered in trade by Country A to Country B (exports to B) will now be cheaper for residents in Country B, because their currency buys more of Country A's currency. From the perspective of residents in Country A, goods and services bought from Country B (imports from B) will now be more expensive because their currency unit buys less of B's currency. In this case, we conclude that country A is becoming more internationally competitive as a result of the nominal exchange rate change. Similarly, if the nominal parity is unchanged between Country A and Country B, but Country A becomes more productive and its costs of production fall, which leads to a decline in its inflation rate, then Country A's international competitiveness will also rise (goods and services exported to other nations will be cheaper).

A situation could arise where a nation's currency is depreciating (which would boost competitiveness) but this is accompanied by an offsetting rise in its inflation rate relative to its trading partners (which would reduce competitiveness) with no net change. The rising inflation could be driven exclusively by the rising import prices (in local currency terms) as the exchange rate depreciates. This is why nations that are experiencing currency depreciation try to 'lock it in' in real terms to benefit from the gain in competitiveness. Governments often try to negotiate deals with trade unions and firms to accept the higher import prices and the resulting drop in real incomes rather than try to recoup the real losses by pushing up wages and/or prices.

Real effective exchange rates take all these factors into account and provide a summary measure of movements in international competitiveness. If the real effective exchange rate rises, then we conclude that the nation is less internationally competitive and vice versa.

Figure 9.1 shows the real effective exchange rates for the Maastricht Treaty nations from March 1979 to December 1994, indexed to 100 in September 1992 (the base period). An index sets all the rates equal to 100 at somc particular point (called the base period) and expresses all following observations as a percentage of the base period value. The use of a common base period aids comparisons of the growth across nations. If there are large differences between real effective exchange rates between nations this will show up in trade imbalances and, if permitted, the nominal exchange rate will adjust to reduce these trade deficits/surpluses. So a nation with a persistent and growing trade deficit as a result of declining international competitiveness will see its nominal exchange rate fall,

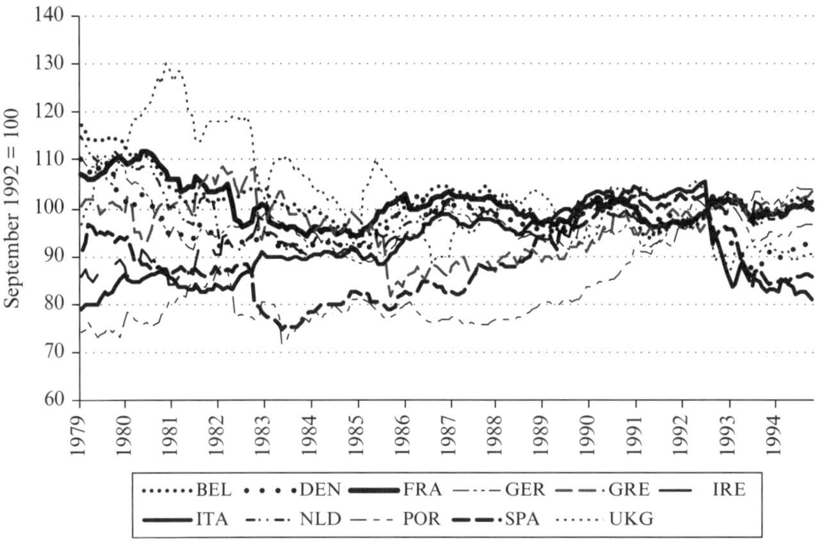

Source: Bank of International Settlements.

Figure 9.1 Real effective exchange rates, Maastricht Treaty nations, March 1979–December 1994, September 1992 = 100

which may improve its trade position as it becomes more competitive. We say 'may' because there are many factors at work, which can complicate the adjustment process following a change in a nation's nominal exchange rate. A nation facing the prospect of a depreciating/appreciating exchange rate as a result of its weak/strong trade position will also endure speculative attacks on its currency, which further push the exchange rate movements.

However, when the nations signed up for the EMS in March 1979, they were all obligated to keep the fluctuations in their exchange rates within 2.25 per cent plus or minus of the agreed parities (Italy was given a higher fluctuation band given its higher inflation and persistent trade deficits following the oil price hikes). This meant that a nation facing reduced international competitiveness had to cut costs (for example, constrain wage rises) to bring its inflation rate down and also constrain domestic demand to reduce growth in national income and GDP, which would lead to reduced spending on imports. It also led to persistently high unemployment. This was the period of the 'Franc Fort' (strong franc), which defined French government economic policy in terms of matching German inflation rates with other nations following suit.

As we have seen in our earlier discussion, the upshot was that there were many forced realignments as the central banks struggled to maintain the exchange rates within the narrow tolerances specified under the EMS rules. These realignments led to sharp fluctuations in real effective exchange rates, which is evident in Figure 9.1 in the early 1980s. After the Basel-Nyborg agreement was signed in 1987, which discouraged exchange rate realignment, nations were forced to rely much more on interest rate adjustments to maintain the parities. By increasing interest rates relative to their trading partners, a nation would attract capital inflow, which would increase demand for its currency and resolve the downward pressure. Of course, the rising interest rates were detrimental to domestic economic activity.

This period of exchange rate stability is also evident in the real effective exchange rates during the second half of the 1980s. But it was a false sense of stability, which didn't reflect any major convergence between the economies in economic performance. Speculative activity in foreign currency markets was more subdued in this period as a result of the perception that central banks were committed to using domestic adjustment rather than exchange rate realignments to resolve trade imbalances.

It should not be forgotten that during this period of relative stability, capital controls were still in place and prevented some of the speculative movements that would have normally destabilised the nations' exchange rates. Italy relied on capital controls extensively and only started to withdraw them in 1988 (Giavazzi and Giovannini, 1989; Eichengreen and Wyplosz, 1993). But the Monetarists hated capital controls because they impinged on their 'free market' ideal, and so they were eventually eliminated as a policy choice for all nations. The Single European Act of 1986 stipulated that all capital controls were to be abolished by 1 July 1990. Exceptions were made for Ireland and Spain (31 December 1992) and Greece and Portugal (31 December 1995).

The abolition of controls eliminated one policy tool that governments had to maintain stability and this became evident in 1992. Eichengreen and Wyplosz (1993), among others, recognised the bind that European governments were getting themselves into, when they coined the term 'The Unstable EMS'. They noted 'that the protracted process of negotiation and ratification allowed doubts to surface about whether the treaty would ever come into effect' (p. 52). They also highlighted the 'perverse incentives built into the treaty' (p. 52) as a further complicating factor. To meet the convergence criteria, nations had to maintain their currencies in narrow bands. But if a speculative attack which forced a nation to devalue (and thus breach the convergence rules) made transition to Stage III impossible, then what incentive did the nation have to maintain its policy austerity? At that point the speculative attacks would become 'self-fulfilling' (p. 52).

Eichengreen and Wyplosz (1993: 57) also argued that the capital controls 'protected central banks' reserves against speculative attacks' by reducing the possibility of the exchange rate being driven below the agreed fluctuation bands (which would require central banks to sell foreign currency in return for its own). This allowed the central banks to 'retain some policy autonomy' (p. 57), in the sense that they could pursue domestic objectives such as economic growth and low unemployment, which may have also meant that a particular nation's inflation rate was higher than its competitors. The capital controls gave them this leverage.

Once capital controls were eliminated, central banks became vulnerable as they had to focus policy on defending the nominal exchange rate parities. And with the rising instability associated with the treaty, this vulnerability became acute. The referendum failure in Denmark on 2 June 1992 brought some reality back into European financial markets by pricking the false bubble of currency stability. It had been true that after the Basel-Nyborg agreement in 1997 there had been no discretionary devaluations. But it was obvious that Italian and British competitiveness had been severely eroded by their higher inflation rates and that their currencies were substantially overvalued, particularly against the mark.

With the large disparities across the 12 Member States in terms of the convergence criteria variables, it was unimaginable that all the components of the convergence agreement could be met. For example, to maintain the exchange rates within the narrow tolerances agreed, some nations would have to increase interest rates, which would violate the undertakings with respect to maintaining narrow interest rate differentials. Exchange rate adjustment was staring the policy makers and politicians in the face but they blithely chose to ignore it. Until September 1992, that is.

The politicians pushing for the EMU saw the dark clouds emerging in the international currency markets as a sign that they had to move more quickly to introduce the single currency and impose harsher fiscal rules on Member States. They drew on the Delors Report (1989a: 11), which urged 'Greater convergence of economic performance' and concluded that 'With full freedom of capital movements and integrated financial markets incompatible national policies would quickly translate into exchange rate tensions and put an increasing and undue burden on monetary policy'.

The Bundesbank didn't help matters when it pushed up interest rates on 16 July 1992 because of its concern for rising inflation associated with the reunification. This had the effect of further reinforcing the view that the mark was undervalued. This was especially the case given that US interest rates had been cut on 2 July 1992 as America battled to avoid recession.

The obvious happened. International currency speculators sold the US dollar, the lira and the pound and shifted massive volumes of funds into the mark.

By pushing interest rates up in Germany, the Bundesbank demonstrated its fundamentally 'conflicted role as the anchor of the mark and simultaneously of Europe's exchange rate mechanism' (Mallaby, 2010: 152). It could not serve both roles. The Bundesbank decisions were particularly problematic for Germany's neighbours because they faced recession and unemployment was already high. The increased German interest rates forced them to increase their own interest rates beyond the levels deemed prudent given their domestic circumstances. Monetary policy was locked into ensuring the exchange rates were stable and higher unemployment was the casualty. The increasing political backlash to the high unemployment raised further doubts in the financial markets as to the commitment by policy makers to maintaining the 'no realignment' policy.

The EMS was now on very shaky ground. The first currency to go into crisis was the Italian lira, after it came under increased speculative scrutiny in mid 1992. The depreciating US dollar had seriously reduced the competitiveness of the European nations, with Italy the most impacted, given its significantly higher inflation rate. Within the logic of the EMS, the correct response would have been for the Italian government to devalue their currency by up to 10 per cent. But the Italian government was deeply divided over how it would go about meeting the convergence criteria and didn't have the political will to act. The Banca d'Italia also resisted devaluation. The Italians instead attempted to maintain the exchange rate parity and raised interest rates sharply on 4 September 1992. At that point, short-term interest rates in Italy were already a growth choking 15 per cent.

But that wasn't enough and the lira plunged below the allowable lower limits as investors continued to move funds from Italy to Germany. This, in turn, placed further pressure on the Bundesbank who had also been defending the lira by selling the mark and buying the Italian currency. The Germans, as expected, felt that the growth in the supply of marks would worsen their inflation and they were reluctant to hold the fort for too long.

Tensions were also high as the French approached the ratification referendum on 20 September. Britain in particular wanted to reduce interest rates without having to devalue the pound as its unemployment was skyrocketing. The European finance ministers and central bankers met in Bath (as UK Chancellor Norman Lamont was chair of the Ecofin committee) over the weekend, 4–5 September 1992. Lamont demanded that Germany cut its interest rates. According to the reports from one German central bank official, Lamont at one stage pounded his fist on the table and shouted at the Bundesbank President, Dr Helmut Schlesinger 'Twelve finance ministers are all sitting here demanding that you lower your interest rates. Why don't you do it?' (Whitney, 1992; Mallaby, 2010). In the following week, Schlesinger made two public statements, which suggested both the lira and pound were overvalued, which further fuelled expectations among the currency traders that there would be realignments (Elliot et al., 1992). This was an explosive intervention.

Over the weekend of 12–13 September 1992, the Italians, at the instigation of the German officials, requested that they be allowed to devalue (Szász, 1999: 173). On 13 September 1992, the lira was duly devalued by 3.5 per cent but this was actually a 7 per cent shift because the other currencies were revalued by 3.5 per cent. Szász (1999: 173) recounts 'telephone conversations' where 'it was decided to devalue the lira . . . by 7 per cent, disguised for reasons of prestige as a devaluation of . . . 3.5 per cent and a revaluation of the other currencies by 3.5 per cent'.

The summer of '92 was also unkind to the British pound, which was under sustained attack from speculators, who were convinced it would have to be devalued because of the declining competitiveness of the British economy and its relatively high inflation. The speculative sales of US dollars, lira and sterling led to massive volumes of funds shifting into the mark. Matters came to a head a few days after the Italians devalued. In his memoirs, Lamont (1999) recounts that while the Italians were negotiating the terms of the devaluation with the Germans, he attended the 'Last Night of the Proms' in London singing 'Rule Britannia' with 'great gusto' (see Mallaby, 2010: 159). Denial.

The British government had initially refused to join the EMS but had during some periods 'shadowed' the movements in the mark, the benchmark currency of the EMS, and kept the pound at around 3 marks (BBC, 2002a). The British government was clearly divided between the pro European camp and the Thatcher camp. The latter correctly saw that membership of the EMU would compromise Britain's policy sovereignty. It was a pity her government used that sovereignty in the way it did. There were also undertones of extreme anti-German sentiment left over from World War II driving Britain's stance against the EMU.

However, with Thatcher's star on the wane and the elevation of the pro European John Major to the role of Chancellor to replace Nigel Lawson, the Tories turned towards joining the ERM. The decision confronted British jingoism (Thatcher's anti-German sentiment) with the ahistorical ideology of Monetarism, which were both in play during the Thatcher years. Drawing on the Monetarist influence, Major and Foreign Secretary Douglas Hurd argued that Britain could expunge the high inflation left over from the oil price shocks if it tied the pound to the German mark, which was equivalent to saying that the Bank of England would passively follow Bundesbank interest rate policy. At the time the Bundesbank was pushing interest rates up beyond the level that would be considered appropriate for a recessed British economy.

Major and Hurd won over Thatcher and Britain joined the ERM on 8 October 1990, while mired in a deep recession with an overvalued currency (2.95 marks per pound). Once Major took over as Prime Minister in November 1990, following Thatcher's demise in the same month, the British Government touted Britain's membership of the ERM and the so-called 'inflation anchor' as the 'centrepiece of the Government's anti-inflation strategy' (Elliot et al., 1992). But it would prove to be a very misguided decision.

While the pound was allowed a 6 per cent fluctuation band as a starting point, informed observers believed that the Bank of England would never be able to sustain the currency within that band. The obvious happened and while tying the pound to the mark lowered inflation, it was at the expense of a deepening recession and worsening unemployment. It was Italy all over again! Britain was also particularly affected by the falling US dollar, which undermined the international competitiveness of its export products. By the summer of '92, the pressure on the pound was unbearable. As in the case of Italy, the Bundesbank was prepared to provide only limited support, given that they were trying to purge inflation from the German economy and to defend the pound would require it to sell more marks and thus increase the money supply by more than they cared.

The foreign currency markets clearly believed that the pound would be devalued despite the ongoing political resistance to the idea. The Government's response was to push up interest rates to 10 per cent and instruct the Bank of England to intervene heavily in the currency markets to maintain strong demand for the pound. This just worsened the recession. It was also a finite strategy because eventually the Bank's international reserves would be depleted if the speculation against the pound continued. By September 1992, the only buyer of the pound in the currency markets was the Bank of England, such was the speculative sentiment against it.

And then Wednesday, 16 September 1992 dawned, and the 'skies became darker' as the day progressed. British Treasury and Bank of England officials agreed to keep buying the pound and purchased £600 million in two interventions before 8.30 am (Mallaby, 2010: 163). But they were up against George Soros's Quantum Fund, who had started an elaborate set of transactions based on the guess that the pound would almost certainly have to be devalued. Mallaby (2010: 163) compared the 'millions' the Bank was buying with the 'billions' that Soros was selling, which then drove 'legions of imitators to sell also'. Ten minutes later, the Bank bought a further £400 million but the pound continued to hover around the lower allowable bound.

This went on throughout the morning until 11.00, at which time the Bank of England pushed interest rates up to 12 per cent in an effort to reverse the ongoing capital outflow. While pondering whether they could withdraw from the ERM, the Bank announced that rates would rise to 15 per cent the next day. But the huge sale of pounds continued in the foreign exchange markets. Macroeconomic policy was, by now, out of control. The obsession with fighting inflation by tying the pound to the mark was leading to frenzied and totally inappropriate changes to domestic policy settings. It was the anathema of responsible government and was being driven by the ideological obsession with Monetarism and the fervent belief in fixed exchange rates.

A Bank of England official recalled later that 'he bought more sterling in four hours that day than anybody had before or since' (Inman, 2012) and all the trades lost money as the pound pushed lower. He also said that the Bundesbank was refusing to play its part under ERM rules to defend the pound. He said that in a conference call later in the day to the Bundesbank officials 'they suddenly didn't speak English, which was extraordinary' (Inman, 2012). Presumably, the German intransigence reflected Schlesinger's view that devaluation was necessary.

At 19:40 that evening, Chancellor Lamont stood outside the Treasury Building in London and announced that Britain has 'suspended' its membership of the ERM. The pound has floated ever since. Overnight, the pound plunged to 2.69 per mark, which was nine pfennigs below its allowable fluctuation band in the ERM (Elliot et al., 1992). During the next day, it continued to fall and devalued around 13 per cent against the mark and 18 per cent against the US dollar between August and October 1992, which freed the Bank of England from following the Bundesbank interest rate policy and spurred growth. Inflation didn't break out as many mainstream economists had predicted.

Szász (1999: 174) pointed out 'Black Wednesday was pre-programmed . . . [and] . . . more than anything else, caused by the UK Government's decision to enter into ERM without accepting its implications.' For many 'Black Wednesday' became 'White Wednesday' because it was the day Britain regained its policy independence and distanced itself from the madness that was going on in Europe, which would become even more insane by the turn of the century.

Why did the Germans and others pressure Britain to join the ERM, given the hostility of the British under Thatcher to the proposed EMU? Szász (1999: 175) recalls a 1987 conversation with the Bundesbank President Pöhl, who said, 'he would not be arguing in favour of British entry if he thought they would listen'. For his part, as Britain was entering the ERM, John Major had apparently dreamed 'aloud' that the sterling would replace 'the German mark as the anchor currency' (Szász 1999: 177). The Groupthink denial was so strong among the political class that it is clear the politicians had a very limited understanding of the consequences of their decisions. Not a lot has changed in Europe it seems.

The proposed rise from 12 to 15 per cent was revoked within a few hours, further reinforcing the view that the policy makers had lost their mojo. The fact is that they never had it and by blindly following the Monetarist pegged currency strategy they had destroyed millions of jobs and handed over more than a billion US dollars in profit to George Soros's Quantum Fund (Kaletsky, 1992). At the time, it was estimated that the Bank of England had lost more than £10 billion of its foreign reserves trying to defend the currency. In 2005, the UK *Financial Times* newspaper sought information under the Freedom of Information Act from the British Treasury about the extent of the losses made by the Bank of England on Black Wednesday 1992. The losses were estimated to have been £3.3 billion (Tempest, 2005).

Next day, the Italian government announced it was withdrawing the lira from the ERM and Spain devalued the peseta by 5 per cent. The rot had set in and the speculators relentlessly attacked most of the European currencies, such that by the summer of 1993, the crisis had resurfaced and Ireland, Portugal and Spain (for the second time within a few months) were forced to devalue.

The 1992–93 crisis demonstrated that the system of fixed exchange rates or even tightly linked exchange rates between economies that were disparate in structure and performance would always fail with mobile capital. The Bank of England governor Robin Leigh-Pemberton wrote in 1993 that the problem for the UK:

> . . . arose because the degree of divergence between the domestic policy needs of Germany on the one hand and those of much of the rest of Europe on the other became wholly abnormal, and it was this quite abnormal tension that tested the margin of tolerance built in the ERM to destruction. (Leigh-Pemberton, 1993: 289)

For Britain, the crisis was a chance to distance itself from the EMU forever. Norman Lamont admitted afterwards that he was 'increasingly unhappy' with the decision to join the ERM in the first place 'as the recession took its toll' in 1992 (Keegan and Brett, 2007). He also said that once the dust had settled on the calamity, the decision to withdraw 'enabled economic policy to be rebuilt "out of the ashes"' (Keegan and Brett, 2007). Apparently, he had a habit of singing in the bath each morning and while he refrained on Black Wednesday, his wife heard him singing one morning a few weeks later on a 'very beautiful morning' (Keegan and Brett, 2007). At a press conference not long afterwards, Lamont summed up his attitude to leaving the ERM with reference to Edith Piaf: 'Je ne regrette rien' (Groom, 2008).

Lamont clearly blamed the Germans for the crisis and the Bundesbank President Schlesinger in particular. The behaviour of the Bundesbank brought back memories of the famous Emminger letter, written by the then Bank President Otmar Emminger to German Chancellor Schmidt on 16 November 1978 (Emminger, 1978). As an aside, the Finance Minister at the time, Hans Matthöfer, a West German trade unionist, described Emminger as a 'miserable know-it-all' (*Der Spiegel*, 2011). The letter sought to confirm an 'agreement' between the Bank and the Federal government such that membership of the proposed EMS would allow for an 'opting out' of the Bundesbank's responsibility to support other exchange rates if 'internal monetary stability is threatened'. Schmidt annotated the letter with a lower case 'r', shorthand for 'richtig' (correct) to signify agreement. In other words, if the Bundesbank thought that it would be undermining its anti-inflation approach by selling marks in order to purchase weaker currencies as part of its intervention obligations under the EMS, this agreement allowed it to simply renege and let the other nations lose reserves and enter crisis.

When Schmidt appeared before the Bundesbank Council on 30 November 1978 to discuss the terms of the letter (that is, to seek the approval of the Bundesbank of Germany's decision to enter the EMS in 1979) he told the Council in relation to the opt out terms that no formal agreement could be made but a 'secret' informal arrangement was understood (Bundesbank, 1978b):

> . . . I have quite severe misgivings about a written specification of this sort, a written specification of the possibility of an at least temporary release from the intervention. Let us first of all assume that it appeared tomorrow in a French or Italian newspaper. What accusations would the newspapers then make in editorials against their own Government who got themselves mixed up with such a dodgy promise with the Germans. A Government which promised them to intervene in the framework of certain rules of the game, but internally put in writing its intention to be able to do otherwise if need be. In the matter itself I agree with you, gentlemen, but I deem it out of the question to write that down.

The Emminger 'opt out' forced the Italians out of the ERM in 1992. The resulting forced devaluation then turned the attention of the financial markets towards the pound and Black Wednesday was the result. It was replayed again when the crisis re-emerged in the summer of 1993 as recession became more entrenched and central banks around Europe were signalling a need to lower interest rates to provide some stimulus support. The constraint they faced was that the Bundesbank would not compromise on its tight monetary policy settings, which were addressing the domestic liquidity consequences of spending associated with reunification. The two positions – high interest rates in Germany and reduced rates elsewhere to fight recession, on the one hand, and maintenance of the agreed exchange rate settings, on the other – were incompatible.

Political pressure on the French government to do something about the rising unemployment became intense as the 1993 summer approached and there were increased calls for France to abandon the EMS. This sort of political instability, especially given the 'petit oui', bred renewed speculative activity. The currency market traders clearly believed the French government would succumb to the domestic pressure to cut rates and devalue the franc. On 29 July 1993, the Bundesbank confirmed they would not cut German interest rates and the currency markets went crazy, selling the franc and other European currencies in huge volumes and making the 2.5 per cent fluctuation bands unsupportable.

The resulting political decision all but ended the EMS. The politicians widened the allowable fluctuation range for all currencies to plus or minus 15 per cent (a 30 per cent overall allowable fluctuation), which made a mockery of the claim that the EMS was maintaining currency stability. The EMS was heading in the same direction as the Bretton Woods system, which collapsed for similar reasons in August 1971. The widening of the bands was called a 'temporary measure' by the politicians who accused the Italians and the British of being too lax in their anti-inflation fight or the Germans of being too lax in their spending on reunification. If the 'fight' against inflation after the oil price shocks in Italy or the UK had been even more stringent, or the fiscal expansion to allow Germany to absorb the East more quickly had been more modest, the result would have been even higher unemployment across Europe than was already the case. The political pressures in that regard would have been intolerable and the speculative attacks on the EMS currencies would have occurred without doubt. The problem was not 'laxity' or excessive fiscal stimulus, but the fact that a fixed exchange rate system such as the EMS (and its predecessor the Bretton Woods system) was incompatible with the economic and political reality. Nations cannot absorb high unemployment for lengthy periods without major consequences such as social instability and increased political extremism. The Germans, above all, should have learned that lesson from the 1930s.

The other reality, beyond the scope of this work, is that a close examination of the Bundesbank behaviour over the life of the EMS reveals that its interventions into foreign exchange markets (buying and selling marks) were 'sterilised' (by simultaneous domestic monetary operations) so that the impact on domestic liquidity (the 'money supply') was relatively neutral. It was never in danger of an uncontrollable outbreak of inflation as a result of honouring its EMS obligations (Gros and Thygesen, 1992). Its claims to the contrary were just posturing.

Far from learning from the mistakes, the politicians claimed that the currency crisis in 1992–93 was evidence of the need to accelerate the move to the single currency. Higgins (1993: 37) illustrated the political denial at the time with an analogy:

> Assume someone embarks upon a trip with only enough gasoline in the car to reach his destination if weather conditions are ideal. If the car were to run out of gas when a strong head wind is encountered, would the driver be justified in blaming bad luck when he has to walk the last few miles? The driver's misfortune was not inevitable, but it could not be said to be totally unexpected. His plan was faulty in that it allowed no margin of safety.

One might make this point more emphatically. Given the disparities of the economies involved it was always likely that the car would 'run out of gas'. The structure of the system was biased toward crisis in the same way that the EMU has resulted in crisis.

While the 'Emminger Doctrine' brought the EMS to its knees in 1992–93, the sentiment and arrogance still resonates in the current crisis. Marsh (2013) noted that Jens Weidmann, the current Bundesbank President, 'has been known to cite Emminger approvingly in his speeches'. Marsh also argued that the 'Doctrine' was invoked during the March 2013 Cyprus crisis when the ECB delivered an 'ultimatum to Cyprus' to agree to the IMF bail out package or go broke. The Cypriots should have 'gone broke' and left the euro. This would have left the resulting mess to Brussels and allowed Cyprus to rebuild its own economy 'out of the ashes', using the freedom that the British gained when they abandoned their membership of the EMS in 1992.

10. The ideological straitjacket

THE ECONOMISTS START BACKFILLING

The design of the EMU agreed on in Maastricht reflected a range of factors, none of which made any real macroeconomic sense. Charles Wyplosz wrote that 'With little experience to rely upon and limited theoretical backing, economists and policy-makers had to invent practically everything in little time. Policy-makers rushed to negotiate a detailed agreement, having no time for detailed economic analysis' (Wyplosz, 2006).

There was one major piece of analysis published by the European Commission in 1990, *One Market, One Money*, which sought to provide some analytical backing to the Delors Plan. The analysis used deeply flawed economic models (including the notoriously poorly performed IMF Multimod model), which generated sympathetic results reflecting the assumptions made. These models are held out as 'neutral' tests of policy propositions but are, in fact, so laden with theoretical biases that they are incapable of providing the role of the 'independent umpire'. The expression GIGO (Garbage In, Garbage Out) is apposite.

Further, the construction of 'macroeconomic stability' in the analysis was solely in terms of 'better overall price stability' (European Commission, 1990a: 9). The authors admitted that while stability (low inflation) and growth would be part of the overall macroeconomic performance of the proposed EMU, a 'quantified estimate of the potential impact of EMU is not feasible' (p. 9). Their modelling could only predict lower output variability rather than stronger growth.

The analysis also asserted that while an independent central bank should be created, 'the case for centralized powers over budgetary policy is much weaker' (p. 13). But it recognised that if tight fiscal rules were used to coordinate national level fiscal policy positions then the ability of nations to absorb 'shocks' in economic activity would be reduced, especially given that the capacity for exchange rate adjustment would be eliminated. Yet they still advocated tight fiscal restrictions.

The report recognised that 'national level stabilization and adjustment in the case of country-specific disturbances' (for example, a collapse in private spending as occurred in many nations in 2008) 'requires flexibility and autonomy, at least within a normal range of sustainable public deficit and debt levels' (p. 23). Fiscal policy has two components: (a) the taxation and spending settings chosen on a discretionary basis by government and deemed suitable to achieve its socio-economic goals in normal times; and (b) the cyclical or automatic stabiliser component, which refers to the impact of economic activity on the fiscal outcome. Thus, when economic activity stalls and employment falls, taxation revenue gained by the government declines and welfare payments associated with unemployment tend to rise. The result is that the fiscal deficit (the difference of overall spending and taxes) rises. Imposing rules on the capacity of fiscal policy to make these adjustments ensures, in most cases, that an economic downturn will cause higher unemployment than is otherwise the case.

Despite that recognition, the Commission report concluded, 'Budgetary discipline, in order to avoid excessively high deficits, will need to be intensified . . .' (European Commission 1990a: 23). In other words, they knew that if there were a major reduction in total spending (from whatever source), the stabilisers built into the national government fiscal policy would be prevented from working in a normal and flexible fashion by the uniform and tight fiscal rules. In that context, they knew that unemployment would rise sharply and persist and fiscal deficits would rise, and the only way that nations could obey the proposed fiscal rules would be to attack domestic wages, pension entitlements and public services and infrastructure provision and further push up unemployment. The economists advising the European Commission knew that but left it unstated and the politicians did not tell the 'people' that this was a likely outcome of what they were doing in their name. The maladministration was stark and the denial was on a grand scale.

The Report's recommendations were also contrary to the available evidence, which suggested that when central banks prioritise inflation over other macroeconomic goals (such as high output and income growth, and lower unemployment) the real losses arising from lower real output growth and higher unemployment are substantial (Ball and Sheridan, 2003). Mitchell and Muysken (2008) argue that this is not due to the way the central bank is organised ('independent' or otherwise). Rather, it is the ideology that accompanies the 'inflation first' monetary policy obsession that damages the real economy because it embraces both high interest rate regimes and a bias towards fiscal austerity. The high interest rates squeeze private spending and the explicit or implicit fiscal rules restrict the capacity of government to maintain adequate levels of spending in the economy. Disinflationary monetary policy and tight fiscal policy can bring inflation down and stabilise it, but it does so by creating mass unemployment (Mitchell and Muysken, 2008).

Further, workers and firms may build expectations of future inflation into wage negotiations and price setting decisions, which means that an inflationary process can become self-fulfilling if all parties think high inflation will persist. This suggests that the fight against inflation has to not only curb cost increases above the capacity of the economy to absorb them, but also break the expectation that inflation will persist no matter what. In this context, one of the principal claims made by economists in favour of the EMU was that central bank independence and the 'credibility bonus' that this allegedly brings would encourage faster adjustment of inflationary expectations to policy announcements. Credibility means that investors trust that the central bank will not succumb to political pressure and abandon the fight against inflation even if unemployment is rising. The major study at the time (Ball and Sheridan, 2003) found no evidence to justify this claim.

A related perceived benefit of the 'inflation first' strategy outlined by proponents of 'independent' central banks was that it would expunge inflationary expectations from the economy. While there is limited research in this area, which uses actual survey data on expectations, the evidence appears to be that the major reductions in both inflation and measured inflationary expectations occur during large recessions (such as in 1991–92) and are unrelated to legislative changes that establish central bank independence and the introduction of formal inflation targeting. The decline in the inflation juggernaut from the 1980s occurred around the 1991 recession in most countries irrespective of the status of their central banks (Mitchell and Muysken, 2008).

While some extreme elements of the profession still deny that a hard-nosed 'inflation first' monetary policy undermines growth, most economists acknowledge that when central banks push up interest rates to keep inflation in check there will be a period of reduced output and increased unemployment (and related social costs). Economists measure these real costs in terms of a quantitative measure known as the 'sacrifice ratio', which is calculated as a percentage loss of initial output expressed as ratio of the accumulated reduction in the inflation rate. While it sounds complex, it is in fact a very easy number to calculate. For example, if the sacrifice ratio was two, it would mean that a one point reduction in the trend inflation rate will be associated with a GDP loss equivalent to 2 per cent of the initial output level before the central bank increased interest rates.

Two major impacts occur when the economy slows down after the central bank increases interest rates. First, actual economic activity (GDP growth) declines and the economy falls below its potential production levels. These income losses may be substantial. Second, when an economy goes into recession and sales dry up, firms are reluctant to invest in new capacity. The potential real GDP growth path also declines. As a result, the long-term capacity of the economy to grow is reduced.

These effects, taken together, typically ensure the real 'sacrifice' of an inflation first strategy will be substantial and endure for decades. Monetarist doctrine predicted that as central banks became more independent and concentrated solely on price stability objectives, sacrifice ratios would decline. There is a vast literature that examines the estimation of sacrifice ratios and the findings typically show that disinflations are not costless and are, in fact, significant. Estimates of sacrifice ratios have increased over several decades contrary to the predictions of the Monetarists (Mitchell and Muysken, 2008).

The economists advising the Commission largely ignored the likelihood that these costs would be substantial for the EMU. They were content to recite the Monetarist doctrine that prioritising a low inflation regime would have little or no negative real output consequences, and would, instead, maximise the growth potential of the economies in question. Contrary evidence was ignored. The economists and politicians also knew that these issues were too complex for even the popular press to pick up on and so the evidence could remain 'buried' in the arcane world of academic journals and books and the public would be none the wiser.

It is also interesting to note that in this era of economic thinking, microeconomic flexibility was promoted as the way to prosperity. The so-called structural reform agenda, which included widespread deregulation of labour and financial markets, was placed at the forefront of the policy agenda. This meant abandoning labour market policies that had helped to level the playing field somewhat between workers and capital in the post World War II period, such that workers had been able to enjoy some semblance of job security and real wages growth consistent with productivity growth. But at the macroeconomic level, flexibility was eschewed and the priority of full employment was dispensed with, despite the fact that all reasonable research studies have demonstrated that the losses associated with mass unemployment dwarf any losses that can be identified with so-called 'microeconomic' inefficiency. The greatest economic inefficiency is mass unemployment.

Yet the 1990 European Commission report, which was the first major attempt at evaluating the costs and benefits of the proposed EMU, concentrated on these lesser costs and benefits and ignored the fact that the system they were designing would inevitably create a major recession with entrenched mass unemployment. Groupthink leads to certain blindness.

Once the Treaty was signed in March 1992, the European Commission and a phalanx of sympathetic economists set about 'backfilling' to justify the arbitrary fiscal rules. They produced a plethora of research papers and reports, which they claimed provided intellectual and evidential authority to justify the decisions that had been made and to 'prove' the Treaty parameters were sound. It was theatre, of the high farce variety.

For example, in 1993, the European Commission's own in-house economics journal, European Economy, published a 'Report of an independent group of economists' on 'Stable money – stable finances', which summarised the more detailed papers presented in an accompanying publication (see European Commission, 1993a, 1993b, respectively). The concept of independence is moot in this case given that the economists they consulted were already caught in the Monetarist web.

A 'core issue' the Report dealt with was 'whether European union will . . . need a big central budget, to make EMU successful and sustainable' (European Commission, 1993a: 3). The Report indicated it was following in the footsteps of the 1977 MacDougall Report, which was the product of a similar exercise whereby the European Commission assembled a group of economists to study how federal systems function in a fiscal context (MacDougall Report, 1977). The comparison doesn't stand scrutiny.

The MacDougall Committee assembled for the first time in April 1975 and met on 14 occasions, finally reporting in April 1977. The 1993 Report was produced after only four meetings of the group of 'experts' over a much shorter time frame.

Both panels sought advice from economists in non-European federal systems. In the case of the 1977 committee, it called on the services of Professor Wallace Oates from Princeton University, who had published some seminal works on public finance, and Professor Russell Mathews, a world expert from the Australian National University. Both Oates and Mathews were Keynesian economists.

Oates's first major piece, published in 1968, was considered the definitive statement on the topic. He argued that:

> . . . the case for the central government to assume primary responsibility for the stabilization function appears to rest on a firm economic foundation . . . local government cannot use conventional stabilization tools to much effect and must instead rely mainly on beggar-thy-neighbour policies, policies which from a national standpoint are likely to produce far from the desired results. The central government, on the other hand, is free to adopt monetary policies and fiscal programs involving deficit finance where it is necessary to fulfil the compensatory function. Thus, the Stabilization Branch must do its job primarily at the central-government level. (Oates, 1968: 44)

In other words, when a federal system is experiencing an economic downturn, perhaps due to a fall in private consumption or investment spending, which may affect the states within the federation unequally, the federal government must be able to use deficit spending to compensate for the loss of private spending. Otherwise, output will fall, unemployment will rise and national income will be lost.

Russell Mathews was a long-time supporter of a strong federal stabilisation function. In his final co-authored book, he argued that Australia's poor economic performance in the late 1970s and into the 1980s was due to the adoption by the Federal government of Monetarist 'fight inflation first' policies, their attacks on public expenditure, and their unqualified belief in the virtue of self-regulating free markets (Mathews and Grewal, 1997).

Contrast that with the non-European economists that the 1993 exercise engaged. First, Canadian economics professor Tom Courchene from the conservative Queens University, a centre of Monetarist thinking in the 1980s and 1990s, promoted the concept of 'hourglass federalism'. He claimed, 'that very generous levels of federal provincial welfare support and interprovincial equalization transfers have created in Canada a version of 'transfer dependency' (European Commission, 1993b: 6). The transfers were also alleged to undermine the 'natural economic adjustments', such that unemployed workers would move to areas where jobs were available in times of recession, a major article of free market doctrine that denies that unemployment can become entrenched. When mainstream economists talk about 'natural' forces they are not considering anything to do with nature or physics. Rather it is code for theoretical free market textbook outcomes that rarely appear in the real world. Courchene also claimed that the design of the EMU with its 'more severe fiscal restraints' (p. 6) relative to Canada would avoid the damage that federal spending causes in federal systems.

The other economist was Cliff Walsh, from the University of Adelaide in Australia and a well-known advocate of the alleged benefits of dismantling regulation and generating government surpluses. He argued that the traditional literature on federalism (for example the work of Wallace Oates) was of 'limited direct application' to the European situation because of the 'unique constitutional and political arrangements in the Community' (European Commission, 1993b: 27). He claimed that unlike 'mature federations' where a 'substantial degree of homogeneity in preferences for core public sector services' exists (p. 49) and supports a strong central fiscal function (a basic finding from the traditional literature), the situation in Europe is different. He surmised that 'the differences in preferences may be sufficiently large in the Community to suggest that to transfer to the Community level many of the functions naturally allocated to central governments . . . elsewhere . . . would impose excessive uniformity costs' (p. 27). He concluded that coordinated fiscal rules across decentralised fiscal units 'may provide the most effective framework for macroeconomic management' (p. 46).

While the 1993 Report was used to justify the Maastricht design for the EMU, the 1977 MacDougall Report provided sufficient analysis and evidence for one to reasonably conclude that this design would fail.

The MacDougall Report involved:

> . . . a detailed and quantitative study of public finance in five existing federations (Federal Republic of Germany, U.S.A., Canada, Australia, Switzerland) and three unitary states of (France, Italy and the U.K.) . . . and in particular the financial relationships between different levels of government and the economic effects of public finance on geographical regions within the countries. (MacDougall Report, 1977: 11)

In other words, the panel sought to work out how a common currency system might operate where there are decentralised government structures with fiscal capacities and a currency-issuing central bank. What sort of fiscal function should be allocated to the federal 'government'?

A close reading of the MacDougall Report will leave one wondering why the Eurozone was ever created. The major issues they highlighted were clearly still relevant in the 1990s as the European political elites rammed through their ill-thought-out plan for a single currency.

The MacDougall Report concluded that (p. 11): 'It is most unlikely that the Community will be anything like so fully integrated in the field of public finance for many years to come as the existing economic unions we have studied.'

The MacDougall panel found that per capita income inequality was 'at least as unequal' between the EC states (nine at the time) and the 72 regions that comprise these states 'as they are on average between the various regions of the countries we have studied' (p. 12). Once the 'equalising effects' of national government spending and taxation was taken into account, 'regional inequalities in per capita income' in the nations studied were reduced 'on average' by 'about 40%' ('by more in Australia and France, by less in the U.S.A. and Germany') (p. 12). But the 'redistributive power between member states of the Community's finances, by comparison, is . . . very small indeed (1%); partly because the Community budget is relatively so small' (p. 12). The:

> . . . redistribution through public finance between regions in the countries studied tends to be reflected to a large extent . . . in corresponding deficits in the balances of payments on current account of the poorer regions, with

> corresponding surpluses in the richer regions. These deficits and surpluses are of a continuing nature. (p. 12)

Significantly, for our purposes, the MacDougall Report concluded that:

> As well as redistributing income regionally on a continuing basis, public finance in existing economic unions plays a major role in cushioning short-term and cyclical fluctuations. For example, one half to two thirds of a short-term loss of primary income in a region due to a fall in its external sales may be automatically offset through lower payments of taxes and insurance contributions to the centre, and higher receipts of unemployment and other benefits. (p. 12)

In other words an effective federation required a strong fiscal presence at the federal level to smooth out economic fluctuations at the sub-federal level. In that regard, the MacDougall Report concluded that (p. 12), 'there is no such mechanism in operation on any significant scale as between member countries, and that is an important reason why in present circumstances monetary union is impracticable.'

The factors that, according to the MacDougall panel of 'experts' in 1977, rendered monetary union 'impracticable' were subsequently built in to the Maastricht Treaty.

The tone of the 1993 Report was very different indeed and reflected the dominance of Monetarist thinking by that time. It concluded, 'Community-wide stabilization should be achieved by the single monetary policy and the coordination of national budget policies' (European Commission, 1993a: 1).

Under the bold heading 'Beware of centralization' (p. 4), the Report claims that it undermines the delivery of public services 'tailored more to the preferences of the population' and that 'democratic control is more effective' at the local level. These propositions were advanced by the new 'public choice theory', which became one of the neo-liberal 'attack dogs' used to undermine the legitimacy of government service provision and deficit spending. It is ironic to consider these claims to democratic superiority of a decentralised EMU, which were used to justify the design of the EMU in the first place, in the context of the austerity regimes imposed by the Troika in recent times on elected Member State governments.

The 1993 Report came up with the conclusion the Commission was looking for under the bold heading 'A small budget will do' (p. 6). The panel concluded that:

> The central message of the report is that a small 'EMU budget' of about 2% of Community GDP is capable of sustaining European economic and monetary union . . . This is clearly contrary to much of the conventional economic

wisdom, reflected in the MacDougall report as well as in the literature on economic and monetary union.

So how did they justify a denial of the evidence base to date? They simply asserted that the 'principle of subsidiarity is applied rigorously' (p. 6), even though we have already learned that a correct understanding and application of that principle would support the MacDougall 'wisdom'. Second, they merely asserted that there would be 'No explicit role for the Community budget in Community-wide macroeconomic stabilization' (p. 6). Why not? Simply because, consistent with the Monetarist religious doctrine, only monetary policy mattered and the creation of the European Central Bank would be more than enough to prevent recession. In addition, they asserted that the coordination of fiscal policies across the Member States would prevent individual governments from undermining the independent monetary policy. They also concluded that the 'shock-absorption mechanism' built into each Member State's fiscal policy (automatic fluctuations in taxation and spending as economic activity varied) would be sufficient 'to provide a cushion against adverse developments' (p. 7). To give you an idea of how unwilling this panel was to address reality, they concluded (p. 7), 'For a shock absorption scheme based on changes in unemployment rates, the group estimates that the average annual expenditure might be of the order of 0.2% of EC GDP.'

The actual fluctuations in 2008 were many times larger than this and would lead to the conclusion that the economists' estimates were comical had they not been part of a regime that has deliberately caused millions of workers to lose their jobs.

THE EMU AND OPTIMAL CURRENCY AREAS (OCA)

In terms of the debate leading up to Maastricht, there was a clear divide among the US-based studies which rejected the viability of the proposed design and thought it unlikely that it would proceed to fruition, on the one hand, and the European based studies, particularly those sponsored in one way or another by the Commission, which were generally positive overall (Wyplosz, 2006).

While playing 'no serious role in the drafting of the Maastricht Treaty' (Wyplosz, 2006: 211), the long-standing concept of an Optimal Currency Area (OCA), which emerged from the work of three economists, Canadians Robert Mundell (1961) and Ronald McKinnon (1963) and American Peter Kenen (1969), became an organising framework for the debate over the viability of the proposed EMU. OCA theory purports to define the conditions under which several independent countries will be better off sharing a currency or, alternatively, fixing their exchange rates. Optimal refers to the collection of geographic units (in the case of the EMU, Member States) that would most effectively enter a monetary union. Too few 'geographical areas' or too many will deliver a sub- or non-optimal arrangement.

In the original formulation, Robert Mundell defined three conditions which, if in existence, would justify the formation of a monetary union as an OCA:

- The economic cycles of the countries move together (up and down) and they face common consequences if hit by a negative shock (for example, a decline in private spending). Thus there should be no major asymmetric shocks, which would affect one region/state significantly more than another. A consequence of this condition would be, for example, that unemployment rates should be similar across the countries in the union;
- There should be a high degree of labour mobility and/or wage flexibility within the group of countries such that if unemployment rose in one country, workers could quickly move elsewhere to find jobs. Mobility also refers to a lack of cultural and institutional barriers (for example, a pension entitlement in one nation would be transferable to another without cost; no language barriers);
- There is a common risk-sharing structure so that fiscal policy can transfer resources from better performing to poorly performing countries without constraints.

Crucially, for Mundell, 'optimality relates to the state of the labor market' such that if 'the currency regime within a given area causes unemployment somewhere in that area (or accepts some other portion of that same area to accept inflation as the antidote to unemployment), it is not optimal' (Kenen, 1994: 41). McKinnon (1963: 717) considered optimality to mean a 'single currency area within which monetary fiscal policy and flexible external exchange rates can be used to give the best resolution of three . . . objectives: (1) the maintenance of full employment; (2) the maintenance of balanced international payments; (3) the maintenance of a stable internal price level . . .'.

Consider the components: both monetary and fiscal policy is deemed important and the goal of full employment is not subjugated to the pursuit of price stability. If a collection of nations cannot combine and use economic policy in this way, then they do not belong together.

McKinnon (1963) added a qualifier to the labour mobility argument.

He noted that if capital was mobile then firms in declining areas might be able to 'retool' to produce products that are currently produced in growing areas and thus overcome labour mobility constraints. Kenen (1969) added that the disparities in labour skills across different regions would make these sorts of transitions (either labour moving to growth areas or capital moving to declining areas) unlikely, suggesting the 'sad certainty that the optimum currency area has to be small' (p. 44). He also considered that if all nations produced a diverse range of goods, then spending fluctuations would not hit a particular region disproportionately.

McKinnon (1963) also considered the 'degree of openness' (how much a nation trades relative to its overall size) to be important. If nations trade extensively between each other then a fixed exchange rate (brought about by a common currency or an EMS type agreement) will be beneficial as it eliminates risk that higher import prices will cause inflation.

In the early 1970s there was a new volley of research on the concept of OCAs, which expanded the initial literature. Mundell (1973) added the additional insight that if capital is mobile between nations, then the exchange rate can easily be attacked and become a source of instability. In this case, monetary union that eliminates exchange rate fluctuations between nations in the union will be beneficial. However, Mundell was assuming that such an arrangement would not also eliminate the capacity of fiscal policy to reduce unemployment when there was a decline in private spending.

The EMU proponents in the late 1980s did not consider the requirements set out in the OCA literature to be significant for their plans. Wyplosz (2006: 212) said that the European Commission 'officials did not waste much time on the issue, which they saw as mainly political'. The Maastricht Treaty was more about making progress towards the adoption of the single currency and the requisite institutional changes that would be required to accommodate this process rather than a deep analysis of whether it would be optimal. Why was the existing economic framework (OCA), which specifically dealt with the issue of when union is desirable and when it is not, ignored? Merely claiming that the policy makers constructed the EMU as a political issue is not sufficient. In fact, it goes much deeper than that.

In the 1990 *One Market, One Money* publication, the European Commission (1990a: 46) concluded that the OCA literature provided a 'rather limited framework whose adequacy for today's analysis is questionable'. They claimed that the 'whole approach ignores policy credibility issues which have been stressed by recent macroeconomic theory' (p. 46), which was code for OCA being associated with the Keynesian view that fiscal policy provides an effective means of stabilising economies hit with private spending fluctuations. The 'policy credibility issues' related to the unproven Monetarist assertions that fiscal policy was ineffective and caused inflation, which can only be controlled with tight monetary policy.

Any serious application of the OCA theory would have been highly inconvenient to the proponents of the EMU. Of the conditions necessary to satisfy the existence of an OCA, only the one relating to openness of trade between the nations could be reasonably met. The other conditions were not satisfied. The Treaty deliberately negated the capacity for a federal fiscal capacity to redress regional unemployment and there was no sense that labour was mobile. Eichengreen (1992: 22) pointed out that 'migration rates within European countries are higher than migration between them . . . [but] . . . low' by US standards. He also suggested that while capital movements would be unimpeded in the EMU, a depressed region could hardly expect job-saving capital inflow. He also noted that adjustments of this type are minor in mature federations. Regional disparities brought about by movements in the economic cycle are resolved more effectively by fiscal transfers rather than labour or capital movement.

Mongelli (2008: 215) noted, 'This message was not pleasing to officials, and dutifully ignored for many years' because their neo-liberal Groupthink didn't entertain any diversions from their vision. De Grauwe (2006) reinforced the view that the EMU cheer squad was ideologically selective in its use of the prevailing knowledge. He noted that while the EMS crisis in 1992–93 demonstrated that 'fixed exchange rates were unsustainable' without monetary union, there 'was also the effect of an intellectual revolution that was started in the 1970s in the academic world and that reached the policy world during the 1980s. This was monetarism . . . [and] . . . In this monetarist vision . . . the costs of a monetary union are small' (De Grauwe 2006). OCA was Keynesian and was to be rejected as a matter of course. The millions that have been unemployed since 2008 are testament to the fallacy of the Monetarist presumptions.

Whichever way you wish to interpret the OCA theory, it is very obvious that the group of nations that entered the EMU did not remotely satisfy the conditions required to ensure that the adoption of a common currency would be beneficial overall. The result was that the only adjustments open to them once a major private spending collapse occurred would be very costly, a point ignored by the EMU proponents.

The 2008 crisis has demonstrated what was already known during the OCA debate in the early 1990s. The ability to absorb external spending shocks, such as the one that arose from the housing collapse in the US in 2007, is very different across the Eurozone countries. The stronger industrial countries like Germany and the Netherlands, which also have the capacity to generate external surpluses, are in totally different situations to the capital importers such as Spain and Greece. The stronger nations can absorb spending shocks much better than the weaker nations of the union.

Further, some Eurozone nations are more closely tied together in trading relationships than others. Finland, for example, retained close cultural and trading ties to Norway and its trade is not linked much with Spain. Ireland maintained strong trading relationships with the UK and less with continental Europe. This also impacts on the capacity of the individual economies to adjust to a major decline in spending.

There is limited labour mobility within Europe because national identities are still strong and language barriers persist. One of the interesting side effects of the coincidence of the recession and the associated collapse in the housing market is that labour mobility in Europe is even lower than it was before the crisis. In bad times, those that can move do so to chase job opportunities elsewhere. However, when there is an accompanying major real estate collapse, this mobility is significantly lower because people cannot afford to move, especially those holding negative equity in their residences.

Financial Times chief economist Martin Wolf (2010) noted that:

> The crisis in the Eurozone's periphery is not an accident: it is inherent in the system. The weaker members have to find an escape from the trap they are in. They will receive little help: the zone has no willing spender of last resort; and the euro itself is also very strong. But they must succeed. When the Eurozone was created, a huge literature emerged on whether it was an optimal currency union. We know now it was not. We are about to find out whether this matters.

Four years later, we have certainly found out that the design of the monetary system matters and the structure chosen at Maastricht has forced millions of people to lose their jobs and suffer increased poverty rates. The most significant deficiency is that fiscal policy is unable to maintain uniformity of outcomes across the monetary union because there is no central fiscal institution, and the imposition of the prohibitive Stability and Growth Pact (SGP) rules has undermined the capacity of the national governments to respond to recession with increased deficits.

How then should we assess this part of the story? Despite the various interpretations that have been made of OCA theory, the fundamental prediction that emerges from it is that if the essential conditions are not in place, then unemployment will rise significantly in some Member States in the face of a large asymmetric decline in spending. This prediction has clearly come to fruition. In other words, the designers of the EMU would have been better advised to heed the general message from OCA before pushing on regardless. Ideology ruled and millions have suffered.

The malevolence goes further though. The neo-liberal economists now use OCA theory as a means to justify attacking labour protections and wage security. They argue that while the requirements for establishing an OCA were irrelevant to the decision to create a monetary union, once the union has been created, there is a need to ensure that the requirements are in place. Suddenly, all the pro-EMU economists started to recognise OCA theory because in this form it was now supportive of their neo-liberal intentions. Frankel and Rose (1998), for example, use this ploy to advance the need for 'structural' reforms, which is code for cutting worker entitlements and creating an environment of income and job insecurity.

11. The Stability and Growth Pact (SGP)

NEITHER GROWTH NOR STABILITY

The SGP was formally adopted in 1997. A Memorandum circulated in November 1995 by the German Finance Minister, Theo Waigel, motivated its final form (Waigel, 1995). Waigel proposed a 'Stability Pact' to restrict government fiscal policy discretion. The Maastricht Treaty had left the fiscal side of the EMU up in the air. The Treaty included articles relating to the coordination and monitoring of Member State budgets and the 'excessive deficit procedure' but suggested that the detail, which was outlined in the Protocol attached to Article 104, would require further legislation and incorporation into the Treaty. The scene was set for further negotiations. The final SGP essentially amended Articles 121 and 126 of the Treaty on the Functioning of the European Union (Treaty of Rome) with reference values specified in the Protocol on the excessive deficit procedure, which is one of the annexes that applies to both the Treaty on European Union (originally agreed in Maastricht) and the Treaty on the Functioning of the European Union, the overarching document that defined the EEC in 1958.

The genus of Waigel's 'Communication' came after the German Federal Constitutional Court ruling on 12 October 1993, which gave the green light to the German Parliament to approve Germany's entry into the EMU on the condition that price stability would be a primary objective of the monetary system, and that the entry conditions would 'not stand in the way of withdrawal from the Community as a last resort if it proves impossible to achieve the stability sought' (German Constitutional Court, 1993: 29). The Court's decision and the publicity that surrounded the case brought home to the German government the degree of public hostility about the impending EMU membership. The national obsession with price stability was at the forefront of the debate within Germany and was focused, initially, on a discussion about the European Monetary Institute (EMI), which would begin operation on 1 January 1994. This was epitomised in Chancellor Kohl's insistence that it be located in Frankfurt near the Bundesbank.

There were also deep suspicions among the politicians and technocrats as to the capacity and, more importantly, the commitment of several prospective European states to fulfil the convergence criteria outlined in the Maastricht Treaty. In 1994, inflation rates in some nations were still persistently high and fiscal deficits were well in excess of the proposed 3 per cent rule.

In an article for the influential *Frankfurter Allgemeine Zeitung* (FAZ, 1994) on 14 February 1994, Waigel responded to the growing public alarm by publicly naming the European nations that he considered were taking the Maastricht convergence criteria seriously (Germany and Luxembourg) and those that he believed were flagrantly abusing them (Greece, Italy, Portugal and Spain). He told the newspaper that he was 'disappointed that the convergence criteria were not respected' by the Southern nations. The Germans felt that the budgetary surveillance by the European Commission was not strict enough to see all prospective nations satisfy the Stage III criteria. At the 26–27 June 1995 European Council meeting in Cannes, it was affirmed that 'it is important for all Member States to make the necessary efforts with regard to convergence, this being a pre-condition for introduction of the single currency' (European Council, 1995a).

The pressure on the German government to do something about the public concern intensified during 1995. Heipertz and Verdun (2004: 7) disclosed how the Bundesbank President Hans Tietmeyer 'engineered' a public intervention in 1995 by the President of the German association of cooperative banks (BVR), Wolfgang Grüge, to demand 'an intergovernmental stability treaty' with tight fiscal rules. Tietmeyer 'did not want to be associated publicly with a new initiative on hardening the EMU regime'. Other interventions from think tanks and the public media pushed the debate along within Germany.

Waigel responded during the Second Reading of the German Budget Bill in the Bundestag on 7 November 1995 by emphasising that each country proposing to go to Stage III had to be in 'strict compliance with words of the Maastricht criteria' (Deutscher Bundestag, 1995: 5671). He said that while his political opponents were talking of 'D-Mark nationalism' in relation to the design of the EMU, the reality was that the Maastricht criteria would be a solid basis for stability as long as the rules were enforced. Waigel said, 'I am proposing a Stability Pact for Europe as a binding commitment by the participants in the third stage of the EMU' (p. 5672). He indicated that the 'Stability Pact' should limit fiscal deficits to 3 per cent (in unfavourable periods). In normal periods, the deficit should never exceed 1 per cent of GDP (p. 5672). His rules represented a tougher approach than had been floated at Maastricht.

On 10 November 1995, Waigel submitted his proposal for consideration at the upcoming Ecofin Council meeting in Brussels on 27 November as a precursor to the December Madrid European Council meeting. Waigel said that 'the stability of the European currency will be reliably and permanently secured through strict budgetary discipline in all the participating countries' and that 'strict observance of the convergence criteria and the institutional safeguards of the Treaty of Maastricht are the preconditions for a successful' EMU. He recommended that the 'stability criteria . . . be precisely stated and operationally defined' (Waigel, 1995).

After considering the Memorandum 'over lunch', the Finance Ministers 'agreed that it was important to pursue policies which would ensure sound budgetary positions' but that they 'should be continued in accordance with the procedures and principles of the Treaty' (European Council, 1995c). The wording was pointed. The view was that all developments would have to be within the existing legal framework of the European Community. Waigel was not only attempting to impose harsher rules, but also proposing to work outside of the normal European Commission institutions. As part of his proposed 'Stability Pact', he wanted to secure an intergovernmental agreement to set up the 'European Stability Council' which would manage the surveillance and compliance processes of the Pact. It would impose harsh penalties (a 'stability deposit') equivalent to 0.25 per cent of GDP on nations that breached the rules. The deposit would become a fine if the breach went beyond two years. He also proposed other sanctions such as 'restricting access to the resources of the structural funds' (Waigel, 1995) for nations that exceeded the upper limit. France immediately rejected the proposal mostly on the grounds of the automaticity of the fines, while Spain and Italy were against the convergence criteria *per se*. The Dutch, as to be expected, sided with Waigel. After debate, the Ministers proposed to water down Waigel's system of automatic fines and bring the process back under the purview of the Commission.

In retrospect, this was never going to be a viable plan for Europe. Waigel failed to demonstrate how the rigid rules he wanted enforced could underpin economic growth and low unemployment. He just maintained the mantra that price stability would reduce the 'transaction costs for business and consumers' (Waigel, 1995), which would encourage investment. Further, the idea that a nation facing a major decline in private spending, which had forced its deficit above 3 per cent, would then face a significant fine was idiotic. The penalty would further reduce the 'offending' nation's capacity to provide fiscal support to the economy in bad times and worsen unemployment.

Despite many European economies suffering under the burden of austerity that had been imposed as they tried to meet the convergence criteria, it was agreed at the Madrid European Council meeting on 15–16

December 1995 that the starting date for Stage III would be 1 January 1999 and that the new currency would be called the 'euro' (European Council, 1995b). But while the politicians' minds were now focused, there was also a growing backlash among some economists who questioned the benefits of creating recession and forcing unemployment up just to meet the artificial standards defined by the convergence criteria. Friend (2001: 67) noted, 'even in Germany, economists and politicians insistently questioned whether employment should be sacrificed to the god of budgetary strictness worshipped by the Bundesbank'.

These tensions came to a head during the European Council meeting in Dublin on 13–14 December 1996. The official conclusions of the meeting were relatively benign and included the recognition that the 'principles and main elements of the Stability and Growth Pact for ensuring budgetary discipline in EMU have been agreed' (European Council, 1996). But the shift from Waigel's 'Stability Pact' to the 'Stability and *Growth* Pact' was not without drama. Friend (2001: 67) wrote that during discussions of Waigel's 'Stability Pact', French President Chirac and German Chancellor Kohl 'were screaming at each other'. Chirac had told a TV show prior to the meeting that the 'Stability Pact' had been conjured up by 'certain German technocrats' (Waigel and German State Secretary Jürgen Stark) (p. 67), and there was an argument between Waigel and his French counterpart Jean Arthuis, which led to the latter railing against the automatic penalties and telling Waigel that 'What you are proposing is a computer that takes the decisions. Policy by Software' (p. 67).

The Franco-German discord continued on the second day of the meeting until a compromise was reached about the triggers for the excessive deficit procedure. The automatic fines were also dispensed with and it was agreed to insert the term 'Growth' into the Pact. So Waigel's 'Stability Pact' became the SGP. Further, the SGP would provide some deficit leeway above the 3 per cent for nations that were enduring a major recession. To satisfy the German technocrats, the Council decided that a nation could exceed the 3 per cent threshold if it was in 'severe recession', which they defined as a decline in GDP of more than 2 per cent.

The inclusion of 'Growth' into the Pact name was a reflection of the fact that unemployment had topped 11 per cent in France during 1996 and the Government of Alain Juppé, elected in May 1995, was starting to flag in the polls. He had already faced humiliation in having to withdraw his so-called Juppé Plan after a series of national strikes had paralysed the country. The Plan had proposed significant cuts to the welfare system and to public sector employment conditions. The rising unemployment only made his popularity decline further. The biggest transport strikes were ongoing as France went to the Dublin Council meeting, and, as a matter of political necessity, France could not be seen to be siding with the German proposal that seemed to negate the capacity of national governments to introduce discretionary spending measures designed to combat recession. The addition of the word 'Growth' to the title of the Pact was a small concession to the French. But in substance it was meaningless because the logic of the Pact remained anti-growth.

After all the haggling was done, the European Council meeting in Amsterdam on 16–17 June 1997 finally agreed on the form that the SGP would take. It was held out as part of the strategy to 'create favourable conditions for economic growth and new job opportunities' (European Council, 1997b). There were two European Council regulations added to the formal resolution.

First, the so-called 'preventative arm' 'on the strengthening of the surveillance of budgetary positions and the surveillance and coordination of economic policies' (European Council Regulation (EC) 1466/97), related to the country-specific medium term budgetary objective (MTO), which would involve each Member State submitting their fiscal plans in 'stability and convergence programmes' on an annual basis to the European Commission. This regulation became operational on 1 July 1998.

Second, the so-called 'corrective arm', 'on speeding up and clarifying the implementation of the excessive deficit procedure' (European Council Regulation (EC) 1467/97), related to the Excessive Deficit Procedure (EDP), which outlined a process for the elimination of so-called 'excessive deficits'. The 3 per cent and 60 per cent rules were central here with various other parameters that we have already discussed in place to define special circumstances. This regulation became operational on 1 January 1999.

In the official resolution it was asserted that 'Adherence to the objective of sound budgetary positions close to balance or in surplus will allow all Member States to deal with normal cyclical fluctuations while keeping the government deficit within the reference value of 3% of GDP' (European Council, 1997c).

There was no credible research to substantiate this claim and plenty of evidence already available to refute it (for example, Eichengreen, 1997). The MacDougall Report (1977) had indicated that a significant European level fiscal function (of at least 5 per cent of total European GDP) would be needed to 'offset asymmetric shocks once monetary independence is lost'. Eichengreen (1997) juxtaposed that realisation with the Delors Report (1989a and b), which considered establishing this capacity would be politically impossible. The Delors alternative, reflected in the Maastricht Treaty (1992), was to impose tight controls on the national fiscal positions in the blind hope that these constraints would allow the ECB to maintain price stability and leave the so-called stabilisation functions at the regional

(Member State) level using the so-called 'automatic stabilisers' that are built into national government fiscal positions (or 'budgets').

THE AUTOMATIC STABILISERS

For any government, the fiscal balance is the difference between total revenue (mostly from taxes) and total outlays (or spending). If total revenue is greater than outlays, the fiscal position is in surplus and vice versa. You might think that if the fiscal deficit is increasing, then the government must be aiming to spend more than its revenue. But what is not often understood is that movements in the fiscal balance do not provide a reliable indication of the policy intent of the government.

A basic rule of macroeconomics is that total spending in the economy generates national income and output of an equal magnitude, which then drives employment growth. If spending increases then production of goods and services will increase and the suppliers of the inputs will receive extra income. This process continues until the economy cannot produce any more goods and services (a state we call full capacity or full employment) and if spending continues to increase after that, inflation will result, because firms will react to the pressure by putting prices up.

If the government spends less than it takes out of the economy via revenue (that is, records a fiscal surplus), its net spending is negative and this will reduce output and income (a 'contractionary' impact). Alternatively, if the government is running a deficit (spending more than it takes out of the economy in revenue), its net spending is positive and this will increase output and income (an 'expansionary' impact).

However, without further information we are not in a position to know whether these positive or negative impacts on growth reflect the chosen policy position of government. The uncertainty arises because there are so-called 'automatic stabilisers', which operate as a result of swings in economic activity.

The fiscal balance at any point in time is the outcome of discretionary policy choices made by the government (tax rates and government spending) and the state of the economy. When the economy is growing strongly and employment is high, tax revenue rises and welfare payments (unemployment benefits) fall. The opposite occurs if growth declines. As these are fiscal shifts that arise purely as a result of the state of the economy, they are called 'automatic stabilisers'.

To understand this further, assume a fiscal balance of zero (that is, government spending equals revenue). If the government maintains its fiscal policy settings but the economy moves into recession, the fiscal balance will move into deficit because tax revenue will fall as less people are employed and company sales fall. Welfare payments will also likely rise, increasing the spending side of the fiscal position. Conversely, if from a starting balance of zero, the economy starts growing strongly, the fiscal position will move into surplus because tax revenue rises and welfare payments fall. Either of these movements would be driven by changes in non-government spending.

This simple example highlights that shifts in the reported fiscal balance can occur without any change in discretionary intent from government. It is easy to imagine a situation where the government was actually intending to slow the economy down by targeting a surplus, but the state of the economy was weak and the loss of tax revenue pushed the fiscal balance into deficit.

The operation of automatic stabilisers attenuates the amplitude in the business cycle by expanding the fiscal deficit during recessions and reducing it during booms. They thus provide a counter cyclical stabilisation function. However, while they lessen the negative impacts of a recession, they do not eliminate them and, if the recession is severe enough, then additional discretionary fiscal measures are necessary to ensure that the output and income losses and the increases in unemployment are kept to a minimum.

STRUCTURAL AND CYCLICAL FISCAL BALANCES

Recognition of the automatic stabilisers also helps us understand the concept of a 'structural' deficit. This is one of those terms that features in the public debate and appears to be significant but which few people, including many of the financial journalists who use it regularly, actually understand very well. As a result, few people appreciate how the concept is misused and manipulated by neo-liberals to provide legitimacy for their austerity policies when such legitimacy or intellectual authority is unwarranted.

We already know that if the fiscal balance goes into deficit or the deficit increases we are unable to unambiguously draw conclusions about the intent of government because of the presence of the automatic stabilisers. To overcome this ambiguity, economists measure the automatic stabiliser impact against some 'full capacity' or potential level of output benchmark. Accordingly, the actual reported fiscal balance can be conceptually separated into that component which is due to specific discretionary fiscal policy choices made by the government (so-called structural decisions) and that which arises because the economic cycle has deviated from the potential level of output.

The 'structural balance' is a hypothetical construction indicating what the fiscal balance would be if the economy was operating at potential or full employment with the tax revenue and spending that would be forthcoming at that level of economic activity. Economists thus conclude that if there is a 'structural' deficit then the overall impact of the discretionary fiscal policy settings is expansionary irrespective of the actual fiscal outcome. That is, the government is intending to stimulate economic growth. If there is a 'structural' surplus, then we conclude that the overall impact of discretionary fiscal policy is contractionary. That is, the government is putting the brakes on economic growth.

Where the controversy (and ideology) enters is in how the 'full employment' or 'potential' benchmark level of output is measured. Full employment used to be considered a state where anyone who wanted a job could find one. Accordingly, the unemployment rate consistent with full employment would be very low and reflect those workers who were moving between jobs at any point in time (referred to as 'frictional' unemployment).

Once the Monetarists assumed dominance in the academy during the 1970s, this concept of full employment was abandoned. Neo-liberal economists now talk about a rather complex sounding concept called the Non-Accelerating Inflation Rate of Unemployment (NAIRU). The NAIRU became a central plank in the front line attack on the use of discretionary fiscal policy by governments to maintain low unemployment rates. This was no surprise given that low unemployment rates help to balance the bargaining power between labour and capital. Higher unemployment swings the balance towards the employers because they can then choose from a bigger pool of desperate workers. There is thus a strong ideological motivation among neo-liberals to inflate the unemployment they claim to be associated with full employment because that will appear to be consistent with a 'desired' state and therefore invoke no government intervention by way of spending increases.

The neo-liberal sophistry claims that full employment does not mean the state where there are enough jobs to satisfy the preferences of the available workforce. Rather, full employment occurs when the unemployment rate is at the level where inflation is stable, neither accelerating or decelerating.

The NAIRU is only a conceptual construct and is not observed. But many fiscal agencies publish estimates of it using various statistical methodologies. Recent history shows us that these estimates are very unreliable with large margins of statistical error. In some cases, we have seen research reports produce estimates that vary between 3 and 13 per cent for the same nation at the same time, which, of course, makes the concept useless for policy purposes. The statistical techniques used to generate these estimates typically just produce results that follow the actual unemployment rate up and down and so the estimates provide little independent 'informational' content. While the neo-liberals hang on to this concept as something meaningful because it serves an ideological purpose in their fight against government spending, a reasonable conclusion is that the NAIRU estimates put out by the IMF or the OECD or other neo-liberal agencies are much higher than any acceptable level of full employment and therefore full capacity.

Once that point is understood, it becomes obvious that the estimates of the 'structural' fiscal balance produced by these organisations and others are biased upwards. Why is it important? The inflated NAIRU estimates set the full employment benchmark used to determine the structural component of the overall fiscal balance. Thus, we might have a situation where the true full employment state is equivalent to an unemployment rate of, say, 2 per cent but the NAIRU estimate is 5 per cent. The economists will then calibrate what they think the tax revenue and welfare spending will be at the 5 per cent level and will call that the 'structural balance'. But if the real full employment level of unemployment is 2 per cent, then this exercise will underestimate the tax revenue and overestimate the spending that would occur at true full employment. As a result, the NAIRU-based estimates of the 'structural' balance will be biased towards predicting higher 'structural' deficits than are really the case. In turn, assessments of the policy stance of government will be biased towards concluding that government is adopting a more expansionary stance than is the case. It could be the case that if we measured the 'structural' position at 2 per cent unemployment (in this example), the 'structural' balance would be in surplus, which would tell us that the government was actually adopting a contractionary position. In the popular debate, governments are judged on the size of the structural deficit. Accusations of 'over spending' or 'laxity' are thus likely to be biased towards the conclusion that governments are spending too much; when in fact it is likely they are not spending enough given the current high unemployment rate.

This is important because the neo-liberals claim that the 'structural' balance should be zero or in surplus. If they systematically estimate this component to be more expansionary than it actually is, then they will be advocating fiscal austerity (a movement towards or into surplus) at times when the 'structural' position of the government might already be contractionary and the actual deficit outcome is just a reflection of weak private spending. This will bias economies to accepting higher than necessary unemployment rates. This sort of bias is endemic in the European Commission's reasoning associated with excessive deficits in the SGP.

STRUCTURAL DEFICITS AND THE SGP FISCAL RULES

This discussion about 'structural' deficits is central to the way we understand the flaws in the SGP and why the fiscal rules bias the Eurozone towards higher unemployment and slower growth than is necessary. The Maastricht outcome was based on the neo-liberal assumption that the 'structural' balance should be always close to zero or in surplus. It was then assumed that even the worst 'cyclical' impacts would, on average, keep the reported deficits below the 3 per cent threshold. In other words, the fiscal rules were deemed to be a reflection of reasonable fiscal policy practice.

Why should a preferred 'structural' balance be close to zero? Is it reasonable to assume that the limits of the automatic stabiliser impact in a severe recession will be 3 per cent of GDP? Could a responsible fiscal position deliver continuous 'structural' deficits? Part III of the book considers these questions in more detail but for now we recognise that the aim of fiscal policy, that is, discretionary government spending and tax decisions, is to achieve the government's macroeconomic policy goals, which include full employment. The responsible goal of fiscal policy is not to achieve some dictated fiscal ratio divorced from the state of the economy. The discussion on automatic stabilisers demonstrated that private sector spending decisions ultimately determine the reported fiscal outcome, which suggests that it is nonsensical for a government to pursue some given deficit outcome.

Fiscal policy positions thus can only be reasonably assessed in the context of the macroeconomic policy goals. Attempting to assess the fiscal outcome strictly in terms of some prior fiscal rule (such as a deficit of 3 per cent of GDP) independent of the actual economic context is likely to lead to flawed policy choices. The 'structural' budget balance thus has to be sufficient to ensure there is full employment. The only sensible reason for accepting the authority of a national government and ceding currency control to such an entity is that it can work to advance the welfare of the citizens.

Firms produce output and pay incomes to workers and others according to their sales volumes. There will be a particular level of national output at any point in time, which we would consider to be sufficient to generate enough jobs to satisfy the preferences of workers for work. Total private spending is typically below the level necessary to support the full employment output level. Economists call this discrepancy a 'spending gap'. Thus the responsible role of government fiscal policy is to eliminate any 'spending gap' by allowing its deficit to rise accordingly. It is unlikely that the automatic stabilisers will be sufficient to provide the required increase in public spending. In other words, the government has to take discretionary decisions to expand its spending and/or cut its tax rates to ensure the 'structural' deficit rises. How much should it rise? The responsible action is to allow it to rise to the level that is sufficient to close the spending gap left by the private spending choices.

Thus there is no predisposition towards a 'small' structural deficit or a surplus. The 'structural' balance should be whatever is required to maintain full employment over time and is conditional on what the private sector spending choices are.

If the government fails to fill that 'spending gap', then persistently high unemployment and underemployment will result. The confidence of the private sector will decline further and cause consumers and firms to make further cuts in their spending. The automatic stabilisers then drive the fiscal outcome towards increasing deficits and stagnation sets in.

Fiscal sustainability is thus about governments ensuring there are no 'spending gaps' so that the levels of economic activity are consistent with full employment. Fiscal sustainability cannot be defined independently of full employment. By introducing fiscal rules that constrain the capacity of government to close these 'spending gaps', policy makers are effectively admitting that they have abandoned the pursuit of full employment (and the accompanying equity advantages), and are instead willing to use mass unemployment to help them achieve erroneous financial outcomes. That is the position that the Eurozone formally took on once it accepted the SGP as its guiding framework. It was denial on a grand scale.

THE SGP AND 'PRO-CYCLICAL' POLICY CHOICES

Eichengreen (1997: 34) concluded that the SGP fiscal rules 'raises the danger that fiscal policy will become increasingly pro-cyclical, as governments are forced to raise taxes and cut spending in downturns to satisfy these restrictions. With neither fiscal nor monetary flexibility, Europe will be helpless in the face of business cycle disturbances.' The anathema of responsible fiscal policy practice is to pursue 'pro-cyclical' policy changes. The terminology is straightforward. The economic cycle goes up and down according to the growth in real GDP (output). The economy cycles between booms (strong growth) and busts (weak growth or recession). If something follows the economic cycle up and down it is said to be 'pro-cyclical', whereas if some variable moves in the opposite direction to the economic cycle it is said to be 'counter cyclical'.

Discretionary fiscal policy changes should be 'counter cyclical' because the role of government is to ensure economic activity remains at levels consistent with full employment. Government deficits should rise when output is falling and vice versa. The worst thing a government can do is to cut spending and/or increase taxes in an attempt to reduce its deficit as private spending falls off and the economy moves towards or into recession. Austerity only makes the recession worse and further undermines the confidence of the private sector. This sort of response is called a 'pro-cyclical' policy change and violates responsible policy practice.

The fiscal rules defined by the SGP bias nations to making 'pro-cyclical' policy decisions. The recent crisis has demonstrated that clearly. As private sector spending collapsed, the deficits rose, not only because there were some attempts at discretionary stimulus, but also because the automatic stabilisers were triggered as tax revenue fell and unemployment increased. For many nations, this 'cyclical' impact was sufficient to breach the upper threshold of 3 per cent, which, according to the nonsensical logic of the SGP, invoked the EDP. Pressure was then imposed on the nations to make discretionary cuts to their spending and/or raise taxes in an effort to offset the automatic stabilisers and maintain the overall fiscal balance below the 3 per cent threshold. That was madness. As the recent experience has so emphatically demonstrated, imposing fiscal austerity on a nation in recession is self-defeating because the attempts to cut the discretionary or 'structural' component of the deficit further undermine the tax base and drive the automatic stabilisers into further deficit as economic growth deteriorates. An unemployed person pays no taxes!

The very fact that the automatic stabilisers are pushing the fiscal deficit up indicates that the government should increase the 'structural' deficit to stimulate growth. The SGP is a source of neither stability nor growth.

FURTHER FLAWS IN THE SGP RULES

Reflecting back to the discussion at the outset of this chapter, we can trace the views of European Commission economists and their consultants from the Maastricht period to the modern day. Several papers in the *One Market, One Money* publication (European Commission, 1990a) used various 'Neo-Keynesian' economic models to compare the role of central budgets in the US and Canada, for example, against what occurred in say

France and Germany. The simulations were deeply flawed. For example, simulations produced by their own economists, Alexander Italianer and Jean Pisani-Ferry (1992), claimed that the new EMU would not need a large federal budget because sufficient 'stabilisation' (via automatic stabilisers) would be forthcoming at the national level.

In a related paper, Pisani-Ferry et al. (1993), using what they admitted was a 'highly simplified' model (p. 519), concluded that the 'model responses followed as expected the standard neo-Keynesian pattern, so there is no need to comment upon simulation results' (p. 521). In other words, as a result of the assumptions and parameters employed in the simulation, the authors basically knew what the results would be before the fact. This was typical of the Groupthink that choked any reasonable debate. These models were not questioned and the results became the gospel for the neo-liberals.

In the aftermath of the GFC, it is now more generally understood how deficient these types of economic models are. For example, the dominant mainstream macroeconomic policy analysis models excluded the banking and financial markets and thus had nothing to say about the likelihood of the financial crisis even though the risks were there for all to see prior to the crash (see Mitchell and Muysken, 2008). Even a mainstream economist like Willem Buiter (2009) considered these models to be 'useless':

> Most mainstream macroeconomic theoretical innovations since the 1970s (the New Classical rational expectations revolution associated with such names as Robert E. Lucas Jr., Edward Prescott, Thomas Sargent, Robert Barro etc., and the New Keynesian theorizing of Michael Woodford and many others) have turned out to be self-referential, inward-looking distractions at best. Research tended to be motivated by the internal logic, intellectual sunk capital and esthetic puzzles of established research programmes rather than by a powerful desire to understand how the economy works – let alone how the economy works during times of stress and financial instability. So the economics profession was caught unprepared when the crisis struck . . .

Buiter's list of economists includes those who were regularly cited as authorities by the European Commission economists and consultants in justifying their support for the Maastricht EMU design.

What do the likes of Pisani-Ferry think now? Pisani-Ferry et al. (2012: 3) noted that while all 'federations have sizeable federal budgets . . . the founders of Europe's monetary union . . . eventually decided that in Europe, stabilisation policy could be exercised at the national level'. The calculations they used assumed that 'automatic stabilisers could fully react to a 6 per cent decline in output before the 3 per cent Maastricht deficit level was reached. It was judged that a 6 per cent decline in GDP was very unlikely' (p. 3). They have now acknowledged that the GFC has proven these assumptions were incorrect and 'When bad times . . . came . . . the buffer proved too small. In the course of two years, from 2007 to 2009, Spain moved from a 2 per cent GDP surplus to an 11 per cent deficit; Ireland went from balance to a 14 per cent deficit' (p. 2).

The experience clearly demonstrated the validity of the insights that were first articulated formally in 1968 by Wallace Oates (Oates, 1968), a consultant to the MacDougall Report, and are basic to Keynesian understanding. Relying on regional governmental units to provide fiscal support when a nation is hit with a major decline in spending will fail to militate against recession. If these flawed neo-liberal models had not been relied on by the European Commission in the early 1990s and the conclusions from Keynesian economists had not been vilified and excluded by the Groupthink that dominated the Maastricht process, then the observations produced by Pisani-Ferry et al. (2012) would have been obvious to all the delegates at the Maastricht conference. The economists that worked outside the Monetarist Groupthink clearly understood in the early 1990s that the Eurozone was being set up to fail.

The Commission was also warned of this before Stage III was finalised by some of its own economists. After the December 1996 Dublin Council meeting signed off on the SGP, three Commission economists performed a 'retrospective' evaluation of how the SGP would have performed in the period between 1961 and 1996 (Buti et al., 1997). In other words they analysed the factual fiscal outcomes over this period against the rigid SGP rules, especially in terms of considering 'what types of recessions' would lead 'Member States into a position of excessive deficit' under the Maastricht rules (p. 1). The point of the exercise is that the earlier work in the 1990s, which sought to give 'authority' to the Maastricht design, claimed that it would be difficult for the SGP rules to be violated without the intent of the government to overspend. That is, they asserted without evidence that it would be nearly impossible for the SGP limits to be violated purely by the impact of the automatic stabilisers.

Buti et al. (1997) found that between 1961 and 1996:

1. There were 24 severe recessions identified among the 15 member states of the EU at the time according to the SGP criteria of a GDP decrease of more than 0.75 per cent. The average decline in real GDP (output) was 2.5 per cent.
2. On average, the output gaps (the departure from trend output) were 5.5 per cent over this period.
3. While the increase in the fiscal deficits varied for each identified episode, the average increase was 3.6 percentage points. Almost all

of the increase was due to the automatic stabilisers (on average 3.5 percentage points).

4. Assuming an average starting point deficit of 2 per cent before the recession struck, in 18 of the 24 episodes identified, the resulting increase in the deficit would have been considered an 'excessive deficit' under the SGP rules.

The authors concluded that the 'risk of incurring an excessive deficit is high in case of protracted recessions' even if the starting point is a balanced fiscal position and that the 'same conclusions can be drawn for exceptionally severe recessions with negative growth of 2% or more' (Buti et al., 1997: 29). The risk of breaching the SGP thresholds was thus identified to be high unless the nations undertook 'a pro-cyclical budgetary stance' (p. 29). Why wasn't that analysis taken seriously?

There were many examples of the way neo-liberal Groupthink promoted flawed analysis that 'justified' the SGP rules. In 2000, the OECD published a paper that aimed to explore the scope that the Maastricht Treaty provided EMU governments to respond to a drop in total spending in their economies (Dalsgaard and de Serres, 2000). In relation to the SGP, the authors claimed that the 'imposition of such debt and deficit ceilings does not necessarily impose a binding constraint on the use of countercyclical fiscal policy because countries can run a structural deficit that is well below 3 per cent of GDP' (p. 116). They recognise that this claim is contingent on assumptions being made about the size of likely spending shocks.

Of course, consistent with the OECD's mission to publish 'research' that supports its neo-liberal agenda, the paper's findings 'validate the "close to balance" rule stipulated by the Stability and Growth Pact' (Dalsgaard and de Serres, 2000: 117). A major problem with their analysis is that it hinged on the output gap estimates they used, which measure the difference between actual output and hypothesised potential output. As we explained earlier, the OECD estimates of these gaps are biased downwards. This bias can be seen in Figure 11.1, which shows the OECD estimates of the output gap for some selected European nations in 2009 and the actual percentage decline in real GDP (actual output) for 2009.

In every case (other than Portugal) the decline in actual output in the first year of the crisis exceeded the OECD measure of the output gap. Even if we assumed that in 2008, at the onset of the crisis, all the economies were producing at full capacity (so real output was equal to potential and the output gap was zero), the actual decline in real production would imply larger output gaps than those published by the OECD. But, of course, with persistently high unemployment in many nations before the crisis,

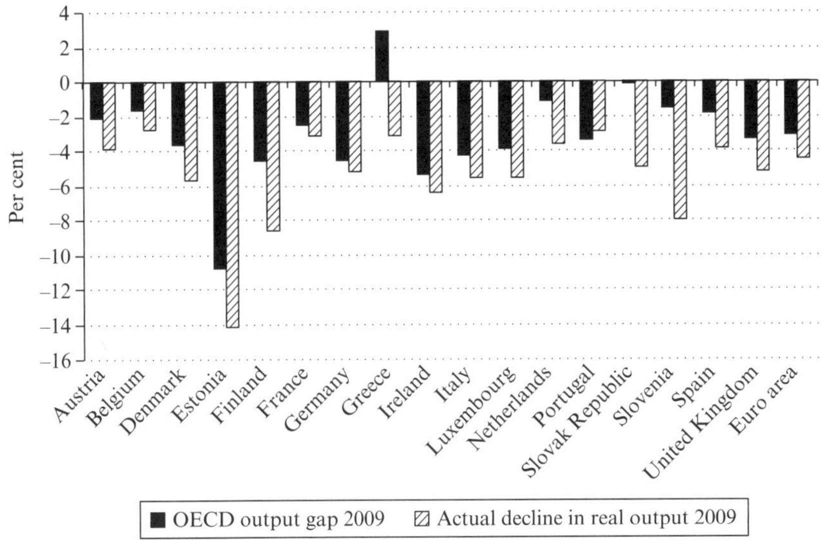

Note: The output gap measure is the deviation of actual from estimated potential as a percentage of the estimated potential whereas the actual decline in real GDP is the percentage change in real GDP between 2008 and 2009.

Source: OECD *Economic Outlook*, Volume 2013, Issue 2, Statistical Annex Table 10; Eurostat National Accounts database.

Figure 11.1 OECD output gap estimates and actual decline in real GDP, 2009

it is far fetched to think they were all operating at full employment and, hence, full capacity. A moment's reflection on the Greek estimate shows the problem. The OECD estimated that Greece was actually producing at around 103 per cent of its capacity in 2008, which is unlikely given that the unemployment rate was still very high at 7.8 per cent.

A possible retort is that the estimate of potential output fell in 2009 as actual output fell, which would explain why the estimated output gap was less than the actual decline in real output. Economists use a concept called 'hysteresis' to capture this possibility. One plausible story about this effect might be that as actual output falls and the economy moves into recession, firms stop investing in new productive capacity and scrap unused capacity, which reduces the potential productive capacity of the economy. While that narrative has strong empirical support, it takes a prolonged downturn before the pessimism of firms leads them to scrap their existing machinery and equipment. The response in the first year of a crisis would be more typically to turn off machines and leave other capacity idle while they ascertained the depth and likely duration of the downturn. In that case, it is highly unlikely that potential output fell sharply in 2009 in these nations.

Further, given that most economies started the downturn with persistently high unemployment rates, the likely widening of the output gaps in 2009 was probably even larger than the actual decline in real output. This also means that a component of the actual fiscal deficit for each country in 2008 was certainly 'cyclical', capturing the deviation from full capacity.

The European Commission and bodies like the OECD also continually argued that given historical output gaps during recessions and estimates of the sensitivity of the automatic stabilisers to changes in these output gaps that shifts in fiscal deficits due to the crisis alone would still be within the 3 per cent limit. Therefore, one could not reasonably challenge the SGP rules.

Figure 11.2 shows the average output gaps during recessions between 1975 and 1997 calculated by Dalsgaard and de Serres (2000) and the actual

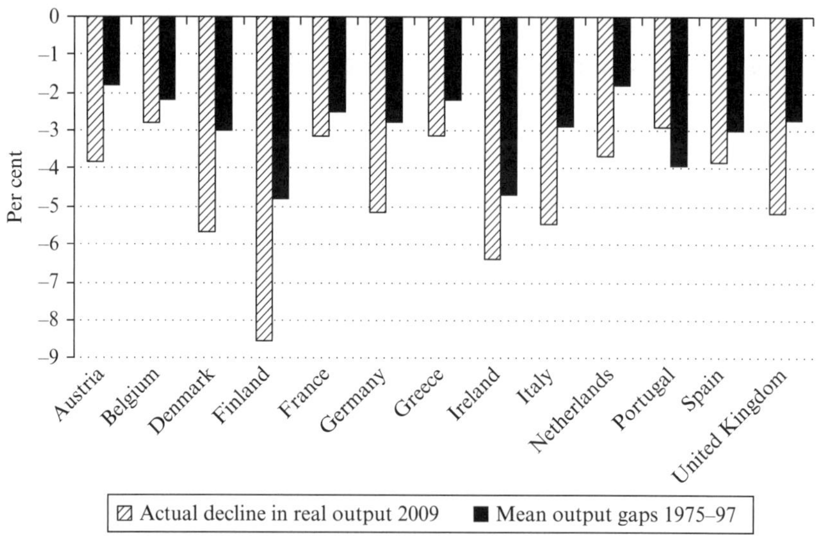

Note: The nations shown are limited by the historical data provided in Dalsgaard and de Serres (2000).

Source: Dalsgaard and de Serres (2000) for historical estimates of output gaps, Eurostat National Accounts database for actual real GDP data.

Figure 11.2 Average output gaps during recessions between 1975–97 and actual decline in real GDP, 2009

decline in real GDP in 2009 for a range of European nations. It is clear that the decline in actual output in 2009 exceeded the average output gaps during recessions in 1975–97, which were used to justify the SGP restrictions, by a considerable margin in all cases except Portugal. This suggests that the SGP was designed on excessively optimistic assumptions about the likely magnitudes of recessions in Europe. The experience of the pre-euro period is also not a sound benchmark because the nations concerned enjoyed the fiscal latitude that comes with being the issuer of one's own currency. This latitude almost assuredly allowed output gaps to be lower than otherwise as nations sought to stimulate their economies in the face of a private spending decline to ensure unemployment didn't rise to politically unacceptable levels.

THE SGP AND THE BOND MARKETS

The SGP also increases the vulnerability of the national governments to the private bond markets. Prior to the 1990s, governments and central banks worked together to ensure that the fiscal plans of the government would always have sufficient funds, even though the governments continued to unnecessarily issue debt to the private bond markets. The convention of issuing debt was continued even though the collapse of the Bretton Woods system freed currency-issuing governments from the need to issue any debt at all. But the convention continued because the dominant conservatism among economists saw it as a means of pressuring governments to run smaller deficits than might be required, with excessive unemployment being the casualty. Shifts in public debt ratios are always a sensitive issue in the public arena, even though most of the financial commentators and the public in general do not understand the meaning or relevance of them.

However during this period, central banks in many European nations regularly purchased government debt directly from the treasuries if they felt that accessing private funds in the bond markets would not be in the interests of the government. This practice was outlawed under the Maastricht Treaty and governments also gave up their currency-issuing sovereignty. Thus once the Eurozone came into operation, all Member States had to seek loans from the private bond markets to fund fiscal deficits. The bond markets were thus elevated in importance. They could dictate the cost of public borrowing to Eurozone governments and had the capacity to withdraw funds altogether and force a Eurozone nation into insolvency.

Most financial commentators regularly discuss Greece or France in the same breath as the United Kingdom or even the United States when considering the response of bond markets to deficits and rising public debt. But the comparison has no validity. The EMU nations are hamstrung as a consequence of ceding their monetary policy authority to the ECB, abandoning their independent exchange rate and their capacity to run an independent fiscal policy. For nations that issue their own currency, the bond markets are impotent given that their central banks can always set the terms (interest rates) on which public debt is issued if they so choose. Governments in these cases only have to pay what the bond markets demand if they concede to the false authority of the markets. Otherwise, the government is fully in charge of the bond issuance process and the markets become compliant recipients of corporate welfare in the form of a guaranteed (risk free) flow of interest payments. The bond markets know that there is no default risk on bonds that are issued in the currency that the central bank creates. We consider that issue in more detail in Chapter 17.

However, the bond investors know that the EMU nations face insolvency risk because they have to borrow to fund their commitments. In the absence of any ECB support, these nations are reliant on the terms set by the bond markets for any debt they issue. The excessive deficit procedure built into the SGP acts as an alarm bell for the bond markets because it unnecessarily invokes a sense of crisis when the real crisis is the loss of employment and output and the responsible response is to support total spending with larger deficits, which almost certainly exceed the SGP threshold. In creating this sense of crisis, the solvency risk of the nations is highlighted. By forcing all the fiscal adjustment onto the Member States and then restricting their capacity to meet an economic crisis, the EMU ensures that recessions will be deeper than they should be and that peripheral crises, such as the refusal of bond markets to lend to governments at reasonable rates, will become more likely.

ASSESSMENT OF SGP

The SGP was designed to place binding constraints on the fiscal capacity of national governments, which has undermined their ability to fulfil their legitimate responsibilities. The motivation for the SGP was a combination of historical enmities and distrust between nations in Europe and the Monetarist dislike of fiscal deficits. The SGP came at the instigation of Germany, which wanted fiscal constraints put on countries like Italy and Spain because they suspected these nations would adopt reckless government spending policies, which would undermine price stability. The SGP was a straitjacket, which aided the transfer of the Bundesbank culture into the wider Europe (see Mitchell et al., 2006; Mitchell and Muysken, 2008).

The constraints have limited the capacity of these governments to respond to crises and the result has been that millions of workers in Europe have unnecessarily lost their jobs as the Troika has bullied governments into adopting 'pro-cyclical' policy changes, which are the anathema of sound fiscal practice.

It is now widely recognised that the fiscal rules that are central to the SGP were purely of arbitrary origin without any solid theoretical foundation or internal consistency (see Mitchell et al., 2006). The rationale of controlling government debt and budget deficits was consistent with the rising neo-liberal orthodoxy that promoted inflation control as the macroeconomic policy priority and asserted the primacy of monetary policy over fiscal policy. Fiscal policy was forced to follow rigid rules, which denied its basic function.

The fiscal rules formalised in the SGP were criticised by many economists at the time of inception. Even relatively conservative economists such as De Grauwe (2003) argued that there was no rationale for zero government debt, which is what a zero deficit would imply in the long run (see also Fitoussi and Saraceno, 2004). They advocated an alternative approach, the golden rule of public finance, which would limit public borrowing to the financing of capital expenditures. Since government invests heavily in infrastructure and other public works that deliver benefits to overlapping generations, it was argued that borrowing would allow future generations to pay for the benefits they receive from such investments (see Buiter and Grafe, 2004). So even within an orthodox classical public finance approach, the SGP constraints were difficult to justify. But these arguments were rejected without reason by the increasingly dominant Monetarist fringe within the European Commission. The Groupthink suffocated debate and reason.

The requirement that fiscal deficits should be zero on average and never exceed 3 per cent of GDP not only restricts the fiscal powers that governments would ordinarily enjoy as a result of issuing their own currencies (so-called 'fiat currency regimes'), but also violates an understanding of the way fiscal outcomes are effectively determined by private spending. Forcing governments to impose harsh austerity on economies suffering from a collapse of private spending exacerbates the intensity and duration of recessions. It further results in rising deficits as tax revenue continues to fall and involves the nations in further SGP rule violations and bond market problems. The vicious circle of spending cuts implied is unsustainable and amounts to fiscal vandalism. In other words, fiscal policy becomes 'pro-cyclical' under the SGP rule, violating any sensible ambitions that are the ambit of responsible fiscal management. That is the major reason that France and Germany refused to comply with the 3 per cent rule in the early years of the EMU.

The SGP rule cannot be seen in isolation from the monetary policy straitjacket that the ECB imposes on economic activity. While the ECB now has a monetary policy monopoly across the EU countries, it is not politically responsible for its actions. The EU countries have voluntarily allowed the ECB to be an unelected and independent body whose sole aim is to control inflation. The fundamental democratic principle that the citizens have the ability to cast judgement on the policies of their representatives at regular intervals has been abandoned in this setup. Former World Bank adviser Joseph Stiglitz (2002: 45) concluded:

> There is a widespread feeling that the ECB exacerbated Europe's economic slowdown in 2001, as like a child, it responded peevishly to the natural political concerns over growing unemployment. Just to show that it was independent, it refused to allow the interest rates to fall, and there was nothing anyone could do about it. The problems partly arose because the ECB has a mandate to focus on inflation, a policy . . . that can stifle growth or exacerbate an economic down turn.

It is often said that the European economies are sclerotic, which is usually taken to mean that their labour markets are overly protected and their welfare systems are overly generous. However, the real European sclerosis is found in the inflexible macroeconomic policy regime that the euro countries chose to contrive. The rigid monetary arrangements conducted by the undemocratic ECB and the irrational fiscal constraints embodied in the SGP, render the Member States incapable of sustaining stable economic growth and low levels of unemployment (see Bofinger, 2003; Buiter, 2006).

The SGP provides neither stability nor growth.

12. The convergence farce: smokescreens and denial

OPERATION SELF-DECEPTION

The convergence criteria specified under Article 109j(1) (Maastricht Treaty, 1992) relating to inflation, interest rates and exchange rate stability were clear and most of the contending nations were likely to have satisfied them as the deadline approached. The sticking point, however, was the rules under Article 104c and Protocol 5, which related to 'excessive deficits'.

The excessive deficit criterion, outlined earlier, was clearly tripping a number of nations up, including Germany. In 1997, France, Germany and Spain had deficits above 3 per cent and could not really appeal to the special circumstances clauses as a way out. Further, the public debt ratios in Germany and Spain were above the 60 per cent threshold and had been increasing since 1995. By contrast, although Italy's public debt ratio was well in excess of the criteria, it had been falling. Further, Belgium was in a similar situation to Italy. Tactically, Germany could not isolate Italy without pleading some special case for Belgium, which of course it attempted without success.

On 2–3 May 1998 the special European Council meeting in Brussels sealed the starting date for Stage III. A week before the meeting, German Finance Minister Waigel upped the ante by demanding that the Council agree to a 'stability declaration'. While his Stability Pact proposal in 1995 concentrated on constraining fiscal deficits, the 'stability declaration' targeted public debt. Germany anticipated that Italy would, by hook or by crook, meet the deficit requirements of the convergence criteria. But even with creative accounting, it knew Italy would not be able to meet the debt limits in time.

Italy was a major headache for the Germans. In 2012, the German newspaper *Der Spiegel* obtained a number of previously secret German government documents via a freedom of information process, which reveal the extent of the German concern over Italy's entry into the EMU. The documents 'prove what was only assumed until now: Italy should never have been accepted into the common currency zone' (Böll et al.,

2012, Part 1). Italy's entry reflected political exigencies 'at the expense of economic criteria' (Böll et al., 2012, Part 1), which is hardly surprising given that the motivation all along was not grounded in sound economics. The only surprising thing is that the issue of political integration was avoided at the Maastricht conference. There was little taste for giving more power to the European Parliament, and Germany caved in to French demands to focus on economic matters almost exclusively.

Der Spiegel characterised the EMU exercise as 'Operation "self-deceit"' (Böll et al., 2012, Part 1). The documents reveal that the German officials and governments were aware of the accounting tricks that Italy was engaging (gold sales and special 'taxes') to bring the deficit down below the Maastricht thresholds. In early 1997, the Italians announced that they had reached the 3 per cent deficit criterion, defying other known measures of their fiscal position provided by the IMF and the OECD. Waigel's state secretary, Jürgen Stark, accused the Italians of having pressured the Banco d'Italia to manipulate the convergence process.

3 PER CENT MEANS 3.0 PER CENT . . . BUT NOT ALWAYS

As 1997 dawned, it was clear that Germany itself might not meet the deficit and public debt thresholds laid out in the convergence criteria. Within Germany, the opposition SPD was making political capital by attacking the German government about its fiscal position. During the October 1996 federal 'budget' debate, Waigel was accused of 'lying and deceiving the public' over the state of the nation's finances (Miller, 1997: 6). SDP leader Gerhard Schröder argued that Stage III should be delayed while Germany sorted out its own economic challenges, which included rising unemployment. Helmut Kohl had a clear political imperative to stitch up the Stage III transition before the 1998 Federal election in Germany.

Externally, the German government's problem was obvious. While the Bundesbank had actually demonstrated some realism about the convergence criteria, with bank President Tietmeyer suggesting that 'countries should be judged less on the exact numbers and more on what he called the sustainability of their economies' (Andrews, 1997a), the German government had been 'Europe's scolding schoolmarm on fiscal and monetary policy, adamantly insisting that countries should not be allowed to take part in the euro unless they meet exact and nonnegotiable numerical targets on a number of issues, including the size of their government budget deficit' (Andrews, 1997a).

So what to do? Waigel had anticipated the problem for some months.

At the 17 March 1997 meeting of Ecofin in Brussels, Germany's convergence program was examined and the European Council 'was well aware of the unique challenges and the difficult economic situation currently faced by Germany' (European Council, 1997a). Waigel apparently told the meeting that Germany should be exempted from the 60 per cent public debt condition and said that while 'I always said that three means three. I never talked about 60' (Cameron, 1997: 9). That sounded as though Germany was seeking flexibility on the debt criteria only.

But the slippage continued. A month later (4–6 April), at the informal Ecofin meeting in the Dutch seaside town of Noordwijk, as the Finance Ministers waxed lyrical about the nature of the fines that would be imposed on nations with excessive deficits, Waigel exhibited shameful hypocrisy. He indicated that Germany was even prepared to be 'flexible' about the 3 per cent threshold. *The Guardian* reported that Waigel had told the meeting that 'I have never nailed myself on the cross of 3 per cent. When I said in the past "3 per cent means 3 per cent" I did not necessarily mean 3.0 per cent' (Palmer, 1997). This was astounding gall.

It was clear that Germany hated the idea of Italy joining the EMU. But it was also weakened by its own inability to meet the criteria and was facing a difficult federal election in 1998. As a result, it would do what it took to push through to Stage III. Waigel's 'softening' at the April Ecofin meeting was in line with Kohl's announcement a few days earlier that he would seek re-election in 1998 and that monetary union would proceed on time in 1999. Waigel's remarks made it clear that there would be no delay in the Stage III transition.

On the domestic front, Germany demonstrated that the accounting tricks were not confined to the nations 'down south'. While Waigel was publicly railing against France, Italy, and Spain for manipulating their public accounts, he privately crafted his own plan to 'cook Germany's books', which looked very similar to those same creative accounting plans deployed by France and Italy. Essentially, Waigel wanted the Bundesbank to revalue its gold reserves at the current market prices rather than at their historical value, and then record the not inconsiderable 'paper profit' in favour of the Government's operating position. This would have wiped off the deficit in that year.

After a public spat with the Bundesbank, which claimed the plan would compromise its independence, the Government was forced to scrap the plan on 4 June 1997 and bear the public humiliation associated with losing out to the bank. Other nations also reasonably noted that Germany was 'resorting to the very same one-time financial manoeuvres that it has loudly denounced in France and Italy' (Andrews, 1997b).

It is ironic that in 2010, Waigel claimed, 'Greece fiddled with the numbers, which is quite a nasty trick' (EurActiv, 2010). This was in reference to the secret loan that Goldman Sachs made to the Greek government in 2001, which allowed Greece to manipulate its books and hide its public debt so as to keep within the EMU rules. The nasty bit was that Goldman produced a transaction of such complexity that Greece 'didn't understand what it was buying and was ill-equipped to judge the risk or costs' (Dunbar and Martinuzzi, 2012).

POLITICS TRIUMPHS AMID THE ECONOMIC HAZE

It was clear though that the final decision on who would enter the EMU would be political and the convergence criteria were really a smokescreen, a sort of delusional security blanket designed to placate the German public and the conservatives elsewhere that the process was disciplined and sustainable.

There was no economic logic, just a set of arbitrary numbers grabbed out of the air, which were then backfilled with a series of spurious 'economic' reports that claimed to represent these numbers as 'economic knowledge'. They were never that. They were always just ideological statements about the Monetarist disdain for government activity.

Kohl's policy advisor Joachim Bitterlich indicated that Germany could not exclude Italy from the EMU because 'We all shared a certain love for Italy', given that Italy had been a foundation member of the Community and was seen as a cooperative member relative to the French and the British, both of which had a long history of tension with Germany (Böll et al., 2012, Part 1).

But even within this political struggle, the 'economic' criteria were being used to undermine the viability of the national economies. The EMI Convergence Report was published in March 1998 as part of the process specified under Article 109j of the Maastricht Treaty (European Monetary Institute, 1998). It assessed that 'further substantial consolidation is warranted in most Member States in order to achieve lasting compliance with the fiscal criteria and the . . . objective of having a budgetary position that is close to balance or in surplus, . . . from 1999 onwards' (p. 7). While the EMI mentioned several nations, including Germany and France, it claimed that there would need to be substantial fiscal 'surpluses in Belgium, Greece and Italy' for 'an extended period of time' (p. 7).

There was no discussion about whether this extended austerity was in any way related to what was actually happening in the economy with respect to economic growth or unemployment. The discussion rendered these important macroeconomic aggregates irrelevant. Public policy was solely being assessed in terms of the arbitrary fiscal criteria that were introduced in Maastricht. It was an extraordinary abandonment of macroeconomic responsibility and the sign of things to come.

The Bundesbank produced its 'Opinion' on the state of convergence in the European Union to the Stage III rules in April 1998 and was more explicit than the EMI Report (Bundesbank, 1998). It expressed 'serious doubts about the long-term sustainability of the financial position' (p. 38) of both Belgium and Italy in relation to their public debt situation. Notwithstanding their recognition of existing austerity plans, the Bundesbank claimed that both nations would have to accept 'further substantial binding austerity commitments' (p. 39).

The problem for Germany was that if it tried to reject Italy's membership on the public debt count, then it would have to reject Belgium's bid. That was impossible. Further, the public debt ratios for both Italy and Belgium had been declining, albeit slowly, while Germany's ratio was also above the 60 per cent threshold and had been rising. Waigel mounted the 'special case' appeal relating to the investment the government had made in the reunification effort as a mitigating circumstance. It was convenient for the political elites elsewhere in Europe to accept that, because then Italy, Belgium, and later Greece could slip through the net without close scrutiny.

Szász (1999: 226) concluded, 'since it was felt to be politically awkward to admit Germany and France despite doubts regarding their performance, while at the same time rejecting the participation of other countries, then it was decided the other countries had to be admitted as well.' Which meant the convergence criteria had to be watered down. In effect, they all agreed to fudge the books and bend the rules they had set for themselves, because the rules themselves were impossible to meet while still maintaining anything like politically acceptable unemployment rates.

The upshot was that 11 nations were deemed to have met the convergence criteria and would enter the EMU. Greece would have to wait a few years. The politicians had demonstrated a spectacular capacity to bend their own rules but there were limits if they wanted to retain any semblance of credibility. Greece was at that stage beyond these limits. But not for long!

PART II

The Path to Crisis

13. The first few years: smug self-congratulation and mass delusion

THE EURO IS BORN

Stage III of the EMU transition covered the period from 1 January 1999 to 1 July 2002, the latter date marking the end of the national currencies. While the convergence process was farcical at best, it remained the case the nations could only 'gild the lily' so far, notwithstanding the amazing scam that Goldman Sachs helped the Greeks to perpetrate in 2001, which facilitated that nation's entry. In other words, the convergence exercise, while fraudulent, still caused considerable self-inflicted damage as the nations imposed fiscal austerity and growth rates fell sharply. Table 13.1 compares the average annual percentage economic growth rates for the decades from 1970, with the last period being 2000 to 2013. The convergence period was clearly damaging for the large European economies

Table 13.1 Real GDP growth rates, 1970–2013, average annual percentage growth, selected periods

	1970–80 %	1980–90 %	1990–2000 %	2000–13 %
Belgium	3.5	2.4	2.4	1.1
Denmark	2.3	2.4	3.0	1.0
Germany	3.1	2.7	2.1	1.1
Ireland	5.5	4.4	10.0	1.7
Greece	5.4	0.8	2.6	0.2
Spain	3.9	3.6	3.1	1.5
France	4.1	2.7	2.1	1.0
Italy	4.0	3.0	1.6	−0.1
Luxembourg	1.5	5.7	5.7	4.5
Netherlands	3.1	2.4	3.7	1.0
Portugal	5.9	4.4	3.8	0.1
United Kingdom	2.0	3.2	3.6	1.6

Source: Eurostat, Annual Macroeconomic Database.

(France, Germany, and Italy), which make up more than 60 per cent of the overall EMU economy. While Ireland was becoming the 'Celtic Tiger' in the early years and the 'darling' of the conservatives, it was also on its way to becoming the mangy cat that it is now.

THE BUSINESS CYCLE IS DEAD! LONG LIVE THE FREE MARKET

But that experience seemed to be ignored by the political elites in Europe. The early days of the EMU coincided with an extraordinary period in economic history, where economic policy makers adopted a sort of smug, self-congratulatory triumphalism, which, in part, would lead them to make policy choices that would eventually multiply the risks inherent in the flawed design of the EMU.

On 20 February 2004, the Governor of the US Federal Reserve Bank, Ben Bernanke, gave a speech to a group of economists in Washington, DC entitled 'The Great Moderation'. He claimed that the liberalisation agenda promoted by the multilateral agencies such as the IMF, the World Bank and central banks and treasuries had 'won' the day. This agenda emphasised the granting of independence to central banks to prioritise 'inflation first' strategies, tight fiscal policy with an obsession for surpluses, and widespread deregulation and privatisation.

Bernanke said that one 'of the most striking features of the economic landscape over the past twenty years or so has been a substantial decline in macroeconomic volatility' (Bernanke 2004). The term 'great moderation', coined by two Harvard economists, James Stock and Mark Watson, referred to this reduction in 'volatility' in output growth and prices in most economies during the 1990s, which tended to suggest that there had been a 'break' in behaviour from the more variable performance experienced in the 1980s. The conservatives were eager to suggest that this 'moderation' was due to financial market deregulation that made credit more accessible and 'improved monetary policy' (Stock and Watson, 2002: 161). Consistent with the dominant neo-liberal narrative, Bernanke claimed that the 'Great Moderation' had delivered numerous benefits to economies because 'recessions have become less frequent and less severe' (Bernanke 2004).

These claims seemed to reinforce the observations made in 1990 by English economist John Williamson who introduced the term 'Washington Consensus' into the public lexicon. The consensus referred to the liberalisation policy agenda broadly pursued by Washington-based institutions such as the IMF, the World Bank and the economic agencies of the US government, the Federal Reserve Board, and the right-wing think tanks (Williamson, 1990). According to Williamson, there were ten pro-growth policy instruments which these agencies mutually supported and promoted, including the neo-liberal agenda based on free market fundamentalism, fiscal austerity, broad-based deregulation of financial and labour markets and privatisation. The narrative suggested that this agenda was responsible for the 'moderation'.

Williamson's 'consensus' terminology seemed to suggest that the economic policy terrain was uncontested. But, there were other, albeit largely ignored, voices at the time. For example, Robert Wade (2004) outlined his own ten-point reform agenda based upon the East Asian experience, which emphasised the centrality of government leadership in managing economic growth. Wade opposed the 'shock therapy' doctrine that the 'Washington Consensus' had advocated and eschewed the use of fiscal austerity. Later, Dani Rodrik (2006) also exposed the failure of the Washington reform agenda.

The underlying neo-liberal narrative that dominated policy making in the 1990s, as the EMU was being crafted, was that if private markets were left free of regulation and central banks were allowed to concentrate on price stability, unfettered by the political process, then economies would be able to maintain long periods of stable output and employment growth. The neo-liberal economists believed this period of 'stability' vindicated their claims that there was no further role for governments to use fiscal policy, the hallmark of Keynesianism, to try to 'stabilise' total spending in search of low unemployment. They prosecuted that view with zeal and arrogance.

KEYNESIANISM WAS DEAD!

One notable demonstration of this arrogance was the 2003 Presidential Address given to the American Economic Association by University of Chicago professor Robert E. Lucas. Lucas (2003: 1) said that:

> My thesis . . . is that macroeconomics in this original sense has succeeded: Its central problem of depression-prevention has been solved, for all practical purposes, and has in fact been solved for many decades . . . I argue that there are gains from providing people with better incentives to work and to save, not from better fine tuning of spending flows. Taking U.S. performance over the past 50 years as a benchmark, the potential for welfare gains from better long-run, supply side policies exceeds by far the potential from further improvements in short-run demand management.

In other words, economic policy should concentrate on further deregulation because the problem of recessions (business cycle downturns) was 'solved'. According to this view, managing total spending with fiscal policy was now redundant. These claims also gave succour to the European politicians who used it as justification for relying on the ECB to provide European level stabilisation.

THE BRUSSELS–FRANKFURT CONSENSUS MERGES WITH THE WASHINGTON CONSENSUS

Clearly, the Washington Consensus dovetailed closely with the policy mentality in Europe that had created the EMU and the growing 'sense of success' that emerged in the early days of the union. In July 2003, the European Commission published the so-called Sapir Report, which was the product of a 'High-Level Group of Independent Experts' who reviewed 'the entire system of EU economic policies' (Sapir et al., 2003: i). Academic economist André Sapir chaired the group meetings. More recently, he was a member of Jose Manuel Barroso's Economic Policy Analysis Group. He also contributes to the public policy debate as 'resident scholar' at the conservative Brussels-based think tank, Bruegel. The latter claims to be 'independent and non-doctrinal' but takes the excessive deficit rules embedded in the SGP as non-contestable, which makes it a biased voice for neo-liberal ideology. Jean-Claude Trichet chairs Bruegel's Managing Board.

The 183-page Sapir Report was very influential and is full of neo-liberal success rhetoric (see Mitchell and Muysken, 2006 for a critique). The Report concluded that the 'three pillars upon which the European economic edifice is now built are fundamentally sound' (p. ii) and that 'there is no doubt that the period of the last 15 years has been a tremendous success' (Sapir et al., 2003: 1). Consistent with its neo-liberal roots, the Report claimed that the remaining policy challenges were at the microeconomic level, to free up more markets and reduce welfare budgets. The Report recommended that the Commission should maintain a 'framework of strengthened budgetary surveillance and . . . should reinforce its surveillance and be given more responsibility to interpret the rules of the SGP. Also, budgetary responsibility would be enhanced by establishing independent Fiscal Auditing Boards in the Member States' (p. 5).

At the time that Sapir and his colleagues were praising the EMU and recommending even harsher fiscal rules, economic growth was slowing and unemployment remained persistently high. It was rather surprising that the ongoing macroeconomic losses that arise from the persistent unemployment, not to mention the massive social and personal costs, were not considered by the Commission to be the most compelling policy problem. It appeared that the politicians and policy makers, aided and abetted by the so-called 'experts' they wheeled in from time to time to produce these self-reinforcing reports, had the totally opposite construction of events. Unemployment was seen, at worst, as an unfortunate and ephemeral consequence of policies that are required to maintain low inflation economies and was largely attributed either to rigidities (overly generous welfare and other regulations and out of touch unions) or to individual choice. This construction provided the political cover for governments in Europe (and elsewhere) to abandon the goal of full employment and replace it with the diminished goal of full employability. It was policy bankruptcy.

The Sapir Report (2003: 41) dubbed this policy framework the 'Brussels–Frankfurt consensus' and summarised it as follows:

> The maintenance of price stability – reflected in low rates of inflation – facilitates achieving higher rates of economic growth over the medium term and helps to reduce cyclical fluctuations. This shows up in a lower variability of output and inflation. In turn, sound public finances are necessary both to prevent imbalances in the policy mix, which negatively affect the variability of output and inflation, and also to contribute to national savings, thus helping to foster private investment and ultimately growth. The latter beneficial effect is magnified as low deficits and debt, by entailing a low interest burden, create the room for higher public investment, 'productive' public spending and a low tax burden. Finally, the beneficial effects of price stability and fiscal discipline on economic performance reinforce each other in various ways. On the one hand, fiscal discipline supports the central bank in its task to maintain price stability. On the other hand, prudent monetary and fiscal policies avoid policy-induced shocks and their unfavourable impact on economic fluctuations while ensuring a higher room for manoeuvre to address other disturbances that increase cyclical instability.

The Washington consensus and the Brussels–Frankfurt consensus thus dovetailed perfectly and the whole world was gripped by the austerity culture and the urgency of deregulation. The pre-conditions for the global crisis, which would manifest a few years later, were being laid, but the creators were blind to their actions, such was their religious conviction and capacity for Groupthink.

The Sapir Report was a classic example of the neo-liberal dogma, asserted as an article of religious faith, and oblivious to evidence. But the world drank the 'Kool-Aid' and we learned to recite the mantra that the creation of independent central banks and the imposition of fiscal austerity would insulate economies from recession. The EMU exemplified this policy utopia. All that was needed was further labour market and financial deregulation, continued suppression of the capacity of workers to maintain real wages growth in line with productivity growth, and a deeper retrenchment of existing welfare safety nets for low-income workers and the unemployed. The confidence exuded by the neo-liberal politicians and their 'hired' economists was only possible because they redefined the mass unemployment that they had created as being 'optimal', a virtue of free choice. They also were blind to the fact that the single monetary policy and financial deregulation were causing massive imbalances in capital flows and trade within Europe.

These imbalances would soon combine with the flawed design of the EMU to amplify the negative consequences of the collapse of the housing market in the US and push the Eurozone to the brink of collapse. Such was the magnitude of the threat to the monetary union that the euro cabal was forced to break its own ban on bailouts, despite continued denials to the contrary. It also forced the ECB to break its taboo on funding government deficits when it bought billions of euros worth of public bonds and maintained the solvency of several EMU national governments. While the ECB denied it was doing that and resorted to opaque explanations about 'managing liquidity requirements', the fact is it was 'funding' deficits and everyone knew it. And, despite all the protestations of economists of the Sapir mould, deflation not inflation emerged as the problem as unemployment skyrocketed.

In a 2011 paper, Sapir and another regular European Commission consultant, Jean Pisani-Ferry, who was one of the so-called 'experts' that produced the Sapir Report, acknowledged that the EMU was beset with destructive imbalances (Darvas et al., 2011). The benefit of hindsight one might say! However, as they waxed lyrical about the way forward for Europe, they largely ignored the role played by Modell Deutschland and, instead, chose to blame nations such as Greece, Ireland, Portugal and Spain for living 'beyond their means by accumulating private and/or public debt and running large current account deficits' (p. 2). They failed to emphasise that the peripheral nations were buying French and German exports using large swathes of capital supplied by German financiers, who were diverting funds away from the stagnant German domestic market. None of the EU cabal thought to tell Greece to stop buying ageing German military equipment to satiate its territorial paranoia about Turkey. What is often forgotten is that for every 'over spending' importer there has to be an 'over supplying' exporter.

It is clear that the ECB considered its interest rates were appropriate and neither the ECB nor Brussels sought to place restrictions on banks and financial engineers who were plying consumers and firms in the weaker states with credit. The massive real estate booms that followed in Ireland and Spain were held out as a sign of EMU success. In 2004, Jean-Claude Trichet said, 'Thanks to Ireland's economic success . . . we can be confident that economic reform works' (Trichet, 2004). And, most importantly, why were the peripheral nations allowed to enter the EMU in the first place when it was obvious that they had not remotely satisfied the convergence criteria? None of those issues were on the minds of Sapir and his colleagues in 2003.

THE IMBALANCES GREW BUT THE EU BOSSES REMAINED OBSESSED WITH FISCAL RULES

The special tenth anniversary edition of the ECB *Monthly Bulletin* (ECB, 2008) was full of self-congratulation about the achievements of the bank in its first decade of operation. The ECB (2008: 10) said it was 'fulfilling its primary objective to maintain price stability' and had delivered 'low interest rates' (p. 15) and 'All in all, good progress has been made' (p. 65) but it urged more deregulation (for example, reduction of employment protections and reduced welfare benefits) to further free up markets and 'to increase incentives to work' (p. 70). On 10 July 2008, ECB President, Jean-Claude Trichet, spoke at a special tenth anniversary conference in Munich and noted:

> The achievements I have just described have accompanied an impressive performance in terms of job creation. From the start of EMU to the end of last year . . . the number of people in employment in the euro area has increased by 15.7 million, compared with an increase of only some 5 million in the previous nine years, and the euro area unemployment rate has fallen to its lowest level since the early 1980s. (Trichet, 2008)

While on the surface the facts were accurate and the employment generation sounded impressive relative to the 'convergence years' prior to formal union, the devil was in the detail. In which countries and sectors were these jobs created? Table 13.2 shows what happened to employment between 1999 and 2007. The nations shown are the original Eurozone nations plus Greece which joined in 2001 and the non-euro nations which joined the European Union but did not adopt the euro as their currency. The employment growth in Ireland and Spain was spectacular over this period while Germany's performance was very poor.

Overall, 15.7 million net jobs were created between 1999 and 2007. Taken together, employment growth in the peripheral Eurozone nations (Portugal, Ireland, Italy, Greece and Spain – the PIIGS) was 2.5 times the rate for the remaining Eurozone nations. The PIIGS accounted for 60 per cent of the total change in total Eurozone employment, while their share in total Eurozone employment in 1997 was just 37 per cent.

Table 13.2 Employment change and growth, selected European nations, 1999–2007, '000s and per cent

Country/group	Change '000s	Growth %
Austria	319.2	8.8
Belgium	392.9	9.9
Finland	140.5	6.1
France	3010.9	13.4
Germany	1654.8	4.6
Greece	478.9	12.1
Ireland	517.4	33.3
Italy	2554.4	12.6
Luxembourg	27.1	15.4
Netherlands	793.5	10.5
Portugal	209.8	4.5
Spain	5693.9	39.2
Euro 12	15793.3	13.1
PIIGS	9454.4	21.0
Non-PIIGS Euro	6338.9	8.4
Denmark	66.4	2.5
Sweden	455.7	11.4
United Kingdom	2068.2	7.8
Total non-Euro EU	2590.3	7.8

Source: Eurostat, Employment by sex, age and economic activity (1983–2008, NACE Rev. 1.1).

But what was happening at the industry sector level in the first eight years of the Eurozone? Table 13.3 shows the growth in employment (per cent) and the shift in employment shares (as a proportion of total for each country) by selected broad industry sectors. The spectacular growth in employment in Ireland and Spain occurred in the Construction sector as a result of the housing boom in both economies. The Construction sector nearly doubled in size between 1999 and 2007 in Ireland (97.9 per cent growth) and grew by 75 per cent in Spain. The Construction sector increased from 9.1 per cent of total Irish employment in 1999 to 13.5 per cent in 2007, and from 10.6 per cent of total Spanish employment in 1999 to 13.3 per cent in 2007. These were radical shifts in the employment mixes in each nation, especially given the speed of the changes.

There was also above average Eurozone growth in the Construction sector in Greece and Italy among the PIIGS, and in Belgium and France. The strongest Eurozone employment growth was in the services sector and

Table 13.3 Employment growth and shares of total employment by sector, 1999 and 2007, per cent

	Industry less construction			Manufacturing			Construction			Services		
	Growth 99–07	Share 1999	Share 2007	Growth 99–07	Share 1999	Share 2007	Growth 99–07	Share 1999	Share 2007	Growth 99–07	Share 1999	Share 2007
AUT	−3.7	21.8	19.3	−3.3	20.6	18.3	10.1	8.2	8.3	14.0	64.2	67.3
BEL	−1.4	19.7	17.6	−1.9	18.6	16.6	21.1	6.3	6.9	12.8	71.8	73.7
FIN	−6.5	21.4	18.8	−5.7	20.2	18.0	15.6	6.4	7.0	12.3	65.8	69.7
FRA	−6.5	19.9	16.4	−6.6	18.9	15.5	21.6	6.4	6.9	19.3	69.5	73.1
GER	−3.0	25.2	23.4	−2.6	23.8	22.2	−20.4	8.7	6.7	12.1	63.3	67.8
GRE	−2.8	16.1	13.9	−2.6	14.5	12.6	36.8	7.3	8.9	23.4	60.3	66.4
IRE	−4.2	19.7	14.1	−6.4	18.6	13.0	97.9	9.1	13.5	40.9	63.6	67.2
ITA	−1.3	25.0	21.9	−0.1	23.8	21.1	24.8	7.6	8.5	19.2	62.2	65.8
LUX	−24.5	13.0	8.5	−25.4	12.1	7.8	9.0	8.9	8.4	23.8	75.7	81.2
NLD	−7.2	15.2	12.7	−7.9	14.5	12.1	7.5	6.1	5.9	16.9	70.7	74.9
POR	−12.6	24.6	20.6	−13.5	23.6	19.5	8.6	11.3	11.7	15.2	54.7	60.3
SPA	10.5	20.2	16.1	10.9	19.1	15.2	74.8	10.6	13.3	48.3	62.1	66.1
E12	−2.4	22.2	19.1	−2.1	21.0	18.2	16.8	8.1	8.4	20.1	64.5	68.6
DEN	−14.5	19.8	16.5	−14.7	19.0	15.8	2.3	7.1	7.1	8.3	69.6	73.5
SWE	−13.2	19.8	15.4	−13.3	18.8	14.6	29.3	5.5	6.4	17.0	72.3	75.9
UKG	−20.4	18.9	14.0	−22.8	17.9	12.8	27.4	7.0	8.2	13.6	72.3	76.2

Note: E12 is the original Eurozone nations.

Source: Eurostat, Employment by sex, age and economic activity (1983–2008, NACE Rev. 1.1).

within that sector the real estate, renting and business activities sub-sector experienced very strong growth, associated with the building boom.

While the house of cards was being built, the only issues that the EU bosses and its coterie of 'hired hand' economists were concerned with in these early days was the violation of their precious fiscal rules by none other than France and Germany in 2003 and the lack of progress in their deregulation agenda. We examine the 2003 SGP crisis next.

14. The 2003 fiscal crisis

THE STABILITY AND GROWTH PACT FAILS ALMOST IMMEDIATELY

After years of negotiating the SGP and the Excessive Deficit Procedures (EDP), in particular, trouble emerged for the EMU almost immediately. Given the poorly conceived nature of the SGP it was no surprise that it would fail its first test. What was surprising was the way the politicians and bureaucrats behaved in the face of what any reasonable assessment would consider to be extraordinary hypocrisy. But then, the way Theo Waigel wriggled and squirmed in the 'convergence period' with his '3 doesn't mean 3.0' and the related slippage in allowing Belgium, Italy, and then Greece to enter had already demonstrated how 'flexible' Germany would be with its 'discipline'. The history of the EMU to date has taught us that if Germany is unable to meet rules, then the rules will be altered. Otherwise, the rules will be used as a blunt weapon to devastate the employment base and living standards of weaker nations without the political clout of Germany.

The EDP is the so-called corrective arm of the SGP and according to the European Commission (2014a) 'begins with a Member State either':

- having breached or being in risk of breaching the deficit threshold of 3% of GDP or
- having violated the debt rule by having a government debt level above 60% of GDP, which is not diminishing at a satisfactory pace. This means that the gap between a country's debt level and the 60% reference needs to be reduced by 1/20th annually (on average over three years).

A rigid procedure is specified for countries 'placed in EDP' with financial penalties imposed for nations who are in 'serious' breach or who fail to meet deadlines imposed by the Commission. The 'EDP is stepped up' for nations that fail 'to take effective action to correct the excessive deficit in time' (European Commission, 2014a). The rules have been strengthened since May 2013 and those developments are discussed in Chapter 16.

The SGP rules and procedures were, in no small way, the product of the demands made by Germany as a pre-condition for surrendering the mark and ceding monetary policy discipline to the ECB. The insistence by Germany that the SGP would be binding was a reflection of its fear that once the single currency was introduced and a common monetary policy was in force, some nations would over borrow and over spend because their debt would be cheaper as a result of the presence of Germany in the EMU. As a consequence, the SGP rules defined a state of 'over spending' and 'over borrowing' without recourse to the normal indicators one would reasonably use to make such assessments, such as the state of the economic cycle, the extent of idle capacity in the economy, including the unemployment rate and the inflation rate.

Ironically, in 2003, Germany was one of the first nations to transgress these rules. Its partner in crime was France. What followed was astounding, especially when we consider how Germany has played it tough with its smaller, more fragile EMU partners in the current crisis.

A CHOICE BETWEEN RIGID OBEDIENCE OR SAVING JOBS IS REQUIRED

By early 2002, the German economy was slowing quickly and the Commission concluded that it was likely that Germany would 'require a substantially higher adjustment effort' to achieve the projected fiscal balance by 2004 (European Commission, 2002a). On 30 January 2002, the Commission, acting under the EDP rules, proposed 'to give Germany an early warning on the basis of Regulation 1466/97 of the Stability and Growth Pact (SGP)', which would be forwarded to the Ecofin Council for its determination (European Commission, 2002a).

At the Ecofin meeting on 12 February 2002, the Finance Ministers concluded that Germany's 'new update broadly complies with the requirements' (European Commission, 2002b: 7) and that Germany was expected to record a balanced fiscal position by 2004. The risk was that economic growth would fall and the automatic stabilisers would push the fiscal balance 'even closer to the 3% of GDP reference value' (p. 8). The Council clearly understood that any further slowdown in the German economy would generate a larger deficit. But it still demanded that 'a balanced budget position must be reached as soon as possible' (p. 8). For these technocrats the rules were binding and Germany would be cited under the EDP if it didn't bring its deficit below the 3 per cent reference value. The likely impact on unemployment and the prosperity of the German population of the enforced austerity at a time when the economy was weak was disregarded. The Council also urged Germany to ensure there was a 'decisive implementation of structural reforms . . . in particular in the labour market and in social security and benefit systems' (p. 8). The neo-liberal mindset was thus firmly in place despite the obvious risk that Germany's insipid growth would falter under the intensified fiscal austerity. The Council determined that the German government had 'effectively responded to the concerns expressed' (by promising more fiscal austerity than previously indicated) and the EDP was closed (p. 9).

At the same Ecofin meeting, the case of France was also considered. A similar narrative was recorded: downside risks of low growth pushing out the deficit; the need to be in balance or surplus by 2004; more fiscal austerity promised by the French government; the need for more cuts 'as soon as possible' in the pension system (p. 15). But there had been no 'early warning' issued to France and so no further determination was deemed necessary.

On 18 October 2002 the Commission President, Italian Romano Prodi, told the French daily newspaper *Le Monde* that 'the SGP was stupid, like all decisions that are rigid and there was a need for a more intelligent tool with more flexibility' (Leparmentier and Zecchini, 2002). The official spin that came out of the Commission's press machine in response emphasised the part of the interview where Prodi indicated that divergent economic policies within the EMU would be 'totally crazy' and that Mr Prodi remained very strong on fiscal discipline (BBC, 2002b).

German growth had stalled completely by the end of 2002 as it tried to rein in its fiscal balance to meet the SGP rules. However, worse would come as the economy moved into recession in 2003. German unemployment, already high in 2001 at 7.9 per cent, rose to new heights over the next four years: 8.7 per cent in 2002, 9.8 per cent in 2003, 10.5 per cent in 2004, and finally peaking at 11.3 per cent in 2005. This was all down to the mindless fiscal austerity that Germany adopted within the recession biases of the SGP. Millions lost their jobs as a result, while others increasingly found their jobs becoming more precarious and their wage prospects suppressed (see Chapter 15 for more discussion). If there was ever a time for reflection on how damaging the EMU structure could be, then this period should have been it.

On 19 November 2002, the Commission again reported on the 'Excessive deficit on Germany'. It noted that Germany's projected fiscal deficit for 2002 would rise from 2.8 per cent of GDP in 2001 to 3.8 per cent and 'therefore, the deficit will exceed the reference value of 3% by a significant margin' (European Commission, 2002c: 2). In addition, its public debt ratio was expected to exceed 60 per cent of GDP and would also breach the SGP threshold. As a consequence, the Commission initiated the EDP against Germany for its 'budgetary slippage' (p. 4). The 'slippage' was due to the recession and the need to expand the fiscal deficit to ensure final spending in the economy was sufficient to arrest the decline. But for the Commission, the 'slippage' was defined solely in terms of the 'reference values', which were the only targets they focused on.

The Commission explained the 'very weak' growth in terms of the decline in the construction sector as a result of the end of the reunification process, 'numerous structural impediments . . . inflexible labour market' (European Commission 2002c: 4) and its welfare system. None of these things caused the move into recession. A responsible government would have realised the reunification construction boom would end and there would be a need for alternative forms of stimulus, given the high propensity of its population to save. But trying to live within the SGP rules forced the government to withdraw any form of spending support for its economy. The 'structure' of the economy had nothing to do with it – Germany had grown at much more robust rates with this 'structure' in the past. The only fundamental 'structural' change that was impacting growth was the imposition of the inane EDP mentality.

The terminology used in the Commission's reasoning was mindboggling. They acknowledged that 'budgetary developments have been adversely affected by continued weakness of economic activity' (European Commission 2002c: 12) plus a one off flood but 'in the sense of the Treaty' the deficits could not be considered 'outside the control of the German authorities, nor . . . the result of a severe economic downturn' (p. 12). The German authorities could have cut its net spending more harshly but growth was already stalling and unemployment was rising quickly. From outside the twisted neo-liberal Groupthink, the downturn was already severe. But the SGP defined the threshold of severity as a decline in real GDP of more than 0.75 per cent in any year. This definition was totally arbitrary, like all the other SGP reference values, which meant that millions could lose their jobs without a downturn being defined as severe.

THE HEAT RISES – GERMANY CAUGHT IN THE TRAP OF ITS OWN MAKING

At any rate, the game was on. Germany was now caught up in the trap it had set for Italy, Greece and other 'suspect' nations. The Commission upped the ante on 8 January 2003 when it concluded that there was an excessive deficit in Germany (European Commission, 2003a) and accused Germany of not respecting the Treaty (European Commission, 2003b: 2). They demanded that Germany 'put an end to the present excessive deficit situation as rapidly as possible' (p. 4) by cutting net spending and retrenching its labour market protections and welfare system. The Council accepted this conclusion a few weeks later and demanded that Germany cut its deficit by 1 per cent of GDP within four months (European Council, 2003a: 4). Had this very large fiscal contraction been successful, the recession in Germany would have deepened with disastrous results. There was also no guarantee that the changes would have reduced the deficit anyway given the loss of tax revenue as economic growth faltered.

The German economy contracted in 2003 and the fiscal balance rose to 4.2 per cent of GDP up from 3.8 per cent in 2002. On 18 November 2003, the Commission recommended to the Council that Germany be declared 'non-compliant' under the EDP, which would require much harsher cuts and fines (European Commission, 2003c). The Commission statement rehearsed the myth of a 'fiscal contraction expansion', which has featured prominently in the current crisis. They claimed that a substantial fiscal reduction would not 'necessarily depress economic activity. A lack of private confidence is a key factor holding back growth . . . [and that] . . . current high saving rates . . . suggest that . . . present income levels are no serious constraint for private consumption. Indeed, consumption is being held back by high uncertainty' (p. 3). This was pure neo-liberal dogma and contrary to evidence.

The Commission failed to mention the growing angst in Germany over the Hartz reforms that had been introduced in early 2003 (see Chapter 15). The rising unemployment associated with the forced fiscal contractions and the increasing attacks on real wages associated with the Hartz reforms had undermined consumer confidence. With further fiscal contraction expected, and worsening unemployment, there were no coherent reasons for consumers to reverse their saving plans and undertake a spending spree. Further, without strong growth in consumption spending, firms could satisfy current sales with the existing capacity and therefore had no imperative or incentive to increase investment. Most firms formed the view that the economy would deteriorate over the next 12 months and yield very few profitable investment opportunities.

Later in its recommendation, the Commission actually acknowledged that 'prolonged stagnation' was more likely for Germany as it sought to cut its deficit and, as a consequence, it extended the deadline for the correction of the 'excessive deficit' by one year to 2005 (European Commission 2003c: 4). As has been the case throughout this saga, it was a case of the blind ideological adherence to the rules coming up against the obvious facts that could not be ignored. The rules were once again being 'bent', as they had been during the convergence process, and as they would be later when the really big crisis hit.

A parallel process had been going on with respect to France. The detail was very similar to the German case – economic downturn, fiscal deficits rising beyond the SGP reference values, enforced austerity, worsening growth and deficits, the technocrats mindlessly applying their rules. On 28 March 2003, the Commission published a report on the French situation, which was intended for the next Ecofin meeting. It followed an 'early warning' being issued to France in January 2003. The Commission considered that France had not taken 'sufficient measures to reduce' (European Commission 2003d: 13) its deficit. It also acknowledged the 'protracted weakness of the economy' (p. 13) but still recommended that the French government ensure the deficit did not exceed 3 per cent in 2003. On 7 May 2003, the Commission determined that there was an excessive deficit in France and the Council was advised accordingly (European Commission, 2003e). The Council agreed on 3 June 2003 (European Council, 2003b) and on 8 October 2003, it determined that France was not responding adequately to its demands for fiscal retrenchment.

A major showdown was looming.

LE PACTE DE STABILITÉ EUROPÉEN N'EST PAS INSCRIT DANS LE MARBRE

The French government was publicly hostile to the process. The problem was that the fiscal rules embedded in the SGP were 'written in stone' despite the protestation to the contrary from Francis Mer, the French Minister for Economic Affairs, Finance and Industry, in June 2003 (House of Lords, 2003). The nations had all signed up to a discipline that they found impossible to maintain if they were to meet their responsibilities to maintain domestic growth and reduce unemployment.

It was obvious that the rising deficits from 2001 were the result of 'persistently poor economic growth and more importantly, consolidation fatigue, which started soon after the launch of the single currency' (Morris et al., 2006: 15). The political reality was that the prosperity of the EMU had been suppressed for years in the race to meet the convergence criteria and there was only so much austerity that could be tolerated by the respective populations.

Further, most of the EMU nations had resorted to a range of 'one off' accounting tricks to render their fiscal balances consistent with the criteria. Once business as usual was resumed, the fiscal balances began to more closely resemble the underlying economic growth realities of the nations, which were largely inconsistent with the rigid SGP fiscal rules.

On Bastille Day 2003, the Ecofin Ministers met in Paris to consider the deficit situation. French President Jacques Chirac had pressured them to relax the fiscal rules to allow some room for growth (*The Economist*, 2003). The hostility among the other EMU partners towards the French call for an easing of the SGP was evident in the reported anger from Dutch Finance Minister Gerrit Zalm who said, 'This is July 14, the day the Bastille was stormed, and now it's the day the stability pact has been stormed. The storming of the Bastille was a better idea' (BBC, 2003). But Germany knew it had the ally in France that it needed to ignore the Commission and manipulate the Council when it came to the crunch later in 2003. Even so the Germans still tried to have it both ways. The German Finance Minister, Hans Eichel, told the press on 14 July 2003 that 'Stability is not the priority right now . . . we need growth' but then claimed that Germany was not calling for a relaxation of the rules (BBC, 2003). The inevitable Franco-German collusion on the deficit question later in 2003 would plunge Europe into crisis.

The naysayers were as usual the central bankers. The ECB was 'vehemently against any revisions' (Howarth and Loedel, 2003: 173) and demanded strict interpretation and enforcement of the Pact. While presenting the ECB's 2002 Annual Report in Strasbourg on 3 July 2003, Wim Duisenberg berated the national governments for 'a lack of ambition in the areas of both fiscal and structural reforms' and stressed 'the need to speed up the pace of structural reforms' (Duisenberg, 2003). He clearly didn't want to admit that the rising deficits reflected the failing growth caused by the imposition of the fiscal rules.

In late August 2003, the French Prime Minister, Jean-Pierre Raffarin, was in Brussels for a European Commission meeting. He called for more flexibility in the application of the SGP. There was fierce resistance within the Commission to this idea. Romano Prodi told the press that there was 'no choice but to apply the rules of the treaty' (Fuller, 2003). Raffarin had a more advanced sense of his responsibilities when he declared that his 'No. 1 duty is to mobilize all of the strengths of our country for growth and employment. And I will do everything in 2004 to make sure that we return to growth and increase employment' (Fuller, 2003).

On 4 September 2003, Raffarin again expressed this sentiment during an interview with French television station TF1, which the *Le Monde* editorial on 6 September said had demonstrated contempt for Europe. Raffarin said that while the SGP was 'important', his 'first duty' was to ensure that there was work for the French and that he was not going to compromise that for some 'accounting equations and to do some maths' to satisfy the bureaucrats in Brussels. He also said that France would not follow Germany into austerity (*Le Monde*, 2003).

THE CRISIS POINT IS REACHED

On 18 November 2003, the Commission recommended to the Council that the response of both the French and German governments to their earlier demands was inadequate under the terms of the Treaty and that further action under the EDP be triggered and a much tighter frame required for resolution. The stakes were now high. The Commission wanted both France and Germany to be sanctioned for their obdurate behaviour with respect to the rules. One should emphasise that by not implementing the scale of the fiscal cutbacks recommended by the bureaucrats, the French and German governments were, at least, saving some jobs from destruction amid the millions that were being retrenched as a result of them playing the game 'somewhat'.

Five days later, the Finance Ministers met in Brussels to vote on these recommendations. Under the Treaty, Ecofin oversaw the process, which was laid out as follows: the Commission was responsible for the surveillance system of Member State fiscal positions and would make recommendations to Ecofin if it considered there was an excessive deficit under the rules. Ecofin would then determine whether that was the case or not and, if it decided that there was an excessive deficit, it would require the offending nation to fix the problem within a short time period. If, after that time, the excessive deficit persisted then Ecofin could impose the very harsh fine.

Further, decisions taken by Ecofin are determined by the quaint construct called a 'qualified majority' (or supermajority), which is a weighted voting system such that the larger nations by population are given more weight (votes) in the process. The aim was to balance the interests of small and large member states. However, the system effectively meant that the 'big police' were able to derail any investigations against them through collusion. The weights used in 2003 were established in the Treaty of Nice, which came into force on 1 February 2003. They have been updated over time as more nations have joined the European Union and the system is now less vulnerable to the so-called 'blocking minority' (now requiring at least four states to be included in the bloc). In November 2003, there were 87 'votes' in total allocated to the 15 EU nations, with Germany, France, Italy and the UK each having ten, Spain eight, Belgium, Greece, the Netherlands and Portugal five each, and so on. A qualified majority amounted to 62 votes out of the 87 (71.3 per cent) and 26 votes (29.9 per cent) constituted a blocking minority. So Germany and France only had to do a deal with the UK or Italy, for example, to run the show in their favour (European Commission, 2012b).

The upshot was that the Ecofin Council rejected the crucial Commission recommendations in relation to both France and Germany. While a simple majority was achieved for each vote, attracting affirmative responses from Belgium, Denmark, Greece, Spain, the Netherlands, Austria, Finland and Sweden or a subset where only Eurozone nations could vote, a qualified majority failed and no decision was adopted (European Council, 2003c). The Council determined that while it had found that an excessive deficit existed in France and had recommended that nation take appropriate measures to reduce the deficit by the end of 2004, there had equally been several 'important economic and budgetary developments' (p. 16) (slower growth and rising unemployment) evident in the third quarter of 2003 which influenced its final conclusion. Accordingly, it decided that it would not act against France 'at this point in time' and would hold the EDP against France 'in abeyance for the time being' (p. 17). The same reasoning was applied to Germany. The Council had not only ignored the recommendation of the Commission, but also suspended any action under the EDP against France and Germany.

The Commission was furious with the Council's decision to let France and Germany off the hook and accused it of not providing an 'adequate explanation' (p. 22). It felt compelled to enter the following statement in the official minutes of the Ecofin meeting (p. 22):

> The Commission deeply regrets that the Council has not followed the spirit and the rules of the Treaty and the Stability and Growth Pact that were agreed unanimously by all Member States. Only a rule based system can guarantee that commitments are enforced and that all Member States are treated equally.
>
> The Commission will continue to apply the Treaty and reserves the right to examine the implications of these Council conclusions and decide on possible subsequent actions.

Where did that leave the whole enterprise? *The Guardian* newspaper in the UK reported soon after the Council had suspended the SGP that, 'Economic stagnation in France and Germany has scuppered the budgetary constraints put in place with the euro' (Tran, 2003). The Council decision to ignore the Commission's recommendation had put the SGP into 'intensive care' (Tran, 2003). Overall, the decision reflected the recognition that 'imposing financial penalties when they're already mired in economic problems made little sense' (Tran 2003). While that is a correct summation, the reality is that it was only because France and Germany were the targets of the action that this sort of recognition came to the fore. It clearly hasn't been a consideration in the case of Greece in 2010 and onwards. On 27 November 2003, Ed Crooks and George Parker wrote in the *Financial Times*:

> France and Germany won: they usually do. But the European Union is assessing the damage of a joyless victory, secured in the small hours of Tuesday

> morning, that did much more than shred the EU's fiscal rulebook ... The message was clear. The European Union has rules, but not everyone has to obey them. France and Germany, long seen as the driving force behind European integration, looked more like a pair of playground bullies. (Crooks and Parker, 2003)

A 2011 ECB paper reflected on the crisis and concluded that the 'first test' of the SGP 'failed' because 'France and Germany, among others, blocked its strict implementation by colluding in order to reject a Commission recommendation to move a step further in the direction of sanctions' (Schuknecht et al., 2011: 10). The ramifications were clear. The rules would have to be renegotiated. But before that process would begin, the 'subsequent actions' noted in the Commission's qualifying statement in the Ecofin minutes were manifested in the form of a challenge by the Commission to have the Council decision annulled by the European Court of Justice (ECJ) on the grounds that the Council had not followed the rules and procedures as set out in the Treaty.

That action began on 24 January 2004 and the ECJ was asked to clarify the powers of each relating to the EDP. On 13 July 2004, the Court brought down its decision. The legal nuances of the action and resulting decision are beyond the scope of this narrative (see Gros et al., 2004 for one account of the legal issues). But the upshot was that the Court made several determinations. First, it declared inadmissible the Commission's request that the suspension of action against France and Germany should be reversed, because a suspension ('hold in abeyance') did not constitute a decision. Second, it annulled the Council decision in favour of France and Germany on the basis that it had used the wrong procedures (European Court of Justice, 2004).

The decision was a small victory for the Commission because the ruling clearly indicated that the EMU partners could not unilaterally ignore the rules that they had formally agreed to. But the 'law breakers' got away with it because the impasse led to a renegotiation of the SGP and no sanction against France or Germany. A Pyrrhic victory nonetheless!

THE THREAT OF THE FINANCIAL MARKETS – NO RESPONSE

It is often claimed that part of the justification for the strict SGP rules is to assuage concerns in the amorphous financial markets so that governments can continue to borrow at affordable interest rates. But even though the Ecofin rejection of the Commission's recommendations plunged the SGP into crisis, there was no reaction from the financial markets to the resulting impasse. The ten-year government bond spreads relative to Germany, which are meant to reflect the risk of government default, moved by less than 0.03 per cent between 2003 and 2005. Even when the Italians threatened to leave the European Union in March 2005 there were no major deviations (Wyplosz, 2006).

The *Financial Times* reported that the financial markets saw the Ecofin rejection of the Commission's recommendation as a positive sign for growth in the EMU (Hargreaves, 2003). Ed Crooks (2003) concluded in a follow-up *Financial Times* report that 'If the European Union's fiscal rules died yesterday – at least in their strictest version – few in the financial markets mourned their passing'. The article quoted a Goldman Sachs executive as saying:

> Our view is that it is not that big a deal. It's a good thing that the stability pact in its strictest interpretation is dead . . . its interpretation is moving in the direction of allowing more cyclical leeway for budget deficits during economic downturns, and that is something we think should have been there from the beginning. (Crooks, 2003)

A DRAWN-OUT TALKFEST BUT NOT MUCH OF SUBSTANCE ACHIEVED

The upshot of this scandal was that the Commission decided to alter the SGP rules. On 3 September 2004, it communicated the intention to the Council and the European Parliament to formally work towards 'refocusing' the SGP (European Commission, 2004a). Behind the scenes, the horse trading that had been going on for months following the disastrous impasse between the Commission and the Council followed the usual script – a protracted, agonising process motivated by the deep national enmities and suspicions.

By the European summer of 2004, ten European Union states were being processed within the EDP. After the Commission-Council impasse and the resulting ECJ decision in July 2004, Germany promised to take measures to reduce its deficit by 2005 and its EDP was terminated. Some would say that its defiance of the initial process that led to the stand off had effectively terminated it anyway. But it is worth noting that Germany actually embraced a much more austere policy stance in 2005 as it started to reap export growth driven by the 'overspending' of its EMU partners.

The case against the Netherlands was also terminated in May 2005, when it recorded a deficit of 2.5 per cent for 2004. The action was stepped up against Greece in February 2005, after Eurostat revised the data for Greece back to 1997 and substantially increased the recorded Greek government deficits for 2003 and 2004. The revised 2004 result of 6.1 per cent of GDP clearly concerned Brussels. This concern was expressed in a report the Commission sent to the Council and the European Parliament, which 'acknowledged deficiencies in the compilation and reporting of fiscal statistics to the Commission' (European Commission, 2004b: 2).

We do not need to concern ourselves with the specific recommendations of that report. Suffice to say that the results led to an improvement in the quality and coverage of the statistics relating to public finances in Europe. The unfortunate aspect is that the data was still being interpreted through a neo-liberal lens and, as a consequence, incorrect inferences continued to be drawn and destructive policies proposed and implemented. The improved data should have been used as part of an overall strategy to render government fiscal policy more effective in dealing with unforeseen cyclical spending variations so that output and employment growth could be maintained. Instead, it was used as input into the continued sledgehammer approach the European Commission adopted to suppress the fiscal capacity of the Member States, which entrenched high unemployment rates as the manifestation of this folly.

An 'intense round of discussions' (European Commission, 2005a: 12) between Ecofin, the European Commission and ECB representatives followed to seek a reformulation of the SGP. Two major criticisms of the SGP emerged, one for each of the two arms of the Pact. First, the fact that a number of nations were caught up in the EDP indicated that the 'preventative arm' was not functioning effectively. Second, with the failure of the 'preventative arm' to keep fiscal balances within the specified band, the 'corrective arm' that was activated by the EDP was considered to be too inflexible and prone to pushing governments into 'pro-cyclical' policy changes – cutting spending and increasing taxes when the economy was already weak.

The French and German fiasco had highlighted the political need, at least, to address these concerns even though there was no real willingness to retreat from the idea that national governments should be significantly restricted in their fiscal latitude. In the wings were the central bankers who didn't want to give an inch. In its 2005 statement on the Ecofin report, the ECB (2005) said that it was 'seriously concerned about the proposed changes to the Stability and Growth Pact'. The ECB was also supported by various conservative academic contributions (for example, Buti et al., 2005). Their general argument was that the rules were fine but needed to be enforced more rigorously. But France and Germany were going to have none of that because they were not willing to subject their economies to the dictates of Brussels unless it was convenient to do so.

An 'extraordinary' Ecofin meeting on 20 March 2005 in Brussels finally signed off on the agreed changes to the SGP (European Council, 2005). The final changes were formalised at the Council meeting on 22–23 March 2005 in Brussels. The Commission press release of 27 June 2005 reported on the Council decision to adopt the 'two modified regulations' to the SGP (European Commission, 2005b). The key aspects of the SGP were left unchanged because otherwise the Treaty would have to be altered. But there were some cosmetic and deeper changes made.

The main changes were as follows (European Commission, 2005b):

- Medium-term budgetary objectives (MTO) will be differentiated to take into account the diversity of economic and budgetary positions and their sustainability. They will range from a deficit of 1% of GDP to a balance or surplus for euro area and ERM II countries.
- Euro area and ERM II countries that have not yet reached their MTO will have to pursue an annual improvement of 0.5% of GDP as a benchmark of their cyclically adjusted balance, net of one-off measures. A higher effort should be pursued in good times.
- Member States having implemented major structural reforms with a verifiable impact on the long-term sustainability of public finances will be allowed to temporarily deviate from the MTO or the adjustment path towards it.

While retaining the 3 per cent and 60 per cent reference values 'without prejudice' they agreed to change the definition of a 'severe economic downturn' from an annual fall in real output of at least 2 per cent to something less defined – an 'excess over the reference value which results from negative growth . . . or from accumulated loss of output during a protracted period of very low growth' (European Commission, 2005b: 33). Further, the new agreement also emphasised that all 'other relevant factors' (p. 34) should be fully considered before an excessive deficit is declared as Stage 1 of the EDP. It also specified the relevant factors that might be considered. The rules now recognised that if a nation had undertaken so-called 'fiscal consolidation efforts in "good times"' (p. 34), that is, had cut government spending when growth was strong, it would be viewed more sympathetically in bad times compared to a government that had not done so. Further, if a nation were implementing the 'Lisbon agenda', then any implications arising from that for its fiscal balance would be taken into account. That issue is considered in the next section.

The changes provided more 'wriggle room' for nations to buy time before an EDP would be invoked. It was a more flexible, but still a rigidly unworkable, framework. The conditionality was defined in such general terms that the Ecofin could be very lenient or very tough depending on the political bargaining power of the nation concerned. While the politicians constructed the changes as 'reforms', the reality was that they had relaxed their rules. But the ideology remained and there was still insufficient fiscal latitude to meet likely changes in economic circumstances. The changed rules and procedures that were finally agreed upon did not alter the fact that, if followed and/or enforced, they biased the Eurozone to crisis.

The changes ensured that Germany and France could largely do what they wanted, which was the objective of the exercise. On the other hand, the changes were sufficiently defined to provide the Council with the power to impose harsh straitjackets on nations such as Greece, which possessed a low weighting in Ecofin's qualified majority voting system.

THE REVISED SGP AND THE EUROPEAN EMPLOYMENT STRATEGY – IDEOLOGICAL PARTNERS

The SGP was also embedded more formally in the dysfunctional labour market strategy that had infested Europe and elsewhere since the release of the OECD's Jobs Study in 1994 (OECD, 1994). The history of the European Union tells us that as one highly promoted strategy for 'sustainable jobs and growth' fails, a new ill-thought-out strategy is announced as the next operational action plan.

The OECD Jobs Study led to governments abandoning their responsibility for achieving and sustaining full employment. Unemployment was no longer considered to be a macroeconomic phenomenon. Prior to the neo-liberal resurgence, mass unemployment was understood, correctly, to reflect a systemic failure to create enough jobs and that the attainment of full employment required that national governments take responsibility for maintaining sufficient total spending to generate the necessary jobs. The neo-liberal era replaced that understanding with the counter factual allegation that unemployment was an individual problem. Accordingly, the unemployed were alleged to have 'chosen' that state, because they had failed to invest in appropriate skill development; or failed to search for available opportunities with sufficient effort or rigour; and/or had become 'work shy' and overly selective in the jobs they would be prepared to accept. The existence of unemployment benefits merely subsidised this sloth.

In this new world, government should only be responsible for the diminished goal of achieving 'full employability', which required it to 'prepare' individuals for work (for example, by forcing participation in training schemes) and to eliminate disincentives to work. With no strong evidence base to justify their claims, the neo-liberals traced these disincentives to income support frameworks and labour market regulation (for example, unfair dismissal legislation). Concerted political campaigns by neo-liberal governments aided and abetted by a capitalist class intent on regaining total control of workplaces, hectored communities into accepting that mass unemployment and rising underemployment was no longer the responsibility of government. The strategy was clear. The politicians and their supporting institutions wanted to break the existing nexus between macroeconomic policy settings and mass unemployment that had defined the post World War II period up to the 1980s. Instead they chose to reconstruct the unemployment 'solution' in terms of an alleged need for income support cuts, labour market deregulation and heavy demands on the unemployed themselves to satisfy 'activity tests' in return for declining real benefit income.

The neo-liberal narrative was formalised in the Jobs Study published in October 1994 by the Paris-based Organisation for Economic Co-operation and Development (OECD). Its main message (OECD, 1994, vii) accurately summarised the state of policy thinking that has dominated since the 1990s:

> . . . it is an inability of OECD economies and societies to adapt rapidly and innovatively to a world of rapid structural change that is the principal cause of high and persistent unemployment . . . Consequently, the main thrust of the study was directed towards identifying the institutions, rules and regulations, and practices and policies which have weakened the capacity of OECD countries to adapt and to innovate, and to search for appropriate policy responses in all these areas . . . Action is required in all areas simultaneously for several reasons. First, the roots of structural unemployment have penetrated many if not all areas of the socioeconomic fabric; second, the political difficulties of implementing several of these policies call for a comprehensive strategy . . . third, there are synergies to exploit if various microeconomic polices are pursued in a co-ordinated way, both with regard to each other and the macroeconomic policy stance.

The Jobs Study also ratified the growing macroeconomic conservatism by articulating that the major task for macroeconomic policy was to allow governments to 'work towards creating a healthy, stable and predictable environment allowing sustained growth of investment, output and employment. This implies a reduction in structural budget deficits and public sector debt over the medium term . . . [together with] . . . low inflation' (OECD 1994: 74).

Prior to the GFC, the OECD consistently claimed that its policy recommendations had been successful in countries that had implemented them. Unfortunately, the reality was (and is) strikingly at odds with this political hubris. Even with more than a decade of fairly stable economic growth in most nations leading up to the crisis, high states of labour underutilisation and low to moderate economic growth were the norm. Further, underemployment became an increasingly significant source of wasted labour and opportunities for youth remained limited. The neo-liberal period has also been marked by significant increases in income inequality, and research now clearly shows that this undermines the potential for growth. The only achievement was that inflation was stabilised, although it was the severity of the 1991 recession that expunged inflationary expectations from the OECD block rather than so-called 'structural' reforms. Since that time, labour costs were kept down by harsh industrial relations deregulation and a concerted attack on the labour unions.

The OECD was following the well-trodden path of the IMF in redefining itself to maintain its hegemony in the public debate. The IMF lost its *raison d'etre* when the Bretton Woods system of fixed exchange rates collapsed in 1971. The IMF was created as a core institution within that system and after 1971 had no meaningful purpose to fulfil. Joseph Stiglitz (2002: 42) provided a fascinating account of how the IMF sought to dominate thinking about economic policy in both developed and developing countries to give it a new role to play. Not only did he strongly criticise the 'one size fits all' nature of the IMF policy prescriptions, but he also observed that:

> The IMF is like so many bureaucracies; it has repeatedly sought to extend what it does, beyond the objectives originally assigned to it. As IMF's mission creep brought it outside its core area of competency in macroeconomics, into structural issues such as privatisation, labour markets, pension reforms and so forth . . .

He argued that the combination of the IMF's fierce promotion of the current dominant neo-liberal ideology in economics, its simplistic yet well-defined policy framework and its good political contacts in the Western world have rendered it a very powerful institution, which often usurped the World Bank's role in its dealing with poor countries. Stiglitz was also critical of the World Bank but that is another story.

Jörg Dostal's (2004) account of how the OECD framed European Union welfare and labour market policies reveals striking similarities to the modus operandi adopted by the IMF. Dostal describes how the OECD deliberately used the 1994 Jobs Study to successfully reposition itself in the policy debate. Dostal (2004: 41) said that, 'preparation for the economic and monetary union separated macroeconomic policy making from the agenda of employment policy . . . [in Europe] . . . Instead, liberal labour market theorists explained unemployment as a structural issue arising from over-regulation of the wage labour relationship and over-generous wage replacement payments'.

The European Commission decided to tailor its own 'jobs strategy' to accord with the OECD agenda. At the European Council meeting in Essen on 9–10 December 1994, it formalised the so-called 'Essen Strategy', which effectively cloned the OECD Jobs Study as European Union policy. This strategy became known as the European Employment Strategy (EES) and was activated under Article 2 of the Treaty of Amsterdam (European Commission, 2012b), which updated the Treaty of Maastricht. The 'Title IX Employment' (Articles 145–150) was formally included in the Treaty of the Functioning of the European Union for the first time and fleshed out the EES. Accordingly, the Member States would 'work towards developing a coordinated strategy for employment and particularly for promoting a skilled, trained and adaptable workforce and labour markets responsive to economic change' (European Commission, 2012b).

The four pillars of the EES closely resemble the key points in the Jobs Study: employability, entrepreneurship, adaptability and gender equality. This is classic OECD speak. Bernard Casey (2004) presented a detailed overview of the similarities between the recommendations of both strategies. He said the recommendations of both reflect a 'structural' interpretation of unemployment, 'symptomatic of an insufficient ability to adapt to change . . . [implying] . . . a focus on policies concerned with labour' (p.5) (see also Mitchell and Muysken, 2006).

The relevant connection here is that the EES was a relatively weak framework, a lot of talk and documentation with little real action and intent. Its impact pales into insignificance when considered against the damage that the SGP was doing to employment in the Eurozone (see also Watt, 2004). The EES was subsumed within the 'Lisbon Strategy' formulated in 2000, which aimed 'to strengthen employment, economic reform and social cohesion as part of a knowledge-based economy' and to make Europe, by 2010, 'the most competitive and the most dynamic knowledge-based economy in the world' (European Council, 2000).

The irony, or should we say the exemplification, of what went wrong with European policy-making circles was revealed in the opening paragraphs of the Lisbon conclusions. On the one hand, the 'Union is experiencing its best macro-economic outlook for a generation . . . [as a result] . . . of stability-oriented monetary policy supported by sound fiscal policies' (European Council 2000). On the other hand, it is stated that these 'strengths should not distract our attention from a number of weaknesses. More than 15 million Europeans are still out of work' and the 'employment rate is too low'. That sort of amazing disconnect could only be made by those blinded by the neo-liberal ideology!

The Lisbon Strategy cloned the Jobs Study narrative about the causes of unemployment and the rejection of active fiscal policy in favour of 'structural policy'. This disconnect was formalised in the changes made in 2005 to the SGP. The European Council 'relaunched' the Lisbon Strategy in March 2005 recognising that it had not achieved its ends, and aimed to better 'interlink' fiscal policy with the employment strategy on the false premise that restricting the flexibility of governments to run fiscal deficits would 'enhance the contribution of fiscal policy to economic growth and support progress towards realising the Lisbon strategy' (European Council, 2005: 22). Recent history has demonstrated that this strategy failed because it was based on false understandings of how the economy operates.

However, this 'interlinking' was accommodated in the revised SGP by allowing Member States to use the progress towards 'structural reforms' as an offset to its current fiscal position under the 'all other relevant factors' clause in the EDP. The idea seemed to be that if a nation had, for example, introduced harsh labour market or welfare system reforms, which increased its fiscal deficit (presumably because total spending fell as incomes were cut and this undermined tax revenue), then it could be excused from the EDP for a time. In the Council's perverted reasoning, these attacks on prosperity would lead to long-term 'fiscal sustainability' (European Council 2005: 12). There was no clear narrative enlightening us on how this strategy would work for all countries together. There were grand statements about how nations would increase competitiveness and become export behemoths! Given the extent of intra Eurozone trade, it was obvious that Germany's export strength, for example, was crucially reliant on other Eurozone nations running external deficits. But the policy makers didn't want to see it that way.

15. The German 'jobwunder'

MODELL DEUTSCHLAND – GERMAN JOBS SHRINK

The German government played a rather particular role in the shift in employment mixes in the early days of the euro. A reasonable argument can be made that Gerhard Schröder helped cause the Eurozone crisis. His government's response to the restrictions that Germany encountered on entering the EMU are certainly one of the least focused upon parts of the story. Before the EMU, the Bundesbank had regularly left the mark undervalued in international currency markets to ensure the German export sector maintained competitiveness. The regular complaint from France and others during the EMS years was that the grossly undervalued mark forced them to reduce domestic demand and increase unemployment in order to maintain the agreed EMS parities.

Upon entering the EMU, Schröder was also under immense political pressure to do something about the high unemployment in the East after reunification. Without the capacity to manipulate the exchange rate, the Germans understood that they had to reduce domestic production costs and inflation rates relative to other nations, in order to retain competitiveness. The Germans thus took the so-called 'internal devaluation' route, that is all the rage in Europe now, well before the crisis; a move which ultimately has made the crisis worse.

On 14 March 2003, Schröder unveiled his Government's 'Agenda 2010', which was aligned in concept, design and timeframe with the EU's Lisbon Strategy, and signified that his coalition government was now unambiguously pursuing a neo-liberal agenda. Agenda 2010 aimed to attack income support systems. It was dressed up in the language of flexibility and incentive, but was based on the mainstream view that mass unemployment was the result of a workforce rendered lazy by the welfare system, rather than the more obvious alternative, that it arose due to a shortage of jobs.

The so-called 'Hartz reforms' were a major plank of the strategy and resulted from a 2002 commission of enquiry, presided over by and named after Peter Hartz, a key Volkswagen executive. Hartz himself was lauded at the time by the neo-liberal cheer squad, but by 2007 was sentenced to a prison term for corruption and in disgrace. The aim of the 'reforms' was clear: unemployment benefits had to be cut and job protections had to go. The recommendations were fully endorsed by the Schröder government and introduced in four tranches, Hartz I to IV, starting in January 2003. The changes associated with Hartz I to Hartz III took place over 2003 and 2004, while Hartz IV began in January 2005. The changes were far reaching in terms of the existing labour market policy that had been stable for several decades. The changes were consistent with those that have been pursued in other industrialised countries, following the agenda outlined in the OECD's Job Study in 1994. The so-called supply-side focus advocated that continued income support should be conditional on a raft of increasingly onerous activity tests and training schemes. Further, governments abandoned their responsibility to reduce unemployment with properly targeted job creation schemes. Public employment agencies were privatised, spawning a new private sector 'industry', the management of the unemployed!

The Hartz reforms accelerated the casualisation of the labour market and increased the precariousness of work. Hartz II introduced new types of employment, the 'mini-job' and the 'midi-job', and there was a sharp fall in regular employment as a consequence. Mini-jobs provide marginal employment with no security or entitlements and allow workers to earn up to 450 euros per month without paying taxes, while the on-costs for employers are significantly lower. While the worker has no tax obligations, they also receive no social security protection or pension entitlements. A job is classified as a 'midi-job' or a 'low wage' job if the monthly wage is between 450 and 850 euros and placed different responsibilities on employers to pay on-costs and workers to pay taxes.

The neo-liberal interpretation of these changes is that Germany underwent a 'jobwunder', or jobs miracle (for example, Caliendo and Wrohlich, 2006). However the speedy increase in employment can also be viewed less optimistically. *The Economist* (2007) concluded that:

> From the bottom of the cycle, in mid 2003, employment grew much less quickly than in previous upturns. And much of the rise took the form of 'mini jobs' . . . By contrast, employment in the 'primary' labour market, where social insurance contributions are compulsory, is still well below what it was seven years ago.

Figure 15.1 shows the growth of mini-jobs in Germany from the start of the scheme in June 2003. In September 2013, there were 7.4 million mini-jobs, which represented 17.4 per cent of the labour force between 15 and 64 years of age. The proportion has been fairly steady since late 2007 after a rapid increase in the earlier years of the scheme. The rapid increase in mini-jobs meant an increasing (and sizeable) proportion of the German workforce has been forced to work in precarious jobs with extremely low

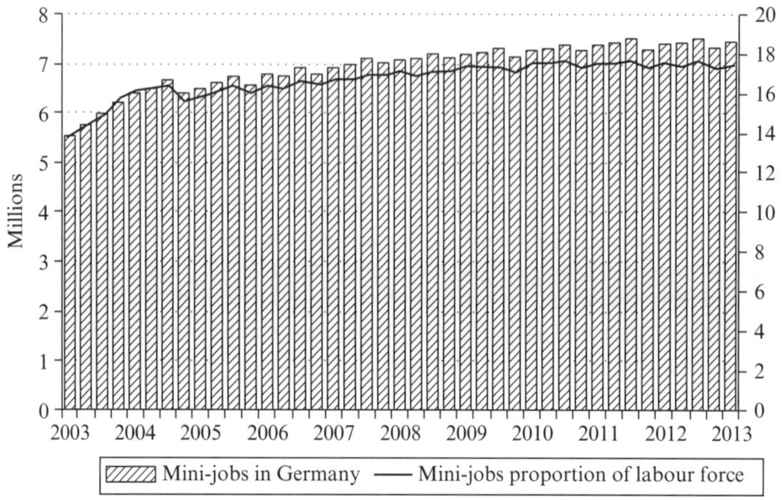

Source: Analyse des Arbeitsmarktes für Frauen und Männer, 2.8 Tabelle: Geringfügig entlohnt Beschäftigte am Arbeitsort nach Geschlecht in Deutschland, Statistik der Bundesagentur für Arbeit. Labour Force data from Eurostat, Table lfsi_act_q.

Figure 15.1 Mini-jobs in Germany, 2003–13, '000s and per cent

pay and is excluded from enjoying the benefits of national income growth and the chance to accumulate pension entitlements. It is also a ticking 'time bomb' because these workers will face long-term poverty once they reach retirement age.

The neo-liberals claim that part time work such as the German mini-jobs provide a greater chance of full time work for those who would otherwise remain unemployed, the so-called 'stepping stone' hypothesis. This hypothesis has several components. First, the mini-jobs provide work experience while unemployment leads to skill atrophy. Second, the mini-job workers signal their ability and willingness to accept work relative to those who remain in unemployment. Third, participating in the mini-jobs enlarges the social network of job seekers, which in turn provides valuable linkages to a wider knowledge of job vacancies. The evidence in Germany (and everywhere else for that matter) refutes all these claims (see Bill et al., 2007).

A joint workshop on transitions from marginal employment in 2010, organised by the Institut Arbeit und Qualifikation (IAQ) at the Universität Duisburg-Essen and der Uni und dem Wirtschafts- und Sozialwissenschaftlichen Institut (WSI) at the Hans-Böckler Foundation, found that while employers are increasingly splitting regular jobs into low paid and insecure mini-jobs, there was no evidence of large scale worker transition from mini-jobs to other, more regular work (Universität Duisburg-Essen, 2010). Mini-job workers are increasingly trapped in this form of marginalised employment.

Further, with no minimum wage in Germany until recently, these structural changes caused pay differentials to widen considerably over the last decade. In a comparative analysis of German low-wage workers with 17 other European nations for 2010, Thomas Rhein, from the Institute for Employment Research (IAB), which is attached to the German Federal Employment Agency, found that the low wage threshold for Germany was 9.54 euros per hour. Rhein (2013: 3) found that 24.2 per cent of German workers in 2010 received less than this hourly rate. Rhein (2013: 3) noted that only Lithuania (27.5 per cent) had a higher proportion of workers in the low wage category.

A MASSIVE REDISTRIBUTION OF NATIONAL INCOME TO PROFITS

In general, German real wages (the purchasing power equivalent of the wages received by workers) failed to keep pace with growth in productivity (how much workers were producing each hour) and as a result there was a massive redistribution of national income to profits. The share of wages as a percentage of GDP in Germany went from 60.6 per cent in 2000 to 55.1 per cent in 2007. Over the same period there was no discernible downward movement for France or the PIIGS (Portugal, Ireland, Italy, Greece and Spain). Figure 15.2 shows the movement in wage shares in national income (indexed to 100 at 2000) from 2000 to 2013 for Germany, France and the PIIGS (average of individual nations). The index numbers are interpreted as deviations in percentages from the base of 100. So by 2007, Germany had reduced its wage share by 9 per cent on its 2000 value. The rise in the shares during the crisis was largely driven by the substantial declines in national GDP (output), the denominator of the ratio.

Why does this matter? Until the early 2000s, real wages and labour productivity had typically moved together in Germany as they did in most advanced nations. If real wages and labour productivity grow proportionately over time, the share of total national income that workers (wage earners) receive remains constant. Indeed, this relationship was so constant that Cambridge economist Nicholas Kaldor listed it as one of six 'stylised facts' about economic growth (Kaldor, 1957). However, once the neo-liberal attacks on the capacity of workers to secure wage increases intensified during the 1980s (and later in Germany), a gap between the

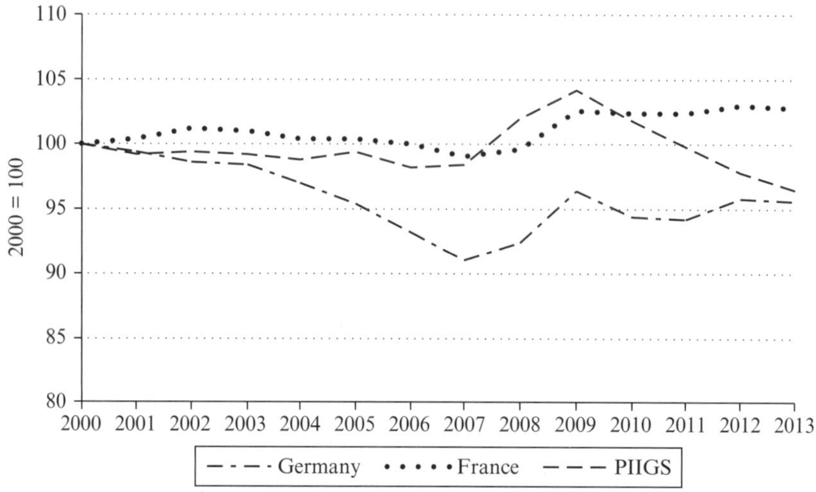

Note: PIIGS are Portugal, Ireland, Italy, Greece and Spain.

Source: Eurostat AMECO database.

Figure 15.2 Index of wage share movements in Germany, France and the PIIGS, 2000–2013, 2000 = 100

growth in real wages and productivity growth widened. This led to a major shift in national income shares away from workers towards profits.

The capitalist dilemma was that real wages typically had to grow in line with productivity to ensure that all the goods produced were sold. If, over time, workers were producing more per hour, then they had to be paid more per hour in real terms to ensure their purchasing power growth was sufficient to consume the extra production being pushed out into the markets. How does economic growth sustain itself when labour productivity growth outstrips the growth in the real wage, especially at the same time as governments were trying to reduce their deficits and thus their contribution to total spending in their economies? How does the economy recycle the rising profit share to overcome the declining capacity of workers to consume?

The neo-liberals found a new way to solve the dilemma. The 'solution' was so-called 'financial engineering', which pushed ever increasing debt onto households and firms in many nations. The credit expansion sustained the workers' purchasing power, but also delivered an interest bonus to capital while real wages growth continued to be suppressed. Households, in particular, were enticed by lower interest rates and the vehement marketing strategies of the financial engineers. It seemed too good to be true and it was.

GERMANY SUPPRESSES DOMESTIC DEMAND

The funds to underwrite this credit explosion came from the redistributed national income towards profits. For some nations, such as Germany, the large export surpluses also provided the funds to loan out to other nations. Germany didn't experience the same credit explosion as other nations but German banks were prominent in the debt build up elsewhere in Europe. The suppression of real wages growth in Germany and the growth in the (very) low wage mini-jobs meant that Germany severely stifled domestic spending up to 2005. Figure 15.3 shows the index of domestic demand (total spending on goods and services by residents, including imports) for Germany, France and the PIIGS (average) from 2000 to 2013. Schröder's austerity policies forced harsh domestic restraint onto German workers, which meant that Germany could only grow through widening export surpluses.

The suppression of consumption in Germany and the reliance on exports to maintain growth was very damaging to the peripheral states.

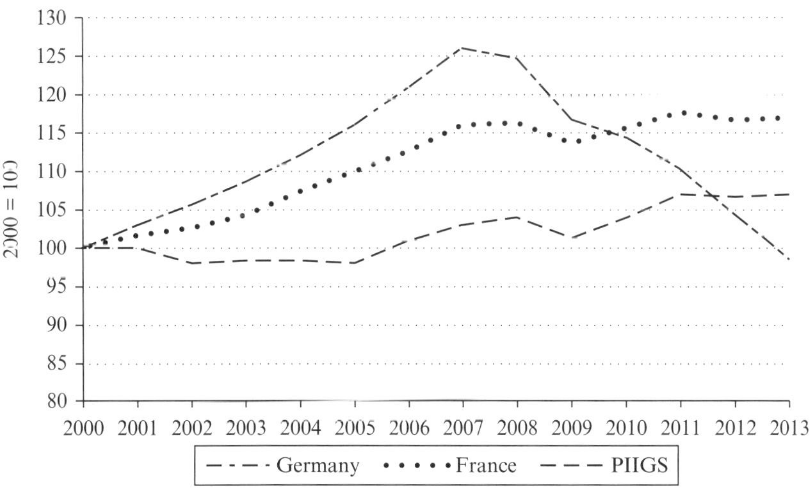

Source: Eurostat, National Accounts.

Figure 15.3 Domestic demand, Germany, France and the PIIGS, 2000–2013, 2000 = 100

The growth in employment in Germany in the lead up to the crisis was not due to a well-functioning monetary union. Rather it reflected its malfunctioning because it depended on widening trade imbalances, huge surpluses in Germany and some of its neighbours against widening deficits in the periphery, covered by unsustainable capital flows from the former to the latter. That sort of unilateralism is not sensible in a monetary union, especially one that deliberately eschewed a federal fiscal transfer system. It not only undermined the welfare of Germany's EMU partners, but also meant that the living standards of German workers were reduced.

EXTERNAL IMBALANCES GROW IN EUROPE AS GERMANY GAMES ITS EMU PARTNERS

The trade imbalances that accompanied the shifts in employment in various nations put the employment data presented in Chapter 13 in context. In the early days of the Eurozone, there were dramatic shifts in the current account balances (which reflect trade and income flows between nations). Germany's 'mercantilist' strategy dominated the early years and they started to record very large external surpluses which were mirrored by expanding external deficits in the peripheral economies (the PIIGS) (Figure 15.4). The two movements were intrinsically linked.

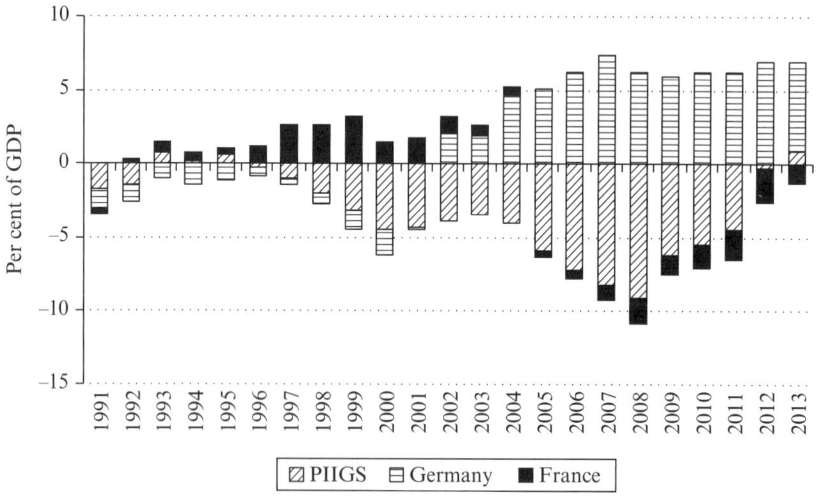

Source: IMF World Economic Outlook database.

Figure 15.4 Current account balances, 1991–2013, per cent of GDP

The German approach overall had overtones of the old canard of federal systems, 'smokestack chasing'. One of the problems that federal systems can encounter is disparate regional development (in states or sub-state regions) driven by tax and other 'business cost' concessions that a state might offer business firms to entice them to locate there. The states thus compete for firms and the concessions granted often end up countering any economic value that the activity might bring to the state. There is a large literature which shows how this practice not only undermines the welfare of other regions in the federal system, but also compromises the position of the state doing the 'chasing'. Germany adopted a similar sort of gaming strategy with its EMU neighbours.

What are these current account imbalances that commentators talk about all the time? For an economy as a whole, imports are real goods and services coming into the nation from abroad and as such represent a real benefit to residents. Conversely, exports are real goods and services that are sold to foreigners. Exports represent a real cost to residents because the real resources (labour, capital and other productive inputs) embodied in them become unavailable to the local residents for their own use. It is obvious that the only motivation for a nation to export is to gain foreign currency, which in turn, allows the nation to purchase imported goods and services that it does not produce itself. If imports exceed exports then a nation is able enjoy a higher material living standard by consuming more goods and services than it produces for foreigners. Transactions between nations also involve financial flows, which are the currency flows in and out of a nation in search of returns on financial assets or other investments (for example, direct investment in a factory in another country).

All transactions between a nation and the rest of the world are recorded in the balance of payments, which national statistical agencies assemble under agreed accounting rules. There are two main accounts in the balance of payments – the current account and the capital account. The former records exports and imports of goods and services and income flows between nations (for example, dividends on investments abroad). If a nation runs a current account surplus, it means that the sum of its exports of goods and services plus investment income received from abroad exceeds the spending on imports and income paid to foreigners. A surplus means that the external sector is contributing to total spending in the domestic economy and helping it grow. A deficit indicates the opposite.

The capital account records the financial side of the current account transactions, including the purchase and sale of financial assets such as shares to foreigners, the purchase and sale of land to foreigners and capital transfers between nations.

What happens if a nation exports more than it imports (ignore, for

16. European Groupthink: denial on a grand scale

THE MELTDOWN BEGINS

Before the crisis really hit Europe, the President of the European Commission, José Manuel Barroso, was more concerned about calls for protection from China by the Member States than the growing financial turmoil in world markets. He told the *Financial Times* in March 2008 that:

> We certainly have no intention at all of having some kind of European super-regulator . . . We think innovation in financial markets is good. It's been good for financial institutions, business and consumers . . . Of course, we cannot be completely immune to the situation in America, but we think there is no rational reason to fear a recession in Europe. (Barber and Barber, 2008)

It was early into his second five-year term as President and he was as wrong as he would ever be. The 'sickly premature baby', an epithet for the euro coined by Gerhard Schröder during the 1998 German Federal election campaign, had already experienced a difficult childhood. But at the time Barroso was exuding his normal political confidence, its very existence was at stake.

The US sub-prime mortgage market showed signs of stress in late 2006 with the sharp increase in defaults. As 2007 unfolded, several of the key mortgage originators such as Countrywide reported a rising incidence of late payments and overall delinquencies, particularly on loans where no prior equity had been provided by borrowers, who often had poor credit ratings and little income. These mortgages were packaged into complex financial products and sold on to other investors, many of whom had no capacity to judge the overall risk of their purchases. The free market mania was unravelling quickly.

On 9 August 2007, the world's financial troubles became more evident when the large French bank BNP Paribas (sixth largest in Europe) froze the accounts of three of its hedge funds (Parvest Dynamic, Euribor and Eonia) worth some $US2.2 billion. The bank said that it had lost the capacity to calculate the value of the funds because they were exposed to unknown risks in the US sub-prime market. In effect it had run out of cash because its assets were becoming untradeable in the financial markets. It was becoming obvious that increasing numbers of US mortgage holders were defaulting on their loans and this was reducing the value of the core assets held by the major banks. Key markets that had been providing funds to banks dried up more or less instantly. Earlier in the same week, the US investment bank Bear Stearns admitted that two of its mortgage hedge funds had collapsed. Within a day, several major investment funds in the US admitted large losses and several of them had to issue statements assuring depositors that they had sufficient liquidity. The statements in many cases would prove false. The dominoes, which had been lining up for some years under the cover of the Great Moderation hubris, were starting to topple.

The response of the US Federal Reserve Bank provides an interesting exposé of how the emerging crisis left the official regulators and officials flat-footed. Two days before BNP Paribas froze the accounts, the Federal Open Market Committee of the Federal Reserve claimed that while there had been some volatility in the financial markets in recent weeks, which had led to tighter credit conditions, the US economy 'seems likely to continue to expand' and the 'Committee's predominant policy concern remains the risk that inflation will fail to moderate' (Federal Reserve Bank, 2007a). Three days later, an updated statement was released saying that the Federal Reserve was 'providing liquidity to facilitate the orderly functioning of financial markets' and that if depository institutions were struggling to get funds 'the discount window' was always 'available as a source of funding' (Federal Reserve Bank, 2007b). On 17 August the Federal Reserve acknowledged that 'Financial market conditions have deteriorated' and that the 'downside risks to growth have increased appreciably' (Federal Reserve Bank, 2007c). At that stage, they cut their lending rate to banks to restore orderly conditions in financial markets. Central banks around the world started to provide billions in various currencies to the private banks in an attempt to head off a 'liquidity crisis', that is, to save the banks from running out of cash. The officials had moved from a state of smug confidence to full-scale panic in just over a week, which indicated how little they had understood the damaging consequences of their misguided financial deregulation agenda.

The UK Northern Rock Building Society typified the madness that prevailed prior to the crisis. It exploited the deregulated and poorly supervised banking environment to grow far beyond its capacities through a series of takeovers of smaller building societies. The expansion strategy involved it borrowing heavily to fund its mortgage growth and then reselling the assets in the international market. That market collapsed in 2007 and Northern Rock was thus unable to service its considerable stock of debt. On 14 September 2007, it had to seek emergency assistance from the Bank of England because it had run out of cash, but once this news became public, its depositors demanded their cash back. It was the first bank run in the UK for 150 years. Early in 2008, the bank was nationalised, like so many other zombie financial institutions throughout the world. At any rate, the GFC had begun.

Despite the massive support to the private banks coming from the central banks in each nation, the crisis worsened in 2008 as many more banks in the US and elsewhere started to collapse. The first large collapse was the California-based IndyMac Bank in July 2008. It had been a large sub-prime lender and could not find buyers for its failing assets. Events unfolded quickly in September and October, when the crisis brought down many major financial institutions (for example, Lehman Brothers, Fannie Mae, Freddie Mac, Washington Mutual, AIG, Wachovia, Citigroup, and Merrill Lynch). Some collapsed completely, others were sold in 'fire sales' to former competitors, and others were nationalised. The September 2008 turmoil in the money markets (massive withdrawals) effectively meant that firms were left unable to service maturing debts. The neo-liberal myth of self-regulating markets delivering efficiency and prosperity was being laid bare. The urgency for large-scale government intervention to prevent a complete financial meltdown and mass bankruptcies of both good and bad companies became obvious. On 3 October 2008, the US government passed the 'Emergency Economic Stabilization Act of 2008', which effectively saw the US Treasury committing to buy up around $US700 billion in failed mortgage-backed assets from investment banks and provide cash to the banks. On 8 October 2008, the British government announced that it had provided a bank bailout package equal to around £500 billion to support the banking system as the turmoil started to impact on the confidence of depositors.

The crisis quickly spread into the so-called 'real' economy as banks stopped lending, consumers stopped spending as their estimates of wealth, particularly their home equity, fell dramatically; firms stopped investing in new capital equipment as sales dried up; and major sectors such as the construction industry nearly collapsed with large scale employment losses. The government bailouts to that point had been concentrated on saving the banks. But what mattered most was maintaining sufficient spending to avoid the huge output and employment losses that would arise. Unfortunately, the fiscal responses were largely insufficient to avoid these losses.

There was also a sense of denial among the European policy makers. On 3 November 2008, the European Commission published its 'Autumn economic forecast 2008–2010', which predicted that 'European Union economic growth should be 1.4% in 2008, half what it was in 2007, and

Table 16.1 Real GDP growth, change in employment and unemployment, selected European nations, 2008–10

	GDP growth (%)		Employment (000s)			Unemployment (% points)		
	2008	2009	2008	2009	2010	2008	2009	2010
EU28	0.4	−4.5	2494.1	−3870.1	−1617.1	−0.2	2.0	0.6
E17	0.4	−4.4	1426.5	−2641.3	−770.5	0.1	1.9	0.6
BEL	1.0	−2.8	65.6	−25.2	68.0	−0.5	0.9	0.4
GER	1.1	−5.2	552.8	−70.4	266.7	−1.2	0.3	−0.7
EST	−4.1	−14.1	1.2	−60.7	−24.9	0.9	8.0	3.2
IRE	−2.1	−6.5	−15.3	−139.9	−79.1	1.7	5.6	1.9
GRE	−0.2	−3.1	49.6	−50.7	−120.1	−0.6	1.8	3.1
SPA	0.9	−3.9	−98.4	−1369.6	−431.5	3.1	6.6	2.0
FRA	−0.1	−3.2	334.4	−251.5	39.8	−0.5	1.6	0.2
ITA	−1.2	−5.5	182.9	−379.7	−152.7	0.6	1.1	0.6
CYP	3.7	−1.9	5.0	0.0	12.3	−0.2	1.7	0.9
LAT	−2.8	−17.7	6.5	−141.4	−42.2	1.6	9.8	2.0
LUX	−0.7	−5.5	−0.5	14.8	3.6	0.7	0.2	−0.5
MAL	3.8	−2.8	3.7	0.8	3.5	−0.5	0.9	0.0
NLD	1.9	−3.7	129.2	3.4	−225.9	−0.5	0.6	0.8
AUT	1.5	−3.8	62.1	−12.4	18.8	−0.6	1.0	−0.4
POR	0.0	−2.9	28.1	−143.7	−75.9	−0.4	2.1	1.4
SLV	3.4	−7.9	10.9	−15.4	−14.7	−0.5	1.5	1.4
SLK	5.8	−4.9	76.0	−67.4	−48.8	−1.6	2.5	2.4
FIN	0.3	−8.5	39.3	−73.6	−9.8	−0.5	1.8	0.2

Source: Eurostat tables, GDP (nama_gdp_k), Employment (lfsi_emp_a) and Unemployment (une_rt_a).

drop even more sharply in 2009 to 0.2% before recovering gradually to 1.1% in 2010 (1.2%, 0.1% and 0.9%, respectively, for the euro area)' (European Commission, 2008: 1). Further, they predicted that 'employment is set to increase only marginally in 2009–2010' and 'unemployment is expected to rise by about 1 pp' (p. 1). Table 16.1 shows the evolution of real GDP growth in 2008 and 2009, the change in employment (000s) and unemployment (points) over 2008, 2009 and 2010. The slowdown in real GDP growth in 2008 was substantially above the forecasts, but worse was to come in 2009 when the EU economy overall shrank by 4.5 per cent and the Eurozone by 4.4 per cent. Further, employment fell substantially in 2008 and 2009. Millions of jobs evaporated and unemployment rose by 2.5 times more than was predicted. The Commission's economic forecasting models, based on neo-liberal economic theories, were clearly deeply flawed.

THE SUCCESS OF FISCAL STIMULUS

There is a simple and well-known policy solution for a nation confronted with a collapse of private spending. The US government knew what to do: ease monetary conditions and introduce a large-scale fiscal stimulus. The Chinese government did the same, as did the Australian government and several others. All the governments that followed the basic rules of macroeconomics that spending equals income, which drives employment, were able to offset, to varying degrees, the private sector meltdown. Australia's fiscal stimulus package was large enough and was introduced early enough to allow it to avoid a recession altogether. Subsequent evaluations by government bodies including the American Congressional Budget Office (CBO), the Australian Treasury and many other economists found that the fiscal interventions were highly successful albeit too conservative (for example CBO, 2011; Blinder and Zandi, 2010a; and Australian Treasury, 2009). The Australian Treasury concluded that discretionary fiscal policy changes were estimated to be around 2.4 times more effective than monetary policy changes, even though the cuts in interest rates were of record proportions.

The fact that many of these same governments sooner or later were bullied by the conservative political lobbies into withdrawing or modifying the stimulus packages, which then undermined the emerging recoveries they had earlier created, doesn't alter the point. The GFC clearly demonstrated that the claims by neo-liberal macroeconomists that the 'business cycle was dead' were far fetched. It also exposed the failure of mainstream economic ideas about efficient markets and deregulation. In turn, the success of the fiscal interventions also demonstrated that the mainstream claims that increasing deficits would only lead to increased inflation were grossly amiss and reflected their ideological preference for small government rather than any evidential knowledge.

Most economists were in denial when the crisis hit. The dominant macroeconomic models used by mainstream economists for research and teaching categorically failed to predict the crisis even though the massive private debt build up prior to the collapse of the US property market made it certain that the global economy would go into a very deep recession. It was only a matter of when and how deep the recession would be. Most economists had no idea of what was happening because the tools that they used on a daily basis in classrooms and in their research provided them with few answers relevant to the real world. There is no doubt that recent history debunks the majority of the macroeconomics that students learn in universities around the world. Fiscal policy was very effective in militating against the private spending collapse and saved the world from a Great Depression 2.0. But despite that, the curriculum being taught by economics departments around the world is resolutely resistant to change and the lessons learned by the crisis have still not been incorporated in any serious way into teaching programs. That is the nature of Groupthink.

The scale of the emerging crisis and the apparent failure of the neo-liberal economists to provide any solutions meant that Keynesian ideas quickly came back in vogue as the obvious and only effective way to deal with the spending collapse. Pragmatism ruled over ideology. Mark Blyth wrote that a 'major reason Keynesianism . . . became the policy du jour was that governing neoliberal ideas denied that such a crisis was possible in the first place' (Blyth, 2013: 101).

However, to characterise the policy response by governments as a return to Keynesian thinking and an abandonment of neo-liberalism would be incorrect. One of the problems in the early recovery stage was that governments all around the world placed too much reliance on monetary policy and failed to give fiscal policy enough scope. While the central banks were able to prevent a collapse of the banking system by providing billions of dollars (or equivalents) in liquidity, the near zero interest rates that have been in place since the crisis began have not provided any significant stimulus to spending.

THE CONSERVATIVES REGROUPED AND RESISTANCE TO STIMULUS GREW QUICKLY

The sullen silence in the early days of the crisis among mainstream economists who had been extolling the virtues of the free market didn't last for long. Some of the leading lights in the economics profession, who had more to lose by way of reputation given their role in perpetuating the neo-liberal myths of self-regulating, efficient markets, expressed their denial in more aggressive terms. At the extreme of this ideological resistance to fiscal stimulus were many well-known economists (such as Robert Barro, Eugene Fama and others) who advocated the so-called laissez faire option to the crisis: letting the 'markets' adjust with zero government intervention. University of Chicago's John Cochrane was representative of this uprising when he wrote:

> Every dollar of increased government spending must correspond to one less dollar of private spending. Jobs created by stimulus spending are offset by jobs lost from the decline in private spending. We can build roads instead of factories, but fiscal stimulus can't help us to build more of both. (Cochrane, 2009)

This assessment was patently wrong but their strategy was simple. If the facts conflicted with their asinine theories, the facts must be wrong.

Fellow Chicago academic Eugene Fama, the best-known proponent of the so-called 'efficient markets hypothesis', which had dominated economic thinking prior to the crisis and had given authority to the financial market deregulation, gave an extraordinary interview in early 2010 to the New Yorker. He claimed the GFC was the result of poor 'government policy . . . not a failure of the market' (Cassidy, 2010). When he was asked what had caused the real economic crisis he replied, 'We don't know what causes recessions. Now, I'm not a macroeconomist so I don't feel bad about that.' The interview transcript notes that Fama was laughing at this point, the arrogance of the ignorant.

The resistance was purely ideological dogma. There was no 'self-correcting' market response possible. The world was plunging very quickly into a total collapse of the magnitude not seen since 1929. The financial markets were collapsing as parties lost the capacity to assess risk on the back of the corrupt and criminal behaviour of many bankers. Blinder and Zandi (2010b: 17) concluded that, despite obvious critical questions that can be asked about any complex stimulus package, 'laissez-faire was not an option'. A failure by the US government to respond in the way they did 'would have left . . . the economy . . . in a far graver condition' (p. 17).

Before long, many economists came out of their holes and began lecturing the public on the evils of budget deficits and the cavalier behaviour of the central banks. Anti-stimulus views started popping up in opinion pieces in the major conservative media outlets such as the *Wall Street Journal*, the *Financial Times*, *The Economist* and Murdoch's Fox TV network. Predictions of an inflationary Armageddon where governments would run out of money and the poor would lose all incentives to seek work as a result of the pitiful welfare cheques that they received became a regular occurrence. The public was told that the 'excessive' deficits would lead to a massive rise in interest rates, which would make home mortgage commitments intolerable. The daily narrative had the US or the UK morphing into Greece.

None of these predictions have come to fruition. If the medical profession had displayed incompetence of this magnitude then authorities would have withdrawn their certificates to practice and large damages claims would have been awarded against them. But an extremely biased, neoliberal media failed to bring these economic zealots to account and the public were increasingly persuaded that the crisis was not one of excessive private debt driven by massive market failure, but was rather a sovereign debt crisis brought on by profligate government spending. At that point, the attack on government fiscal activism became almost manic in its intensity and the politicians bought into the fray. Why was there so much resistance to abandoning the failed economic theories? The mainstream economics paradigm is more than a set of theories. Blyth (2013: 100) notes that these mainstream economic theories 'enshrine different distributions of wealth and power and are power resources for actors whose claims to authority and income depend upon their credibility', which explains, in part, why there was such resistance to abandoning them even though it was clear that they were bereft of any evidential standing.

Blyth characterised the policy makers as 'Twelve-Month Keynesians' (Blyth, 2013: 100) as their resolve to continue the growth process increasingly gave way to confused narratives about the need for growth-friendly fiscal consolidation, which of course was a classic example of the law of contradiction. The two propositions (growth) and fiscal consolidation (austerity) could not coincide given the collapse of private spending.

By 2010, there was an amazing reversal in the political rhetoric. At the Pittsburgh meeting of the G20 leaders in September 2009, the communiqué talked about the sufficiency and quality of jobs. The Leaders' Statement acknowledged that 'the national commitments to restore growth resulted in the largest and most coordinated fiscal and monetary stimulus ever undertaken' (G20, 2009: 1) but that the 'conditions for a recovery of private demand are not yet fully in place . . . [and] . . . We pledge today to sustain our strong policy response until a durable recovery is secured . . . We will avoid any premature withdrawal of stimulus' (pp. 1–2). There was even a proposal put forward by the British Prime Minister, Gordon Brown, to radically reform the IMF, to ensure its resources were used to help nations rather than load them up with debt and onerous conditionality programs (Morris and Grice, 2009).

Less than a year later, the political leaders were advocating austerity policies, which would push unemployment rates up further and increase poverty. This is in the context of dramatic increases in global poverty rates in 2009 due to income losses associated with entrenched unemployment (ILO, 2010). At the June 2010 G20 Toronto Summit, the narrative emphasised 'the importance of sustainable public finances and growth-friendly plans to deliver fiscal sustainability . . . countries with serious fiscal challenges need to accelerate the pace of consolidation' (G20, 2010a: 1). Later that year, in South Korea, the annual G20 Finance Ministers and Central Bank Governors' Meeting concluded that monetary policy should aim to 'achieve price stability', which thereby 'contributes to recovery' (G20, 2010b: 1) and that 'ambitious and growth-friendly medium-term fiscal consolidation plans' be implemented (p. 1). The emphasis on fiscal consolidation and the need for 'structural reform' (also known as labour market deregulation) was affirmed at the G20 Leaders' Meeting in Seoul in November 2010 (G20, 2010c). The tide had turned and the anti-stimulus lobby had won the day.

The rapid retreat from fiscal stimulus is exemplified by the UK macroeconomic policy response. The UK was on the road to recovery courtesy of its fiscal stimulus package until the Conservative Cameron government took office in May 2010 and set about pushing Britain down the austerity path. The British economy then laboured under continuous recession until modest growth returned in the first quarter of 2013. Six years after the crisis, the size of the economy (measured by real GDP) was still below the peak before the crisis. Germany followed up the G20 meeting in South Korea by proposing an austerity plan. German Finance Minister Wolfgang Schäuble said the measures might have to be 'stricter than necessary' (*The Guardian*, 2010).

The conservative economics and financial press provided a daily arena for this anti-deficit mania. For example, in May 2010, *The Economist* magazine, never known for its balanced coverage, claimed, 'thanks to incompetence and impotence, governments may become the problem that will drag the world economy down' (*The Economist*, 2010a). On 22 July 2010, ECB President Jean Claude Trichet published an opinion piece in the *Financial Times* imploring governments around the world to 'address our fiscal fragilities', failing, of course, to differentiate between the currency issuing governments such as Britain, Japan and the US, which can never run out of money, and the Eurozone nations, which had opted to use a currency they didn't issue. Moreover, Trichet rehearsed the growing conservative mantra that fiscal austerity, far from 'jeopardising the economic recovery', would become a 'decisive component of economic stability and sustainable global growth' (Trichet, 2010a).

The public was now being bombarded with a myth drawn from the depths of mainstream economic theory that even most economists failed to fully understand, the so-called Ricardian Equivalence Theorem or, in more common parlance, the fiscal contraction expansion. In contradiction to everything we know about the real world, this arcane piece of reasoning claims that if the government cuts its spending, private consumers and firms will increase their own spending and more than fill the gap so that growth accelerates. The theory assumes people have 'rational expectations', which means that on average we accurately predict the future and know exactly what government policy is going to be for the rest of our lives. The theory claims that people associate higher fiscal deficits with higher future taxes and so we save up to ensure we can meet the higher tax obligations. Thus when the government announces it is cutting the deficit we spend more because we believe our future tax obligations will be lower.

The ECB was a prominent exponent of this discredited theory. They claimed the 'beneficial effects of fiscal consolidation are undisputed' because 'consumers anticipate benefits arising from fiscal consolidations for their permanent income and consequently increase private consumption' (ECB, 2010a: Box 6, 83–85). Jean-Claude Trichet made many memorable interventions into the debate in his last years as ECB boss in the style of an evangelical minister. At the Jackson Hole gathering of central bankers in August 2010, he told the audience he didn't believe the argument that cutting government spending would damage growth because 'the strict Ricardian view may provide a more reasonable central estimate of the likely effects of consolidation. For a given expenditure, a shift from borrowing to taxation should have no real demand effects as it simply replaces future tax burden with current one' (Trichet, 2010b).

Not to be outdone, the French Finance Minister and soon to be IMF boss, Christine Lagarde, told the American ABC program *This Week* on 10 October 2010 that:

> If we do not reduce the public deficit, it's not going to be conducive to growth. Why is that? Because people worry about the public deficit. If they worry about it, they begin to save. If they save too much, they don't consume. If they don't consume, unemployment goes up and production goes down. (ABC, 2010)

This was, of course, pure nonsense. To deduce the 'Ricardian' outcome, the proponents of the theory have to rely on several assumptions that never hold in the real world. Further, the theory has never worked out in practice. But the zealots have never been too bothered by the facts.

With the ECB–IMF–German–French alliance firmly committed to fiscal austerity as the way forward, the prospects for an early return to growth in Europe were effectively doomed.

THE EUROPEAN RESPONSE

The most responsible strategy for Europe, given the severity of the crisis and the particular exposure of some European economies and banks, would have been for the Council to immediately suspend the SGP provisions and for the ECB to announce that it would support all necessary fiscal deficits to offset the private spending collapse. The former decision could have been justified under the 'exceptional and temporary' circumstances provision of Article 126 of the TFEU relating to the EDP. It was clear that the situation was 'exceptional' and with appropriate policy action would have been 'temporary'. The Council had already demonstrated a considerable propensity to bend its own rules. The ECB could have immediately announced a program such as the Securities Markets Program (SMP) whereby it promised to buy up unlimited volumes of national government debt in the secondary markets. If the SMP had been introduced in 2008 rather than 2010 and without the conditional austerity attached, things would have been very different. No Treaty change would have been required for either of these ad hoc arrangements to be put in place. While obviously inconsistent with the European Groupthink, these policy responses would have saved the Eurozone from the worst. Fiscal deficits and public debt levels would have been much higher but in return there would have been minimal output and employment losses and private sector confidence would have returned fairly quickly. The response of the private bond markets would have been irrelevant.

The European policy makers did exactly the opposite and guaranteed the economic collapse would be deeper and longer than otherwise. By 2009, the Council had determined that 16 of the 17 Eurozone nations had 'excessive deficits' under the meaning given in Articles 104.6 and 126.6 of the Treaty. Only Luxembourg escaped the net. The fact that virtually the whole Eurozone was in default of the fiscal rules should have told the political leaders that the rules were poorly calibrated in relation to likely scenarios. But instead millions of Europeans lost their jobs and prosperity unnecessarily because of the policy folly that ensued.

The first mistake the European policy makers made was to claim that excessive government spending had caused the crisis. In the early days of the collapse, the news media was full of stories of lazy Greeks who didn't pay taxes and a lax government, spending beyond its means. This was meant to explain why private bond investors were pushing up public borrowing costs. But that occurred because the bond investors had realised that Eurozone governments were at risk of insolvency because they had surrendered their currency sovereignty. The real cause of the crisis was the spiralling and unsustainable private debt build up and the exposure of the European banks to that debt. This was pushed quietly to the background by the Troika and only occupied their minds when they forced the Spanish, Irish and Greek taxpayers to foot the bills necessary to keep the big French and German banks from failing. The fact that these 'bailout loans' were added to the outstanding sovereign debt of these nations only exacerbated the situation. Further, there was no evidence that government spending among the Member States was in any way 'out of control'. Greece alone was running larger deficits than most. But Spain and Ireland were exemplars of fiscal prudence as defined by the nonsensical SGP rules.

Yet it was in the ideological interests of the neo-liberals to deny and blur the reality so that they could reconstruct the private debt crisis in Europe (and elsewhere) as a public debt crisis, which they could claim had its roots in out-of-control government spending. Fiscal austerity was then the obvious solution. The SGP rules provided the cover for these zealots to impose the austerity. Important things such as real GDP, employment and unemployment were considered expendable. There was a mindless zeroing in on the SGP rules and financial numbers, with the understanding of what was driving the rising deficits and debt ratios ignored.

A reasonable interpretation of what was going on in Europe and the UK is that the GFC was an inconvenient disruption to the pre-crisis neo-liberal program of deregulation, retrenchment of government welfare programs, and income redistribution away from workers towards capital. The GFC had conveniently provided some very high fiscal numbers, which the conservatives sought to use as evidence for their case that government spending is bad. The public was encouraged by daily media headlines and interviews with economists and political leaders to believe that the low growth was the result of the high deficits, rather than the other way around. As Mark Blyth noted, 'treating it as a crisis brought about by debt fuelled consumption and profligate state spending is to confuse correlation (they happened at the same time) with causation (out-of-control spending caused the crisis)' (Blyth, 2013: 97). The return to austerity under the smokescreen of the fiscal crisis allowed the neo-liberals to resume business as usual.

The language of morality also became prominent, which reflected the religious nature of the crusade against fiscal stimulus. *Financial Times* journalist Wolfgang Münchau abhorred the September 2009 decision by the French government to abandon any aim to reduce its fiscal deficit to below 3 per cent by 2012 and claimed other governments (Greece, Italy, Portugal and Spain) were similarly recalcitrant. In contradistinction, Münchau (2009a) said 'Germany . . . has committed itself to the virtuous path.' German economist Otto Issing, a former European Central Bank executive board member, claimed that Greece 'wasted potential savings in a spending frenzy' (Issing, 2010). German Finance Minister Wolfgang Schäuble told the press before a two-day summit in Brussels in March 2010 on whether there should be Community support for Greece that 'an automatic system that hurts those who persistently break the rules' was needed to punish the 'fiscal sinners' (Traynor, 2010). Even Australian journalists felt compelled to lecture the world about the 'decadence' and 'depravity of modern Greece' in relation to its fiscal deficit and public debt ratio (Sheehan, 2010). The importance of language and framing in reinforcing the continuity of Groupthink is examined in more depth in Chapter 18.

APPEASING THE BOND MARKETS

The willingness of the political leaders in Europe to elevate the bond markets to deity status became a repetitive theme from the early days of the crisis. ECB boss Trichet claimed that the 'first necessary' thing the Eurozone nations had to do was 'to adopt a fiscal policy that would enable them to convince all market participants' (Trichet 2010a). Austerity was promoted as the only way to keep bond markets investing in the governments. The corollary of this view, also often repeated, was that country X (say America or the UK) would soon be heading down the Greek path if it didn't radically cut its fiscal deficit. The so-called historian Niall Ferguson was often featured by the conservative media claiming that the 'situation of the United Kingdom in fiscal terms is in fact worse than the situation of Greece . . . Britain has a massive fiscal crisis that is just about to break' (Daily Dish, 2010). It was a pity that most of these commentators, including Ferguson, could not understand the difference between a nation that issues its own currency and can never run out of money and the Eurozone nations that had rendered themselves vulnerable to insolvency as a result of adopting the euro. The true problem was the euro itself rather than the size of the deficits.

As the hysteria reached crescendo proportions, London banker Steven Major wrote in the *Financial Times* that a spreading of the Eurozone public debt crisis to countries such as the US, UK and Japan is 'not going to happen . . . because the obsession with public debt ratios fails to distinguish between different levels of sovereignty. The US, UK and others can maintain high public debt ratios for longer, especially given the amount of deleveraging being carried out by the private sector' (Major 2010). The likes of Ferguson and company had consistently demonstrated a flagrantly ill-conceived view of how monetary systems operate. The reason that the 'UK cannot turn into Greece' is that 'US, UK, Japan and Canada are examples of what I call "true sovereigns". For these countries there is zero default risk. Investors should not worry about credit fundamentals, as they will always receive their coupons and original investment on redemption' (Major, 2010). Chapter 17 demonstrates that a nation that issues its own currency and floats it on international currency markets will always be able to repay debt denominated in that currency. Bond markets can never bully such a government. Chapter 21 examines why such a government can always spend its own currency without recourse to borrowing.

The debt 'spreads' (the interest paid on debt relative to the interest paid on German government bonds) for many Eurozone governments rose sharply as the crisis unfolded because the bond investors were worried about default. Major (2010) concluded, 'The countries that adopted the single currency immediately relinquished some policy sovereignty'. The problem was (and is) the flawed design of the EMU including the unworkable fiscal restrictions. Given the overriding 'cultural' loathing of any ECB support for deficits, the Eurozone governments can never run deficits large enough to meet major cyclical fluctuations and challenges to their banking systems.

THE BAILOUTS – ON A HIDING TO NOTHING

> On a hiding to nothing . . . to be trying to do something when there is no chance that you will succeed. (Cambridge Dictionary, Cambridge University Press).

Faced with nations unable to fund themselves but with pending liabilities maturing, the focus turned to bailouts. A new European bully formed, the so-called Troika (the European Union, the ECB and the IMF), to spearhead the austerity push. Once again the unelected and unaccountable IMF felt its role was to trample on the democratic rights of citizens in Greece and elsewhere. While these interventions initially protected Greece and other nations from insolvency, they imposed destructive conditionality, which made it impossible for the nations to grow.

On 9 May 2010, the European Council (through Ecofin) resolved to create the European Financial Stability Facility (EFSF), which would be its bailout vehicle in cooperation with the IMF. It was replaced in October 2012 by the permanent rescue vehicle, the European Stability Mechanism (ESM). Both institutions shared the same flaws.

The very idea of a bailout seemed at odds with Article 125 of the Treaty, the 'no bailout' clause. If the Treaty was so rubbery, why impose the SGP rules in the first place, given their severe negative consequences for economic growth and living standards? Such inconsistencies among European policy makers were rife during the crisis as the ideologues who designed the rules came up against the reality of the system collapsing from the application of these rules. A desperate pragmatism reigned supreme but was so tainted by ideology (the unsustainable conditionality) that the bailouts just made matters worse.

The first major bailout came in May 2010 when Greece was given a three-year €110 billion loan from the Troika with strict conditions attached. The austerity package was breathtaking in its harshness. Greece was compelled to reduce its deficit by 15 per cent of GDP within three years, which was an impossible task. The terminology was that the fiscal policy changes were 'frontloaded with measures of 7½ per cent of GDP in 2010, 4 per cent of GDP in 2011, and 2 per cent of GDP in 2012 and 2013, each, to turn around the fiscal position and help place the debt ratio on a downward path' (IMF, 2010: 1). It was obvious that the austerity plan would, in fact, increase the deficits given the loss of tax revenue that would accompany the output and employment losses.

British journalist Larry Elliot described the bailout conditions as an 'austerity package of eye watering severity. The news from Athens last week could mean only one thing: the International Monetary Fund had been in town' (Elliot, 2010). The Troika demanded that public sector pay be cut by around 18 per cent and pensions cut by 10 per cent, that wages and pensions be subject to a three-year freeze, that taxes on fuel, alcohol and tobacco be increased by 10 per cent and across the board VAT increases of 2 per cent be imposed, among other measures. When announcing the terms of the bailout to the Greek people, Prime Minister George Papandreou wore a dark purple-coloured tie, the colour that Greeks wear to funerals. But his days were numbered. Soon afterwards the Troika got rid of Papandreou and put one of 'their men' into the role, the central banker Lucas Papademos. It didn't matter what the people who vote might think!

Key personnel in the Troika were unflinching in their claims that austerity would be good for Greece. Soon after the bailout was pushed onto Greece, the centre-left Parisian daily newspaper Libération published an interview with Trichet. He was asked whether the austerity plans 'pose the risk of killing off the first green shoots of growth' (Quatremer, 2010). He replied:

> It is an error to think that fiscal austerity is a threat to growth and job creation. At present, a major problem is the lack of confidence on the part of households, firms, savers and investors who feel that fiscal policies are not sound and sustainable. In a number of economies, it is this lack of confidence that poses a threat to the consolidation of the recovery. Economies embarking on austerity policies that lend credibility to their fiscal policy strengthen confidence, growth and job creation.

The IMF had the audacity to put numbers to this Ricardian nonsense and predicted that by 2012 Greece would return to increasingly robust growth. The IMF (2010: 8–9) predicted growth would follow a 'V-shaped pattern' and that 'the frontloaded fiscal contraction in 2010–11 will suppress domestic demand in the short run; but from 2012 onward, confidence effects, regained market access, and comprehensive structural reforms are expected to lead to a growth recovery. Unemployment is projected to peak at nearly 15 per cent by 2012.'

Table 16.2 shows the IMF growth forecasts against the reality. The forecasts they had used to justify their harsh austerity package for Greece were very inaccurate. Moreover, the actual outcomes were more in keeping with what a reasoned assessment, which was uncontaminated by neo-liberal ideology, would have suggested. Cuts that deep and that quick were always going to devastate both public and private spending and lead

Table 16.2 IMF forecasts for Greece and reality

	Real GDP growth (%)			Unemployment rate (%)		
	IMF forecast	Actual outcome	Error	IMF forecast	Actual outcome	Error
2010	−4.0	−4.9	−0.9	11.8	12.6	1.2
2011	−2.6	−7.1	−4.5	14.6	17.7	3.1
2012	1.1	−7.0	−8.1	14.8	24.3	9.5
2013	2.1	−4.2	−2.1	14.3	27.3	13.0

Source: IMF (2010), Eurostat.

to a depression with very high unemployment. By April 2014, the national unemployment rate in Greece remained at 26.5 per cent.

There is a sequel to this part of the story. As the Troika were busily imposing austerity on beleaguered European nations such as Greece and Portugal, the IMF consistently claimed that their 'modelling' showed that if governments cut their fiscal deficits quickly, private sector spending would respond and growth would soon return. But the IMF admitted in its October 2012 World Economic Outlook that its past recommendations for fiscal austerity in Europe, which conditioned, for example, the harsh terms embedded in the Greek bailout packages, were based on 'modelling errors'. They admitted 'that actual fiscal multipliers have been larger than forecasters assumed' (IMF, 2012: 43). Fiscal multipliers tell us what will happen to total spending (both public and private together) for every extra $1 of public spending. The IMF had assumed that they were very low (below 1) so that cutting public spending would actually lead to higher total spending. In October 2012, they admitted that the 'multipliers' were well in excess of 1, which means that if the government cuts spending by 1 euro, the total decline in spending and output will be well in excess of that. The reality told us that would be the case. More credible economic analysis told us that would be the case. But the neo-liberal biases in the IMF models simply refused to allow for that outcome because it would have undermined their ideologically motivated desire to cut deficits and reduce the size of government. So the combination of the IMF incompetence and the usual European Groupthink justified policies that have led to millions of people unnecessarily losing their jobs.

In June 2013, the IMF released a suite of new reports on Greece. At the press conference accompanying the release, the head of the IMF Greek Mission, Poul Thomsen, was asked 'Is it true that the IMF admits mistakes on the Greek bailout?' (IMF, 2013b). Thomsen replied:

> Sure. There is in this bundle of papers, there is a discussion of the past and, in the context of the Article IV Consultation, a full report . . . And, sure, in reviewing what we have done the whole time, there are certainly things we could have done differently. We already had that debate six months ago on these multipliers and that if we should do it again, we would not use the same multipliers.

The accompanying report (IMF, 2013c) admitted that the IMF had altered its own rules in order to provide the bailout. It was clear to them from the outset that the austerity program would not reduce Greece's public debt ratio, which was one of four criteria that the IMF dictate must be satisfied in order for them to provide funding. They proceeded not as a result of any concern for what the austerity would do for Greece, but 'because of the fear that spillovers from Greece would threaten the euro area and the global economy' (p. 10). Defending the interests of international capital has always been a priority of the IMF even if the welfare of ordinary citizens is compromised. Extraordinarily, the IMF also admitted that, in retrospect, Greece actually failed to meet three of the four criteria for funding (p. 29), which indicates how poor the initial assessment was, in part, because the 'negotiations took place in a very short period of time' (p. 49). The IMF has a history of parachuting officials into nations who, within a day or so, come up with radical structural adjustment programs, which ravage the local economy. The neo-liberal free market paradigm is seen as being a 'one size fits all' solution, irrespective of the circumstances.

Finally, the IMF's huge forecasting errors in relation to Greece were not one-off incidents. While forecasting errors are a fact of life, the IMF and other major neo-liberal inspired organisations produce systematic errors, that is, they consistently make the same errors, which are easily traced to the underlying ideological biases which shape the way they create their economic models. The IMF typically overstates the benefits of austerity and understates the costs. Further, it also overstates the inflationary impact of fiscal deficits. Each systematic error reinforces its free market approach. Yet each systematic error also demonstrates the poverty of that approach. In the case of Greece, the damage caused by the IMF malpractice has been massive. Some IMF officials, at the very least, should have gone to prison given the damage the institution caused, which dwarfs that of fraudsters such as Bernie Madoff who was sentenced to 150 years imprisonment for his criminality.

The Greek government was also forced into a €50 billion privatisation program. And it was here that things turned decidedly nasty with the 'ugly German' coming to the fore. While the Greek government was undermining its own citizens' welfare in return for the bailout funds, the Germans considered the austerity measures were 'not even a drop in the bucket' (Bild, 2010). The headlines in the downmarket German tabloid Bild demanded that the bankrupt Greeks should sell their islands and the Acropolis (Bild, 2010). Josef Schlarmann, a senior politician in Angela Merkel's Christian Democrats, captured the German sentiment when he likened the Greek situation to that of a bankrupt individual, arguing that Greece should sell its buildings, companies and uninhabited islands (Bild, 2010). Obviously, Dr Schlarmann didn't realise that a nation can never be like a private company. Regardless of any (imprudent) voluntary arrangements the government has entered into, such as pegging its currency, borrowing in foreign currency, or joining the EMU, it can withdraw whenever it chooses and reintroduce its own currency and redenominate all liabilities in that currency. That was an option the Germans didn't want Greece to take, given the exposure of the German (and French) banks to the Greek government debt. By 2011, this 'crass populism' (*The Economist*, 2011a) had become the standard 'sell, sell, sell' rhetoric of Europe's finance ministers, led by none other than Christine Lagarde. The IMF was relatively silent at this point given that its boss, Dominique Strauss-Kahn, was languishing in an American gaol on sexual assault charges. But its delegation to Greece earlier in the year had stressed that more 'structural reforms' were required and that an acceleration of the 'privatization program' was essential (IMF, 2011).

Ireland received its bailout loan of €85bn in late November 2010 (of which the Irish government contributed €17.5 billion from the National Pension Reserve Fund). A sum of €35bn would be allocated to bail out its zombie banks, which was the main aim of the exercise. In return, the Troika demanded it make drastic public spending cuts, cut pensions (4 per cent) and the minimum wage by €1 per hour, impose a swathe of tax increases, and implement extensive retrenchments to working conditions. In total, Ireland committed to cutting €15 billion from its net spending, which was double its original 2009 austerity plan. It amounted to a cut of around 26 per cent.

Ireland was the first Eurozone nation to introduce a harsh austerity program. In early 2009, the Irish Prime Minister said that a primary consideration was that Ireland had to address the crisis 'in a way which would be seen to be credible by international markets' (Cowan, 2009). The priorities in favour of the amorphous 'bond markets' were clear and the Irish citizens would suffer as a result. Before the crisis, the so-called Celtic Tiger was held out as the poster nation for others to follow, particularly in terms of deregulation and tax concessions to foreign businesses. The British shadow Chancellor, George Osborne, wrote:

> A generation ago, the very idea that a British politician would go to Ireland to see how to run an economy would have been laughable. The Irish Republic was seen as Britain's poor and troubled country cousin, a rural backwater on the edge of Europe. Today things are different. Ireland stands as a shining example of the art of the possible in long-term economic policy making, and that is why I am in Dublin: to listen and to learn. (Osborne, 2006)

That assessment was as ludicrous then as are the claims that Ireland represents the austerity template for other nations to follow now. After more than five years of austerity, the Irish Central Statistics Office (CSO) tells us that GDP growth was negative in 2013, as were net exports; employment was more than 13 per cent lower than it was in 2008; and the unemployment rate was at 11.7 per cent. However, given the labour force participation rate in 2013 was well below its 2007 peak, the real unemployment rate is closer to 18.6 per cent. The CSO also reported that in the year to April 2013 'among Irish nationals, net outward migration is estimated to have increased significantly, rising from 25,900 to 35,200' (CSO, 2013). The young and the skilled have left Ireland in search of work in Australia, Canada and elsewhere. The hollowing out of the productive workforce will undermine Ireland's growth potential in the future. Taken together, the Irish experience only looks like a template on what not to do when confronted with a major banking and spending collapse. Peter Boone and Simon Johnson (2010) showed that the Irish growth 'miracle' prior to the crisis was a mirage 'driven by clever use of tax-haven rules' and that '20 per cent of Irish gross domestic product is actually "profit transfers" that raise little tax for Ireland and are owned by foreign companies'. They considered the decision to impose austerity was 'making things ever worse' and concluded that 'adjustment to this awful situation would be far easier outside the euro zone' (Boone and Johnson, 2010). It is hard to disagree with that assessment, both then and now.

In March 2011, Portugal received 78 billion euros from the Troika. The Government had already been pressured by Brussels to implement a harsh austerity program encompassing tax increases, cuts to public sector wages and conditions while unemployment soared. The bailout conditions made matters worse. The spread on ten-year Portuguese government bonds went astral early in 2012, reflecting the lack of confidence the bond markets had in the austerity strategy. In his best-selling book *Why We Should Leave the Euro*, Portuguese economist João Ferreira do Amaral described the adjustment programs imposed on Portugal by the Troika as absurd (Ferreira do Amaral, 2013, Chapter 5.1) because imposing austerity upon austerity would exacerbate the economic and social collapse, without solving the problem of funding. He described the European Commission as Germany's new foreman (Chapter 5.1). The translation of the synopsis provided by the publisher places the modern calamity alongside Portugal's 60 years of colonial repression under Phillip II of Spain:

> In 1581 Portugal surrendered to Spain. In 1992 it laid itself at the feet of a European Commission increasingly answering to Germany's tune. There was no referendum, the voters were never consulted. The Portuguese elites, who hoped to benefit richly from European Structural Funds, cavalierly handed over our currency – and with it our monetary sovereignty. The rest is history. From 2008 onwards, the European Commission broke with tradition and became an organ at the service of a new power. The Portuguese economy succumbed, choked by the new Mark. The tragedy was widely foretold in advance. In the 1990s several voices had alerted us to the dangers of joining the single currency. (Ferreira do Amaral 2013: Chapter 5.1)

As economic and social conditions deteriorated in Greece, it became obvious that the country would not be able to meet its ongoing liabilities without further financial assistance and would be forced into default by March 2012. After an emergency summit of European leaders in July 2011, the tenth in 18 months concerning Greece, a second Greek bailout package was proposed. This bailout was the first to suggest that the private banks and other private bond holders would provide some of the debt relief (European Council, 2011). The so-called 'haircut' or private sector involvement (PSI) proposed that investors would either roll over their stock of maturing Greek government bonds or sell the bonds back to the government at a discount. In return, the Greek government agreed to even harsher austerity measures including further tax increases, more public sector job cuts, a 20 per cent cut in workers' wages, pension cuts and reduced trade union rights. In September, the Greek parliament passed some of the tax increases but civil unrest was mounting. On 19 October, the day before the vote on the rest of the austerity measures in parliament, a national strike began supporting large-scale protests in Athens. Amidst violent riots outside the parliament, the Government passed the bill.

On 26 October 2011 the details were fully worked out between the parties. The Troika would extend €130 billion to Greece in return for more austerity, and all private Greek government bond holders would be invited to accept lower yields and discounts on the face value of their assets. The total bailout sum included an estimated €30 billion in revenue, which the Troika hoped Greece would get from the large-scale privatisation plan it had agreed on as part of the first bailout. Further, some 40 billion euros of the bailout sum would go to buying back debt (safeguarding banks) or recapitalising zombie Greek banks. In other words, the interests of capital were privileged. Virtually no new funds were made available to support spending in the Greek economy to stimulate employment. Further, for all the angst surrounding the negotiations, it was estimated that the deal would not provide any significant debt relief anyway (Spiegel et al., 2011). While the political leaders and the ECB did not refer to this as a default, it was clearly that. The German government once again dominated the negotiations by constructing the plan, which forced the private banks to take some of the loss. The French and the ECB had been opposed to such a move.

It was not smooth sailing though. The social unrest translated into political instability. Greek Prime Minister Papandreou, who up until then had been a pliant conduit for the Troika, faced major political resistance from an electorate already reeling from the austerity package associated with the first bailout in 2010. As a political stunt, he indicated that he would take the second bailout package to a popular vote, a move that sent shock waves among the political elites in Europe. They knew the Greek people would reject the package and an exit from the Eurozone would then be inevitable. A plan had to be devised. On 3 November 2011, Papandreou withdrew the referendum threat after being 'dressed down' by G20 leaders at the November Cannes Forum. He claimed that the back-down was because the opposition parties decided they would support the package after all. But the neo-liberal New Democracy Party, which had been holding out against any ratification of the second bailout package for political gain, denied that was the case (Donadio and Kitsantonis, 2011). Papandreou, in desperation, promoted the idea of a 'national unity' government with New Democracy, as a last desperate effort to preserve his political position. He resigned on 6 November 2011. Four days later, a deal driven by New Democracy and heartily endorsed by the Troika saw an unelected Lucas Papademos installed as the Prime Minister of Greece. He was a neo-liberal central banker totally supportive of the Troika. He soon became the mouthpiece for the Troika, berating the Greek population that unless they were prepared to accept major cuts in their incomes the Government would have to default and exit the Eurozone. He claimed that if forced to exit 'the country would be unable to pay salaries and pensions and keep schools and hospitals running' (Granitsas and Stevis, 2012). Of course, that claim was an absolute lie. Once the Greek government regained its own currency it could pay for anything that was for sale in that currency including all the workers' wages and pensions.

All parties finally agreed to the deal on 21 February 2012 including the 53.5 per cent 'haircut' on the face value of any bonds held. The Troika demanded that the Greek government set up a special 'off budget' escrow account which had to be prioritised and contain enough cash at all times to service its liabilities. The Germans and French had at one stage proposed that a European Commissioner take over running economic policy in Greece. Douzinas (2012) noted that this plan 'was more than a little insensitive for a country that has suffered a brutal Nazi occupation'. Facing increasing hostility, the Troika decided to create a 'task force' of inspectors who would rough ride over the democratic process to make sure that the Troika got their pound of flesh. Later in 2012, the Greek government was forced to ratchet up the austerity cuts in order to receive the next instalment from the Troika. By June 2013, the Government closed its public broadcaster, marking a further blow to democracy. Greece was now more or less a German colony.

The reality was that Greece could never fulfil its obligations under the agreement given the harshness of the austerity measures, which guaranteed that it would remain in depression for many years to come. Even with the reduced debt burden, insolvency was a continual threat and increasing poverty was a certainty. The bailout conditions were so harsh and doomed to fail that *Guardian* journalist Larry Elliot (2012) suggested 'whatever eurozone finance ministers were smoking in their all-night marathon talks it must have been something strong'.

There were other bailouts that followed the same pattern, money to prop up private banks in return for massive austerity being imposed on the citizens. Not a great bargain! Cyprus became another Troika zombie state in late 2012 when it agreed to steal depositors' funds to 'save' the banks. Spain never formally entered a bailout agreement with the Troika. Instead, it borrowed €41 billion from the EU to prop up its zombie banks. The Government was forced to count these funds against its public debt, which worsened its position in relation to the SGP procedures after Germany refused to allow the loans to be 'off budget'. It would have been much better if the Spanish government had allowed the banks to crash and provided depositor guarantees within newly nationalised structures with ECB backing. But the twisted Bundesbank logic would have constructed that as monetising fiscal deficits. The IMF had also bullied Spain into imposing austerity. On 24 May 2010, the IMF demanded that Spain continue to aggressively cut its deficit and radically deregulate the labour market (removing job protections and cutting wages).

THE SIX-PACK, THE TWO-PACK AND THE FISCAL COMPACT

By the time the European Council met in Brussels in March 2010, the shape of the response that the political leaders would take was clear. The official statement said that the 'current situation demonstrates the need to strengthen and complement the existing framework to ensure fiscal sustainability in the euro zone . . . For the future, surveillance of economic and budgetary risks and the instruments for their prevention, including the Excessive Deficit Procedure, must be strengthened' (European Council, 2010: 2). The German agenda was clearly to make the SGP conditions even more onerous so as to further constrain discretionary fiscal policy, which ensured that only nations with strong export positions would have any chance of sustained growth. Conservative German academic Hans-Werner Sinn called for a new SGP, 'one that would be formulated to impose ironclad debt discipline. What is needed are modified debt rules, hefty sanctions, and most of all, a system of rules that automates the levying of penalties, leaving no room for political meddling' (Sinn, 2010).

The European Union's response to this pressure was embodied in three new 'governance' measures – the Six-Pack, the Two-Pack and the Fiscal Compact. All three initiatives sought to further restrict the fiscal flexibility of the national governments. All three took the monetary union further into the mire and further away from an effective solution to its woes. The presumption was that if the fiscal rules were tighter and behaviour more closely monitored and controlled, the SGP would be enforceable and the so-called fiscal crisis would dissipate. The European leadership was clearly prepared to let higher unemployment and poverty become the adjustment mechanism rather than government spending.

In late 2011, the Commission proposed a major revision of the SGP, which was approved by the Member States and the European Parliament in October 2011. The so-called 'reinforced Stability and Growth Pact (SGP)' became operational on 13 December 2011 (European Commission, 2011). The Official Memorandum said the so-called 'Six-Pack' comprised 'five regulations and one directive' (p. 1). The innovation was the creation of a new 'Macroeconomic Imbalance Procedure', which was described as a 'new surveillance and enforcement mechanism' (p. 3). Essentially nations would move into the EDP more quickly and there would be harsher sanctions for compliance failure. The Six-Pack specified a more rigorous imposition of financial sanctions if a nation fails to follow 'specific recommendations' (p. 1) to get its deficits below 3 per cent of GDP. Further, if the '60% reference for the debt-to-GDP ratio is not respected' then the EDP will begin 'even if its deficit is below 3%' and the nation will have to reduce the 'gap between its debt level and the 60% reference . . . by 1/20th annually (on average over 3 years)' (p. 2). The Six-Pack also introduced 'expenditure benchmarks' which will enforce 'a cap on the annual growth of public expenditure according to a medium-term rate of growth' (p. 2). Finally, a series of interventions were detailed under the so-called Excessive Imbalances Procedure (EIP), which aims to reduce macroeconomic imbalances (particularly unit costs and so on) and will force nations to submit 'a clear roadmap and deadlines for implementing corrective action' (p. 3). The whole system is subject to a huge surveillance operation (EU monitoring) with rigorous enforcement (fines equal to 0.1 per cent of GDP) and central intervention in a nation's budgetary process.

The Two-Pack, which became enforceable on 30 May 2013, extended the surveillance mechanisms by requiring national governments to submit detailed fiscal plans to the Commission prior to their own enacting legislation. The Commission would not have the right to veto the plan, but could warn a national government of potential for breach. Further, any government receiving bailout money or in an EDP would be subject to more detailed scrutiny by the Commission. In other words, more centralised bullying.

These changes provide no extra capacity for the national governments to defend their economies against recession. The GFC proved that the existing SGP fiscal rules were too restrictive and so-called automatic stabilisers (mainly lost tax revenue due to recession) were enough to breach the Treaty reference values. More flexibility is required if the Member States are to fulfil their responsibilities to advance the welfare of their citizens. The restrictions effectively redefine the purpose of government to one of satisfying two arbitrary and unworkable financial ratios at the expense of all that really matters. That is a very strange vision for a prosperous Europe. These new rules invoke visions of a nasty controlling, big brother sort of world where the worker in the village in Greece or the Netherlands will basically be casting a vote in futility if their respective governments stay in the Eurozone, because at any time a European Commission official will be able to intervene and coerce the elected government into following the Troika dictates rather than their elected mandate.

But the Eurozone leaders were still not satisfied with these new restrictions. They decided to introduce an even more onerous set of fiscal rules under the guise of the Treaty on Stability, Coordination and Governance in the Economic and Monetary Union (TSCG), also known as the 'Fiscal Compact' (European Union, 2012b). These changes were driven by the Germans, who in 2009 enshrined a 'balanced budget rule' or 'debt brake' in their Basic Law (Constitution). From 2016, the rule will make it illegal for the federal government to run a structural deficit larger than 0.35 per cent of GDP, while from 2020 the German states are prohibited from running any deficits. This effectively means that once operational, that outstanding public debt will eventually disappear. Previously there were debt limits in place to guide German economic policy but after 2016 the ceiling cannot be breached. Only in exceptional and rare situations, which are beyond the control of the government, can the rules be temporarily breached but any deficits incurred would have to be offset by surpluses soon after.

Predictably, the Bundesbank (2011: 15) considered the move to be 'a very welcome development and a clear improvement'. Consistent with their deflationary bias, they recommended that all levels of government 'incorporate a safety margin below the constitutional ceiling' to avoid 'the need for short-term adjustments that could have a procyclical impact, particularly given unexpected adverse developments'. In other words, they wanted the government to run fiscal surpluses as a matter of course, imparting a constant fiscal drag on economic growth independent of the state of the economy. In the context of German domestic policy, this means the only source of growth would be net exports. The export issue is discussed later in the chapter. A debt brake means that all investment in public infrastructure has to come out of current revenue, which violates the basic economic principle that the costs and benefits of such provision should be spread out over time so the current generation doesn't bear the costs and the future generation enjoy the benefits. Further, it works on the assumption of symmetrical economic cycles, such that any deficits incurred in a downturn can be more than offset by surpluses in periods of stronger growth. But cycles are typically asymmetric and deep recessions can require extended fiscal deficits to sustain the recovery.

The problems pertaining to the SGP are magnified under a 'balanced budget rule'. In particular, the techniques used by the multilateral agencies to estimate the structural component of the fiscal balance always produce biased results, overstating the size of the deficit. In other words, they always suggest the cyclical component is smaller than it actually is. The application of fiscal rules based on these estimates will then always ensure policy settings are excessively restrictive in the context of private spending and thus biases economic outcomes towards slower growth and higher unemployment, if not worse. Even conservative *Financial Times* journalist Wolfgang Münchau considered that the policy 'is going to be hugely damaging to the eurozone', either because 'the German economy would become a structural basket case, and would drag down the rest of Europe for a generation' or because 'economic and political tensions inside the eurozone are going to become unbearable' as a result of diverging trade imbalances (Münchau, 2009b).

The Fiscal Compact adopted by the European Union, unfortunately, embodied much of the German approach, including the preference that the 'balanced budget rule' be binding and embedded into permanent 'constitutional provisions' (p. 5). Article 3 of the Treaty specifies that a 'balanced budget' would be normally defined as a structural deficit under 0.5 per cent of GDP. Member States can only exceed this in 'exceptional' circumstances. The so-called 'independent' surveillance and monitoring bodies would quickly refer infractions to the Court of Justice of the

European Union, which under Article 8, was given 'radical new powers to ensure compliance with permanent austerity in the eurozone and most of the not-so-eurozone (the UK and the Czech Republic excepted)' (Phillips, 2013). Phillips (2013) concludes that:

> The reason the court was given these powers was to remove the exiguous remaining sliver of democratic control over such matters. EU leaders of course don't put it quite this way. They say instead that giving the court these powers will 'depoliticise such decisions'. But it is exactly the same thing. De-politicise = de-democratise.

Portugal has already witnessed this tendency to disregard national institutions. When the Portuguese Constitutional Court, which seemed to understand the limits of how far the government can undermine the wellbeing of pensioners and those on sickness benefits and others, declared the 2013 national budget illegal, all hell broke loose. This fiscal package incorporated the harsh 2011 bailout requirements. The neo-liberal Portuguese government then determined that it would meet the spending cut targets imposed on it by the Troika by forcing larger cuts in health and education expenditure to get around the Court's ruling. The response from the European Commission was swift and clear. On 7 April 2013, it said, 'The European Commission welcomes that, following the decision of the Portuguese Constitutional Court on the 2013 state budget, the Portuguese Government has confirmed its commitment to the adjustment programme, including its fiscal targets and timeline' (European Commission, 2013). This exposed an interesting hierarchy. The Court of Justice of the European Union was now the supreme arbiter on national economic policy and the national courts set up to defend the constitutional rights of the citizens in any country would be largely by-passed by agreements between co-opted national governments and the bullies in Brussels. And all the time, Germany would be watching what they were all doing.

The schizoid nature of the Treaty is seen when comparing Article 3, which defines the harsh fiscal rules, and Article 9, which says that all parties:

> . . . shall take the necessary actions and measures in all the areas which are essential to the proper functioning of the euro area in pursuit of the objectives of fostering competitiveness, promoting employment, contributing further to the sustainability of public finances and reinforcing financial stability. (European Union, 2012b, Article 9: 17)

What exactly is the goal of government in this vision? Why is the 'sustainability of public finances' a separate objective given that fiscal policy should always be in service of prosperity, which at least requires that full employment and price stability be achieved? It is clear that obedience to the fiscal rules under Article 3 will severely compromise the capacity of a government to promote sustained employment growth. Fiscal policy parameters have to be flexible enough up and down to allow a government to maintain adequate levels of total spending in the economy.

Finally, the 'Macroeconomic Imbalance Procedure' embedded in the Six-Pack exposes the inherent, anti-people biases that dominate European policy making. The stated aim of the MIP surveillance mechanism is 'to identify potential risks early on, prevent the emergence of harmful macroeconomic imbalances and correct the imbalances that are already in place' (European Commission, 2012a: 4). The so-called MIP Scoreboard uses ten 'early warning' indicators that provide information about 'macroeconomic imbalances and competitiveness losses' which are easy to compute and communicate (p. 4). Threshold values (positive and negative) are provided to assess when there is an imbalance. A detailed examination of the indicators is beyond the scope of our narrative but the priorities are clear. A nation that had endured an unemployment rate of say 9.9 per cent for the last three years is not considered to be imbalanced, given the warning threshold is 10 per cent. The Commission chose this very high threshold due to a 'focus on adjustment in labour markets and not on cyclical fluctuations' (p. 23). In other words, they do not consider the unemployment problem in terms of insufficient jobs being caused by deficient levels of spending but rather consider the only policy concern to be so-called 'structural' issues. This in turn concentrates their attention on 'market impediments', the standard neo-liberal, supply side bias that has failed since it became the dominant approach in the early 1990s. In the Commission's annual 'Alert Mechanism Report', which is based on a review of the MIP scoreboard, any reference to unemployment is usually accompanied by some conclusion that wages are too high and need to be reduced in line with productivity growth. There is no recognition that the enduring recession has caused both productivity growth to slump and jobs to disappear due to a lack of spending. The European policy makers are thus 'content' with very high levels of unemployment yet they hide their intent in a language of deception.

Another bias is evident in the way they deal with current account deficits and surpluses. They conclude that 'sustained current account surpluses do not raise the same concerns about the sustainability of external debt and financing capacities, concerns that can affect the smooth functioning of the euro area' (p. 6) as do current account deficits. The MIP thus accords 'a greater degree of urgency' to 'countries with large current account deficits and competitiveness losses' (p. 6). The upper warning threshold (for a surplus) is 6 per cent of GDP. If the balanced budget rule is satisfied by a nation sitting on the current account surplus threshold, then its private domestic sector will be saving overall 6 per cent of GDP. Where will those savings go? We have previously discussed how Germany maintained its external competitiveness once it could no longer manipulate the exchange rate. The Hartz reforms reduced the capacity of workers to share in the productivity growth of the economy and suppressed domestic demand. Profitable investment opportunities were limited in the German economy as a result and capital sought profits elsewhere. The persistently large external surpluses (and 6 per cent is large) were the reason that so much debt was incurred in Spain and elsewhere.

In the 'Alert Mechanism Report 2014', issued on 3 March 2014, the European Commission concluded that Germany had a macroeconomic imbalance as a result of its current account surplus being above the 6 per cent threshold. The Commission acknowledges that the large surpluses have been, in part, due to the suppression of domestic spending and hence imports. But it praises the surpluses because they 'provide savings to be invested abroad' (European Commission, 2014b: 9–10). The conclusion is that Germany will have to find ways to 'strengthen domestic demand and the economy's growth potential' (p. 14). However, it dodges the main issue. Higher domestic demand will require faster wages growth both to boost the very modest consumption performance and to attract investment into the domestic market. But such a change would be at odds with the mercantile mindset that dominates the nation because it would reduce the competitive advantage that Germany enjoys over other nations that have treated their workers more equitably.

This also raises the question of inequality. There is no indicator for national income or wealth inequality in the MIP Scoreboard. Despite the neo-liberal denial, income inequalities undermine economic growth. Even the IMF has now acknowledged 'countries with more equal income distributions tend to have significantly longer growth spells' (Berg and Ostry, 2011: 16). According to the German Socio-Economic Panel (SOEP), which is a wide-ranging representative longitudinal study of private households, located at the German Institute for Economic Research, DIW Berlin, income inequality in Germany has risen sharply since it joined the Eurozone. While the poorest 10 per cent of income earners in Germany achieved 15 per cent gains in their annual median incomes between 1997 and 2008, the richest 10 per cent enjoyed gains of 28 per cent (Inequality Watch, 2012). The Hartz reforms and the export imperatives were an important part of this rising inequality. A substantial redistribution of income is required within Germany if domestic spending is to increase.

THE EXPORT-LED GROWTH MANIA

The release of the United Nations Conference on Trade and Development (UNCTAD) annual Trade and Development Report in September 2010 (UNCTAD, 2010) provided some sober assessment of the dominance of export-led growth strategies among policy makers and multilateral agencies such as the IMF and the OECD. UNCTAD considered that a reliance on such strategies combined with the imposition of fiscal austerity would worsen growth and increase poverty. UNCTAD concluded that a fundamental rethink was needed to reorientate policy towards stimulating domestic demand and employment creation. UNCTAD considered that an expansion of fiscal policy in Europe was essential to avoid an extended period of recession and economic stagnation.

The current policy orthodoxy in the Eurozone is at odds with that advice. The European policy makers have conjured up the argument that if government deficits are cut and so-called 'internal devaluation' is pursued (which means cuts to wages, pensions and other production costs), two sources of growth will emerge as a result. First, there will be a 'Ricardian' private domestic spending boom, discussed earlier. Second, even if domestic spending does not pick up, the process of wage and price deflation brought on by the 'internal devaluation' will increase the nation's external competitiveness and spawn export-led growth.

The evidence suggests internal devaluation does not provide a sound basis for growth. First, it is a 'race to the bottom' strategy that attempts to drive down unit costs via cuts in wages, which undermine domestic spending. But if workforce morale also falls as a result of the wage cuts, it is likely that industrial sabotage and absenteeism will rise, undermining labour productivity. Further, overall business investment is likely to fall in response to declining spending, which also erodes future productivity growth. There is thus no guarantee that there will be a significant fall in unit labour costs. There is robust research evidence to support the notion that by paying high wages and offering workers secure employment, firms enjoy higher productivity growth and the nation improves its international competitiveness as a result. Eurostat data shows that between 2008 and 2013, labour productivity per hour worked rose by 1.8 per cent in Germany, but fell in Greece, the worst hit by the austerity, by 8.5 per cent and in Italy by 0.7 per cent. So not only does the internal devaluation approach fail to lift competitiveness, it locks in a low productivity path, which undermines increases in real living standards. The massive costs for nations being subjected to these austerity programs in the form of millions of lost jobs and the very high youth unemployment are much higher in the long term than any benefits that might arise. Second, the imposition of domestic austerity and a reliance on net exports for growth cannot work for all nations. To understand that point, we need to understand the concept of a fallacy of composition, which is discussed later.

Does internal devaluation boost external competitiveness? Recall the BIS 'real effective exchange rate indices' (REER) discussed in Chapter 9, which are internationally accepted measures of international competitiveness that adjust nominal exchange rates with other data on domestic inflation and production costs. If the real effective exchange rate rises (falls) for a nation, then it signals a loss (gain) in its international competitiveness.

Figure 16.1 shows movements in real effective exchange rates since January 2009 until April 2014 for selected Eurozone nations and Iceland. Two sub-samples are shown: January 1999 to December 2007 and January 2008 to April 2014, roughly coinciding with the period of growth and the period of recession. The data shows that following the introduction of the euro, international competitiveness for all the nations shown declined except in the cases of France and Germany. Further, Germany made relative gains on the rest. Following the crisis, the general tendency has been for real effective exchange rates to decline. However, the real effective exchange rate for Greece was only 1.9 per cent lower in April 2014 than

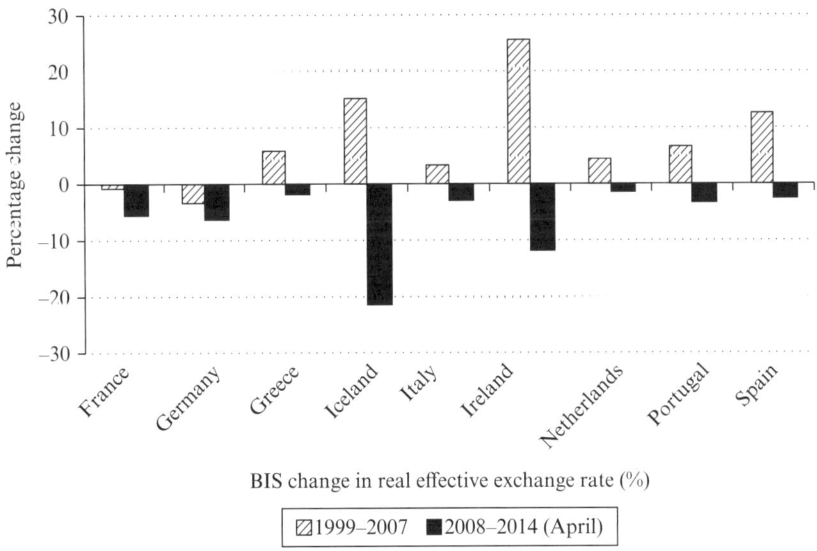

Source: BIS Real Effective Exchange Rates, http://www.bis.org/statistics/eer/index.htm.

Figure 16.1 Movements in international competitiveness in the Eurozone, 2007–14

in January 2008 despite the massive austerity program it has endured. By comparison, the real effective exchange rate for Germany fell by 6.1 per cent since the beginning of 2008. Of these Eurozone nations, only Ireland has improved its position relative to Germany since the onset of the crisis.

The comparison of these fixed exchange rate euro nations with Iceland is striking. The fundamental differences between the Eurozone nations and Iceland are threefold: (a) Iceland issues its own currency while the other nations use a foreign currency; (b) Iceland enjoys a floating exchange rate; and (c) Iceland sets its own interest rate. These are the characteristics that differentiate sovereign from non-sovereign nations in terms of the currency in use. Iceland has experienced a massive gain in its international competitiveness in recent years with less austerity. The results for Iceland are actually conservative because its percentage gain in competitiveness from its maximum index value (November 2005) and April 2014 was 31.5 per cent. Ireland was next gaining 15 per cent on its maximum index value in June 2008. Third best was Germany, improving by 9.3 per cent on its maximum value in January 1999 compared to April 2014.

The exchange rate depreciation in Iceland made its exports cheaper and demand for them grew rapidly at the same time as import demand fell because of the rise in prices in the local currency. The same sort of dynamic assisted Argentina in growing after it allowed its exchange rate to drop significantly in 2002. Iceland's real effective exchange rate evened out after its initial plunge. That is a common pattern. After an initial plunge, the nominal exchange rate stabilises as growth returns. The scaremongers who claim that the weaker euro nations would experience massive and ongoing currency plunges are in denial of history.

Iceland's approach to the crisis has been less painful and more effective. Greece and other weaker euro nations could have enjoyed similar improvements in their external competitiveness if they had exited the EMU and allowed their currencies to float. Internal devaluation has clearly not been an effective route to increasing international competitiveness despite all the neo-liberal claims to the contrary. The costs of such a strategy have been huge in terms of lost output, mass unemployment and social breakdown.

The second issue is whether an almost exclusive reliance on net exports provides a sustainable growth strategy. The austerity approach strips away the capacity of the government to contribute to growth. In the current context, private demand is also very weak because households and firms are trying to reduce their debt exposure and also fear the risk of unemployment and the weak sales that follow. In other words, the only remaining source of growth for Eurozone nations is net exports. That is the logic of the internal devaluation approach. However, not all nations can enjoy current account surpluses, which are required if the external sector is to be a positive contributor to economic growth. Germany, for example, relies on other nations running current account deficits so that it can maintain strong exports growth. It also suppresses its imports, which impact on the capacity of other nations to export. Austerity also undermines the capacity of nations to import. These observations tell us that generalised austerity is another example of the concept of a fallacy of composition.

The 'fallacy of composition' is an important notion in macroeconomics that is often forgotten by the neo-liberal mainstream when they advocate wage cutting and fiscal austerity. It is a concept drawn from logic, which the Oxford Dictionary says is the 'error of assuming that what is true of a member of a group is true for the group as a whole.' While this is not a book about the history of macroeconomics, the identification by John Maynard Keynes in the 1930s that free market economic theory was riddled with these compositional errors was a central aspect in the development of modern Keynesian theory and macroeconomics (the study of the whole economy). Up until then, it was assumed that everything could be understood at the single consumer or firm level (so-called microeconomics) and if economists wanted to talk about the economy as a whole they claimed they could just add up all the individual elements. This led to the identification of the so-called 'aggregation problem', which meant that such an addition could not be reasonably accomplished to generate a meaningful whole. To overcome that problem, the free market economists invented what they called a 'representative household', which behaved as if it was a single household/consumer, and a 'representative firm', which behaved like a single firm. Thus, one firm and one household represented the entire economy. Together they bought and sold a 'composite good'. In other words, all the theories that were developed to explain how an individual firm might decide on their employment and production levels, and the like, were assumed to apply at the aggregate or macroeconomic level.

The classic example of the fallacy of composition in this sort of reasoning was the famous 'paradox of thrift', which describes how individual virtue can become a public vice. In simple terms, if an individual decided to increase his/her individual saving, they would probably succeed if they were disciplined enough. But if all individuals tried to do this *en masse*, then the decline in consumption spending would force firms to cut output and employment and national income would fall, perhaps plunging the economy into recession. Total saving rises (falls) with national income. So if everyone tried to save more, the economy overall would generate lower saving. The paradox tells us that what applies at a micro level (ability to increase saving if one is disciplined enough) does not apply at the macro level (if everyone increases saving). The term paradox of thrift entered the nomenclature during the Great Depression as Keynes and others saw this particular problem as providing a *prima facie* case for government deficit spending which could replace the lost consumption as the non-government sector sought to increase its saving.

Another classic fallacy of composition that Keynes exposed related to the recommendation by the free market economists that wage cuts were the solution to unemployment and low growth. This argument obviously remains relevant to the resolution of the Eurozone crisis. The free market economists claim that if a particular business firm cuts its wages then it will employ more workers because its costs will fall. The argument assumes that the firm's sales will not be affected by the wage cuts, which is a reasonable assumption. Applying this logic to the economy as a whole, the standard economics textbook then says that a general wage cut will lead to higher employment. However, if all firms cut wages, total spending will fall dramatically and destroy jobs. Wages are both a component of costs and a significant source of income. The mainstream economists ignore the income side of the wage deal. If workers have less income, they spend less. The fallacy, then, is in trying to draw conclusions at the economy-wide level on the basis of individual experience.

What has all this to do with export-led growth strategies? The IMF has been pushing export-oriented growth strategies onto developing countries for years, usually supplemented with so-called 'structural adjustment programs' (SAPs), which are similar to the austerity programs that the Troika has imposed on Greece and Portugal and has urged other Eurozone nations to implement. It is worth noting that the IMF was initially conceived at the UN Monetary and Financial Conference at Bretton Woods, New Hampshire in 1944 as one of the two major international institutions (along with the World Bank) to rebuild the damaged economies after the Second World War and to ensure (in the case of the IMF) that there would be no return to the Great Depression. The IMF was empowered to be an unconditional lender to nations in trouble to ensure there would not be another collapse. It quickly morphed into ensuring the fixed exchange rate system was sustained by providing foreign reserves to nations who were having trouble defending their exchange rates. The free market credentials that characterise the present day institution were not in evidence then.

The collapse of the fixed exchange rate system in 1971 meant that the IMF had no role to play. With considerable deftness it exploited the increasingly neo-liberal milieu provided by the popularity of Monetarism to reinvent itself as the overseer of poor nations who faced pressures to repay foreign debts. The IMF used its lending capacity to become a neo-liberal enforcer. Its lending became increasingly conditional on a country's willingness to accept these SAPs, which emerged as a response to the debt crisis that engulfed the world in the late 1970s; a crisis that was significantly related to IMF loans in the first place. The debt crisis was really a crisis for the first world banks and the IMF made sure that the SAPs forced the poorest nations to transfer resources to the richest to maintain the profits of these big banks. The SAPs forced nations to adopt free market policies, which involved widespread privatisation of state assets, cuts to education and health services, cuts to public sector employment and wages, the elimination of minimum wages, and banking deregulation aimed at allowing speculative capital to come and go more easily. Policies to give private capital privileged access to the nations' resources were also encouraged. These are the same sort of policy changes that created the GFC. The SAPs typically increased unemployment and poverty and led to greater income and wealth inequality.

The obvious measure of the failure of this approach has been that the IMF programs have not decreased world poverty. The IMF has a long history of damaging the poorest nations. There are many mechanisms through which the SAPs increased poverty. First, fiscal austerity is almost always targeted at cutting welfare services to the poor. Moreover, the cuts prevent sovereign governments from building public infrastructure and directly creating public employment. Areas such as the military, which do little to enhance quality of life, are rarely included in the IMF cuts, in part because these expenditures benefit the first world arms exporters. Second, public assets are typically privatised. Foreign investors often benefit significantly by taking ownership of the valuable resources. Third, contractionary monetary policy forces interest rates up, and this often discriminates against women who survive by running small businesses. But the higher interest rates promote speculative investment (hot money) that fails to augment productive capacity. Fourth, export-led growth strategies transform rural sectors, which had traditionally provided food for subsistence consumption, into 'cash for trade' crops. Smaller landholdings are concentrated into larger cash crop plantations or farms aimed at penetrating foreign markets. When international markets are over supplied and prices drop below those required for servicing the debts, the IMF steps in with further loans. Some nations pillaged their natural resources to create export products (for example, timber) to the point where they exhausted their export potential but were still burdened by the onerous IMF loans. Massive environmental damage is often created in the process. Further, the transformation undermines the viability of the subsistence sector and food poverty increases. Fifth, user-pays regimes are typically imposed which increase costs of health care, education, power, and, in some notable cases, reticulated clean water, and exclude the poorest cohorts. Sixth, trade liberalisation involves reductions in tariffs and capital controls.

Often the elimination of protection reduces employment levels in exporting industries. Further, in some parts of the world child labour becomes exploited so as to remain 'competitive'.

The Japan Bank for International Cooperation published a detailed study of the impact of SAPs on poverty reduction in low-income countries in 2003. The study concluded that in the period where export-led growth strategies were being intensively implemented by the IMF in tandem with SAPs:

> Low-income countries experienced little per capita economic growth during 1981–2000 . . . Between program and nonprogram countries, the overall macroeconomic performances of the former have fallen below those of the latter. Compared to nonprogram countries, program countries have achieved a lower level of real GDP per capita . . . accumulated larger external debt as a share of GDP, borne a heavier debt service burden relative to exports, held fewer months of foreign reserves, and adopted a lower pace of trade openness (measured by the sum of exports and imports as a share of GDP). (Shirai, 2003: 4)

Former World Bank official William Easterly (2000: 3) wrote that when growth occurred in nations under IMF and World Bank adjustment lending, the 'economic expansions benefit the poor less'. While the earlier manufacturing export strategies of the Asian tigers (which pre-dated the IMF SAPs onslaught from the late 1970s) were successful and required massive public sector involvement, the research evidence clearly demonstrated that most poor nations went backwards under the IMF programs.

This rich history of failed export-led growth strategies where nations suppress domestic spending through austerity and dismantle their public sectors and then hope for a net exports boom is a cautionary tale for modern European policy makers. While there are clear differences between the poor subsistence nations of Africa that the IMF likes to intimidate and the advanced economies of Europe, the principle remains the same. Not all nations can simultaneously run trade surpluses to external markets, especially when they are often all trying to penetrate the same markets and, more significantly, a high proportion of their trade is intra-EMU. Further austerity kills world trade and stifles innovation.

The export-led growth proponents like to use the 1990s experience of Canada and Sweden to justify their claim that fiscal austerity can still be consistent with growth. But even neo-liberal leaning *The Economist* (2010b) saw through that ruse:

> The advocates of austerity exaggerate more dangerously still. They base their argument on cases in the 1990s, when countries such as Canada to Sweden cut their deficits and boomed. But in most of these instances interest rates fell sharply or the country's currency weakened. Those remedies are not available

> now: interest rates are already low and rich-country currencies cannot all depreciate at once. Without those cushions, fiscal austerity is not likely to boost growth.

While Canada may have, in isolation, been able to offset the public spending cuts by an improving external sector helped along by increased competitiveness via exchange rate adjustments, this solution cannot work if all countries engage in austerity. That is the fallacy of composition. An export-led growth strategy cannot apply for all nations, which are simultaneously cutting back on their domestic demand. The only reliable way to avoid a fallacy of composition like this is to maintain adequate fiscal support from spending while the private sector reduces its excessive debt levels via saving. That strategy is also likely to be the best one for stimulating exports because world income growth will be stronger, which stimulates imports. Austerity not only undermines the rights and welfare of the citizens, but also undermines the source of the export revenue, domestic spending. UNCTAD (2010: I) concluded, 'not all countries can rely on exports to boost growth and employment; more than ever they need to give greater attention to strengthening domestic demand'.

THE SECURITIES MARKET PROGRAM SAVED THE EUROZONE

When the Greek government effectively lost access to the private bond markets, it was almost certain that Greece would have to default on its maturing liabilities and exit the Eurozone. The fears were that the Greece exit would be the first domino of several to fall. Further, given the exposure of the big French and German private banks to Greek government debt and the linkages between these banks and other banks throughout the European financial system, it was also considered likely that a default would trigger a general financial collapse. There were mixed views on this among the political elites in Europe.

By 2012, German Finance Minister Wolfgang Schäuble considered a Greek exit was preferable and would allow the rest of the nations to 'create a firewall' without the distraction of the Greek bailout sagas. Schäuble met US Treasury boss Timothy Geithner in July 2012 and indicated, 'with Greece out of the picture, Germany would be in a position to provide financial assistance to the rest of the eurozone as the German people would be less reticent about this than they were about bailing out the Greeks' (Ekathimerini, 2014). While the doomsday claims about the consequences of a Greek exit were nonsense and designed to advance the neo-liberal agenda (see Part III), there is no doubt that the integrity of the Eurozone was under threat in early 2010 as the Greek government approached insolvency.

Moreover, the bailout programs were never going to be sufficient to ensure Greece or any other nation remained solvent. Given the structure of the monetary system, it was obvious that a major 'fiscal like' intervention was going to be required to keep the nations solvent in the face of growing private bond market uncertainty and withdrawal. But while the ratings agencies, whose behaviour leading up to the GFC had been exposed as incompetent and corrupt by US Congressional hearings, were circling with downgrades and issuing all manner of spurious briefings about likely insolvency to investors, it became obvious in May 2010 that the ECB would use its 'currency issuing' capacity to ensure no Member State became insolvent. Effectively, a massive 'fiscal operation' was introduced, seemingly in violation of the Treaty rules. But, without any doubt, it saved the Eurozone, for the time being.

On 14 May 2010, the ECB established its Securities Markets Program (SMP), which opened the possibility that the ECB and the national central banks could 'conduct outright interventions in the euro area public and private debt securities markets' (ECB, 2010b: 8). This is central bank speak for the practice of buying government bonds in the so-called secondary bond market in exchange for euros, which the ECB could create out of 'thin air'. Government bonds are issued to selective institutions (mostly banks) by tender in the primary bond market and then traded freely among speculators and others in the secondary bond market. The SMP also permitted the ECB to buy private debt in both primary and secondary markets. To understand this more fully, the decision meant that private bond investors (including private banks) could offload distressed state debt onto the ECB. The action also meant that the ECB was able to control the yields on the debt because by pushing up the demand for the debt, its price rose and so the fixed interest rates attached to the debt fell as the face value increased. Competitive tenders then would ensure any further primary issues would be at the rate the ECB deemed appropriate (that is, low).

Figure 16.2 shows the history of the SMP program, which was formally replaced on 6 September 2012 when the ECB introduced the Outright Monetary Transactions (OMT) program. The bars show the weekly debt purchases while the line shows the cumulative asset holdings associated with the program (in billions of euros). Clearly the ECB accelerated its purchases at times when the difference between the yields on some Member State government bonds against the benchmark bond, the German bund (the 'spreads'), were widening significantly. The initial

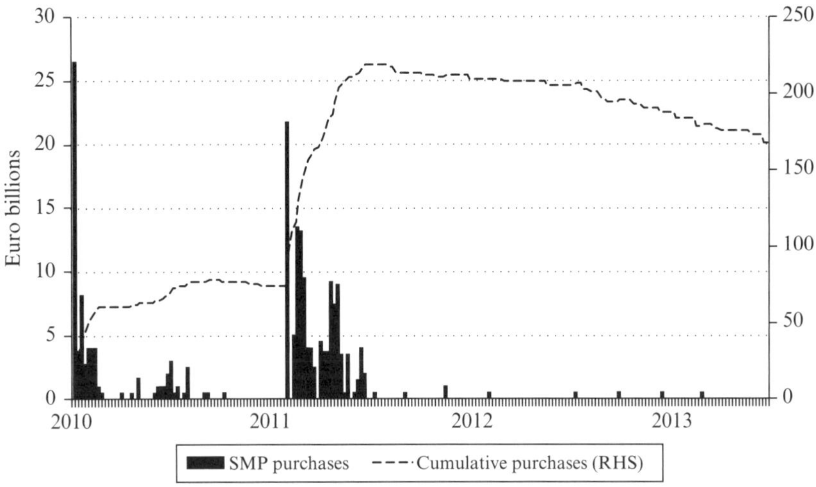

Source: ECB, Open Market Operations, Ad-hoc communications, http://www.ecb.int/mopo/implement/omo/html/index.en.html.

Figure 16.2 ECB SMP activity, 15 May 2010 to 12 May 2014, euro billions

spike from May 2011 was associated with the escalation in spreads on bonds issued by Greece, Ireland, Portugal and Spain. The second, larger acquisitions began in August 2011 and were mostly associated with the sharp rise in the spread on Italian government bonds, which went from 1.5 percentage points in April 2011 to a peak of 5.2 percentage points in November 2011. The large scale ECB buying stabilised the Italian bond spreads by the end of 2011 and by April 2014 they had fallen back to 1.77 percentage points. Given the size and importance of the Italian economy to Europe, the ECB was clearly not going to allow the Italian spreads to rise as quickly or as far as the Greek spreads had risen. Of course, the SMP purchases effectively allowed the relevant governments to ignore the bond markets, which meant that the size of the spreads were moot anyway.

After the SMP was launched, a number of ECB's official members gave speeches claiming that the program was necessary to maintain 'a functioning monetary policy transmission mechanism by promoting the functioning of certain key government and private bond segments' (González-Páramo, 2011). In other words, by placing the SMP in the realm of normal weekly central bank liquidity management operations, they were trying to disabuse any notion that they were funding government deficits. This was to quell criticisms, from the likes of the Bundesbank and others, that the program contravened Article 123 of the EU Treaty. In early 2011, the fiscally conservative boss of the Bundesbank, Axel Weber, who was being touted to replace Trichet as head of the ECB, announced he was resigning, ostensibly in protest at the SMP and the bailouts offered to Greece and Portugal. When the SMP was introduced, Weber breached ECB 'etiquette . . . [and] . . . stridently voiced his dissent on decisions' made by the ECB council since May 2010 (Ewing, 2010). In a notable speech on 12 October 2010, Weber claimed that the SMP was largely ineffective but risked 'blurring the different responsibilities between fiscal and monetary policy. As the risks associated with the SMP outweigh its benefits, these securities purchases should now be phased out permanently as part of our non-standard policy measures' (Weber, 2010: 2). Another ECB Executive Board member, Jürgen Stark, also resigned in protest over the SMP in November 2011. Stark told the Austrian daily *Die Presse* that the ECB was heading in the wrong direction by pushing aside the crucial no bailout clauses that provided the bedrock of the EMU (Schellhorn and Jilch, 2012). He also said that the ECB had panicked by caving in to the pressure from outside of Europe (Schellhorn and Jilch, 2012). Weber's successor as head of the Bundesbank, Jens Weidmann, maintained the criticism, albeit in a more muted manner. As the ECB accelerated its SMP purchases in 2011 to quell the rising bond yields on Italian government debt, Weidmann gave a speech in Berlin (Weidmann, 2011), which reiterated the Bundesbank's obsession with inflation:

> One of the severest forms of monetary policy being roped in for fiscal purposes is monetary financing, in colloquial terms also known as the financing of public debt via the money printing press. In conjunction with central banks' independence, the prohibition of monetary financing, which is set forth in Article 123 of the EU Treaty, is one of the most important achievements in central banking. Specifically for Germany, it is also a key lesson from the experience of the hyperinflation after World War I. This prohibition takes account of the fact that governments may have a short-sighted incentive to use monetary policy to finance public debt, despite the substantial risk it entails. It undermines the incentives for sound public finances, creates appetite for ever more of that sweet poison and harms the credibility of the central bank in its quest for price stability. A combination of the subsequent expansion in money supply and raised inflation expectations will ultimately translate into higher inflation.

Whatever spin one wants to put on the SMP, it was unambiguously a fiscal bailout package. Weidmann was correct in that sense. The SMP amounted to the central bank ensuring that troubled governments could continue to function (albeit under the strain of austerity) rather than collapse into insolvency. Whether it breached Article 123 is moot but largely irrelevant. The SMP reality was that the ECB was bailing out governments by buying their debt and eliminating the risk of insolvency. The SMP demonstrated that the ECB was caught in a bind. It repeatedly claimed that it was not responsible for resolving the crisis but at the same time, it realised that as the currency issuer, it was the only EMU institution that had the capacity to provide resolution. The SMP saved the Eurozone from breakup.

The ECB officials further tried to reduce the inflationary fears by distancing the SMP from so-called Quantitative Easing (QE) and the 'printing money' connotation by 'sterilising' the intervention. This amounted to all the funds spent by the ECB in the SMP being 're-absorbed on a weekly basis so as to specifically neutralise the programme's liquidity impact' (González-Páramo, 2011). In other words, the ECB was purchasing bonds in the secondary bond market with euros created out of 'thin air' and then, on a weekly basis, it would open a tender to offer deposits with the ECB (with a ceiling of 1.25 per cent yield) up to the volume of outstanding SMP bond purchases. So they were swapping the euros they 'spent' in purchasing the bonds for an interest-earning account with the ECB instead of leaving the interest-earning bond in the hands of the private sector. Economists call this type of swap a 'sterilisation operation' because it neutralises the liquidity of the initial bond purchases 'by draining the same amount of money from the banking system' (González-Páramo, 2011).

But an astute mind will see the smoke and mirrors. First, QE was never about giving the banks more money to loan out. Bank lending is never constrained by a lack of reserves. Rather lending requires credit worthy customers seeking loans. At the height of the crisis as banks tightened their lending criteria in the face of increasing financial uncertainty, there was a dearth of such customers. Quantitative easing is just an asset swap designed to bid up the prices of assets in certain maturity ranges and thus keep interest rates in those maturity segments lower. The only way it would have helped alleviate the crisis is if the lower rates stimulated investment growth. However, with the crisis so deep and consumers hunkering down for fear of unemployment and insolvency (given the debt overhang), firms have been able to satisfy demand with existing capacity.

Further, the fact that most central banks have been offering a return on excess bank reserves means that the SMP is virtually indistinguishable from QE. Both strategies keep bond yields lower than otherwise by strengthening demand in the private bond markets and both provide an interest-bearing alternative to the bond holders. QE added bank reserves (cash) and the relevant central bank then paid interest on the excess reserves created, whereas the 'sterilisation' functions associated with the SMP merely shunted the excess euro reserves created by the bond purchases into a separate ECB account which earned interest.

Weidmann's inflation fears were unfounded and reflected the fact that

German economists (in the main) and economic policy makers have become locked in a time warp that centres on the 1920s. The neutralising of the SMP purchases was another trick that played on the sort of misunderstandings that the likes of Weidmann perpetuate. Mainstream economists claim that by draining the reserves via the 'sterilisation' operation, the central bank has reduced the ability of banks to lend them out, which reduces the money supply and the inflation threat. This is a common misunderstanding. When a government spends and issues a bond to cover that spending (borrows back what it has spent) the reserves in the private banking system are reduced by the bond sales but the net worth of the private sector is not altered. Only the composition of the asset portfolio held in the non-government sector changes. There are more bonds and less euro reserves. If no debt is issued then there will be excess reserves in the banking system. If the central bank decides to pay interest on the excess reserves there is still no change in the net worth of the non-government sector.

Inflation is caused by aggregate spending growing faster than real output capacity of the economy. The banks are able to create credit if they can find credit-worthy customers. All components of total demand carry an inflation risk if they become excessive, which can only be defined in terms of the relation between spending and productive capacity. But the sterilisation operations associated with the SMP didn't reduce that risk. By offering an interest return on the excess reserves it was identical in outcome to issuing a bond. These issues are considered in more detail in Chapter 21.

While the SMP saved the Eurozone from breakup, it remained a failed vision for European prosperity because it didn't address the core problem: Southern Europe was in depression and the only way out was for fiscal deficits to expand. The ECB clearly signalled a willingness to buy unlimited quantities of government bonds if there was the risk of insolvency. But this intervention required that the countries succumb to a fiscal austerity package that ensured their growth prospects are minimal.

PART III

The Options for Europe

17. A monetary framework for fiscal policy activism

> The mind likes a strange idea as little as the body likes a strange protein, and resists it with a similar energy. It would not perhaps be too fanciful to say that a new idea is the most quickly acting antigen known to science. If we watch ourselves honestly, we shall often find that we have begun to argue against a new idea even before it has been completely stated. I have no doubt that that last sentence has already met with repudiation—and shown how quickly the defence mechanism gets to work. (Trotter, 1941)

BREAKING OUT OF THE NEO-LIBERAL GROUPTHINK

The austerity consensus that holds the Eurozone in a straitjacket is not grounded in any logical understanding of the modern monetary system and deliberately ignores many of the actual options that are available to fiat currency-issuing governments. European politicians and their supporting bureaucracies are paralysed by a destructive Groupthink that defines policies, which are incapable of restoring and sustaining prosperity. This is because their fundamental macroeconomic assumptions are not ground in reality. The aim here is to outline a new way of thinking about the economy, which demonstrates the actual options and responsibilities that apply to modern governments that issue a fiat currency. The conceptual framework provides policy makers with an effective way to break out of the neo-liberal Groupthink. This monetary framework, which is called Modern Monetary Theory (MMT), provides a coherent basis for fiscal activism and provides a real alternative to the austerity and stagnation that besets the Eurozone at present. The principles of MMT provide insights for reform within the existing common currency arrangement, and a basis for understanding the consequences of breaking up the monetary union and restoring individual currencies.

Most people are unaware that a major historical event occurred in 1971, when President Nixon abandoned gold convertibility and ended the system of fixed exchange rates. Under that system, which had endured for about 80 years (with breaks for war), currencies were convertible into gold, exchange rates were fixed, and governments could expand their spending only by increasing taxes or borrowing from the private sector. After 1971, most governments issued their own currencies by legislative fiat; the currencies were not convertible into anything of value, and were floated and traded freely in foreign currency markets. A flexible exchange rate releases monetary policy from defending a fixed parity against a foreign currency. Fiscal and monetary policy can then concentrate on ensuring domestic spending is sufficient to maintain high levels of employment. A consequence of this is that governments that issue their own currencies no longer have to 'fund' their spending. They never need to 'finance' their spending through taxes or selling debt to the private sector. The reality is that currency-issuing governments such as those of Australia, Britain, Japan and the US can never run out of money. These governments always have the capacity to spend in their own currencies.

Most of the analysis appearing in macroeconomics textbooks, which filters into the public debate and underpins the cult of austerity, is derived from 'gold standard' logic and does not apply to modern fiat monetary systems. Economic policy ideas that dominate the current debate are artefacts from the old system, which was abandoned in 1971. Students of macroeconomics are misled very early in their studies. Their textbooks typically use the flawed analogy between the household budget and the sovereign government 'budget' to argue that the same principles that constrain the former apply similarly to the government. The analogy is false at the most elemental level. The government issues the currency, which the households use. As a consequence, households have to seek funds before they can spend. Fiscal surpluses do not give a government any greater future spending capacity and fiscal deficits do not limit that capacity.

In the context of the EMU, the Treaty deliberately separated the currency-issuance capacity held by the ECB from the fiscal responsibilities retained by the Member States. The Member States effectively use a foreign currency, much like a state in the US or Australia and thus they *do* face the risk of insolvency. Thus the Member States are constrained. The ECB, however, can never run out of euros nor become insolvent.

MODERN MONETARY ECONOMIES USE FIAT CURRENCIES

The starting point is to understand the central role that government can play in a modern monetary economy. Modern monetary economies use money as the unit of account to pay for goods and services. An important notion is that money is a fiat currency, that is, it is convertible only into itself and not legally convertible by government into gold, for instance, as it was under the gold standard. The monetary unit (currency) has no intrinsic worth unlike so-called commodity money (gold and silver coins).

Why do we use the currency? It is obviously convenient for us to use the government's currency because we know it will be widely acceptable in exchange for goods and services. But that doesn't explain why it has that status.

The viability of the currency is guaranteed, because it is the only unit acceptable for payment of taxes and other financial demands of the government. The private sector *has* to get hold of the currency to meet its tax obligations, which requires the government to 'spend the currency into existence'. In most nations, the currency issuer is the central bank, which works closely with the national government treasury department responsible for fiscal policy (spending and taxation).

HOW DOES A GOVERNMENT SPEND? WHAT IS A FISCAL DEFICIT?

Governments typically have cash operating accounts with the central bank from which they spend and receive receipts (tax revenue) on a daily basis. So, in this sense, the central bank is the government's banker. We don't need to get into too much detail in this book about accounting jargon such as 'debits' and 'credits'. Suffice to say that the electronic records that describe the relationship between the treasury arm of government, the central bank (which sets interest rates), and the private banking system use the standard conventions of the accounting profession. To maintain an accounting record of government spending, the treasury asks the central bank to transfer funds out of its account (a debit) and into private banking sector accounts identified as spending recipients (a credit). This signifies that a payment has been made. The numbers entered indicate to Treasury the funds the private sector can draw upon as public outlays. Deposits thus show up in a number of commercial banks as a reflection of the government spending. The central bank may issue a cheque and post it to someone in the private sector whereupon that person will deposit the cheque at his or her bank, but this would have the same effect as if the transaction had occurred electronically.

Similarly, when the tax department receives revenue it asks the central bank to record the receipts in its central bank account. The private banking sector facilitates a transaction that reduces the funds available in the bank account of the taxpayer.

No printing presses are involved in either transaction. Computer operators in the central bank and the private banks just type numbers that are recorded by the electronic accounting systems in the various banks to signify how much the government wishes to spend and/or how much it has received. It is a very orderly process and goes on hour by hour, day by day, and year by year. All government spending is enacted in this way.

You will note that:

- Governments do not spend by 'printing money'. They spend by creating deposits in the private banking system. Some printed currency notes are in circulation but that is a separate process from the daily spending and taxing transactions that define what we call fiscal policy;
- There has been no mention of where the 'credits' and 'debits' in the private banking system that define government spending and taxation come from. Central banks create money by an act of decree. There is no limit to how much money a government-controlled central bank can create in this way.

A government fiscal (aka budget) deficit occurs when its spending exceeds its taxation revenue, whereas a fiscal surplus occurs when government spending is less than its taxation revenue.

A CURRENCY-ISSUING GOVERNMENT IS NOT A LARGE HOUSEHOLD

When British Prime Minister David Cameron said in June 2011 that 'If you have maxed out your credit card, if you put off dealing with the problem, the problem gets worse' (*The Telegraph*, 2011), he was inferring that the government deficit is just like credit card debt and that Britain was facing bankruptcy. He was misleading susceptible voters by invoking the false neo-liberal analogy between national government budgets and household budgets. This analogy resonates strongly with voters because it attempts to relate the more amorphous finances of a government with our daily household finances. We know that we cannot run up our household debt forever and that we have to tighten our belts when our credit cards are maxed out. We can borrow to enhance current spending, but eventually we have to sacrifice spending to pay the debts back. We intuitively understand that we cannot indefinitely live beyond our means. Neo-liberals draw an analogy between the two, because they know we will judge government deficits as reckless. In submitting to this logic we unknowingly reinforce a dangerous lie.

Economics students are misled because the differences between private household budgets and the government fiscal position are deliberately blurred in their textbooks. For example, Nobel Prize winner Robert Barro from Harvard University wrote in his text that 'we can think of the government's saving and dissaving just as we thought of households' saving and dissaving' (Barro, 1993: 367). Just like a household has a 'budget constraint' that they cannot disregard, the textbooks introduce the 'government budget constraint' framework (GBC) to analyse three alleged forms of public finance: (1) Raising taxes; (2) Borrowing from the private sector; and (3) Instructing the central bank to 'print money'.

Textbooks construct various scenarios to show that deficits are inflationary if central banks 'print money' to fund them. Students are led to believe that to avoid the inflation that would accompany money printing, the government has to raise taxes or borrow to get money in order to spend. Bell (2000: 617) said that the erroneous understanding that a student will gain from a typical macroeconomics course is that 'the role of taxation and bond sales is to transfer financial resources from households and businesses (as if transferring actual dollar bills or coins) to the government, where they are re-spent (i.e., in some sense "used" to finance government spending).'

But if we cut through all this pseudo-science then it is obvious that the government is not a big household. The government can consistently spend more than its revenue because it creates the currency. As private citizens we are required, for the most part, to use the government's money. Our access is constrained by the sources of available funds, including income from all sources, asset sales, and borrowings from external parties. Whereas households have to save (spend less than they earn) to spend more in the future, governments can purchase whatever they like, as long as there are goods and services for sale in the currency they issue. Budget surpluses provide no greater capacity to governments to meet future needs, nor do budget deficits erode that capacity. Governments always have the capacity to spend in their own currencies.

Why? Because they are the issuers of their own currencies. Governments like Britain, the United States, Japan and Australia can never run out of money. Remember that after President Nixon abandoned what had been called the gold standard (or US dollar standard) in 1971, governments no longer had to raise taxes or borrow from the private sector in order to spend. After 1971, the gold stocks held by the central bank of a nation did not limit the stock of money that could be issued at any point in time and national governments no longer had to 'fund' their spending.

Neo-liberal textbooks sometimes admit that the government doesn't need to raise taxes or borrow in order to spend. For example, the current

IMF chief economist Olivier Blanchard wrote in his macroeconomics text that government:

> . . . can also do something that neither you nor I can do. It can . . . finance the deficit by creating money . . . with the central bank's cooperation, the government can in effect finance itself by money creation. It can issue bonds and ask the central bank to buy them. The central bank then pays the government with money it creates, and the government in turn uses that money to finance the deficit. (Blanchard, 1997: 429)

This option, which is also termed Overt Monetary Financing (OMF), is quickly dismissed and considered to be taboo because Blanchard erroneously claims that it causes severe inflation. OMF, which is often referred to as the 'printing money' option, is considered in detail in Chapter 21.

IF GOVERNMENTS ARE SO FREE WHY ARE THERE FISCAL CONSTRAINTS?

When proponents of MMT say that a currency-issuing government is not revenue constrained, a common response is that governments continue to issue debt and have elaborate accounting structures, which require them to have funds in particular accounts before they can spend. It is also noted that many governments prohibit the central bank from directly purchasing government bonds. The debates in recent years in the US about debt ceilings are also used to support the argument that governments appear to be very revenue constrained. How then does MMT deal with these claims?

Under the Bretton Woods system of fixed exchange rates and gold convertibility that was in place prior to 1971, governments were, indeed, limited in their spending capacity by the value of the gold held by the central bank. This was because the outstanding stock of money that the central bank would issue was proportional to its gold reserves; if a government wanted to spend more, it had to reduce the money held by the non-government sector using taxation and/or bond sales. Clearly, the decision to enter this type of monetary system was voluntary, but once the decision had been taken, the government was bound to operate in that manner. Institutional machinery was then established to facilitate the issuing of bonds to the private markets, although central banks could still purchase government debt. In some periods, central banks purchased significant amounts of government debt.

However, once governments started to adopt fiat currency monetary systems in the 1970s, these conventions became irrelevant. All the spending caps and debt limits that had some operational significance prior to the adoption of fiat currencies were now meaningless. Intrinsically, these governments were now free of revenue constraints. They could spend as much as they wanted up to the volume of goods and services available for sale in their currency. The spending constraint shifted from a financial limit to a real limit – there had to be real goods and services available for sale.

The breakdown of the Bretton Woods system and the rise of Monetarism occurred around the same time. During this period there was intense pressure on governments to retain the various behaviours and supporting institutional structures that limited their spending capacity. Governments thus continued to issue debt even though this was no longer financially necessary. They continued to put spending caps on themselves and preach fiscal discipline because it was consistent with the Groupthink within which they had become trapped. MMT shows that these rules, and the restrictive accounting procedures that have been retained and in many cases made more severe, are just voluntary constraints that have been inherited from the gold standard days. In the era of fiat currency systems, the rules have been perpetuated by the mainstream economics ideology to constrain government and to give more latitude for private market activity. The lunacy of this thinking is that the private sector actually does better when there is a strong fiscal involvement in the economy through provision of first class public infrastructure and a highly educated, healthy, and employed workforce.

The public debt limits that governments accept are a classic example of a voluntary constraint that could be easily legislated out of existence if the public truly understood how the monetary system operates.

The US social security debate demonstrates how these voluntary restrictions cloud the public understanding of an important issue. The US social security system set up during the Great Depression requires that specially identified payroll taxes be levied to help pay for social security. If there is an excess of revenue raised in any year it goes into the Social Security Trust Fund, which is the responsibility of the US Treasury. Normally revenue exceeds payouts and the law requires that the surpluses are invested in 'special series, non-marketable U.S. Government bonds' (DeWitt, 2005), which mainstream economists claim indicates that the payroll taxes (that is, the Social Security Trust Fund) 'finance' US federal government net spending (deficit). The Trust Fund can be supplemented from the US government at any time it likes (subject to legislation). The only time this has happened was in 1982 when the accounting assets of the Trust Fund were close to being depleted and the US Congress allowed the Old Age and Survivors Insurance Trust Fund (OASI), which is the largest of the funds, to borrow from elsewhere in the federal system (Board of Trustees, 1982). But these 'Funds' are simply a labyrinth of elaborate accounting structures. The bottom line is that US federal government can always fund its social security obligations and any other nominal obligations that it faces. There is no need for these elaborate arrangements to 'store up' spending capacity.

Similarly, the EMU is itself a system of voluntary constraints that are reflected in legal statements, all of which could be changed via appropriate legislation. There is nothing irrevocable about the euro, and the debt ceiling in the US is simply a political contrivance expressed in legal processes that allows conservatives to create embarrassing headlines when deficits rise.

GOVERNMENT DEFICIT EXACTLY EQUALS NON-GOVERNMENT SURPLUS

Macroeconomists simplify the myriad of transactions and relationships that comprise a socio-economic system by focusing on broad sectors, which aggregate all these transactions. If, for simplicity's sake, we split the economy into two sectors – government and non-government – then the impact of fiscal deficits and surpluses can be seen more clearly. The former is comprised of the central bank and treasury and the latter encompasses households, firms, private banks and all the transactions with the rest of the world (exports and imports of goods and services and financial (money) flows).

A very simple example of such an economy, which captures the essence of the relationship between the government and non-government sectors, is an economy with a population of just two; one person being government and the other deemed to be the non-government sector (see Nugent, 2003). If the government runs a balanced fiscal position (spends 100 dollars and taxes 100 dollars) then non-government accumulation of fiat currency (money) is zero in that period and the non-government budget is also balanced. Thus there is no non-government saving in the currency. Say the government spends 120 and taxes remain at 100, then the non-government surplus is 20 dollars, which can accumulate as financial (monetary) assets and represents an increase in the non-government sector's net worth or wealth. The non-government saving of $20 initially takes the form of non-interest bearing money holdings. The government may decide to issue an interest bearing bond to encourage saving but operationally it does not have to do this to finance its deficit. An interest bearing bond is just a piece of paper that says the government will repay a certain amount (the face value) at some specified time (maturity date) and will pay an interest premium in addition (the yield or coupon rate). The non-government sector exchanges cash for the bond if it wants to earn interest and has no use for the liquid funds, which may be held as deposits in private banks. The government deficit of 20 is exactly the non-government savings of 20. Now if government continued in this vein, accumulated non-government savings would equal the cumulative fiscal deficits. However, should government decide to run a surplus (say spend 80 and tax 100) then the non-government sector would owe the government a net tax payment of 20 dollars and would need to run down its prior savings or sell interest bearing bonds back to the government to get the needed funds. The result is the government generally buys back some bonds it had previously sold.

Either way accumulated non-government saving (financial wealth) is reduced dollar for dollar when there is a government surplus. The government surplus thus has two negative effects for the non-government private sector: (a) the stock of financial assets (money or bonds) held by the non-government sector, which represents its wealth, falls; and (b) non-government disposable income also falls in line with the net taxation impost. Some may retort that government bond purchases provide the non-government wealth holder with cash. That is true but the fiscal surplus forces the non-government sector to liquidate its wealth to resolve its shortage of cash that arises from the tax demands exceeding current income. The cash from the bond sales pays the government's net tax bill. The result is exactly the same when expanding this example by allowing for non-government income generation, private firms and production, and a banking sector.

GOVERNMENT TRANSACTIONS ARE THE ONLY SOURCE OF NET FINANCIAL ASSETS

There is another important aspect of the relationship between the government and non-government sectors that is often misunderstood but crucial to understanding the suite of options available to a currency-issuing government. In any monetary system there are financial assets and liabilities. These are specified in monetary terms and can take a multitude of forms. A financial asset could be a bank deposit, some money in your pocket, a government bond, or a corporate bond. A financial asset is different from a real asset, such as property holdings or an art work because it has no tangible expression. For example, a bank deposit is a virtual statement of wealth. A financial liability is usually a bank loan or some other debt that is owed. The difference between total financial assets and total financial liabilities is called net financial assets. It is different to total net wealth or net worth in that it excludes real assets.

Financial transactions within the non-government sector cannot create new net financial assets or destroy previous net financial positions. For example, when a bank agrees to a loan it creates a deposit that the borrower can draw upon to fund spending. The loan is an asset to the bank but an equal and offsetting liability for the borrower. There is no net gain in financial assets for the non-government sector *as a whole* from this transaction. Transactions within the non-government sector may alter who owns the financial assets and the form those assets are held in, but they do not alter the net position of that sector overall. For example, a household might use some cash it holds in a bank deposit to purchase a corporate bond. The person's financial asset is now a bond rather than cash and the liability shifts from the bank to the corporation that has borrowed the funds. But there is still the same quantity of assets and liabilities in the non-government sector overall.

For the non-government sector to accumulate net financial assets (financial wealth) or lose net financial assets, there has to be a source of financial assets that is 'outside' the non-government sector (Johnson, 1969). This can only be the government sector. In this context, the government sector is considered to be the consolidation of the treasury function (fiscal policy) and the central bank (monetary policy), despite claims that central banks are largely independent of government. Consolidating the currency-issuing arm of government (central bank) and the spending and taxing arm (treasury) allows for a better understanding of how net financial assets can enter and exit the non-government sector. It is the transactions that are conducted between the consolidated government sector and the non-government sector which determine the level of net financial assets (denominated in the money unit) that are held by the non-government sector.

Only these transactions can create or destroy net financial assets in the non-government sector. In our simple two-person economy, the fundamental principle is that the non-government sector can only accumulate net financial assets if the government runs a fiscal deficit. We can now more fully appreciate that result. For example, when the treasury department purchases some equipment for a school, it will instruct the central bank to put funds into the bank account of the private supplier of the equipment. The bank entry is created because the government required it to be created. In effect, the entry was created 'out of thin air'. The private supplier now has a higher bank account balance (an increased asset) but there is no offsetting liability within the non-government sector. Net financial assets have increased in that sector as a result of the government spending. Conversely, when the government extracts tax revenue from the non-government sector, the taxpayer will, depending on the arrangements within the tax system, see more income extracted on pay day or an existing bank deposit reduced by the amount of the tax liability. Either way, financial assets decline in the non-government sector without any corresponding decline in liabilities. As a result net financial assets decrease.

But note that the intrinsic logic of a fiat monetary system is that taxes do not finance government spending, even if the government has accounting structures that make it look like they do. While taxes reduce balances in private sector bank accounts, the government doesn't actually get anything it needs. The reductions are accounted in the 'books' but do not enhance the capacity of the government to spend. Thus the concept of a fiat-issuing government saving in its own currency is of no relevance. Governments may use their net spending to purchase stored assets (for example, Norway's sovereign fund) but that is not the same as saying that government surpluses allow the government to spend more in the future. That concept is erroneous.

These transactions occur every day and if the government spends more than it receives by way of tax revenue (a deficit) then net financial assets in the non-government sector will rise. The main thing to keep in mind about taxes is that they reduce liquidity in the private sector. Fiscal deficits thus increase the financial wealth of the non-government sector. Fiscal surpluses, clearly, have the opposite effect. They destroy net financial assets and financial wealth in the non-government sector.

Two more points can be made. First, while the treasury policies may deliver fiscal surpluses (destruction of net financial assets) this could be countered by a deficit (of, say, equal magnitude) as a result of central bank operations (for example, a foreign exchange transaction involving the purchase of foreign currency held by residents using the domestic currency). This particular combination would leave a neutral net financial position for the non-government sector in the currency of issue. The two arms of government (treasury and central bank) work closely together in the real world on a daily basis and impact on both the stock of accumulated financial assets in the non-government sector and the composition of these assets. The government deficit (treasury operation) determines the cumulative stock of financial assets in the private sector. Central bank decisions then determine the composition of this stock in terms of notes and coins (cash), bank reserves (clearing balances) and government bonds. We analyse that last impact more fully further on.

However, most central bank operations merely shift non-government financial assets between bank reserves and government bonds, so for all practical purposes the central bank is not involved in altering net financial assets. The exceptions include the central bank purchasing and selling foreign exchange and paying its own operating expenses. Extending the model to distinguish the foreign sector makes no fundamental difference to the analysis and as such the private domestic and foreign sectors can be consolidated into the non-government sector without loss of analytical insight. Foreign transactions are largely distributional in nature, which means they alter the ownership of assets and liabilities between the nation and the rest of the world.

We will see how important these results are for understanding why mass unemployment occurs.

WHY DO GOVERNMENTS BORROW?

If currency-issuing governments do not need to borrow in order to run fiscal deficits then why do they continually issue debt? Under the gold standard governments had to borrow to spend more than their tax revenue. But since 1971 that necessity has lapsed. Now governments issue debt to match their deficits only as a result of pressure placed on them by neo-liberals to restrict their spending. Conservatives know that rising public debt can be politically manipulated and demonised, and they do this to put a brake on government spending. Interestingly, conservatives are schizoid on the question of public debt: public borrowing provides corporate welfare in the form of risk-free income flows to the rich because it allows them to safely park funds in bonds during uncertain times and provides a risk-free benchmark on which to price other, riskier financial products. The fact that bond yields have remained low throughout the latest economic crisis (reflecting strong demand for public debt) tells you that the parasitic bond markets do not buy the neo-liberal rhetoric. They know that national governments (outside the Eurozone) have no solvency risk.

WHAT ARE BANK RESERVES?

All the major banks have some money in so-called reserve accounts that they are obliged to keep with the central bank. The central bank may pay interest on positive balances kept in these accounts but some do not (for example, prior to the GFC, the Bank of Japan and the US Federal Reserve Bank offered no interest return on funds kept in reserve accounts). Banks also hold cash in their vaults, which is counted among their reserves. What do these 'reserves' do? Every day a myriad of transactions occur through the banking system as cheques are written against and deposited in the various banks in the system. The central bank acts as a clearinghouse for all these different financial claims to ensure no cheque is dishonoured. A bank will maintain what they consider to be a desirable level of reserves based on their expectation of the normal daily claims that will be made on it to honour cheques written by their customers and given to clients of other banks and the flow of funds it will expect from cheques written in favour of their customers by clients of other banks. These accounts typically have to have positive balances at the end of each day, although during the day a particular bank might be in surplus or deficit, depending on the pattern of the cash inflows and outflows. There is no reason to assume that these flows will exactly offset themselves for any particular bank at any particular time.

At the end of each day, the banks have to appraise the status of their reserve accounts. If a bank has more reserves than it believes it needs to meet its clearing obligations (that is, 'excess reserves') and does nothing, then it will earn the overnight rate offered by the central bank, which will typically be below the commercial rates at which it lends money. As noted, in normal times, many central banks pay a zero return on excess reserves. Clearly it is better for banks with excess reserves to lend them to other banks who might be short of reserves on that day in the hope they can get a market return above the rate the central bank pays. These transactions occur in the so-called interbank market, which is only accessible to banks, and loans are usually on a 24-hour settlement basis. The interbank rate of interest is the cost that banks pay to borrow reserves from other banks.

However, there may be several banks with excess reserves and competition between these banks for custom from other banks in need of reserves puts downward pressure on the interbank interest rate (sometimes called the overnight rate). If there is an overall excess of reserves in the banking system, the transactions between banks cannot eliminate it and the competitive process will drive the interbank rate down to the rate the central bank offers on overnight reserve balances, which could be zero. We will examine what this means for the conduct of monetary policy by the central bank in the next section.

What can a bank do if it cannot redress its shortage of reserves by borrowing in the interbank market? Any bank can *always* borrow the required funds from the central bank at a penalty interest rate (usually higher than the short-term interest rate). There can thus never be a shortage of reserve funds in the system as a whole because the central bank acts as a lender of last resort to the banks.

Another important point to understand is that banks do not loan out reserves to ordinary citizens. In Chapter 21, we will examine this point in detail and explain why the claim by mainstream economists and financial commentators that banks have greater lending capacity when they have more reserves is erroneous.

Finally, it is important to comprehend the link between fiscal policy outcomes (deficits or surpluses) and movements in bank reserves to fully grasp the impact of fiscal policy on interest rates. We have seen that when the government spends, increased deposits (credits) appear in various bank accounts (whether directly via electronic transfer or indirectly as cheques are posted and deposited). At the same time, the central bank also increases the reserves held by the relevant bank(s) by the amounts of the deposits created so that the bank will be able to cover cheques drawn on the new deposit by the beneficiary of the government spending. Taxation payments work in the opposite way. A fiscal deficit will therefore be associated with increasing bank reserves, which, in turn, has implications for the central bank's monetary policy stance.

THE CENTRAL BANK SETS THE SHORT-TERM INTEREST RATE AND GOVERNMENT DEBT FUNCTIONS TO SUPPORT IT

In most countries, the central bank conducts monetary policy by setting the short-run interest rate, which is an expression of how cheaply it wants money to be available in the economy to borrowers. This rate, sometimes called the policy or target rate, sets the benchmark for the longer-term commercial interest rates, such as home mortgage rates. If the central bank wants to make it more expensive for people to borrow from banks then it will increase the policy rate and vice versa. In normal times, the private loan and deposit rates will be tightly linked to the central bank's rate, deviating according to assessments of risk and expectations of future inflation, among other factors.

The central bank then has to manage its policy rate to ensure that developments in the private banking system do not undermine it. The central bank aims to keep the interbank rate in line with the policy rate. The rate at which a bank will extend loans is influenced by the price it has to pay for reserves. If that price falls, then it can still profit from offering loans at a lower interest rate. Building on the earlier discussion, if there are excess reserves in the system and the competitive process in the interbank market drives the price of these reserves down, then the policy rate would cease to discipline the market cost of gaining funds and the monetary policy stance of the central bank would falter.

To keep the interbank rate close to the policy rate, the central bank has a number of options. First, it can intervene into the interbank money market to manage the daily supply of and demand for reserve funds using so-called 'open market operations' (OMOs), which involve the buying and selling of government bonds. When there is an overall excess of reserves and the competitive pressures in the overnight funds market would drive the interbank rate below the desired policy rate, the central bank sells government bonds to the banks in return for reserves and thus 'drains' the excess liquidity. The banks prefer the interest earning government bonds to the lower returning excess reserve funds. The sale of government debt to the private sector allows the central bank to maintain its policy interest rate target. It has no connotation of raising funds for government spending. Second, the central bank can simply offer to pay the banks the policy rate on excess reserves, which also eliminates the incentive for banks to loan them out in the interbank market. In the GFC, most central banks exercised this option and as a result the volume of bank reserves rose sharply.

A related myth that students of macroeconomics are indoctrinated to believe is that government deficits accompanied by borrowing pushes up interest rates, which 'crowd out' private expenditures. We have seen that the central bank sets the short-run interest rate and is not subject to direct market forces. The orthodox macroeconomic approach argues that persistent deficits 'reduce national savings . . . [and require] . . . higher real interest rates and lower levels of investment spending' (DeLong, 2002: 405). Unfortunately, proponents of this logic fail to understand that the central bank can choose to set and leave the interest rate at 0 per cent, regardless, should it consider it desirable for the longer-term commercial lending rates to be lower. The 'crowding out' myth is considered in more detail in Chapter 21.

UNEMPLOYMENT OCCURS WHEN THE GOVERNMENT DEFICIT IS TOO LOW

We are now in a position to understand how mass unemployment arises and why government is central to its solution. There is no unemployment in traditional non-monetary economies or in non-monetary segments of a modern economy. For example, an unpaid child carer can never be unemployed. In monetary economies, the output of goods and services responds to spending. Firms and other organisations do not produce if they are not confident of selling their output. The production process generates a flow of income (paid to the various inputs to production). One person's spending is another person's income. A basic macroeconomic rule is that total spending must equal total income (whether actual income generated in production is fully spent or not in each period) for all the goods and services produced in any period to be sold. If total spending in a period is less than the total income generated, then firms will have unsold output in the form of unwanted inventory accumulation and will reduce future production and employment.

Why would total spending fall below total income in any period? A simple reason might be that households desire to save some of their income for future use or purchase imports, which means income generated in the domestic economy is spent abroad. The result of this spending deficiency is a rise in involuntary unemployment, which is idle labour offered for sale with no buyers at current wages. In this situation, making labour cheaper (cutting wages) will not reduce the unemployment, unless those cuts somehow increase total spending. Clearly, wages are an important component of total income and spending is dependent on income. Cutting wages is likely to worsen a spending shortfall.

In our simplified two-sector economy, if the non-government sector desires to save overall, it will spend less than its income. That shortfall in each period has to be eliminated by the government spending more than it receives in revenue to prevent a rise in mass unemployment. There is another complication. The non-government sector may desire to save overall but it also has to pay taxes from its income, which further reduces the amount that can be recycled back into the non-government spending stream each period. The imposition of taxation thus reduces the spending power of the non-government sector. That gap also has to be filled by government spending, which means 'taxes in aggregate will have to be less than total government spending' (Wray, 1998: 81). Thus, in general, deficit spending is necessary to ensure high levels of employment. Where there are high levels of unemployment, we could say that government spending is too low relative to the current tax receipts, or that taxes are too high relative to the level of government spending, after taking into account the overall saving desires by the non-government sector that have to be matched by government deficits.

The conclusion that mass unemployment is the result of the government deficit being too low also defines the limits on responsible government spending. It is clear that government spending has to be sufficient to allow taxes to be paid. In addition, net government spending is required to meet the non-government desire to save (accumulate net financial assets). The government should aim to maintain total spending such that firms are willing to produce and employ at levels sufficient to fully employ the available labour resources. Not a penny more need be spent by government.

This logic also allows us to see why the pursuit of government fiscal surpluses will be contractionary. Pursuing fiscal surpluses is necessarily equivalent to the pursuit of non-government sector deficits. They are two sides of the same coin. For a time, inadequate government deficits can continue without rising unemployment. In these situations, as is evidenced in many countries in the pre-GFC period, GDP growth can be driven by an expansion in private debt. The problem with this strategy is that when the private debt service levels reach some threshold percentage of income, the private sector will 'run out of borrowing capacity' as incomes limit debt service and banks become risk adverse. Typically, this will then provoke efforts to reduce the debt exposure (so-called 'balance sheet restructuring') and render the household and/or firm finances less precarious. As a consequence, total spending from private debt expansion slows and unemployment rises unless the government increases its deficit. If the government refuses to show this fiscal leadership then recession follows.

In the next two chapters, concrete applications of this MMT framework are explored as a precursor to framing the options that are available to the Eurozone at present. The array of myths that are used by neo-liberals to undermine the use of this fiscal freedom are also critically analysed.

18. Framing the debate: two alternative visions of the economy

> . . . there really is no alternative. (Margaret Thatcher, British Prime Minister, Press Conference for American correspondents in London, 25 June 1980)

> There is no alternative to the monetary union. (Wolfgang Schäuble, German Finance Minister, *Deutschland Financial Times*, 12 March 2010)

THE TINA MYTH

When considering the options that Europe faces, it is important to frame the debate in an acceptable economic framework. While poor political motivation cannot be ignored, a major part of the problem that currently besets the EMU nations arises from the application of a flawed macroeconomic framework that has been used by officials and their political masters since the 1980s. The gap between the 1970 Werner Report and the 1977 MacDougall Report, on the one hand, and the Delors Report (1989) on the other, reflected a fundamental shift in economic thinking towards Monetarism and its current neo-liberal manifestation. This shift reflects the re-emergence of the free market ideology rather than any superior appeal to evidential authority.

This chapter confronts the TINA ('there is no alternative') mantra that has been a powerful organising framework for conservatives to promote the myth that fiscal discipline and widespread deregulation will allow a free market to maximise wealth for us all. A significant part of this chapter is drawn from the work of Connors and Mitchell (2013) and also draws on the theoretical framework that was developed in Chapter 17. The argument rehearsed is fairly simple even if the concepts that underpin it are not. The neo-liberal economic framework, promoted vigorously by many economists, the multinational agencies such as the IMF and the OECD, and conservative politicians including the Eurozone establishment in Brussels and Frankfurt, blinds the public eyes to realistic alternatives by deliberately confining the boundaries of the public debate through the use of selective priorities, incorrect causalities, and scandalous misrepresentations of reality. Thus, before one can really appreciate the alternatives, we need to reframe the underlying economics. Otherwise, some of the actual and superior alternatives to the current fiscal austerity are too easily dismissed as being naïve, unrealistic or just downright crazy, if they are viewed and assessed through the neo-liberal economic lens. Chapter 17 outlined an alternative economics that is grounded in reality and has strong evidential support, in contradistinction to the dominant neo-liberal economics, which is grounded in conservative ideology and lacks empirical support. The task of this chapter is to apply this alternative approach to learn a new way of thinking and speaking about economics, which will condition our understanding of the various options that the Eurozone has available to it. With a new economic approach, a whole new world is open to us.

Macroeconomic concepts, such as real GDP, inflation and unemployment rate, the fiscal deficit, and the interest rate make headlines on a daily basis. Finance segments on national news broadcasts increasingly discuss macroeconomic issues with frequent recourse to complex terms that are not well understood by the majority of media commentators or the public. Consequently, the public discourse reflects significant errors that render it almost impossible for participants to make informed assessments of macroeconomic developments independent of the politics involved.

Economic concepts such as the government 'budget' deficit contain nuances that make unambiguous assessment of their meaning difficult. One cannot conclude, for example, that a deficit equal to 2 per cent of GDP signals that the government is trying to stimulate the economy more (a more expansionary fiscal stance) than if it was running a deficit half the size. These complexities are lost to the public but are fundamental to an accurate understanding of the issues.

Social media exacerbates this problem. The so-called blogosphere is populated with self-styled macroeconomic experts who make claims about such things as the state of the government finances that are erroneous at best. Reliance on 'common sense' logic or intuition becomes a dangerous guide in these cases and not all opinion should be given equal privilege in public discourse. Our propensity to generalise from personal experience, as if the experience constitutes general knowledge, continually leads these social media macroeconomic debates into combative dead ends of false reasoning.

Problems in communicating the complexities of economic concepts and evidence are amplified by the ideological assumptions that dominate the public debate. Economics as an academic discipline and profession has come to be defined by a set of beliefs that are associated with the dominant free market paradigm. The consequence of this is a narrow debate that excludes the lessons of history and alternative economic paradigms that offer realistic insights into current economic conditions and related policy options.

Conservative think tanks and media outlets produce an array of 'research' or 'policy' reports such that the public understanding has become straitjacketed by orthodox concepts and conclusions that in themselves are erroneous, but also lead to policy outcomes that undermine prosperity and subvert public purpose. The willingness to tolerate mass unemployment, rising income inequality and poverty is a manifestation of this syndrome.

Prior to the GFC, mainstream economists pronounced the business cycle dead and declared that we had entered a period of 'great moderation' (Stock and Watson, 2002; Lucas, 2003). These economists categorically failed to foresee the catastrophic consequences of the labour market and financial deregulation they promoted. The global economic crisis exposed the neo-liberal promise that markets can self-regulate and deliver sustained prosperity for all as a lie. But that doesn't seem to have registered with governments, which have, without exception, built their responses to the crisis on a series of myths, the same myths that caused the crisis.

The crisis was the culmination of three decades of policy choices made by governments infested with this neo-liberal lie. The Great Depression showed that markets fail badly if left unregulated and that governments have a strong role to play as an employer and a spender. Unfortunately, in the 1980s, governments abandoned these responsibilities and introduced widespread deregulation. This unleashed the destructive dynamics of capitalism, which mixed greed, criminality (for example, Enron, Libor scandal) and incompetence into a lethal cocktail, and ultimately manifested as the crisis. Our discussion has shown that European politicians added their own eccentricity to this neo-liberal mess by creating a monetary system that was doomed to fail and then imposed policy responses once the crisis unfolded that exacerbated the situation.

Now with millions unemployed, youth jobless rates in excess of 60 per cent in some advanced nations, inequality and poverty rates rising, and massive daily losses of national income being endured, governments have claimed that there is no alternative but to impose more austerity by cutting fiscal deficits and enforcing widespread cutbacks to social welfare systems. The unquestioned dominance of neo-liberal ideology has not only homogenised the political debate, but also obscured the only credible route to recovery. A correct assessment of the current state indicates that fiscal deficits have to increase. Austerity is exactly the opposite policy response to the one that is required. All the evidence is telling us that.

The extraordinary events in world financial markets in 2007 and 2008, which undermined the basis of monetary capitalism, initially led to massive injections of public spending. The stimulus packages promoted early recovery, which negated the claims by mainstream economists that fiscal policy (public spending minus taxes) was ineffective. The glaring defects of mainstream macroeconomic theory upon which the EMU was built were laid bare.

However, the neo-liberals soon began to reassert their dominance and what began as a problem of unsustainable private debt growth, driven by an out-of-control financial sector aided and abetted by government deregulation, has now mysteriously been reconstructed as an alleged sovereign debt crisis. Now conservatives, some of whom were direct beneficiaries of bailout packages in the early days of the crisis, tell us that our governments are bankrupt, that rising public debt burdens are enslaving our grandchildren and that hyperinflation is imminent. Governments are being pressured to cut deficits despite strong evidence that public stimulus has been the major source of economic growth during the crisis and that private spending remains subdued.

The crisis was created by a lie and the current solution, fiscal austerity, is making matters worse because it is built on the same lie. Public deficits do not necessarily cause inflation, nor do they impose crippling debt burdens on our children and grandchildren. Deficits do not cause interest rates to rise, choking private spending. Governments cannot run out of money unless the central bank in the relevant monetary system is voluntarily constrained such that support is prohibited. The greatest lie, endlessly repeated by neo-liberal economists and uncritically echoed by the mainstream media, is the claim that if governments cut their spending, the private sector will 'crowd in' to fill the gap.

In April 2013, some shoddy (at best) spreadsheet work by two high profile American economists was discovered. These economists had promoted the famous 90 per cent threshold on public debt, beyond which they erroneously claimed growth would contract and solvency would be threatened. Policy makers used this threshold to justify harsh cutbacks in public spending, which in turn have caused economic ruin. Together with the weight of empirical evidence, the simple discovery of this spreadsheet incompetence, some say fraud, has highlighted the fact that there are no credible grounds for the disastrous austerity that the IMF and the OECD have promoted and which many advanced nations have implemented. The fact that some flawed spreadsheet analysis became so influential among policy makers and the financial journalists helps us to understand why the crisis occurred and why many nations are still enduring massive daily output losses and rising unemployment. It is a triumph of ideology over evidence.

A sustained recovery in the Eurozone and elsewhere requires a categorical rejection of mainstream macroeconomic theory and practice. Economists should seek to understand how the monetary system actually works, not how they might wish it to work. MMT, which is ground in the operational realities of the system, not only predicted the crisis, but also provides credible recovery strategies that reject the austerity paradigm.

The fact that mainstream macroeconomics has retained its hegemonic status in the face of its failure to resonate with reality is, in no small way, due to the way economic debates are framed in the public discourse. Framing refers to the way an argument is conceptualised and communicated by speakers and listeners. Processes of conceptualisation proceed by way of adaptive reasoning on the basis of models and representations. Research in cognitive philosophy and cognitive linguistics suggests that the models that constrain our thinking operate at a largely unconscious level, and that the abstract concepts we draw on are 'largely metaphorical', 'imaginative', and 'emotionally engaged' (Lakoff and Johnson, 1999: 3–4).

Proponents of neo-liberal macroeconomics have been extremely successful in their use of common metaphors to advance their ideological interests. What is, in fact, a myth that is designed to advance a narrow ideological interest is constructed and accepted by the public as a verity. Thus ideology triumphs over evidence and we accept falsehoods as truth.

Recent psychological studies have highlighted the extent to which pre-existing biases influence the way in which we interpret factual information, including straightforward statistical data (for example, Kahan et al., 2013). This presents a problem for the communication of research outcomes that bear on public policy design, particularly where findings may be counterintuitive, or may challenge a dominant or controversial discourse, as in the case of economic austerity or climate change.

The communication of progressive points of view is complicated by the tolerance of diversity that characterises progressive politics: this diversity is reflected in extremely fragmented rhetoric. Often the language that is used to advocate a progressive alternative actually serves to reinforce conservative myths (see Lakoff, 2010; Wray, 2013). Shenker-Osorio (2012) considers the progressive side has no coherent story to tell and has been diverted by its failure to adopt a progressive language.

This chapter examines some of the basic metaphors that are used to advance the austerity agenda and confronts them with the basic MMT principles that were developed in Chapter 17. We argue that MMT has a coherent story to tell about the operations of the macroeconomy and provides new insights into the opportunities available to a government and its citizens concerning full employment, accessible high quality health, education and other infrastructure. The poverty of the EMU debate and its failure to embrace the coherency of MMT in its design and policy implementation is in no small way due to:

1. An incomplete understanding of key macroeconomic terms amongst economic commentators, especially journalists, and the wider community (lack of education); and
2. The deployment of key macroeconomic terms (incorrectly) in the context of pervasive cultural metaphors to support policy interventions that effectively benefit a privileged few at the expense of the majority.

TWO VISIONS OF THE ECONOMY

Shenker-Osorio (2012) juxtaposed two models of the economy. Figure 18.1 represents the conservative view, where the basic assumption is that 'people and nature exist primarily to serve the economy' (Shenker-Osorio, 2012: Location 439). This narrative tells us that a competitive, self-regulating economy will deliver maximum wealth and income if 'allowed' to operate with minimum intervention. The economy is figured as a deity that is removed from us though it recognises our endeavours and rewards us accordingly. We are required to have faith (confidence), work hard and make the necessary sacrifices for the good of the 'economy': those who do not are rightfully deprived of such rewards.

The economy is also figured as a living entity. If the government

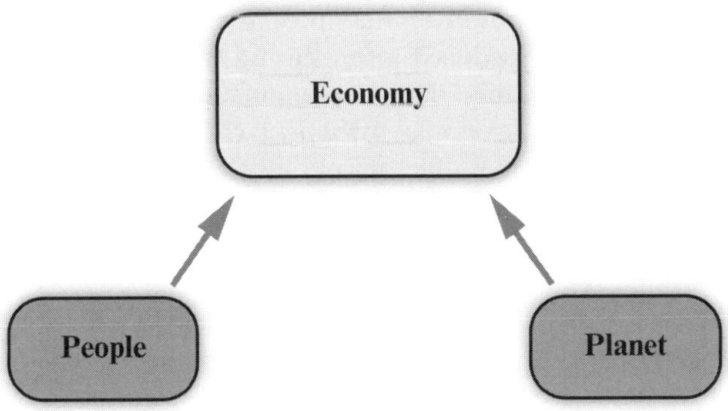

Source: Shenker-Osorio (2012).

Figure 18.1 The conservative economic construction

intervenes in the competitive process and provides an avenue where the undeserving (lazy, and so on) can receive rewards then the system becomes 'sick'. The solution is to restore the economy's natural processes (its health), which entails the elimination of government intervention such as minimum wages, job protection, and income support.

The key messages are 'self-governing and natural', which force the obvious conclusion that 'government "intrusion" does more harm than good, and we just have to accept current economic hardship' (Shenker-Osorio, 2012: Location 386). Although subscribers to this view would have us believe this is a rational narrative, in fact it represents a type of 'magical thinking' more appropriately associated with medieval views on the relationship between individuals and the world.

In the orthodox view, the hallmarks of a successful country are whether real GDP growth is strong irrespective of whether 'this comes at the expense of air quality, leisure time, life expectancy, or happiness . . . all of these are secondary' (Shenker-Osorio, 2012: Location 439). In the EMU context, price stability has been elevated to the top of priorities and the politicians judge success according to adherence to arbitrary financial ratios. They tolerate mass unemployment as if there is no choice. Discipline and sacrifice are eulogised even as poverty rates rise and a generation of youth is rapidly becoming dislocated from the normal pathways that provide for individual prosperity and maintain social stability.

The narrative teaches us that our own outcomes are dislocated from the success of the system and so success and failure are both represented as due primarily to our own efforts. Similarly, the unemployed are seen as being responsible for their jobless status, when in reality a systemic shortage of jobs explains their plight.

This narrative is so powerful that progressive politicians and commentators have become seduced into offering 'fairer' alternatives to the mainstream solutions rather than challenging mainstream assumptions root and branch. For example, progressives timidly advocate more gradual fiscal austerity when they should be comprehensively rejecting it on the basis of evidence that it fails, and advocating larger deficits to solve the massive rates of labour underutilisation that burden most economies. The euro Groupthink is so strong that progressives design all sorts of solutions to the crisis that will preserve the euro, when in fact it is the euro that is the problem.

Progressives and conservatives are hostage to the same erroneous beliefs about the way the economy operates; yet the public is compelled to believe there is no alternative to the damaging economic policies being introduced.

Figure 18.2 represents an alternative view of the economy, where the economy works for us as our construction and people are organically

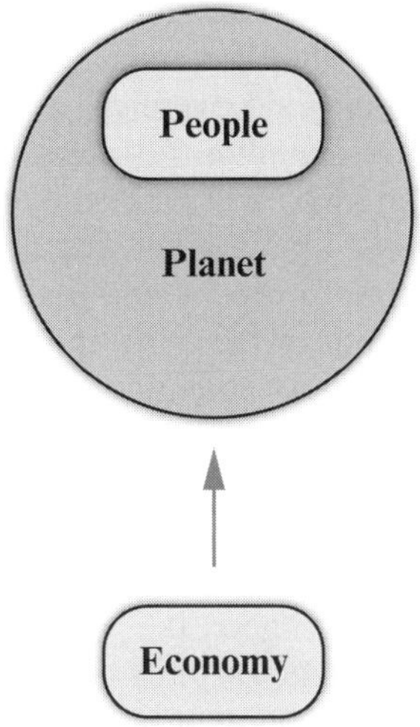

Source: Shenker-Osorio (2012).

Figure 18.2 The economy is us

embedded and nurtured by the natural environment. Shenker-Osorio (2012: Location 1037) says:

> This image depicts the notion that we, in close connection with and reliance upon our natural environment, are what really matters. The economy should be working on our behalf. Judgments about whether a suggested policy is positive or not should be considered in light of how that policy will promote our well-being, not how much it will increase the size of the economy.

In this view, the economy is seen as a 'constructed object' and policy interventions should be appraised in terms of how functional they are in relation to our broad goals, which a progressive vision would articulate in terms of advancing public wellbeing and maximising the potential for all citizens within the limits of environmental sustainability. The focus shifts to one of placing our human goals at the centre of our thinking about the economy. This perspective echoes the principles of functional finance (Lerner, 1943), which we examine in Chapter 19. Consistent with this, MMT highlights the irrelevance of a narrow focus on the fiscal balance without reference to a broader human context.

In this narrative, people create the economy. There is nothing natural about it. Concepts such as the 'natural rate of unemployment', which imply that it should be left to its own equilibrating forces to reach its natural state, are erroneous. Governments can always choose and sustain a particular unemployment rate. We create government as our agent to do things that we cannot easily do ourselves and we understand that the economy will only serve our common purposes if it is subjected to active oversight and control. The EMU was created by human effort and can be dismantled accordingly. The union is not irrevocable and the euro is not irreplaceable. The claim that Europe would plunge back into a new 'dark age' if a single nation abandons the euro and restores its own currency sovereignty is simply Groupthink polemic.

The two visions of the economy can be summarised in value terms as individualistic (Figure 18.1) and collectivist (Figure 18.2). For a progressive, collective will is important because it provides the political justification for more equally sharing the costs and benefits of economic activity. Progressives have historically argued that government has an obligation to create work if the private market fails to create enough employment. Accordingly, collective will means that our government is empowered to use net spending (deficits) to ensure there are enough jobs available for all those who want to work.

The contest between the two visions outlined in Figures 18.1 and 18.2 has spawned a long-running debate in the academy. It played out during the Great Depression, which taught us that policy intervention was elemental in order to rein in the chaotic and damaging forces of greed and power that underpin the capitalist monetary system. We learned that so-called 'market' signals would not deliver satisfactory levels of employment and that the system could easily come to rest and cause mass unemployment. We learned that this malaise was brought about by a lack of spending and that the government had the spending capacity to redress these shortfalls and ensure that all those who wanted to work could do so.

From the Great Depression, and responses to it, we learned that the economy was a construct, not a deity, and that we could control it through fiscal and monetary policy in order to create desirable collective outcomes. The Great Depression taught us that the economy should be understood as our creation, designed to deliver benefits to us, not an abstract entity that distributes rewards or punishments according to a moral framework. The government is therefore not a moral arbiter but a functional entity serving our needs. Our experiences during the period of the Great Depression led to a complete rejection of neo-classical macroeconomics (the forerunner of the modern neo-liberal variant).

The OPEC oil price hikes in the 1970s provided the switch point that saw the conservative ideas represented in Figure 18.1 regain ascendancy (see Mitchell and Muysken, 2008), despite them being cast into disrepute during the 1930s by the work of Keynes and others.

The ways in which governments around the world have responded to the GFC, in contrast to responses to the Great Depression, offer insights into the extent to which orthodox economic rhetoric has come to define economics as a profession and the public's understanding of the policy options that flow from this, guiding societies away from a model of the economy that serves to maximise collective wellbeing.

The resurgence of the free market paradigm has been accompanied by a well-crafted public campaign where framing and metaphor triumph over operational reality or theoretical superiority. This process has been assisted by business and other anti-government interests, which have provided significant funds to emergent conservative, free market 'think tanks' (Quirk, 2011). Beder (1999: 30) argues that these institutions fine tuned 'the art of "directed conclusions", tailoring their studies to suit their clients or donors' (Beder, 1999: 30). Politicians parade these so-called 'independent' research findings as the authority needed to justify their deregulation agendas. Multilateral organisations such as the IMF also continue to distort policy debates with their erroneous claims and, in the case of the IMF, incompetent and error-prone modelling.

DOMINANT METAPHORS IN ECONOMIC COMMENTARY

Connors and Mitchell (2013) provide an overview of the assumptions that underpin cognitive linguistics and cognitive philosophy, which help explain why it has been difficult to mount a coherent challenge to orthodox macroeconomic views. The mainstream theoretical models in macroeconomics that reinforce the conception of the economy represented by Figure 18.1 do not embrace the basic characteristics of the real world economy. The public in general is not aware of the impoverished status of mainstream economic theory and this limits the debate concerning options for the EMU.

Prior to the GFC, the dominant neo-liberal economic models (so-called New Keynesian models) ignored any mention of banks and assumed that financial markets would always deliver the best outcomes for all. Willem Buiter (2009) writes that the shortcomings of the mainstream approach to financial markets that underpin the neo-liberal conception of the world 'was obvious to virtually all those whose cognitive abilities had not been warped by a modern Anglo-American Ph.D. education' (see also Mitchell and Muysken, 2008).

The dominance of mainstream macroeconomics narratives in the EMU debates is achieved through a series of linked myths that are reinforced

Table 18.1 Examples of neo-liberal macroeconomic metaphors

Focus of attack	Metaphor	Intent
Government spending	Living beyond means	Excess, sacrifice needed Cuts needed immediately
	Nation has maxed out its credit card	Run out of money Irresponsible spending
	Spending like a drunken sailor	Wanton irresponsibility, delinquent
Fiscal balance	Budget black hole	Astronomical analogy Collapse of massive star
	Deteriorating state of the budget	Health analogy – illness, emergency TINA – surgery
	Mushrooming budget deficit	Out of control and unbalanced
	The nation has run out of money, it is broke	Government budget is like a household budget – the economy is like us
	Ballooning deficits and debt	Out of control
Public debt	The US is bankrupt	Nation is a badly managed insolvent firm
	The debt mountain	Huge, insurmountable, significant
	Burdening our grandchildren	Undermining family values
	Mortgaging the future	Undermining future
Income support	Welfare dependency	Drug addiction, ill health
	Dole bludgers, skivers	Laziness, undeserving
	Working families	The paragon

with strong metaphors. Table 18.1 shows some of the popular examples of metaphors used by mainstream economists and commentators to focus their attack on government spending, deficits, public debt and income support payments for the most disadvantaged workers. These metaphors are designed to reinforce the main core values that the neo-liberals seek to promote, such as self-discipline, independence, ambition, wealth and sacrifice (see Figure 18.1).

These metaphors obscure the truth and lead us to support policies that make us worse off even when there are alternatives that would make us all, in a collective sense, better off. They support the TINA narrative when in fact there are very real and demonstrably superior options for Europeans, some of which retain the euro while others would abandon it.

FACE TO FACE – MAINSTREAM MACROECONOMICS AND MODERN MONETARY THEORY

Metaphors, such as those in Table 18.1, reinforce a series of propositions promoted by mainstream economists and conservative commentators to focus their attack on government intervention. They are at the core of the European Groupthink that claims the euro has to be retained at all costs. We juxtapose them against the relevant operational reality presented by MMT, which we developed in considerable detail in Chapter 17.

Proposition 1 The government faces the same budget constraints as a household.

The household budget analogy is false. Households use the currency and must finance their spending. A sovereign government issues the currency and must spend first before it can subsequently tax or borrow. A household cannot spend more than its revenue indefinitely because continuously increasing private debt is unsustainable. The budget choices facing a household are thus limited and prevent permanent deficits. A currency-issuing government can never be revenue constrained in a technical sense and can sustain deficits indefinitely without solvency risk.

The euro nations are an exception. They surrendered currency sovereignty and thus have to borrow to cover deficits, which makes them dependent on bond markets (in lieu of ECB support) and exposes them to solvency risk. The currency monopoly in the Eurozone is at present made up of the ECB and the national governments, although that is an ineffective way to organise the currency. Further, the rules and policy practice that have been deliberately put in place actually thwart any chance that currency monopoly can function effectively. To ensure there is financial stability, confidence in the banking system and prosperity, the regulations governing the ECB should be changed to allow it to underwrite the national government deficits in lieu of a federal fiscal authority being established.

Implications

- The household budget analogy is inapplicable.
- Our own personal budget experience generates no knowledge relevant to consideration of government matters.
- An alternative narrative must highlight the special characteristics of the government's currency monopoly.

Proposition 2 Fiscal deficits are bad and fiscal surpluses are good.

Once we reject the household budget analogy, we need to be careful with language, a point taken up in more detail in the next section. Throughout this book we have used the term 'fiscal' instead of 'budget' to refer to government spending and taxation. So a fiscal deficit (surplus) is when spending exceeds (falls short of) tax revenue. Fiscal deficits are neither good nor bad and, in accounting terms, equal the non-government surplus. In behavioural terms, they are required when spending intentions of the non-government sector are insufficient to ensure full utilisation of available productive resources. The context matters because the fiscal balance is a vehicle for achieving socio-economic goals rather than an end in itself.

Similarly, fiscal surpluses are neither good nor bad and may be harmful in some circumstances. Conversely, for a nation with strong net exports, quality public services, and national income levels sufficient to support the private sector's saving desires, a surplus may be required to contain nominal aggregate demand and avoid inflation.

There are two problems with using the summary term fiscal deficit to describe the state of affairs in a nation. First, the fiscal outcome is determined by the state of overall activity and is, largely, beyond the control of government. This militates against the use of arbitrary and rigid fiscal rules. If private spending is weak then the deficit will typically rise as tax revenue declines irrespective of what the government does. Movements in the fiscal balance are thus ambiguous. A given fiscal outcome can signal that the deficit is 'good', if it has arisen as a result of discretionary fiscal policy decisions by government to maintain full employment given the spending and saving decisions of the non-government sector; or 'bad', if it has arisen because non-government spending has fallen and the automatic stabilisers have led to a decline in tax revenue and an increase in unemployment. When private spending collapses and the deficit rises, the correct response is to increase discretionary net public spending, not cut it.

Second, the term 'deficit' has a negative connotation because it signifies a shortfall, which while accurate in an accounting sense, is highly misleading in the context of the positive contribution that a deficit makes to non-government sector net financial wealth. Government deficits are the sole source of net financial assets for the non-government sector. All transactions between agents in the non-government sector net to zero. This accounting reality means that if the non-government sector wants to net save in the currency of issue, then the government has to be in deficit.

The sectoral balances derived from the national accounts generalise this result and show that the government deficit (surplus) *always* equals the non-government surplus (deficit). The systematic pursuit of government surpluses is necessarily manifested as systematic declines in non-government overall savings. Fiscal surpluses either destroy private wealth by forcing the private sector to liquidate its wealth to get cash, or destroy liquidity (debiting reserve accounts), which is deflationary. With an external deficit, fiscal surpluses result in increasing private domestic sector debt levels.

This cannot be a viable long-term growth strategy because the financially constrained private domestic sector is unlikely to be able to sustain ongoing deficits. Ultimately, the decision by the private domestic sector to increase its net saving and reduce its debt levels will interact with the fiscal drag coming from the surpluses and force the economy into recession. The cyclical component of the fiscal balance will then push the deficit back into a (bad) deficit.

Implications

- Understanding the context in which a particular fiscal outcome occurs is crucial to a reasoned assessment of the appropriateness of the fiscal position.
- The fact that a fiscal deficit allows the non-government sector to save overall and a fiscal surplus destroys non-government wealth should be promoted.

Proposition 3 Fiscal surpluses contribute to national saving.

A currency-issuing government does not save in its own currency. Fiscal surpluses do not represent 'public saving', which can be used to fund future public expenditure. Saving is an act of foregoing current spending to enhance future spending possibilities and applies to a financially constrained non-government entity, such as a household.

A currency-issuing government never needs prior funds in order to spend and thus never needs to 'save'. Fiscal surpluses provide no greater capacity to governments to meet future needs, nor do fiscal deficits erode that capacity. The constraints on government spending are not financial but are defined by the availability of real resources that are available for sale in the currency that the government issues (see Proposition 7). Clearly, this also holds in the Eurozone if we consider the ECB to be the central banker to the national governments and would hold if a fully functional federal fiscal authority were established. The current operational framework in the Eurozone deliberately undermines the capacity of fiscal policy to serve the function for which it is designed.

Implications

- Fiscal surpluses destroy non-government wealth.
- Fiscal deficits increase non-government wealth.

Proposition 4 The fiscal outcome should be balanced over the economic cycle.

Recognising that the fiscal outcome is endogenous means that the government cannot realistically target a fiscal outcome because changes in private spending, for example, can thwart any efforts made by the government to achieve that target. The responsible strategy for a government is to allow its fiscal outcome to adjust to the level of net spending (deficit) required to achieve full employment, given the spending decisions of the non-government sector, irrespective of the state of the economic cycle.

The national accounts tell us that for a nation with an external deficit, a 'balanced budget rule' is tantamount to requiring the private domestic sector record a deficit of equal magnitude to the external deficit. This is unlikely to be a sustainable strategy.

Further, a counter cyclical fiscal strategy does not require the government to achieve a surplus. The concept of counter cyclicality more correctly refers to the direction of change rather than the level of the fiscal outcome. The government should not increase its discretionary net spending if the economy is already at full capacity and it is satisfied with the private spending mix. Such an expansion would be pro-cyclical. But holding a steady deficit where the external deficit is steady and the private domestic sector is saving overall and content with that outcome is desirable.

Implications

- Fiscal rules defined in terms of public debt or deficit ratios are unlikely to be consistent with the responsible management of fiscal policy.
- A currency-issuing government should pursue functional targets and allow its fiscal outcome to adjust accordingly.

Proposition 5 Fiscal deficits drive up interest rates and crowd out private investment because they compete for scarce private saving.

This is a specific version of Proposition 2. There is no competition for finite savings between public and private borrowers. First, government deficits stimulate growth and private savings as national income grows. Second, the funds that the government borrows from the non-government sector ultimately originate from the net financial assets created by past deficits. Third, bank lending is not 'reserve constrained' and banks will extend loans to any creditworthy customer. If the banks are short of reserves then they borrow from each other in the interbank market. Ultimately, they can always borrow from the central bank.

History shows that Japan has run large deficits since the early 1990s while simultaneously maintaining zero interest rates and low inflation. Further, budget deficits have risen sharply in recent years in most nations but interest rates have remained close to zero. The reality is that the central bank sets interest rates, not the market.

Moreover, deficits place downward pressure on interest rates. Debt issuance serves to allow the central bank to maintain a positive target interest rate by providing investors with an interest bearing asset that drains the excess reserves in the banking system that result from deficit spending. If these reserves were not drained (that is, if the government did not borrow) then in an environment of government deficits, the overnight interest rate would fall (due to competition by banks to rid themselves of the non-profitable reserves) and this might compromise the central bank's target interest rate, unless it offered a return on excess reserves, which most do.

A related claim is that the sovereign issuer of currency is at risk of default if the public debt ratio rises above some threshold (often construed as 80 or 90 per cent). As long as the government only issues debt in its own currency and provides no assurances about convertibility into another currency, the default risk is zero. Again, this proposition highlights the deficiency of the Eurozone design. Each of the national governments is forced to issue debt in a foreign currency. A way forward while retaining the euro would be to establish a federal fiscal authority and link it intrinsically with the ECB, such that its debt was always guaranteed by the currency issuer and thus risk free. This is quite apart from the discussion in Chapter 21 on overt monetary financing, which eschews the very issuance of debt. Clearly, historical, political and cultural constraints will prevent the proper links between a federal fiscal authority and the ECB from being created, which helps explain why the monetary union became crisis prone in the first place.

Implications

- Public debt is used as part of an interest maintenance strategy by central banks and does not fund government spending.

- There is no default risk for debt issued by a government in its own currency.
- Currency-issuing governments do not need to borrow.

Proposition 6 Fiscal deficits mean higher taxes in the future.

Taxes serve many purposes (for example, reducing private sector purchasing power, reducing consumption of harmful goods and services such as tobacco, and so on) but none of these purposes relate to funding government spending.

In a fiat monetary system, where the currency has no intrinsic worth, the government needs to transfer real goods and services from the non-government to the government sector to facilitate its economic and social program. In this context, a primary function of taxation is to promote offers from private individuals to the government of goods and services in return for the necessary funds to extinguish tax liabilities. The crucial point is that the funds necessary to pay the tax liabilities are provided to the non-government sector by government spending. Accordingly, government spending, if sufficient, provides the paid work, which eliminates the unemployment created by the taxes.

Another way of expressing this role of taxes is to recognise that by depriving the non-government sector of purchasing power, they can attenuate aggregate demand so that government spending has the real resource space necessary without incurring inflation.

Importantly, every generation can freely choose the level of taxation it pays because it determines, through the political process, the size of government and the real resource space it will utilise. Past fiscal deficits never need to be paid back by the current generation. A related proposition that taxpayer money should not be wasted is flawed as a result of the erroneous causality implied that taxes fund government spending.

Implications

- Taxpayers do not fund government spending.
- Taxes are required to reduce the capacity of the non-government sector to command real goods and services so that government can utilise them.

Proposition 7 The government will run out of fiscal space (money).

This is related to Propositions 1, 5 and 6. Conservative politicians and media commentators often claim the government will run out of money if it does not curb spending. They attempt to give this statement authority by appealing to our intuition and experience, that is, they draw on the household budget analogy and claim that governments, like households, have to live within their means. This analogy resonates strongly with voters because it attempts to relate the more amorphous finances of a government with our daily household finances. We know that we cannot run up our household debt forever and that we have to tighten our belts when our credit cards reach our borrowing limit. We can borrow to enhance current spending, but eventually we have to sacrifice spending to pay the debts back. We intuitively understand that we cannot indefinitely live beyond our means.

As we have seen, a currency-issuing government has no financial constraints and can never run out of money. Fiscal space is thus more accurately defined as the real goods and services available for sale in the currency of issue. These are the 'means' available to government to fulfil its socio-economic charter. The currency-issuing government can always purchase whatever is for sale in its own currency. Even a national government within the Eurozone would enjoy that status if the ECB acted as an efficient currency issuer whose primary responsibility was to support full employment *and* price stability.

This is also related to the intergenerational (ageing) population claims that pension and health care systems will be unsustainable in the future. There are no financial constraints on a currency-issuing government providing first class health care and/or pensions in the future. The challenge of rising dependency ratios will be whether productivity growth ensures there are adequate real goods and services available to maintain growth in living standards with fewer workers available. These are not financial constraints.

A variation on this proposition is that public debt imposes intergenerational burdens when past fiscal deficits have to be paid back. Deficits are not 'paid back' and intergenerational burdens are linked to the availability of real resources. For example, a generation that exhausts a non-renewable resource imposes a burden on the next generation.

Implications

- Fiscal space is not defined in terms of some given financial ratios (such as a public debt ratio).
- Fiscal space refers to the extent of the available real resources that the government is able to utilise in pursuit of its socio-economic program.

Proposition 8 Government spending is inflationary.

All spending (private or public) is inflationary if it drives nominal aggregate demand faster than the real capacity of the economy to absorb it. Increased government spending is not inflationary if there are idle real resources that can be brought back into productive use (for example, from unemployment).

Related propositions include the claims that issuing bonds to the central bank, the so-called 'printing money' option, devalues the currency whereas issuing bonds to the private sector reduces the inflation risk of deficits. Neither claim is true. First, there is no difference in the inflation risk attached to a particular level of net public spending when the government matches its deficit with bond issuance relative to a situation where it issues no debt, that is, invests directly. Bond purchases reflect portfolio decisions regarding how private wealth is held. If the funds that we used for bond purchases were spent on goods and services as an alternative, then the fiscal deficit would be lower as a result. Second, the provision of credit by the central bank (in return for treasury bonds) will only be inflationary if there is no fiscal space (see Proposition 7).

Hyperinflation examples such as 1920s Germany and modern day Zimbabwe do not support the claim that deficits cause inflation. In both cases, there were major reductions in the supply capacity of the economy prior to the inflationary episode. We consider that issue in more detail in Chapter 21.

Implications

- All spending carries an inflation risk and issuing treasury bonds does not mitigate the risk associated with public spending.
- Government deficits should seek to bring idle resources back into productive use.
- The limits of non-inflationary public spending are defined by the fiscal space available.

Proposition 9 Fiscal deficits lead to big government.

Fiscal deficits may reflect large or small government. Even small governments will need to run continuous deficits if there is a desire of the non-government sector to save overall and the policy aim is to maintain full employment levels of national income.

Economic theory does not specify an optimal size of government. This reflects an ideological commitment with no basis in economic theory. The size of government will reflect the preferences of the population for public provision of goods and services and infrastructure.

Implications

- The size of government is a political choice rather than an economic necessity.
- Even small governments will typically run continuous deficits to maintain full employment.

MOVING TOWARDS BETTER OPTIONS FOR EUROPE

While MMT provides an internally consistent and empirically robust account of the way the economy works and demonstrates the effective (and ineffective) way to construct the currency monopoly, it also clearly challenges the way in which humans think about macroeconomic concepts. The task is to frame a progressive macroeconomics narrative, based on MMT concepts, which can overcome these challenges. While MMT provides an accurate description of how the capitalist monetary system operates and can support policy prescriptions consistent with either the individualistic or collective value systems, we prefer to situate this challenge within a collective vision of public purpose.

A related advantage for progressives of promoting public awareness in MMT is that the ideological basis of conservative policy agendas would become more transparent. It could no longer be said that fiscal austerity needs to be imposed because the government has run out of money. In the Eurozone context, it would become obvious that the millions of jobless were the direct result of preventing the ECB from acting as an effective central bank. It is anticipated that if the public were to have a better understanding of how the system actually works and could correctly distinguish between fiscal space constraints and ideological constraints, it would demand an end to austerity and require policy responses that enhanced collective and individual wellbeing. No reasonable person would be prepared to tolerate increased poverty and mass unemployment if they knew that its source was an irrational religious/ideological belief that 'markets' are superior.

The progressive starting point has to be the social purpose of government policy rather than a view of the economy as a natural entity, separated from us, which gets sick if government attempts to alter its natural course. The social purpose of government policy should be articulated and narrated in ways that will resonate with and activate the frames in our brains that constrain the way we interpret information. That exercise should pre-date the presentation of the facts about the way the economy actually works.

As an example, the New Zealand Mayors Taskforce for Jobs developed its policy interventions and said it was 'working towards the "zero waste" of New Zealanders' (see http://www.mayorstaskforceforjobs.co.nz/). They promoted their mission with slogans such as 'Our Youth, Our Future'. These objectives can easily be generalised to embrace all citizens, with additional goals being defined for those that are not able to work.

Importantly, these mission statements cannot be a reflection of general goals that have almost universal desirability but no associated concrete actions. The debate between conservatives and progressives is not about whether there should be full employment but what that means in action. For example, does full employment mean 5 per cent unemployment or 2 per cent? Who is responsible for its attainment? How should it be attained?

We might think that 'Jobs for all that want to work' is a desirable purpose. Almost everyone would agree on that. But progressives have to relate this generality to a policy action, aggregate demand has to rise by x per cent and y million jobs have to be created. Progressives have to invoke event-causation structures to force the debate to move beyond generalities such as 'free markets will grow the economy and create jobs'. They have to clearly articulate why mass unemployment occurs and how it will not naturally cure itself. Further, by implicating the government as part of the solution they have to counter such claims that governments do not create jobs by detailing public employment initiatives that clearly create productive work.

PROGRESSIVE LANGUAGE AND METAPHOR

The progressive challenge is in two parts: (a) a need to better educate the public regarding macroeconomic matters in ways that our learning skills can absorb; (b) develop language that appeals to our intrinsic frames, which foster concern and action (such as economic justice/rights) and connect people with the economy rather than reinforce the Figure 18.1 idea that the economy is a natural construct that we should fear. In this vein, a progressive narrative has to use, according to Lakoff (2010), 'insight into the nature of unconscious reason and the role of language' to frame the message. While this topic is part of a larger research project this author is engaged in, here are some examples of how we might proceed.

The primary metaphor Purposes are Destinations relates to the subjective judgement that we want to achieve purposes and we succeed when we reach a destination.

Progressives must define the destination in terms of people rather than in terms of an independent 'economy' or 'how to save the euro'. For example, we might define our purpose as having 'zero waste of people'. This destination is then reached not when the public debt ratio is x per cent but when unemployment is at 2–3 per cent and there is zero underemployment and other forms of precarious work. Rather than complain about high unemployment, we must always specify the desired destination, which links with the Purposes are Desired Objects metaphor. Accordingly, debating financial ratios such as the size of deficits merely reinforces the conservative frames about sacrifice, solvency, rectitude, and drunken sailors. Progressives must always focus on the desired objects that relate directly to the intrinsic frames.

A key issue concerns language and terminology. As Shenker-Osorio notes, the term 'spending' may be problematic because to 'spend' means to 'use up'. This implies that what is spent has then gone and is no longer with us. This language supports erroneous assumptions about what a government that issues its own currency does with its money (Shenker-Osorio, 2012: Location 452). Our language needs to reinforce the reality that government spending injects financial assets into the system, which not only meet 'critical human needs' but 'change hands again and again . . . [and] have their efficacy multiplied through exchange' (Shenker-Osorio, 2012: Location 452).

We might thus say:

Governments invest to enhance our purposes (rather than spend).

Invest is a term we readily relate to wealth creation – that is, 'building up' not 'using up'.

This invokes the More is Up metaphor, which works in reverse for something that is considered 'bad'. We noted that the term 'fiscal deficit' has a negative connotation because it signifies a shortfall. In part, this relates to Proposition 1 – the household analogy. Using 'budget' with 'deficit' triggers this analogy immediately. We should thus only use the term 'government deficit (surplus)' or 'fiscal deficit (surplus)' and eschew the use of the accompanying qualifier 'budget'.

The term deficit is clearly accurate in an accounting sense, but highly misleading in the context of the contribution that a deficit makes to non-government sector net financial wealth. But trying to replace the term deficit would almost certainly result in a total loss of meaning, further complicating the challenge to win over the public debate. We thus consider that the progressive challenge is not to invent a new term for deficit, but rather to exploit the More is Up metaphor to advantage. First, the household analogy should be debunked regularly; we can run out of money but how can the government? Even a Eurozone government can only run out of euros if the ECB allows it to. This means a thorough debate about the role of the ECB is required rather than hiding behind amorphous statements about the sanctity of central bank independence and safeguarding the currency. A related issue that needs to be debunked is the linked connotation to inflation and 'printing money'. That issue is discussed in Chapter 21.

Second, we can exploit the More is Up metaphor by always relating the government deficit to its non-government manifestation: the rising net financial assets that a deficit provides.

So we should say:

The government deficit rose and generated higher levels of wealth for households and firms.

This type of language also more aggressively invokes the Event-Structure metaphor, which constructs 'purposes as destinations to be reached' (Lakoff and Johnson, 1999: 94). The destination must be prominent in the narrative and then we must specify the causal chains through which the purposes are achieved. Causation is linked to concepts of forced movement where, for example, we might say that the government deficit is the application of a force (the injection of net financial assets), which causes a change of state (higher income, employment, or wealth).

Lakoff and Johnson (1999: 91) say the concept of forced movement suggests to us that the 'movement would not have occurred without the application of the force' (that is, the economy is a construct rather than a natural equilibrating system beyond us) and that the improvement in national income or employment was the direct result of the cause (the government stimulus).

People respond to the logic where 'causes are forces' and 'causation is forced movement'. In the 'economy as a natural system or deity' approach, government regulations and interventions are unnecessary and damaging. In the progressive alternative, the same actions force movement towards our desired destinations and, without the force, the current state does not change and the goals are thus not achieved.

We want government to act on our behalf to move us from State A (less desirable) to State B (closer to our purpose). It is important to note that the economy has no goals. They are *our* goals and *we* use, manage, and control the economy to achieve our goals. There are always alternatives.

Further, careful choice of frames to promote in the public debate is important. For example, while conservatives focus on concepts such as 'tax relief' to attack government, progressives should frame the debate by emphasising the need for 'unemployment relief', a frame that makes unemployment painful and a reduction in the pain a desired goal.

Relatedly, progressives should avoid debating within the frames that conservatives use. For example, attacking the British government's pursuit of fiscal austerity as being 'too fast' implies that the desirable alternative is more gradual (managed) reduction in the government deficit. The frame is that the fiscal deficit is bad and has to be reduced. The more productive progressive frame would be to explicate the functional role of government deficits. Progressive rhetoric must continually reference the costs to people of conservative policies. A demand for 'relief' from high unemployment reframes the debate and focuses on the failure by conservative forces to reach the desired destination (access to employment). Every statement must reinforce purposes and destinations that define how we feel about policy.

FISCAL SPACE

Propositions 2 and 6 show that the government deficit always equals the non-government surplus, and the government surplus always equals the non government deficit. For most nations, the combination of external deficits and a desire by the private domestic sector to save overall, means that the non-government sector will act as a drain on overall spending in relation to income flows. This means a continuous fiscal deficit is required to sustain a given level of activity.

A progressive macroeconomics agenda thus has to recognise that a normal state will require continuous government deficits over each economic cycle rising and falling with fluctuations in non-government sector net spending. Rarely will a government surplus be appropriate. Further, government deficits are not just appropriate in times of recession or slow growth. They are required whenever there is a non-government desire for a surplus, which is the typical case.

We might thus continually reinforce the frame:

Government deficits are normal, surpluses are atypical.

This means that 'balanced budgets over the cycle' type arguments, which progressives use in order to appear responsible, 'deficits in bad times, surpluses later when times are better', are destructive and fall into the misleading 'deficits are bad' frame. Progressives should thus frame the concept of fiscal space in terms of the idle real resources that can be brought into productive use via higher government spending and/or lower taxation. The idle resources signal that the government deficit is too low or the surplus is too large. The desired destination is zero waste and the required action is a larger deficit.

In the Eurozone there is thus massive fiscal space available for governments to expand their deficits. In calibrating that space in mainstream terms, it is likely to exceed the fiscal limits specified by the SGP by a substantial margin. But of course, such rules have no application in a correct assessment of what fiscal space is available.

COSTS OF A PUBLIC PROGRAM

The emphasis on real resource availability as the demarcation of fiscal space is also related to a frame relating to cost.

We often hear or read statements such as:

- Cost to taxpayer
- The new school cost . . .
- The nation cannot afford the cost of that . . .

If we were to take a public employment program that required government to spend $x billion in wages, capital equipment, administration and oversight, we might reasonably ask about the cost of that program. The conservative frame tells us that the cost is $x (the figure that appears in the annual budget documents against the program).

The progressive frame considers the $x in the 'budget' papers to be of little interest. The actual cost of the program is the change it causes in the usage of real resources, more consumption by the unemployed workers, some equipment, and so on. An additional cost would be the opportunity costs of such a program (that is, the resources that are diverted from other uses as a result of it) which are minimal given the unemployed are idle. These costs are excluded from the conservative frame.

When we ask whether the nation can afford an initiative that a currency-issuing government wishes to implement, we should ignore the $x and consider what real resources are available, as in levels of unemployment, equipment etc. Those available resources constitute the fiscal space. Whenever we talk about fiscal policy it should always be in relation to the fiscal space rather than centred on $x. The fiscal space should then always be related to the purposes to which we aspire and the destination we wish to reach.

SUMMARY

MMT provides an accurate description of how the monetary system actually operates. It remains an accurate account of the macroeconomy regardless of whether the policy framework the economy supports is driven by an individualistic or a collectivist value system. Responsible economic management does not entail a commitment to an orthodox economic model, or to a positive or negative figure in a fiscal balance.

The decision to pursue a policy framework consistent with Figure 18.1 is purely ideological. Orthodox economic rhetoric associated with Figure 18.1 trades on an incomplete understanding of macroeconomic realities and exploits powerful metaphors to ensure that these realities and related policy opportunities are obscured from vision.

When this economic reality is understood and framed in an accessible way, it is anticipated that decisions to cut spending on welfare and other public goods will be seen not as responsible economic management, but ideologically motivated decisions that deprive our children of a future and rob the most vulnerable members of our society of the opportunity to thrive.

19. The basic principles of functional finance

> Many of our publicly minded men who have come to see that deficit spending actually works still oppose the permanent maintenance of prosperity because in their failure to see *how* it works they are easily frightened by fairy tales of terrible consequences. (Lerner, 1943: 38)

Important aspects of MMT are derived from the work of economist Abba Lerner, who emphasised that the conduct and evaluation of economic policy should be intrinsically linked to the aim of advancing social purpose. As in Figure 18.2, economic policy cannot be assessed without regard to the functions it serves. Trying to assess whether the economic policy settings are 'good' or 'bad' in terms of whether the fiscal deficit is below or above 3 per cent of GDP is meaningless.

In 1943, Abba Lerner provided a roadmap for governments aiming to eliminate 'economic insecurity' (Lerner, 1943: 38). The Second World War was raging and Lerner was worried about the 'threat to democratic civilisation' (p. 38) posed by Fascism. He wanted to understand how nations might resist falling prey to extremist ideologies, especially when it is clear that these extreme positions emerge when there is hardship and mass unemployment.

Lerner wanted to further elucidate the 'principles by which appropriate government action can maintain prosperity' (p. 38). These principles had emerged from the work of John Maynard Keynes and others during the Great Depression and demonstrated the poverty of the so-called 'Classical' ideas that had dominated the period prior to the 1930s. The 'Classical' approach extolled the virtues of the free market and fiscal austerity. Keynes and others demonstrated beyond doubt that these principles not only were flawed from a theoretical perspective but also failed the evidence test. They simply didn't describe the way the world worked and the policies that were derived from the flawed theories often made matters worse. It should not escape you that this orthodoxy that Keynes and others convincingly debunked during the Great Depression is the same neo-liberal orthodoxy that dominates today. For many decades following the Great Depression, however, the 'Classical' ideas were not considered to be credible or worthy of any status in policy circles.

Lerner understood that people are 'easily frightened by fairy tales of terrible consequences' (p. 38) when new ideas are presented. The sense of fright is driven by a lack of education that leaves people unable to comprehend how the economy actually operates. Neo-liberals magnify that sense of fright, by demonising what are otherwise sensible and viable explanations of economic matters. They know that by elevating these ideas into the domain of fear and taboo, they increase the probability that political acceptance of the ideas will not be forthcoming. That strategy advances their ideological agenda. The basic rules that should guide government fiscal policy are, as Lerner noted, 'extremely simple' and 'it is this simplicity which makes the public suspect it as too slick' (p. 29). Neo-liberals who have vested interests in ensuring that the public does not understand the true options available to a government that issues its own currency manipulate that suspicion. In the place of these simple truths, neo-liberals advance a sequence of myths and metaphors that they know will resonate with the public and become the 'reality'.

Lerner (1941 reproduced in 1951) introduced the 'steering wheel' metaphor. The economy is a vehicle we can control to achieve collective wellbeing. This is in contrast to the neo-liberal concept of the economy as a self-regulating mechanism, which demands us to act as sacrificial lambs to maintain its 'health'. Lerner used the 'steering wheel' metaphor to juxtapose the laissez faire approach where the car zig-zags across the road, often out of control and producing multiple wrecks, with the alternative, where judicious steering can ensure the car travels safely and smoothly along the road towards its desired destination. Lerner considered fiscal and monetary policy to be the government's steering wheel to avoid the crises that the free market approach creates (for example, the Great Depression then and the GFC now).

Lerner (1951: 4–5) noted that people accept the need to use the steering wheel for orderly driving:

> But are they as reasonable about other things as they are about the desirability of steering their automobiles? . . . Do they not allow their economic automobiles to bounce from depression to inflation in wide and uncontrolled arcs? Through their failure to steer away from unemployment and idle factories are they not just as guilty of public injury and insecurity as the mad motorists . . .

Significantly, Lerner distinguished between what he called 'functional finance' and 'sound finance', the latter being the orthodoxy he confronted (which is consistent with the vision shown in Figure 18.1). 'Sound finance', which also dominates the public debate in the current period, is usually expressed in terms of some defined fiscal and monetary policy rules. For example, governments should aim for a fiscal balance or not allow deficits to exceed 3 per cent of GDP. Equally, the central bank should only allow the money supply to increase in line with the rate of output growth. These rules, which are rarely challenged, usually disguise an underlying conservative morality about the role of government (for example, deficits are characterised as 'living beyond the means'). The SGP rules, which are also now taken as given, exemplify the idea of 'sound finance'.

By way of departure, Lerner considered a government should always use its policy capacity to achieve full employment and price stability and thought that fiscal or monetary policy rules based on conservative morality were not likely to help in that regard. In contrast to 'sound finance', Lerner (1943: 39–40) said:

> The central idea is that government fiscal policy, *its* spending and taxing, its borrowing and repayment of loans, its issue of new money and its withdrawal of money, shall all be undertaken with an eye only to the *results* of these actions on the economy and not to any established traditional doctrine about what is sound and what is unsound . . . The principle of judging fiscal measures by the way they work or function in the economy we may call *functional finance*. The first responsibility of the government (since nobody else can undertake the responsibility) is to keep the total rate of spending in the country on goods and services neither greater nor less than that rate which at the current prices would buy all the goods that it is possible to produce. If total spending is allowed to go above this there will be inflation, and if it is allowed to go below this there will be unemployment. The government can increase total spending by spending more itself or by reducing taxes so that taxpayers have more money left to spend. It can reduce total spending by spending less itself or by raising taxes so that taxpayers have less money left to spend. By these means total spending can be kept at the required level, where it will be enough to buy the goods that can be produced by all who want to work, and yet not enough to bring inflation by demanding (at current prices) more than can be produced. (Emphasis in original)

This statement of purpose, Lerner's 'first law of Functional Finance', recognises the basic rule of macroeconomics that spending equals income and output, which drives the demand for labour. Unemployment results from insufficient spending, making it a macroeconomic problem. The neo-liberal claims that unemployment arises because for various reasons, individuals do not seek work hard enough, totally misses the point. An individual cannot search for jobs that are not there! When there is a lack of jobs, an unemployed individual can do nothing to resolve that shortage.

In other words, the government responsibility should be to adjust its spending and taxation to ensure that all production is purchased and that this level of production generates jobs for all, such that the society cannot produce any more goods and services with its current available inputs.

What are the financial implications of this? Lerner noted that if in fulfilling its responsibilities, the government recorded a fiscal deficit, then it 'would have to provide the difference by borrowing or printing money. In neither case should the government feel that there is anything especially good or bad about this result' (p. 40). The goal is to 'concentrate on keeping the total rate of spending neither too small nor too great, in this way preventing both unemployment and inflation' (p. 40). Importantly, assessments of 'good' or 'bad' are defined purely in terms of whether the government is achieving its goals. Obviously, moral considerations enter at the stage of setting goals. It is clearly a values-based position to aim for a state where everyone who desires work can find it. Once agreed that this will be the societal goal, then we should be indifferent if, in different circumstances, a deficit of 1 per cent of GDP or a deficit of 5 per cent of GDP is required to meet that goal. Thinking in this way flushes out the role of ideology. The neo-liberals obscure their disregard for mass unemployment by claiming that the 5 per cent deficit is dangerous and unsustainable. If the public truly understood that the 5 per cent deficit is as sustainable as the 1 per cent deficit, then the neo-liberals would be forced to debate their preference for mass unemployment. Clearly, the public would not generally accept that ideological preference and that is why the neo-liberals have to obfuscate their true motivations and hide behind the financial myths concerning the sustainability of government deficits and erect the metaphorical defence structures.

Lerner's 'simple' ideas thus represent a very powerful organising framework for the conduct of government policy, which appear to be totally alien to the type of considerations and priorities that drive the policy-making process in the EMU. The message is that governments should act to advance welfare and, at a minimum, this requires that it achieve and sustain full employment; that it has an array of policy tools available to pursue that goal (spending, taxation, debt issuance, money creation); and that the mix of tools used should be appraised in terms of how effective they are in advancing the mission of the government. *No tool is taboo*. The use of each depends on what the government is trying to achieve on our behalf and the circumstances in which it finds itself at any point in time.

Economic policy making is about a means to an end: a functional endeavour. It is not a sacred, religious activity where abstract concepts of virtue and sacrifice rule behaviour and choice. Within functional finance there is no meaning that can be applied to the SGP rule that 'the deficit must not exceed 3% of GDP' without reference to the functional outcome with which any particular deficit is associated.

In this regard, Lerner proceeded to debunk the myths of 'sound finance' with respect to the roles of taxation, the issuance of public debt, and 'money printing' operations conducted by the central bank in relation to government spending and deficits. In Chapter 17 we learned that students of macroeconomics are misled from the outset of their studies into believing that currency-issuing governments are subject to the same financial constraints as a household. Lerner understood that such an analogy was inapplicable. He noted, 'taxing is *never* to be undertaken merely because the government needs to make money payments' (p. 40). Lerner was only concerned with the effects of taxation, which are twofold: 'the taxpayer has less money left to spend and the government has more money' (p. 40). While true, he then observed that the 'second effect can be brought about so much more easily by printing the money' (p. 40), which means we only should think of taxation inasmuch as it reduces the capacity of the private sector to spend and should 'be imposed only when it is desirable that the taxpayers shall have less money to spend' (p. 40).

The 'second law of Functional Finance' relates to the issuance of debt by governments. MMT explains that such practices have no role to play in 'funding' government spending and, instead, may facilitate monetary operations (for example, interest rate management by the central bank), although, even then, they are unnecessary artefacts left over from the old gold standard monetary systems. Lerner said the 'government should borrow money only if it is desirable that the public should have less money and more government bonds, for these are the *effects* of government borrowing' (p. 40). His explanation is consistent with the discussion in Chapter 17 about how central banks might sell government bonds to drain away excess bank reserves to prevent interbank competition from driving the interest rate below the chosen policy interest rate.

The upshot of this discussion is that if there is a deficit and there is no reason for the private sector to have more public debt, then the excess 'must be met by printing new money' (p. 41). Contrast this insight with the rigidity that was expressed in Article 123 of the Treaty on the Functioning of the European Union, which prohibits the 'monetisation' of fiscal deficits. The use of the term 'prohibits' immediately intends to cast such behaviour as taboo. But in functional finance, a government should use all the policy tools that are available to it, including, as Lerner would have it, 'printing money'.

As noted in Chapter 17, the term 'printing money' is not used in MMT because it is not descriptive of the actual process that underpins government spending. The term also invokes irrational emotional responses about hyperinflation with the Weimar Republic or Zimbabwe immediately entering the conversation, and reasoned debate then becomes impossible. We consider those episodes in more detail in Chapter 21. Lerner was keenly aware that the conservative economists considered the 'printing money' option to be taboo. He remarked that the 'almost instinctive revulsion that we have to the idea of printing money, and the tendency to identify it with inflation, can be overcome if we calm ourselves and take note that this printing does not affect the amount of money *spent*' (p. 41). To put it another way, the only reason the government would increase its deficit would be to fill a widening shortfall between the total spending required to maintain full employment and current private spending. Chapter 17 showed that this would not be inflationary if the sales boost allows firms to maintain their current levels of production and eliminate unsold inventory. If governments expanded the deficits beyond that point then inflation would threaten. But the inflation risk lies in the spending growth rate, not whether the government matches its deficit with debt issuance or new money. If the non-government sector, upon receipt of this new money, decided to reduce its current savings rate and to spend more, then the deficit would have to be lower to avoid higher inflation. Equally, holders of government bonds could decide to liquidate their stocks and spend more. In the same way as before, this would require a lower deficit. The choice of debt issuance or new money creation is separate to the desire to avoid a surge in inflation.

Once we understand these principles, it is easy to understand why Lerner wrote (p. 41): 'In brief, Functional Finance rejects completely the traditional doctrines of "sound finance" and the principle of trying to balance the budget over a solar year or any other arbitrary period.'

Lerner's work also contains a very clear message for progressive thinkers who are reluctant in the current debate to think outside of the confines that the neo-liberals have created. For example, the Labour politicians in the United Kingdom confront the austerity debate with claims that they would 'fix the budget' over a longer time period to avoid the massive damage that immediate austerity brings. Of course, even debating the 'health' of the fiscal position in terms of some financial ratios is ceding ground to the conservatives, ground that is illegitimate. Lerner (1951: 15) called progressives who argued in this way 'proponents of organized prosperity' and said:

> A kind of timidity makes them shrink from saying anything that might shock the respectable upholders of traditional doctrine and tempts them to disguise the new doctrine so that it might be easily mistaken for the old. This does not help much, for they are soon found out, and it hinders them because in endeavoring to make the new doctrine appear harmless in the eyes of the upholders of tradition, they often damage their case. Thus instead of saying that the size of the national debt is of no great concern . . . [and] . . . that the budget may have to be unbalanced and that this is insignificant when compared with the attainment of prosperity, it is proposed to disguise an unbalanced budget (and

therefore the size of the national debt) by having an elaborate system of annual, cyclical, capital, and other special budgets.

Progressives should first and foremost seek to educate the public about how the economy and money actually operate and what opportunities the government has to act on our behalf to advance our wellbeing. If we think in this way, then options that have been constructed by the neo-liberals to be 'dangerous', 'radical' or 'taboo' will start to appear reasonable and grounded in reality. The next step is that they eventually become the mainstream orthodoxy. Progressives should avoid petty conversations that lead to statements such as 'we will reduce the deficit more slowly than you but we will still reduce it'. Perhaps at a point in time a deficit reduction will be functional. But that will never be the case when there is mass unemployment of the scale that besets Europe at present.

Lerner (1951: 16) addressed the problem of progressives who present their arguments in a conservative way because the public might not understand the fundamentals of functional finance:

> The scholars who understand it hesitate to speak out boldly for fear that the people will not understand. The people, who understand it quite easily, also fear to speak out while they wait for the scholars to speak out first. The difference between our present situation and that of the story is that it is not an emperor but the *people* who are periodically made to go naked and hungry and insecure and discontented – a ready prey to less timid organizers of discontent for the destruction of civilization. (Emphasis in original)

One of the goals of this book is to educate and provide progressive thinkers and activists a knowledge basis on which the destructive neo-liberal orthodoxy can be challenged and abandoned.

Of course, developing comprehension is just the first step. A bold confidence is also required to withstand the vilification that comes with expressing ideas that are contrary to the neo-liberal norms.

20. The federal solution

THE LACK OF A FEDERAL FISCAL CAPACITY

An obvious economic solution for the Eurozone is to bring the fiscal policy responsibilities (spending and taxation) in line with the monetary issuing capacity and allow the federal fiscal authority to run deficits commensurate with the non-government spending gap. The necessity of this alignment was recognised by the Werner Committee in 1970 and the MacDougall Study Group in 1977 but was ignored, for ideological reasons, by the Delors Committee in 1989. Reflecting on our earlier discussion, the Werner Report concluded that for EMU cohesion 'transfers of responsibility from the national to the Community plane will be essential' (Werner Report, 1970: 10). Moreover, the:

> . . . transfer to the Community level of the powers exercised hitherto by national authorities will go hand in hand with the transfer of a corresponding Parliamentary responsibility from the national plane to that of the Community. The centre of decision of economic policy will be politically responsible to a European Parliament. (p. 11)

In a similar vein, the MacDougall Report (1977: 12) concluded in relation to the need for a mechanism to cushion 'short-term and cyclical fluctuations' that 'because the Community budget is so relatively very small there is no such mechanism in operation on any significant scale, as between member countries, and this is an important reason why in the present circumstances monetary union is impracticable.' In the context of the current crisis, Pisani-Ferry et al. (2012: 1) argue that 'a monetary union requires some form of budget for fiscal stabilisation in case of shocks, as a backstop to the banking union'. Belgian economist Paul De Grauwe also argues that abandoning the common currency 'would have devastating consequences' but the only other choice for salvation is to 'move toward fiscal union' even though he considers it to be a 'distant prospect' (De Grauwe, 2013).

The current design of the Eurozone determines that the Member State governments are not 'sovereign' in the sense that they are forced to use a foreign currency and must issue debt to private bond markets in that foreign currency to fund any fiscal deficits. Their fiscal positions must then take the full brunt of any economic downturn because there is no 'federal' counter-stabilisation function. The EMU is a federation without the most important component. The Member State governments thus can run out of money and become insolvent if the bond markets decline to purchase their debt. Among other things, this means the elected governments cannot guarantee the solvency of the banks that operate within their borders. De Grauwe notes that Eurozone governments 'cannot provide a guarantee to bondholders that the cash will be available to pay them at maturity' (De Grauwe, 2013). It is a basic characteristic of any monetary system that government can only create risk-free liabilities if they are denominated in its own currency. The fact that the political leaders chose this design was astounding given it stood no chance of withstanding a major event such as the GFC. The design of the Eurozone ensured it was a disaster waiting to happen.

THE CREATION OF A FEDERAL FISCAL AUTHORITY (FFA)

The establishment of a full fiscal union would require the creation of a Federal Fiscal Authority (hereafter FFA), which would have the capacities that were outlined in Chapter 17 and adopt fiscal principles discussed in Chapter 19. This would certainly offer a relatively speedy solution to the economic mess. The FFA would preferably deploy Overt Monetary Financing (OMF), which is discussed in Chapter 21. Combined with the abandonment of the SGP, the FFA could set about restoring domestic demand in the Member State economies through a combination of direct employment schemes, investment in improved education, health and training capacity, increased pension and fixed income entitlements where appropriate, and major public infrastructure projects including better and greener ports, airports and public transport systems. The spending injections would kick start the regional economies, increase household and business confidence and inspire a private spending recovery as incomes and jobs became more secure. It is likely that the FFA would have to run fiscal deficits significantly higher than those allowed for under the SGP for an extended period, which means that any attempt to impose such fiscal rules would be self-defeating.

The establishment of a FFA would address the major current constraints on recovery. First, it would directly redress the stagnant spending conditions across the Eurozone. Second, it would mesh perfectly with the proposal to create a full banking union. The FFA would be uniquely equipped to ensure that bank deposits were not vulnerable. Consistent with the observations made by the Werner Committee that a loss of national fiscal power to the centre should not undermine democratic processes, the FFA should become responsible to the European Parliament. There should be no capacity for the European Commission or Council of Ministers (Ecofin) to dominate this new 'governmental' body. In Australia, for example, the Federal government regularly meets with the Premiers and Treasurers of the State governments, but the latter group are not part of the federal treasury nor do they have any role in the economic and finance ministries. The role of the FFA is to take a federal view of things rather than be a forum for deal mongering, which primarily reflects national level intrigues and enmities.

The notion of a FFA also has implications for how public debt is issued and who is responsible for it. While OMF would be the preferable way to consolidate the fiscal policy responsibilities and operations of the FFA with the monetary policy obligations and related liquidity management functions of the ECB, we will assume that the FFA issues its own debt to the private bond markets to match its fiscal deficits. The FFA would thus have to possess the capacity to issue federal bonds, which would carry no default risk because they would be backed by the currency-issuing capacity of the ECB. The FFA euro bonds would have the same risk-free status as debt issued by the Japanese, US, UK, Australian and other 'sovereign' governments. Debt issued by the Member States, for their own projects, would still carry default risk, but that could be significantly reduced through guarantees provided by the FFA. Another option could be that the FFA uses its superior borrowing capacity to raise funds on behalf of the Member States using some sort of federal state partnership agreement. All of these arrangements are, however, nuances of the overall fact that the creation of a FFA with its own debt-issuance capacity would solve the so-called sovereign debt crisis in the Eurozone immediately. The ECB could also easily subsume all the outstanding Member State debt and write it off as a new beginning. If there were a truly federal spirit operating, none of the 'better off' Member States would begrudge this sort of debt redemption.

The FFA would replace the existing European Stability Mechanism (ESM), which is not equipped to fulfil the required fiscal role. While the necessary changes to the Treaty were being made, the European Parliament could set up the FFA and establish its mission and operational capacities. In the transition phase, the ECB could continue to guarantee all Member State debt via the Outright Monetary Transactions (OMT) Program, which was introduced in September 2012 to replace the Securities Markets Program (SMP). Both programs had the same intent – the ECB would stand ready to buy up Member State government bonds in the secondary markets to ensure that demand was always strong and, hence, yields (interest rates) were low. The SMP was flawed because the ECB imposed so-called 'conditionality' on the governments in question before it would support its debt. The conditionality (also known as growth-sapping austerity) had two effects. First, it locked the nation into recession with rising unemployment. Second, the ongoing economic stagnation made it difficult for the fiscal position of the nation to meet the SGP rules, which led to further calls for austerity. It was a vicious cycle of stupidity. The OMT could easily support increased fiscal deficits at the Member State level while the Treaty was being changed to allow the FFA to take over. Thereafter Member State fiscal initiatives would be considerably diminished and reflect an agreement about federal state responsibilities. The OMT program (or similar) is a very effective device to render the private bond markets powerless to influence bond yields. The ECB can effectively buy up all the debt as it is issued and deal private sentiment out of the picture. This is the capacity that any central bank has in a more traditional federation. The ECB should definitely use that power without imposing self-defeating austerity as a qualifying condition for support.

THE FFA SOLUTION IS NOT POLITICALLY OR CULTURALLY TENABLE

The problem is that the FFA option is not politically or culturally tenable as the MacDougall Study Group clearly understood. An essential requirement for an effective monetary system with multiple tiers of government is that the citizens have to be tolerant of intra-regional transfers of government spending and not insist on proportional participation in that spending. The other side of this coin is that a particular region might enjoy less of the income it produces so that other regions can enjoy more income than they produce. To achieve that tolerance there has to be a shared history, which leads to a common culture and identity. For example, are the citizens of Berlin Germans or Europeans in the first instance? Language is an aspect of this, but not necessarily intrinsic. In a successful federation such as Australia, people in the states of NSW and Victoria might occasionally complain that the smaller state of Tasmania gets a disproportionate amount of government assistance relative to its 'tax base'. However, there is no serious discussion that these federal transfers should stop or that the states with the weaker economies should be forced to endure a lower material standard of living than any other state. Further, when there is a major dilemma facing one state (perhaps a natural disaster or a significant economic downturn), it is assumed, without question, that the federal government will offer financial assistance to the beleaguered state. The point is that the citizens within an effective federal system have to share a common sense of purpose and togetherness to ensure that the monetary system works for all states/regions rather than those that have powerful economies. That capacity and required tolerance is largely non-existent in the Eurozone, which is why talk of a fiscal union will be largely inconsequential.

An example of this political and cultural shortfall in Europe is the fact that politicians think it is appropriate to refer to large economies such as Spain and Italy as 'peripheral' nations. The 'core-periphery' nomenclature came out of development economics, and the periphery referred to nations or regions which were underdeveloped or less developed, without basic infrastructure or human capital. Referring to rich civilisations such as Italy and Spain in this way indicates a deep malaise (Soros, 2013).

Moreover, it is not just the historical and cultural differences that are at odds with the idea of a fully integrated economic and political union. For the FFA to provide effective fiscal support for growth and prosperity in the Eurozone, a major paradigm shift in economic thinking is required. When the old hatreds and suspicions in Europe combined with the emergence of neo-liberal economic thinking, the outcome was the Delors Report and the subsequent unworkable design of the Maastricht Treaty. That mindset biases the Eurozone towards stagnation. A new way of economic thinking, such as was outlined in Chapter 17, which recognises the opportunities that a truly sovereign federal government has if it utilises its currency appropriately, is required. If that way of thinking could emerge, then the design of the FFA and its operational charter would follow easily. The expectation would have to be, however, that there will be no paradigm shift in economic thinking forthcoming on a European-wide scale, such is the grip that neo-liberalism has on the economics profession and the policy makers. In that context, it will be easier for a single nation to exit and build a new culture of growth with a new economic policy-making approach.

In that context a number of what we might call 'hybrid' federal schemes have been proposed as the way forward. However, they mostly offer compromises to the status quo, which means that they will not be able to deliver lasting prosperity and reduced vulnerability.

THE HYBRID PROPOSALS FOR FEDERALISM

There are a number of hybrid proposals which acknowledge that transition towards a full fiscal union is desirable but unlikely in the time frame necessary to militate against the ravages of the crisis. These schemes are broadly organised in terms of proposals that seek to add cyclical responsiveness (increasing the 'automatic stabilisers') and, hence, provide European level support to regions in crisis, and proposals that seek to reorganise and reclassify government debt to reduce the vulnerability of the EMU to private bond markets. They are all what might be called 'austerity' proposals in that they offer palliative care solutions ('band aids') to stop the breach. In that sense, they fail to address the cause of the breach itself, the lack of a fully functioning fiscal authority and the bias towards pro-cyclical fiscal policy as a result of the SGP rules.

Boosting the Automatic Stabilisers within the European Tax and Transfer System

The so-called 'asymmetric shocks' (spending contractions not evenly spread across the monetary union) are particularly damaging to a monetary union comprised of relatively disparate economies. When a particular state or region succumbs to a major downturn in economic activity, investment declines as sales plummet, unemployment rises, and new capital is hard to attract as it seeks profitable opportunities elsewhere. The asymmetry of economic performance across a monetary union also highlights one of the major shortcomings of monetary policy: it cannot be spatially targeted. The main policy tool at the central bank's command is to set the interest rate, which is a one-size-fits-all tool. The experience of the EMU prior to the crisis illustrates this problem. Given the fiscal policy settings, the ECB interest rates were too low for economies such as Spain and Ireland, which were undergoing unsustainable and, ultimately, destructive property booms. But some of the other economies, such as Germany and the Netherlands, were experiencing modest growth, which would have been undermined by higher interest rates.

In these instances, only a fiscal policy stimulus can provide the overall spending boost necessary to counteract the fall in private demand. The question then turns to what mix of fiscal policy tools is appropriate. There are two sources of stimulus that fiscal policy can provide: (a) discretionary changes to the spending and/or taxation settings; and (b) the operation of the in-built automatic stabilisers, which refers to the inherent sensitivity of taxation revenue and spending to changes in economic activity. Thus when economic activity falls and employment declines, the government automatically receives less taxation revenue and increases spending by way of welfare benefits. No discretionary changes to the policy settings are needed for this second effect to work. The upshot is that the automatic stabilisers will push the fiscal deficit up and provide a modicum of spending support to the local economy. In recessions, both sources of stimulus will typically be needed to ensure unemployment doesn't escalate. Reliance on the automatic stabilisers alone only moderates the contraction, but will usually not provide sufficient stimulus to prevent the recession from occurring. Müller (2013) notes that a major advantage of these automatic spending buffers 'is that they come into action reliably due to rules established in advance and without the necessity for further political decisions'.

The design of the EMU deliberately reduces the potency of these automatic stabilisers. As Müller (2013) notes, 'the EU budget is too small and its transfer mechanisms (such as the structural and regional funds) are too rigid to enable a short-term adjustment of different cyclical development'. In 2013, the German Young European Federalists proposed that a European level unemployment benefit system be established to 'partly replace the national insurance systems' (Müller, 2013). The scheme would bolster the so-called 'automatic stabilisers' at the European level, which would provide some support to Member States suffering 'asymmetric shocks'. The scheme would be 'funded through non-wage labour costs' (for example, a small levy on all payrolls) and provide support for workers for 12 months at half pay (Müller, 2013). While the devil would be in the detail, the proponents claim there 'would not be much of a change' in payments for the unemployed. This raises the question as to how the scheme actually would generate a higher level of total income in crisis regions, especially when it is acknowledged that 'the national insurance systems are already higher than the ones the European Unemployment Insurance would provide' (Müller, 2013).

Further, the proposal is essentially political rather than economic given that the support would evaporate after 12 months, thus ensuring that there would not be a 'permanent financial redistribution among the member states' (Müller, 2013). However as the current crisis has demonstrated, severe downturns, especially those related to private balance sheet imbalances, take many years to resolve and require long-term fiscal support while the private sector reduces its debt levels. Successful federations, such as Australia, allow for ongoing redistributions of tax revenue, for example from states with strong growth to those with weaker performance. But the limits on the transfers proposed by the German scheme reveal the conservative, neo-liberal nature of the proposal. The aim is to ensure that over the 'whole economic cycle, the fiscal net balance would . . . be almost evened out' (Müller, 2013). Why is that a desirable goal? What the desirable federal fiscal balance should be depends on the circumstances. At times, a balance might be desirable. At other times, a deficit or a surplus might be desirable and these circumstances may or may not coincide with a complete economic cycle.

Enderlein et al. (2012) also proposed boosting the automatic 'cyclical response' capacity in Europe. Their reasoning is symptomatic of the Groupthink among European economists that led to the problem in the first place. Many of the authors of this report were involved in various studies that gave rise to the design of the EMU. Now, as the system they lauded has failed, their approach is to patch it up with various ad hoc measures, all of which are ringfenced by the austerity mentality. They refused to 'even consider the option to abandon the euro' (p. 3) and are, instead, guided by the principle: 'As much political and economic union as necessary, but as little as possible' (p. 3). They continue to maintain that the 'principle of subsidiarity', which we examined in detail earlier, justifies this minimalist approach to fiscal union. They advocate what they call a 'sui generis form of fiscal federalism', which is driven by an implicit assumption that the national economies to be involved in this union are not remotely interested in surrendering their fiscal autonomy to the centre. Of course, the SGP and the austerity packages forced onto many of the Eurozone economies during this crisis have already severely compromised the so-called fiscal autonomy of these nations. It seems that democracy and autonomy can be violated when the Troika is imposing the terms, but in other cases they are upheld as a sacrosanct principle that cannot be compromised.

This sort of hypocrisy has woven its way through the entire debate about economic and monetary integration in Europe and will continue to deliver sub-par outcomes. Enderlein et al. (2012: 7) propose a simple rule for the limits of democracy, 'sovereignty ends when solvency ends', which is astounding if you think about it. The application of this rule inevitably leads to a violation of democracy because the risk of insolvency is intrinsic to the flawed design of the monetary system. Member States are forced to issue debt in a currency they have no control over and the ECB is formally precluded from giving any guarantees (although of course it has violated that prohibition via programs such as the SMP). Default risk and insolvency are always lurking, waiting for the next major economic downturn to arrive. Thus as soon as a nation falls into crisis, its citizens lose the capacity to influence their own destiny and are, instead, at the behest of unelected officials in the European Commission, the ECB and the IMF. That doesn't appear to be a road map for a sustainable and prosperous Europe.

Enderlein et al.'s preferred approach to 'cyclical divergences' (2012: 26) is to 'enhance the real exchange rate channel' (p. 28), which is code for making internal devaluation more responsive through increased labour mobility and wage cuts in declining regions. The authors thus invoke the standard neo-liberal approach – workers from recessed regions should move to growing regions and those who stay should work harder for less pay. The virtue of stable social communities built on family structures and community spirit is ignored. The economy rules and workers are considered meagre pawns in the decisions by management on where to locate industry. One would think a primary aim for any durable solution to the European crisis is to keep regions viable, especially as the authors recognise that 'Linguistic and cultural barriers are certainly important' (p. 8). Labour mobility is also unlikely to be of sufficient magnitude to provide any semblance of equalisation in unemployment rates within the Eurozone. A recent OECD study found that between 2009 and 2011 there was no discernible movement among citizens who were already resident within the Eurozone. The major 'labour market adjustment in Europe during the crisis was driven primarily by citizens from outside the eurozone, such as the recent EU accession countries or non-EU-27/EFTA countries' (Jauer et al., 2014: 23). While the study found some net in-migration to Germany from Italy, Portugal and Spain between the middle of 2012 and the middle of 2013, Greek migration to Germany declined.

To supplement their 'structural' emphasis, which they admit would be 'unlikely to solve the inherent difficulties' (p. 30), Enderlein et al. (2012) propose 'a cyclical adjustment insurance fund'. This fund would be managed by Eurozone finance ministers and build its kitty from contributions from nations experiencing above the Eurozone growth rates and pay out to nations in crisis to 'reduce pressure on public finances' (p. 31). The scheme would thus force nations to reduce their domestic spending in times of buoyant economic growth and provide some relief in bad times. Significantly, the authors stress the 'the system cannot become a hidden instrument for permanent transfers' (p. 31) and nations might only be permitted to 'take out what they once paid in' (p. 32). Once again the presumption is that the 'federal' redistribution would be neutral across the economic cycle and across space, a proposition for which there is no rationale other than fiscal conservatism.

Pisani-Ferry et al. (2012) propose a similar type of transfer system such that in times of recession, nations would enjoy increased 'federal' income and be forced to pay it back in better times. Their 'relatively simple rule' would again exploit the 'current fiscal framework' and require income support payments to flow whenever there are absolute and large output gaps (p. 5). The authority administering the scheme would borrow funds during a recession. It is unclear how the debt would be serviced or relinquished. The proponents claim that a 'natural way to pay the debt incurred in recessions would be to extract payments from countries with output above potential in good times' (p. 5). But an examination of the historical record suggests that nations find themselves in that position neither often nor for long. The scheme also depends on how one measures the output gap. As Chapter 11 demonstrated, the estimates of the output gap provided by multilateral organisations such as the OECD and the IMF are biased downwards because their adopted estimates of full employment unemployment are too high (that is, unemployment could be reduced substantially below the levels assumed by the neo-liberals to constitute full capacity). In this environment, the income support scheme proposed would provide inadequate spending support to nations in recession and would be of limited duration. The economies would be deemed to be back at full employment, while in reality they were still enduring persistently high unemployment and private spending gaps.

Solutions that Propose Manipulating and Massaging Public Debt

There has also been a swathe of proposals that start with the observation that the Eurozone cannot progress while the Member States have high public debt. They all claim that Europe is trapped in a sovereign debt crisis, which can only be solved by rapid reductions in the debt ratios. De Grauwe (2013) suggests that a first step towards a fiscal union should address the basic flaw in the EMU, whereby 'member governments issue debt in euros, a currency that they cannot control.' A proposed solution is to pool government debts so as to better align the capacity to pay with the responsibility for the liability. As usual, any discussion of a 'federal' development opens up the 'moral hazard' debate. In this context the issue would be how to stop the Member States from running up too much 'pooled' debt. But De Grauwe also raises the issue of interest rate imbalances, whereby nations such as Germany would be forced to pay higher interest on their debt as a result of absorbing some of the risks associated with the weaker economies. This sort of concern highlights the reason why these nations should never have entered a monetary union in the first place.

De Grauwe's solution is for a Eurozone debt mutualisation scheme that would: (a) limit how much debt could be pooled by each Member State; (b) penalise the weaker nations so that the stronger nations do not have to pay higher costs; and (c) create a federal surveillance body that would discipline government spending. Following the proposal from Enderlein et al. (2012) to reduce democratic rights of nations under threat of insolvency, De Grauwe suggests that 'rule-breaking governments should gradually lose control over their own national budgetary processes'. Of course, what constitutes a 'fiscally responsible' position is not a matter of fact but a matter of opinion and heavily tainted by ideology. The rule driven approach that De Grauwe and his colleagues favour is associated with an ideology that appears to only produce stagnation.

But debt mutualisation schemes started jumping out of the woodwork as the crisis deepened. In 2010, Jacques Delpla and Jakob von Weizsäcker proposed what they called the 'Blue Bond Proposal' (BBP), which they claim would be an 'incentive-driven and durable way out of' the debt dilemma (Delpla and von Weizsäcker, 2010: 1). There are a number of derivative plans in the literature, which share similar characteristics and shortcomings. The BBP would pool up to 60 per cent of each nation's public debt (the allowable amount under the SGP) into a common 'Blue Bonds' fund, with 'joint and several liability' (p. 1), which would reduce 'the borrowing cost for that part of the debt' (p. 1). The remaining 'Red Debt' would be subordinated to the Blue Bonds and its servicing costs would rise, thereby providing the incentive to reduce the debt to the Maastricht threshold. Further rules are proposed to tie down governments participating in the scheme, all of which would reduce the options available to Member States and reinforce the austerity straitjacket. For example, the proposal might allow nations such as Germany to add the full 60 per cent of its debt to the pool while nations such as Greece would be restricted to borrowing much lower proportions. Given the immediate problem is mainly one of default risk, the proposal's perverse incentives (punish those most at risk) would not seem to be part of any viable solution.

There is also a sense that the authors think all debt above the Maastricht threshold is due to the pursuit of unsustainable fiscal policies. The authors claim that the financial markets failed Greece by 'continuing to provide cheap funding while fiscal policy was reckless' (p. 2). How do they also assess the situations of Spain and Ireland, which were models of fiscal rectitude leading up to the crisis? But moreover, imagine that China continues to slow and the world is plunged into a further economic spending crisis. Under current arrangements, Eurozone public debt levels and fiscal deficits will rise sharply again, even though the governments are locked into the austerity mentality. It is likely that many nations would go beyond the 60 per cent debt threshold given the elevated debt levels already in place due to the GFC. The proponents of the BBP state that the 60 per cent threshold is the 'debt level deemed sustainable for any EU member state according to the Maastricht Treaty' (p. 6). But in the event of a sequence of slowdowns, exacerbated by the austerity bias, the BBP proposal would punish many nations, even if they were following the mindless fiscal path specified by the Treaty. It is hard to see how that can represent a viable solution. These schemes implicitly deny that the Eurozone is biased towards crisis. As discussed earlier, the reference values in the SGP were considered to be 'safe' given the expected output gaps that might occur in a serious downturn. Those expectations were tied up with the 'Great

Moderation' narrative and the denial that private spending collapses could still devastate growth and employment. The same sort of arrogance underpins this approach. The GFC was the first major crisis to hit the Eurozone, but it won't be the last!

Economists Yanis Varoufakis and Stuart Holland proposed a variant of the BBP scheme under their so-called 'Modest Proposal'. The title recalls Jonathan Swift's satire of the same name, published in 1729, in which Irish parents were encouraged to ease their economic travails by selling their children as food to provide culinary pleasure to the rich. Varoufakis and Holland have updated their proposal a number of times since 2010. The latest version (July 2013) was co-authored with American economist James Galbraith. The aim of the proposal is to address four 'interrelated' problems: a banking crisis, involving banks that are the responsibility of the national governments, who do not have the currency capacity to guarantee deposits; a debt crisis where nations cannot borrow from private bond markets; an investment crisis, where both the level of investment has fallen sharply and the imbalance between the trade surplus and deficit nations has widened; and a social crisis, with high unemployment, rising homelessness and poverty, and falling incomes. Like all the 'hybrid' schemes, they are motivated by the assertion that 'a Eurozone breakup would destroy the European Union, except perhaps in name' which would pose a 'global danger' (Varoufakis et al., 2013: 2). Such dramatics are dealt with in Chapter 22. It is also hard to see how a proposal that involves no fiscal transfers or changes to the Treaty can provide a lasting solution to the mess.

Their 'modest' proposal seeks 'immediate solutions' that are 'feasible within current European law and treaties' (p. 2). There is some virtue in trying to sidestep the 'dyadic choices' that 'imprison thinking and immobilise governments' in Europe (p. 10) and operate within a time frame that can deliver immediate, if only palliative, care to those most in need. But the modesty of the proposal is its shortcoming. It will not solve the inherent problems within the Eurozone, which are defined by the very political constraints that the authors recognise force them to adopt these 'modest' proposals in lieu of more effective and lasting solutions. The political constraints they identify include those that prevent the ECB from funding governments directly (see Chapter 21 for a discussion), the inability to issue euro bonds, the impasse over the creation of a 'properly functioning federal transfer union' (p. 3), and the time delays that would be involved in activating any Treaty changes, once agreed.

Their debt manipulation proposal aims to reduce the debt-servicing costs and default risk vulnerability of Member States under the current arrangements. Varoufakis et al. (2013) propose what they term a 'Limited

Debt Conversion Programme (LDCP)' or a 'tranche transfer' (see earlier version, Varoufakis and Holland, 2011), whereby:

- Participating Member States would agree to an 'accounting transfer' to the ECB of their so-called Maastricht Compliant Debt (MCD), that is, public debt up to 60 per cent of GDP. The ECB would not buy any bonds from the Member States nor provide any debt guarantees; thus, according to the proponents, it would remain faithful to its Treaty obligations.
- In recognition of this 'transfer', the ECB would issue its own debt (ECB bonds) in the private bond markets at a risk-free interest rate. The Member States and the ECB then would 'swap' payments. The ECB would 'finance' the servicing costs of the transferred debt and assume any default risk, while the Member State involved in the 'transfer' would be liable for the servicing costs on the ECB bonds, which would be lower than the rates that they could gain themselves in the private markets.
- Upon maturity of the debt, the investor would have a choice: take the terms of the original debt (for which the Member States would be responsible) or roll the debt over at the 'lower, more secure rates offered by the ECB' (p. 4).
- If the Member State defaulted on its payments the European Stability Mechanism would provide the funds.

The obvious question is why bother? The ECB's SMP, which began in May 2010, demonstrated that they could deal the private bond investors out of the equation when it came to setting yields on government bonds. The replacement program (OMT) means that the ECB stands ready to purchase unlimited volumes of government debt and any private bond trader that tried to take a counter position against any Eurozone government would lose if the ECB exerted its power. The ECB can effectively set yields at any level it desires including zero, which means that a Member State can only run out of money if the ECB refuses to exercise its power to buy unlimited volumes of the government's debt. The SMP program kept the Eurozone together, but by imposing austerity as a pre-condition for participation, it failed to address the core problem that Southern Europe is in depression and the only way out is for budget deficits to expand. The most direct way forward is for the ECB to invoke its OMT facility and facilitate increased government spending.

Varoufakis et al. (2013: 5) acknowledge that the OMT program 'has succeeded in taming interest rate spreads within the euro-zone' but conclude that the implicit threat against bond markets, described above, is 'non-credible'. Allegedly, bond dealers will eventually call the ECB's bluff and expose the OMT program as a paper tiger. This criticism is without foundation. How exactly can the private bond markets 'test the ECB's resolve'? (p. 5). The ECB has unlimited euro capacity to purchase all the secondary market bonds it desires. Of course, at present it is the announcement rather than any action that has had the impact, given that the ECB has so far purchased no bonds under the program. The OMT announcement:

> . . . was a game changer in the euro-zone. It had dramatic effects. By taking away the intense existential fears that the collapse of the euro-zone was imminent the ECB's lender of last resort commitment pacified government bond markets and led to a strong decline in the spreads of the Eurozone countries. (De Grauwe and Ji, 2013)

But the gymnastics involved in the 'Modest Proposal' seem unnecessary given that the SMP showed that the ECB can control yields and 'fund' governments, albeit indirectly. The OMT program would have equivalent success if enacted.

There is some uncertainty surrounding the OMT as a result of the decision on 7 February 2014 by the German Constitutional Court (BVerfG) to refer the program to the Court of Justice of the European Union (CJEU) for a preliminary ruling, the first time this has happened. The referral reflects the reality that BVerfG knows the operations of the ECB have to be assessed with the legal structure of the Treaties rather than the German Basic Law. That alone amounted to a rejection of the Bundesbank position, which had opposed the program. While the BVerfG found that there was a good case to be made that the program was outside of the ECB's legal charter, it also recognised that the CJEU, known for its 'federalist'-type interpretations, could find the OMT program to be legal (German Constitutional Court, 2014). The BVerfG considered the program could be construcd as an economic policy intervention rather than the ECB's claim that it was a liquidity management operation. Interestingly, it was the inclusion of the 'conditionality', which clearly went beyond any notion of liquidity management, that provoked the Court's concern that the program was infringing on the core Treaty responsibilities of the Member States. Of further relevance, under the heading 'Violation of the Prohibition of Monetary Financing of the Budget', paragraphs 84–98 of the Decision make it clear that the BVerfG considers that any ECB measures which have the same impacts as the purchase of a primary bond issue (for example, holding down bond yields) should be treated as 'dem unmittelbaren Erwerb von Staatsanleihen gleichkommt' ('equivalent to the direct purchase of government bonds'). This discussion would also impact negatively on the bond-buying trickery that forms the core of the 'Modest Proposal'.

It is also difficult to see the 'Modest Proposal' as being consistent with Article 104 of the Treaty if a Member State failed to make payments as agreed. In that case the ECB would have to fund the deficiency, which would be equivalent to offering the prohibited 'overdraft facility' to the state.

The 'Modest Proposal' would also probably promote perverse bond market behaviour and deliver massive corporate welfare to the investment banks. The debt policy would see the ECB take bank reserves out of the system in return for ECB bonds. It wouldn't take long for the bond markets to work out that they could ask for a premium on the ECB bonds and the ECB would be under pressure to concede. With interest rates low, the private banks could then borrow from the ECB to buy the bonds, which would pay a return higher than the short-term cash.

Conservatives will attack the 'Modest Proposal' for exposing the ECB to insolvency risk because it might find itself holding huge quantities of zombie debt, which would amount to it losing all its capital. This is not a valid criticism of the 'Modest Proposal' or any other that involves the ECB taking on massive quantities of high-risk debt. The fact is that neither the ECB nor any central bank can ever go broke. The days when economist Walter Bagehot, an early editor of *The Economist* magazine, wrote about the solvency risks of the Bank of England in the 1870s are long gone. A private bank needs capital for satisfying prudential regulations and covering potential losses to avoid insolvency. It does not have a currency-issuing capacity in its own right. While the ECB has an elaborate formula for determining the contributions of capital that each national member bank is required to provide, at an intrinsic level, it has no need for capital. It could operate forever with negative capital, a state that would signal insolvency for a private bank.

Willem Buiter (2008: 7) wrote that:

> . . . the central bank can always bail out any entity – including itself – through the issuance of base money – if the entity's liabilities are denominated in domestic currency and nominally denominated (that is, not index linked). If the liabilities of the entity in question are foreign currency denominated or index linked, a bail out by the central bank may not be possible.

This reflects the basic MMT propositions that there is no solvency risk for a consolidated government sector (comprising the central bank and treasury) as long as it only issues liabilities denominated in its own currency. If it issues liabilities (for example, takes on debt) denominated in a foreign currency, then insolvency becomes a possibility. In the case of the Eurozone, where there is no fiscal authority, the pecking order is that the member state treasuries are deemed to guarantee their own national central banks which 'own' the ECB and which provide lender of last resort facilities to their own banking systems. No fiscal authority backs the ECB but despite all the legal complexities involved in how the national central banks might carry out their lender of last resort duties, the reality is that the ECB is the ultimate lender of last resort in the EMU. In fact, the ECB could purchase all the outstanding public debt if it wanted to and, if it lost capital as a result, it could simply replenish it by issuing new currency. It alone issues the euro.

A RARE PROPOSAL TO STIMULATE AGGREGATE DEMAND

The 'Modest Proposal' contained one sensible component. Varoufakis et al. (2013) recognise that creating a bank union and reducing the servicing costs of public debt in the Eurozone will not be sufficient to remedy the crisis. They acknowledge that there has been a dramatic slump in private investment in productive infrastructure as a result of a loss of confidence and poor sales, which 'threatens its living standards and its international competitiveness' (p. 2). Further, they realise that monetary policy innovations have been unable to revive the Southern European economies from depression. Their solution is to promote a large scale, Europe-wide 'Investment-led Recovery and Convergence Programme' (IRCP). It is one of the few proposals that explicitly seeks to reverse the austerity mindset by increasing total spending and, as a consequence, directly addresses the core short-run problem of stagnant growth. Figure 20.1 shows the extent of the investment collapse. By 2013, gross capital formation (investment) in the Eurozone (18 nations) had fallen by 22 per cent relative to its 2007 level. For Germany the decline has been 6.9 per cent; Ireland 53.7 per cent (to 2012); Greece, a staggering 60.5 per cent; Italy 29.9 per cent; Spain 38.4 per cent; and Portugal 37.4 per cent. Adjustments of this magnitude are almost beyond belief and a testament to the total failure of the policy framework that the Eurozone leaders put in place to respond to the crisis.

The IRCP proposal would divert borrowed funds raised by 'bonds issued jointly by the European Investment Bank (EIB) and the European Investment Fund (EIF)' (Varoufakis et al., 2013: 6). The debt would not be counted against any Member State. The authors note (p. 6) that 'the joint bonds can be serviced directly by the revenue streams of the EIB–EIF funded investment projects', although it is entirely unclear from the proposal what proportion of the funds would go to public infrastructure

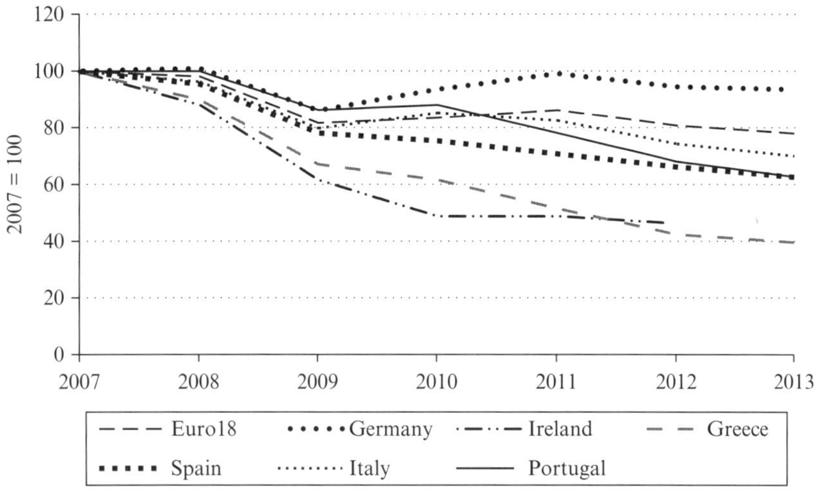

Source: Eurostat, Annual National Accounts.

Figure 20.1 Gross capital formation in the Eurozone, 2007–13, 2007 = 100

projects, which provide social returns as opposed to investment in private, profit-making ventures. It would be unfortunate if the public investments were valued on the basis of so-called 'commercial returns', which are inapplicable to the public sector that aims to deliver public service. Further, would the monetary returns on the remaining projects be sufficient to service and repay the debt? In responding to the criticism that the debt could be expensive given the risk, the authors claim that there is a surplus of savings in the global markets that are 'seeking sound investment outlets' (p. 6). They merely assert that these projects would be desirable targets for such investment. The reality is that the investment climate is very uncertain at present because of the mass unemployment, falling incomes and cutbacks in public spending. The capacity of the projects to generate sufficient monetary return to cover borrowing costs, notwithstanding the likelihood that the EIB and EIF could access capital markets at lower rates, is debatable. An obvious question is, if there are such substantial profitable investment opportunities available, why haven't the entrepreneurial class seen that? What sort of myopia is operating to prevent the capitalists seizing on these opportunities?

This reality, which the authors admit 'would be entirely within the central bank's remit and charter' (Varoufakis et al., 2013: 13), once again raises the question as to whether this process would be better than the

Member States determining their own spending priorities and kick-starting their own economies with similar secondary bond market assistance from the ECB. The retort is that the IRCP proposal would avoid any further rise in the debt levels of the Member States. But, again, that is buying into the false claims that the debt levels are really the constraint on growth. With ECB support through, say, the OMT, the bond markets have no capacity to undermine the spending choices of the Member States. Of course, then we get into the Excessive Deficit Mechanism debate, which the IRCP would avoid, and that is acknowledged. It is also clear that the ECB could play a part by purchasing the EIB-EIF bonds in the secondary market, thus driving the cost of borrowing down close to zero if it so wanted.

The argument that substantial new investment could kick-start growth if put into productive use is sound. It mimics the emergency responses that marked the New Deal in the US between 1933 and 1937. The questions are whether the scale of the program would be sufficient to generate a recovery, given how large the output gaps are at present, and whether a massive investment program could be absorbed without creating damaging imbalances. The authors merely assert that the scale of the program would be sufficient. If Germany is excluded, real GDP in 2013 for the remaining Eurozone nations was some 4 per cent below its 2007 level (some 253 billion euros). Similarly, investment was about 27 per cent lower. Even assuming a very generous spending multiplier, the injection that would be required to make up that gap would dwarf the previous allocations that the EIB has handled.

Further, investment has a dual characteristic; it adds to spending in the current period but also to the supply capacity of the economy in the subsequent periods. Would the growth in consumption spending pick up quickly enough to absorb the new capacity? While the authors have characterised their proposal as akin to the New Deal (see Varoufakis et al., 2013), it should be remembered that the US program was heavily weighted towards providing relief to unemployed and impoverished citizens in the form of cash payments and direct public sector job creation. This sort of relief is outside of the ambit of the 'Modest Proposal' and thus it is questionable whether an investment-led answer to the deficient total spending will generate the gains necessary to lift household consumption in, say, Greece, where in 2013 it was around 25 per cent below its 2007 value.

ASSESSMENT

There are a plethora of schemes that propose a way out of the Eurozone crisis. Some are more adventurous than others but most involve gymnastic manipulations of debt classifications, dual currencies, or pension plans to work around the obvious problem that most refuse to recognise. Virtually all of the plans seek to work within the SGP straitjacket, appealing to political realities as the justification, without wanting to admit that the political realities are part of the problem and, until they change, little will be done to progress the situation.

The debt manipulation schemes such as we have examined and others, like the proposal for GDP indexed bonds, all assume there is something sacrosanct about the 60 per cent Maastricht threshold. The only relevance of the 60 per cent limit is that it is a reference value specified in the Treaty. It has no economic meaning or other authority. The Treaty has to be changed to move forward and in the meantime the sort of flexibility that was given to France and Germany in 2003 and 2004 via the Excessive Deficit Mechanism needs to become the norm. The short history of the euro has already demonstrated that there is enough generality in the rules for them to be stretched far and wide.

We did not consider the dual currency proposals. They all fall foul of Gresham's Law or the Copernicus Law, which tells you how long we have known that such schemes do not work. Yet they keep coming back. In the Eurozone context, they are proposed because there is a denial that it is the design of the monetary system that is the problem. In effect, the asserted problem is that nations, lacking international competitiveness, encounter rigidities that prevent them from cutting wages far enough. The dual currency proposals, where the euro (which denominates most contracts and trade transactions) operates in tandem with a local depreciated currency (in which wages are paid), is just a ruse to cut real wages. They assume that the workers are blinded by what economists call 'money illusion', which is just a fancy term for assuming that workers are too stupid to know the purchasing power of their weekly wage and think they are better off than they actually are. Cutting wages will not help the Eurozone crisis unless it can be demonstrated that the policy will somehow increase consumption spending and reduce the propensity to save. The historical evidence tells us, repeatedly, that such strategies do exactly the opposite and make the spending shortage worse.

There is no doubt that a coordinated and large-scale investment strategy should be part of the revival of Europe that has been sabotaged by the neo-liberal austerity policies. But there has to be a recognition that no lasting recovery will come unless fiscal deficits rise and are held at elevated levels for an extended period.

The front line for progressives has to be an attack on the entire austerity culture. There has to be a concerted and coordinated challenge to the very existence and design of the Eurozone rather than effort being put into working out clever ways of working within the neo-liberal straitjacket. It is clear that Treaty change will be a drawn-out process – everything in Europe is. Also clear is the depth of the crisis: the growing hunger among the poor, the crisis in the medical and health care systems, the rising youth unemployment, increasing social instability and growing political extremism all demand immediacy in the policy response. In the next two chapters we consider two proposals, one of which would retain the euro but dramatically restructure the monetary system, while the other would abandon the union and restore currency sovereignty to the individual nations and allow their democratically elected governments to work in the interests of their citizens without falling prey to the dictates of unelected cabals in Brussels, Frankfurt or Washington.

21. Overt Monetary Financing

Taboo *noun* . . . a social or religious custom prohibiting or forbidding discussion of a particular practice or forbidding association with a particular person, place or thing; *adjective* . . . prohibited or restricted by social custom; *verb* . . . place under prohibition. (Oxford Dictionary)

We have to ensure that the prohibition of monetary financing is respected. (Jens Weidmann, President of the Deutsche Bundesbank, interview with MNI, 21 March 2014)

As the story goes, the British explorer Captain Cook introduced the word taboo into the English language after observing Tongan society in 1777. There is a very detailed and diverse literature on the concept of taboos in western society. We learn early in life the things we can say and do in polite company, and those things that will attract opprobrium as forbidden behaviour. We isolate individuals who step over these rather indistinct lines and consider their behaviour aberrant. Taboos are ways in which the status quo reinforces itself and resists change. But taboos are not inscribed in marble and as social values evolve so does the list of taboos. Further, while there are some things that all societies and cultures consider to be taboo, there are other things that are culturally specific. Dominant hegemonies also isolate options as taboos if they consider they would undermine their capacity to maintain ideological control over public policy.

The question asked in this chapter is this: how can a relatively simple monetary operation between a central bank and its corresponding treasury department (both part of what we call the 'consolidated' government sector) possibly be considered a taboo? This simple operation is called 'monetary financing' or 'debt monetisation'. In the current debate in Europe it has been called 'Overt Monetary Financing' (OMF), which simply means that, in some form or another, the treasury arm of government tells the central bank it wants to spend a particular amount and the latter then ensures those funds are available for use in the government's bank account. Various accounting arrangements might accompany that action. For example, the treasury might sell some government bonds to the central bank to match the value of the funds that are placed in the treasury's bank account. None of these accounting arrangements should cloud, in the words of Bundesbank chief Jens Weidmann, 'the fact that central banks can create money out of thin air' (Weidmann, 2012), a capacity he thinks 'many observers are likely to find surprising and strange, perhaps mystical and dreamlike, too – or even nightmarish'. That is, they can create as much money as they like but to do so is taboo. Why?

DIE ANGST VOR DER INFLATION

The mere mention of the term OMF creates apoplexy among the current crop of central bankers. Weidmann recently quoted from the classic German story Faust, which recounts how the evil Mephistopheles tricks the Emperor into signing some paper to create money. Immediately, the money multiplies and people become happy as their town 'half-dead once, and decaying' is now 'alive, enjoying life . . .' (von Goethe, 1888: Act 1, Scene IV). In other words, when new money is spent into an economy, which has been mired in recession and has plenty of idle capacity available, new commerce is stimulated and people are happier, presumably because unemployment is lower and incomes higher. But, in Faust, the Emperor and his supporters realise the advantages of fiat currency but not its dangers and start spending it without regard to the capacity of the economy to respond to the higher spending by increasing output. The result unsurprisingly is inflation. It should not be forgotten that von Goethe was making a satirical statement about the monetary behaviour of the French government during the French Revolution.

What von Goethe's example can tell us is that human folly leads to undesirable consequences. What else is new? However, Weidmann thinks that the message from von Goethe is more sinister, given that Mephistopheles is none other than the devil's agent. He thinks that it tells us that money creation 'degenerates into inflation, destroying the monetary system' (Weidmann, 2012). If you think about this for more than a moment you will wonder why central bankers would keep pumping out liquidity for the government to spend once the economy was beyond full employment and was no longer able to increase output? Are central bankers so irrational that they need to be placed in a straitjacket to stop their destructive tendencies? These questions might seem ludicrous or crass but they are merely responding at the logic level that maintains the taboo.

However, it is clear that the taboo of monetary financing permeates deeply into the German psyche. On 23 September 2012, the well-respected *Frankfurter Allgemeine* carried a story 'Die Angst vor der Inflation' (The Fear of Inflation) which documents a sort of national neurosis. The article advanced the view that the 'Securities Market Program' introduced by the ECB in May 2010 (see Chapter 16) would result in higher inflation.

The conjecture was clearly wrong but the article signalled how deeply ingrained the fear of inflation is in Germany, which has been a major influence on the way the Eurozone was designed and the policy choices available to resolve the crisis.

The report indicated that the fear of inflation in Germany has reached extraordinary dimensions. Surveys indicate that more people are afraid of inflation than they are of getting a serious illness, being victims of brutal crimes, separating from their partners, loneliness in old age, or even war. And the fear has been rising even though inflation was running at a steady 2.6 per cent at the time of the survey.

Irrationality is not a good basis for designing economic policy.

WINDS OF CHANGE IN EUROPE – QUANTITATIVE EASING IS MOOTED

On 31 March 2014, Eurostat released the latest inflation data for the euro area, which showed that annual inflation fell in March 2014 to 0.5 per cent. A year earlier (March 2013), the euro area annual inflation rate was 1.7 per cent, and it fell progressively over the year, signalling that Europe was approaching a dangerous deflationary situation (Eurostat, 2014a). The next day, Eurostat released new data showing that the Eurozone unemployment rate was 11.8 per cent and hadn't moved since October 2013 (Eurostat, 2014b).

Data releases such as these have promoted a rethink of monetary policy in Europe as the policy makers begin to realise that the EMU is not only failing to grow at any acceptable level but that inflation is also decelerating. There is even talk of deflation (price levels falling rather than the rate of increase slowing), which is extremely damaging for asset holders and firms. Both facts indicate a dramatic shortfall in total spending relative to productive capacity. While the economic policy debate has been mired in calls for increased 'structural reform' (also known as cutting wages and working conditions and reducing the generosity of pension and income support schemes), there can be no reasonable structural explanation for this coincidence of outcomes.

On 21 March 2014, the Bundesbank President, Jens Weidmann, was interviewed by the press agency Market News International (MNI) and, in what was seen as a 'radical' departure from Bundesbank rhetoric, he claimed that the ECB could purchase 'top-rated' private assets and even government bonds as long as this was in 'conformity with the Maastricht Treaty' (MNI, 2014). In other words, he was giving the nod to the ECB engaging in so-called Quantitative Easing (QE).

It is questionable whether the ECB would have been prepared to openly consider such a policy direction without the Bundesbank imprimatur. When the ECB President, Mario Draghi, addressed the press on 3 April 2014 to announce the monthly interest rate decision he made it clear that QE had 'explicitly' entered the discussions at the Governing Council for the first time at the April meeting. Draghi said that in light of 'the broad-based weakness of the economy', the ECB 'is unanimous in its commitment to using . . . unconventional instruments within its mandate in order to cope effectively with risks of a too prolonged period of low inflation' (ECB, 2014a). The IMF also ratcheted up pressure on the ECB when its Director told a gathering in Washington that the 'low-flation' economies 'particularly in the Euro Area' are in danger of suppressing spending and output growth and that 'More monetary easing, including through unconventional measures, is needed' (Lagarde, 2014).

QE, however, has been of limited success where it has been tried and is not the appropriate answer to the ongoing malaise in the Eurozone. As we saw in Chapter 16, QE involves the central bank exchanging a non- or low interest bearing asset (that is, adding funds to bank reserve accounts) for some higher yielding and longer-term assets (for example, ten-year government bonds or commercial bonds). It is nothing more than a simple asset swap between the central bank and the private sector. Proponents of QE claim that by giving the banks more reserves it will stimulate bank lending to the private sector with commensurate higher rates of investment and economic growth.

Financial journalists regularly claim that QE involves 'printing money' to ease a 'cash starved' banking system. Invoking the evil sounding 'money printing' terminology to describe QE is deliberately emotive (for example, it stokes our irrational fears of Weimar hyperinflation scenarios). It is also highly misleading. All transactions between the government sector (treasury and central bank) and the non-government sector involve the creation and destruction of net financial assets ('money') denominated in the currency of issue. Typically, when the government buys something from the non-government sector it just credits a bank account somewhere. That is, numbers denoting the size of the transaction appear electronically in the banking system. These numbers signify a new financial asset has been created to the favour of the recipient of the spending. The reverse is true when taxes are paid. There are no printing presses involved! We discuss this later in the chapter.

Does QE work? The mainstream belief is that it will stimulate the economy sufficiently to put a brake on the downward spiral of lost production and the increasing unemployment. It is based on the erroneous belief that a bank is an institution that accepts deposits in order to build up reserves, which, in turn, provides it with the funds to on lend at a margin in order to profit. But this is not how banks operate. Bank lending is not 'reserve constrained'. Banks lend to any credit-worthy customer they can find without, initially, worrying about how much funds they have in their reserve accounts. They know that if they are short of reserves (their reserve accounts have to be at least in positive balance each day) then they borrow from each other in the so-called 'interbank market'. If that is not possible, then they know they can borrow from the central bank, which always stands ready to provide funds to meet reserve shortfalls. Ensuring there are adequate reserves (liquidity) in the system is part of the central bank's charter to maintain financial stability. If the central bank refused to supply bank reserves on demand (at a price) then cheques might fail to clear and the financial system would be plunged into turmoil.

The ECB itself debunked the myth that banks need reserves before they will make loans in its Monthly Bulletin for May 2012. In considering whether 'a large increase in central bank liquidity . . . necessarily implies rapid broad money and credit growth', the ECB said (ECB, 2012a: 20–24):

> The occurrence of significant excess central bank liquidity does not, in itself, necessarily imply an accelerated expansion of . . . credit to the private sector . . . The Eurosystem, however, as the monopoly supplier of central bank reserves in the euro area, always provides the banking system with the liquidity required to meet the aggregate reserve requirement . . . the Eurosystem always provides the central bank reserves needed on aggregate, which are then traded among banks and therefore redistributed within the banking system as necessary. The Eurosystem thus effectively accommodates the aggregate demand for central bank reserves at all times and seeks to influence financing conditions in the economy by steering short-term interest rates.

In sum, holdings of central bank reserves are thus not a factor that limits the supply of credit for the banking system as a whole. Ultimately, the growth of bank credit depends on a set of factors that determine credit demand and on other factors linked to the supply of credit.

The Bank of England also rejected the idea that bank lending is constrained by prior reserve holdings. It concludes that the 'reality of how money is created today differs from the description found in . . . economics textbooks' (Bank of England, 2014: 14). Banks do not 'receive deposits' and lend them out. Rather 'bank lending creates deposits' (p. 14).

The point is that building bank reserves will not increase the bank's capacity to lend, which has been a central premise of those advocating QE. The reality is that loans create deposits, which then generate reserves, not the other way around. Banks have to have sufficient reserves to meet their obligations but they know they can get them anytime they need them. The reason that bank lending is restrained at present is because there is a dearth of credit-worthy customers. In the current climate the assessment of what is credit worthy has become very strict compared to the lax days prior to the crisis and there are fewer people/firms wanting to take out loans.

It is also important to understand that QE does not change the net financial position of the private sector. When the central bank exchanges one type of financial asset (an increase in a private bank's reserve balance) for another type of financial asset (private holdings of bonds, and so on), the net financial assets in the private sector are unchanged although the portfolio composition of those assets is altered. Typically there will be more short-term assets in the mix, a shift referred to as maturity substitution (short for long in this case). QE thus increases central bank demand for so-called 'long maturity' assets held in the private sector (for example, ten-year bonds), which reduces their 'yields' in the market place and, in turn, makes interest rates on longer-term loans cheaper. This might increase aggregate spending overall given the cost of investment funds is likely to drop. But, on the other hand, the lower rates reduce the interest income of savers who will reduce consumption (demand) accordingly. Further, by taking income-earning bonds from the private sector, QE undermines an income source for the holders. How these opposing effects balance out is unclear. The central banks certainly don't know! Overall, this uncertainty points to the problems involved in using monetary policy to stimulate (or contract) the economy. It is a blunt policy instrument with ambiguous impacts.

The current debate about monetary policy evokes a strong sense of déjà vu, given that these points were well understood during the 1930s. On 16 December 1933, as the Great Depression was worsening and policy makers were relying on monetary policy solutions similar to the emphasis in the current crisis, British economist John Maynard Keynes, who is often credited with the 'pushing on a string' analogy, wrote an 'Open Letter to President Roosevelt', and said:

> Some people seem to infer from this that output and income can be raised by increasing the quantity of money. But this is like trying to get fat by buying a larger belt. In the United States today your belt is plenty big enough for your belly. It is a most misleading thing to stress the quantity of money, which is only a limiting factor, rather than the volume of expenditure, which is the operative factor. (Keynes, 1933)

In that context, he said that the government 'must be called in aid to create additional current incomes through the expenditure of borrowed or printed money'. In other words, economic growth requires that money be *spent* into the economy, not stored in bank reserves.

In a similar vein, on 18 March 1935, the US House of Representatives Committee on Banking and Currency considered the introduction of the Banking Act of 1935, which was designed to 'provide for the sound, effective, and uninterrupted operation of the banking system' (Committee on Banking and Currency, 1935). On that particular afternoon, the Federal Reserve Bank Chairman, Marriner Eccles, was interrogated by Congressman Thomas Alan Goldsborough about what the central bank could do to address the parlous state of the US economy. The US economy was mired in a deep depression, not unlike the situation that the Eurozone finds itself in today. The US unemployment rate was around 21 per cent.

Their exchange was clear (p. 377):

> Governor Eccles: Under present circumstances, there is very little, if anything, that can be done.
> Mr Goldsborough: You mean you cannot push on a string.
> Governor Eccles: That is a very good way to put it, one cannot push on a string. We are in the depths of a depression and as I have said several times before this committee, beyond creating an easy money situation through reduction of discount rates and through the creation of excess reserves, there is very little, if anything, that the reserve organization can do toward bringing about recovery . . .

The expression 'pushing on a string' describes the situation where central banks may be able to inhibit credit creation by the commercial banks (by making the price it provides reserves prohibitive) but it cannot force the banks to lend.

QE also pushes against a string and is not a sensible anti-recession strategy. What will motivate consumers to borrow if they are scared of losing their jobs? Why would a company borrow if it expects its sales to remain depressed? The major problem facing the Eurozone and elsewhere at present is that the private sector is not willing to spend as robustly as it did before the crisis and governments are being prevented from offsetting that private spending decline. The only way to fill the resulting spending gap is for governments to increase their deficit spending. Relying on an export boom will not work for most nations.

While QE will not resolve the current crisis, the ECB can still play an important role in the recovery process. In this context, the idea of OMF has entered the European debate, which would put the ECB at centre stage in stimulating growth. The aim of this chapter is to consider whether OMF is a viable option for a Eurozone recovery and to outline how it might work in practice. At the outset, it is a strategy that can save the single currency. In Chapter 22, we show that it is also a preferred strategy should any or all Member States restore their own currencies and exit the EMU.

The discussion initially focused on QE to ensure that it is not confused with OMF. While QE is an asset swap that does not alter the net financial assets held by the non-government sector, OMF is a monetary operation conducted by the central bank and coordinated with fiscal policy changes, which increases the net financial assets held by the non-government sector. It thus increases private wealth rather than alters the mix of the existing wealth (between short- and long-term assets). OMF is a supportive operation conducted by the central bank to ensure government deficits can rise without any commensurate increase in public debt.

WHAT IS OVERT MONETARY FINANCING?

From an MMT perspective, OMF is a desirable option that allows the currency issuer to maximise its impact on the economy in the most effective manner possible. But in the neo-liberal world of taboo, 'monetary financing' is seen as a radical suggestion. It wasn't always so. Abba Lerner's second law of functional finance (see Chapter 19) advocated the central bank 'printing money' to match government deficit spending sufficient to achieve and sustain full employment. The idea is very simple and does not actually involve any printing presses at all. While the exact institutional detail can vary from nation to nation, governments typically spend by drawing on a bank account they have with the central bank. An instruction is sent to the central bank from the treasury to transfer some funds out of this account into an account in the private sector, which is held by the recipient of the spending. A similar operation might occur when a government cheque is posted to a private citizen who then deposits the cheque with their bank. That bank seeks the funds from the central bank, which writes down the government's account, and the private bank writes up the private citizen's account. All these transactions are done electronically through computer systems. So government spending can really be simplified down to typing in numbers to various accounts in the banking system.

When economists talk of 'printing money' they are referring to the process whereby the central bank adds some numbers to the treasury's bank account to match its spending plans and in return is given treasury bonds to an equivalent value. That is where the term 'debt monetisation' comes from. Instead of selling debt to the private sector, the treasury simply sells it to the central bank, which then creates new funds in return. This accounting smokescreen is, of course, unnecessary. The central bank doesn't need the offsetting asset (government debt) given that it creates the currency 'out of thin air'. So the swapping of public debt for account credits is just an accounting convention.

Some OMF proponents have invoked the 1948 article by Milton

Friedman as evidence that even arch free market economists support the money financing approach. There is a sort of security in this approach because it suggests the radical idea is not that radical at all. But this is a negative approach for progressives to take. The preferred option is to explain that OMF merely recognises that a currency-issuing government never needs to borrow or tax in order to spend. Friedman (1948: 5) wrote, 'government expenditures would be financed entirely by tax revenues or the creation of money, that is, the use of non-interest bearing securities. Government would not issue interest bearing securities to the public.' Adair Turner, the former Chairman of the British Financial Services Authority, suggested that serious consideration be given to the 'extreme option' of 'overt money finance (OMF) of fiscal deficits', which would involve the 'permanent monetisation of government debt' (Turner, 2013: 2). He channelled Friedman's claim 'that government deficits should always be financed in that fashion' (Turner, 2013: 3). However, former Australian Treasury official Richard Wood (2013a) correctly points out that Friedman's proposals were part of what was known as the Chicago Plan (emanating out of the free market bastion at the University of Chicago), which proposed a broad regime change where private banks would be prevented from creating new money and public deficits would be the only source of new money. Equally, the government would run a balanced fiscal position over the cycle and destroy the money created in the downturn when they ran offsetting surpluses in the upturn. This is a very different proposition to the current suggestion for OMF.

OMF is seen by an increasing number of economists and commentators as a way to get out of the 'mess' (Turner, 2013). OMF supports fiscal expansion, which directly stimulates the economy by putting extra dollars of spending into the economy. Paul McCulley, former managing director of the large bond trader PIMCO, convincingly argues that a reliance on monetary policy to resolve the crisis will fail, especially when fiscal policy is forced by the austerity mania to act in a pro-cyclical fashion (McCulley and Pozsar, 2013). The correct policy response in circumstances of low or falling inflation and massive spending shortages is to ensure 'monetary stimulus is paired with fiscal stimulus', a coincidence they refer to as a 'helicopter drop' (p. 26). The former US Federal Reserve Chairman, Ben Bernanke, revived the idea of a 'helicopter drop' in 2002. In a speech to the National Economists Club in Washington about methods to avoid deflation, Bernanke advocated a 'money-financed tax cut' (Bernanke, 2002), which he said was equivalent to Friedman's anti-deflation proposal to drop money from helicopters in order to stimulate spending (Friedman, 1969: 4). Bernanke said that when total spending collapses, a nation endures rising unemployment and ultimately deflation, as 'producers cut prices on an ongoing basis in order to find buyers' (Bernanke, 2002). As the recession deepens, interest rates drop to zero, which reduces the flexibility of monetary policy. Even from the conservative eye of Ben Bernanke, these situations call for a significant increase in fiscal deficits to stimulate spending and confidence, with the central bank issuing new money to support the deficits. From the perspective of MMT, a helicopter drop is equivalent to an increase in the fiscal deficit in the sense that new financial assets are created and the net worth of the non-government sector increases.

McCulley and Pozsar (2013: 16) consider that 'unconventional and radical policies' such as QE and similar policies are not effective because they are 'independent of the fiscal policy stance', and so the imposition of fiscal austerity kills any growth potential that these monetary policies might have. Instead, they propose that monetary policy has to go 'nuclear' (p. 16) (reflecting the strength of the taboo) as part of what they call 'fiscal-monetary cooperation ("FMC")' (p. 16). FMC means that monetary policy works to 'support the fiscal authority in raising nominal demand, not to stimulate private borrowing *per se*' (p. 17) by funding the deficit. They qualify their support for this policy option by suggesting that to overcome what they call technical constraints (by which they mean the voluntary constraints that force governments to issue debt to the private sector), the central bank can 'underwrite government spending . . . by buying on the secondary market the same amount of bonds that the government has issued to fund the stimulus' (p. 18). Readers will note that this is exactly what the ECB was doing under the aegis of the SMP. From the MMT perspective, the preferred approach would be to eliminate any of the voluntary constraints on central banks so they could directly underwrite the fiscal deficits without the need for governments to engage in primary issuance of debt to the private markets.

Richard Wood said that the austerity approach in Europe was a 'self-defeating exercise' (Wood, 2012: 1), which had 'failed to restore the levels of sustainable growth needed to substantially reduce unemployment and to prevent the public debt burden spiralling upward' (p. 1). In the Eurozone context, Wood claimed the two major problems are 'deficient aggregate demand, and high and rising public debt' (p. 1). Wood argued that because the current situation is grave, 'policymakers will be required to consider the widest set of policy instruments to succeed' and the current failed orthodoxy 'will need to be jettisoned' (p. 2). In that vein, Wood outlined two policy options, which he said were in the 'general policy zone of monetisation of spending' and would provide stimulus but not increase the level of outstanding public debt (p. 4): 'Option A is a pure 'helicopter drop' of new money by the central bank into private bank accounts. Option B is the creation of new money to directly finance the budget deficit.'

Wood concurred with the view that a helicopter drop is not a very targeted strategy and in the case of the Eurozone would run 'parallel' with the ongoing fiscal deficits. In that sense, it would not break the institutional nexus between rising deficits and rising public debt levels. For those reasons, he advocated Option B, which from hereon we will refer to as the OMF option (see also Wood, 2013b; Bossone and Wood, 2013). It is exactly what Abba Lerner was advocating back in the 1940s, and has been the basis of MMT since it became a coherent body of theory in the 1990s.

In April 2012, Biagio Bossone said that OMF was a 'radical action' to address the problems in the Eurozone without the need to abandon the single currency (Bossone, 2013a, 2013b). He examined whether OMF could be consistent with Article 123 of the Treaty, which prohibits so-called monetary financing. He concluded that the existing Emergency Liquidity Assistance (ELA) facility would allow OMF to fund government deficits on an ongoing basis. The ELA allows the ECB to provide 'central bank money' to any solvent financial institution 'facing temporary liquidity problems, without such operation being part of the single monetary policy' (ECB, 2014b: 1). While the rules prohibit the ELA being used to provide 'overdraft facilities for official bodies', or 'purchase government bonds' (Bossone, 2013a), Bossone pointed to precedents in the current crisis (for example, Belgium, Ireland and Greece) where the ELA facility 'has been used . . . as a source of additional bailout funding'. However, when the Italian Ministry of Finance sought permission for the Banca d'Italia to use the ELA in 'a guarantee scheme for the liabilities of Italian banks' (ECB, 2012b: 1), the ECB only agreed on the proviso, among others, that 'the Banca d'Italia must comply with the monetary financing prohibition in Article 123 of the Treaty' and 'all the guarantees must be financed from the State's budget' (p. 5).

Bossone (2013a) was cognisant of the issue and suggested that the ECB could 'extend its legal interpretation' of the ELA to allow it to be used as 'last-resort demand management tool to fight local recessions and preserve monetary and financial stability in the Eurozone'. It is unlikely, however, that the ECB could extend that 'flexibility' without coming up against Article 123 of the Treaty. It is more likely that a Treaty change would be required to allow OMF to be used on an ongoing basis. In the interim, the ECB could ramp up its OMT program to provide indirect support to the expanding deficits in the Member States. Clearly, OMF requires both a paradigm shift in European politics and an intellectual shift of a similar magnitude in the academy.

The idea of OMF was given further impetus in the public arena in March 2013 when the well-respected conservative Adair Turner proposed it as a solution. He considered the pre-crisis emphasis on inflation targets was misguided and any recovery should be based on policies that explicitly give weight to achieving low unemployment as well as price stability. In addition to more aggressive use of fiscal policy, Turner said that he supported OMF because it allowed a fiscal stimulus to directly enter 'the income stream' (p. 25), which means that the impact of the spending is immediate, a dollar of extra government spending is immediately a dollar of extra income and output in the private sector. This is in contrast to monetary operations such as interest rate cuts and QE, which indirectly rely on consumers and firms responding to the lower costs of borrowing. The impact is always uncertain and drawn out.

OVERT MONETARY FINANCING ENTERS THE EUROPEAN PARLIAMENTARY DEBATE

On 24 April 2014, the ECB presented its Annual Report 2012 (ECB, 2012c) to the Committee on Economic and Monetary Affairs (ECON) of European Parliament. ECON considered the Report on 11 June 2013. The Rapporteur of the Committee and Deputy President of the Parliament, Gianni Pittela, tendered a draft ECON response (Committee on Economic and Monetary Affairs, 2013a), which was intended to motivate discussion and provide the basis for their final Report.

The draft ECON report contained two interesting paragraphs (nine and ten) under the heading 'Monetary Policy' (Committee on Economic and Monetary Affairs, 2013a: 4–5):

> 9. Considers that the monetary policy tools that the ECB has used since the beginning of the crisis, while providing a welcome relief in distressed financial markets, have revealed their limits as regards stimulating growth and improving the situation on the labour market; considers, therefore, that the ECB could investigate the possibilities of implementing new unconventional measures aimed at participating in a large, EU wide pro-growth programme, including the use of the Emergency Liquidity Assistance facility to undertake an 'overt money financing' of government debt in order to finance tax cuts targeted on low income households and/or new spending programmes focused on the Europe 2020 objectives;
> 10. Considers it necessary to review the Treaties and the ECB's statutes in order to establish price stability together with full employment as the two objectives, on an equal footing, of monetary policy in the Eurozone . . .

These proposals resonate strongly with the foundation principles of MMT and would serve to redress some of the social and economic damage that the implementation of austerity has caused.

The Draft Report received lengthy Committee scrutiny, which resulted in 247 amendments (Committee on Economic and Monetary Affairs, 2013b). By the time the Final Report (Committee on Economic and Monetary Affairs, 2013c) was released on 13 November 2013, we had learned a lot about European politics and why the current monetary system is unworkable. The Final Report bore little relation to the Draft Report and is a largely innocuous document that will engender no significant changes.

A lot can be learned about European Groupthink by studying the ECON amendment process. For example, Amendment 116, proposed by German conservative Werner Langen as a replacement for Paragraph 9 (Committee on Economic and Monetary Affairs, 2013b: 54):

> Considers that the monetary policy tools that the ECB has used since the beginning of the crisis may have provided welcome relief in distressed financial markets in the short term, but the easy money policy has done nothing to bring about a lasting economic recovery; considers, therefore, that the only way to promote growth is through sustainable economic policy and purposeful structural reforms, that the ECB must concentrate primarily on the goal of price stability, and that ECB financing of government debt is unlawful and must be prevented at all costs . . .

In the context of the debate, where unemployment was rising to record levels, youth unemployment in some nations had risen to around 60 per cent and the EMU was in a state of protracted stagnation, the claim that the ECB must resist OMF 'at all costs' is an extraordinary statement of priorities. But that is the nature of this taboo. The simple idea that a central bank should facilitate government deficits through money creation invokes hysterical claims about inflation and, within the European context, strikes at the heart of the paranoia among Germans about hyperinflation.

The proposed Amendment 136 to Paragraph 10 from Dutch-born libertarian politician Derk Jan Eppink, who was a Belgian member affiliated with the right wing List Dedecker party, was also illustrative of the way conservatives in Europe prioritise policy ends. The proposed change eliminated any reference to full employment as a policy target 'on any footing' with price stability: 'Underlines that the primary mandate of the ECB is to maintain price stability in the Euro area, and that the achievement of this mandate overrides subordinate objectives such as supporting economic growth and job creation' (Committee on Economic and Monetary Affairs, 2013b: 64).

It was clear that the conservatives were obsessed with inflation control and believed it was necessary to sacrifice the jobs and incomes of millions of European workers to pursue that end. For them, price stability and full employment are trade-offs. In Chapter 17 we learned that both policy objectives could be simultaneously achieved with appropriate fiscal interventions. Chapter 23 provides a policy framework to achieve that simultaneity.

WHY IS OVERT MONETARY FINANCING CONSIDERED TABOO?

The substantive criticism of OMF is the obvious one. All economics students are hard wired to recite that inflation follows an expansion of the money supply. This is one of the most basic and sacred of all the myths that mainstream economists use to dissuade the public of the benefits of fiscal activism, and particularly if they can imply this requires that the money printing presses would be running at ever increasing speeds.

There are many misconceptions as to what inflation actually is. Many media commentators, for example, think that a pay rise for workers constitutes inflation. Others (of perhaps a different political persuasion) think that inflation occurs when companies increase their prices. Some people think inflation occurs when the local prices of imports rise after the exchange rate depreciates. A depreciating exchange rate means that the local currency becomes less valuable in relation to other currencies and foreign-sourced goods and services typically become more expensive to local buyers. But is this inflationary? Similarly, some commentators think inflation occurs when the government increases a particular tax (say, a value added tax on goods and services) by x per cent and this is passed on by firms in the form of higher prices for goods and services. None of these examples constitute inflation. Given they all involve a rise in prices, each example would constitute what we call a necessary condition for an inflationary episode. But none of these examples represent a sufficient condition.

Inflation is the *continuous* rise in the price level. If the price level rises by 0.1 per cent every month, for example, then we would be observing an inflationary episode. In this case, the inflation rate would be considered stable. If the price level was rising by 0.1 per cent in month one, then 0.15 per cent in month two, then 0.2 per cent in month three and so on, then we would be observing an accelerating inflation. Alternatively, falling or decelerating inflation occurs when the price level rises by, say, 0.1 per cent in month one, 0.05 per cent in month two and so on. A deflationary episode occurs when the price level starts to continuously fall. The term hyperinflation is reserved for inflationary episodes, which rapidly exponentiate. There have been few instances of hyperinflation in recorded history.

We might also define a normal price level as being the prices firms are willing to supply at when they are operating at normal capacity. However, the economic cycle fluctuates around these 'normal' levels of capacity utilisation and firms not only adjust to the flux and uncertainty of total spending by adjusting output but, in some cases, will vary prices. This is particularly the case during a recession. When sales are depressed, firms might offer discounts to increase capacity utilisation and/or clear unsold inventories. They temporarily suppress their profit margins as a means of maintaining their market share. As demand conditions become more favourable the firms start withdrawing the discounts and prices return to normal levels. We would not consider these price increases to be inflation.

With that cleared up, why do economists claim that OMF would lead to out of control inflation? Whenever governments increase their deficits, mainstream economists and their pawns in the financial media make claims about the likely inflation that they say will result. The large fiscal and monetary stimulus packages introduced by many governments to offset the GFC have not resulted in the predicted inflation. It isn't the first time that the doomsayers have been proven wrong. When QE was first introduced in Japan in the 1990s, mainstream economists rushed to predict that the massive expansion in central bank reserves would be inflationary. Students in every mainstream macroeconomics class, and that means almost all students, would have predicted, based on the non-sense they were learning, that the high deficits and high public debt ratios in Japan at the time should have driven interest rates sky high, that bond markets should have stopped buying government bonds, that the government should have run out of money, and all the time that these disasters were unfolding that inflation should have been galloping towards hyper-inflation. Nothing like that happened. Neo-liberal economists wrote off their mistakes by claiming that Japan is 'so strange' that it is a 'special case' and therefore not generally applicable. Their ad hoc defence was convenient because the Japanese experience with sustained high fiscal deficits, the world's largest public debt-to-GDP ratio, close to zero interest rates and *deflation*, was totally at odds with their economic theories. It was a mind-boggling failure to explain reality.

Undaunted by their failure to understand Japan, the neo-liberals rehearsed the same logic when governments around the world introduced massive stimulus packages to combat the GFC. The economists were once again quoting from their undergraduate macroeconomics textbooks and predicting that it was only a matter of time before these nations would be heading down the Zimbabwean path. Despite the significant increase in deficits and central bank reserves, inflation has been stable or falling. The economists were wrong again!

There are two arcane textbook notions that render OMF taboo for neo-liberals. One is just plain wrong while the other has limited applicability during a recession. The first notion is the rather technical sounding concept of the 'money multiplier', which links so-called central bank money or the 'monetary base' to the total stock of money in the economy (called the money supply). The second notion then links the growth in that stock of money to the inflation rate. The combined causality then allows the mainstream economists to assert that if the central bank expands the money supply it will cause inflation, which is their prima facie case against OMF (see Figure 21.1). As is often the case, many financial commentators who wax lyrical about the dangers of OMF do not even fully understand the theoretical route that is alleged to link central bank monetary expansion with inflation.

For our purposes, the 'monetary base' would be enlarged by OMF because the quantity of bank reserves held in accounts with the central bank would increase (see Chapter 17). Macroeconomics students around the world rote learn the mantra that the money multiplier times the monetary base determines the money supply. The money multiplier is just some number that scales up the monetary base to give a larger number, which according to the textbooks is the money supply. The causality embodied

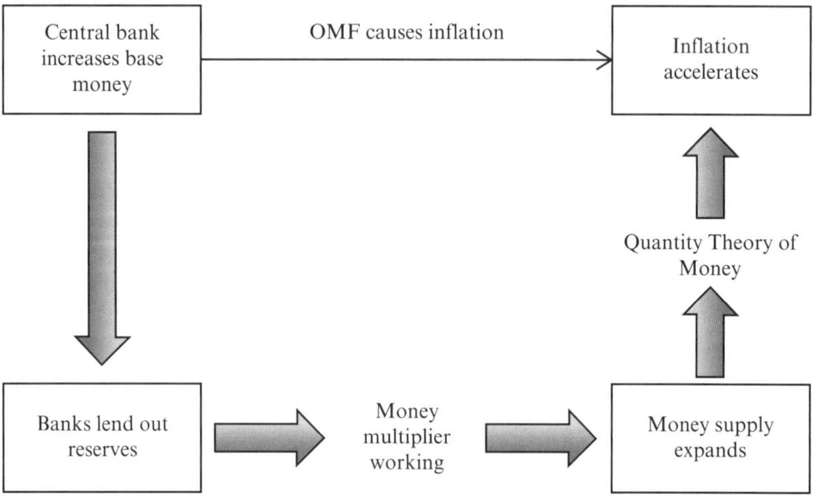

Figure 21.1 The alleged OMF inflation chain

in this mantra is an article of religious faith among mainstream economists and underpinned the attempts in the 1980s by central banks, infested with the emerging Monetarist thinking, to attempt to introduce so-called 'monetary targets'. They were just projections of the growth in the measured money supply, which the central banks claimed would be their primary policy vehicle for controlling inflation. That policy approach failed badly because central banks soon found out that they did not actually have control over the money supply. But the theory persisted. We will return to that issue later. But first we need to briefly understand the myth of the 'money multiplier'.

The Myth of the Money Multiplier

Students are introduced to the money multiplier early in their studies. It is an article of faith in mainstream thinking. It is asserted, erroneously, that by manipulating the monetary base the central bank can control the money supply. Milton Friedman, the father of Monetarism, once said in relation to the US monetary system that 'the Federal Reserve System essentially determines the total quantity of money; that is to say, the number of dollars of currency and deposits available for the public to hold. Within very wide limits, it can make this total anything it wants it to be' (Friedman, 1959a: 4; also Friedman, 1959b). Later, in 1968, as the Monetarists were gaining traction in the public debate, Friedman said that the central bank should publicly adopt 'the policy of achieving a steady rate of growth in a specified monetary total . . .' (Friedman, 1968: 16). Unfortunately, like most aspects of the Monetarist doctrine, the theory doesn't match the reality.

The 'monetary base' is measured as the notes and coins in circulation or in bank vaults plus bank reserves held at the central bank. It is understood that central banks can add 'money' to the bank reserve accounts whenever they choose. They create money 'out of thin air'. The money supply is defined in a range of ways – from very narrow (a small number of components) to broad (more components). The narrowest measure, M1, includes only notes and coins in circulation and bank and cheque account deposits on demand (that is, funds that can be withdrawn instantly). Broader measures such as M3 include items such as longer-term deposits, which require more than 24-hours' notice before withdrawal is permitted. The definitions also vary across nations.

The money multiplier is then defined as the money supply divided by the monetary base. The textbook argument goes that the central bank controls the 'base money' in existence and then the act of credit creation in the private banking system multiplies this base up to create the money supply. The determinants of the money multiplier need not concern us here but relate to various parameters in the banking system (for example, the quantity of notes and coins that depositors wish to hold and any required reserves that the banks must hold). A simple story to get the concept across is that someone deposits a sum in a bank to earn some interest. The bank then keeps some of that deposit in reserve to meet the daily withdrawal behaviour and lends the rest out at a higher interest rate in order to profit. The recipient of the loan spends the money, which ends up as a deposit in some bank or another. That bank, in turn, lends most of this new deposit out and the process continues. The resulting money supply expands as these deposits multiply.

The conception of the money multiplier is really as simple as that. There are two major flaws. First, the empirical evidence clearly shows that empirical estimates of the money multiplier are not constant and so can hardly be used to make predictions. Second, the stylised textbook model of the banking system isn't remotely descriptive of the real world.

Figure 21.2 shows the estimates of the 'money multiplier' for the US and the Eurozone using the so-called M1 measure of the money supply. The pattern would be the same if we had used a broader measure of the money supply. If one is to postulate a causal relationship between the monetary base and the money supply mediated by this so-called money multiplier then the multiplier would have to be stable or predictable. The multiplier has not exhibited stability in either the US or the Eurozone and thus serves no useful basis for predicting the money supply. Mainstream commentators attempted to argue that with QE driving up excess reserves

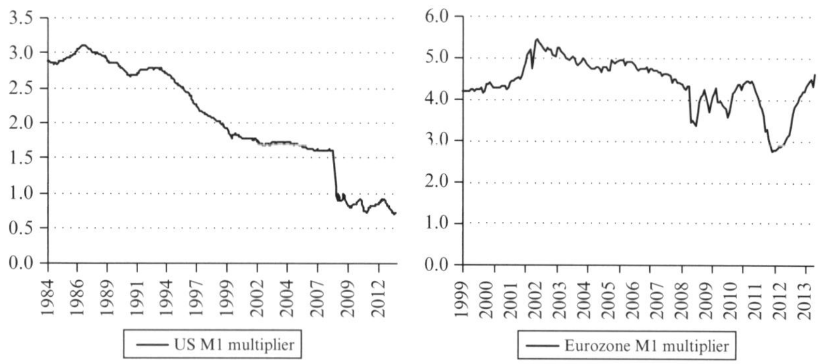

Source: ECB, M1/base money, US Federal Reserve, M1/monetary base.

Figure 21.2 Money multiplier estimates, US and Eurozone, various periods

in the banking system, the multiplier fell, which was an attempt to explain the sudden drops you can see in Figure 21.2. However, this defence is an example of the ad hoc reasoning that permeates economic theory. Whenever the mainstream paradigm is confronted with empirical evidence that appears to refute its basic predictions, it creates an exception by way of response to the anomaly and continues on as if nothing had happened (see Gordon, 1972). Students are not told that the measured multiplier is a moving feast and moves around like a Mexican jumping bean. Moreover, the measured multiplier was clearly unstable in the pre-crisis period, which means the special crisis case explanation for the instability fails.

In our earlier discussion of QE, it was noted that banks do not wait for depositors to provide reserves before they make loans. Rather, they aggressively seek to make loans to credit-worthy customers in order to profit. These loans are made independent of a bank's specific reserve position at the time the loan is approved. A separate department in each bank manages the bank's reserve position and will seek funds to ensure it has the required reserves in the relevant accounting period. They can borrow from each other in the interbank market but if the system overall is short of reserves these transactions will not add the required reserves. In these cases, the bank will sell bonds back to the central bank or borrow from it outright at some penalty rate. At the individual bank level, certainly the 'price' it has to pay to get the necessary reserves will play some role in the credit department's decision to loan funds. But the reserve position *per se* will not matter. For its part, the central bank will always supply the necessary reserves to ensure the financial system remains functional and cheques clear each day. The upshot is that banks do not lend out reserves and a particular bank's ability to expand its balance sheet by lending is not constrained by the quantity of reserves it holds or any fractional reserve requirements that might be imposed by the central bank. Loans create deposits, which are then backed by reserves after the fact.

In recent years, in the face of all this hyperinflation angst, several central banks published articles which showed how far fetched the monetary theory is that is taught to students and espoused by mainstream economists and financial commentators. They showed that real world banking doesn't operate in the way the textbooks claim. Among the enlightening reports was the Bank of England article 'Money creation in the modern economy'. The two central conclusions were (Bank of England, 2014: 14):

> The reality of how money is created today differs from the description found in some economics textbooks:
>
> - Rather than banks receiving deposits when households save and then lending them out, bank lending creates deposits.

- In normal times, the central bank does not fix the amount of money in circulation, nor is central bank money 'multiplied up' into more loans and deposits.

These conclusions are devastating for mainstream economics. The Bank of England further notes that 'in reality . . . commercial banks are the creators of deposit money . . . the reverse of the sequence typically described in textbooks' (p. 15) and that the 'money multiplier theory . . . is not an accurate description of how money is created in reality' (p. 15). Central banks do not control the quantity of reserves and implement monetary policy 'by setting the price of reserves – that is, interest rates' (p. 15). These insights lead to the conclusion that 'neither are reserves a binding constraint on lending, nor does the central bank fix the amount of reserves that are available' (p. 15). In terms of the determinants of the broad money supply, the Bank of England ratifies the MMT argument that 'lending creates deposits' (p. 15), which then creates money.

The Bank of England also highlighted the 'related misconception . . . that banks can lend out their reserves' and concluded that 'Reserves can only be lent between banks' (p. 16) and 'consumers do not have access' (p. 16) to central bank reserve accounts. This insight is also confirmed in an interesting article published in September 2008 by the Federal Reserve Bank of New York in their Economic Policy Review entitled 'Divorcing money from monetary policy' (FRBNY, 2008). Commercial banks require bank reserves for two main reasons. First, from time to time, central banks will impose reserve requirements, which means that the bank has to hold a certain non-zero volume of reserves at the central bank. Most nations only require the banks to keep their reserves in the black on a daily basis. Second, the FRNBY states that 'reserve balances are used to make interbank payments; thus, they serve as the final form of settlement for a vast array of transactions' (p. 42). Chapter 17 explained that there is daily uncertainty among banks surrounding the payments flows in and out as cheques are presented and other transactions between banks are accounted for. The banks can get funds from the other banks in the interbank market to cover any shortfalls, but also will choose to hold some extra reserves just in case. If all else fails the central bank maintains a role as lender of last resort, which means they will lend reserves on demand from the commercial banks to facilitate the payments system.

When the central bank adds funds to these reserve accounts (for example, when conducting QE or OMF), 'the new reserves are not mechanically multiplied up into new loans and new deposits as predicted by the money multiplier theory' (Bank of England, 2014: 24). The fact is that the existence of new reserves, even if they are well in excess of the banks' requirements to operate an orderly clearing system, 'do not, by themselves . . . change the incentives for the banks to create new broad money by lending' (p. 24).

The question then is: why are students in our universities forced to learn material that has no foundation in the system they are purporting to understand? The answer is that the educational opportunity is replaced by a propaganda exercise to suit ideological agendas.

Central Banks Do Not Control the Money Supply

This also reflects on the Monetarist claim that the central bank controls the money supply. The Bank of England concludes 'it does not directly control the quantity of either base or broad money' (p. 25). This insight is also confirmed by the FRBNY (2008: 41):

> In recent decades, however, central banks have moved away from a direct focus on measures of the money supply. The primary focus of monetary policy has instead become the value of a short-term interest rate. In the United States, for example, the Federal Reserve's Federal Open Market Committee (FOMC) announces a rate that it wishes to prevail in the federal funds market, where overnight loans are made among commercial banks. The tools of monetary policy are then used to guide the market interest rate toward the chosen target.

Thus, monetary policy is not practised through attempts by the central bank to control the 'money supply' but rather through its capacity to set the short-term interest rate, the rate that gains all the headlines each month.

The reality is that the demand for credit by individuals and firms from their banks determines the money supply. Business firms seek credit to meet working capital needs to produce goods and services to meet their expectations of sales. Consumers also seek loans for a variety of purposes. These loans appear as bank deposits and so the 'money supply' expands. When the credit is repaid the money supply shrinks. These flows are going on continuously and so fluctuations in the money supply measures published by central banks are just arbitrary reflections of the credit circuit: the borrowing and repayment of loans. Central banks clearly do not determine the volume of deposits held each day. Rather they determine the price at which it will supply reserves on demand by the banks (see Lavoie, 1984). A far better depiction of reality is that instead of the money supply being a multiple of the monetary base (the money multiplier story), the money supply brings forth the demand for bank reserves and so the monetary base responds accordingly. The causality is thus reversed.

Money Spent Can Buy Goods and Services Rather than Cause Inflation

The second flawed aspect of the antagonism against OMF relates to the mainstream theory of inflation captured by the so-called Quantity Theory of Money (QTM). In Figure 21.1, the QTM links the expansion of the money supply with accelerating inflation. It is the most intuitive part of the neo-liberal story and the one that resonates with the public. This theory has a central place in the Classical economics literature but we can still get the idea without having to delve too deeply into that murky terrain. Suffice to say, while the QTM was formulated in the 16th century, the idea still forms the core of what became known as Monetarism in the 1970s and is the principle reason for the taboo against OMF.

First, a small bit of theory. The QTM postulates the following relationship: M times V equals P times Y, which can be easily described in words as follows. M is a symbol for how much money there is in circulation, that is, the money supply. V is called the velocity of circulation in the textbooks but simply means how many times per period (say a year) the money supply 'turns over' in transactions. To understand velocity, think about the following example. Assume the total stock of money is $100, which is held between the two people that make up this hypothetical economy. In the current period, Person A buys goods and services from Person B for the $100 it currently holds. In turn, Person B uses the $100 to buy goods and services from Person A. The total transactions equal $200 yet there is only $100 in the economy. Each dollar has thus been used 'twice' over the course of the year. So the velocity in this economy is two. When we make transactions we hand over money, which then keeps being circulated in subsequent purchases. The result of M times V is equal to the total monetary transactions in the economy per period, which is a flow of dollars (or whatever currency is in use). The P times Y is the average price in the economy (P) times real output produced (Y), which sums to what we call nominal Gross Domestic Product (GDP). The national statistician estimates the total sum of all the goods and services produced to get real GDP and then values this in some way using the price level to get a monetary measure of total production. How they do that is beyond this discussion but there are well-defined procedures that all government statistical agencies such as Eurostat use. So P times Y is the total money value of the output produced in the period.

At this level, the relationship M times V equals P times Y is nothing more than an accounting statement that says that the total value of spending (M times V) in a period must equal the total monetary value of output (P times Y), that is, a truism. It is true by definition and thus totally unobjectionable. How does the QTM become a theory of inflation? The answer is that the inflation theory uses a sleight of hand. The Classical economists, who pioneered the use of the QTM, assumed that the labour market would always be at full employment, which means that real GDP (the Y in the formula) would always be at full capacity and thus could not rise any further in the immediate future. They also assumed that the velocity of circulation (V) was constant (unchanged) given that it was determined by customs and payment habits. For example, people are paid on a weekly or fortnightly basis and shop, say, once a week for their needs. These habits were considered to underpin a relative constancy of velocity. These assumptions then led to the conclusion that if the money supply changed, the only other thing that could change to satisfy the relationship M times V equals P times Y was the price level (P). The only way the economy could adjust to more spending when it was already at full capacity was to ration that spending off with higher prices. Financial commentators simplify this and say that inflation arises when there is 'too much money chasing too few goods'.

The problem with the theory is that neither of the required assumptions holds in the real world. First, there are many studies which have shown that velocity of circulation varies over time quite dramatically. Second, and more importantly, capitalist economies are rarely operating at full employment. The Classical theory essentially denied the possibility of unemployment. The fact that economies typically operate with spare productive capacity, and often with persistently high rates of unemployment, means that it is hard to maintain the view that there is no scope for firms to expand the supply of real goods and services when there is an increase in total spending growth. If a firm has poor sales and lots of spare productive capacity, why would it hike prices when sales improved?

Thus, if there was an increase in availability of credit and borrowers used the deposits that were created by the loans to purchase goods and services, it is likely that firms with excess capacity will respond by increasing the supply of goods and services to maintain or increase market share rather than push up prices. In other words, an evaluation of the inflationary consequences of OMF should be made with reference to the state of the economy. If there is idle capacity then it is most unlikely that OMF will be inflationary. At some point, when unemployment is low and firms are operating at close to or at full capacity, then any further spending, whether funded by OMF or some other scheme, will likely introduce an inflationary risk into the policy deliberations.

Would OMF Increase the Inflation Risk?

This brings us to a further misconception that is associated with the claim that OMF would predispose a nation to inflation. The mainstream macroeconomic textbooks all have a chapter on fiscal policy, which introduces the so-called 'Government Budget Constraint (GBC)'. The claim is that governments face funding constraints in the same way as a household and thus have to raise income via taxation or borrowing to finance their spending. It is acknowledged that governments are not quite like households because they can create money out of thin air, a capacity that no household possesses. But that option is eschewed and vilified for the reasons we have discussed. To further the case against money creation, the textbooks claim that the expansionary impact of a fiscal deficit in terms of total spending in the economy is lower if the government matches the deficit by borrowing from the private sector relative to if it just creates money. In other words, the inflation risk is much higher under OMF. The reason advanced is that when the government issues debt it not only drains the excess reserves in the banking sector created by deficit, and thus takes private purchasing power out of the monetary system, but, further, by 'competing' for funds with other private borrowers it pushes the interest rate up, which chokes off some private spending. This is the so-called 'financial crowding out' effect of 'debt finance'.

In presenting a case in support of OMF, Wood (2013b) seems to be operating within this mainstream paradigm. He advocates OMF as an option 'where public debt is already high and "conventional" government bond sales are used to finance the budget deficits' because he claims issuing further debt will push interest rates up. In this regard, he concluded that:

> Fiscal multipliers and marginal propensities to consume ordinary goods and services would be relatively larger under *overt money financing* than under *quantitative easing/new bond financing* of budget deficits. Overt money financing offers the most powerful combination of monetary and fiscal policies to combat the dual problems of recessions/depressions and high public debt. (Emphasis in original)

This is straight out of the mainstream macroeconomics textbook and presents an erroneous depiction of what happens in the real world. First, the 'financial crowding out' argument, which is a central plank in the mainstream economics attack on government fiscal intervention, is based on a totally false construction of the financial system. The Classical economists advanced the so-called 'loanable funds doctrine' which claimed that the so-called loanable funds market mediates saving and investment via interest rate variations. The theory claimed that household saving (supply of funds) responds positively to rising interest rates because savers can get a higher return and increase their future consumption possibilities. Investment (demand for funds) declines with the interest rate because higher interest rates increase the costs of funds and render marginal investment projects unprofitable. Demand and supply forces thus mean that shortages of funds available for lending would push up interest rates and vice versa. It is then alleged that if the government borrows more to 'fund' a rising deficit, interest rates have to rise because there are now more borrowers in the market competing for the same scarce savings. The higher interest rates then choke off some private investment spending. The public spending is deemed to 'crowd out' private spending.

John Maynard Keynes demolished the 'crowding out' hypothesis in the 1930s, when he noted that in the real world total saving rises when national income rises. In other words, when the government deficit rises, it not only increases national income because output is higher but total saving also rises. In other words, the assumption that there is a finite pool of funds available for investment is flawed.

Deficit spending also increases private bank account balances once all the transactions (purchases and sales) that arise from the initial spending impulse are accounted for. The extra bank account balances may be used to buy the newly issued government bonds. In this way, the sale of debt by the government is really 'borrowing' funds that the government has already spent into existence when it ran the deficit. The sale of bonds just alters the composition of the portfolio of assets that are held by the non-government sector (more interest bearing bonds and less bank deposits). In that context, it makes no sense to say that government borrowing rations finite 'savings' which could alternatively finance private investment.

What would happen if the government didn't borrow and used OMF instead? Like all government spending, the treasury would spend by instructing the central bank to put money into the bank accounts of the recipients of the spending, which would involve 'crediting' the reserve accounts held by some commercial banks at the central bank. As we learned in Chapter 17, the assets of these commercial banks would rise (reserves increase) and their liabilities would also increase because a deposit would be made on behalf of the recipients of the government spending. The recipients of the government spending enjoy increased assets (bank deposits) and thus their net worth (wealth) rises. Taxation does the opposite. Thus when the government runs a fiscal deficit (spending greater than taxation) total bank reserves rise and private wealth increases.

The increased deficit spending would most likely create excess reserves in the banking system, which then raises issues for the central bank about its liquidity management. The aim of the central bank is to 'hit its policy target', that is, maintain the policy interest rate. Recalling Chapter 17, the central bank has to ensure that competitive forces in the interbank market do not compromise that target. For a commercial bank, excess reserves constitute dead money unless the central bank pays a return on them. If there is no return on the excess reserves held overnight, the banks with excess reserves scurry around seeking interest earning opportunities by loaning to other banks in the interbank market, which might have a shortage of reserves. The excess reserves put downward pressure on the overnight interest rate because banks will accept anything above a zero return. But the competition to get rid of excess reserves can only redistribute the excess, not eliminate it. Faced with this situation, the central bank has to sell government bonds to the banks to soak the excess reserves up and maintain liquidity at a level consistent with the target interest rate. Some central banks offer a return on overnight reserves, which reduces the need to sell debt as a liquidity management operation. The 'penalty' for the central bank that doesn't pay interest on reserves would be a Japan-like zero interest rate. Should a default support rate be paid on excess reserves, the interest rate would converge on that support rate. Any economic ramifications (like inflation or currency depreciation) would be due to lower interest rates (stimulating excessive nominal growth rates relative to the real capacity of the economy) rather than any notion of OMF.

What would happen if the government borrowed to match its fiscal deficit? All that happens is that the bank's reserves are reduced by the bond sales as the bank balances used to purchase the assets decline. In other words, the composition of the asset portfolio held in the non-government sector changes, leaving the net worth of the non-government sector unaltered. The only difference between the treasury borrowing from the central bank (as in OMF) and issuing debt to the private sector is that the central bank has to use different liquidity operations to maintain its policy interest rate target. If public debt is not issued to match the deficit then it has to either pay interest on excess reserves (which most central banks are doing now anyway) or let the target rate fall to zero (the Japan solution). There are no differences in the impact that the fiscal deficits have on net worth in the non-government sector or on total spending in the economy.

Mainstream economists claim that by draining the reserves, the central bank reduces the ability of banks to lend. But in the real world, building or draining bank reserves does not increase or decrease the ability of the banks to lend. The banks will lend to credit-worthy customers, knowing they can access bank reserves after the fact from a number of sources with a guarantee that they can source them from the central bank if all other options fail. The banks are able to create credit whenever they can find credit-worthy customers irrespective of the central bank liquidity operations that accompany government spending. Bank loans simultaneously create new deposits, which borrowers can then use to invest in capital formation (building productive capacity). Even if the government borrowing drained all the bank reserves that the initial government spending created, the central bank is always standing by to provide the desired reserves to the commercial banks to ensure the integrity of the payments system. Thus, there can be no squeeze on private investment arising from government borrowing.

Ultimately, private agents may refuse to hold any more cash or bonds. The private sector at the micro level can only dispense with unwanted cash balances in the absence of government bond sales by increasing their spending levels. Given the current tax structure, this reduced desire to net save would generate a private spending expansion and reduce the fiscal deficit because tax revenue would rise on the back of the increased economic activity.

All Spending Creates an Inflation Risk

Bossone and Wood (2013) also claimed that the concerns with OMF about 'any potential inflation threat are misplaced' because the 'new money can be withdrawn from the economy (sterilised), if liquidity is adequate'. This is again related to the claim that the inflation risk is higher with OMF than with government spending matched by borrowing. It should be emphasised that fiscal deficits do carry inflation risk. To explain that point requires us to further expose the myths taught in macroeconomics. The approach taught to students fails to explicate and reinforce the fact that government spending is performed in the same way irrespective of these accompanying monetary operations (taxation, bond sales or money creation). More telling is that the inflation risk of fiscal deficits is embedded in the spending function of government and issuing bonds to the private sector does not alter that risk. Governments spend by crediting bank accounts (issuing cheques which are then deposited is equivalent). All the accounting institutions that might be put in place whereby 'tax' funds go into a certain account, which is then drawn down when governments spend, are just a chimera of the underlying reality.

But, more generally, all components of total spending, private consumption expenditure, private investment, exports and government consumption and investment spending carry inflation risk if they become excessive. Inflation is caused by total spending growing faster than the capacity of the economy to produce real goods and services in response. In that situation, firms have no flexibility to increase production and thus 'ration' off the spending growth by putting up prices. Significantly, the reserve position of the banks is not functionally related to that process. The central bank can 'sterilise' the liquidity impacts of the deficit spending by selling bonds to the private sector. But that doesn't reduce the inflation risk of the initial spending. It just means the private sector has more bonds and less deposits. The government spending has already occurred. Of course, no responsible government would desire to expand the economy beyond its real limit given the political problems it would face should inflation rise sharply.

THE HYPERINFLATION MYTH

This chapter opened by noting the German 'Angst vor der Inflation'. Mark Blyth (2013: 103) terms it the 'German Ideology', a 'collective historical neuralgia over the inflation of the 1920s, which inevitably leads German policy makers to the conclusion that "throwing money around" is never a good idea'. The perversity of the current ideological trap that the Germans are imposing on the rest of Europe is that it is informed by a particular period of history that is generally misunderstood. The Germans are obsessed with the hyperinflation of the Weimar years in the 1920s and have ingrained into their cultural fabric an ill-constructed version of what actually happened during those years. The modern Germans have also forgotten that in the 1930s, the gross and indecent acts of the Nazis aside, their economy prospered on the back of strong fiscal interventions. They also have forgotten the period after World War II when their economy was repaired via a massive fiscal injection, in part due to the Marshall Plan.

There is also a new pariah to fuel the hyperinflation paranoia: Zimbabwe is the new Weimar Republic. The financial press is awash with articles claiming that Zimbabwe is the modern day demonstration of the proposition that government deficits and OMF generate hyperinflation. When one understands what really happened in Zimbabwe the only reasonable conclusion is that it is an African country which has laboured under a dysfunctional government. There is nothing in the Zimbabwean experience that militates against the use of fiscal deficits accompanied by OMF.

But while any hint of OMF sends economists into apoplexy, it is a pity that their appreciation of history and causality doesn't match the intensity of their hysteria. The Weimar Republic of the 1920s and Zimbabwe in the modern era are distinct cases of hyperinflation. Let us briefly explore each instance in order to understand what really caused the hyperinflation.

The economic problems in the Weimar Republic began long before the hyperinflation in 1922. Inflation rose throughout Europe with the onset of World War I as import prices increased, as exchange rates depreciated, and as investors sought safer currencies, such as the US dollar. By war's end, Germany, like many of the warring nations, was dealing with elevated inflation rates (see Feldman, 1997).

The Treaty of Versailles, signed in June 1919, was particularly harsh to Germany, not only in terms of its reputation but also in terms of the reparations and loss of territory that were required as part of the peace settlement. While the loss of repute and position in Europe was probably justified given the aggression Germany showed to Belgium and France after Austria-Hungary declared war on Serbia to reclaim disputed territory in the Balkans, the scale of the reparations and the loss of territory are reasonably considered to have been an unwise response by the victors. The harshness of the reparations may have given France some consolation after it had been forced to pay massive compensation to Germany under the terms of the 1871 Treaty of Frankfurt, but it also directly contributed to Germany's martial behaviour, which led to World War II.

The reparations had to be made in gold Marks, which involved regular cash payments and equivalent in kind deliveries of 'coal, timber, chemical dyes and pharmaceutical drugs' (Marks, 1978: 233). There were other items involved, such as transfer of state-owned Saar coalmines and the return of some art treasures and materials, machinery and equipment to replace the booty stolen as the Germans retreated towards the end of the war (Marks, 1978). Between 1919 and 1922, the German mark depreciated significantly and this placed further strain on its export revenue and accelerated the inflation rate. The reparation payments schedule squeezed the German government's capacity to pay and eventually they were unable to meet the terms. They had been lagging behind on payments throughout 1921, and in 1922 were declared to be in default on agreed timber deliveries, an act that was interpreted by the Allies to be a show of 'German governmental bad faith' (Marks, 1978: 240). Then in early 1923, Germany defaulted on agreed coal deliveries and the Belgian and French armies responded by occupying the industrial area of the Ruhr, Germany's mining and manufacturing heartland. The military occupation was supported by Belgian, French and Italian engineers who were intent on extracting the coal (Bergmann, 1927). The Germans, in turn, engaged in a campaign of strikes and production ground to a halt. The German workers of the 1920s were more worried about unemployment than inflation (Smith, 1981). To encourage the local resistance among workers, the German government kept paying their wages in local currency despite limited production being possible. The inflation rate escalated as a result and export income fell sharply (Bergmann, 1927).

While the political struggles between the French and Germans, in particular, were considered to be 'an extension of World War I', the economics of the situation was simply that the supply capacity of the German economy fell sharply below the spending capacity and inflation was the obvious relief valve. Many commentators claim that the German central bank funded the continued spending (for example, the wage payments to the Ruhr workers) and this caused the hyperinflation. But if the supply capacity of the economy had not been curtailed, there would not have been the same issue with rising prices. The final crunch came when the export trade stalled and the only way the German government could keep paying its obligations was to keep spending. The high inflation morphed, not unexpectedly, into hyperinflation.

The causality is clear: excessive spending growth in the face of a declining output capacity will result in accelerating inflation. Clearly, the growth in spending had to be radically constrained for Germany to have avoided the hyperinflation and that was politically impossible, particularly as the national government was fragile and under attack from the Communists (Smith, 1981). It was a very abnormal situation and not related in any way to the case where a currency-issuing government spends to fill the gap left by the saving plans of the non-government sector in order to keep employment and output levels high. Mark Blyth (2013: 104–5) concludes that:

> Today, this specter of hyperinflation is invoked by German and ECB policy makers whenever they want to either curtail criticism of austerity measures or go on the offensive against stimulus proposals. Yet, it seems an odd argument to make when the classic case of hyperinflation haunting the policy memory of Europe's most powerful country was singularly not caused by a deliberate monetary stimulus attempting to arrest an economic slump.

The collapse of the supply potential of the economy is also relevant for understanding the Zimbabwean hyperinflation. Imagine an agrarian-based economy that is growing steadily with farm output at levels sufficient to supply the demands of both the export and domestic markets. Then a dictator comes along and starts taking land off the original farmers (who were productive) and gives it to those who do not understand how to farm or have no real interest in farming. The result would be that the overall capacity of the economy to produce goods and services would contract. The current spending levels in this economy would now be excessive in relation to the dramatically reduced supply potential and inflation would result on the back of rising food prices.

This is almost exactly what happened in modern day Zimbabwe. The white racist regime that ruled prior to 1980, and which had broken away from the colonial arrangements with Britain, created such an unfair sharing of land between the whites and blacks that a backlash was always going to occur once minority rule ended. From the inception of Colonial rule in the 1890s, the minority white population had conspired in various ways to keep 'the black farmers poor' (*The Guardian*, 2000). By 1970, the white population constituted around 5 per cent of the population (Jakobsen, 2012) but owned more than 70 per cent of 'the most fertile lands' (*The Guardian*, 2000). After the civil war of the 1970s, the newly independent nation under President Mugabe experienced improved growth with relatively stable inflation. The economy underwent a severe drought in 1992–93, which pushed the inflation rate up, but it soon fell back to usual levels (World Bank, 1995). There were no signs of the disaster that followed.

During the 1980s and 1990s, land reform was a central topic in Zimbabwe and the 'need for land reform in Zimbabwe . . . [was] . . . generally acknowledged, even by representatives of the commercial farming sector' (Human Rights Watch, 2002: 2). The problem was that while many foreign governments were eager to assist the restructuring of the Zimbabwean economy in the early years of independence and provided funds, 'conditions were put on the way that the money handed over could be used' (p. 3). In particular Britain, which had brokered the transition to majority rule, was 'protective of white farming interests in Zimbabwe' (p. 3) and the World Bank imposed an 'Economic Structural Adjustment Plan', which had 'damaging social consequences, in particular by increasing poverty' (p. 4). The debate became bogged down as to whether the support should be provided 'on the basis . . . of historical obligation rather than development assistance' (p. 4). None of these interactions were solving the basic problem whereby the 'Colonial policies of expropriation . . . [had] . . . established ownership patterns in which white farmers in Zimbabwe possess large, fertile farms while black rural dwellers barely subsist' (p. 4).

The problems came to a head in 2000 when President Mugabe introduced the 'fast track' land reforms to speed up the process of equality and break through the resistance from international donors (such as the World Bank and the IMF). The reaction to the stark inequality in land holdings and wealth in general was understandable but the way the government implemented the policy was not very sensible in terms of maintaining an economy that could continue to produce at reasonably high levels of output and employment. The revolutionary fighters that gained Zimbabwe's freedom were allowed to take over productive, white-owned commercial farms, sometimes violently, and in many cases the local farm workers were expelled (Human Rights Watch, 2002). No compensation was provided. These farms had hitherto fed the population and were the largest employers in the economy. From an economic perspective, the farm takeover and collapse of food production was catastrophic.

In December 2001, the United Nations Food and Agriculture Organization (FAO) reported:

> ... the already tight food supply situation has deteriorated as a result of reduced cereal production and general economic decline. Serious food difficulties are reported in the south, east and extreme north where production was reduced by dry weather or excessive rains. A recent vulnerability assessment indicated that 705000 people in rural areas are at risk of food shortages. In addition, 250000 people in urban areas are experiencing food difficulties due to a sharp increase in food prices, while some 30000 farm workers have lost their jobs and are left without means of subsistence. (FAO, 2001)

A major drought in the 2000–01 growing season combined with the farm takeovers to produce a decline in total agricultural output by 12.9 per cent in 2001 (AfDB/OECD, 2003). Real GDP fell by 9.3 per cent in 2002, 16.8 per cent in 2003, 6.1 per cent in 2004 and 5.6 per cent in 2005 (IMF, 2014). By 2005, unemployment had risen to 80 per cent and many of those who had managed to remain employed were forced to scratch around for a part time, low wage existence.

The land reforms represented the first big contraction in potential output (supply) and around 45 per cent of the food output capacity was destroyed. A rapid contraction in total spending (demand) was required but impossible to implement politically. The situation then compounded as other infrastructure was trashed, which further constrained the supply chain. For example, the National Railways of Zimbabwe (NRZ) had decayed to the point that its capacity to transport mining output to export markets fell substantially (Mbohwa, 2008).

Manufacturing output declined by 29 per cent in 2005, 18 per cent in 2006 and 28 per cent in 2007. In 2007, only around 19 per cent of Zimbabwe's industrial capacity was being used. This reflected a range of factors including raw material shortages. But, overall, the manufacturers blamed the central bank for stalling their access to foreign exchange, which was needed to buy imported raw materials (Confederation of Zimbabwe Industries, 2009). The Reserve Bank of Zimbabwe was using foreign reserves to fund the purchase of imported food to ease the food crisis. The causality was clear. The land reforms undermined the domestic food supply, which introduced a reliance on imported food. This, in turn, squeezed importers of raw materials who could not get access to foreign exchange. So not only had the agricultural capacity been destroyed, but also the manufacturing capacity was being barely utilised. Further, significant volumes of imported goods and services were also prevented from flowing in because many importers abandoned goods at the border when they were hit by exorbitant import duties.

Given these circumstances, the hyperinflation was inevitable. But the Zimbabwean experience is not remotely like a situation where a currency-issuing government uses OMF associated with permanent fiscal deficits to close a private spending gap so as to maintain full employment. In other words, there can be no threat of hyperinflation if the total growth of spending in the economy matches the capacity of the economy to produce real output.

Conversely, when a nation so comprehensively mismanages the supply side of its economy, as in the case of Zimbabwe, the only way it can avoid inflation is to severely contract total spending to match the new lower capacity. Had the government of Zimbabwe adopted that strategy, more people would have died from starvation than already was the case. In the situation that Zimbabwe found itself in, even a surge in private sector investment would have triggered a severe worsening of the inflation situation until the growth in supply capacity caught up with the spending growth.

22. Abandoning the euro

Reuters news agency reported the Italian Welfare Minister, Roberto Maroni, saying that Italy 'should consider leaving the single currency and reintroducing the lira'. The Minister said the euro was a 'disaster' and 'has proved inadequate in the face of the economic slowdown, the loss of competitiveness and the job crisis'. His remedy was to 'to give control over the exchange rate back to the government' and empower the Italian government to 'defend national industry from foreign competition' (Reuters, 2005). The news report was from June 2005. His reasoning remains sound today. However, whenever someone proposes 'Grexit' or 'Spexit' or 'Exit' generally, hysteria erupts. Predictions of devastation, catastrophe, hyperinflation, financial market lock out, the end of Europe, and more are heard at the mere mention of the prospect that a nation or nations would be better off abandoning the euro and restoring their own currencies. What the political leaders hate the most is when the word 'Argentina' also enters the exit debate, followed a little later by Italy. The Troika can bully Greece because it is small, insecure in its own identity, and receives more from the European Union budget than it contributes. Italy is a different beast altogether not only because of its size and sense of place in Europe and the world, but also because it is a net contributor, by a large margin, to the European Union budget.

Argentina has become a bogey nation for neo-liberals and there are now concerted attempts to disabuse any notion that Argentina provided a credible, alternative path to crisis resolution when it defaulted on its international debt obligations in 2002 and floated its currency. For example, Goodhart and Tsomocos (2010) claim:

> . . . neither Greece nor any other country in a similar position could sensibly leave the eurozone (indeed any sniff of thinking about that would cause an immediate banking crisis). Apart from the immediate effects on wages, prices and interest rates, existing debts are denominated in euros and any attempt to renege on that would, very likely, result in seizure of Greek assets abroad and expulsion from the eurozone, in addition to a cessation of European Union net transfers. In this respect Greece is far more constrained than Argentina was.

This assessment is typical of the mainstream catastrophe viewpoint that ignores the opportunities that would be provided to the Eurozone states if they restored their own currency and took some heed of what Argentina was able to achieve when it ignored the warnings and threats of the IMF and the international bankers and restored its own sovereignty.

There is nothing irrevocable about the euro or the Eurozone. While there are no formal exit mechanisms established in the relevant Treaties, short of military occupation, Greece and Italy and any other nation can do what it likes. Argentina showed in the early 2000s that it could take on the big financial market lenders and the multilateral bullies (such as the IMF) and restore its sovereignty for the benefit of its people. Argentina's derring-do approach humiliated the global power elites and invoked all manner of threats and scaremongering, none of which really gained any traction. Far from cowering to the demands of the IMF and the financial markets, Argentina took several bold steps to resolve its crisis through domestic expansion and employment creation. It largely worked. Why do you suppose that there is an expanding literature being pumped out by conservatives extolling the so-called 'failure' of Argentina? The reason is that the big neo-liberal players who desire to ensnare nations in onerous financial obligations and penury do not want it to become too obvious that a nation can restore its own currency and deal with its external and foreign currency denominated debts to its own advantage and prosper while doing so. There are clear differences between Greece, for example and Argentina, not least the latter's capacity to export a broader range of commodities and agricultural produce, in particular, to lucrative markets. But the general point remains valid: a nation that restores its own currency increases its options and alters the balance of power between itself and the financial markets. A nation can force foreign lenders to come bidding for a deal rather becoming captive to a Troika of predators working in the interests of the investment bankers and other corporate interests without regard for the nation's population.

In this chapter, we examine what an exit from the Eurozone might involve. Would it be a disaster? How might it happen? What are the costs and benefits? One retort is that things couldn't get much worse for some of the Eurozone nations and so the assessment should be in terms of how quickly a recovery can be engineered. In considering an abandonment of the euro and a restoration of currency sovereignty, there would be a difference between what we might term an orderly, planned dismantling of the currency union while reinforcing the political union through the European Parliament, on the one hand; and a disorderly exit by one or a few nations (for example, Greece or Italy), on the other hand. The obvious solution for one nation is not necessarily the best solution for all. The conjecture entertained in this chapter is that an orderly exit would be in the best interests of all nations even though there would be significant costs involved in making the adjustment back to full currency sovereignty. But, given the political situation in Europe, it is more likely that a single nation would have to make a disorderly exit to get free of the euro. Further, it is argued that the exit by a single nation would have relatively minor consequences for the remaining nations but enhance the prospects for recovery of the exiting country, notwithstanding rather massive adjustment costs. However, the larger the current malaise, the lower would be the relative costs of exit.

European politics and policy making are caught in two very powerful and destructive vices at present. The first is the age-old Franco-German rivalry. A corollary to this rivalry is a disdain for the 'Latinos' who by geographic proximity cannot be ignored, much to the angst of those further north. The second is the domination of free market economics, the Groupthink, which, though empirically deficient and riddled with internal theoretical inconsistencies, still rules the academy and, through its graduates, the policy-making sphere. How the economics profession has been able to convince the rest of us that by 'counting angels on a pinhead' and then not being able to correctly sum the angels they claim to see (their so-called 'economic models') they have anything to say about enhancing societal wellbeing is a study in itself and constitutes one of the biggest frauds of the 20th century and beyond. All the evidence from psychology and behavioural studies tells us that the mainstream economic assumptions about human motivation and decision making are devoid of reality.

The rise of Monetarism, which originated out of the academy in the US, created a 'post-national' tension among the politicians which cut across the old state-based rivalry between the nations in Europe. Whereas the early discussions about union placed the national state at the forefront, by the time Delors and his Committee met the global capture by the financial elites of the policy process was well entrenched and the promotion of Monetarist economic ideology aided their agenda. Recall that Delors excluded the national finance ministers from his panel to ensure that the Monetarist perspective would emerge quickly and not become derailed by national political hankering. It was imperative that the supranational entities, which were created as part of the union, were consistent with this post-national ideology. That is why the fiscal role of the state was so restricted and the primacy of the depoliticised ECB elevated. The old national rivalries have persisted but their expression has become increasingly channelled by the free market narrative, which created the monster that is the EMU.

Neither of these vices will release their destructive grip on European affairs easily. The cultural and historical aspects of the Franco-German rivalry are permanent constraints on European progress. When the Gauls and the Prussians began hating each other is a matter of history, but it was a long time ago. Historians create all sorts of revisionist narratives to suit their own angle, but it is clear that the two 'nations' were at odds after Napoleon incorporated German-speaking areas such as the Rhineland during the First Republic. His disdainful treatment of the German aristocracy, including the various German-speaking monarchs, spawned German nationalism and led to the Franco-Prussian War in 1870. German unification was motivated, in part, by a desire for a German-speaking power to rival the domination of France (Wetzel, 2001).

It is true that this 'enmity' evolved in the post World War II period. The diplomacy is less chauvinistic and the prospect of another major European war is minimal. Some have even considered the relationship between the two great European nations to be one of 'amitié franco-allemande'. But despite the handshakes at official meetings and smiles for the cameras, there is always a simmering clash of culture and the memory of World War II is still strong. While the rivalry was intense and open under President de Gaulle, which held back European integration, later the rivalry was expressed from the French side as a desire to neutralise German power, and the only way to do that was to create a European state where France dominated. From the German side, whether anyone wants to talk about it or not, a deep and silent shame gripped the nation as a result of its actions during the 1930s and 1940s. The only source of national pride became Germany's economic acumen, its technical and organisational skills and the discipline of its workers. The stereotype of the 'clever German' arose to replace that of the 'ugly German'. European integration became a way the German nation could win back some respect by demonstrating that it could be part of a peaceful Europe. Reunification accelerated that desire but accentuated the paranoia in the rest of Europe about the 'German question'. This rivalry and divergent ambitions and motivations dominated the path to monetary union over many decades. When finally Mitterand and Schmidt seemed to be working together, the motivations and cultural baggage remained as disparate as they had been when Monnet and Schuman first proposed the 'European Project'.

These differences suggest that both of the large European nations would be better off pursuing their own economic destinies. But they can only do that if they also free themselves from the vice-like grip of neo-liberal economics. The dominance of free market thinking has so perverted the European Project that the failure of the economic plan is now endangering the beneficial political and legal aspects that have accompanied the formation of the European Union. The true value of the European Project is in its capacity to deliver a rule of law throughout Europe and engender multilateral co-operation on matters such as immigration, climate change, human trafficking and global concerns that single nations cannot solve alone. Abandoning the euro would not undermine that sort of cooperation.

THE PATH TO A DISORDERLY EXIT

Several models have been put forward to describe how a nation such as Italy or Greece might unilaterally exit the monetary union. There was even the 'Wolfson Economics Prize 2012', which offered £250,000 'to the person who is able to articulate how best to manage the orderly exit of one or more member states from the European Monetary Union' (Policy Exchange, 2012). Any exit scheme has to address the same issues: how to handle the euro-denominated public and private debt that is outstanding; how to handle bank deposits denominated in euros within the exiting nation; how to ensure financial stability is maintained; how to introduce the new currency (for example, unilaterally or as an interim dual currency); how to manage the inevitable large currency depreciation and to minimise the resulting inflation risk and protect real living standards; how to reduce speculative capital flows (for example, using capital controls); how to deal with any changes to the legal framework governing cross-border trade if the nation also is expelled from the EU, among other issues.

The estimated likely overall consequences that have been put forward also, crucially, depend on the economic framework that underpins them. Neo-liberal macroeconomics, which downgrades the importance of fiscal policy and currency sovereignty, not surprisingly provides the basis for the catastrophe predictions. These economists project massive and ongoing currency depreciation leading to an uncontrollable surge in inflation, which debases the currency. They predict the nation's banking system would collapse in the face of large capital outflows, debt delinquency and the state's incapacity to defend the capital base of its banking system. They predict that there would be massive outflows of skilled labour, which would undermine the future productivity of the nation. They predict that the nations would have to default on their debt obligations, which would not only force the nation into a costly, drawn out legal morass, but would also see it being shunned by international capital markets. As a consequence, they claim that the government would not be able to fund itself and would run out of money. Further, they predict that credit would also become unavailable to the private sector, and businesses and the housing market would collapse. The catastrophe scenario sees the nation mired in depression, poverty and isolation. Civil anarchy would erupt and give way to totalitarian regimes with vicious secret police departments enforcing order through torture and death squads. This future would surely be many times worse than a future within the Eurozone. All of these predictions have been rehearsed in the literature. Almost every day someone will write something along those lines.

Conversely, adopting the MMT framework as the basis for analysis would lead to dramatically different projections. It should be made clear that no one really knows for sure what would happen. It would be hard to project the costs of the exit. But we can deduce several things based on historical experience. It is highly likely that the benefits of exit would outweigh the costs, if the exit decision is, simultaneously, accompanied by a decision to reject the flawed neo-liberal, austerity approach in favour of a fiscally active policy stance that seeks to maximise wellbeing of the citizenry. If the exiting nation continues its idolatry of financial markets and considers it can 'do' austerity in a more gradual manner, then the exit will likely be even more costly than provided for by the current outlook. Abandoning the culture of austerity and restoring currency sovereignty would provide the exiting government with numerous opportunities to bring idle resources, including the unemployed, back into productive use. Real economic growth would be immediate. The bond markets would become supplicant when faced with a currency-issuing nation because the central bank could control interest rates and force investors out of the market whenever it chose. Whether investors chose to buy any new public bonds issued in the new currency would become irrelevant. The newly empowered state would still be able to spend and purchase anything that was available for sale in its own currency. The new state would be able to protect the capital of its banking system and guarantee deposits in the local currency.

LESSONS FROM THE ARGENTINEAN DEFAULT

In April 1991, Argentina adopted a rigid peg of the peso to the US dollar and guaranteed convertibility under this arrangement. This meant that the central bank stood by to convert pesos into dollars on demand at the pegged parity. This decision was totally unsuited to the reality of Argentina's trade and production structure relative to the US. In the same way that the EMU countries do not constitute an optimal currency area, Argentina never looked like it could be a member of an optimal US dollar area. Argentina regularly faced quite different external pressures compared to those that the US economy had to deal with. The US predominantly traded with countries whose own currencies fluctuated in line with the US dollar. Given the relatively closed nature and large size of its non-traded goods sector, the US economy could thus benefit from nominal exchange rate swings and use them to balance the relative price of its traded and non-traded goods. Conversely, Argentina was a very open economy with a small non-tradables domestic sector, which meant its domestic economy had to take the brunt of swings in the terms of trade (export prices relative to import prices), which made the management of domestic policy very difficult.

The IMF supported convertibility as a way of disciplining domestic policy, which imposed a permanent sort of austerity. The Argentine central bank could only issue pesos if they were backed by holdings of US dollars (with a tiny, meaningless tolerance range allowed). So US dollars had to be earned through net exports, which would then allow the domestic policy to expand. While Argentina had suffered from high inflation in the 1970s and 1980s, the correct solution was not to impose a US dollar peg because the arrangement unnecessarily constrained both monetary and fiscal policy. After the peg was introduced, the neo-liberals made matters worse with wide-scale privatisation programs, harsh cuts to social security and deregulation of the financial sector, the latter burdening the economy with massive amounts of foreign currency denominated debt.

Things came unstuck in the late 1990s as export markets started to decline and the peso became seriously over valued (as the US dollar strengthened) with subsequent loss of Argentinean export competitiveness. Argentina was lumbered with massive foreign currency debts, so the decline in competitiveness was lethal and, as the new millennium approached, the domestic economy was mired in recession with the unemployment rate around 16 per cent. The international bond traders then introduced a 'Greek scenario' when they realised the nation would face insolvency as exports collapsed and its capacity to generate US dollars declined. As a result, investors required ever increasing interest returns (yields) on any funds they loaned the government. In 2000, under direct orders from the IMF (with the threat of refusal to maintain financial assistance), the Argentinean government tried to appease the bond markets by implementing a harsh program of fiscal austerity (mainly through tax increases), which damaged an already decimated domestic economy. The government believed the rhetoric from the IMF and others that this would reinvigorate capital inflow and ease the external imbalance. But at the time it was obvious that convertibility would soon collapse because the Banco Central de la Republica Argentina (BCRA) couldn't hold the flood waters back indefinitely.

In December 2000, an IMF bailout package was negotiated with foreign reserves being exchanged for further austerity imposed, but there was no observed increase in net capital inflow. Why would anyone want to invest in a place mired in recession and unlikely to be able to pay back loans in US dollars anyway? The resonance with the Greek tragedy and that of other crisis-ridden EMU nations in the current period is powerful. Any observer who understood the way monetary systems operate would have predicted that insolvency was approaching. But that possibility was ignored by the IMF forecasts. Just as in the current crisis the IMF's modelling has proven to be destructively error prone, so it was in the case of Argentina. The IMF then pushed the Argentinean government into announcing that it would maintain the peg against the US dollar, but also extend it to the euro once the two achieved parity. This meant that it was guaranteeing convertibility in both major world currencies, an impossibility given its export volatility. Pure neo-liberal dogma was thus exacerbating the crisis that it had created in the first place.

Economic growth continued to decline and the foreign debts piled up. In April 2001, the Argentinean government forced local banks to buy government bonds (it changed prudential regulation rules to allow them to use the bonds to satisfy liquidity rules), which further exposed the local banks to the foreign debt problem. The bank run started in late 2001, with the oil bank deposits being the first to be put under pressure. This led to the freeze on cash withdrawals in December 2001 and the collapse of the payments system. The riots in December 2001 brought home to the government the folly of its strategy. In early 2002, it defaulted on all government debt and abandoned the peg and associated institutional arrangements (known as the 'currency board'). All US-dollar denominated financial contracts were compulsorily redenominated into pesos and terms renegotiated such that short-term obligations were converted into longer-term commitments to give the government more breathing space. Initially, foreign direct investment (FDI) dried up completely when the default was announced.

The default has been largely successful. It was clear that the Argentinean government could not service the debt as its foreign currency reserves were gone, and it additionally realised, to its credit, that borrowing from the IMF would have required an austerity package that would have precipitated a revolution. As it was, riots broke out as citizens struggled to feed their children. Despite stringent criticism from the world's financial power brokers (including the IMF), the Argentine government refused to back down and in 2005 completed a deal whereby around 75 per cent of the defaulted bonds were swapped for others of much lower value with longer maturities.

The crisis was engendered by faulty (neo-liberal) policies in the 1990s and exemplified by the peg and convertibility. Once Argentina abandoned the fixed exchange rate and convertibility arrangements, its exchange rate was no longer tied to the US dollar's performance; its fiscal policy was no longer held hostage to the quantity of US dollars the government could accumulate; and its domestic interest rate came under control of its central bank. As part of the resolution of the 2001 crisis, the government realised it had to adopt a domestically oriented growth strategy. One of the first policy initiatives taken by newly elected President Kirchner was a massive job creation program that guaranteed employment for poor heads of households. Within four months, the Plan Jefes y Jefas de Hogar (Head of Households Plan) had created jobs for 2 million participants, which was around 13 per cent of the labour force. This not only helped to quell social unrest by providing income to Argentina's poorest families, but it also put the economy on the road to recovery. Conservative estimates of the multiplier effect of the increased spending by Jefes workers are that it added a boost of more than 2.5 per cent of GDP. In addition, the program provided needed services and new public infrastructure that encouraged additional private sector spending. Without the flexibility provided by a sovereign, floating currency, the government would not have been able to promise such a job guarantee.

Argentina demonstrated something that the world's financial masters didn't want anyone to know about. The lesson was that a country with huge foreign debt obligations can successfully default and enjoy renewed fortune almost immediately based on domestic employment growth strategies and more inclusive welfare policies without an IMF austerity program being needed. The clear lesson is that sovereign governments are not necessarily the hostage of global financial markets. A strong recovery path can be defined, which directly benefits the population and insulates the most disadvantaged workers from the devastation that recession brings.

Figure 22.1 shows the so-called real effective exchange rate (REER) for Argentina from January 1994 to April 2014. Recall from earlier chapters that the REER is a measure of international competitiveness and takes into account both movements in the nominal exchange rate on world markets and relative inflation rates. A falling REER indicates an increase in competitiveness relative to the nation's trading partners. The REER for Argentina peaked in October 2001 at an index value of 100, just before the crisis really began, and by January 2002 it had fallen to 62, a massive real devaluation. The low point came in June 2002 (index number was 34.8), after which it rose and stabilised around 45. Almost all of the gain in competitiveness was due to the depreciation of the peso once it floated.

The nominal depreciation created a major change in the fortunes of the traded goods sector of the economy. Argentinean exports became much cheaper in world markets and demand for them grew rapidly at the same time as spending on imports fell because of the rise in prices in the newly restored local currency. The growth in China also helped Argentina via

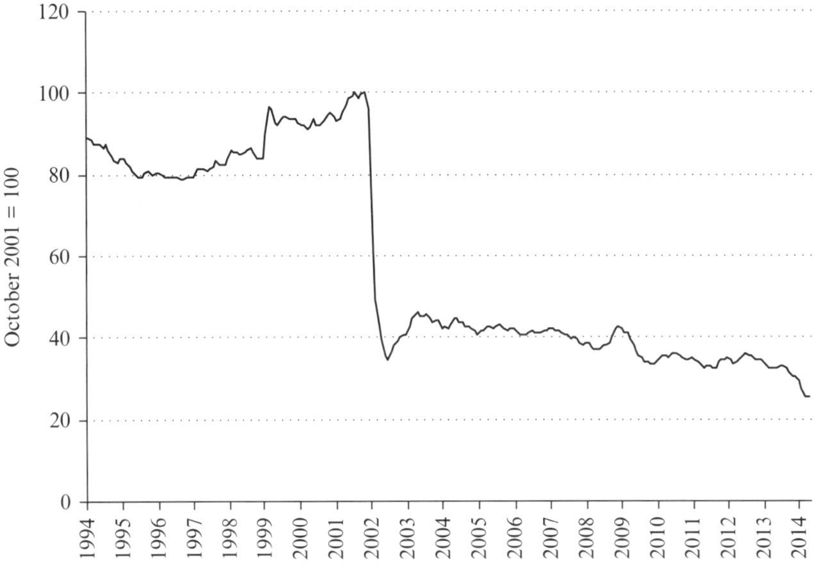

Source: Bank of International Settlements.

Figure 22.1 Real effective exchange rate, Argentina, January 1994 to April 2014, October 2001 = 100

soya bean exports, which helped stabilise the currency. In general, agriculture boomed. The tourism industry also grew rapidly as a result of the currency depreciation. The government sought to take advantage of the massive shift in the terms of trade by providing incentives for import substitution to stimulate local employment and relieve the cost pressure on local citizens.

Before long, the peso started appreciating again. But by then, the domestic economy was on a solid growth footing with strong social welfare spending to maintain domestic demand supported by a booming export sector. In the mid 2000s the government actually had to take measures to stop the peso appreciating further given the size of its trade surplus. The central bank acquired huge stockpiles of foreign reserves (US dollars mainly) by selling pesos in the foreign exchange market. The exchange rate stabilised at the higher value (BCRA, 2007). There has been some easing in recent years but nothing of the magnitudes encountered in the crisis.

The claims by the scaremongers that nobody would want the Argentinean peso once it depreciated were proven to be false. It is clear that people still wanted to buy the Argentinean currency on foreign exchange markets even with the massive default (BCRA, 2007). By 2007, international buyers of the depreciating currency were many. Further, after nearly running out of US dollar reserves in 2002, the BCRA had quadrupled its holdings by early 2007 (p. 7). Between 2003 and 2007, the foreign exchange market transactions between Argentina and the rest of the world (measured in US dollars) rose from $22.3 billion to around $64.5 billion. The total traded volume was very healthy and mostly involved transactions between local private banks and foreign banks (pp. 4–5).

The evidence failed to support any of the predictions from those who vehemently opposed the restoration of Argentina's currency sovereignty, the default and the float. There are many lessons from Argentina's experience that are applicable to Greece and other EMU nations contemplating exiting the Eurozone and restoring their own currencies.

THE EXIT PROCESS

There are several factors that a nation must consider when deciding whether to exit a monetary union. There are historical precedents, which help us to understand likely pitfalls and desired strategies. The following points summarise the process that a nation might undertake to exit the Eurozone:

- Secrecy – all decision making and planning would have to be done in secrecy to minimise the costs of the resulting exit. All announcements would be made on a weekend or another day when the banks are closed.
- Reintroduction of national currency to be used within national borders – all levels of government would require tax obligations to be met in this currency. Major improvements in tax law enforcement would be required to reduce the increased participation in 'black market' activities.
- Float the currency on international foreign exchange markets – this would follow redenomination of all monetary amounts at a stated parity (perhaps one to one or the parity that ruled on 31 December 2001).
- Restore central bank sovereignty – negotiate the transfer of monetary policy and prudential functions of the ECB to the national central bank, with the nation's contribution to the ECB capital reserves, bank notes and foreign currency reserve equivalents (and share of accrued profits) returned.

- Capital controls – imposition of capital and foreign exchange controls for some indeterminate period.
- Redenomination – all bank account balances and all debts incurred under national law would be redenominated into the national currency. Banks would be closed for a day or so following the announcement. Current public sector debt is typically issued under national law and so-called 'place of payment' rules support a nation's capacity to offer legal payments in the national currency.
- Maintain dual currency – euro payments for transactions permitted for a limited period as in the dual system between 1999 and 2002 but euros would exchange at the parity determined on foreign exchange markets. New currency notes and coins would progressively eliminate the need to transact in euros.
- Focus on reducing domestic strife – provide an immediate fiscal stimulus to restore growth and reduce the danger of social unrest. The government would announce the introduction of a national Job Guarantee, which would offer anyone wanting a job a position at a socially acceptable minimum wage, thus buttressing domestic demand (see Chapter 23 for discussion of employment guarantees).

WHY THE NEED FOR SECRECY?

At first blush, the notion that all decision making and planning associated would require secrecy to minimise the costs of the resulting exit is at odds with the idea of participatory democracy. On the surface, this unilateralism would appear to be similar in effect to the way the Troika has imposed harsh austerity measures on nations and influenced the appointment of senior government officials.

The problem is that policy surprises are necessary at times if the cost of total transparency is high. It is clear that the transition costs that individuals and business firms would incur as a result of an exit could be significant. The prospect of the likely losses from a depreciated currency would instigate efforts by households and firms to hoard euros and/or transfer euro deposits to banks and other institutions elsewhere in Europe or swap for other more stable currencies. Secrecy is required to minimise the losses rather than to compromise democracy. There is a temporal perspective that should not be forgotten. The restoration of the national currency makes the elected government fully responsible for national economic and social policy and, with regular electoral cycles, the citizens are in a much better position to hold the government accountable for its actions.

ISSUING THE NEW CURRENCY

By exercising the sovereignty embodied in its own constitution, the exiting European nation would reintroduce its own currency and immediately require all tax and other public contractual obligations within the nation to be denominated in that currency. The strategic operations that would accompany this reissuance do not really concern us. Clearly, a covert operation involving a weekend, the announcement of a bank holiday and the imposition of capital controls for a period would be involved. The announcement would then come into effect on the first business day of the new week.

The new currency would be empowered because the citizens and corporate entities would have to use it to extinguish their ongoing tax obligations. The private sector would have to acquire that currency, notwithstanding any decisions or preferences it might have for another currency in which it might store wealth. Even if there is a second 'trading' currency in use, the local currency will always be in demand as long as the national government can enforce its tax laws. One of the major shortcomings of the several 'dual currency proposals' recently put forward as a way to resolve the Eurozone crisis is that they still insist that state taxes and charges be paid for in euros, thus giving rise to continued demand for that currency at the expense of the local currency (for example, Goodhart and Tsomocos, 2010).

The actual practicalities of creating the new currency (minting coins and printing bank notes) would involve minimal changes because under the current system, the national central banks are already responsible for this function. All the euro Member States already produce large quantities of euro currency. With sufficient forward planning, the new currency tokens could be issued on the first day of the new system. Scott (2012: 19) suggests that because the existing euro notes and coins have 'the unique national identifying marks' or other identifiable symbolism, the urgency to introduce new distinctive tokens would be reduced. However, the logistics of introducing the new tokens are relatively trivial and that would be the preferable way forward to avoid confusion and the need to physically stamp the existing currency 'with an identifying mark' (p. 19).

The more significant issue is to decide at what parity the new currency will be introduced, relative to the euro and other currencies. The net benefits of exiting the Eurozone would be increased if the losses embodied in the process of redenomination and subsequent (expected) depreciation were also minimised. The preferred option is to fully float, but some analysts have argued in favour of pegging the new currency to the euro, which would involve participating in a new version of the Exchange Rate

Mechanism (ERM II). Proponents of this option argue that the decision to peg would reduce the capital outflow and provide a way of 'coordinating its economic policy with other E.U. Member States' (p. 35). Accordingly, the national central bank would be expected to intervene in the foreign exchange market if the new currency was in danger of breaching the agreed upper or lower bands within which the currency was allowed to fluctuate. We have traversed the problems of this type of arrangement in the earlier chapters. Effectively, the central bank would lose discretion over monetary policy and the interest rate would be dictated by the ECB policy rate. Further, history tells us that the currency would become hostage to financial market speculators and this volatility would be beyond the capacity of the central bank to control given it would soon run out of foreign reserves. Sure enough, in theory, the ECB could provide an 'unlimited swap line' (p. 38) to allow the national central bank to maintain the fixed exchange rate, but that would be resisted by the Bundesbank among others because it would mean an expansion of euro currency stocks and increase the fear of inflation. This likelihood was exactly the reason the Bundesbank refused to operate in a symmetric manner during the Snake and the first iteration of the ERM in the 1980s to help weaker currencies avoid devaluation.

While the depreciation that followed the launch of the new currency would initially be significant, the scaremongering that suggests it would be bottomless, leading to hyperinflation, is unfounded. We can be guided, in part, by what happened to the Argentinean peso in the years after the Argentinean government floated it during the 2001–02 crisis. Greece, for example, would suffer the same short-term collapse in the value of its new currency once it was traded on foreign exchange markets. It is true that the nations such as Greece do not have the large quantities of natural resources that Argentina enjoyed, but it is equally untrue to say they have no desirable assets that are exchange rate sensitive. Of importance is that Argentina created new export capacity given the competitive boost it received from the depreciation. For example, Greece would likely experience a tourism boom, notwithstanding the fact that the crisis has run down its capacity somewhat. The positive change in the direction of the current account would also put a floor into the downward spiral of the new currency as it did in Argentina's case. Further, in the same way that Argentina had to bear a major inflation impulse as its currency depreciated, which eroded real living standards, the reversal in standards was just as swift as the currency started to appreciate on the back of renewed growth. Greece would experience the same dynamic as Germans flooded into the sunny Greek islands to escape the Berlin winter and enjoy the dramatically cheaper vacations.

THE INFLATION THREAT

It is often argued that the 'key danger for countries departing the euro is hyperinflation due to poor fiscal and monetary policies' (Tepper, 2012: 136). Most of the commentary surrounding the risk of hyperinflation following an exit concentrates on scenarios where the government is unable to access private debt markets as a result of a depreciating currency (and other stability concerns), and instead enters the 'taboo' world of OMF. We dealt with the myths surrounding this taboo in Chapter 21. Tepper (2012: 136), like many commentators, dodges around after introducing the taboo by claiming that the risk was that OMF could 'potentially' generate hyperinflation. We emphasise 'potentially', which is in the same class of scaremongering as 'might' and 'may'. We have already learned that any increase in spending, whether it is private or public, carries a risk of inflation if it pushes the economy beyond its capacity to respond by increasing the production and sales of goods and services. For nations mired in recession with large quantities of idle resources, it is highly unlikely that increased deficits will invoke a major inflationary spiral. That situation certainly describes the state of many European nations in the aftermath of the GFC and the imposed austerity.

The main source of inflation would be the rising prices of imported goods and services in terms of the local currency as a result of the depreciation. History tells us that such depreciations are short and sharp. Argentina is an example. However, more recent 'European' experience is also available to guide our thinking. When Iceland's financial system collapsed in 2008, the government refused to bail out the private banks and instead restructured domestic bank deposits within newly nationalised banks, pushing all foreign exposure into the bankruptcy process. The Icelandic disaster was another demonstration of the perils of neo-liberalism. Its banking crisis had its roots in deregulation and privatisation of the banks which saw them expand 'their balance sheets many times over between 2004 and 2008' (Central Bank of Iceland, 2010: 7). They were aided by flawed credit rating reviews and consulting reports provided by hired academics, who waxed lyrical about the solid state of the economy. One of those academics was Columbia University's Frederick Mishkin, who featured in the 2010 movie *Inside Job* and was paid a considerable sum by the Iceland Chamber of Commerce in 2006 to produce the report 'Financial stability in Iceland'. At the same time that Mishkin and his co-author were giving the financial system in Iceland a clean bill of health, the Icelandic banks were engaged in elaborate and not so elaborate growth schemes based on refinancing debt with extra borrowing using 'fake capital' (and 'illegal market manipulation') to evade scrutiny which allowed them to 'enter the big-bank league' (Wade and Sigurgeirsdottir, 2010). *Inside Job* highlighted that the payment to Mishkin was not initially disclosed and thus his report appeared to be independent academic research, which gave it considerably more gravitas. After the crisis broke, Mishkin was caught changing his CV by renaming the paper 'Financial instability in Iceland'. When *Inside Job* challenged him about this during an interview, he stumbled, in a dissembling fashion, and eventually managed to get it out that it must have been a 'typo'.

Just before the collapse, total bank assets in Iceland were 'around 11 times GDP' (Central Bank of Iceland 2010: 8) and a large majority of the banks' operations were in foreign currencies, which meant the central bank was unable to provide any security as a lender of last resort. International markets started to get the jitters in early 2008 and capital inflow dried up, which led to a weakening of the króna, and inflation began to accelerate due to the rising price of imports including petrol (Central Bank of Iceland, 2008). In early October 2008, 'nearly nine-tenths of Iceland's banking system collapsed in a single week' (Central Bank of Iceland, 2010: 8) and the government stepped in with emergency legislation to save the economy from total collapse. The Central Bank of Iceland notes that as 'a share of GDP the Icelandic banking system is the largest banking system ever to have collapsed' (p. 9). The bank collapse exacerbated the currency crisis and the króna depreciated by 50 per cent over 2008 in terms of the euro. This was particularly difficult for Icelandic households who were heavily indebted in foreign currencies and there were 'enormous losses of private sector wealth, and a steep drop in disposable income' (p. 10). This was compounded 'because of widespread inflation-indexed debt' (p. 10).

But the decline was finite. In the first half of 2010, the króna had appreciated by nearly 10 per cent and by October 2010 the inflation rate, which had peaked at 21.9 per cent in January 2009, was back down to the central bank's '4% threshold band' (p. 12) (Figure 22.2). While the IMF became involved under a Standby Arrangement and the government was prevented from introducing a full scale discretionary fiscal stimulus, the 'automatic stabilisers were allowed to work fully in 2009' (p. 10), which cushioned the loss of total spending. Moreover, the government, realising it was partially constrained by the IMF program, freed up rules relating to private pension savings and, relative to GDP, 'the size of the pension withdrawal scheme is broadly similar to fiscal stimulus packages that many other countries adopted in response to the crisis' (p. 10). In other words, blanket austerity was not imposed on the economy and the spending growth led to an early recovery.

In order to minimise the costs and maximise the benefits of the shift to the floating exchange rates, it is crucial that the exiting government can

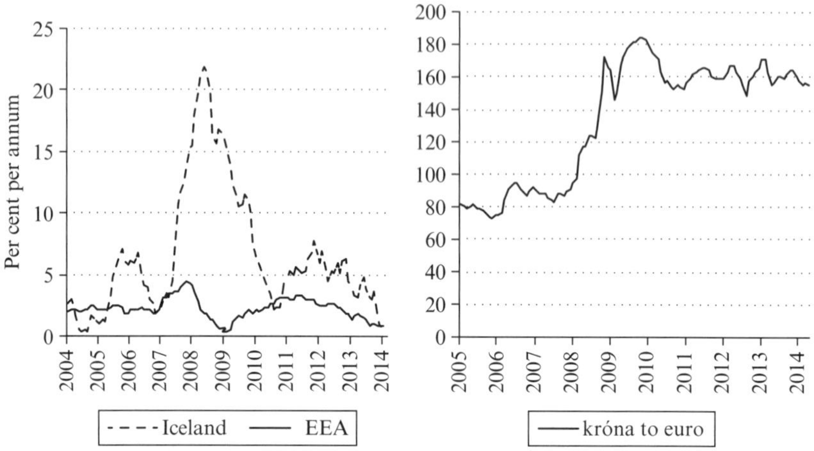

(a) Inflation rate (b) Nominal exchange rate

Note: Exchange rate is the monthly average. The European Economic Area (EEA) comprises three member states of the European Free Trade Association (EFTA) (Iceland, Liechtenstein and Norway).

Source: Statistics Iceland, Central Bank of Iceland.

Figure 22.2 Iceland inflation rate and exchange rate, January 2005–May 2014

ensure that the nominal exchange rate depreciation leads to a real depreciation (that is, the real exchange rate has to fall). The real income loss arising from the rising import prices is one of the costs of exit and the government should ensure that the burden is equitably shared. But if domestic wages and profits are fully compensated for the rise in import prices, then the nation will not enjoy any competitive gain from the depreciation. It is clear that real standards of living have to fall in terms of traded goods for the nominal depreciation to 'stick'. It is politically easier to engineer a real depreciation via a nominal exchange rate decline than it is to undertake so-called 'internal depreciation', which involves cutting the money wages that workers receive.

Keynes long ago understood the reasons workers resist nominal wage cuts. First, wages are not only a component of income but also indicate our social standing. People think in relative terms and we value our place in the wage structure. If inflation outstrips the growth in money wages then our purchasing power (real wages) falls, but our relative position in the wage structure will not be threatened because the real wage cut is across the board. However, if one group of workers takes a money wage cut then that alters their relative position and it is unlikely that they will regain that status when the economy recovers. Thus, there is little incentive to accept nominal wage cuts even if the resulting real wage cut is identical to that achieved through inflation or exchange rate depreciation. Second, our most important contractual obligations are specified in nominal rather than real terms. When we take out a mortgage at the bank we rarely have indexed contracts. Most of us are obligated to pay a certain number of dollars per month to service the debt. Thus, cuts in our nominal income may undermine our capacity to service these obligations and lead to insolvency. While a decline in real income arising from inflation is difficult to deal with, we are still able, within limits, to alter our consumption mix (for example, reduce discretionary entertainment, dining out and so on) and still maintain our nominal contractual obligations. This feature of wage rigidity, while criticised by mainstream economists, is, in fact, a source of stability in the economy. It prevents widespread bankruptcies from occurring and the associated fall out. Firms also resist cutting wages because they do not want to be seen as being capricious employers. They know that when times are good they will find it hard to attract labour if they have behaved badly in the downturn when their relative bargaining power was higher.

There are thus solid reasons why it is difficult and undesirable for economies to cut nominal wages during a downturn. Further, even if an across the board cut in money wage levels can be accomplished, the problem then is that competition for market share between firms is likely to lead to price cuts as their unit costs fall, which means that the purchasing power equivalent of the wages (the so-called real wage) might not fall much if at all. In this case, no gains in competition will occur with exchange rates fixed.

Moreover, reducing real wages and profits by 'internal depreciation' is likely to undermine total spending in the economy and exacerbate the recession as people reduce their consumption and firms constrain their investment spending in the face of falling sales and rising unemployment. But if the same fall in real living standards is accomplished via exchange rate depreciation (through the impact on import prices), the economy will experience an increased capacity to export due to the rise in international competitiveness, which may reduce or even offset the decline in domestic demand. The decline in domestic demand can also be minimised through fiscal policy stimulus.

Proponents of the 'internal devaluation' path cite Latvia as an example. Between 2008 and 2010, Latvia's monthly labour costs fell by a staggering 34.4 per cent in total (public sector by 30 per cent and private sector by 37.3 per cent) (Latvijas Statistika, 2014). This signifies a very large internal deflation. Over the same period, the employment to population ratio fell from 68.1 per cent to 58.5 per cent and the unemployment rate rose from 4.5 per cent in 2007 to 14.5 per cent in 2010. In 2013, Latvia's unemployment rate (9 per cent) remained at double its 2007 value and would have been much worse had there not been the staggering 9.2 per cent decline in the population since 2007 (Latvijas Statistika, 2014) as a result of massive out migration of citizens searching for employment elsewhere. In 2010, net out migration was running around 36 thousand people per month. The decline in real GDP between 2007 and 2010 was around 21 per cent and by 2013 the economy was about 9 per cent smaller than it was in 2007. Its recent growth up to 2013 has not been due to a major surge in exports and gross capital formation (investment) remained negative in 2013. The modest growth has been supported mainly by private and public consumption combined with declining imports. It is hardly a testament for the benefits of 'internal deflation'.

RESTORING CENTRAL BANK SOVEREIGNTY AND THE RELATIONSHIP WITH THE ECB

An essential but relatively straightforward part of the exit strategy would involve the re-establishment of the sovereign national central bank. First, the existing national central banks retained most of their prior functions and structure when they entered the so-called Eurosystem. Second, there are already well-defined structures in place between the Eurosystem and the European System of Central Banks (ESCB), which is composed of the ECB and the central banks of all 28 EU Member States. This structure allows nations outside the Eurozone to conduct independent monetary policy (that is, set their own interest rates) but still allows for close cooperation through the General Council of the Eurosystem.

The first priority for the central bank would be to introduce a viable payments system to facilitate the new currency. A payments system:

> . . . refers to arrangements which allow consumers, businesses and other organisations to transfer funds usually held in an account at a financial institution to one another. It includes the payment instruments – cash, cheques and electronic funds transfers which customers use to make payments – and the usually unseen arrangements that ensure that funds move from accounts at one financial institution to another. (RBA, 2014)

A legal framework defining operating procedures and standards backs this system up. There are two types of systems: wholesale (for large transactions) and retail (for consumer related transactions).

Introducing a robust wholesale payments system would not be a major issue. The central banks already had functional systems in place when they entered the Eurozone. Further, in terms of the Eurozone's TARGET2 system, non-euro nations such as Denmark already voluntarily link their national central banks to this system. There are also alternative systems operating in Europe, which process euro-denominated transactions (for example, the system run by the European Banking Association). The retail system would be even easier given the widespread use of the so-called Single European Payments Area (SEPA), which is a system for simplifying bank transfers in euros. Even non-EU nations (Iceland, Liechtenstein, Norway, and Switzerland) are members, as are Monaco and San Marino.

Second, the new central bank would have to redefine its relationship with the ECB. It would now set its own policy interest rate and be responsible for so-called official transactions, which include foreign exchange market interventions. Much of this expertise remains in the national central banks, given the structure of the Eurosystem.

Third, the exiting nation would expect its capital and foreign reserve contribution to the ECB to be returned. The so-called 'capital key' of the ECB was formed by contributions from the Member States, the first being at the start of stage three of EMU on 1 January 1999. The contributions were based on the size of the population and the economy, reflecting a 'capacity to pay'. There have been six adjustments to the ECB capital since that time as a result of specified five-yearly updates and also due to new EU accessions. As at January 2014, the total capital of the ECB stood at €10 825 007 069 61. The euro area national central banks (NCBs) had contributed a total of €7 575 155 922 19 or 70 per cent of the total capital (ECB, 2014c).

There are no legal provisions for these capital contributions to be refunded in the relevant Treaties but, from an operational sense, procedures are already in place whereby funds are transferred back and forward between the national central banks and the ECB. Some commentators claim that the ECB would not be able to absorb the losses and would be insolvent without major contributions from the remaining national central banks and non-euro participating banks. A central bank that issues the currency in which its capital is defined can never 'go broke'. It is not like a commercial bank that requires capital for solvency. The ECB could function with negative capital forever without missing a heartbeat. The ECB could also write off all its holdings of Member State public debt, thus reducing the liabilities of these governments dramatically, without any negative consequences arising in relation to its normal operations. The actual amount that should be refunded would also depend on whether the nation remained part of the EU or not. Already, EU nations outside the Eurozone, such as Bulgaria, Denmark, Poland and several others, provide a small amount of capital to support the ECB as part of their membership of the European System of Central Banks.

There is also the question of contributed reserves. On January 1999, the national central banks of the Member States transferred the equivalent of 50 000 million euros in foreign reserve assets to the ECB. Those assets now stand in euro-equivalent terms at around 40 553 million euros. As in the case of the capital contributions, the new central bank would expect to have these assets refunded.

TRANSACTION COSTS INVOLVED IN EXIT

Chapter 3 of the European Commission's 'One Market, one money' report, released in 1990, estimated the 'transaction costs' of moving from the 12 national currencies to the euro to be equivalent to 'about 0.4% of Community GDP' (European Commission, 1990a: 63). The major part of these savings would result from the 'disappearance of the exchange margin and commission fees paid to banks'. The analysis recognised that the savings would vary across the Member States such that the gains for a nation 'whose currency is extensively used as a means of international payments and belongs to the ERM may be of the order of between 0.1% and 0.2% of national GDP' and that 'small open and less developed economies of the Community may stand to gain around 1% of their GDP' (p. 63). The Commission published a follow-up report in 1998, which estimated 'that transaction costs of about 0.8% of EU GDP may be saved through EMU' (IFO Institute, 1998: 46). The study provided no estimates for the individual nations. A later study, using a different methodology, found the estimates to be higher at both the Community and national levels but noted they were upper bounds (Mendizábal, 2002). The estimates of these studies would be lower if they had been conducted in 2014 given the increased sophistication of banking and other financial institutions and the increased emphasis on electronic transactions via credit cards and the like.

As an aside, the financial market cost savings conjectured in the 1990s by these studies failed to foresee the massive and irrational explosion of financial market transactions that led to the GFC. Far from reducing the claim on GDP, the financial markets (banks and related institutions), aided and abetted by financial market deregulation, a lack of oversight from the regulators of the remaining rules, and plainly illegal business practices, rapidly increased its share of world income. The mess that this frenzy created has cost multiples of GDP relative to the savings alleged to be forthcoming from the shift into one currency. Further, the imposition of austerity, which has blighted growth for years in the Eurozone, has also forced nations to incur massive losses, which dwarf the estimated savings in these Commission Reports. While not denying the existence of transactions costs when nations trade with different currencies, the retention of a nation's own currency and the capacity to manage fluctuations in private spending would have delivered huge net gains relative to the austerity route with one currency.

Further, however much we reduce the earlier estimates to reflect 2014 reality, they are still not applicable to the situation where one nation exits the EMU. The estimates were arrived at on the assumption that the multitude of currencies would be collapsed into the euro. If, for example, Italy were to re-introduce the lira, then the transaction costs associated with lira-euro exchanges would be minimal. Further, for any exiting nation, the extra transaction costs would be directly related to the openness of its economy and the proportion of intra-EMU in its total trade. A less open economy with a higher proportion of trade outside the EMU will experience smaller increases in transaction costs as a result of abandoning the euro. The United Nations Conference on Trade and Development (UNCTAD) propose an Index of Openness based on the trade-to-GDP ratio, whereby the sum of the current value of exports and imports of goods and services are expressed as a percentage of GDP. The higher the ratio, the more open the economy is. Care is needed when making cross-country comparisons because a nation such as Belgium has much less opportunity to trade within its own borders than, say, China or the United States. Nations such as Greece, Italy, Spain and Portugal are relatively closed when compared to the average EU nation. According to Eurostat, 53 per cent of Italian exports are bought within the EU while around 40 per cent are absorbed by EMU nations. For Greece, around 53 per cent of its exports go to the EU with about 37 per cent being sold to EMU nations. Nations such as Belgium, Spain, France, Netherlands and Portugal are more heavily dependent on intra-EMU exports. The dramatic increase in German openness since 2000 is notable and reflects the deliberate suppression of domestic demand (Hartz reforms) and the reliance on net exports for growth. This strategy has created the imbalances within the euro area that have exacerbated the impacts of the crisis.

LEX MONETAE AND REDENOMINATION

Lex monetae is a well-established legal principle, backed up by a swathe of case law across many jurisdictions, and is internationally accepted. It states broadly that the government of the day determines what the legal currency is for transactions and contractual obligations within its national borders. There is thus no question that a nation currently using the euro could abandon it, introduce its own currency, and require all taxes to be paid and all contracts to be denominated in that currency. *Lex monetae* also has been taken to mean that if, say, an Italian had borrowed US dollars from a London bank operating under English law, the definition of the 'currency' for the purposes of resolving this contract is governed by US law. Finally, the principle also means that if a government changes its currency and redenominates at some given parity, all contracts must be honoured at the redenominated rate.

The euro nations have practical experience with the sort of legislation that would be required for redenomination having performed the same feat less than 15 years ago. They already understand the processes that are required and the issues that might arise. They understand that people might get stuck in car parks, and vending machines would need to be recalibrated, among the myriad of conversions that would be required.

At what rate should the redenomination be made? If the currency is to float, then the initial conversion rate is moot. The foreign exchange markets will sort out the levels quickly enough. Floating will give the domestic policy instruments (fiscal and monetary) maximum scope to pursue domestic aims including restoring growth and creating jobs. However, the possibility of the so-called 'rounding up' problem where converted prices are pushed up to the next finite currency unit does suggest some thought needs to be given to the parity (Capital Economics, 2012).

Some financial market commentators have suggested that the new currency should be initially pegged against the euro at the 31 December 2001 parity. The European Council Regulation No. 2866/98, effective from 31 December 1998, established the conversion rates between the euro and the currencies of the Member States which would adopt the euro. It was amended by Regulation No. 1478/2000 of 19 June 2000 to allow for the fact that Greece had 'satisfied' the conditions for entry and would adopt the euro from 1 January 2002. Rounding up, unless declared illegal, would be more likely in this case. Others have argued that to avoid the rounding problem, a one for one parity against the euro be adopted (Capital Economics, 2012: 29).

Application of the *lex monetae* principle becomes blurred or dual in nature when considering the Eurozone because the euro persists even if a nation exits and introduces a new currency. Capital Economics (p. 26) notes that:

> . . .it may be uncertain whether any reference to the 'euro' should be interpreted as meaning the national currency of Greece at the time that payment is due, and hence as the new drachma, or as the common international currency of the EU as a whole, in which case it would remain the euro.

The complication is likely to apply more to private contracts than the public debt, which typically recognises that a government issues liabilities in the currency of use. The exception is that the Troika forced the Greek government to issue liabilities under English law in order to gain further bailout assistance, thus anticipating the application of *lex monetae*, in the case of an exit. Notwithstanding that act of bastardry, the discussion suggests that all public debt would be redenominated into the local currency at the going parity on day one.

Capital Economics (p. 26) noted that the 'government could also legislate to redenominate all private sector debt governed by local law from euros to the new domestic currency' but considered this might be confined to financial sector debt 'to reduce the risk of a banking sector collapse' (p. 26). The crucial issue is what will happen to private sector debt if the local currency becomes the unit in which wages are paid, prices are set and tax obligations are relinquished? We will return to that issue presently. We do not explore the deeper legal issues involved in redenomination in this book. No doubt complex legal cases would drag out for years should the parties decide to take the 'costly' rather than the practical option.

REDENOMINATION AND DEFAULT

The general principle is that to fully regain currency sovereignty it is better to redenominate than default, even if the creditors would consider the two options to be equivalent. On 6 June 2011, German Finance Minister Wolfgang Schäuble wrote a letter to the ECB, the IMF and his Ecofin finance ministers, which expressed doubt that Greece could meet the terms of the bailout conditions in place and return 'to the capital markets within 2012' (Reuters, 2011). He knew the IMF would oppose further funding in these circumstances but predicted that without 'another disbursement of funds before mid July, we face the real risk of the first unorderly default within the euro zone'. He then judged that 'any additional financial support for Greece has to involve a fair burden sharing between taxpayers and private investors', which introduced the idea of the PSI (private sector involvement) at the highest levels. He called for a 'substantial contribution of bondholders to the support effort', which should be achieved 'through a bond swap leading to a prolongation of the outstanding Greek sovereign bonds by seven years' (Reuters, 2011). This set in place what would become a major default by the Greek government on its privately held debt liabilities. Thus the fear that an exit would lead to a nation defaulting on its outstanding liabilities is somewhat moot given the Troika has already managed a major Greek default as part of a strategy to retain the euro.

The Greek government debt held by the ECB (its largest creditor), the national central banks (also large creditors) and the European Investment Bank (a smaller creditor) were excluded from the 'haircut'. Various tricky legal mechanisms were put in place to ensure the default was not subject to further legal challenges (for example, to cope with debt issued under English law). The details of the PSI need not concern us here but suffice to say, the 'present value of the haircut of the Greek debt exchange was in the range of 59–65 per cent' (Zettelmeyer et al., 2013: 19). The question is why should it be preferable to force a restructuring of public debt to the detriment of the investor instead of managing a negotiated withdrawal with the liabilities being redenominated and possibly losing value due to depreciation? The PSI was a Troika-managed and -imposed loss for private investors who had presumably acted in good faith. A forced 'haircut' gives the financial community no option. The loss is imposed upon them and the accompanying austerity that is imposed on the defaulting nation increases the likelihood of further defaults. Everyone loses and the losses magnify over time.

By way of contrast, the losses from redenomination only arise if the new currency depreciates significantly. This provides the holders of the redenominated assets an incentive to work to ensure the depreciation is contained and that there is confidence in the new currency. For example, the ECB could offer the central bank of the exiting nation an unlimited, say, euro-lira swap line, which would help to buffer the depreciation. In the extreme case, the ECB could manage a peg on behalf of the exiting nation until growth resumes and confidence in the currency returns. However, as we have seen, the depreciated currency provides a more effective way to increase a nation's international competitiveness than the present method of 'internal devaluation', which ensures there will be long periods of economic stagnation and hardship.

There are many reasons why exit and redenomination is a superior path when compared to remaining with the Eurozone with debt default. Scott (2012: 41) concluded that the opposition to exit 'cannot be allowed to obscure the *economic* reality that redenomination is at least a marginally better solution than restructuring – and in certain circumstances, a markedly better solution' (emphasis in original). First, the nation gains full access to its fiscal and monetary policies and can stimulate growth immediately. Structural adjustments and managing large private debt exposures are more easily accomplished in a growth environment. Second, redenomination alters nothing with respect to contracts except the unit of account (the currency). There is no need for lengthy renegotiations and delays in payment flows. Third, Scott argued convincingly that redenomination avoids the problem of 'holdout creditors' (p. 4). Fourth, redenomination doesn't advantage any creditor over another: they all face the same adjustment. There would be no 'super priority creditors'.

Redenomination is simple depending on which jurisdiction is being considered. Within a nation's own legal system, under the principle of *lex monetae*, a government could determine that all contractual liabilities currently specified in euros would now be valued in the new currency. The legal matters relating to this are not straightforward but are not likely to be prohibitive (see Thieffry, 2005; Proctor, 2006; Scott, 1998, 2012). In the case of liabilities whose legal status lies outside of the national legal system, the situation becomes murkier. This uncertainty is less likely to burden public debt, which is mostly issued under national law (Capital Economics, 2012; Scott, 2012). Further, for a nation borrowing in its own currency, depreciation presents no real problems because the government can always service its liabilities and the value of the debt in the local currency remains unchanged. For foreigners who hold this debt, the depreciation means that the value of the bonds in their currency falls. For a euro nation, the debt is already effectively denominated in a foreign currency, that is, one they do not issue and cannot control. This exposes any euro-using nation to insolvency risk if it cannot generate enough euros to service its debt obligations. Exiting the EMU and restoring its own currency does not alleviate this problem for euro-denominated liabilities. Furthermore, the value of its outstanding euro-denominated debt rises for the exiting nation once the currency depreciates. The local currency equivalent of the public debt-to-GDP ratio would rise, perhaps quite substantially, which could trigger further falls in the confidence in the currency. It is thus essential that the government only issues debt (if at all) in the new currency with no convertibility guarantees and redenominates all outstanding debt accordingly.

However, in the case of private debt obligations the legal issues are likely to be thorny, which is why some commentators recommend taking a 'laissez faire' approach and leaving these obligations outside the redenomination net (Capital Economics, 2012). According to this argument, apart from the avoidance of legal issues, the evidence from the Asian financial crisis and the Russian default is that the private sector was 'able to resolve these issues without governments becoming heavily involved' (p. 41).

However, given that all local wages and prices would be paid in the new currency, it would become difficult for a household to service an ongoing euro liability. All bank deposits could remain outside the redenomination net but they would soon be exhausted and the debtor would then have to convert local currency into euros at the going price to facilitate payments. Widespread bankruptcies would be inevitable, which would then place severe strains on the banks. Capital Economics (2012) recognises this 'systemic' risk as justifying government decreed redenomination. They also see scope for multilateral negotiations between governments to legislate to recognise the redenomination.

Scott (2012) also suggests that an international approach should be adopted in these cases, similar to the way the euro was brought into being. While the probability of loss through exchange rate fluctuations was minimal in that transition, the point is that when confronted with a total loss (default) or somewhat of a loss (depreciation), there would be an incentive to minimise the loss. These incentives should be enough to induce a process of Treaty change which, as a result of the more streamlined processes introduced in the Treaty of Lisbon, would not take that long should there be a general view that it was in the best interests of all for these negotiated settlements to be allowed. That would clearly be a preferable route to take than unilateral exit. If Italy led the way then it would be likely that the nations would cooperate rather than pillory the exiting nation.

Scott (2012) also raises the issue of vulture funds (or holdout creditors), which hunt around and purchase non-performing public debt and then sue if there is default. Various legal precedents have been established whereby courts rule that 'commercial activity' usurps sovereign immunity. Then the issue is to get the funds. *The Economist* (2011b) noted, 'Getting the country to cough up is another matter. Unlike companies, countries cannot officially go bust so their creditors don't have the benefit of a clear insolvency framework'. Accordingly, the plaintiffs may 'have rights but may not have remedies.' In the current proceedings against the Government of Argentina, the vulture funds have hit a dead end because a large proportion of the government's off shore reserves are deposited with the BIS. The Swiss Federal Supreme Court (Schweizerisches Bundesgericht) ruled in 2010 that the BIS has immunity from any claims for embargoes (Schweizerisches Bundesgericht, 2010, para 4.3). However, there are still avenues that these profit-seeking funds can pursue and these might be disruptive for extensive economic connections between European nations. Scott (2012: 43) concludes that 'redenomination provides the clear advantage of making holdouts simply impossible' because the 'haircut' via depreciation does not constitute any legal claim. With the cooperative approach outlined above, redenomination is vastly superior to outright default.

WOULD THE NATION NEED TO IMPOSE CAPITAL CONTROLS?

Some commentators claim that an exit would instantly destroy the Greek banking system (for example, Buiter, 2011). It is a moot point whether the European banking system, particularly in nations such as Ireland or Greece, is actually solvent anyway. But that point aside, capital controls are policies that place restrictions on the free movement of capital in or out of a nation. Like OMF, capital controls are another one of those 'taboo' topics for mainstream economists. They hate the idea of anything that interferes with the so-called free market. The reason nations impose controls, despite traditional opposition from multilateral agencies such as the IMF, is that the financial markets are, in fact, highly irrational and behave nothing like the way the economics textbooks would like us to believe. Despite the claims to the contrary, governments impose such controls because they are effective. There are many types of controls, ranging from outright prohibitions to market-based incentives, which increase the cost of cross-border transactions (see Ariyoshi et al., 2000). In the context of a nation exiting the EMU, capital controls could limit the extent of the currency depreciation. If targeted to short-term capital transactions they could also serve 'to counter speculative flows that threaten to undermine the stability of the exchange rate and deplete foreign exchange reserves' (p. 18). In short, they allow a nation to 'buy time' (p. 18).

There are many other examples where such policies can reduce foreign exchange market pressures. While the breakup of the Austro-Hungarian Monetary Union in 1919 also provides some insights into the strategies that a government can employ to avoid bank runs ('overstamping' existing banknotes; forced loans to government; restrictions on travel) one should not rely heavily on that experience. The capacity to make electronic transfers now means that people do not have to get on intercontinental trains with suitcases full of banknotes to protect themselves from currency depreciation (see Eichengreen, 2010). More recent examples demonstrate, however, that capital controls can be effective. Malaysia imposed a range of controls on capital outflows during the 1997–99 Asian financial crisis, which 'helped to stabilize the exchange rate' (Eichengreen, 2010: 24). When the Czech and Slovak governments decided to abandon their short-lived monetary union in early 1993, cross-border currency movements were prohibited while new Slovak banknotes were issued. The old Czech banknotes were 'stamped' and were in use in Slovakia until August 1993. Capital controls were very effective in protecting the Slovak banking system. More recently, Iceland also imposed capital controls in 2008, which limited the extent of the depreciation of the currency.

While mainstream economists claim that the financial markets will always subvert capital controls, development economist Dani Rodrik (2010) adopts a more realistic assessment:

> Even if true, evading the controls requires incurring additional costs to move funds in and out of a country – which is precisely what the controls aim to achieve. Otherwise, why would investors and speculators cry bloody murder whenever capital controls are mentioned as a possibility? If they really couldn't care less, then they shouldn't care at all.

Without any cross-border restrictions on financial flows, households and firms in a nation abandoning the EMU may seek to relocate their euro deposits and other financial assets to other Eurozone nations or even into another currency. The exiting government could employ a range of measures (for example, freeze bank withdrawals; restrict electronic transfers, and so on) to prevent runs on the banks. While it is likely that there have already been substantial cross-border movements in deposits and other financial assets in nations such as Greece, the fact remains that there are still substantial deposits remaining in the Greek banking system. Data from the Central Bank of Greece shows that deposits in Greek banks held by domestic residents peaked at 246 210 million euros in September 2009 and then fell steadily to a low of 158 580 million euros by June 2012. They have subsequently risen to 177 203 million euros by March 2014. The decline in deposits was mainly due to reductions in household savings as a result of the depression. The deposits held in Greek banks by 'other euro area residents' have not significantly declined.

The imposition of capital controls should be seen as part of a broader agenda of bank reform once the exit is consolidated. Local banks should play no role in facilitating the entry of speculative short-term flows. The only useful thing a bank should do is to facilitate a payments system, accept deposits, and provide loans to credit-worthy customers. First, banks should only be permitted to lend directly to borrowers. All loans would have to be shown and kept on their balance sheets. This would stop all third party commission deals, which might involve banks acting as 'brokers' and on selling loans or other financial assets for profit. It is in this area of banking that the current financial crisis has emerged and it is costly and difficult to regulate. Second, banks should not be allowed to accept any financial asset as collateral to support loans. The collateral should be the estimated value of the income stream on the asset for which the loan is being advanced. This will force banks to appraise the credit risk more carefully. Third, banks should be prevented from having 'off balance sheet' assets, such as finance company arms, which can evade regulation. Fourth, banks should never be allowed to trade in credit default insurance. Fifth, banks should be restricted to the facilitation of loans and not engage in any other commercial activity.

It is unlikely that the banking union reforms that are slowly working their way through the tortured European processes will go anywhere near introducing these fundamental changes. A nation with its own currency restored and its own central bank and prudential law will be better able to restructure its banking system.

DOES EMU EXIT MEAN EU EXPULSION?

As part of the threats to dissuade nations from considering abandoning the euro, it is claimed that any nation which unilaterally exits the EMU would simultaneously have its EU membership revoked. Given the transfers systems within the EU, a nation that receives a net benefit might think twice about the costs of exit if this would mean it would be expelled from the EU. Greece, for example, received net benefits from the EU equal to about 2.4 per cent of its gross national income in 2012.

There is no doubt that a nation can freely exit any international treaty whenever it chooses. Neil MacCormick (1999: 127) noted that 'Sovereign power is that which is enjoyed, legally, by the holder of a constitutional power to make law, so long as the constitution places no restrictions on the exercise of that power . . . .' The Treaty of Lisbon finally caught up with this obvious fact. Neither the EMU nor the EU is a federal state! While the Treaty remained silent on the question of whether a nation could exit the EMU, the updated Treaty on European Union added Article 50, which holds that 'Any Member State may decide to withdraw from the Union in accordance with its own constitutional requirements' (European Commission, 2012b: 43). There is a negotiated process listed under this article but if there is a failure to agree on terms then the terms of the Treaties lapse after two years. Even the German Constitutional Court has ruled on more than one occasion that (following Maastricht and Lisbon) national law is sovereign. In its decision on whether the Lisbon Treaty was consistent with German Basic Law, the Court reasserted its view that the EU Member States remain 'Masters of the Treaties' (German Constitutional Court, 2009: Paragraph 150). It also concluded that any of the provisions of the European Treaties are considered to be 'abgeleitete Grundordnung' (Paragraph 231), that is, a derived basic law.

They are derived from the constitutional law of the Member States, which remains supreme. The Court also refused to recognise a situation where any Member State would allow the EU the freedom to create powers unilaterally (Paragraph 233).

Thus to eliminate all uncertainty, any Eurozone nation could unilaterally abandon the currency and exempt itself from the provisions of the relevant Treaties any time it chose. It appears that a nation could not easily remain in the EU if it chose to reintroduce its own currency, notwithstanding the fact that there are non-euro EU nations (Athanassiou, 2009). But even that is far from clear. Scott (2012: 6) raises the possibility that in the absence of anything explicit, the principle of 'the greater power includes the lesser' holds, which means that as Article 50 of the Treaty on European Union allows a nation to leave the EU, it 'necessarily creates a unilateral right to euro area-only withdrawal' (p. 6).

Whether retaining EU membership is desirable is another matter. Nations such as Norway, Switzerland and Greenland do not seem to suffer from being outside the EU. Norway and Switzerland have never been members, but Greenland was part of the EEC courtesy of Denmark's membership. Once it attained self-rule in 1979, strong domestic opposition against the EEC (particularly over fishing rights) led to Greenland formally leaving the EEC in 1985. Nothing obviously bad has happened to it as a consequence. Interestingly, as part of its exit, Greenland negotiated the so-called 'Greenland Treaty', which allowed the nation to remain subject to some of the provisions of the European Treaties by dint of its status under the 'Overseas Countries and Territories' provision within the Treaty on the Functioning of the European Union. Therefore it seems possible that any EU nation, for example Italy, could abandon the euro unilaterally, negotiate to leave the EU, but, on exit, sign a special 'Italian Treaty', which could, if there was the political will and the sense of mutual benefit, leave the nation within the EU scope. It can also be argued that Iceland, another non-EU nation, has recovered from its financial collapse much more quickly and robustly as a result of exercising its own sovereignty. It is highly unlikely that, had it been part of the Eurozone, it would have navigated through the crisis as well as it did. The Troika would have surely imposed draconian austerity on it, forced it to prop up the zombie banks and carry the resulting financial burden, and demanded it to pay the spurious claims made by the British and Dutch governments for recompense for the losses their citizens incurred during the bank collapses.

However, a nation such as Italy could show leadership in this uncertain world of Treaties and constitutional law. As a foundation member of the European Coal and Steel Community, which was established by the

Treaty of Paris in 1951 at the start of the European Project, Italy has a status that Spain and Greece, for example, do not enjoy. In 2012, Italy was the fourth largest net contributor to the EU budget and the fourth largest economy (European Commission, 2012e). Neither point can be ignored by the other EU nations in the same way they might brush off any claims by Greece for a 'special' Greece Treaty. While Italy should abandon the euro, restore the lira and allow it to float in international currency markets, it should also use its position in Europe to negotiate a Treaty change such that nations could remain in the EU while restoring their own currencies. This would establish symmetry in the status of all EU nations such that a nation that had entered the EMU could enjoy the same status as those that negotiated to remain outside of it (that is, the UK and Denmark).

CONCLUSION

The costs of the crisis, which have been exacerbated by the mindless fiscal austerity, have been huge. Greece has lost 25 per cent of its economy, and austerity has created a generation of youth that have no connection with work and will enter adulthood having never worked. The loss of opportunities to gain experience are extremely damaging for that socially dislocated cohort. The experience in many other countries in the EMU is similar.

The evidence presented in this book suggests that while the costs of exit will be huge, the long-term costs of more or less permanent austerity will be greater. The EMU nations will eventually resume growth. But they will be prone to a further crisis each time the world economy slows given the SGP rules and their use of the foreign euro.

An orderly exit would be the superior path for each nation to take. Italy should lead the way, given its size and relative importance within Europe, and the terrible damage that is being done to its social structure as a result of the austerity.

23. Employment guarantees

A central idea in economics is efficiency, which means getting the best out of what you have available. The concept is extremely loaded and is the focus of many disputes. But economists of all persuasions are united in saying that developing theories about how efficiency is to be attained at any level is a core activity of their profession. At the macroeconomic level, an economy is deemed to be operating at its maximum level if all productive resources are fully engaged. In more simple terms an efficient economy is one where there is full employment, where everyone can find a job that wants one. This concern about full employment was embodied in the policy frameworks and definitions of major institutions all around the world in the period following World War II.

In his 1987 Ely Lecture to the American Economics Association, Princeton economist Alan Blinder described the failure to provide productive employment for all those willing and able to work as one of the 'major weaknesses of market capitalism'. He argued that the failure had been 'shamefully debilitating' since the mid 1970s, and that the associated costs make 'reducing high unemployment a political, economic and moral challenge of the highest order' (Blinder, 1989: 139). In 2013, Blinder said there was still an emergency, 'five years after the worst . . . we have this titanic loss of output . . . something we number crunching economists tend to emphasize. But more regular people care more about the misery that the unemployed have to endure.' (Blinder, 2013: 1). The solution? Blinder said we 'can hire people directly into government jobs . . . try to induce businesses to hire more . . . The point is, we can still do these things' (p. 4). The following year, Blinder wrote that Reaganomics, the precursor to what we now put under the banner of 'fiscal austerity', 'marked the beginning of the federal government's conversion from fighting poverty to fighting the poor (and the middle class)' (Blinder, 2014). Blinder is no particular champion of the poor and remains locked in the world of mainstream economics. But as a more moderate member of that fraternity he can see the blight of unemployment; the fact that government can do something about it; and that governments have adopted ideological positions to punish the unemployed and the poor rather than reduce their distress.

Sadly, Blinder's 1987 challenge to the economics profession in the US remains acutely relevant to the Eurozone policy makers, which have allowed massive inefficiency to endure in the form of mass unemployment. Neo-liberal Groupthink has blinded them to the options.

A GOVERNMENT HAS TWO BROAD CHOICES

The government has two broad ways to maintain price stability and the use of 'buffer stocks' is involved in each even if the public might not recognise that, nor the politicians dare admit to it. A buffer stock is a fancy term to describe a fluctuating quantity of some stored thing that can be used to stabilise prices. In the agricultural context, the Australian government used to buy wool when it was being oversupplied to the market to ensure the price remained within an agreed limit, which would stabilise incomes for Australian wool growers. The consequence was that it amassed large stockpiles of wool in good seasons, a 'buffer stock' of wool, which it kept in large wool stores spread around the nation. In poor seasons, the government would release wool from its stores into the market to keep the price stable in the face of the wool shortage. The government's buffer stock of wool would thus fluctuate up and down according to the vagaries of demand and supply in the wool market, but the price of wool would remain more or less constant. The scheme exploited the well-known principle that a commodity can be stored if in surplus production or released from store if in shortage in order to stabilise prices and preserve incomes (Graham, 1937).

In general terms, the two broad buffer stock approaches that a government can use to stabilise prices are:

1. *Unemployment buffer stocks* Inflation is controlled using a combination of high interest rates and/or fiscal austerity, which creates a buffer stock of unemployment. The unemployment dampens wage demands and the accompanying subdued sales reduce the capacity of firms to push up prices. Deliberately creating unemployment to reduce inflationary pressures is a very costly and unreliable approach. This is the current mainstream approach employed in the Eurozone and elsewhere.
2. *Employment buffer stocks* The government makes an unconditional offer of employment at a socially acceptable minimum wage to anyone who cannot find a job, thereby creating a buffer stock of jobs. The jobs pool would fluctuate according to how strong the rest of the economy was. The job offer does not compete with the labour demand elsewhere in the economy and is thus non-inflationary. The

Job Guarantee (JG) approach is an example of an employment buffer stock policy approach (Mitchell, 1998).

UNEMPLOYMENT BUFFER STOCKS AND PRICE STABILITY

The modern policy framework is in contradistinction to the practice of governments in the post World War II period to the mid 1970s which sought to maintain levels of spending in the economy using a range of fiscal and monetary measures that were sufficient to ensure that full employment was achieved. Continuous fiscal deficits were common and the idea that a government should pursue some preconceived fiscal balance irrespective of what that might mean for the level of unemployment was alien. Unemployment rates were at very low levels throughout this period.

Our earlier discussion of the so-called 'Great Moderation' emphasised how politicians increasingly came under the hold of the Monetarist free market ideology, which asserted that there is no discretionary role for government fiscal policy to regulate total spending. The neo-liberals claimed that mass unemployment was a structural problem arising mostly because individuals are not motivated enough to seek work or are subsidised to halt job search by excessively generous income support measures provided by government. Accordingly, the policy debate became increasingly concentrated since the late 1970s on deregulation of financial and labour markets (particularly job protection and trade union involvement), privatisation, and reductions in welfare support. Macroeconomic policy became concentrated on using interest rates to control spending with a bias towards excessively high rates supported by fiscal austerity. Governments abandoned full employment as a policy goal. Instead, they deliberately manipulated unemployment buffer stocks to suppress price pressures. Unemployment rates have been significantly higher ever since.

The fear of job loss that accompanies periods of high unemployment suppresses price pressures because workers are discouraged from seeking higher wages. Further, firms have reduced ability to push up prices when their sales decline. Taken together, the rising unemployment keeps a lid on inflation. Several nations also introduced extensive labour market deregulation, which spawned new forms of labour underutilisation making it harder for workers to secure wage rises. For example, underemployment, the state where a part time worker desires more hours of work but cannot find them, has joined unemployment as a major problem and adds to the underutilised pool of labour, which acts as a wage constraint.

However, neo-liberal policy makers do not characterise their approach in this way. Instead, they claim that full employment follows naturally from the maintenance of price stability, even though this approach to price stability requires the maintenance of an unemployed buffer stock. In other words, they conveniently redefine full employment as being consistent with any unemployment rate where inflation is stable, even if that rate is high and variable. The high unemployment is then dismissed as being of structural origin, with the additional assertion that if governments try to reduce it with increased deficit spending, they will only generate accelerating inflation. The evidence is not consistent with this view. Big jumps in unemployment always occur during major recessions when no significant changes in the so-called structural influences cited by neo-liberals to explain high unemployment are observed. Also, whenever economic growth picks up, firms start hiring and unemployment drops. Further, in the pre-GFC period, several nations drove unemployment well below these 'estimated' full employment levels while inflation also fell and remained low. The ad hoc response from the neo-liberals was that the 'full employment' level had shifted down but there was no convincing 'structural' explanation for that shift.

The only reasonable explanation was that increased total spending created more sales and gave firms an incentive to increase employment. MIT academic Michael Piore (1979: 10) had earlier noted the same phenomenon in the US:

> Presumably, there is an irreducible residual level of unemployment composed of people who don't want to work, who are moving between jobs, or who are unqualified. If there is in fact some such residual level of unemployment, it is not one we have encountered in the United States. Never in the post war period has the government been unsuccessful when it has made a sustained effort to reduce unemployment.

The tolerance of high levels of unemployment, a relatively recent phenomenon, exemplifies the policy dominance of neo-liberal ideology. The empirical evidence is clear that most OECD economies have not provided enough jobs since the mid 1970s and neo-liberal austerity policies have forced the unemployed to engage in an involuntary fight against inflation.

It is clear that the experience of OECD nations since 1975 suggests that deflationary policies, including fiscal austerity, are effective in bringing inflation down but impose huge unemployment costs on the economy generally, and on certain demographic groups specifically, which are rarely computed or discussed in official circles. These costs include:

- Loss of current output and income;
- Social exclusion and the loss of freedom;
- Skill loss;
- Psychological harm;
- Ill health and reduced life expectancy;
- Loss of motivation;
- The undermining of human relations and family life;
- Racial and gender inequality; and
- Loss of social values and responsibility.

While the unemployed and their families are certainly aware of these massive losses, the rest of society is less aware. For example, we might notice rising crime rates in our neighbourhoods but not associate them with higher unemployment. In part, this is because neo-liberalism has changed the way we think about unemployment. In the past we understood clearly that it arose as a result of a shortage of jobs. In recent decades, we have been conditioned by relentless government campaigns supported by a largely co-opted media to perceive unemployment as an individual problem. The upshot is that we are lulled into accepting the popularised narrative that the unemployed are lazy; have poor work attitudes; refuse to invest in appropriate skills; are subject to disincentives arising from misguided government welfare support, and all the rest of the arguments that the mainstream use to obfuscate the social and economic problem.

Further, there is evidence that the 'quality' of the unemployed buffer stock (defined in terms of its capacity to discipline price pressures) deteriorates over time. Just as soggy rotting wool is useless in a wool price stabilisation scheme, the quality of labour resources can deteriorate if unemployed for lengthy periods. The more employable are the unemployed, the greater is the price level discipline of the unemployment buffer stock. There is overwhelming evidence that the skill losses and related circumstances associated with long-term unemployment undermine the quality of the jobless buffer stock and require higher and higher levels of unemployment to be created to maintain the same downward pressure on prices.

For these reasons, it is difficult to argue in cost benefit terms that this approach could possibly be a superior way to maintain price stability. This is especially so when we realise that the currency-issuing government can create a buffer stock of jobs which allow workers to maintain a continuous involvement in paid work, which in turn leads to improved physical and mental health, more stable labour market behaviour, reduced burdens on the criminal justice system, more coherent family histories and useful output, if well managed. It is also the case that training in a paid work environment is more effective than training schemes that are isolated from work. The latter have become the fashion under the active labour market programs pursued by governments in all countries over the last two decades.

EMPLOYMENT BUFFER STOCKS AND PRICE STABILITY

Once the neo-liberal myths about macroeconomics are exposed and the implications completely understood (see Chapters 17 and 18), it becomes obvious that a better alternative would be to utilise an employment buffer stock approach. The Job Guarantee (JG) is an example of this approach and is considered the best way to maintain price stability while avoiding the massive costs of unemployment. Between 1945 and the mid 1970s, western governments realised that with deficit spending supplementing private demand, they could ensure that all workers who wanted to work could find jobs. Although private employment growth was relatively strong during this period, governments were important employers in their own right, and also maintained a buffer of jobs for the least skilled workers: for example, in the major utilities, the railways, local public services and major infrastructure functions of government. By absorbing workers who lost jobs when private investment declined, government jobs acted as an economic safety valve. British economist Paul Ormerod (1994: 203) noted that the economies that avoided high unemployment in the 1970s maintained a '. . . sector of the economy which effectively functions as an employer of last resort, which absorbs the shocks which occur from time to time, and more generally makes employment available to the less skilled, the less qualified'. He concluded that societies with a high degree of social cohesion (such as Austria, Japan and Norway) were willing to broaden their concept of costs and benefits of resource usage to ensure that everyone had access to paid employment opportunities.

It is in that context that the JG can be understood. The JG is a simple concept with far reaching consequences. The JG would involve the government making an unconditional job offer to anyone who is willing to work at a socially acceptable minimum wage and who cannot find work elsewhere. The buffer stock of jobs would expand (decline) as private sector employment declined (expanded). To avoid disturbing private sector wage structures and to ensure the JG is consistent with stable inflation, the JG wage rate should be set at the minimum wage level, defined to ensure the worker is never socially excluded. The minimum wage should be an expression of the aspiration of the society of the lowest acceptable material standard of living. Since the JG wage would be open to everyone, it would functionally become the national minimum wage. JG workers would enjoy stable incomes and their increased spending would boost confidence throughout the economy and underpin a private spending recovery.

The JG Provides a Powerful Automatic Stabiliser

The JG would thus become a powerful, additional 'automatic stabiliser'. The JG would fulfil an absorption function to minimise the employment and income losses currently associated with the flux of private sector spending. When private sector employment declines, public sector employment and spending would automatically rise. The nation would remain fully employed, with only the mix between private and public sector employment fluctuating as it responded to the spending decisions of the private sector. In this respect, the JG would maintain what is referred to as 'loose' full employment because the government would be offering jobs to workers who are not currently in demand by the market. The increased government spending, therefore, would not compete with other resource users. The JG would thus recruit labour 'off the bottom of the market' in contradistinction to general government spending, which involves the government competing with other purchasers for resources including labour at market prices. By not competing with the private market for resources, the JG would avoid the inflationary tendencies of traditional Keynesian pump priming, which attempts to maintain full capacity utilisation by 'hiring off the top', that is, competing for resources at market prices and relying on so-called spending multipliers to generate extra jobs necessary to achieve full employment. The latter approach fails to provide an integrated full employment price anchor policy framework. Further, under a JG the government knows that the last person who seeks a job on any particular day defines how much government spending is required to ensure there are enough jobs available. It is also true that because it would be impossible to run a JG matching all the skills to jobs, the employment buffer stock would comprise 'loose' full employment in the sense that there would be some skills-based underemployment remaining when the pool was large. In better times, as the JG pool shrank and was predominantly occupied by workers who would typically be the last employed by any private firm (if ever), the gap between 'loose' and 'true' full employment would approach zero.

If the business community or anyone else thought the fiscal deficit associated with the JG at any time was 'too high' or that there were 'too many' workers in the JG pool then there is a simple remedy available. The JG pool and government spending will fall if private spending rises (for example, invest more in productive capacity). In that sense, the size of the JG would always be determined by private sector spending.

The JG is a Qualitatively Superior Inflation-Fighting Approach

The anti-inflation mechanisms of a JG are easy to understand. If inflationary pressures developed in the private sector as it reached full capacity, the government would manipulate fiscal and monetary policy settings to constrain private sector spending to prevent the economy overheating. Labour would be transferred from the inflating private sector to the 'fixed wage' JG sector and eventually this would resolve the inflation pressures. In general, there cannot be inflationary pressures arising from a policy that sees the government offering a fixed wage to any labour that is unwanted by other employers (see Mitchell, 1998; Mitchell and Muysken, 2008).

The JG buffer stock is a qualitatively superior inflation-fighting alternative to the unemployed buffer stock. Some disagree by arguing that workers may consider the JG to be a better option than unemployment. Without the threat of unemployment, wage-bargaining workers then may have less incentive to moderate their wage demands notwithstanding the likely disciplining role of unemployment in skilled labour markets. But JG workers would retain higher levels of skill than those who are forced to succumb to lengthy spells of unemployment, and therefore would constitute a more credible threat to the current private sector employees. When wage pressures mount, an employer would be more likely to exercise resistance if she could hire from the fixed price JG pool.

The JG Helps Maintain Wellbeing and Socio-Economic Stability

The JG is a minimum spending approach to full employment. It does not replace conventional use of fiscal policy to achieve social and economic outcomes. The government would supplement the JG wage with a wide range of social wage expenditures, including adequate levels of public education, health, and child care. Further, the provision of large-scale public infrastructure remains crucial.

Some JG proponents have referred to it as an 'employer of last resort' scheme for workers in the same way that central banks function as lender of last resort to the banks. However, while the central bank's capacity to provide reserves to the commercial banks should be seen as a true last resort, the JG should be one of the first policies introduced. The JG would be much more than a public sector job creation strategy because it would provide a macroeconomic stability framework designed to deliver full employment *and* price stability based on the buffer stocks principle where job creation is but one component.

The Job Guarantee is Not Workfare

A popular misconception is that the JG would simply be a version of 'workfare' or so-called 'work for the dole' schemes. Unlike workfare schemes, the JG would not jettison economic security, social justice and the traditional objectives of wage setting in order to build an efficient and productive economy. Workfare does not provide secure employment with conditions consistent with norms established in the community with respect to non-wage benefits and the like. Workfare does not ensure that stable living incomes are provided to the workers. Workfare is a program where the State extracts a contribution from the unemployed for their welfare payments. The State, however, takes no responsibility for the failure of the economy to generate enough jobs. In a JG economy, the state would assume this responsibility and provide acceptable rewards to the workers for their work. Most unemployed workers would exit the JG pool as soon as they could. But low skilled workers, with a history of job instability and lengthy spells of unemployment, would benefit from a guaranteed, secure job and might prefer to remain in the JG forever. That option is not typically permitted under workfare schemes.

Existing unemployment benefits schemes could be maintained alongside the JG program, depending on the government's preference and conception of mutual responsibility. Without the continued provision of unemployment benefits, the concept of mutual obligation from the workers' side would become straightforward because the receipt of income by the unemployed worker would be conditional on taking a JG job. The JG wage could be paid to anyone who turned up at some designated government JG office even if the office had not yet organised work for that person. A person might be permitted a short period of non-work to sort out their affairs before starting a JG job. This period would be covered by full JG pay. It might be argued that in the European context, where unemployment benefits are paid from an insurance fund as some proportion of the worker's last earned wage, unemployed workers would be disadvantaged if the JG replaced the unemployment insurance schemes. It would depend on the worker's past history and the generosity of the scheme, but both schemes could coexist with no loss of effectiveness of either.

The JG Provides Jobs that are Inclusive to the Most Disadvantaged

Gregg and Layard (2009: 2) recognise that there is a 'mass of low tech maintenance which needs to be done on public housing, schools, hospitals and roads, by . . . [the long-term unemployed] . . . given 1–2 weeks' training.' Extensive research has been done in a number of countries to identify suitable JG jobs (see CofFEE, 2008). The jobs have to be accessible to the least skilled workers, who typically bear the greatest burden of unemployment. The jobs should ideally not substitute for existing government or private employment. Within those constraints, JG workers could still contribute in many socially useful activities including urban renewal projects and other environmental and construction schemes (reforestation, sand dune stabilisation, river valley erosion control, and the like), personal assistance to pensioners, and other community schemes. For example, creative artists could contribute to public education as peripatetic performers.

The investment in the JG would thus create a safety net that automatically fluctuates with private sector spending. In that sense, it would avoid the unemployment that is currently associated with the flux and uncertainty of private spending. It is almost unbelievable that citizens tolerate governments which deliberately force millions of people around the world into unemployment for want of some funding that the government can always provide.

The fluctuating nature of the JG jobs pool would have to be reflected in the design of the jobs and the functions they fulfilled. Projects or functions requiring critical mass might face difficulties as the private sector expanded, and it would not be sensible to use only JG employees in functions considered essential. Thus in the creation of JG employment, it can be expected that the stock of standard public sector jobs, which is identified with conventional Keynesian fiscal policy, would expand, reflecting the political decision that these were essential activities. The JG would be integrated into a coherent training framework to allow workers (by their own volition) to choose a variety of training paths while still working in the JG. However, if they chose not to undertake further training, no pressure would be placed upon them.

It is also highly likely that the introduction of the JG would place pressure on private employers, particularly in the low skill service sectors, to restructure their workplaces to overcome the discontent that their underemployed workers feel. A full time, secure JG position at wages not significantly different from those offered in low paid, casualised and insecure private service sector jobs would be an attractive option to workers. In this regard, the JG would offer flexibility to workers and become a source for dynamic efficiency. Some workers would prefer part time jobs while others would seek full time JG jobs. To retain their marginal workers, private firms would be motivated to invest in new work processes, which would generate higher productivity and justify higher wages being paid. It would be very easy to design the JG in such a way that workers with child care needs can be accommodated. Disabled workers can also be incorporated within this flexible environment whereas private firms have demonstrated an unwillingness to provide jobs to this cohort.

The JG would be Green

Future labour market policy must consider the environmental risk factors associated with economic growth. Possible threshold effects and imprecise data covering the life cycle characteristics of natural capital suggest a risk-averse attitude is wise. Indiscriminate (Keynesian) expansion fails in this regard because it does not address the requirements for risk aversion. It is not increased demand *per se* that is necessary, but increased demand in certain areas of activity. The JG would thus be 'green' because it would provide jobs in environmentally sustainable activities, which are unlikely to be produced by traditional private sector firms.

The JG is Not a Universal Panacea

The JG would not be a universal panacea. It would provide safety net employment capacity and an inflation anchor for the economy and, in that sense, would represent the minimum policy structure that a responsible government should put in place. But it should not stop a government introducing other spending measures to improve the scope and quality of public infrastructure, to ensure that first class education and health care services are available, and to provide career opportunities for skilled workers.

The value of the JG is that the government always knows that if total spending levels come up against the real capacity of the economy, then they are able to tighten fiscal policy without creating unemployment. In normal times, the JG would be a very small program but essential to those who would otherwise be excluded by private employers.

EMPLOYMENT GUARANTEES ENTER THE MAINSTREAM DEBATE IN EUROPE

On 14 April 2009, the German newspaper *Die Welt* ('The World') reported on a proposal whereby the German Federal Employment Agency would create so-called 'transfer companies' which could 'park' workers that firms could no longer currently afford (Evert and Neumann, 2009). These firms would guarantee to re-employ them again once their economic outlook improved (also *Der Spiegel*, 2009). The scheme would be government funded and pay workers 67 per of their current wage for a period of two years. It would also pay social insurance contributions and offer training opportunities for up skilling. The proposal was framed in the context of deteriorating economic conditions in Germany and a fear among trade unions and firms that the government-funded shorter hours scheme would not be sufficient to avoid an unemployment crisis. These transfer companies would thus provide a 'buffer stock' function to absorb workers at times when firms could no longer justify employing them on the basis of their sales. The politicians rejected the scheme claiming it would be too costly.

The idea of an employment guarantee was also floated in Britain, by academics Paul Gregg and Richard Layard. They proposed that a 'job guarantee' should be introduced to reduce the likelihood that the current crisis will create an entrenched pool of disadvantaged long-term unemployed, which then allegedly 'makes it difficult to have a quick recovery that is not also inflationary' (Gregg and Layard, 2009). The idea that the long-term unemployed present a bottleneck to non-inflationary growth is one of Layard's persistent messages but is highly contested and outside the scope of this discussion. The empirical evidence suggests that whenever spending in the economy is strong enough, the resulting growth draws labour from both the short- and long-term pools of unemployment.

It suited Layard to make this claim because he was one of the principle architects of the OECD *Jobs Study* (1994), which formalised the abandonment of full employment as an objective of governments in place of a diminished 'supply side' concept of 'full employability' (Layard et al., 1991). Governments following the OECD agenda launched attacks on the unemployed and welfare recipients on the presumption that so-called 'supply side' rigidities undermined the capacity of economies to adjust, innovate and be creative. The proposed reform agenda was introduced in many countries at the same time as central banks were increasingly concentrating on price stability and governments were adopting fiscal conservatism as the norm (Mitchell and Muysken, 2008).

The Layard–OECD narrative supported the view that unemployment was an individual problem rather than the result of a systemic failure to create enough jobs, the latter having been the dominating policy view since the Great Depression ended. The whole thrust of the so-called active labour market policy was predicated on the belief that the long-term unemployed represented a structural bottleneck that could only be addressed by supply initiatives like training and cuts to welfare entitlements (OECD, 1994). Layard (1998: 27) argued that:

> . . . in the very bad old days, people thought that unemployment could be permanently reduced by stimulating aggregate demand . . . This belief has died everywhere . . . these ideas did not address the fundamental problem . . . The only way to address this problem is to make all the unemployed attractive to employers . . . Nothing else will do the trick.

He believed in what economists know as 'Say's Law' or, crudely, supply creates its own demand, which is an arcane idea from the 19th century that denied that there could ever be a shortage of spending and unsold goods. This claim underpinned the view that there could never be any sustained unemployment. Layard's version of the idea was that new jobs follow an increase in a more trained pool of unemployed and 'the mechanism is simple enough. If the labour supply increases and the number of jobs does not, inflation starts to fall; this makes possible an increase in aggregate demand in the economy, which in turn increases employment in line with the increase in the labour supply' (p. 26). Keynes knew this argument was false in the 1930s, just as Marx had years earlier referred to Say's Law as '"preposterous", "childish babble"', and thought Say himself was 'inane', 'miserable', 'thoughtless', 'dull', and a 'humbug' (Sowell, 2006: 173). The evidence doesn't support the view that the production of output creates its own sales or that the creation of skills creates jobs. In the period after the OECD *Jobs Study* was released and before the crisis ensued, the advanced economies continued to generate high unemployment rates and broader forms of labour underutilisation (for example, underemployment) increased. The crisis has since exacerbated these elevated levels of labour underutilisation and it is difficult to see what has been achieved by the supply side labour market policies other than to punish the most disadvantaged workers within our communities.

As the Maastricht 'convergence process' was sustaining persistently high levels of unemployment in Europe, there were mixed messages coming out from Layard and his colleagues, seemingly struggling to reconcile their 'theoretical' position with the contrary evidence. As an example of this tension, Layard (1997: 202) expressed doubts about the supply side labour market policies that he had initially promoted and which had been so zealously taken up by governments around the world:

> If we seriously want a big cut in unemployment, we should focus sharply on those policies which stand a good chance of having a really big effect. It is not true that all policies which are good in general are good for unemployment. There are in fact very few policies where the evidence points to any large

> unambiguous effect on unemployment and some widely advocated policies for which there is little clear evidence.

In this vein, he argued that further cuts in the duration of benefits, a key neo-liberal policy strategy, would only increase employment at the costs of the creation of an underclass with an 'ever-widening inequality of wages' (p. 192). He then admitted to seeing a role for government job creation, which would allow people to reacquire 'work habits – to prove their working capacity . . . [and to restore] . . . them to the universe of employable people. This is an investment in Europe's human capital' (p. 192).

Further, in 2001, another member of the LNJ team, Stephen Nickell wrote (Nickell and Quintini, 2001: 5) in relation to cutting income support benefits:

> . . . simply because a change in the benefit system reduces equilibrium unemployment . . . [by making unemployment less attractive] . . . it does not necessarily imply that it is a good thing. It is arguable, for example, that the current benefit system is simply too mean. In fact, to have a system which operates well, it is not necessary to plunge households into poverty should the sole breadwinner lose his or her job.

The point is that this group of researchers have been at the centre of the neo-liberal policy attack on workers and supported policies, which culminated in the GFC. Layard's call for a job guarantee should be seen as part of this history of failed ideas and policies and a history of trying to remain at the centre of the debate despite that failure. The Gregg and Layard proposal calls on the British government to 'offer an ultimate guarantee that a job will be there' and reflects the view that 'Common humanity requires us to offer meaningful activity when the regular economy does not' (Gregg and Layard, 2009: 1). No doubt you will see the tension between this position and some of Layard's earlier claims about jobs being generated if there is an effective labour supply.

Mainstream economists are notorious for selective citations and rarely refer to other social science research in their own work (Zuckerman, 2003). Despite the concept of a job guarantee having a specific and decades-long tradition in the Institutionalist and then MMT literature, Gregg and Layard (2009: 1) said that we 'should use a new term "The Job Guarantee" which will resonate with people, rather than have headline talk about modifications to the New Deal, which is pretty arcane to most people.' At the time they released their paper, I wrote to Layard questioning his claim to be authoring a 'new term' and further noting that their concept of an employment guarantee was a very limited conceptualisation of the JG outlined earlier in this chapter, which has been a central element of MMT. No reply was forthcoming.

Gregg and Layard's proposal can be summarised as a very short-term job for people after they have been in an active labour market program for 12 months. Unemployed 18–25 year olds would be churned through various labour market programs first, and then, if they had not succeeded in gaining employment, they would be offered a six-month paid job. For the over 25s, access to six months of guaranteed employment would not be provided until they had been churned through 18 months of these humiliating and useless labour market programs.

Significantly, as noted earlier, Gregg and Layard (2009) recognise that there are many jobs that could be done to improve public infrastructure and advance wellbeing that could be adequately performed by anyone with a few weeks' training. One wonders how this squares with Layard's view that the long-term unemployed represent a bottleneck, which constrains the capacity of the economy to grow. It is clear that these types of jobs are available in all economies if the government is willing to fund them. The private sector will not provide them because the private costs outweigh the private benefits, which means they cannot make a profit from them. But it is also clear that the social benefits outweigh the social costs, which justifies government involvement. These jobs would be of overwhelming benefit to society.

If these jobs can be productively performed with limited extra training then why submit unemployed workers to months or years of so-called 'training' on pitiful income support levels if they can be immediately productive, provide a beneficial service to society, and exit the welfare system? The answer is governments have become obsessed with fiscal austerity and think the 'cost' of these jobs is 'too high'. The reality is the British government like other currency-issuing governments can always afford to hire everyone who wants a job at a minimum wage. Gregg and Layard fall into the fiscal austerity trap by proposing a highly limited program that would only provide temporary relief after a person had been unemployed for a long period. To extract the full benefits of a true JG approach the job offers have to be unconditional and unlimited. It is only then that the buffer stock dynamics ensure that all those who want to work can do so and that price stability will be maintained.

THE EUROPEAN COMMISSION YOUTH GUARANTEE INITIATIVE

In June 2012, the International Labour Conference in Geneva adopted a youth employment resolution calling for decent job creation with policy to be focused on increasing aggregate spending; increased spending on education and training; targeted support for disadvantaged youth; entrepreneurship and business support for young people; and ensuring rights at work are protected (ILO, 2012: 43). The resolution aimed to provide 'guiding principles' to 'tackle the youth employment crisis' (p. 43) where 'the situation facing youth has become unsustainable and threatens to erode social cohesion' (p. 45).

Some European nations had responded to this crisis with specific youth guarantee programs, although the Scandinavian countries have a long history with policies that attempt to keep youth engaged in schooling, training or work. In 2007, for example, Sweden introduced a 'new job guarantee scheme for young people' (Eurofound, 2012a: 1) while Finland introduced a similar scheme in 2005 but revised it twice in 2010 and 2013 as the crisis mounted. These schemes aim 'to reduce the time young people spend in unemployment and inactivity', using the Public Employment Service (PES) to provide 'personalised needs assessment and an employment plan, followed by the guarantee' (p. 1). The latter takes the form of 'either the offer of a job or a study opportunity (academic or vocational), or some other activation measure' (p. 1). The evidence suggests that schemes of this type improve the chances of a participant finding a job quicker relative to older workers not given the same intensive care. But this difference 'tended to dissipate during the economic crisis' (p. 2). In other words, when there is jobs growth these schemes shuffle the unemployment queue such that those given intensive help move closer to the front of the queue. But when a recession strikes, and the job vacancies disappear, the queue lengthens again and no amount of 'supply side' initiative will create the necessary employment. People cannot search for jobs that are not there!

On 22 October 2012, the European Foundation for the Improvement of Living and Working Conditions (Eurofound) published a report which sought to estimate the monetary cost of the growing incidence of youth classified as NEETs (not in employment, education or training) in Europe. The aim was 'to broaden understanding of the benefits accruing from re-engaging young people in employment and education' and to stimulate 'governments and social partners to prevent the disengagement of young people from the labour market and education' (Eurofound, 2012b: 65). Eurofound's 'conservative approach' to estimating these costs still found that in:

> . . . 2008, the 26 Member States lost almost €120 billion, corresponding to almost 1% of European GDP. When the recent economic crisis and the increase in the NEET population between 2008 and 2011 is taken into account, it is

> likely that this loss has been even greater . . . It was estimated to be €153 billion, corresponding to more than 1.2% of GDP in Europe. (p. 81)

For several nations including Greece, Italy, and Ireland, the losses were estimated to be 'equal to 2% or more of each country's GDP' (p. 1). For example, for Greece the estimated losses in 2011 were over EUR 7 billion or 3.28 per cent of GDP.

The ILO (2012: 48) estimated that the annual cost of implementing 'a young guarantee programme across the Eurozone would not exceed 21 billion euros . . . which represents around 0.45 per cent of Eurozone government spending, a modest figure vis-à-vis expected benefits', although it is hard to know what implementation would mean. Certainly, when the European bureaucrats talk about 'youth guarantees' they are not conceiving that governments will ensure that their young citizens will receive an on going guaranteed job if they are not in schooling or training. There is still political resistance to that idea. The reality is that when job opportunities are scarce as a result of inadequate total spending in the economy, young workers will always be at the back of the queue due to their lack of experience, along with other disadvantaged groups such as those with physical and mental disabilities. Only an unconditional JG improves the job prospects for those groups under these circumstances.

When Eurostat released the unemployment estimates for October 2012, the data showed that youth unemployment had increased sharply over the previous 12 months across the European Union and in some nations (for example, Greece 57 per cent; Spain 55.9 per cent) was beyond what might be termed alarming levels. It was clear that the policy framework in Europe was failing. The European Commissioner for Employment, Social Affairs and Inclusion, László Andor, responded to these disastrous unemployment statistics by announcing the Commission's intention to introduce a Youth Guarantee scheme. He said that the high:

> . . . youth unemployment has dramatic consequences for our economies, our societies and above all for young people. This is why we have to invest in Europe's young people now . . . This Package would help Member States to ensure young people's successful transition into work. The costs of not doing so would be catastrophic. (European Commission, 2012c)

In other words, the situation had reached emergency proportions requiring a response of commensurate proportions.

In December 2012, the Commission presented a proposal to the European Council for a European-wide Youth Guarantee (European Commission, 2012d). The Council adopted the recommendation on 22 April 2013 (European Council, 2013). The Youth Guarantee was taken to mean:

> . . . a situation in which young people receive a good-quality offer of employment, continued education, an apprenticeship or a traineeship within a period of four months of becoming unemployed or leaving formal education. An offer of continued education could also encompass quality training programmes leading to a recognised vocational qualification. (European Council, 2013: 1)

The Council had determined at its 8 February 2013 meeting to allocate 'EUR 6 billion for the period 2014–20 to support the measures set out in the Youth Employment Package' (p. 3), which included the Youth Guarantee.

The fact that the Commission considered this policy initiative marked somewhat of a change in thinking amidst the doom and gloom that austerity had created. The task, however, was to break out of the austerity straitjacket and introduce a policy that would represent a real opportunity for European youth caught in the despair of joblessness. The Youth Guarantee Initiative is a good idea but unfortunately fails to make that break.

The scale of the program has austerity written all over it. The allocation of just 6 billion euros to the Youth Employment Initiative (YEI) between 2014 and 2020 does not match the scale of the problem. The European Investment Bank Group also has committed to spend the same amount on youth employment initiatives but not necessarily on the Youth Guarantee. Where will the remaining funds come from? The answer is the Member State governments, which are being forced to reduce net spending overall to bring their fiscal balances into line with the SGP and the six-pack. How will it be possible to avoid the catastrophe with such a minimal funding commitment? If the Member States really allocate significant amounts to the program, then the funds will be at the expense of other programs. Austerity means a net retreat of the public sector no matter what changes are made to the mix of the public spending. The lack of any serious funding commitment really highlights the Eurozone disaster. Comparing this 6 billion euro allocation to the Eurofound's estimates that at least €153 billion or nearly 3 billion euros a day are being wasted as a result of the NEET problem alone exemplifies the Commission's distorted sense of priorities.

The official documentation (for example, European Commission, 2012d) provides details of the sort of activities that would be funded under the Youth Guarantee. These activities can be clustered under headings such as information provision, training and wage subsidies/self-employment support. But there is not a job in sight! The program is clearly not an adequate response to the 'catastrophe' and continues the bias towards failed supply side measures, which were defined by the OECD Jobs Study in 1994. The evidence from the last 20 years doesn't support the principle tenets of the 'activation' approach. First, training programs that are divorced from the paid work environment tend to be ineffective. Second, building new information systems to reduce mismatch between job seekers and firms is only an effective strategy if there are jobs available. Third, proposals to address poor signalling (for example, improving interview techniques, CV presentation) are ineffectual if there is a shortage of jobs. Fourth, wage subsidies have a long record of failure and operate on the flawed assumption that mass unemployment is the result of excessive wages. There is no consistent evidence that supports the idea that private firms will provide millions of jobs to the European youth as a result of wage subsidies (100 per cent or otherwise). If firms cannot sell the extra output, they will not hire extra workers. They may, however, hire youth and sack adults and pocket the cost differential if productivity considerations allow. So the problem is just shifted.

The overwhelming problem with the Youth Guarantee proposal is that it skirts around the main issue, a lack of jobs. It continues the emphasis on full employability, that is, preparing youth for work rather than ensuring there are enough jobs available to ensure there is full employment. What is needed in Europe is a large-scale job creation program for those who are not in formal education or formal apprenticeship programs. Within that job creation program, various training ladders can be included where appropriate and where the participants' desires lie.

It is telling that the most recent document available from the Commission on the Youth Guarantee initiative (European Commission, 2014c) is a glossy brochure filled with photos that show young people in employment and training situations. The photos are copyrighted to Shutterstock, the stock photography agency based in New York. In other words, the brochure is filled with photos downloaded from the internet, which are designed to send a positive message in lieu of any actual job experiences for youth in Europe being available to the bureaucrats in Brussels.

EMPLOYMENT GUARANTEES VERSUS INCOME GUARANTEES

Many progressive commentators advocate the introduction of a Basic Income Guarantee (BIG) as the primary policy weapon against poverty and consider employment guarantees to be coercive. They highlight the fact that if there is a lack of employment alternatives available to citizens then the provision of a BIG, set at some 'liveable' level and payable to all citizens, is the most direct means of addressing income insecurity. Mitchell and Watts (2004) presented a detailed critical comparison of employment guarantees and income guarantees. In this section, their argument is summarised. In brief, they concluded that the BIG conception of income insecurity and unemployment is highly problematic. Key BIG advocates (for example, Belgian Phillipe Van Parijs) typically claim that unemployment is caused by wages being above the free market optimum. Trade unions and government minimum wage legislation is blamed for creating this scarcity of jobs. There is no recognition that mass unemployment is always the result of a deficiency of total spending in the economy. Further, the BIG proponents adopt the neo-liberal assumption that governments are financially constrained and thus propose to fund the income guarantees by taxing those who enjoy employment because their excessive wages deny the unemployed a chance to work. The unemployed are thus considered to be 'allowing' those in employment to enjoy being employed and as a result should be rewarded for their sacrifice.

The mainstream BIG proponents advocate the introduction within a 'fiscal neutral' environment in order to allay the criticism of the neo-liberals who eschew government deficits. One of the sensitive issues for BIG proponents is thus its perceived 'cost'. Under fiscal neutrality, the maximum sustainable BIG would be modest. Aggregate demand and employment impacts would be small and, even with some redistribution of working hours, high levels of labour underutilisation would persist. Overall this strategy does not enhance the rights of the most disadvantaged, nor does it provide work for those who desire it.

Persistent unemployment could be avoided if the BIG was sufficient to motivate the unemployed to drop out of the labour force and take the income guarantee. This would require a substantial government stimulus (deficit). But then the implied concept of full employment is bizarre. Mass unemployment would be solved by engineering an artificial withdrawal of the available labour supply, so that some of the unemployed are reclassified as not in the labour force and in receipt of a basic income allotment.

But then a further quandary emerges. The more generous BIG would probably stimulate total spending such that there would be a shortage of labour at 'full employment', resulting from the artificial reduction of the full employment level of employment, which then compounds the inflationary pressure. The alternative is that the excess demand for goods would be increasingly met via imports with consequential effects for the exchange rate and the domestic price level, which would accentuate the inflationary pressure.

In contradistinction, the JG creates a buffer employment capacity in the economy by hiring at a fixed price in exchange for hours of work and does not compete with private sector wages. Employment redistributions between the private sector and the buffer stock can always be achieved to stabilise any wage inflation in the non-JG sector. The JG addresses the problem of unemployment at its root cause, a lack of jobs. The solution is direct: provide as many jobs as are required.

There is an additional and important contrast to be drawn between employment guarantees and income guarantees. The JG is predicated on the view that participation in work remains central to our identity and independence, and persistent unemployment remains the central cause of social exclusion. The benefits of work go well beyond the provision of income. Individuals achieve social standing from work, and the social networks that emerge through workplaces provide many of the opportunities that define the quality of life. Further, the JG recognises that work remains intrinsic to human existence. Humans seek to transform nature to live. Certainly, history has evolved to the stage where the organisation of that effort under capitalism is oppressive and the anathema of liberation, despite the wage form making it look as though we have freedom to choose. But we need to separate the specific form of work organisation from the intrinsic meaning of work for people. Most unemployed workers indicate in surveys that they prefer to work rather than be provided with income support.

If the vast majority of workers prefer to work then the systemic failure to provide a sufficient quantum of jobs imposes harsh costs that can be reduced by the introduction of a JG. In this regard, the JG is a source of freedom from the oppression of unemployment, the capitalist property relations notwithstanding.

The future of paid work is clearly an important debate. The traditional moral views about the virtues of work, which are exploited by the capitalist class, need to be recast. Clearly, social policy can play a part in engendering this debate and help establish transition dynamics. However, it is likely that a non-capitalist system of work and income generation is needed before the yoke of the work ethic and the stigmatisation of non-work is fully expunged.

In contradistinction, while the introduction of a BIG has superficial appeal in that it allows individuals to subsist without work, the approach effectively denies these social (non-income) aspects of work. BIG individuals are reduced to being 'consumption' units. The government's responsibilities are limited to providing these workers with enough income to allow them to maintain some basic consumption levels. Payment of a BIG would signify a further withdrawal by the State from its responsibility to manage economic affairs and care for its citizens by ensuring that there were sufficient jobs for all. Young people must be encouraged to develop skills and engage in paid work rather than be the passive recipients of social security benefit. The failure to ensure there is enough paid work excludes the unemployed from participating in economic, social and cultural life, which has highly detrimental consequences. There are substantial social benefits that arise from the provision of stable work with decent wages, health and retirement benefits.

Further, with job opportunities declining due to technological change, a central question is to determine how society can broaden the definition of productive work and reduce the stigma of not being engaged in traditional work. BIG advocates consider their approach provides for this transition but it is hard to see how the stigma of being unemployed disappears when one is not working and receiving an income guarantee. Clearly, there is a need to embrace a broader concept of work in the first phase of decoupling work and income. However, current social norms are unlikely to digest this new culture of non-work very easily. The patent resentment of the unemployed will only be transferred to the 'surfers on Malibu' (Van Parijs' model BIG recipient)! By way of contrast, the JG would provide a means to establish a new employment paradigm where community development and other non-traditional jobs would become valued. Over time, and within this new JG employment paradigm, public debate and education can help broaden the concept of valuable work until activities which we might construe today as being 'leisure' would become considered to be 'gainful' employment. Ultimately, struggling musicians, artists, surfers, thespians, and the like, could be working within the JG. In return for the income security, the surfer might be required to conduct water safety awareness for school children; and musicians might be required to rehearse some days a week in school halls and thus impart knowledge about band dynamics and increase the appreciation of music to young school children. Thinking laterally a bit more, community activism could become a JG job. For example, organising and managing a community garden to provide food for the poor could be considered a paid job. We would see more of this sort of beneficial activity if it were rewarded in this way.

In other words, society can begin to re-define the concept of productive work well beyond the realms of 'gainful work' which, in current parlance, specifically relates to activities that generate private profits for firms. Over time, productivity would become more of a social, shared, public concept, and only limited by one's imagination. In this way, the JG would be an evolutionary force, which provides income security to those who want it, but also allows us to broaden the very concept of work!

Social attitudes take time to evolve and are best reinforced by changes in the educational system. The social fabric must be rebuilt over time. The change in the mode of production through evolutionary means will not happen overnight, and concepts of community wealth and civic responsibility that have been eroded over time, by the divide and conquer individualism of the neo-liberal era, have to be restored. The traditional moral views about the virtues of work, which are exploited by the capitalist class, need to be recast. Clearly, social policy can play a part in engendering this debate and help establish transition dynamics. However, it is likely that a non-capitalist system of work and income generation is needed before the capitalist work ethic and the stigmatisation of non-work is fully expunged.

The BIG approach creates a dependency on passive welfare payments and hence a stigmatised cohort. It also treats people who are unable to find adequate market-based work as 'consumption' entities and is satisfied to meet their basic consumption needs. However, the intrinsic social and capacity-building role of participating in paid work is ignored and hence undervalued. It is sometimes said that beyond all the benefits in terms of self-esteem, social inclusion, confidence building, skill augmentation and the like, a priceless benefit of creating full employment through job creation is that the 'children see at least one parent going to work each morning'. In other words, it creates an intergenerational stimulus that the BIG approach can never create.

Unlike the BIG model, the JG model meets these conditions within the constraints of a monetary capitalist system. It is a far better vehicle to rebuild a sense of community and the purposeful nature of work. It is the only real alternative if intergenerational disadvantage is to be avoided. It also provides the framework whereby the concept of work itself can be broadened to include activities that many would currently dismiss as being leisure. The JG also allows for capacity building by integrating training and skills development into the paid work environment.

References

Abeille, G. (2010) 'A l'origine du déficit à 3% du PIB, une invention 100% . . . française', *La Tribune*, 1 October.

AfDB/OECD (2003) *African Economic Outlook 2003/2004*, Paris, African Development Bank and Organisation for Economic Co-operation and Development.

Allers, R. (2013) *The Challenges of European Integration (1966–1974)*, Luxembourg, Centre Virtuel de la Connaissance sur l'Europe.

American Broadcasting Company (ABC) (2010) 'Interview with Christine Lagarde', *This Week*, 10 October.

Andrews, E.L. (1997a) 'Germany Set to Revalue Gold Reserve', *New York Times*, 29 May.

Andrews, E.L. (1997b) 'German's Slick Bookkeeping to Meet Euro Goal is Scrapped', *New York Times*, 4 June.

Ariyoshi, A., Habermeier, K., Laurens, B., Otker-Robe, I., Iván Canales-Kriljenko, J. and Kirilenko, A. (2000) 'Capital Controls: Country Experiences with their Use and Liberalization', Occasional Paper 190, International Monetary Fund, 17 May.

Assemblee Nationale (1971) *Journal Officiel de la République Française, Debats Parlementaires*, 13 May.

Athanassiou, P. (2009) 'Withdrawal and Expulsion from the EU and EMU: Some Reflections', Legal Working Paper Series, European Central Bank, No. 10, December.

Australian Treasury (2009) 'The Return of Fiscal Policy', presentation to the Australian Business Economists Annual Forecasting Conference, Sydney, 8 December.

Ball, L. and Sheridan, N. (2003) 'Does Inflation Targeting Matter?', NBER Working Paper No. 9577, March.

Balladur, E. (1988) 'Mémorandum sur la construction monétaire européenne', *ECU*, No. 3, Brussels, March.

Balleix-Banerjee, C. (1997) 'La France et la Banque Centrale Européenne: débats politiques et élaboration de la décision, janvier 1988–septembre 1992', PhD thesis, University Panthéon-Assas, Paris II, 10 January.

Banco Central de la Republica Argentina (BCRA) (2007) 'Single Free Exchange Market (MULC) Transactions and the Foreign Exchange

Balance in the First Quarter of 2007', available at: http://www.bcra.gov.ar/pdfs/estadistica/MULC1trim07i.pdf, accessed 14 May 2014.
Bank of England (2014) 'Money Creation in the Modern Economy', *Quarterly Bulletin*, Quarter 1.
Bank of International Settlements (BIS) (1969) *Thirty-Ninth Annual Report*, Basel, 8 June.
Bank of International Settlements (BIS) (1970) *Fortieth Annual Report*, Basel, 8 June.
Bank of International Settlements (BIS) (1971) *Forty-First Annual Report*, Basel, 14 June.
Bank of International Settlements (BIS) (1972) *Forty-Second Annual Report*, Basel, 12 June.
Bank of International Settlements (BIS) (1973) *Forty-Third Annual Report*, Basel, 18 June.
Bank of International Settlements (BIS) (1974) *Forty-Fourth Annual Report*, Basel, 10 June.
Bank of International Settlements (BIS) (1980) *Fiftieth Annual Report*, Basel, 9 June.
Bank of International Settlements (BIS) (1985) *Fifty-Fifth Annual Report*, Basel, 10 June.
Bank of International Settlements (BIS) (1988) *58th Annual Report*, Basel, 13 June.
Barbash, J. (1982) 'The Guilds of Academe', *Challenge*, **25**(1), March–April, 50–54.
Barber, L. and Barber, T. (2008) 'Barroso warns on protectionist pressures', *The Financial Times*, 2 March.
Barre Report (1969) *Commission Memorandum to the Council on the Co-ordination of Economic Policies and Monetary Co-operation within the Community*, Secretariat of the Commission of the European Communities, Brussels, 12 February.
Barro, R.J. (1993) *Macroeconomics*, 4th edn, New York, Wiley.
Baun, M.J. (1996) 'The Maastricht Treaty as High Politics: Germany, France, and European Integration', *Political Science Quarterly*, **110**(4), 605–24.
Beder, S. (1999) 'The Intellectual Sorcery of Think Tanks', *Arena Magazine*, **41**, June/July, 30–32.
Bell, S. (2000) 'Do Taxes and Bonds Finance Government Spending?', *Journal of Economic Issues*, **34**(3), September, 603–20.
Berg, A.G. and Ostry, J.D. (2011) 'Inequality and Unsustainable Growth: Two Sides of the Same Coin?', *IMF Staff Discussion Note*, SDN/11/08, 8 April.
Bergman, U.M. (1999) 'Do Monetary Unions Make Economic Sense?

Evidence from the Scandinavian Currency Union, 1873–1913', *Scandinavian Journal of Economics*, **101**(3), 363–77.
Bergman, M., Gerlach, S. and Jonung, L. (1993) 'The Rise and Fall of the Scandinavian Currency Union 1873–1920', *European Economic Review*, **37**, 507–17.
Bergmann, C. (1927) *The History of Reparations*, Boston, Houghton Mifflin.
Bernanke, B. (2002) 'Deflation: Making Sure "It" Doesn't Happen Here', Speech to the National Economists Club, Washington, DC, 21 November.
Bernanke, B. (2004) 'The Great Moderation', speech presented to the Eastern Economic Association, Washington, DC, 20 February.
Beveridge, W. (1944) *Full Employment in a Free Society*, London, Allen and Unwin.
Beyer, A., Gaspar, V., Gerberding, C. and Issing, O. (2009) 'Opting out of the Great Inflation, German Monetary Policy After The Breakdown of Bretton Woods', ECB Working Paper Series No. 1020, Frankfurt am Main.
Bild (2010) 'Verkauft doch eure Inseln, ihr Pleite-Griechen', 27 October.
Bill, A., Mitchell, W.F. and Welters, R. (2007) 'Labour Reform and Labour Mobility within Cities: Have the Hartz Reforms Succeeded?', Working Paper No. 07-16, Centre of Full Employment and Equity, University of Newcastle.
Bindi, F. (2011) *Italy and the European Union*, Washington, DC, Brookings Institution Press.
Bindi, F. (2013) 'Even in Death, Giulio Andreotti Defeated Margaret Thatcher One Last Time', *The Huffington Post*, 5 July.
Bini-Smaghi, L., Padoa-Schioppa, T. and Papadia, F. (1994) 'The Transition to EMU in the Maastricht Treaty', *Essays in International Finance, No. 194*, November, Department of Economics, Princeton University.
Bitsch, M.-T. (2007) *La construction européenne: enjeux politiques et choix institutionnels*, Brussels, Paul Lang.
Blanchard, O.J. (1997) *Macroeconomics*, New York, Prentice Hall.
Blanchard, O. (2008) 'The State of Macro', NBER Working Paper No. 14259, National Bureau of Economic Research, August.
Blinder, A.S. (1987) *Hard Heads, Soft Hearts*, Reading, MA: Addison-Wesley.
Blinder, A.S. (1988) 'The Fall and Rise of Keynesian Economics', *Economic Record*, **64**(187), 278–94.
Blinder, A.S. (1989) *Macroeconomics Under Debate*, London, Harvester Wheatsheaf.

Blinder, A.S (2013) 'A Bold Approach to the Jobs Emergency', keynote addresses to the 'Rediscovering Government' Conference, Roosevelt Institute, Washington, DC, 4 June.

Blinder, A. (2014) 'How Government Wages War on the Poor', *The Wall Street Journal*, 13 January.

Blinder, A. and Zandi, M. (2010a) 'How the Great Recession Was Brought to an End', mimeo, Princeton University, 27 July.

Blinder, A. and Zandi, M. (2010b) 'Stimulus Worked', *Finance and Development*, December, 14–17.

Blyth, M. (2013) *Austerity: The History of a Dangerous Idea*, New York, Oxford University Press.

Board of Trustees (1982) *1982 Annual Report*, Board of Trustees, Federal Old-Age and Survivors Insurance and Disability Insurance Trust Funds.

Bofinger, P. (2003) 'The Stability and Growth Pact Neglects the Policy Mix between Fiscal and Monetary Policy', *Intereconomics*, **38**(1), 1–7.

Böll, S., Reiermann, C., Sauga, M. and Wiegrefe, K. (2012) 'Operation Self-Deceit: New Documents Shine Light on Euro Birth Defects', *Der Spiegel*, 8 May.

Boone, P. and Johnson, S. (2010) 'Irish Miracle – or Mirage?', *New York Times*, 20 May.

Bordo, M.D. and Jonung, L. (2003) 'The Future of EMU: What Does the History of Monetary Unions Tell Us?', in Capie, F.H. and Wood, G. (eds), *Monetary Unions: Theory, History, Public Choice: International Studies in Money and Banking, Vol. 18*, London, Routledge, pp. 42–69.

Bossone, B. (2013a) 'Time for the Eurozone to Shift Gear: Issuing Euros to Finance New Spending', *VoxEu*, 8 April.

Bossone, B. (2013b) 'Italy, Europe: Please Do Something!', *EconoMonitor*, 19 April.

Bossone, B. and Wood, R. (2013) 'Overt Money Financing of Fiscal Deficits: Navigating Article 123 of the Lisbon Treaty', *EconoMonitor*, 22 July.

Boughton, J.M. (2001) *Silent Revolution: The International Monetary Fund 1979–1989*, Washington, DC, International Monetary Fund.

British Broadcasting Corporation (BBC) (2002a) 'Not While I'm Alive, He Ain't – Part 4', transcript from *The Westminster Hour*, Sunday 21 April.

British Broadcasting Corporation (BBC) (2002b) 'Row Over "stupid" EU Budget Rules', 17 October 2002.

British Broadcasting Corporation (BBC) (2003) 'Chirac's Budget Plea Creates EU Storm', 15 July.

Buiter, W.H. (2006) 'The "Sense and Nonsense of Maastricht" Revisited:

What Have We Learnt about Stabilization in EMU?', *Journal of Common Market Studies*, **44**(4), 687–710.

Buiter, W.H. (2008) 'Can Central Banks Go Broke?', *Policy Insight, No. 24*, Centre of Economic Policy Research, May.

Buiter, W.H. (2009) 'The Unfortunate Uselessness of Most "State of the Art" Academic Monetary Economics', *The Financial Times*, 3 March.

Buiter, W.H. (2011) 'A Greek Exit from the Euro Area: A Disaster for Greece, a Crisis for the World', *Global Economics View*, Citigroup, 13 September.

Buiter, W.H. and Grafe, C. (2004) 'Patching Up the Pact: Suggestions for Enhancing Fiscal Sustainability and Macroeconomic Stability in an Enlarged European Union', *Economics of Transition*, **12**(1), 67–102.

Bundesbank (1968) *Monthly Report of the Deutsche Bundesbank*, November/December, Frankfurt am Main.

Bundesbank (1969) *Monthly Report of the Deutsche Bundesbank*, October, Frankfurt am Main.

Bundesbank (1971) *Monthly Report of the Deutsche Bundesbank*, May, Frankfurt am Main.

Bundesbank (1978a) *Monthly Report of the Deutsche Bundesbank*, February, Frankfurt am Main.

Bundesbank (1978b) 'Transcript of Meeting of the Bundesbank Council', 30 November, Frankfurt am Main.

Bundesbank (1979) *Monthly Report of the Deutsche Bundesbank*, January, Frankfurt am Main.

Bundesbank (1998) 'Stellungnahme des Zentralbankrates zur Konvergenzlage in der Europäischen Union im Hinblick auf die dritte Stufe der Wirtschafts- und Währungsunion', April, Frankfurt am Main.

Bundesbank (2011) 'The Debt Brake in Germany – Key Aspects and Implementation', *Monthly Report of the Deutsche Bundesbank*, October, Frankfurt am Main.

Bundesbankgesetz (1997) Sixth Act Amending the Bundesbank Act of 22 December 1997, *Federal Law Gazette*, p. 3274.

Buti, M., Eijffinger, S. and Franco, D. (2005) 'The Stability Pact Pains: A Forward-Looking Assessment of the Reform Debate', CEPR Working Paper, No. 5216.

Buti, M., Franco, D. and Ongena, H. (1997) 'Budgetary Policies during Recessions – Retrospective Application of the "Stability and Growth Pact" to the Post-War Period', *Economic Papers*, **121**, 1–33.

Caliendo, M. and Wrohlich, K. (2006) 'Evaluating the German "Mini-Job" Reform Using a Natural Experiment', Working Paper, German Institute for Economic Research (DIW), Berlin.

Cameron, D.R. (1997) 'Economic and Monetary Union: Transitional

Issues and Third-Stage Dilemmas', paper presented at European Policy Paper Series, 4.
Cangelosi, R. and Grassi, V. (1996) *Dalle comunità all'unione. Il trattato di Maastricht e la conferenza intergovernativa del 1996*, Milan, Franco Angeli.
Capie, F. (2010) *The Bank of England: 1950s to 1979*, New York, Cambridge University Press.
Capital Economics (2012) 'Leaving the Euro: A Practical Guide', submission for the Wolfson Economics Prize MMXII, 5–115.
Carchedi, G. (2001) *For Another Europe: A Class Analysis of European Economic Integration*, London, Verso.
Carli, G. (1993) *Cinquantíanni di vita Italiana*, Rome, Editori Laterza.
Case 95/81 (1982) *Commission v. Italy* [1982] ECR 2187, available at: http://eur-lex.europa.eu/LexUriServ/LexUriServ.do?uri=CELEX:61981CJ0095:EN:PDF, accessed 6 February 2014.
Casey, B.H. (2004) 'The OECD Jobs Strategy and the European Employment Strategy: Two Views of the Labour Market and of the Welfare State', *European Journal of Industrial Relations*, **10**(3), 329–53.
Cassidy, J. (2010) 'Interview with Eugene Fama', *The New Yorker*, 13 January.
Central Bank of Iceland (2008) *Economic Indicators*, September.
Central Bank of Iceland (2010) *Economy of Iceland 2010*, 6 October.
Central Statistics Office (CSO) (2013) 'Population and Migration Estimates', *CSO Statistical Release*, 29 August.
Centre of Full Employment and Equity (CofFEE) (2008) 'Creating Effective Local Labour Markets: A New Framework for Regional Employment Policy', University of Newcastle, November.
Cochrane, J. (2009) 'Fiscal Stimulus, Fiscal Inflation, or Fiscal Fallacies?', mimeo, 27 February.
Committee for the Monetary Union of Europe (1988) 'Report on Economic and Monetary Union in the European Community', Brussels.
Committee of Governors of the Central Banks (1971) 'Minutes of the 47th Meeting, 06/03/71 (Proces-Verbal)'.
Committee of Governors of the Central Banks (1987) 'Compte rendu de la rêunion du Comité des Gouverneurs du 8 septembre 1987 consacrée à la finalisation du rapport sur le renforcement du SHE', 10 September.
Committee on Banking and Currency (1935) Banking Act of 1935, Hearings before the Committee on Banking and Currency, House of Representatives, Seventy-Fourth Congress, First Session, H.R. 5357, Washington.
Committee on Economic and Monetary Affairs (2013a) 'Draft Report

on the European Central Bank Annual Report for 2012', European Parliament, ECON/7/12316, 11 June.

Committee on Economic and Monetary Affairs (2013b) 'Amendments 1-247 – Draft Report on the European Central Bank Annual Report for 2012', European Parliament, ECON/7/12316, 12 July.

Committee on Economic and Monetary Affairs (2013c) 'Report on the European Central Bank Annual Report for 2012', European Parliament, ECON/7/12316, 13 November.

Confederation of Zimbabwe Industries (2009) *Manufacturing Sector Survey 2009*.

Congressional Budget Office (CBO) (2011) 'Estimated Impact of the American Recovery and Reinvestment Act on Employment and Economic Output from October 2010 through December 2010', Washington, DC, February.

Connors, L. and Mitchell, W.F. (2013) 'Framing Modern Monetary Theory', in Wrightson, G. (ed.), *Reconstructing the Full Employment Narrative*, '14th Path to Full Employment Conference' and '19th National Conference on Unemployment', December, pp. 22–40.

Cowan, B. (2009) 'Leaders' Questions', *Dáil Eireann Debate*, **677**(4), 11 March, p. 4.

Crooks, E. (2003) 'Europe's Stability Pact: EU May Yet Feel the Bite of the Paper Tiger', *The Financial Times*, 26 November.

Crooks, E. and Parker, G. (2003) 'The Growth and Stability Pact May Not Be Mourned by Many But the Eurozone Needs Fiscal Discipline', *The Financial Times*, 27 November.

Daily Dish (2010) 'Is the UK Worse than Greece?', *The Atlantic*, 3 May.

Dalsgaard, T. and de Serres, A. (2000) 'Estimating Prudent Budgetary Margins for EU Countries: A Simulated SVAR Model Approach', *OECD Economic Studies*, **30**, 115–47.

Danescu, E.R. (2013a) 'Economists v. Monetarists – Agreement and Clashes in the Drafting of the Werner Report', Centre Virtuel de la Connaissance sur l'Europe, Luxembourg.

Danescu, E.R. (2013b) 'The Werner Report in the International Media of the Time', Centre Virtuel de la Connaissance sur l'Europe, Luxembourg.

Danescu, E.R. (2013c) 'The Werner Report and the Delors Report,' Centre Virtuel de la Connaissance sur l'Europe, Luxembourg.

Danescu, E.R. (2014a) 'Pierre Werner's Appointment as Chairman of the Committee of Experts – Three Different Accounts', Centre Virtuel de la Connaissance sur l'Europe, Luxembourg.

Danescu, E.R. (2014b) 'The Work of the Werner Committee', Centre Virtuel de la Connaissance sur l'Europe, Luxembourg.

Danescu, E.R. (2014c) 'The Difficulties of the Monetary Snake and the EMCF', Centre Virtuel de la Connaissance sur l'Europe, Luxembourg.

Darvas, Z., Pisani-Ferry, J. and Sapir, A. (2011) 'A Comprehensive Approach to the Euro-Area Debt Crisis', *Bruegel Policy Brief*, 2011/02, February.

De Boissieu, C. and Pisani-Ferry, J. (1995) 'The Political Economy of French Economic Policy in the Perspective of EMU', *Document de travail no. 95-09*, Centre d'Etudes Prospectives et d'Informations Internationales, October.

De Cecco, M. (2007) 'Italy's Dysfunctional Political Economy', *West European Politics*, **30**(4), 763–83.

De Grauwe, P. (2003) *The Stability and Growth Pact In Need of Reform*, CEPS.

De Grauwe, P. (2006) 'What Have We Learnt about Monetary Integration since the Maastricht Treaty?', *Journal of Common Market Studies*, **44**(4), 711–30.

De Grauwe, P. (2013) 'Debt Without Drowning', *Project Syndicate*, 9 May.

De Grauwe, P. and Yuemei Ji, Y. (2013) 'Panic-Driven Austerity in the Eurozone and its Implications', *Voxeu*, 21 February.

Della Sala, V. (1997) 'Hollowing Out and Hardening the State: European Integration and the Italian Economy', *West European Politics*, **20**(1), 14–33.

DeLong, J.B. (2002) *Macroeconomics*, Burr Ridge, IL: McGraw-Hill Higher Education.

Delors, J. (1989a) 'Regional Implications of Economic and Monetary Integration', in European Commission (1989b) *Collection of Papers Submitted to the Committee for the Study of Economic and Monetary Union*, pp. 80–89.

Delors, J. (1989b) 'Address at the College of Europe, Bruges, October 17, 1989', Centre Virtuel de la Connaissance sur l'Europe, Luxembourg.

Delors, J. (1991) 'The Principle of Subsidiarity: Contribution to the Debate', in *Subsidiarity: The Challenge of Change, Proceedings of the Jacques Delors Colloquium*, Maastricht, European Institute of Public Administration, pp. 7–18.

Delors Report (1989a and b), see European Commission (1989a and b).

Delpla, J. and von Weizsäcker, J. (2010) 'The Blue Bond Proposal', *Bruegel Policy Brief*, Issue 2010/03, 6 May.

Democracy Now! (2007) 'The Conscience of a Liberal: New York Times Columnist Paul Krugman on Healthcare, Tax Cuts, Social Security, the Mortgage Crisis and Alan Greenspan', 17 October.

Der Spiegel (2009) 'New Idea to Keep Unemployment Down: Germany

Mulls "Parking" Unwanted Labor in New State-Funded Firms', 14 April.
Der Spiegel (2011) 'Saving the Euro: Germany's Central Bank against the World', 15 November.
Deutscher Bundestag (1970) *Drucksachen und Plenarprotokolle des Bundestages, Plenarprotokoll Nr. 06/77*, 6 November.
Deutscher Bundestag (1989) 'Zehn-Punkte-Programm 1989', *Streifzug durch die Geschichte*.
Deutscher Bundestag (1995) 'Stenographischer Bericht Plenarprotokoll 13/66', Bonn, 7 November.
DeWitt, L. (2005) 'Research Note #20: The Social Security Trust Funds and the Federal Budget', *Research Notes and Special Studies by the Historian's Office*, US Social Security Administration.
Die Zeit (1971a) 'Die Dollar-Krise wird bedrohlich', 13 August.
Die Zeit (1971b) 'Report Aus Bonn', 27 August.
Donadio, R. and Kitsantonis, N. (2011) 'Greek Leader Calls Off Referendum on Bailout Plan', *New York Times*, 3 November.
Dostal, J.M. (2004) 'Campaigning on Expertise: How the OECD Framed EU Welfare and Labour Market Policies – And Why Success Could Trigger Failure', *Journal of European Public Policy*, **11**(3), June, 440–60.
Douzinas, C. (2012) 'What Now for Greece – Collapse or Resurrection?', *The Guardian*, 5 March.
Duchaussoy, V. (2010) 'De la relance à la rigueur La Banque de France et le début de l'ère Mitterrand (1981–1983)', *La Lettre No. 32*, Institute François Mitterrand, 22 June.
Duisenberg, W.F. (1989) 'The ECU as a Parallel Currency', in European Commission (1989b) *Collection of Papers Submitted to the Committee for the Study of Economic and Monetary Union*, pp. 185–89.
Duisenberg, W.F. (2003) 'Presentation of the ECB's Annual Report 2002 to the European Parliament', Strasbourg, 3 July.
Dunbar, N. and Martinuzzi, E. (2012) 'Goldman Secret Greece Loan Shows Two Sinners as Client Unravels', *Bloomberg News*, 6 March.
Dyson, K. (1994) *Elusive Union: The Process of Economic and Monetary Union in Europe*, London, Longman.
Dyson, K. and Featherstone, K. (1996) 'Italy and EMU as Vincolo Esterno: Empowering the Technocrats, Transforming the State', *South European Society and Politics*, **1**(2), 272–99.
Easterly, W. (2000) 'The Effect of IMF and World Bank Programs on Poverty', *World Bank*, 31 October.
Economic and Social Committee (1991) 'Additional Opinion of the Economic and Social Committee on Economic and Monetary Union', Brussels, 21 February.

Eichengreen, B.J. (1992) 'Should the Maastricht Treaty be Saved?', *Princeton Studies in International Finance*, **74**, December.

Eichengreen, B.J. (1997) 'Saving Europe's Automatic Stabilisers', *National Institute Economic Review*, **159**(1), 92–98.

Eichengreen, B.J. (2007) *The European Economy Since 1945: Coordinated Capitalism and Beyond*, Princeton, NJ, Princeton University Press.

Eichengreen, B.J. (2010) 'The Breakup of the Euro Area', in Alesina, A. and Giavazzi, F. (eds) *Europe and the Euro*, National Bureau of Economic Research, Chicago, University of Chicago Press, pp. 11–51.

Eichengreen, B. and Wyplosz, C. (1993) 'The Unstable EMS', *Brookings Papers on Economic Activity*, **1**, 51–143.

Einaudi, L. (2000) 'From the Franc to the "Europe": The Attempted Transformation of the Latin Monetary Union into a European Monetary Union, 1865–1873', *Economic History Review*, **53**(2), 284–308.

Ekathimerini (2014) 'Geithner Describes Alarm at Schaeuble Plan for Greek Euro Exit in New Book', 14 May.

Elliot, L. (2010) 'IMF Has One Cure for Debt Crises – Public Spending Cuts with Tax Rises', *The Observer*, 9 May.

Elliot, L. (2012) '€130bn Plaster Leaves Greece Independent in Name Only', *The Guardian*, 21 February.

Elliot, L., Hutton, W. and Wolf, J. (1992) 'September 17 1992: Pound Drops Out of ERM', *The Guardian*, 17 September.

Emminger, O. (1978) 'Stellungnahme des Zentralbankrats zum künftigen EWS', 16 November, Deutsche Bundesbank.

EMU Group (1990) 'Minutes EMU Group Meeting, Tuesday 19th June', Brussels, European Commission.

Enderlein, H., Bofinger, P., Boone, L., de Grauwe, P., Piris, J.-C., Pisani-Ferry, J., Rodrigues, M.J., Sapir, A. and Vitorino, A. (2012) 'Completing the Euro. A Road Map towards Fiscal Union in Europe', *Notre Europe*, Jacques Delors Institute, June.

Endo, K. (2001) 'Subsidiarity and its Enemies: To What Extent is Sovereignty Contested in the Mixed Commonwealth of Europe?', EUI Working Papers, RSC No. 2001/24, Robert Schuman Centre for Advanced Studies, European University Institute.

EurActiv (2010) 'Theo Waigel: Greek Crisis Exposed EU Weaknesses', 13 September.

Eurofound (2012a) 'Youth Guarantee: Experiences from Finland and Sweden', 12 June.

Eurofound (2012b) 'Young People Not in Employment, Education or Training: Characteristics, Costs and Policy Responses in Europe', 22 October.

European Central Bank (ECB) (2005) 'Statement of the Governing Council on the ECOFIN Council's Report on Improving the Implementation of the Stability and Growth Pact', 21 March.

European Central Bank (ECB) (2008) *1998–2008: Monthly Bulletin 10th Anniversary of the ECB*, Frankfurt am Main.

European Central Bank (ECB) (2010a) *Monthly Bulletin June*, Frankfurt am Main.

European Central Bank (ECB) (2010b) 'Decision of the European Central Bank of 14 May 2010 Establishing a Securities Markets Programme', *Official Journal of the European Union*, L 124/8, 20 May.

European Central Bank (ECB) (2012a) *Monthly Bulletin May*, Frankfurt am Main.

European Central Bank (ECB) (2012b) 'Opinion of the European Central Bank of 24 January 2012 on a Guarantee Scheme for the Liabilities of Italian Banks and on the Exchange of Lira Banknotes', CON/2012/4, Frankfurt am Main.

European Central Bank (ECB) (2012c) 'Annual Report 2012', Frankfurt am Main.

European Central Bank (ECB) (2014a) 'Introductory Statement to the Press Conference (with Q&A)', Mario Draghi, President of the ECB, Frankfurt am Main, 3 April.

European Central Bank (ECB) (2014b) 'ELA Procedures', Frankfurt am Main.

European Central Bank (ECB) (2014c) 'Capital Subscription', available at: https://www.ecb.europa.eu/ecb/orga/capital/html/index.en.html, accessed 1 May 2014.

European Commission (1970a) *Report to the Council and the Commission on the Realization by Stages of Economic and Monetary Union in the Community*, Luxembourg, 8 October, also known as the Werner Report.

European Commission (1970b) 'Communications et informations', *Journal officiel des Communautés européennes*, 13e année, no. C151, 27 December.

European Commission (1970c) 'The Summit Conference' at the Hague, Statements made by the Heads of State or Government on 2 December 1969, reproduced from the *Bulletin of the European Communities*, **12**, Brussels.

European Commission (1971) 'Résolution du Conseil et des représentants des gouvernements des États membres, du 22 mars 1971, concernant la réalisation par étapes de l'union économique et monétaire dans la Communauté', *Journal officiel des Communautés européennes*, 14e année, no. C28, 27 March.

European Commission (1972) 'Resolution concernant la réalisation par étapes de l'union économique et monétaire dans la Communauté', *Journal officiel des Communautés européennes*, 15e année, no. C38, 18 April, pp. 0003–0004.

European Commission (1973a) 'Regulation (EEC) No. 907/73 of the Council of 3 April 1973 Establishing a European Monetary Cooperation Fund', *Official Journal* L089, 5 April, pp. 0002–0005.

European Commission (1973b) 'EC Monetary Cooperations Fund Begins Operations', European Community Information Service, 6 April, available at: http://aei.pitt.edu/43306/1/123.pdf, accessed 28 January 2014.

European Commission (1973c) 'European Monetary Cooperation Fund: Increase in Credit Potential and Joint Management of Reserves', Memo by the Italian Members, EC Monetary Committee, 2 March.

European Commission (1974) 'Compensatory Monetary Amounts, the Monetary Crisis and Common Agricultural Policy', *Common Agricultural Policy Digests, No. 25–26*, April–May, European Commission and Ministry of Agriculture and Rural Development, France.

European Commission (1977) *Report of the Study Group on the Role of Public Finance in European Integration*, Volume 1: General Report, Brussels, April, also known as the MacDougall Report.

European Commission (1989a) *Report on Economic and Monetary Union in the European Community*, Brussels, 17 April, also known as the Delors Report.

European Commission (1989b) *Collection of Papers Submitted to the Committee for the Study of Economic and Monetary Union*, 17 April, also known as the Delors Report Appendix.

European Commission (1989c) 'Preparatory Document for the "Guigou" High-Level Group on EMU', 15 September.

European Commission (1989d) 'Compte rendu de la réunion du groupe ad hoc UEM (Guigou)', 25 September.

European Commission (1990a) 'One Market, One Money. An Evaluation of the Potential Benefits and Costs of Forming an Economic and Monetary Union', *European Economy*, **44**, October.

European Commission (1990b) 'European Parliament, Rapid Information Note, SP (91) 2669, 21–25 October 1991 Plenary Session', 25 October.

European Commission (1991a) 'Resuming Progress Towards Convergence of Economic Policies and Performances in the Community', SEC (91) 1291 final, Brussels, 4 July.

European Commission (1991b) *Economic and Monetary Union: Europe on the Move 1991*, Brussels, European Commission.

European Commission (1991c) 'Intergovernmental Conferences:

Contributions by the Commission', *Bulletin of the European Communities*, Supplement 2/91, Luxembourg, also known as the Christophersen Report.
European Commission (1993a) 'Stable Money – Sound Finances. Community Public Finance in the Perspective of EMU', *European Economy*, **53**, January.
European Commission (1993b) 'The Economics of Community Public Finance', *European Economy – Reports and Studies*, No. 5.
European Commission (1999) *Pierre Werner – Testimonies at the Threshold of the 21st Century*, documentary film produced by European Commission, Brussels.
European Commission (2002a) 'Commission Assesses the German Stability Programme Update (2001–2005)', Brussels, 30 January.
European Commission (2002b) '6108/02 (Presse 28)', 2407th Council Meeting, ECOFIN, Brussels, 12 February.
European Commission (2002c) 'Report from the Commission: Excessive Deficit in Germany', Report prepared in accordance with article 104, paragraph 3 of the Treaty, SEC (2002) 1245 final, Brussels, 19 November.
European Commission (2003a) 'Recommendation for a Council Decision on the Existence of an Excessive Deficit in Germany – Application of Article 104(6) of the Treaty Establishing the European Community', SEC (2003) 9 final, Brussels, 8 January.
European Commission (2003b) 'Recommendation for a Council Recommendation to Germany with a View to Bringing an End to the Situation of an Excessive Government Deficit – Application of Article 104(7) of the Treaty', SEC (2003) 10 final, Brussels, 8 January.
European Commission (2003c) 'Recommendation for a Council Decision Giving Notice to Germany, in Accordance with Article 104(9) of the EC Treaty, to Take Measures for Deficit Reduction Judged Necessary in Order to Remedy the Situation of Excessive Deficit', SEC (2003) 1317 final, Brussels, 11 November.
European Commission (2003d) 'Report from the Commission: Excessive Deficit in France', Report prepared in accordance with Article 104(3) of the Treaty, ECFIN/91/03-EN, Brussels, 28 March.
European Commission (2003e) 'Commission Opinion on the Existence of an Excessive Deficit in France, Application of Article 104(5) of the Treaty Establishing the European Community', SEC (2003) 514 final, Brussels, 7 May.
European Commission (2004a) 'Strengthening Economic Governance and Clarifying the Implementation of the Stability and Growth Pact', COM (2004) 0581 final, Brussels, 3 September.

European Commission (2004b) 'Towards a European Governance Strategy for Fiscal Statistics', COM (2004) 832 final, Brussels, 22 December.
European Commission (2005a) 'Public Finances in EMU 2005', *European Economy*, No. 3, Brussels.
European Commission (2005b) 'Stability and Growth Pact Reform: Commission Welcomes Agreement on New Regulations', Press Release, IP/05/798, Brussels, 27 June.
European Commission (2008) 'Autumn Economic Forecast 2008–2010', IP/08/1617, Brussels, 3 November.
European Commission (2009) *Building Parliament: 50 Years of European Parliament History 1958–2008*, Luxembourg.
European Commission (2011) 'EU Economic Governance "Six-Pack" Enters into Force', MEMO/11/898, Brussels, 12 December.
European Commission (2012a) 'Scoreboard for the Surveillance of Macroeconomic Imbalances', Occasional Papers No. 92, Brussels, February.
European Commission (2012b) 'Consolidated Versions of the Treaty on European Union and the Treaty on the Functioning of the European Union', *Official Journal of the European Union*, Volume 55, C326, 26 October.
European Commission (2012c) 'Youth Employment: Commission Proposes Package of Measures', Press Release, 5 December.
European Commission (2012d) 'Proposal for a Council Recommendation on Establishing a Youth Guarantee', *Commission Staff Working Document*, COM (2012) 729, 5 December.
European Commission (2012e) *EU Budget 2012, Financial Report*, Luxembourg.
European Commission (2013) 'Statement by the European Commission on Portugal', MEMO/13/307, Brussels, 7 April.
European Commission (2014a) 'The Corrective Arm', available at: http://ec.europa.eu/economy_finance/economic_governance/sgp/corrective_arm/index_en.htm, accessed 9 April 2014.
European Commission (2014b) 'Alert Mechanism Report 2014', COM (2014) 150, Brussels, 3 March.
European Commission (2014c) 'Leaflet – The Youth Guarantee: Making It Happen', Brussels, April.
European Council (1970) 'Final Communiqué of the Conference of Heads of State or Government on 1 and 2 December 1969 at the Hague', *Bulletin of the European Communities*, Supplement 7/1970, 18–19.
European Council (1978a) 'The Results of the European Council in

Bremen, 6–7 July 1978', *Bulletin of the European Communities*, No. 6, 17–21.
European Council (1978b) 'Conclusions of the Sessions of the European Council, Brussels, 4 and 5 December 1978', *Bulletin of the European Communities*, No. 12, 113–21.
European Council (1978c) 'The European Council in Brussels – Outcome and Follow-Up', *Bulletin of the European Communities*, No. 12, 7–14.
European Council (1979) 'Conclusions of the Presidency of the European Council', Final, Brussels, 5 December 1978.
European Council (1983) 'Decision 83/298/EEC of 16 May 1983 Concerning a Community Loan in Favour of the French Republic', *Official Journal of the European Communities*, L153/44, 11 June, p. 0044–45.
European Council (1986) 'Compendium of Community Monetary Text', Monetary Committee, Brussels.
European Council (1987) 'Report by the Chairman of the Alternates', Monetary Committee Annexe, 7 September.
European Council (1988) 'Conclusions of the Presidency', European Council, Rhodes, 2 and 3 December.
European Council (1989a) 'Conclusions of the Presidency', European Council, Madrid, 26 and 27 June.
European Council (1989b) 'Conclusions of the Presidency', European Council, Strasbourg, 8 and 9 December.
European Council (1990a) 'Requirements for the Achievement of Closer Convergence of Public Finance in the Member States', Economic Policy Committee, Brussels, 22 May.
European Council (1990b) 'Conclusions of the Presidency', European Council, Rome, 27–28 October.
European Council (1990c) 'Monetary and Fiscal Policy in the EMU: Contribution of the Italian Treasury to the Debate in the Monetary Committee', Monetary Committee, Brussels, 1 March.
European Council (1991) 'Report by the Alternates on the Excessive-Deficit Procedure', Monetary Committee, Brussels, 12 April.
European Council (1992) 'Conclusions of the Presidency', European Council, Edinburgh, 11 and 12 December.
European Council (1995a) 'Conclusions of the Presidency', European Council, Cannes, 26 and 27 June.
European Council (1995b) 'Conclusions of the Presidency', European Council, Madrid, 15–16 December.
European Council (1995c) 'Press Release', Press: 341, Nr 12026/95, European Council Economic and Financial Affairs Committee (Ecofin), Brussels.

European Council (1996) 'Conclusions of the Presidency', European Council, Dublin, 13 and 14 December 1996.
European Council (1997a) 'Press Release: 1994th Council Meeting – ECOFIN – Brussels', 17 March.
European Council (1997b) 'Conclusions of the Presidency', European Council, Amsterdam, 16 and 17 June.
European Council (1997c) 'Resolution of the European Council on the Stability and Growth Pact Amsterdam, 17 June 1997', *Official Journal of European Community*, C236, 2 August, p. 0001–0002.
European Council (2000) 'Presidency Conclusions, Lisbon European Council', 23–24 March.
European Council (2003a) 'Council Recommendation with a View to Bringing an End to the Situation of an Excessive Government Deficit in Germany – Application of Article 104(7) of the Treaty', 5540/03 ECOFIN 23, UEM 32, Brussels, 28 January.
European Council (2003b) 'Council Decision on the Existence of an Excessive Deficit in France, Application of Article 104(6) of the Treaty Establishing the European Community', *Official Journal of the European Union*, L165/29, 3 June.
European Council (2003c) '2546th Council Meeting, Economic and Financial Affairs', Council Press Release, 14492/1/03 REV 1 (en) (Presse 320), Brussels, 25 November.
European Council (2005) 'Improving the Implementation of the Stability and Growth Pact', 7423/05, UEM 97 ECOFIN 104, Brussels, 21 March.
European Council (2010) 'Statement by the Heads of State and Government of the Euro Area', Brussels, 25 March.
European Council (2011) 'Statement by the Heads of State or Government of the Euro Area and EU Institutions', 23 July.
European Council (2013) 'Council Recommendation of 22 April 2013 on Establishing a Youth Guarantee', *Official Journal of the European Union*, C120/1, Brussels, 26 April.
European Court of Justice (2004) 'Press Release No. 57/04', 13 July.
European Monetary Institute (1998) 'Convergence Report', March.
European Parliament (1989) 'Minutes of the Sitting of Friday, 14 April 1989', *Official Journal of the European Communities*, No. C95/1, 17 April.
European Parliament (1990) 'Minutes of the Sitting of Wednesday, October 10, 1990', *Official Journal of the European Communities*, No. C284/01, 12 November.
European Parliament (1994) 'Resolution on the Constitution of the European Union', *Official Journal of the European Communities*, No. C61, 28 February.

European Union (2012a) 'Consolidated Versions of the Treaty on European Union and the Treaty on the Functioning of the European Union', *Official Journal of the European Union*, No. C326, Volume 55, 26 October.

European Union (2012b) 'Treaty on Stability, Coordination and Governance in the Economic and Monetary Union', available at: http://www.lexnet.dk/law/download/fiscal-c/Scg-2012.pdf, accessed 26 December 2014.

Eurostat (2014a) 'Euro Area Annual Inflation Down to 0.5%', *Flash Estimate March 2014*, published 31 March.

Eurostat (2014b) 'Euro Area Unemployment Rate at 11.9%', February, published 1 April.

Evert, H. and Neumann, P. (2009) 'Tarifparteien fordern Staatsgeld gegen Jobkrise', *Die Welt*, 14 April.

Ewing, J. (2010) 'Central Banker Takes a Chance by Speaking Out', *New York Times*, 1 November.

Fauvet, J. (1979) 'Dix ans de montants compensatoires', *Le Monde*, 8 March.

Federal Law Gazette I (2010) *Basic Law for the Federal Republic of Germany in the Revised Version Published in the Federal Law Gazette Part III*, classification number 100-1, as last amended by the Act of 21 July 2010 (Federal Law Gazette I, p. 944).

Federal Reserve Bank (2007a) 'Press Release', 7 August.

Federal Reserve Bank (2007b) 'Press Release', 10 August.

Federal Reserve Bank (2007c) 'Press Release', 17 August.

Federal Reserve Bank of New York (FRBNY) (2008) 'Divorcing Money from Monetary Policy', *Economic Policy Review*, September, 41–56.

Feldman, G. (1997) *The Great Disorder: Politics, Economics and Society 1914–1924*, Oxford, Oxford University Press.

Ferreira do Amaral, J.F. (2013) *Porque Devemos Sair do Euro*, Lisbon, Lua de Papel.

Fitoussi, J.P., Atkinson, A.B., Blanchard, O., Flemming, J., Malinvaud, E., Phelps, E.S. and Solow, R. (1993) *Competitive Disinflation. The Mark and Budgetary Politics in Europe*, Oxford, Oxford University Press.

Fitoussi, J.P. and Saraceno, F. (2004) 'The Brussels–Frankfurt–Washington Consensus: Old and New Tradeoffs in Economics', *Document de Travail 2004-02*, Paris, Observatoire Français des Conjunctures Economiques.

Flandreau, M. (1995) 'Was the Latin Union a Franc Zone?', in Reis, J. (ed.) *The International Monetary System in Historical Perspective*, London, Macmillan, pp. 71–90.

Flandreau, M. (2000) 'The Economics and Politics of Monetary Unions: A Reassessment of the Latin Monetary Union, 1865–71', *Financial History Review*, **7**(1), 25–43.

Flandreau, M. and Maurel, M. (2005) 'Monetary Union, Trade Integration and Business Cycles in 19th-Century Europe', *Open Economies Review*, **16**, 135–52.

Food and Agriculture Organisation (FAO) (2001) 'Food Supply Situation Tightening in Southern Africa', *Africa Report No. 3*, United Nations, December.

Frankel, J. and Rose, A. (1998) 'The Endogeneity of the Optimum Currency Area Criteria', *Economic Journal*, **108**, 1009–25.

Frankfurter Allgemeine Zeitung (FAZ) (1994) 'Nur zwei Länder erfüllen die Maastricht-Kriterien', 15 February.

Frankfurter Allgemeine Zeitung (FAZ) (2012) 'Die Angst vor der Inflation', 23 September.

Fratianni, M. (2000) 'The International Monetary System after the Euro', in Prakash, A. and Hart, J.A. (eds) *Responding to Globalization*, London and New York, Routledge, pp. 151–70.

French Planning Office (1950) 'Neuvième projet pour le Plan Schuman (projet définitif)', 6 May, available at: http://www.let.leidenuniv.nl/pdf/geschiedenis/eu-history/EU_05.doc, accessed 15 January 2014.

Friedman, M. (1948) 'A Monetary and Fiscal Framework for Economic Stability', *American Economic Review*, **38**, June, 245–64.

Friedman, M. (1959a) 'Statement and Testimony', Joint Economic Committee, 86th US Congress, 1st Session, 25 May.

Friedman, M. (1959b) *A Program for Monetary Stability*, New York, Fordham University Press.

Friedman, M. (1968) 'The Role of Monetary Policy', *American Economic Review*, **58**(1), 1–17.

Friedman, M. (1969) *The Optimum Quantity of Money, and Other Essays*, Chicago, Aldinc Publishing Company.

Friend, J.W. (2001) *Unequal Partners: French–German Relations, 1989–2000*, Westport, CT, Praeger Publishers Inc.

Fuerxer, J. (2003) *Raymond Barre à la loupe: Le barrisme est-il une des facettes du libéralisme?*, Tomc I, Editions Le Manuscrit.

Fuller, T. (2003) 'France Defends its Flouting of Europe's Rules on Deficits', *New York Times*, 28 August.

G20 (2009) 'G20 Leaders Statement', The Pittsburgh Summit, 24–25 September.

G20 (2010a) 'G20 Toronto Summit Declaration', 26–27 June.

G20 (2010b) 'Communiqué, Meeting of Finance Ministers and Central Bank Governors', Gyeongju, Republic of Korea, 23 October.

G20 (2010c) 'The G-20 Seoul Summit Leaders' Declaration', 11–12 November 2010.

Garton Ash, T. (1994) *In Europe's Name: Germany and the Divided Continent*, New York, Vintage (re-issue, first published 1993).

Genscher, H.D. (1998) *Rebuilding a House Divided: A Memoir By the Architect of Germany's Reunification*, New York, Broadway (translated from the 1995 German edition).

Gerbet, P. (2014) 'The Intergovernmental Conference (IGC) on Economic and Monetary Union', Centre Virtuel de la Connaissance sur l'Europe, Luxembourg.

German Constitutional Court (1993) 'Judgment of 12 October 1993 – 2BvR 2134/92 and 2 BvR 2159/92', *Decisions of the Bundesverfassungsgericht*, Vol. 89, 155.

German Constitutional Court (2009) 'Entscheidungen: Lissabon-Urteil', 2 BvE 2/08 vom 30.6.2009.

German Constitutional Court (2014) 'Entscheidungen: über die Verfassungsbeschwerde . . . gegen 1 den Beschluss des Rates der Europäischen Zentralbank vom 6. September 2012 betreffend Outright Monetary Transactions (OMT) und die fortgesetzten Ankäufe von Staatsanleihen auf der Basis dieses Beschlusses und des vorangegangenen Programms für die Wertpapiermärkte' (Securities Markets Programme – SMP), BvR 2728/13, 7 February.

Giavazzi, F. and Giovannini, A. (1989) *Limiting Exchange Rate Flexibility: The European Monetary System*, Cambridge, MA, MIT Press.

Giavazzi, F. and Pagano, M. (1988) 'The Advantage of Tying One's Hands: EMS Discipline and Central Bank Credibility', *European Economic Review*, **32**(5), 1055–75.

González-Páramo, J.M. (2011) 'The ECB's Monetary Policy during the Crisis', Closing speech at the Tenth Economic Policy Conference, Málaga, 21 October.

Good, K. (1988) 'Institutional Reform Under the Single European Act', *American University International Law Review*, **3**(1), 299–322.

Goodhart, C. and Tsomocos, D. (2010) 'The Californian Solution for the Club Med', *The Financial Times*, 24 January.

Gordon, D.M. (1972) *Theories of Poverty and Underemployment*, Lexington, MA: Heath, Lexington Books.

Graham, B. (1937) *Storage and Stability: A Modern Ever-Normal Granary*, New York, McGraw Hill.

Granitsas, A. and Stevis, M. (2012) 'Greek Party Leaders Urge Yes Vote on Austerity', *Wall Street Journal*, 12 February.

Gregg, P. and Layard, R. (2009) 'A Job Guarantee', mimeo, London School of Economics, 16 March.

Grim, R. (2009) 'Priceless: How the Federal Reserve Bought the Economics Profession', *Huffington Post*, 13 May.

Groom, B. (2008) 'Darling – Time to Sing in the Bath', *The Financial Times*, 19 February.

Gros, D. and Pisani-Ferry, J. (1989) 'Costs and Benefits of EMU', *EMU Work Program*, 11 October.

Gros, D. and Thygesen, N. (1992) *European Monetary Integration*, New York, Longman.

Gros, D., Mayer, T. and Ubide, A. (2004) *The Nine Lives of the Stability Pact*, Brussels, Centre of European Policy Studies.

Gross, C.C. (2008) 'Three Before Their Time: Neuroscientists Whose Ideas Were Ignored by Their Contemporaries', *Experimental Brain Research*, **192**(3), January, 321–34.

Guigo, P.-E. (2013) 'Pierre Mauroy et le dit "tournant de la rigueur"', *Huffington Post*, 19 June.

Haas, P.M. (1992) 'Introduction: Epistemic Communities and International Policy Coordination', *International Organization*, **46**(1), 1–35.

Hagemann, H. (2000) 'The Post-1945 Development of Economics in Germany', in Coats, A.W. (ed.), *The Development of Economics in Western Europe since 1945*, London, Routledge, pp. 119–28.

Hargreaves, D. (2003) 'Market Insight: A Kickstart for the Eurozone?', FT.Com, 25 November.

Heipertz, M. and Verdun, A. (2004) 'The Dog that Would Never Bite? What We Can Learn from the Origins of the Stability and Growth Pact', CGPE Working Paper 04-06, January.

Henning, C.R. (1994) *Currencies and Politics in the United States, Germany, and Japan*, Washington, DC, Peterson Institute.

Henrikson, I. and Kaergard, N. (1995) 'The Scandinavian Currency Union 1875–1914', in Reis, J. (ed.) *The International Monetary System in Historical Perspective*, London, Macmillan, pp. 91–113.

Hetzel, R.L. (2002) 'German Monetary History in the Second Half of the Twentieth Century: From the Deutsche Mark to the Euro', *Federal Reserve Bank of Richmond Economic Quarterly*, **88**(2), Spring, 29–64.

Hiepel, C. (2003) 'In Search of the Greatest Common Denominator. Germany and the Hague Summit Conference 1969', *Journal of European Integration History*, **9**(2), 63–82.

Higgins, B. (1993) 'Was the ERM Crisis Inevitable?', *Economic Review*, Fourth Quarter, Federal Reserve Bank of Kansas City.

Hoffmeyer, E. (2000) 'Decision Making for European Economic and Monetary Union', Occasional Papers No. 62, Group of Thirty, Washington, DC.

Holtferich, C.-L. (1993) 'Did Monetary Unification Precede or Follow

Political Unification of Germany in the Nineteenth Century?', *European Economic Review*, **37**, 518–24.
Houben, A. (2000) *The Evolution of Monetary Policy Strategies in Europe*, Dordrecht, Springer.
House of Commons Hansard (1990a) 'European Council (Rome)', *HC Deb*, 30 October, vol. 178, cc869–92.
House of Commons Hansard (1990b) 'Personal Statement', *HC Deb*, 13 November, vol. 180, cc461–5.
House of Lords (2003) 'Debate', *Hansard*, 4 June.
Howarth, D.J. (2000) *The French Road to European Monetary Union*, Basingstoke, UK, Palgrave Macmillan.
Howarth, D.J. and Loedel, P. (2003) *The European Central Bank: The New European Leviathan?*, Basingstoke, UK, Palgrave Macmillan.
Human Rights Watch (2002) *Fast Track Land Reform in Zimbabwe*, March.
IFO Institute (1998) 'Currency Management Costs', *The Single Market Review, Subseries III, Volume 6*, Commission of the European Communities.
Independent Evaluation Office (IEO) (2011) *IMF Performance in the Run-Up to the Financial and Economic Crisis: IMF Surveillance in 2004–07*, Washington, DC, International Monetary Fund, 9 February.
Inequality Watch (2012) 'The Evolution of Income Inequalities in Germany', 4 June.
Inman, P. (2012) 'Black Wednesday 20 Years On: How the Day Unfolded', *The Guardian*, 13 September.
International Labour Organization (ILO) (2010) 'Recovery and Growth with Decent Work', International Labour Conference 2010, 99th Session, Geneva, 18 June.
International Labour Organization (ILO) (2012) 'Eurozone Job Crisis: Trends and Policy Responses', Geneva, International Labour Organization.
International Monetary Fund (IMF) (2010) 'Greece: Staff Report on Request for Stand-By Arrangement', IMF Country Report No. 10/110, May.
International Monetary Fund (IMF) (2011) 'Statement by the European Commission, the ECB and IMF on the Fourth Review Mission to Greece', Press Release No. 11/212, 3 June.
International Monetary Fund (IMF) (2012) *World Economic Outlook (WEO)*, October, Washington, DC.
International Monetary Fund (IMF) (2013a) 'Factsheet: Special Drawing Rights', available at: http://www.imf.org/external/np/exr/facts/pdf/sdr.pdf, accessed 26 December 2014.

International Monetary Fund (IMF) (2013b) 'Transcript of a Conference Call on Greece Article IV Consultation', Washington, DC, 5 June.

International Monetary Fund (IMF) (2013c) 'Greece: Ex Post Evaluation of Exceptional Access under the 2010 Stand-By Arrangement', IMF Country Report No. 13/156, June.

International Monetary Fund (IMF) (2014) *World Economic Outlook*, April, database.

Issing, O. (2010) 'Europe Cannot Afford to Rescue Greece', *The Financial Times*, 15 February.

Italianer, A. and Pisani-Ferry, J. (1992) 'Systèmes budgétaires et amortissement des chocs régionaux: implications pour l'union économique et monétaire', *Economie prospective internationale*, **51**, 49–69.

Jakobsen, T.G. (2012) 'The Fall of Rhodesia', *Popular Social Science*, 19 October.

James, B. and Friedman, A. (1998) 'Show of Support for Rome's EMU Bid', *New York Times*, 20 January.

Janis, I.L. (1982) *Groupthink: Psychological Studies of Policy Decisions and Fiascoes*, 2nd edn, New York, Houghton Mifflin.

Jauer, J., Liebig, T., Martin, J.P. and Puhani, P. (2014) 'Migration as an Adjustment Mechanism in the Crisis? A Comparison of Europe and the United States', Organisation for Economic Co-operation and Development, January.

Jeffries, S. (2005) 'The Prophet of Anti-Globalism', *The Guardian*, 9 June.

Jenkins, R. (1977) 'Europe's Present Challenge and Future Opportunity', Jean Monnet Lecture, Florence, 27 October.

Johnson, H.G. (1969) 'Inside Money, Outside Money: Income, Wealth, and Welfare in Monetary Theory', *Journal of Money, Credit and Banking*, **1**(1), 30–45.

Journal Officiel de La République Française (1976), *Débats Parlementaires Assemblée Nationale*, 5 October.

Judt, T. (2005) *Postwar: A History of Europe Since 1945*, London, Penguin Books.

Kaelberer, M. (2001) *Money and Power in Europe*, Albany, NY, State University of New York Press.

Kahan, D.M., Peters, E., Dawson, E. and Slovic, P. (2013) 'Motivated Numeracy and Enlightened Self-Government', Public Law Working Paper No. 307, Yale Law School.

Kahn, G.A. and Jacobson, K. (1989) 'Lessons from West German Monetary Policy', *Economic Review*, Federal Reserve Bank of Kansas City, April, 18–35.

Kaldor, N. (1957) 'A Model of Economic Growth', *The Economic Journal*, **67**(268), 591–624.

Kaletsky, A. (1992) 'How Mr. Soros Made a Billion', *The Times*, 26 October.

Keegan, W. and Brett, A. (2007) 'Mr Lamont's Dark History', *The Guardian*, 22 July.

Kenen, P.B. (1969) 'The Optimum Currency Area: An Eclectic View', in Mundell, R.A. and Swoboda, A.K. (eds) *Monetary Problems of the International Economy*, Chicago, University of Chicago Press, pp. 41–60.

Kenen, P. (1994) *Exchange Rates and the Monetary System: Selected Essays of Peter B. Kenen*, Aldershot, UK, Edward Elgar.

Keynes, J.M. (1933) 'An Open Letter to President Roosevelt', *New York Times*, 31 December.

Kinzer, S. (1991a) 'France and Germany Warn Britain on Europe', *New York Times*, 16 November.

Kinzer, S. (1991b) 'Kohl Calls the Path to European Unity Irreversible', *New York Times*, 14 December.

Krugman, P. (2009) 'How Did Economists Get It So Wrong?', *New York Times*, 2 September.

Kuhn, T.S. (1996) *The Structure of Scientific Revolutions*, 3rd edn, Chicago, University of Chicago Press.

Lagarde, C. (2014) 'The Road to Sustainable Global Growth – the Policy Agenda', Speech to the School of Advanced International Studies, Johns Hopkins University, Washington, DC, 2 April.

Lagayette, P. (1988) 'Les perspectives monétaires à l'horizon 1992', *Politique étrangère*, **2**, 53rd year, 443–52.

Lakatos, I. (1970) 'Falsification and the Methodology of Scientific Research Programmes', in Lakatos, I. and Musgrave, A. (eds) (1990) *Criticism and the Growth of Knowledge*, Cambridge, Cambridge University Press, pp. 91–195.

Lakoff, G. (2010) 'Untellable Truths', *Huffington Post*, 10 December.

Lakoff, G. and Johnson, M. (1999) *Philosophy in the Flesh: The Embodied Mind and its Challenge to Western Thought*, New York, Basic Books.

Lamfalussy, A. (1989) 'Macro-Coordination of Fiscal Policies in an Economic and Monetary Union in Europe', in European Commission (1989b) *Collection of Papers Submitted to the Committee for the Study of Economic and Monetary Union*, pp. 93–125.

Lamont, N. (1999) *In Office*, London, Little, Brown.

Larosière, J. de (1989) 'First Stages Towards the Creation of a European Reserve Bank. The Creation of a European Reserve Fund (October–December 1988)', in European Commission (1989b) *Collection of Papers Submitted to the Committee for the Study of Economic and Monetary Union*, pp. 177–84.

Latvijas Statistika (2014) Table DIG02, Annual Labour Costs and their Structure, various years.

Lavoie, M. (1984) 'The Endogenous Flow of Credit and the Post Keynesian Theory of Money', *Journal of Economic Issues*, **18**, 771–97.

Lawson, D. (1990) 'Saying the Unsayable About the Germans', *The Spectator*, 14 July.

Layard, R. (1997) 'Preventing Long-Term Unemployment', in Phillpott, J. (ed.), *Working for Full Employment*, Routledge, London, pp. 190–203.

Layard, R. (1998) 'Getting People Back to Work', *Centrepiece Magazine*, **3**(3), Autumn, 24–27.

Layard, R., Nickell, S. and Jackman, R. (1991) *Unemployment, Macroeconomic Performance and the Labour Market*, Oxford, Oxford University Press.

Le Figaro (2007) 'Les petites phrases de l'ancien premier ministre', 20 November.

Le Monde (2003) 'Contre l'Europe, Editorial', 6 September.

Le Monde diplomatique (2011) 'Maniere de voir, No. 116', April–May.

Le Parisien (2012a) 'L'incroyable histoire de la naissance des 3% de déficit', 28 September.

Le Parisien (2012b) '3% de déficit: "Le chiffre est né sur un coin de table"', 28 September.

Lefèvre, S. (2002) 'Les ministères de l'Économie et des Finances allemand et français dans la mise en place de la CEE: politiques et compétences', in *Le rôle des ministres des Finances et de l'Économie dans la construction européenne (1957–1978)*, Comité pour l'Histoire économique et financière de la France, Vol. I, Paris, pp. 73–84.

Leigh-Pemberton, R. (1993) 'The UK Perspective', in Temperton, P. (ed.) *The European Currency Crisis: What Chance Now for a Single European Currency?*, Cambridge, Probus.

Leparmentier, A. and Zecchini, L. (2002) 'La France sera en minorité si elle n'est pas le levain de l'Europe', *Le Monde*, 18 October.

Lerner, A. (1943) 'Functional Finance and the Federal Debt', *Social Research*, **10**(1), 38–51.

Lerner, A. (1951) *The Economics of Employment*, New York, McGraw Hill.

Lind, J. (2011) *Sorry States: Apologies in International Politics*, Ithaca, NY, Cornell University Press.

Lindenlaub, D. (2011) 'Ten Years: United Towards Stable Money – The Bundesbank in the History of European Monetary Integration', Frankfurt am Main.

Longworth, R.C. (1990) 'Ridley's (Oops) Believe It Or Not', *Chicago Tribune*, 13 July.

Loriaux, M. (1991) *France After Hegemony: International Change and Financial Reform*, Ithaca, NY, Cornell University Press.

Lübke, A. (2008) 'Medium-Term Financial Planning in the Federal Republic of Germany', *Presupuesto y Gasto Público*, **51**, 133–144.

Lucas, R.E. Jr (2003) 'Macroeconomic Priorities', *American Economic Review*, **93**(1), 1–14.

Ludlow, N.P. (2003) 'An Opportunity or a Threat? The European Commission and the Hague Council of December 1969', *Journal of European Integration History*, **9**(2), 11–26.

Maastricht Treaty (1992) 'Treaty on European Union', *Official Journal of the European Communities*, No. C191.

MacCormick, N. (1999) *Questioning Sovereignty*, Oxford, Oxford University Press.

MacDougall Report (1977) see European Commission (1977).

Maes, I. (2002) 'On the Origins of the Franco-German EMU Controversies', Working Paper No. 34, National Bank of Belgium, Working Paper Research Series.

Major, S. (2010) '"True sovereigns" Immune from Eurozone Contagion', *The Financial Times*, 16 August.

Mallaby, S. (2010) *More Money Than God: Hedge Funds and the Making of a New Elite*, New York, The Penguin Press.

Market News International (MNI) (2014) 'Interview with Jens Weidmann', 21 March.

Marks, S. (1978) 'The Myths of Reparations', *Central European History*, **11**(3), 231–255.

Marsh, D. (2013) 'The Emminger Letter Reappears', *OMFIF Commentary*, 2 April.

Martens, W. (2009) *Europe: I Struggle, I Overcome*, Dordrecht, Springer.

Mathews, R.L. and Grewal, B.S. (1997) *The Public Sector in Jeopardy: Australian Fiscal Federalism from Whitlam to Keating*, Melbourne, Centre for Strategic Economic Studies, Victoria University.

Mbohwa, C. (2008) 'Operating a Railway System within a Challenging Environment: Economic History and Experiences of Zimbabwe's National Railways', *Journal of Transport and Supply Chain Management*, **2**(1), November, 25–40.

McAllister, R. (2009) *European Union: An Historical and Political Survey*, New York, Taylor & Francis.

McCulley, P. and Pozsar, Z. (2013) 'Helicopter Money: Or How I Stopped Worrying and Love Fiscal–Monetary Cooperation', *Global Society of Fellows*, 7 January.

McKinnon, R.I. (1963) 'Optimum Currency Areas', *American Economic Review*, **53**, 717–25.

Mendizábal, H.R. (2002) 'Monetary Union and the Transaction Cost Savings of a Single Currency', *Review of International Economics*, **10**(2), 263–77.

Miller, V. (1997) 'The European Politics of Economic and Monetary Union: Developments in Germany, France, Italy and Spain', Research Paper 97/36, House of Commons Library, 19 March.

Millon-Delsol, C. (1992) *L'etat subsidiaire: ingérence et non-ingérence de l'état: le principe de subsidiarité aux fondements de l'histoire europeéenne*, Paris, Presses Universitaires de France.

Minister of Reconstruction to Parliament (1944) *Employment Policy*, London, His Majesty's Stationery Office.

Ministry of Economic Affairs (1989) 'The Danish Government's Official Report on EMU', Copenhagen, 27 November.

Mitchell, W.F. (1998), 'The Buffer Stock Employment Model – Full Employment without a NAIRU', *Journal of Economic Issues*, **32**(2), 547–55.

Mitchell, W.F. and Muysken, J. (2006) 'The Brussels–Frankfurt consensus: An Answer to the Wrong Question', in Mitchell, W.F., Muysken, J. and Van Veen, T. (eds) (2006) *Growth and Cohesion in the European Union*, Cheltenham, UK and Northampton, MA, USA, Edward Elgar, pp. 3–31.

Mitchell, W.F. and Muysken, J. (2008) *Full Employment Abandoned: Shifting Sands and Policy Failures*, Aldershot, UK, Edward Elgar.

Mitchell, W.F. and Watts, M.J. (2004) 'Comparison of the Macroeconomic Consequences of Basic Income and Job Guarantee Schemes', *Rutgers Journal of Law and Urban Policy*, **2**, 1–24.

Mitchell, W.F., Muysken, J. and Van Veen, T. (2006) *Growth and Cohesion in the European Union*, Cheltenham, UK and Northampton, MA, USA, Edward Elgar.

Modigliani, F. (2000) 'Europe's Economic Problems', *Carpe Oeconomiam Papers in Economics*, 3rd Monetary and Finance Lecture, Freiburg, 6 April.

Mongelli, F.P. (2008) 'European economic and monetary integration and the optimum currency area theory', *European Economy Economic Papers*, 302, February.

Moravcsik, A. (1998) *The Choice for Europe. Social Purpose and State Power from Messina to Maastricht*, London, UCL Press.

Morris, N. and Grice, A. (2009) 'Brown's Assignment for Next G20 Meeting: A Blueprint for IMF Reform', *The Independent*, 4 April.

Morris, R., Ongena, H. and Schuknecht, L. (2006) 'The Reform and Implementation of the Stability and Growth Pact', Occasional Paper Series No. 47, June, European Central Bank, Frankfurt am Main.

Müller, M. (2013) 'EU Unemployment Insurance: Getting the Eurozone Back on Track', thenewfederalist.eu, 5 July.

Münchau, W. (2009a) 'Diverging Deficits Could Fracture the Eurozone', *The Financial Times*, 4 October.

Münchau, W. (2009b) 'Berlin Weaves a Deficit Hair-Shirt For Us All', *The Financial Times*, 21 June.

Mundell, R.A. (1961) 'A Theory of Optimum Currency Areas', *American Economic Review*, **51**, 657–65.

Mundell, R. (1973) 'Uncommon Arguments for Common Currencies', in Johnson, H.G. and Swoboda, A.K. (eds) *The Economics of Common Currencies*, London, George Allen and Unwin, pp. 114–32.

Nickell, S. and Quintini, G. (2001) 'The Recent Performance of the UK Labour Market', talk given to Economics Section of the British Association for the Advancement of Science, Glasgow, September.

Notulen Ministerraad (1967), Top Secret Memo, Ex. Nr. 29, 27 October, available at: www.historici.nl/pdf/europa/C00103.pdf, accessed 10 January 2014.

Nugent, T.E. (2003), 'The Budget Deficit/The Budget Surplus: The Real Story', available at: http://www.mosler.org/docs/docs/budget_deficit_real_story.htm, accessed 18 August 2007.

Oates, W. (1968) 'The Theory of Public Finance in a Federal System', *Canadian Journal of Economics*, **1**, 37–54.

Organisation for Economic Co-operation and Development (OECD) (1994) *Jobs Study*, Paris, Organisation for Economic Co-operation and Development.

Ormerod, P. (1994) *The Death of Economics*, London, Faber and Faber.

Osborne, G. (2006) 'Look and Learn from Across the Irish Sea', *The Times*, 23 February.

Palmer, J. (1997) 'Bonn Softens Stance on EMU Entry Criteria', *The Guardian*, 7 April.

Phillips, L. (2013) 'Portugal vs the Joffrey Baratheon of Economic Policies', *EUobserver*, 8 April.

Piodi, F. (2012) 'The Long Road to the Euro', European Parliament, Directorate-General for the Presidency, Archive and Documentation Centre, 8 February.

Piore, M.J. (1979) *Unemployment and Inflation, Institutionalist and Structuralist Views*, White Plains, NY, M.E. Sharpe, Inc.

Pisani-Ferry, J., Italianer, A. and Lescure, R. (1993) 'Stabilization Properties of Budgetary Systems: A Simulation Approach', in *The Economics of Community Public Finance*, European Economy, Reports and Studies, 5.

Pisani-Ferry, J., Vihriälä, E. and Wolff, G. (2012) 'Options for a Euro-Area Fiscal Capacity', *Bruegel Policy Contribution*, Issue 2013/01, January.

Pöhl, K.O. (1989a) 'The Further Development of the European Monetary System', in European Commission (1989b) *Collection of Papers Submitted to the Committee for the Study of Economic and Monetary Union*, pp. 131–53.

Pöhl, K.O. (1989b) 'Aktuelle Fragen der Währungspolitik', speech to the Banking Federation in Bonn, 6 October.

Policy Exchange (2012) 'Wolfson Economics Prize 2012', available at: http://www.policyexchange.org.uk/component/zoo/item/wolfson-economics-prize-2012, accessed 26 December 2014.

Pope Pius XI (1931) *Quadragesimo Anno*, Vatican, Rome.

Proctor, C. (2006) 'The Future of the Euro – What Happens if a Member State Leaves?', *European Business Law Review*, **17**(4), 909–37.

Quatremer, J. (2010) 'Interview with Jean-Claude Trichet, President of the ECB, and Libération, conducted by Jean Quatremer', 8 July, European Central Bank.

Quirk, V. (2011) 'The Political Constraints on Full Employment', unpublished PhD thesis, University of Newcastle.

Renard, F. (1987) 'M. Balladur veut accélérer la construction de l'Europe monétaire', *Le Monde*, 8 January.

Reserve Bank of Australia (RBA) (2014) 'About the Payments System', available at: http://www.rba.gov.au/payments-system/about.html, accessed 7 May 2014.

Reuters (2005) 'Italy Minister Says Should Study Leaving Euro-Paper', 3 June.

Reuters (2011) 'TEXT-German Schaeuble's Letter on Greece to IMF, ECB, Euro Peers', 8 June.

Rhein, T. (2013) 'Deutsche Geringverdiener im europaeischen Vergleich', *IAB-Kurzbericht*, Issue 15.

Richter, R. (1999) 'European Monetary Union: Initial Situation, Alternatives, Prospects – in the Light of Modern Institutional Economics', Economic Series No. 9908, University of Saarland, May.

Riding, A. (1990) 'France Urges West Germany to Speed Unification', *New York Times*, 21 March.

Rodrik, D. (2006) 'Goodbye Washington Consensus, Hello Washington Confusion?', *Journal of Economic Literature*, **44**(4), 973–87.

Rodrik, D. (2010) 'The End of an Era in Finance', *Project Syndicate*, 11 March.

Rueff, J. (1950) 'L'Europe se fera par la monnaie ou ne se fera pas', *Revue Synthèses*, **45**, 386–88.

Sachs, J., Wyplosz, C., Buiter, W., Fels, G. and de Menil, G. (1986) 'The Economic Consequences of President Mitterand', *Economic Policy*, **1**(2), 261–322.

Sapir, A., Aghion, P., Bertola, G., Hellwig, M., Pisani-Ferry, J., Rosati, D., Viñals, J. and Wallace, H. (2003) 'An Agenda for a Growing Europe: Making the EU Economic System Deliver', report of an independent high-level study group established on the initiative of the President of the European Commission, Brussels. Later published by Oxford University Press, 2004. Also known as the Sapir Report.

Schellhorn, F. and Jilch, N. (2012) 'Stark: "EZB bewegt sich außerhalb ihres Mandats"', *Die Presse*, 22 September.

Schiller, R.J. (2008) 'Challenging the Crowd in Whispers, Not Shouts', *New York Times*, 2 November.

Schmidt, H. (1974) 'Regierungserklärung von Bundeskanzler Helmut Schmidt vom 17. Mai 1974'.

Schmidt, H. (1995) 'Deutsches Störfeuer gegen Europa', *Die Zeit*, No. 40, 29 September.

Schönfelder, W. and Thiel, E. (1994) *Eine Markt – Eine Währung, Die Verhandlungen zur Europäischen Wirtschafts- und Währungsunion*, Baden-Baden, Nomos Verlagsgesellschaft.

Schuknecht, L., Moutot, P., Rother, P. and Stark, J. (2011) 'The Stability and Growth Pact: Crisis and Reform', Occasional Paper Series No. 129, September, European Central Bank.

Schweizerisches Bundesgericht (2010) 'Appeal in Civil Matters, 12 July 2010, BGE 136 III 379'.

Scott, H.S. (1998) 'When the Euro Falls Apart', *International Finance*, **1**(2), 207–28.

Scott, H.S. (2012) 'When the Euro Falls Apart – A Sequel', Working Paper, Harvard Law School, January.

Sheehan, P. (2010) 'Greece Laid Low by its Decadence', *Sydney Morning Herald*, 15 May.

Shenker-Osorio, A. (2012) *Don't Buy It: The Trouble with Talking Nonsense about the Economy*, New York, PublicAffairs (E-book references).

Shirai, S. (2003) 'The Impact of IMF Economic Policies on Poverty Reduction in Low-Income Countries', JBICI Discussion Paper Series, No. 4, Japan Bank for International Cooperation, August.

Sievert, O. (2003) 'Vom Keynesianismus zu Angebotspolitik', in *Sachverständigenrat zur Begutachtung der gesamtwirtschaftlichen Entwicklung*, Statistiches Bundesamt, Wiesbaden, 33–46.

Sinn, Hans-Werner (2010) 'How to Save the Euro', *The Wall Street Journal*, 20 April.

Smith, A. (pseudonym of Goodman, G.J.W.) (1981) *Paper Money*, New York, G.K. Hall.
Soros, G. (2013) 'How to Save the EU from the Euro Crisis', *The Guardian*, 10 April.
Soutou, G. (1996) *L'alliance incertaine, Les rapports politico-stratégiques franco-allemands, 1954–1996*, Paris, Fayard.
Sowell, T. (2006) *On Classical Economics*, New Haven, CT, Yale University Press.
Spiegel, P., Peel, Q., Jenkins, P. and Milne, R. (2011) 'EU Leaders Agree €109bn Greek Bail-Out', *The Financial Times*, 21 July.
Stead, D. (1990) 'Magazine of the Right that Tripped Up a Tory', *New York Times*, 19 July.
Stiglitz, J.E. (2002) *Globalization and Its Discontents*, London, Penguin Group.
Stock, J. and Watson, M. (2002) 'Has the Business Cycle Changed and Why', *NBER Macroeconomics Annual*, 159–230.
Stoltenberg, G. (1988) 'Statement by Mr Gerhard Stoltenberg to the Interim Committee of the IMF, Washington, April 14, 1988', Twenty-Ninth Activity Report of the Monetary Committee of the European Communities, pp. 37–40.
Szász A. (1999) *The Road to European Monetary Union*, Basingstoke, UK, Palgrave Macmillan.
Tempest, M. (2005) 'Treasury Papers Reveal Cost of Black Wednesday', *The Guardian*, 9 February.
Tepper, J. (2012) 'A Primer on the Euro Breakup: Default, Exit and Devaluation as the Optimal Solution', Wolfson Economics Prize MMXII, Policy Exchange, 133–38.
Thatcher, M. (1993) *The Downing Street Years*, London, Harper Collins.
The Economist (2003) 'Chirac Storms the Stability Pact', 17 July.
The Economist (2007) 'Back Above the Bar Again', 12 July.
The Economist (2010a) 'Fear Returns: Governments Were the Solution to the Economic Crisis. Now They Are the Problem', 27 May.
The Economist (2010b) 'Austerity Alarm', 1 July.
The Economist (2011a) 'Sell, Sell, Sell', 16 May.
The Economist (2011b) 'Argentina's Debt Default – Gauchos and Gadflies', 22 October.
The Guardian (2000) 'Land Redistribution is Not Robbery, But a Necessity', 19 April.
The Guardian (2010) 'Germany Joins EU Austerity Drive with €10bn Cuts', 7 June.
The Spectator (1944) 'Sir William Beveridge on Employment', 6 July.

The Spectator (1979) 'The Failure of Raymond Barre', 8 September.

The Telegraph (2011) 'David Cameron: Tax Cuts Would Make Economic Situation Worse', 16 June.

Théron, M. (1972) 'Comité des Gouverneurs des Banques centrales des Etats membres de la Communauté économique européenne, Pre-rapport du Groupe d'experts présidé par M. Théron', 8 January.

Thieffry, G. (2005) 'The Not So Unthinkable – The Break-Up of the European Monetary Union', *International Financial Law Review*, July.

Tietmeyer, H. (2003) 'From the Werner Report to the Euro', Pierre Werner Lecture, Luxembourg, 21 October.

Toniolo, G. (2005) *Central Bank Cooperation at the Bank for International Settlements, 1930–1973*, Cambridge, Cambridge University Press.

Tran, M. (2003) 'What is the Stability and Growth Pact?', *The Guardian*, 27 November.

Traynor, I. (2010) 'Eurozone Leaders Lock Horns Over Whether to Rescue Greece's Economy', *The Guardian*, 25 March.

Trichet, J.C. (2004) 'Structural Reforms and Growth, as Highlighted by the Irish Case', keynote address delivered at the Whitaker Lecture organised by the Central Bank and Financial Services Authority of Ireland, Dublin, 31 May.

Trichet, J.C. (2008) 'The Current State of the Euro Area and its Future', speech delivered at the conference 'The Euro's 10th Anniversary: History and Presence of the Euro', Munich, 10 July.

Trichet, J.C. (2010a) 'Stimulate No More – It is Now Time for All to Tighten', *The Financial Times*, 22 July.

Trichet, J.C. (2010b) 'Central Banking in Uncertain Times: Conviction and Responsibility', speech at the Symposium on 'Macroeconomic Challenges: The Decade Ahead', Jackson Hole, Wyoming, 27 August.

Triffin, R. (1960) *Gold and the Dollar Crisis: The Future of Convertibility*, London, Oxford University Press.

Trotter, W. (1941) *The Collected Papers of Wilfred Trotter F.R.S.*, Oxford, Oxford University Press.

Tsoukalis, L. (1977) *The Politics and Economics of European Monetary Integration*, London, Allen and Unwin.

Tsoukalis, L. (1989) 'The Political Economy of the European Monetary System', in Guerrieri, P. and Padoan, P. (eds) *The Political Economy of the European Integration: States, Markets and Institutions*, New York, Harvester Wheatsheaf, pp. 58–84.

Turner, A. (2013) 'Debt, Money and Mephistopheles: How Do We Get Out of This Mess?', speech to Cass Business School, London, 6 February.

UNCTAD (2010) *Trade and Development Report, 2010*, New York, United Nations Conference on Trade and Development.

Ungerer, H. (1997) *A Concise History of European Monetary Integration: From EPU to EMU*, London, Quorum.

Ungerer, H., Evans, O. and Nyberg, P. (1983) 'The European Monetary System: The Experience, 1979–82', Occasional Paper No. 19, International Monetary Fund.

Ungerer, H., Hauvonen, J.J., Lopez-Claros, A. and Mayer, T. (1990) *The European Monetary System: Developments and Perspectives*, Washington, DC, International Monetary Fund.

Universität Duisburg-Essen (2010) 'Workshop: Wege aus der geringfügigen Beschäftigung, Minijob mit Nebenwirkungen', March.

US Energy Information Administration (2013) *Monthly Energy Review*, December.

Valeurs actuelles (2007) 'Raymond Barre ou le courage d'être impopulaire', 30 August.

van der Harst, J. (2003) 'The 1969 Hague Summit: A New Start for Europe?', *Journal of European Integration History*, **9**(2), 5–10.

van der Ploeg, F. (1991) 'Macroeconomic Policy Coordination Issues during the Various Phases of Economic and Monetary Integration in Europe', in European Commission (1991) 'The Economics of EMU: Background Studies – One Market, One Money', *European Economy*, **44**, Special Edition No. 1, 136–64.

Van Rompuy, P., Abraham, F. and Heremans, D. (1991) 'Economic Federalism and the EMU', in European Commission (1991) 'The Economics of EMU: Background Studies – One Market, One Money', *European Economy*, **44**, Special Edition No. 1, 107–35.

Varoufakis, Y. and Holland, S. (2011) 'A Modest Proposal for Resolving the Eurozone Crisis', Policy Note 2011/3, Levy Economics Institute of Bard College.

Varoufakis, Y., Holland, S. and Galbraith, J.K. (2013) 'A Modest Proposal for Resolving the Eurozone Crisis, Version 4.0', July.

Vedel, G. (1972) 'Report of the Working Party Examining the Problem of the Enlargement of the Powers of the European Parliament', *Bulletin of the European Economic Community*, April, No. 4, Luxembourg: Office for Official Publications of the European Communities.

Verde, A. (2004) 'La Lira dal Crollo di Bretton Woods alla fluttuazione: Una Ricostruzione degli Schemi Teorici del Comportamento delle Autorità Monetarie Italiane', *Studi e Note di Economia*, **2**, 47–67.

Verdun, A. (1999) 'The Role of the Delors Committee in the Creation of EMU: An Epistemic Community?', *Journal of European Public Policy*, **6**(2), 308–28.

von Cramen-Taubadel, S. and Thiel, H. (1994) 'EU Agriculture: Reduced Protection from Exchange Rate Instability', *Intereconomics*, November/December, 263–68.

von Goethe, J.W. (1888) *Faust: A Tragedy*, London, Ward Lock and Co.

von Hagen, J. (1989) 'Monetary Targeting with Exchange Rate Constraints: The Bundesbank in the 1980s', *Federal Reserve Bank of St. Louis*, September/October, 53–69.

Wade, R. (2004) *Governing the Market*, 2nd edn, Princeton, NJ, Princeton University Press.

Wade, R. and Sigurgeirsdottir, S. (2010) 'Lessons from Iceland', *New Left Review*, **65**, September–October.

Waigel, T. (1995) 'Stability Pact for Europe', Communication to the Ecofin Council, November.

Walsh, J.I. (1999) 'Political Bases of Macroeconomic Adjustment: Evidence from the Italian Experience', *Journal of European Public Policy*, **6**(1), 66–84.

Watt, A. (2004) 'Reform of the European Employment Strategy after Five Years: A Change of Course or Merely of Presentation?', *European Journal of Industrial Relations*, **10**(2), 117–37.

Weber, A. (2010) 'Monetary Policy after the Crisis – A European Perspective', speech presented to the Shadow Open Market Committee (SOMC) symposium, New York City, 12 October.

Weidmann, J. (2011) 'Managing Macroprudential and Monetary Policy – A Challenge for Central Banks', speech to SUERF/Deutsche Bundesbank Conference 2011/IMFS – The ESRB at 1, Berlin, 8 November.

Weidmann, J. (2012) 'Money Creation and Responsibility', speech at the 18th Colloquium of the Institute for Bank-Historical Research (IBF), Frankfurt, 18 September.

Werner Report (1970) see European Commission (1970a).

Wetzel, D. (2001) *A Duel of Giants: Bismarck, Napoleon III, and the Origins of the Franco-Prussian War*, Madison, WI, The University of Wisconsin Press.

Whitney, C.R. (1992) 'Bundesbank Chief is at Eye of Currency Storm', *New York Times*, 8 October.

Williamson, J. (1990) 'What Washington Means by Policy Reform', in Williamson, J. (ed.) *Latin American Readjustment: How Much has Happened*, Washington, DC, Peterson Institute for International Economics, Chapter 2.

Wolf, M. (2010) 'The Eurozone's Next Decade Will Be Tough', *The Financial Times*, 5 January 2010.

Wood, R. (2012) 'The Economic Crisis: How to Stimulate Economies

Without Increasing Public Debt', *Policy Insights*, No. 62, Centre for Economic Policy Research, August.

Wood, R. (2013a) 'Conventional and Unconventional Fiscal and Monetary Policy Options', *EconoMonitor*, 20 June.

Wood, R. (2013b) 'Overt Money Financing and Public Debt', *EconoMonitor*, 3 September.

World Bank (1995) 'Zimbabwe Achieving Shared Growth', *Country Economic Memorandum Volume 1: Overview*, Report No. 13540-ZIM, 21 April.

Wray, L.R. (1998) *Understanding Modern Money: The Key to Full Employment and Price Stability*, Cheltenham, UK and Northampton, MA, USA, Edward Elgar.

Wray, L.R. (2013) 'A Meme for Money', Working Paper No. 736, Levy Economics Institute.

Wyplosz, C. (1991) 'Monetary Union and Fiscal Policy Discipline', in European Commission (1991) 'The Economics of EMU: Background Studies – One Market, One Money', *European Economy*, **44**, Special Edition No. 1, 165–84.

Wyplosz, C. (2006) 'European Monetary Union: The Dark Sides of a Major Success', *Economic Policy*, **21**(46), April, 207–47.

Zettelmeyer, J., Trebesch, C. and Gulati, M. (2013) 'The Greek Debt Restructuring: An Autopsy', Working Paper Series, WP13-8, Peterson Institute for International Economics.

Zuckerman, E.W. (2003) 'Some Notes on the Relationship between Sociology and Economics (and Political Science): Cross-Disciplinary Citation Patterns over the 20th Century', mimeo, MIT Sloan School of Management, 14 October.

Index